Lecture Notes in Computer Science 4317

Commenced Publication in 1973
Founding and Former Series Editors:
Gerhard Goos, Juris Hartmanis, and Jan van Leeuwen

T0224421

Sanjay K. Madria   Kajal T. Claypool
Rajgopal Kannan   Prem Uppuluri
Manoj Madhava Gore (Eds.)

Distributed Computing and Internet Technology

Third International Conference, ICDCIT 2006
Bhubaneswar, India, December 20-23, 2006
Proceedings

 Springer

Volume Editors

Sanjay K. Madria
University of Missouri-Rolla, Department of Computer Science
Rolla, MO 65401, USA
E-mail: madrias@umr.edu

Kajal T. Claypool
Oracle Inc.
Nashua, NH 03062, USA
E-mail: kajal.claypool@oracle.com

Rajgopal Kannan
Louisiana State University, Department of Computer Science
Baton Rouge, LA 70803, USA
E-mail: rkannan@bit.csc.lsu.edu

Prem Uppuluri
Radford University, Department of Information Technology
Radford, VA 24060, USA
E-mail: puppuluri@radford.edu

Manoj Madhava Gore
M N National Institute of Technology
Department of Computer Science and Engineering
Allahabad 211004, India
E-mail: manoj.gore@gmail.com

Library of Congress Control Number: 2006938407

CR Subject Classification (1998): D.1.3, C.2.4, D.2, F.2, H.3, H.4, D.4.6, K.6.5

LNCS Sublibrary: SL 3 – Information Systems and Application, incl. Internet/Web
and HCI

ISSN	0302-9743
ISBN-10	3-540-68379-8 Springer Berlin Heidelberg New York
ISBN-13	978-3-540-68379-7 Springer Berlin Heidelberg New York

Springer is a part of Springer Science+Business Media

springer.com

© Springer-Verlag Berlin Heidelberg 2006
Printed in Germany

Typesetting: Camera-ready by author, data conversion by Scientific Publishing Services, Chennai, India
Printed on acid-free paper   SPIN: 11951957   06/3142   5 4 3 2 1 0

Message from the General Chair

ICDCIT was initiated with the idea of providing a forum for researchers around the world for discussing the challenges in the areas of computing, communication and control. As challenges due to the fusion of computing, communication and control lie in collaborative programming/computing and integration of technologies, the focus ICDCIT 2006 was on the following themes: network centric, program centric and data centric.

A right measure for the conference is the material being presented and also the participation. I was delighted to see a wealth of material represented, which was broadly categorized into the following tracks: (1) Net Centric, (2) Program Centric, and (3) Data Centric. In addition to these tracks, various tutorials were planned in the emerging areas, particularly for students from engineering colleges. This conference is a forum that attempts not only to understand the impact but also reshape it for the Indian context. It was a delight to see the enthusiastic participation of researchers from a large number of countries around the world. A very interesting feature of the conference is that it was held in the academic environment of a typical college in India. This facilitated a large participation of students from Orissa and other parts of India.

It is a pleasure to thank the plenary keynote speakers Vivek Sarkar, IBM T.J. Watson Research Center, Yorktown Heights. In addition, I thank the Track Chairs, invited speakers of various tracks, and authors of contributed papers for joining us in making the conference a success.

I would like to thank Sanjay Madria, PC Chair, for compiling such an excellent program. I would like to express my sincere thanks to all the Program Committee members and reviewers who did an excellent job in arriving at an attractive programme.

It is a pleasure to thank the Kalinga Institute of Industrial Technology (KIIT), Bhubaneswar, who took the responsibility of the organization of ICDCIT 2006. My special thanks go to Achyuta Samanta Chancellor, and Prashanta K. Mishra, Pro-Vice Chancellor, of KIIT (Deemed University), for all their organizational efforts and also to the innumerable dedicated volunteers who were responsible for the organization of the conference. Finally, I thank Springer for accepting to publish the proceedings in their LNCS series.

December 2006

R.K. Shyamasundar
IBM India Research Laboratory, New Delhi

Message from the Program Chair

It gives me great pleasure to welcome you to the Proceedings of the Third International Conference on Distributed Systems and Internet Technology (ICDCIT 2006). Continuing the rich tradition of the previous two ICDCITs, this year's technical program presents a collection of excellent papers representing the three themes: Network Centric, Program Centric and Data Centric. This ICDCIT 2006 technical program stimulated future research in this area and brought leading researchers to enhance the intellectual atmosphere of the conference attendees.

I would like to thank the three theme Chairs, Kajal Claypool, Raj Kannan, and Prem Uppuluri, for managing the review process. This year the International Program Committee in consultation with the theme Chairs and the Program Chair recommended 24 full papers and 10 short papers, thus a total of 34 papers out of 200 were selected for the presentation. I would like to thank members of the PC who were instrumental in putting a strong technical program for ICDCIT 2006. Also, thanks to all the authors who submitted their papers to ICDCIT 2006.

In addition, this year's program included one keynote talk and five invited papers. The keynote speaker was Vivek Sarkar from IBM Research Lab, USA, and the topic of his talk was "The Role of Programming Languages in Future Data-Centric and Net-Centric Applications."

I would like to thank all the authors for coming to this conference to present their work and discuss their ideas with peers. The papers presented simulated further discussion and hopefully excited some students to further participate in the areas of research represented by ICDCIT.

I would like to thank Hrushikesha Mohanty, University of Hyderabad, and R.K. Ghosh from IIT Kanpur for their valuable suggestions and guidance. I would like to thank various other Chairs and members of the Organizing Committee for their tireless work to make this symposium a success. In particular, thanks to Kaushik Sahu, Rashmi and their team for managing the conference secretariat, and promptly handling the Web site and other issues, and finally, Manoj Gore for handling the proceedings.

As the founder of this conference series, KIIT University (Kalinga Institute of Industrial Technology), Bhubaneswar, has been very supportive in hosting ICDCIT 2006. In particular, I would like to thank the Chancellor and the Pro-Chancellor of KIIT University, Achyuta Samanta and P. K. Mishra, respectively, for their uninterrupted support.

I hope you find the papers in this volume intellectually stimulating and enjoyable.

Sanjay Madria
University of Missouri-Rolla, USA

Messages from the Theme Chairs

Net Centric

Net-centric computing is an emerging paradigm encompassing modern distributed and embedded systems. The goal of Net-centric technology is to develop open and robust achitectural solutions for converging computing, communication and content. In this spirit, the focus of this year's Net-Centric Track was on networking and quality of service issues. We received an outstanding set of paper submissions addressing various net-centric problems. I would like to thank all of the authors who submitted papers, our invited speaker and the members of the Technical Program Committee.

The net-centric track received around 102 submissions from around the world, of which we were able to select 18 high-quality papers organized into four sessions. The main focus of this year's selected papers was wireless sensor and ad-hoc networks and quality of service. Each paper was first reviewed for relevance to the track theme and reviewed by at least two referees from the Program Committee.

I would like to thank Arun Somani for contributing an outstanding invited paper on the central track theme (Net-centric technologies). I would also like to thank the Program Committee members for doing an excellent job during the review process. The committe members were drawn internationally from universities and research labs in North America, Europe, Asia and Australia. The quality of the program reflects positively on their expertise and dedication.

December 2006   Rajgopal Kannan

Program Centric

I would like to thank all the Program Committee members and reviewers for providing excellent and critical reviews in a timely manner. This track received over 37 papers ranging from issues in load scheduling to papers on e-commerce. Thanks to all the authors for their continued support of this conference by choosing it as an avenue to publish their original research results.

In keeping with the tradition of the previous ICDCIT conferences, the acceptance rate was 18 in this track. These papers were complemented by a invited paper on "Application Level Checkpointing Techniques for Parallel Programs" by Vipin Chaudhury of State University of New York at Buffalo.

With the growth of the Internet fueled by powerful and inexpensive desktop computers, there is renewed interest in several areas of distributed computing which aim to harness this power. I believe this conference was a rewarding opportunity for all of us working or planning to work in the area of distributed computing with emphasis on the program-centric portions. Furthermore, it provided all of us with avenues to meet other researchers both from industry and academia.

Finally, I would like to thank KIIT for their continued support of this conference.

December 2006   Prem Uppuluri

Data Centric

This year's distributed data management track included work on Web and distributed databases, data mining, spatio-temporal databases, and information security and privacy, and it attracted researchers from both academia and industry.

We were honored to have Tsae-Feng Yu of Oracle Inc. Nashua, NH, Aparna Verde of Virginia State University, Petersburg, Virginia, and Gillian Dobbie from University of Auckland, New Zealand as our invited speakers. Tsae-Feng has had numerous contributions in the area of materialized views, data partitioning and query rewriting, and brought a rich industry perspective to the conference. Aparna Verde's strengths have been in applying data-mining techniques for discovering artifacts in the area of material science, and more recently in the area of nanotechnology. Gillian Dobbie's expertise is in managing semistructured data models.

This year, we received approximately 55 submissions from all over the world, and we accepted 10 for publication, 8 as full-length papers and 2 as short papers. The quality of submitted works was high, making this a great year for ICDCIT and ensuring its growing status as a reputed conference. Every submitted paper received three reviews, and further scrutiny by the chairs. We are grateful for the hard work of our Technical Program Committee—they did an outstanding job. The participation of stellar researchers on the TPC is a complement to the previous ICDCIT conferences.

December 2006   Kajal Claypool, Oracle Inc.

Conference Organization

Patrons
Achyuta Samanta, KIIT-DU, Bhubaneswar, India
C. R. Mishra, KIIT-DU, Bhubaneswar, India
P. K. Mishra, KIIT-DU, Bhubaneswar, India

General Chair

R. K. Shyamasunder, IBM India Research Lab, India

Business Committee
Gerard Huet, INRIA, France
Goutam Chakraborty, IP University, Japan
R. K. Ghosh, IIT Kanpur, India
S C DeSarkar, KIIT-DU, India
Sanjiva Prasad, IIT Delhi, India

Steering Chair

Hrushikesha Mohanty, University of Hyderabad, India

Program Chair

Sanjay K. Madria, University of Missouri-Rolla, USA

Theme Chairs

Net Centric:
Raj Kannan, LSU, USA
Program Centric:
Prem Uppuluri, UMKC, USA
Data Centric:
Kajal Claypool, UMass-Lowell, USA

Publication Chair

M. M. Gore, MNNIT Allahabad, India

Publicity Chair

Rahul Banerjee, BITS-Pilani, India

Organizing Chair

Kaushik Sahu, KIIT-DU, India

Finance Chairs
M. N. Das, KIIT-DU, India
S. Mishra, KIIT-DU, India

Program Committee Members

Albert Burger, Heriot-Watt University, UK
Andreas Koeller, Oracle, USA
Antonio Badia, University of Louisville, USA
Anup Kumar, University of Louisville, USA
Anwitaman Datta, EPFL, Switzerland
Arnab Ray, UMCP, USA
Arunabha Sen, Arizona State University, USA
Atul Negi, University of Hyderabad, India
B. S. Panda, IIT-Delhi, India
Bhabani Sinha, ISI, Kolkata, India
Bhed Bahadur Bista, Iwate-Pref. Univ, Japan
Bikram Sengupta, IBM Research Labs, India
Cindy Chen, UMass Lowell, USA
D. Mukhopadhyay, Techno Kolkata, India
David Wei, Fordham University, USA
Debasish Chakraborty, Tohoku Univ, Japan
Dipti Kalyan Saha, SUNY Stony Brook, USA
Erdal Cayirci, University of Stavanger, Norway
Gajanan Chinchwadkar, Sysbase, USA
Glenn Mansfield, Cyber Solutions, Japan
Gruenwald Le, University of Oklahoma, USA
Guna Seetharaman, AFIT, USA
Hong Jiang, University of Nebraska, USA
Hong Su, Oracle, USA
Hwajung Lee, Radford University, USA
J. Indulska, University of Queensland, Australia
Jun Zheng, University of Ottowa, Canada
Kalpdrum Passi, Laurentian University, Canada
L. Lilien, Western Michigan University, USA
Li Chen, San Diego Super Computing, USA
Maciej Zawodniok, UMR
Mohammed Hefeeda, SFU, Canada
Murali Mani, Worcester Polytech. Institute, USA
N L Sarda, IIT Bombay, India
Nabanita Das, ISI Kolkata, India
O.B.V. Ramanaiah, JNTU, Hyderabad, India
P. Roop, University of Auckland, New Zealand
Partha Dasgupta, ASU, USA
R. C. Hansdah, IIS, Bangalore, India
R. Kettinuthu, University of Chicago/ANL, USA
R. Wanker, University of Hyderabad, India

Program Committee Members Contd.

Rahul Agarwal, SUNY Stony Brook, USA
Richard Brooks, Clemson University, USA
Rosario Uceda-Sosa, IBM T.J. Watson Research Center, USA
S. Iyengar, Louisiana State University, USA
S. Krishnaswamy, Monash University, Australia
S. Nandi, IIT, Guwahati, India
Samik Basu, Iowa State University, USA
Sandip Das, ISI Kolkata, India
Sanjeev Aggarwal, IIT, Kanpur, India
Shuangqing Wei, LSU, USA
Sibabrata Ray, Google Inc., USA
Sourav Bhowmick, NTU, Singapore
Takahiro Hara, Osaka University, Japan
V. N. Sastry, IDRBT, Hyderabad, India
V. N. Venkatakrishnan, UIC, USA
Vasu Chakravarthy, AFRL-WPAFB, USA
Viktor K. Prasanna, USC, USA
Vipin Chaudhury, Wayne State, USA
Wee Keong Ng, NTU, Singapore
Yifei Dong, University of Oklahoma, USA
Yugi Lee, University of Missouri-KC, USA

External Reviewers

Baek Yong Choi, UMKC, USA
Janaki Ram, IIT Madras, India
Jerolynn Hebert, LSU, USA
Krishnendu Mukhopadhyaya, ISI Calcutta, India
Promita Chakraborty, LSU, USA
Sandeep Madamanchi, UMKC, USA
Subhas Chandra Nandy, ISI Calcutta, India

Host Institution

Kalinga Institute of Industrial Technology, KIIT-DU, Bhubaneswar, India

Table of Contents

Mobile AdHoc Networks – Security and Reliability

Quality of Service I

Quality of Service II

Grid and Distributed Computing

Web Services and E-Commerce

Web Databases

Data Mining

Spatio-temporal Databases

The Role of Programming Languages in Future Data-Centric and Net-Centric Applications

Mukund Raghavachari and Vivek Sarkar

IBM Thomas J. Watson Research Center
raghavac@us.ibm.com, vsarkar@us.ibm.com

Abstract. The primary mechanism for developing current data-centric and net-centric applications is through software frameworks that extend mainstream languages with runtime libraries. While library-based approaches can be pragmatic and expedient, we assert that programming language extensions are necessary in the long run to obtain application software that is robust, maintainable, and efficient. We discuss, through case studies, how programming language extensions can increase programmer productivity over library-based approaches for data-centric and net-centric applications.

1 Introduction

Over the last decade, there have been significant advances in application frameworks and middleware for net-centric and data-centric applications. These advances include the emergence of application servers and middleware (including BEA's WebLogic™, IBM's WebSphere™, and Microsoft's .NET™), XML-based standards for data interchange, and new standards for web services construction, composition, and choreography. Recently, the increased interest in service-oriented architectures has led to the development of common multi-vendor frameworks such as the Service Component Architecture [4].

We observe that the primary mechanism in use today for delivering middleware functionality to application developers is through *libraries*. A library-based approach is a convenient and pragmatic way to extend a programming model, and is the most expedient option in many situations. However, there are many issues that arise with an increased dependence on the use of libraries. First, the semantics guarantee offered by a library call is usually limited to a *weak checking of types* in the host language for the library, thereby lowering the fidelity of programmer-viewable types. Second, *problem determination* becomes complex in the presence of interface and contract failures in API calls to libraries. Third, *performance analysis* becomes challenging in the presence of libraries. Finally, the *syntactic verbosity* of library calls usually reduces productivity, and can be a major source of software defects when multiple API calls are necessary to perform a common task.

In this paper, we take the position that *programming languages* need to play a larger role in the construction of future net-centric and data-centric applications.

S. Madria et al. (Eds.): ICDCIT 2006, LNCS 4317, pp. 1–13, 2006.

Legacy languages such as C and Cobol are especially brittle in this regard because of their lack of portability, and their low-fidelity mechanisms for network and data access. Modern object-oriented languages such as Java^{TM}and C#, and modern scripting languages such as JavaScript, PHP, and Ruby, offer a more usable foundation compared to the legacy languages, but they still encapsulate network and data accesses as opaque low-level library calls. In contrast, the integration of higher-level abstractions for data and network access in new programming languages could offer multiple benefits. First, the language will have more flexibility in supporting *alternate and changing implementations*, compared to a library-based approach. Second, important properties of programs written in the new language can be *checked statically* via an enriched type system and program analysis. Third, *higher-level optimizations* can be enabled when new capabilities are integrated into the language. Finally, an *ecosystem of tools and frameworks* can be built more readily in support of programming language constructs compared to libraries.

One drawback of language-based extensions is that the overhead of design is greater than that of library-based frameworks. For common patterns of programming, however, this investment of effort can be justified through increased programmer productivity and robustness of applications. We believe that data access (of XML and relational data) and asynchronous invocations are two examples of common programming patterns that are better served by language-based extensions than by library-based approaches. In this paper, we examine this point in greater detail through two case-studies of specific language-based approaches that address these issues.

The rest of the paper is organized as follows. In Section 2, we outline some of the challenges that arise in designing a programming model for data-centric or net-centric applications. In Section 3, we present a case study of how programming language integration can improve the development of XML-centric applications. In Section 4, we consider how improved abstractions for concurrency and cluster programming can facilitate the development of applications. Finally, in Section 5, we discuss our conclusions.

2   Challenges

We consider some of the challenges faced in designing a programming model that facilitates the development of data-centric and net-centric applications. The list discussed is not meant to be exhaustive, but a sample of some of the key issues.

2.1   Multiple Data Models

Data are represented in a variety of data models, which differ significantly in representation, type systems, etc. Traditionally, programming languages have been weak in supporting the development of applications that process non-native data models. A typical solution is to provide a runtime library that supports generic operations on foreign data models, ignoring the non-native type system. For example, DOM is a generic API for processing XML data that reduces all XML data into generic classes such as `Node, Element`, etc. It is the programmer's responsiblity to ensure that the operations performed on XML data are correct with respect to the XML Schemas governing the data. As another example, consider JDBC, which reduces all relational data to generic classes such as `ResultSet`. In effect, programs written using such APIs are written in a reflective style (imagine writing a program in Java using only reflection), with the fragility and tediousness that comes with such a style.

Data-binding approaches address some these problems by providing tools that map heterogeneous type systems into the native type system. For example, consider JAXB where an XML Schema is converted into a set of Java classes or many of the available Object-Relational technologies. The advantage of these approaches is that by carefully designing the mapping from the foreign type system into the native one, one can achieve some static type checking (for example, that a reference to the child of an XML element is correct). On the other hand, the differences in the type systems cannot be hidden — they eventually manifest themselves in the form of *impedence mismatches*. To achieve the right semantics or to avoid significant performance penalties, often, a programmer must reason about both the foreign type system and the mapping, and restructure applications to avoid problems. While these approaches are satisfactory in certain cases, in general, they do not attain their goal of shielding a programmer from the heterogeniety of data models.

Recently, there has been increased interest in the development of *pluggable* type systems [7]. In this approach, the foreign type system is not hidden from the programmer, but the programming language is designed so that it can be extended with declarative specifications that control how foreign data types are to be integrated into the language. For operations on heterogeneous data, the compiler ensures that the accesses are correct and appropriate with respect to the foreign type system governing the data. There remain many research issues to be resolved, some of which we will discuss. It is worthwhile to note, however, that while there are many data models, XML and relational data are the most prevalent. While a general pluggable type system may be difficult to achieve, a solution that focuses on these two data models might address many common programming patterns and be more amenable. This is the approach we are pursuing in the DALI (Data Access Language Integration) project. We have integrated XML and the XML Schema type system (in an extensible manner) into the Java language (see Section 3), and are currently exploring how relational data access can be integrated in a similar fashion.

2.2 Querying

For many data sources, especially relational and XML data, querying is a natural technique for recovering and processing data. On closer inspection, many programming patterns may be better expressed with a declarative query rather than more imperative traversals. As a result, the integration of queries in programming languages has attracted significant attention, generally in the form of comprehensions as in Scala [16] or a deeper integration of queries, as in

Microsoft's LINQ [3]. What is unknown is whether a single query langauge will be sufficient to address common programming patterns. A common query language has the advantage of consistency — a programmer uses the same constructs to query all data, whether they be objects, XML, relational, etc. On the other hand, as in the data-binding approach above, one is relying on the compiler to map the query to the underlying query language (for example, SQL and XQuery). The open question, and an active area of research, is whether this mapping can be done efficiently for the majority of programs. The alternative is to have an extensible syntax in the programming language that can support many different query languages. Examples of such embedded languages exist for particular query languages, for example, SQLJ [9] in Java. The problem with the embedded language approach is that it is unclear how to extend it to handled multiple query languages, and to express queries that span data models (for example, a join across XML and relational data).

2.3   Transactions

The issue of updates of external data is one of the most difficult to address in a programming language. Currently, it is mostly the programmer's responsibility to manage updates to distributed data sources and ensure that, where required, the ACID (Atomicity, Consistency, Isolation, and Durability) properties are met. Several researchers have noted that some of these features, such as atomicity, consistency, and isolation are essential concepts of concurrent programming and have studied the introduction of language constructs based on these notions [8,13]. Durability is essentially persistence, whose integration into programming languages has also been studied in some depth [5]. What is yet to be resolved is a holistic integration of transactions into a programming language, that is amenable to the varying semantics of updates in different data models, and the varying notions of recovery or compensation from transactions.

2.4   Asynchrony

Mainstream programming languages have emphasized synchronous procedure or method calls over asynchronous message patterns. Recently, there has been increased interest in asynchronous programming patterns, which seem to suit the disconnected loosely-coupled nature of web. Many abstractions have been proposed for simplifying the development of asynchronous applications : futures [8], continuations [11,2], asynchronous join calculus [6], etc. It is not clear which of these constructs is best suited for current programming paradigms.

3   Case Study: XJ as a Foundation for Web Services

Web Service programming, or service-oriented computing in general, has become increasingly important. The development of applications using standards-based interface specifications such as WSDL and interoperable interchange formats based on XML Schema and XML promise to facilitate the development of flexible web-based applications. The methodology for building these applications is still somewhat immature — in this section, we examine alternative programming models for Web Service development.

3.1   Data-Binding Approaches

The current approach for developing Web Service programs in mainstream languages is based on data binding. One can summarize the approach as follows: a tool is used to generate a set of Java classes from a WSDL specification and programmers develop applications using the generated classes. This situation essentially covers how programmers can interact with existing Web Services. For the other aspect, defining Web Services based on existing Java code, programmers can create new Web Services by annotating existing methods in Java code as being part of the service. Using the annotations, tools can generate WSDL from the Java code automatically, as well as, the proxies needed to convert XML data into the Java model. In both cases, the marshalling and demarshalling of data to and from XML data is handled by generated Java code transparently.

At some level, this approach is attractive. A Java programmer need not learn new programming paradigms, but can interact with Web Services using existing Java-based tools and programming patterns. Unfortunately, while data-binding based techniques are satisfactory for certain cases, the differences in the data models for XML and Web Services and Java (the so-called Object-XML impedance mismatch) results in greater programming complexity in general.

Object-XML impedance mismatch has been studied in depth [14,15]. Due to space limitations, we do not repeat the arguments here, but refer interested readers to these studies. Some of the salient causes of the mismatch are:

– Objects are inherently a graph-based model, whereas XML is a tree model.
– Object models do not handle mixed content or order (in general) properly.
– Mainstream languages do not support choices (as in XML Schema) well.
– Namespaces, substitution groups and XML Schema subtyping are not naturally expressed in object models.
– Construction of XML data cannot be validated statically (or only be validated partially).

The effect of the Object-XML impedance mismatch is that the data-binding abstraction is not as clean as desired. A programmer must understand the mapping rules of the data binding approach and work around its idiosyncracies to ensure that the XML generated by the underlying system will be correct (according to the Web Service specification). Furthermore, since the goal is to compile these Java-based programs with a standard Java compiler, there is little scope for compiler static analysis and optimizations, which are necessary for practical XML processing.

```
1   import aws.*;
2   import com.ibm.xj.io.XMLOutputStream;
3
4   public class AmazonClient {
5     public static final String amazonId = "...";
6
7     public static void main(String[] args) {
8       AWSECommerceServicePortType svc =
9                         new AWSECommerceServicePort();
10
11      ItemSearch iRq = new ItemSearch(
12        <ItemSearch xmlns="...">
13          <SubscriptionId>{amazonId}</SubscriptionId>
14          <Request>
15            <Keywords>computer</Keywords>
16            <SearchIndex>Books</SearchIndex>
17          </Request>
18        </ItemSearch>);
19      ItemSearchResponse response = svc.ItemSearch(iRq);
20      new XMLOutputStream(System.out).println(response);
21    }
22  }
```

Fig. 1. Sample XJ Web Service application

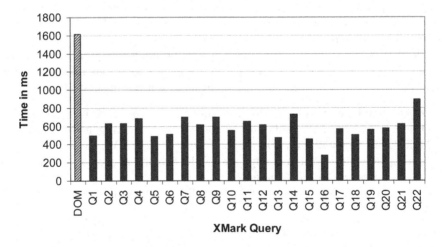

Fig. 2. Comparison of document construction time on a 10MB XMark file. The first column shows the cost of constructing a DOM in-memory instance. The remaining columns provide construction times for the various queries.

3.2   A Language-Based Approach

Given the fact that in data-binding approaches, the programmer is never oblivious of the underlying XML model, and given the increasing relevance of XML as a data interchange format, we propose a language-based approach for the development of Web Services. At the core of our proposal is the introduction of XML as a first-class construct in Java, much like the `java.lang.String` class has special semantics in Java.

We introduce an extension for Web Service programming to the XJ programming language [12] through an example in Figure 1. The example is based on the Amazon Web Services [1], which allows programmatic interaction with the Amazon catalog. First, the import statement of Line 1 is interpreted in a nonstandard way. If a Java class or package cannot be found to satisfy an import statement using the Java rules, then the compiler searches the classpath for either an XML schema (with a file extension ".xsd") or a WSDL specification (with a file extension ".wsdl"). In this case, the compiler parses the Amazon WSDL specification, the effect of which is that a programmer may refer to Ports and PortTypes declared with the WSDL as if they were Java types. So, for example, on Line 8, `AWSEcommerceServicePortType` is a type declared within the Amazon WSDL. In XJ, a port is treated similarly to a Java interface — specifically one can invoke methods on it such as the `ItemSearch` method on Line 19.

The second point to note is that a programmer can use XML literals to construct XML data. The compiler ensures that the constructed XML is consistent with respect to the declared types. In this example, it guarantees that the `ItemSearch` method is passed a value of the right type. XML literal construction can be dynamic, in that it contains expressions that will be evaluated at runtime. For example, on Line 13, the braces "{" "}" delimit an expression (in this case, a reference to a local variable) whose value will be substituted at runtime.

Advantages of this tight language integration of WSDL and XML are:

– The programmer does not have to work through mappings whose demarshalling into XML may not be clear — the programmer programs directly in terms of the XML that needs to be produced. This XML could be cut-and-pasted directly into the program from samples on the Web.
– The compiler guarantees that the program is correct with respect to the relevant interface specifications.
– The compiler can perform optimizations that improve the performance of the serialization / deserialization.
– The program is easier to maintain. If the Amazon interface were to change, the compiler would detect exactly the portion of the program that needs to be changed.

Aside from the tight integration of XML Schema, WSDL, and XML literals into the language, XJ also supports the integration of XPath expressions. Rather than writing explicit traversals over XML data, programmers can write declarative XPath expressions to navigate XML data. The use of XPath expressions allows programs to be more concise and readable, but also allows the compiler to perform optimizations that may not be possible otherwise. In Figure 2, we show the effect on performance of one such optimization — a compiler can analyze a program statically and generate code that only loads those portions of a document that are necessary for the processing of the program. The end result is that the cost of materializing, querying and serializing XML data tends to be significantly lower. In the figure, we show the time taken for loading an entire document using DOM, versus that for loading only the portions of the document needed for specfic queries. Further details can be found in [10].

4   Case Study: X10 as a Foundation for Asynchronous Computing

As mentioned earlier, one of the key challenges in net-centric and data-centric applications is the increased role of *asynchronous computing*. Asynchronous invocation of web services has now become as important as the synchronous variant. Similarly, just as asynchronous I/O has increased in importance for file access, we believe that the asynchronous invocation of queries will also increase in importance for database access. Any attempt to implement asynchronous invocation using low level concurrency mechanisms such as threads and locks usually leads to significant pitfalls due to common concurrency errors, especially for less-skilled mainstream programmers.

In this section, we provide a brief summary of v0.41 of the X10 programming language, as described in [8]. The goal of X10 is to introduce a core set of new language constructs that address the fundamental requirements for asynchrony and concurrency required by parallel systems at all scales, ranging from multi-core processors to network-connected clusters. We focus on four core concepts in X10 — *places, async, finish,* and *atomic*. An important safety result in X10 is that any program written with async, finish, atomic can never deadlock. (This result also holds with the addition of *foreach, ateach,* and *clock* constructs [8]).

The most important concept in X10 from the viewpoint of net-centric applications is that of a *place*. A place is a collection of resident (non-migrating) mutable data objects and the activities that operate on the data. Each mutable location and each activity is associated with exactly one place, and places do not overlap. A scalar object in X10 is allocated completely at a single place. In contrast, the elements of an array or of any other collection may be distributed across multiple places. X10 supports a *global name space* that is partitioned across places.

Places are *virtual* — the mapping of places to physical nodes in the network is performed by a deployment step that is separate from the X10 program. Though objects and activities do not migrate across places in an X10 program, an X10 deployment is free to migrate places across physical locations based on affinity, load balance, and fault tolerance considerations. While an activity executes at the same place throughout its lifetime, it may dynamically spawn activities in remote places.

Async is the X10 construct for creating or forking a new asynchronous activity. The statement, *async (⟨place-expr⟩) ⟨stmt⟩*, causes the parent activity to create

a new child activity to execute ⟨*stmt*⟩ at the place designated by ⟨*place-expr*⟩.
X10 permits the use of async's to create multiple distributed nested activities inline in a single method. Execution of the async statement returns immediately
i.e., the parent activity can proceed immediately to its next statement. The
async is local if the destination place is same as the place where the parent
is executing, and remote if the destination is different. Local async's are like
lightweight threads. A remote async can be viewed as an active message, since
it involves communication of input values as well as remote execution of the
computation specified by ⟨*stmt*⟩.

The X10 statement, *finish* ⟨*stmt*⟩, causes the parent activity to execute ⟨*stmt*⟩
and then wait till all sub-activities created within ⟨*stmt*⟩ have terminated globally. If async is viewed as a fork construct, then finish can be viewed as a join
construct. However, as discussed below, the async-finish model is more general
than the fork-join model. X10 distinguishes between *local termination* and *global
termination* of a statement. The execution of a statement by an activity is said
to terminate locally when the activity has completed all the computation related to that statement. For example, the creation of an asynchronous activity
terminates locally when the activity has been created. A statement is said to
terminate globally when it has terminated locally and all activities that it may
have spawned (if any) have, recursively, terminated globally.

Consider the following X10 code example of async and finish constructs. The
goal of this example is to use two activities to compute the sums of the odd
and even numbers in the range $1 \ldots n$. This is accomplished by having the main
program activity use the *async for (int i ...) ...* statement to create a remote
child activity to execute the for-i loop and compute oddSumResult.val, while
the main program activity proceeds in parallel to execute the for-j loop and
compute evenSum. Finally, the main program activity waits for its child activity
to finish so that it can print the result obtained by adding oddSumResult.val
and evenSum.

```
final int n = 100;
double evenSum = 0;
finish {
  async ( oddSumResult )  {
    // Compute oddSum in child activity at place where
    // oddSumResult is located
    for (int i = 1 ; i <= n ; i += 2 ) oddSumResult.val += i;
  }
  // Compute evenSum locally in parent activity
  for (int i = 2 ; i <= n ; i += 2 ) evenSum += i;
} // finish
// The remote value of oddSumResult.val can be read directly
System.out.println("Sum = " + (oddSumResult.val + evenSum));
} // main()
```

In addition to waiting for global termination, the finish statement plays an important role with regard to exception semantics. An X10 activity may terminate

normally or abruptly. A statement terminates abruptly when it throws an exception that is not handled within its scope; otherwise it terminates normally. While it may seem that an obvious solution is to propagate exceptions from a child activity to a parent activity, doing so is problematic when the parent activity terminates prior to the child activity. Since we want to permit child activities to outlive parent activities in X10, the finish construct is a more natural collection point for exceptions thrown by descendant activities. X10 requires that if statement S or an activity spawned by S terminates abruptly, and all activities spawned by S terminate, then finish S terminates abruptly and throws a single exception formed from the collection of all exceptions thrown by S or its descendant activities. There is an implicit `finish` statement surrounding the main program in an X10 application. Exceptions thrown by this statement are caught by the runtime system and result in an error message printed on the console. This provides more robust exception handling support for multithreaded programs compared to the Java model in which an exception is simply propagated from a thread to the top-level console instead of propagation to an appropriate handler in an ancestor thread.

It is instructive to compare how this distributed computation would have been written in standard Java. First, the storage model for distributed Java is one of independent JVMs with local address spaces communicating via Remote Method Invocation (RMI). In contrast, X10 supports a global name space partitioned across places. Second, to perform a synchronous RMI call in Java, the server must create an instance of a remote object class that implements `java.rmi.Remote`, the client must locate the remote object and then invoke an `execute()` method on it by passing an instance of a "task" object that implements `java.io.Serializable`. To get the effect of asynchronous invocation, these steps will need to be performed in the context of Java threads, which would add another significant level of complexity. In contrast, X10 supports asynchronous remote invocation by just using the `async` statement. Finally, the parameter passing convention for Java RMI is that remote objects are passed by reference, and local objects are passed by copy (using object serialization) For X10, mutable objects are passed by reference, and immutable objects are passed by value.

The finish statement guarantees that the child activity terminates globally before the print statement is executed. Note that the result of the child activity is communicated to the parent in a shared object, oddSumResult, since X10 does not permit a child activity to update a local variable in its parent activity. It is also worth noting that the X10 memory model is weak enough to allow oddSumResult.val to be allocated to a register during the execution of the entire for-i loop.

Figure 3 shows pseudocode for an example X10 program and its corresponding X10 activity invocation tree. As illustrated in the figure, each X10 activity or part of an activity has a unique parent finish operator (identified by the dashed line) which serves as the point for notifying termination and also as the collection point for any exceptions thrown by the activity. X10's async-finish model is more general than fork-join because it does not require a parent activity to wait till a

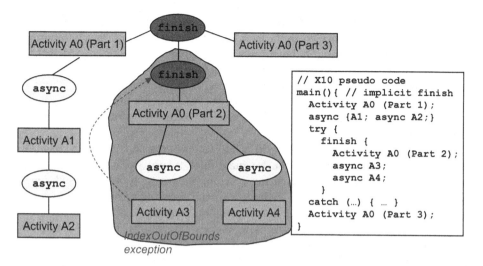

Fig. 3. Example of an X10 Dynamic Activity Invocation Tree

child activity completes. In the example, it is possible for activity A2 to continue executing after activity A1 terminates; notification of A2's termination only needs to be communicated to its parent finish operator and not to its parent activity.

The atomic construct in X10 is used to coordinate accesses by multiple activities to shared data at a single place. Even if net-centric applications are single-threaded in principle, the ability for multiple nodes to create asynchronous activities at the same place effectively creates multiple threads at the destination.

The X10 statement, *atomic ⟨stmt⟩*, causes ⟨stmt⟩ to be executed atomically i.e., its execution occurs as if in a single step during which ⟨stmt⟩ executes and terminates locally while all other concurrent activities in the same place are suspended. Compared to user-managed locking, the X10 user only needs to specify that a collection of statements should execute atomically and leaves the responsibility of lock management or alternative mechanisms for enforcing atomicity to the language implementation. Commutative operations, such as updates to histogram tables and insertions in a shared data structure, are a natural fit for atomic blocks when performed by multiple activities. An atomic block may include method calls, conditionals, and other forms of sequential control flow. For scalability reasons, blocking operations like finish and force are not permitted in an atomic block.

5   Conclusion

In this paper, we adopt the position that new programming language support will be necessary to address the challenges faced by future net-centric and data-centric applications. As examples, we showed how the XJ language can be used as a foundation for building web service applications and the X10 language as a foundation for asynchronous computing. In both cases, the language extensions were designed for the Java language, but they could just as well have been designed for some other modern object-oriented language. By building on Java, we are able to carry forward the portability, productivity, and security benefits of Java, while also leveraging its maturity and ubiquity with respect to runtime environments, tools, and a large existing skill base.

There are many challenges that still need to be addressed to further raise the abstraction levels supported in the language. For future work, it is important to extend the type-based specification of components to protocol-based specifications that are amenable to extended static checking. Another important direction for future work is to define a common semantic foundation for integrating strongly-typed infrastructure languages such as Java, XJ, and X10 that are designed for building robust long-lived software components, with scripting languages that are designed for rapid application development and rapid application integration.

Acknowledgments

The authors would like to thank members of the XJ and X10 project teams at IBM for their contributions to the ideas expressed in the paper. In addition, we woudl like to thank Bob Blainey, Doug Lea, Vijay Saraswat and Jan Vitek for discussions related to the role of new languages for modern net-centric and data-centric applications.

References

1. Amazon web services. `http://www.amazon.com/AWS-home-page-Money/b?ie=UTF8&node=3435361`.
2. Links. `http://groups.inf.ed.ac.uk/links/`.
3. Microsoft Linq. `http://msdn.microsoft.com/data/ref/linq/`.
4. Service component architecture. `http://www-128.ibm.com/developerworks/library/specification/ws-sca/`.
5. M. P. Atkinson and O. P. Buneman. Types and persistence in database programming languages. *ACM Computing Surveys*, 19(2):105–170, 1987.
6. N. Benton, L. Cardelli, and C. Fournet. Modern concurrency abstractions for c#. *ACM Trans. Program. Lang. Syst.*, 26(5):769–804, 2004.
7. G. Bracha. Pluggable type systems. In *OOPSLA Workshop on Revival of Dynamic Languages*, 2004.
8. P. Charles, C. Donawa, K. Ebcioglu, C. Grothoff, A. Kielstra, C. von Praun, V. Saraswat, and V. Sarkar. X10: An object-oriented approach to non-uniform cluster computing. In *OOPSLA 2005 Onward! Track*, 2005.
9. A. Eisenberg and J. Melton. Sqlj part 0, now known as sql/olb (object-language bindings). *SIGMOD Rec.*, 27(4):94–100, 1998.
10. R. Fernandes and M. Raghavachari. Inflatable XML trees. In *Middleware*, LNCS. Springer, 2005.

11. P. T. Graunke, S. Krishnamurthi, S. van der Hoeven, and M. Felleisen. Programming the web with high-level programming languages. In *European Symposium on Programming*, 2001.
12. M. Harren, M. Raghavachari, O. Shmueli, M. Burke, R. Bordawekar, I. Pechtchanski, and V. Sarkar. XJ: Facilitating XML processing in Java. In *Proceedings of World Wide Web (WWW)*, pages 278–287, May 2005.
13. T. Harris, S. Marlow, S. Peyton-Jones, and M. Herlihy. Composable memory transactions. In *PPoPP '05: Proceedings of the tenth ACM SIGPLAN symposium on Principles and practice of parallel programming*, pages 48–60, New York, NY, USA, 2005. ACM Press.
14. R. Lammel and E. Meijer. Revealing the X/O impedence mismatch. `http://homepages.cwi.nl/ ralf/xo-impedance-mismatch`, 2006.
15. S. Loughran and E. Smith. Rethinking the Java SOAP stack. Technical Report HPL-2005-89, HP Labs, HP Laboratories Bristol, May 2005.
16. M. Odersky and M. Zenger. Scalable component abstractions. *SIGPLAN Notices*, 40(10):41–57, 2005.

Net-Centric Computing: The Future of Computers and Networking

Arun K. Somani and Shubhalaxmi Kher

Dependable Computing and Networking Lab
Iowa State University
Ames, Iowa 50011
{arun, shubha}@iastate.edu

Abstract. Futuristic computers will only be thought of in the context of their ubiquitous connectivity. Net-centric computing isn't communications or networking per se, although it certainly includes both. With the changes in the computing and networking environment we need a different paradigm for distributed computing. The area of net-centric computing encompasses the embedded systems but is much larger in scope. In the near future, many hardware devices will be interconnected in large and highly dynamic distributed systems, using standard communication protocols on standard physical links [1] [3] [5] [6] [7] [8]. Such types of systems exist only for computers interconnected by TCP/IP networks, or for hardware devices interconnected in small areas by using specific protocols for the physical link, such as Bluetooth, Ethernet or X-10.

In this paper we review Net-Centric computing in the perspective of Hardware requirements, Embedded system design, Middleware, Control, IT and provide an insight into the issues and challenges ahead.

1 Introduction

The underlying principle of Net-Centric Computing (NCC) is a distributed environment where applications and data are downloaded from servers and exchanged with peers across a network on as as-needed basis. NCC is an ongoing area of interest to a wide-variety of software engineering researchers and practitioners, in part because it is an enabling technology for modern distributed systems (e.g., Web applications) [4]. As such, knowledge of NCC is essential requirement in architecting, constructing, and evolving the complex software systems that power today's enterprizes.

The widespread interest in Ubiquitous and Pervasive Computing systems will give a new impulse to Net-Centric Computing (NCC) systems. Solutions such as OSGi have the capability to become the foundation of a new middleware for NCC systems and offer the possibility to browse the physical world in the same way as the web content is browsed.

The activities for Net-Centric Technology consists of three layers.

- The Information Service Layer pertains to the abstraction of objects. The focus here is on the quality, security, auditability and control.

S. Madria et al. (Eds.): ICDCIT 2006, LNCS 4317, pp. 14–26, 2006.
© Springer-Verlag Berlin Heidelberg 2006

- The Network Service Layer pertains to all aspects of communications, particularly configuration, fault management, security, performance and accounting.
- The Component Control Layer pertains to the development, acquisition and implementation of components that form the infrastructure for distributed computing.

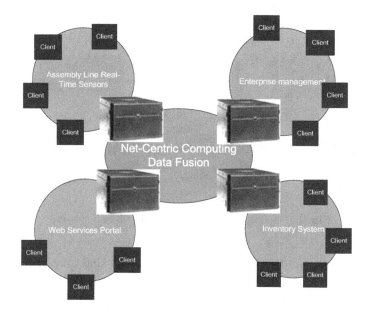

Fig. 1. Net-centric Computing and Data Fusion

Figure 1 shows the environment for Net-centric computing. For several years, business and technology observers have been talking about the major changes being brought by universal networking capabilities, such as the Internet. Today's technology solutions are what we can call "convergence" solutions: They represent the convergence of computing power, communications capability and content the information, data or knowledge that forms the "stuff" of the solution. At the heart of the solution, however, is the network. Hence the term network-centric, or "netcentric," solution is used. Net-centric computing refers to an emerging technology architecture and an evolutionary stage of client/server computing. The common architecture of netcentric computing supports access to information through multiple electronic channels (personal and network computers, cell phones, kiosks, telephones, etc.). This information is made accessible to many more users not just an organization's workforce but also its customers, suppliers and business partners through technologies that employ open, commonly accepted standards (Internet, Java, Web browsers and so forth).

Figure 2 shows how Distributed computing is different than Net-Centric computing. Netcentric computing is a common architecture built on open standards

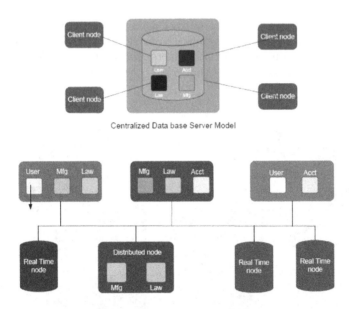

Fig. 2. Net-centric computing vs Distributed systems

that supports many different ways for many different kinds of people to collaborate and to reach many different information sources [2]. The evolutionary yet radical nature of netcentric solutions can be seen in many of those already implemented. The robust architecture of netcentric computing has the ability to evolve as new channels and functionality become available. Netcentric computing links technological capability and strategic opportunity, helping to open today's new markets and provide the flexibility to meet tomorrow's business challenges. It can also add complexity and risk to information systems. Net-centric computing is like a box. Open the box; inside, there is technology that seems both familiar and new. Something that will do great things for a business. It can enable true e-commerce capabilities. For any business/organization, it can link customers, suppliers, employees and other business partners to its information systems, and thus to its entire business anywhere in the world. It can maximize the flow of information inside any organization, allowing people to share data and knowledge, to collaborate more effectively. This will, in fact, redefine the industry and create new markets.

It is easy to recognize pieces of it: your client/server system, your legacy applications, your network. Yet, taken as a whole, it represents a new kind of technology infrastructure for your organization that links, perhaps for the first time, technology capability with new business opportunity. When you read or hear today of companies opening up new markets, engaging in e-commerce, delighting their customers with unprecedented levels of services or streamlining their internal processes by encouraging the sharing of information and data, that's netcentric computing in action.

1.1   Flow Computing Model

In this context of net-centric computing we propose a new distributed computing paradigm [8] called flow computing in which nodes comprising the internet can be dynamically contracted to perform the required computing tasks. With the increasing computing capabilities of the router nodes or by specifically deploying additional computing facilities, some of the end hosts (client or server) computation may be delegated to the intermediate nodes (INs). The instructions about how to do the processing may be provided by the end hosts. Thus internet is converted into a large distributed computing environment, we call this paradigm flow Computing because data are processed on the fly enroute from source to destination. Only a few nodes may be equipped to support such Flow computing. Figure 3 shows a flow computing model.

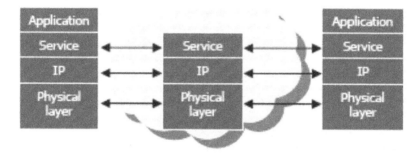

Fig. 3. Flow computing model

Individual nodes may be designed to provide specific or general computing services. To facilitate such a facility, we propose to develop a reliable transport layer protocol, called Intermediate Processing Protocol (IPP) for processing within the internet. The protocol design makes provisions for connection set up handshake, processing capability reservation, intermediate processing, data acknowledgement, buffering and retransmission, flow and congestion control, ordered delivery and security issues.

Flow computing is different than Peer to Peer computing and grid computing environment models where the computing nodes are known in advance with the help of certain services. In our model, the end nodes need not be aware of location of such services and no centralized or distributed directory services are maintained. Figure 4 shows components of a flow computing model. The broader impact of flow computing approach is to allow a large number of different kinds of hosts to be integrated into the internet computing environment and provide ubiquitous services to a large class of small devices and reduce need for large and or centralized servers. Some of the major advantages of flow computing are: full CPU/memory utilization; new business model for ISPs; simplified client and server implementation; support for new multimedia applications for wireless

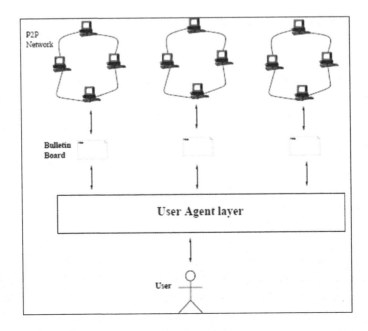

Fig. 4. Components of Flow model

clients; and new distributed computing paradigm by way of merging/processing data as it flows from various sources to clients.

In a flow computing model, application flows are meaningfully processed to satisfy end host requirements, and efficiently utilized for computing and network resources. Due to the support for intermediate processing this model would be a generalization of other distributed object models like grid computing, peer to peer computing and client server computing. Our flow computing model has the advantages of both P2P and grid computing as it enables data sharing and processing by treating the entire network as a reliable computing engine, including the intermediate routers or enhanced routers with little additional overhead.

Flow computing proposes to use a new transport layer protocol that seamlessly integrates with the widely used TCP/IP protocol suite. The idea in this work stems from the observation that there is an increasing number of devices with varying computing powers and energy sources being connected to the internet. End hosts may or may not be able to perform all the computations whose results are of interest to them due to unavailability of computation power or need for energy conservation. The data source may not be able to provide such computing services, but may get overloaded due to a large number of such clients. Moreover in certain environment all raw data may be stored on large data repositories such as disk farms that may be optimized towards streaming data from disks to networks to be processed by servers located elsewhere. Related is a scenario where data needed for processing may be distributed such as sensor networks. In such cases it would be more prudent to assign computing task to some intermediate node rather than to a single source/server.

One such environment is Enterprize computing, with a secured networking environment; Consider a scenario an executive of a company would like to view total sales data for a specific product line on his cell phone. The computation needs to obtain raw sales data from the data server and after processing display the result. If the data server does not have the needed processing power and cell phone would not like to manage this data, who should provide the service? Our goal is that either the cell phone host on the forward path or the data server on the backward path during establishment of connection should have contracted this service out to some intermediate node who is a willing participant and has idle capacity available at the time the request is being processed.

2   Aspects of Net-Centric Computing

2.1   Architectures

CompuP2P. CompuP2P given in [7] is an architecture for sharing of computing resources in Internet-scale computational grids. It provides idle resources, such as processing power, memory storage etc., of computing engines that have Internet connectivity and are under-utilized most of the time to user applications that might require them. It achieves this objective by allowing owners of idle resources to sell to those who need them. Thus applications, like scientific simulations and data mining, requiring large processing requirements, can tremendously benefit from potentially unlimited availability of compute power provided by CompuP2P. Likewise, database applications, requiring huge storage, can harness the disk capacity of virtually millions of machines connected to the Internet.

Fig. 5. ComP2P architecture

CompuP2P shown in Figure5 uses light-weight protocols for building and operating dynamic computing resource markets, where sellers and buyers can come together to negotiate transfer (usage) of resources from seller to buyer nodes. To meet the resource sharing requirements, the lookup of such markets and the availability of resources are robust even in the face of several nodes entering or leaving the network at the same time. CompuP2P uses ideas from game theory and microeconomics to devise incentive-based schemes for motivating users to share their idle computing resources with each other. The trading and pricing of resources is done in a completely distributed manner without requiring any trusted centralized authority to oversee the transactions.

Pricing Structure and Incentive Based Allocation. Pricing in CompuP2P markets, where buyers (clients) pay to sellers (computing nodes) and intermediaries (MOs) that facilitate the transactions, can be a non-trivial issue. Unlike in real-world, there likely will be no well established protocols (government rules and policies), and institutions and infrastructure (such as stock exchanges) in an Internet-scale computational grid setting that can govern the parameters (such as the price charged, the place of occurrence etc.) of the transactions. Due to such constraints several non-trivial issues need to be addressed - setting resource prices, determining payoffs to intermediate, preventing cheating etc. We again borrow ideas from game theory and microeconomics for developing appropriate pricing strategies, which addresses the above issues to some extent. Utilizing the model that a transaction involving the trading of resources can be modeled as a one-shot game and using the results from game theory (the classical Prisoner's dilemma problem), we observe that long-term collusion among resource sellers (and MO) is unlikely to occur. In one-shot Prisoner's dilemma game, non-cooperation is the only unique Nash equilibrium strategy for the players. In fact, the model of Bertrand oligopoly suggests that sellers (irrespective of their number) would not be able to charge more than their marginal costs (MCs) for selling their resources. In Bertrand oligopoly sellers strategy is to set "prices" (as opposed to "outputs" in Cournot oligopoly) and is thus more reasonable to assume in the context of CompuP2P. This is because in CompuP2P all the sellers in a market sell the same kind (volume) of a resource. As a consequence, sellers (irrespective of how many there are in a market) in CompuP2P set prices equal to their marginal costs only.

2.2   Embedded Systems Design

Embedded designers were among the first to pick up on the significance of the Internet and the World Wide Web and start using them. This is one of the largest markets in the embedded arena is, of course, networking and data communications. The nature of this market is changing from the use of a computer as a data processing or control engine to a data flow engine, moving data from "in here" to "out there" and vice versa. Combined with the higher bandwidths and the large numbers of users, the network processors embedded in the router-and-switch fabric are essentially multiprocessor applications, not loosely coupled, but tightly coupled. This situation is causing some developers to worry about parallel programming issues - a can of worms with no satisfactory methodologies that are widely accepted.

2.3   Middleware Technology in Net-Centric Computing

One of the key components of NCC technology is middleware. It is the "glue" that connects disparate components in a heterogeneous environment across a network. Middleware is a well-established research topic in software engineering. In an NCC context, middleware functionality informs the decisions made by all stakeholders, since applications must be engineered within the constraints of the available technology [6].

As NCC applications become more pervasive, the need for new developments in middleware technology becomes apparent. The unique requirements of today's NCC operational environment, such as the need to incorporate security policies across all aspects of the system, expose gaps in current offerings. The identification of such shortcomings in turn provides opportunities for novel developments in the area in the coming years.

2.4   Control Objective for Net-Centric Technology

As distributed computing systems grow to hundreds or even thousands of devices and similar or greater magnitude of software components it will become increasingly difficult to manage them without appropriate support tools and frameworks. For example: In distributed applications, single transactions may span multiple hosts and multiple processes. However, applications must still guarantee the atomic integrity of transactions (that is, a unit of work). In distributed environments, both users and their applications can move. Users can access applications from just about anywhere and system administrators enjoy the luxury of moving applications/components among various machines based on such factors as load, hardware failure, performance and others. Applications no longer deal with only simple data types. Current technologies allow system designers to incorporate enhanced objects such as video, audio and multimedia into even the most basic applications [3].

3   Role of Net-Centric Computing in Enterprize Integration Architectures

Enterprize integration has the goal of providing timely and accurate exchange of consistent information between business functions to support both strategic and tactical business goals in a seemingly seamless manner [9]. Although there have been some success, in general there is no clear roadmap for how to achieve effective integration of information systems [5]. Full scale integration efforts tend to focus on integration across an organization's information systems, or in B2B applications between organizations. However, smaller scale efforts can focus on integration at different levels of granularity.

3.1   Net-Centric Scenarios

Example 1. NBTel, the telecommunications provider for the Canadian province of New Brunswick, had an existing customer self-service application, installed in the early 1990s, that enabled customers to conduct transactions and make inquiries by phone. As NBTel moved to enhance this application, netcentric computing allowed the organization to evolve this approach to a richer multimedia environment through interactive channels, including the Internet. Today, NBTel's Interactive Phone Store gives customers access, through their personal computers, to fully interactive service over the organization's broadband and Internet network. Interactive television access is also planned. Rockwell Collins has extensive domain knowledge in net-centric computing due to its participation, along with General Dynamics, in developing the Integrated Computer System (ICS) for the U.S. Army's Future Combat System (FCS).

Today's netcentric solutions would not be possible if we were still in the era of proprietary architectures and incompatible technologies, software and standards. The common architecture of the netcentric approach solves a number of information technology issues, such as systems interoperability, and provides the benefits of moving to an open computing environment and common standards, linking everything between the desktop and the Internet. The benefits of this openness can be seen in most netcentric solutions today.

Example 2. Commerzbank, the fourth largest bank in Germany. Commerzbank wanted to push the technology envelope in order to reach a younger, more profitable customer base without incurring the costs of a branch delivery system. Its solution: COMLINE, a "virtual" bank subsidiary designed to attract new, high-income customers between the ages of 25 and 50 with a range of direct-banking services never before offered. The new bank needed to provide a unique combination of flexibility, capability and convenience. This is possible with Net-centric computing.

Outside the enterprise, the reach of netcentric computing allows an organization to link its employees, customers, suppliers, partners and others, irrespective of time, location or device. But reach applies inside the enterprise as well among its departments and business units, at home and around the world. It enables the sharing of information and allows everyone to tap into the organization's brain power.

An important netcentric initiative that extends internal reach has come from Motorola. Motorola designed a self-service network, or Enet, that gives its employees 24-hour access to basic information. This helps them put HR personnel to address higher value added work. This network is accessible through the organization's intranet, as well as through stand-alone corporate kiosks. It not only provides information on demand but is integrated with the organization's human resources system as well.

Netcentric computing is today's enabler of major business capabilities. Perhaps for the first time in the history of computing, people are defining an evolutionary stage in the industry, not just by pointing to a new set of hardware components, but by telling stories about what their business is now capable of doing, and about the value being derived from netcentric solutions.

Example 3. A US-based utility that manages a pool of retail electricity suppliers for all or parts of six states. The utility today handles almost 8 percent of the electric power in the United States. As a result of deregulation, electricity customers were given a choice of electricity provider. This meant that the industry needed to think in new ways about how to schedule and provide service. The utility's business strategy was to operate the first bid-based regional energy market in the United States. The netcentric technology enabler for that business strategy was the first Internet-based retail contract and scheduling application in the United States electric power industry.

The system enables participants to buy and sell energy, schedule bilateral transactions and reserve transmission service; it also provides accounting and billing services for these transactions. The system allows more than 30 retail electricity suppliers to manage their energy services to residents in their area. The utility has since become one of the most liquid and active energy markets in the United States.

Example 4. Figure 6 gives an example scenario to show how a long distance customer can get connected to a manufacturer/vendor in a Net-centric computing to order custom made cars. Accenture has been working on a systems development project for a large automotive manufacturer. They recently reviewed the technical infrastructure for a centralized system that was to be integrated with local dealer systems and asked the organization executives, What if, at some point in the future one or two years from now the way in which the business is transacted changes? What if, for example, somebody walked into a dealership on a Thursday or Friday, interacted with the system (that is, created a customized car, selected the color, looked at the finance or lease package) but then said, "I want to go away and think about this for the weekend." Then suppose the organization had a 24-hour call center. That same customer could call and, by speaking to a customer-service representative about the details of the package designed at the dealership, talk through the deal on a Sunday afternoon. Right there, the customer could make some adjustments and close the transaction over the phone. Of course, being a 24-hour operation, the call center could be based anywhere in the world.

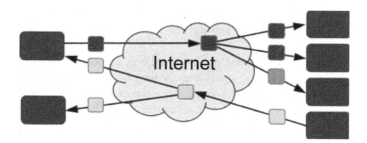

Fig. 6. Scenario for Automotive Manufacturers

This would be a new way to buy cars not dramatically different, perhaps, but it would have a big impact on the technology infrastructure of the business. All of a sudden, the entire context of the transaction from the showroom conversation on Thursday or Friday would have to be made available to a call center three days later, potentially on the other side of the world.

We asked our client if this scenario was within the realm of possibility. It was. Would there be a significant impact on the infrastructure if we did not design and build in that potential capability today? Yes. Netcentric architectures provide the flexibility and resiliency required in such scenarios.

Features of Netcentric Computing:

- It creates a more resilient architecture that evolves and extends over time.
- It enables companies to transition their legacy systems into a new environment.

Flexibility also becomes the key to how an organization plans for developing future netcentric capabilities. A critical point for companies today is that even if their current business solutions do not involve netcentric computing, it is vital to maintain the flexibility in technical architecture that will permit a move to netcentric computing in the future.

4   Risks and Challenges

Hardware Complexity

Netcentric computing presents new complexities and risks involved in building netcentric infrastructures. If we view it in the context of mainframes where we may have had three or four major infrastructure components: the database, the CPU, a network and some terminals. Two or three suppliers provided all those major components, so choices were limited. Also that there were only six to eight combinations of all components and vendors, the complexity was manageable. During the client/server computing, infrastructure components increased from five six to some more : workstation, workgroup server, enterprise server, a database and a couple of networks. Each had five to seven possible suppliers. So instead of six to eight combinations, we were looking at up to 40. The size of the problem was bigger, and the nature of the computing solution got more complex.

With netcentric or flow computing, if we add only 20 percent more components and, let us say, 30 percent more providers, we may have between 40 combinations to up to 100. It is more exciting to see that the components and providers change practically every day. The vendors are numerous, and the products are younger the "average version number" is much lower.

This complexity can be managed through the use of a proven architectural approach. Experience from client/server development clearly demonstrated that technology architectures can isolate and manage risk. They permit the development of consistent, reliable and high-quality applications that are also better integrated within and between an organization's business units. The netcentric architecture framework again, an evolution from client/server architectures helps neutralize technology complexity by managing the explosion of new technologies.

Component	Net-Centric Computing	Traditional Client-Server computing
Thin Client Devices	10	-
Middleware(metal Frame)	1(with 10 user license)(1 server)	-
Number of Processors	A dual processor(server)	10(client)1(server)
Hard disks	A @12 GB server	@2GB(10 clients)+1 Server
Memory	1(144Mb RAM)(server)	@32MbRAM(10 clients)+1 server
Disk Drives	1(server)	10 Client+1 server
Monitor, keyboard, mouse	10 clients + 1server	10 Client+1 server

Fig. 7. Hardware requirements in Net-Centric Computing

The framework has been successfully used by hundreds of companies to deliver new business capabilities across a wide range of industries and environments.

In a net centric environment the challenges include performance, security, reliability, and usability. The vendor claims that it is faster, cheaper and easier. Our framework accomplishes two major things. First, it helps manage the development of the netcentric solution, serving as a guide and a completeness check, allowing one to assess more easily the types of services and products needed for any specific situation. Second, the framework is a logical representation of the environment in which the business problem will be addressed by the computing solution. It is a tool that allows development teams to break the problem down into component parts and reassemble a solution.

5   Conclusions

From a technical point of view, netcentric computing is breaking down the hierarchy of command and control that was implicit in earlier technologies. It is moving intelligence to the edge of the network and flattening the hierarchy, while it creates new strategic opportunities. Today's opportunity, however, is tomorrow's necessity. Innovators in netcentric computing today can redefine their markets and seize the advantage. Tomorrow's imitators will be forced toward these new technologies simply to stay in business.

In all, the capabilities of net-centric computing provide greater flexibility, enabling companies to rapidly adopt new technology to support innovative marketplace solutions.

References

1. Bernard Conrad Cole,The Emergence of Net-Centric Computing: Network Computers, Internet Appliances, and Connected PCs,Prentice Hall (January 1999)(Hardcover).

2. Hugh W. Ryan et.al, Netcentric Computing: Computing, Communications, and Knowledge, Auerbach Publications (1997).
3. ISACA(Society that leads in IT security, assurance and control); Control objective for Net-Centric Technology, IEEE Press.
4. STEP 2005 workshop on Net-Centric Computing (ncc2005).
5. Dennis Smith, and Scott Tilley; On the role of Net-Centric Computing in enterprise Integration Architectures, ASERC Software Architecture workshop 2001.
6. Thierry Bodhuin, Italy Gerardo Canfora, Italy Rosa Preziosi,an Italy Maria Tortorella, "Open Challenges in Ubiquitous and Net-Centric Computing Middleware," 13th international workshop on engineering and practice (STEP O5).
7. R. Gupta, and A. K. Somani, "CompuP2P: An Architecture for Sharing of Computing Resources In Peer-to-Peer Networks With Selfish Nodes," In Online Proceedings of Second Workshop on the Economics of Peer-to-Peer Systems, Harvard University, June 2004.
8. Arun K. Somani, "Proposal on Internet as Distributed Computing Environment," personal.
9. Dennis Smith, and Scott Tilley, "On the role of net centric computing in enterprise integration architecture"', ASERC Softaware Workshop 2001.

Optimisation Problems Based on the Maximal Breach Path Measure for Wireless Sensor Network Coverage

Anirvan DuttaGupta[1], Arijit Bishnu[2], and Indranil Sengupta[2]

Department of Computer Science and Engineering
Indian Institute of Technology, Kharagpur - 721302, India
[1] anirvan@cse.iitkgp.ernet.in, [2] {Arijit.Bishnu, isg}@iitkgp.ac.in

Abstract. Coverage is a central issue in the design of wireless sensor networks. There are many measures for coverage, based on what aspect of surveillance quality we wish to address. Designing a network that achieves desired standards in terms of the measure chosen is a non-trivial problem. In this paper we take the *Maximal Breach Path* measure and formulate the sensor-network design problem as a geometric optimisation problem. We present improved polynomial time algorithms for computing the aforesaid measure for a given sensor network. Also, as a first step toward solving the optimisation problem posed in this paper, we present a geometric transformation on a given configuration of sensors that brings the maximal breach to a "local optimal" - in the sense that the resulting *breach* is the best we can get keeping the topology of the starting configuration intact.

1 Introduction

In recent times wireless sensor networks have found wide-ranging practical applications - from forest-fire detection to securing battlefields against enemy infiltration [1]. Coverage and quality of surveillance are of prime importance in the design of these networks. In the forest fire example, for instance, one might want to determine the precise segments where local fires might go undetected. In a battlefield, the sentinels would want to anticipate the movements of a *well-informed* intruder. Both these problems address the notion of *coverage*, which is, broadly speaking, a measure for how well a network of sensors monitors each and every point of the *field* it is designed to protect.

The coverage problem can be viewed from two angles - from the point of view of the *intruder* and that of the *defender*. In the battlefield example, these entities translate to *enemy* and *sentinel* respectively. Given a complete knowledge of the arangements of sensors in the field, the intruder needs to determine the *safest* means of infiltration, i.e., the *weakest* sections of the field. The defender, on the other hand, would like to make things difficult for the intruder *even when the latter is armed with complete information*. In other words, the defender needs to identify and secure the weakest sections of the field. Sections 3 and 4 deal with these two angles.

S. Madria et al. (Eds.): ICDCIT 2006, LNCS 4317, pp. 27–40, 2006.

The main contributions of this paper are: We have posed the coverage problem as an optimisation problem, the solution to which will arm the designer with a tool for building secure sensor networks. We have theoretically derived a procedure that solves this problem partially by finding a local optimum. We have developed upon the geometric and graph-theoretic approach of [1] and proposed two asymptotically efficient, centralised, exact and easy-to-implement algorithms for computing a specific measure of coverage (maximal breach), complete with proofs of correctness and analysis. The first of our algorithms is directly adapted from a maximal breach algorithm presented in [1] and removes two of its flaws: the tacit assumption of integral weights and a complexity figure depending upon the *magnitudes* of weights. We have used *Network Flow* concepts to derive our second algorithm, which is the one of the first polynomial time centralised algorithms for this problem.

The rest of this paper goes as follows: Section 2 introduces *Maximal Breach*, the measure of coverage that acts as the central focus of this paper, followed by the formulation of the optimisation problem. Section 3, which views the coverage problem from the intruder's view-point, presents two algorithms for computing maximal breach. Section 4 presents a procedure that takes the *breach* to a local-optimum and is useful from the defender's point of view. Finally, in Section 5 we provide some pointers to future work.

2   Background and Related Work

The coverage problem is, in general terms: *Given a number of sensors, how to deploy them so as to achieve the maximum degree of coverage at every point on the field.* [5] gives a precise statement of this problem. However, we emphasize this should be viewed as a *class* of problems rather than a single one. Till now we have left the notion of *coverage* deliberately vague. We need *concrete* measures to quantify coverage based on the requirements at hand. k-Coverage, as defined in [5], is one such measure. *k-Barrier-Coverage* [4] is another. In terms of these measures we can formulate optimisation versions of the coverage problem. The number, cost and sensing ranges/angles of the sensors can act as constraints; the objective is to minimise/maximise the measure chosen.

Our measure of interest is defined in [1]. A number of sensors, with identical sensing/transmission radii, are deployed in a unit-square field. The sensors are not directional. To estimate the quality of surveillance a deployment scheme provides to the defender, two measures are proposed - *worst-case* and *best-case* coverage. In what follows, we assume that the intruder knows the exact coordinates of all the sensors and tries to traverse the field from an initial point I to a final point F (Figure 1).

2.1   Worst-Case Coverage

Consider a path P through the field from I to F.

Definition 1. *[Breach] The quantity* breach *is defined as the minimum Euclidean distance from P to any sensor in the field.*

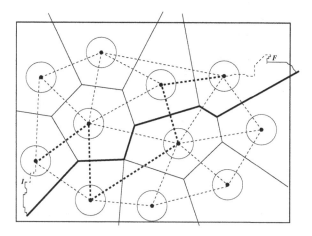

Fig. 1. Maximal Breach and Support Paths. The sensors are depicted as circles with prominent centres. The continuous line segments are the edges of the Voronoi Diagram, and the dashed ones are the edges of the Delaunay triangulation. The segments drawn in bold type signify maximal breach and support paths.

For every point p on P, we measure the distance of p from the nearest sensor, and finally take the *minimum* of all these distances.

Definition 2. *[Maximal Breach Path] Among the infinitely many paths connecting I and F, one that has the* maximum breach value *is called a* maximal breach path, P_B.

From the point of view of the *intruder*, this is the *safest* path to take, because along P_B the distance from the nearest sensor is maximised. But, for the *defender*, along this path, the chances of detecting the intruder are minimum, hence the term worst case. It has been established in [1] that

Theorem 1. *At least one maximal breach path must lie along the edges of a* bounded Voronoi diagram[7] *determined by the sensor nodes (points) and the boundaries of the field.*

The solid bold path in Figure 1 is a maximal breach path.

2.2   Best-Case Coverage

This is, in geometric terms, the dual of the previous measure.

Definition 3. *[Support] The measure* support *for a path P connecting I to F is defined as the maximum Euclidean distance from P to the nearest sensor.*

For every point p on P, we measure the distance of p from the nearest sensor, and finally take the *maximum* of all these distances. Clearly, the chances of detecting an intruder along some path improves when the *support* value for that path is *low*.

Definition 4. *[Maximal Support Path] P_S, the* maximal support path *is defined as the one with the* lowest *value of support among all possible paths.*

For the intruder, this is the worst possible path to take, but for the defender this is the path along which the surveillance quality is the highest. Hence the term *best-case*. The dashed bold path in Figure 1 is a maximal support path.

[1] proposes that at least one maximal support path must lie along the edges of the Delaunay Triangulation [7] of the sensor nodes. (Figure 1). [3] presents a proof for this proposition.

2.3   Optimisation/Decision Versions of the Worst- and Best-Case Coverage Problems

We now frame the following geometric optimisation/decision problems, as promised:

Problem 1. We have N sensors at our disposal. Given a threshold value (upper bound) for *breach*, can we arrive at a deployment scheme, *deterministically*, that satisfies the threshold?

Problem 2. A possibly harder version: Given the breach threshold, can a deployment scheme be determined that minimises the number of sensors used while satisfying the threshold?

The preceding formulation of the coverage problem is concrete, precise and mathematical, and consequently, amenable to algorithmic techniques. To the best of our knowledge, provably correct solutions to Problems 1 and 2 are as yet undiscovered. [1] deals with a close variant: starting from a *random* arrangement they compute the maximal breach and run heuristics that add sensors so as to reduce breach. We present a *partial* solution (Section 4).

3   Algorithms for Computing Maximal Breach

[1] presents a centralised algorithm for computing the maximal breach path, given the coordinates of the sensors within the unit square. A rough description follows:

1. From the Voronoi diagram for the sensor nodes, a weighted, undirected graph (which we shall call henceforth *the associated graph*) G is built: For each Voronoi *vertex*, there is a *node* in the associated graph, and for each Voronoi *edge*, there is an *edge* in the associated graph weighted by a quantity proportional to the minimum distance of any point on the edge to the closest sensor[1].
2. Maximal breach is computed using a combination of binary search and *BFS* on the associated graph. The minimum and maximum edge weights are computed and a search-criterion, *breach_weight* is set to the mid-point of this range. At every iteration,

---

[1] When the line segment joining two sensors S_1, S_2 cut the Voronoi edge they share, the weight is proportional to the length $S_1 S_2$. Otherwise, the weight is proportional to the distance of S_1 to the *nearer* of the two Voronoi edge endpoints.

(a) All edges in the associated graph with weights *greater* than *breach_weight* are dropped.

(b) Through *BFS*, if a path can be found between the nodes corresponding to I and F, the search is continued with *breach_weight* shifted to the mid-point of the interval $[min\_weight, breach\_weight]$. Otherwise, the search is continued with *breach_weight* shifted to the mid-point of $(breach\_weight, max\_weight]$. Observe, however, that binary search is performed on the *range* of weights, rather than the actual weights.

This algorithm has the following difficulties:

1. **Time Complexity.** Pruning of edges and *BFS* run in time linear in the number of nodes and edges of the associated graph. From [6], we know that the latter are $O(N)$. Thus, each search iteration runs in $O(N)$ time. However, since binary search is performed on the range $[min\_weight, max\_weight]$, we might need, in the worst case, $\log C$ iterations, where $C = max\_weight - min\_weight$. This makes the overall complexity of the algorithm, excluding the voronoi diagram construction part, $O(N \log C)$. Thus, the time-complexity is indirectly dependent on the *magnitudes* of weights - the larger the range, the more the runtime, even for topologically identical graphs. This is only a *theoretical* objection, though.

2. **Exact results only for integral weights.** For the same reason, the algorithm finds *exact* value of the maximal breach *only* if the edge weights are all *integral* - but this is an unreasonable assumption, since the weights are derived from euclidean distances.

3.1 A Centralised, Exact, Polynomial-Time Algorithm: *BfsBreach*

A straight-forward modification of the foregoing algorithm removes both the difficulties. Instead of running binary search on the range of edge weights, do it on a sorted list of edge weights. Algorithm 1 describes **BfsBreach**.

For the correctness and time-complexity of Algorithm 1, we state and prove the following

Theorem 2. *Algorithm 1 computes the maximal breach in time* $O(N \log N)$.

Proof. For correctness, it is sufficient to show that

1. If *BFS* succeeds for some value of *candidate*, then the actual value of maximal breach is at least as large as *candidate*. Thus, it make sense to increase our estimate of *candidate* to $(max\_weight - candidate)/2$ for the next iteration.

2. If, on the other hand, *BFS fails* for some value of *candidate*, maximal breach is *strictly less* than *candidate*. Thus, we must carry out the next pruning with the *smaller* value $(candidate - min\_weight)/2$.

For the first part, since *BFS* succeeded, there *is* a path P_1 in the pruned graph between I and F. Let e_1 be the edge in P_1 with the minimum weight. $w(e_1) \geq candidate$, because all edges lighter than *candidate* have been dropped. It follows from Definition 2 that the actual value of maximal breach cannot be less than *candidate*.

For the second part, observe that failure of *BFS* implies that the pruned graph has become disconnected. Thus *all* paths P between I and F *must* have at least one edge e with $w(e) < candidate$. This implies maximal breach is strictly less than *candidate*.

To complete the proof, we observe that there are $O(N)$ edges, and thus binary search entails $O(\log N)$ iterations. In each iteration, we do a pruning ($O(N)$) and a BFS ($O(N)$). This makes the overall complexity $O(N \log N)$.   □

Algorithm 1. BfsBreach.

Input: The associated graph G built from the Voronoi diagram for the sensor locations.

Output: The maximal breach W, and the critical edge e.

1. **Sort.** Sort the edges of G in ascending order of weights and store the results in an array *Edges*.
2. **Initialise.** $lb \leftarrow 0$, $ub \leftarrow Edges.size()$.
3. **repeat**
   (a) $mid \leftarrow (lb + ub)/2$.
   (b) $candidate \leftarrow Edges[mid].weight$.
   (c) **Prune** G. Drop all edges from G that have weight larger than *candidate*. Let G' be the resulting graph.
   (d) Run *BFS* on G' starting from node I. If node F is reachable from I, report *success*, else report *failure*.
   (e) **if** *success* **then** $W \leftarrow candidate$, $e \leftarrow Edges[mid]$, $lb \leftarrow mid + 1$.
       else $ub \leftarrow mid - 1$.
4. **until** lb and ub cross over.
5. **return** W and e.

3.2 Another Fast Centralised Algorithm: *McaBreach*

We start with some standard terminology from *Network Flow* [9].

Definition 5. *In a flow network, given a path P between the source s and sink t, the* bottleneck capacity *of P is defined as the* minimum *capacity among all edges of P.*

Definition 6. *The* maximum bottleneck path *in a flow network is a path with the largest bottleneck capacity among all paths that connect the source s and sink t.*

Definition 7. *The* maximum bottleneck capacity *of a flow network is the bottleneck capacity of its maximum bottleneck path.*

Consider the associated graph G derived from the bounded Voronoi diagram for the sensor locations. If we view G as a *flow network* with edge weights acting as the *capacities* of the links (edges), then it is hard to miss the correspondence between Definitions 2 and 6. Thus:

Observation 1. *The* maximal breach path *for a given sensor configuration is nothing but the* maximum bottleneck path *of the associated graph G derived from the bounded Voronoi diagram, where G is viewed as a flow network with source I, sink F, and edge weights acting as the link capacities.*

Now we propose a greedy algorithm **McaBreach** (Algorithm 2) for computing the maximal breach path from the associated graph G. It basically follows the relaxation step of Dijkstra's shortest path algorithm. The principal merits of this algorithm are:

1. It does not assume integral weights, and its runtime is independent of the range of weights.
2. It is **fast**. With a good implementation e.g. one using Fibonacci heaps [9] - it out-performs Algorithm 1.
3. What makes this algorithm **significantly more useful** than Algorithm 1 is that it computes the actual maximal breach *path* on the fly, at no extra cost in terms of time and space. Algorithm 1 returns only the maximal breach and the critical edge; it does *not* compute the breach path.

Algorithm 2 runs just like Dijkstra's algorithm. The node set V of G is partitioned into S and $V - S$, where at any point of time, S contains all the nodes that have been relaxed - the maximum bottleneck path from I to any node u in S is known exactly. At every iteration, a new node j is picked from $V - S$ with the highest bottleneck capacity, and, if it so happens that via j, the bottleneck of some adjacent node u improves, $bottleneck[u]$ is updated. For justification, we turn to the following recursive relations. Figure 2 shows a flow network along with the bottleneck capacities of all the nodes computed from the designated source node.

1. $bottleneck[I] = 0$
2. Let u be a node adjacent to I such that for any other adjacent node x, $w(I, u) \geq w(I, x)$. Then $bottleneck[u] = w(I, u)$
3. Let u and v be adjacent nodes. The bottleneck of v can be improved via u as follows:
$$bottleneck[v] = MAX(bottleneck[v], MIN(bottleneck[u], w(u, v)))$$

Here, I denotes the source node, and $bottleneck[u]$ denotes the best known estimate of the maximum bottleneck capacity of node u over all paths from I.

The proof of correctness Algorithm 2 mirrors that of Dijkstra's shortest path algorithm.

Lemma 1. *At the end of any iteration, S, the set of relaxed nodes has the property that the maximum bottleneck capacity from I to any node in S is correctly known and does not change henceforth.*

Proof. The loop invariant is in force at the end of the first iteration, because at this point $S = I$ and $bottleneck[I] = 0$, which is correct by definition.

The invariant also holds at the end of the second iteration. Note that, after iteration 1, all nodes u with direct edges from I were marked with $bottleneck[]$ estimates equal to $w(I, u)$. Suppose node v is picked, which implies $bottleneck[v] \geq bottleneck[u]$ $\forall u$ adjacent to I. Suppose $bottleneck[v]$ is not the correct (final) maximum bottleneck for node v. Then, there must exist some other path P from I to v, such that $bottleneck(P) > bottleneck[v]$. Since one of the other nodes adjacent to I, say u, must lie on P, this implies $bottleneck[u] \geq bottleneck(P) > bottleneck[v]$ - a contradiction.

Algorithm 2. McaBreach.

Input: The associated graph G.
Output: The maximal breach W, the critical edge e and the *maximal breach path P*.
Variables: The following *vectors* are used:

- $bottleneck[j]$: stores the maximum bottleneck over all paths from the source to node j;
- $isRelaxed[j]$: flags whether node j has been relaxed;
- $path[j]$: stores the predecessor of node j in the maximum bottleneck path from the source to j;
- $critEdge[j]$: stores the critical edge among all paths from the source to node j.

1. **Initialise.** In what follows I and F will denote the graph nodes corresponding to points I and F respectively. Set all elements of $bottleneck[]$ and $path[]$ to *unassigned*, *isRelaxed* to $false$ and $critEdge[]$ to *unassigned*.
2. $path[I] \leftarrow I$, $bottleneck[I] \leftarrow 0$.
3. $critEdge[I] \leftarrow (I, I)$;
   forall nodes j *adjacent to* I, $critEdge[j] \leftarrow (I, j)$.
4. **repeat**
   (a) Pick a node, j, that is *un-relaxed* and has the maximum $bottleneck[]$ value among all un-relaxed nodes[2]. $isRelaxed[j] \leftarrow true$.
   (b) **forall** *un-relaxed* nodes u adjacent to j **do**
      i. **if** j is the source node I **then** $potentialBottleneck \leftarrow w(j, I)$.
      ii. **else** $potentialBottleneck \leftarrow MINIMUM(bottleneck[j], w(j, u))$.
      iii. **endif**
      iv. **if** $potentialBottleneck > bottleneck[u]$ **then** update $bottleneck[u]$:
         A. $bottleneck[u] \leftarrow potentialBottleneck$;
         B. $path[u] \leftarrow j$;
         C. **if** $w(j, u) > potentialBottleneck$ **then** $critEdge[u] \leftarrow critEdge[j]$ **else** $critEdge[u] \leftarrow (j, u)$.
      v. **endif**
   (c) **end for**.
5. **until** *all* nodes have been relaxed.
6. Reconstruct the maximal breach path P from I to F from the predecessor array $path[]$.
7. $W \leftarrow bottleneck[F]$, $e \leftarrow critEdge[F]$.
8. **return** W, e and P.

Suppose the loop invariant holds at the end of the kth iteration, and during the $(k+1)$th iteration, node v is picked. Suppose, again, that $bottleneck[v]$ is *not* the maximum bottleneck for v and there exists an alternate path P from I to v that satisfies $bottleneck(P) > bottleneck[v]$. Let x be the first node from $V - S$ that lies on P. Since $bottleneck[x] \geq bottleneck(P) > bottleneck[v]$, node x should have been picked instead of v - a contradiction. □

Theorem 3. *Algorithm 2 computes the maximal breach path in $N \log N$ time.*

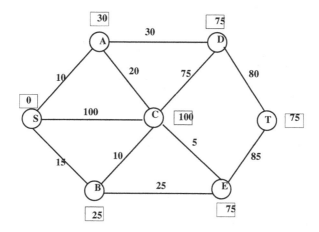

Fig. 2. Maximum Bottleneck Capacity. S is the source, so $bottleneck[S] = 0$. (S, C) has the highest capacity among all links incident on S; so $bottleneck[S] = 100$. $bottleneck[B] = 25$ because the maximum bottleneck path from S to B is S, C, D, T, E, B.

Proof. It is sufficient to prove that Algorithm 2 correctly computes the maximum bottleneck capacity from source I to sink F. First, the algorithm *does* terminate, because exactly one node is relaxed at every iteration, and we run the algorithm only as long as there is an un-relaxed node. Thus, by the loop invariant proved in Lemma 1, the maximal breach path from I to F is known when the algorithm terminates.

The complexity of this algorithm is the same as that of Dijkstra's shortest path algorithm - $O(|V| \log |V| + |E|)$ with a Fibonacci heap implementation [9] - which translates to $O(N \log N)$ here. □

3.3   A Note on the Implementation

There is one small, but significant, aspect in which our implementation of the foregoing algorithms differs from that of [1]. Consider the scenario of Figure 3(a), where the sensors are clustered near the centre of the field. An intruder with knowledge of these coordinates would never walk along the Voronoi edges in this case - he would rather walk right, and then up, along the boundary of the field, in order to maximise his distance from any of the sensors. This illustrates a special case in which the maximal breach path does *not* lie along Voronoi edges. [1] fails to consider, or at least mention, this special case. Our implementation takes care of this - along with the Voronoi edges, we insert edges into the associated graph corresponding to the segments on the bounding box that are created by intersections with Voronoi edges. Figure 3(b) depicts a general scenario where the sections of the maximal breach path comprise a mix of Voronoi edges and segments on the bounding box. Also, we have always taken $I = (0, 0)$ and $F = (1, 1)$.

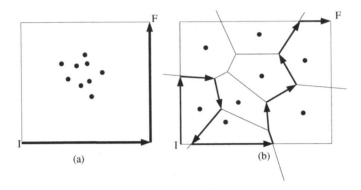

Fig. 3. (a) Sensors clustered near the centre. The intruder won't walk along the Voronoi edges at all. **(b) A more general scenario.** The maximal breach path lies along the Voronoi edges as well as on sections of the bounding box.

3.4   Experimental Data

Table 1 shows a comparison of the running times (in μsecs) of Algorithms 1 and 2 for random configurations of 25, 50, 75 and 100 sensors respectively. Because of the integral weights problem of the original algorithm of [1], we do not compare it directly with Algorithm 2. We have used the *LEDA* [8] package throughout our programmes. The data corroborates our claim that the latter algorithm outperforms the former, with the added feature of computing the maximal breach *path* at no extra cost.

Table 1. A Comparison of the Running Times of Algorithms 1 and 2. All figures are in μseconds.

# Sensors	CPU Time of Algorithm 1	CPU Time of Algorithm 2	% Gain
25	349308	192398	44.9
25	366147	40268	89.0
25	223421	185185	17.1
50	1243582	802282	35.5
50	738003	482315	34.6
50	1252359	478352	61.8
75	2297251	1098142	52.2
75	2016794	1065805	47.4
75	2118170	1214090	42.7
100	3118262	2005446	35.7
100	3107053	1294002	58.4
100	3251317	3408833	−4.8
100	3058631	681152	77.7
100	3388012	2399938	29.2

4 Tightening an Existing Configuration Without Disturbing the Topology

Suppose we are given a random arrangement of a number of sensors over the square field. Refer to Figure 4. Keeping the topology of this configuration intact, how far can we reduce the maximal breach value? This is the question we set out to answer in this section. *topology* in this context refers to the adjacency relationships between pairs of sensors as defined by the edges Voronoi Diagram with the sensor locations as point set. The local perturbation we are going to apply will *not* alter the Voronoi edges: pairs of nodes that shared an edge *before* the perturbation will still share an edge *after* it is applied.

We start with an assumption:

Assumption 1. *In the point set defined by the sensor locations, no three points are collinear, no four points cocircular.*

Suppose the sensors S_1 and S_2 are brought just a bit closer to each other along the line joining them. We are about to put an upper bound on the distance by which each sensor can be moved. Since the only points that move are S_1 and S_2 and *all* other sensors remain static, the following observation is true:

Observation 2. *When two sensors (sharing a Voronoi edge) are moved closer along the straight line joining them by a small distance, the only Voronoi polygons that get affected are the ones bordering upon the Voronoi polygons of the sensors moved.*

We know that the average number of edges per Voronoi face is strictly less than 6 [6]. In other words the average number of faces neighbouring upon any given face is less than 6. This, together with Observation 2, implies that less than 12 Voronoi faces are affected when the sensors across the critical edge are moved towards each other along the straight line joining them. This leads us to the following result.

Theorem 4. *The expected combinatorial complexity of the structure affected by our local perturbation is $O(1)$.*

From Assumption 1, we infer that any maximum empty circle encloses at most 3 points [6]. Consider the two maximum empty circles, C_1 and C_2, passing through S_1 and S_2 (the sensors flanking the critical edge AB). The next result follows from Figure 5.

Observation 3. *Due to our local perturbation, the two maximum empty circles containing the sensors in question strictly reduce in size.*

But since

a. The union of *Delaunay Triangles* of a point set covers the convex hull of the point set; and,
b. Each maximum empty circle circumscribes the corresponding Delaunay triangle (*empty circle property* of Delaunay triangles);

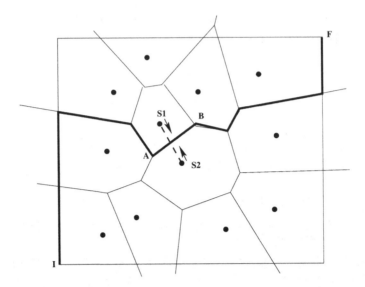

Fig. 4. Tightening a configuration locally. Given an arbitrary configuration of sensors, the Voronoi Diagram is drawn and the maximal breach path is computed. AB is the critical edge, $S1$ and $S2$ are the corresponding sensors. If we bring $S1$ and $S2$ nearer, the maximal breach will go down, but only upto a certain point.

we can conclude that the maximum empty circles *cover* [10] the convex hull of the sensor locations. Thus, if C_1 and C_2 shrink, there should be a point when the neighbouring empty circles must *grow* to fill up the holes left by the two shrinking circles. But the neighbouring circles can only grow to the extent possible without enclosing a fourth site point. This in turn places a bound on the extent to which

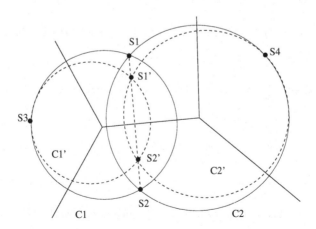

Fig. 5. Shrinking maximum empty circles. When S_1 and S_2 are moved closer, the maximum empty circles C_1 and C_2 shrink (dashed circles C_1' and C_2').

the circles C_1 and C_2 can shrink, and consequently, a bound on the distance by which S_1 and S_2 can be shifted.

However, this is not the only force that limits the extent of our local perturbation. Recall that the maximal breach path P has the property that the weight of the *lightest* edge along P is greater than or equal to the weight of the lightest edge of any other path P' connecting I and F. Arbitrary reduction of this weight will merely alter the maximal breach path. Let P_s be the path with the second highest breach value, W_s (W being the current maximal breach). The distance between the critical pair can be reduced only by the amount $W - W_s$; further reduction will make P_s the new maximal breach path.

The foregoing discussion suggests procedure **LocallyPeturb** (Algorithm 3) for arriving at a locally tight and topologically intact configuration, given an arbitrary configuration of sensors.

The check in line 6(c) can be done in linear time: just iterate through the Voronoi edges and check whether the adjacent site-pairs are the same as before.

Algorithm 3. LocallyPerturb.

Input: An arbitrary configuration of sensors.
Output: A locally tight configuration.

1. Using Algorithm 2, compute the maximal breach path P, the critical edge e and the maximal breach value (same as the weight of e) W.
2. Let W_{min} be the weight of the lighest edge in the associated graph. Update the weight of e to a value $W' < W_{min}$.
3. Run Algorithm 2 on the modified graph. This will return the second maximal breach path P_s, and correspondingly e_s and W_s.
4. Let $\Delta = W - W_s$.
5. Let K = maximum number of iterations and $\delta = \Delta/K$.
6. **while** $numIterations \leq K$ **do**
   (a) Reduce the distance between S_1 and S_2 by δ.
   (b) Recompute the Voronoi diagram.
   (c) **if** topology is altered **then** *STOP*.
   (d) **else** Increment $numIterations$; **goto** Step 6.
7. **end while**

---

5   Conclusion

In this paper we have examined the coverage problem of wireless sensor networks from two angles - those of the intruder and the defender. We have given a precise formulation in the form of a geometric optimisation problem with a useful coverage measure as the objective function. We have presented efficient algorithms for computing the objective function. We have also derived a transformation that brings the objective function to a local minimum. But we need to investigate into the hardness of this problem and find efficient algorithms that solve this problem exactly or approximately, as the case may be.

References

1. Megerian, S., Koushanfar, F., Potkonjak, M., Srivastava, M.B.; *Worst and Best-Case Coverage in Sensor Networks*; IEEE Transactions on Mobile Computing, vol.4, no.1, pp. 84- 92, Jan.-Feb. 2005. [3]

2. S. Meguerdichian, F. Koushanfar, M. Potkonjak, M.B. Srivastava; *Coverage Problems in Wireless Ad-hoc Sensor Networks*; April, 2001; Proceedings of the 20th Annual Joint Conference of the IEEE Computer and Communications Societies, IEEE INFOCOM 2001.

3. Xiang-Yang Li, Peng-Jun Wan, Frieder, O.; *Coverage in Wireless Ad-hoc oc Sensor Networks*; IEEE Transactions on Computers, vol.52, no.6, pp. 53- 763, June 2003.

4. Santosh Kumar, Ten H. Lai, Anish Arora; *Barrier Coverage with Wireless Sensors*; August 2005; Proceedings of the 11th annual international conference on Mobile computing and networking, MobiCom 2005.

5. Chi-Fu Huang, Yu-Chee Tseng; *The Coverage Problem in Wireless Sensor Networks*; September 2003; Proceedings of the 2nd ACM international conference on Wireless sensor networks and applications.

6. M. de Berg, M. Van Kreveld, M. Overmars, O. Schwarzkopf; *Computational Geometry Algorithms and Applications*; Springer-Verlag, 1997.

7. F. Aurenhammer; *Voronoi Diagrams - A Survey of a Fundamental Geometric Data Structure*; ACM Computing Surveys, Vol. 23, No. 3, September 1991.

8. K. Mehlhorn, S. Näher; *The LEDA Platform of Combinatorial and Geometric Computing*; Cambridge University Press, 1999.

9. T.H. Cormen, C.E. Leiserson, R.L. Rivest, C. Stein; *Introduction to Algorithms, 2nd Edition*; MIT Press, 2001.

10. H. Melissen; *Packing and Covering with Circles*; Ph.D. thesis, University of Utrecht, 1997.

---

[3] Actually, there are two versions of this paper - a 2001 conference paper [2] and a 2005 enhanced journal paper [1]. [3] refers to [2].

Energy-Aware Improved Directed Diffusion Algorithm for Area Event Monitoring in Wireless Sensor Network

Bin Guo, Zhe Li, and Dan Li

Institute of Telecommunications and Information Systems, College of Information
Science & Engineering, Northeastern University, ShenYang, P.R. China 110004
lizhe@mail.neu.edu.cn

Abstract. In this paper, we devise and evaluate an Energy-aware Improved
Directed Diffusion (EIDD) algorithm for area event monitoring in wireless
sensor network. Through Diffusion of different type interest, a gathering node is
chose to build an aggregate tree to gather and aggregate data in the event area.
Meanwhile, we improve the way using to build the gradient field in original
Directed Diffusion. The new way can find more logical route by taking residual
energy as a key element. The simulation results show that EIDD gains better
energy efficiency, data collection efficiency and lesser transmission delay
compared with original Directed Diffusion.

Keywords: Directed Diffusion; Energy-aware; wireless sensor networks; area
event.

1 Introduction

With the developments of microprocessors and wireless communication technology,
more and more cheap wireless sensor nodes with high-performance can be achieved.
Wireless sensor networks have broad application prospects in the military applications,
environmental monitoring, and medical fields. Sensor nodes are usually powered by
battery, energy is limited. Therefore how to extend the network lifetime is the primary
consideration in the design process of routing [1]

Area events monitoring application is more common in wireless sensor network
implementation [2]. In this kind of application, source nodes usually locate in adjacent
region. Utilizing this feature, we improve the query-based Directed Diffusion routing.
Through Diffusion of different type interest, a gathering node is chose, the gathering
node build an aggregate tree to gather and aggregate data in the event area. Meanwhile,
we improve the way using to build the gradient field in original Directed Diffusion. The
new way can find more logical route by taking residual energy as a key element.

2 Motivation

Directed Diffusion is a query-based routing paradigm [3]. The course of its work is
shown as figure 1. Sink node send out query task through broadcasting interest

S. Madria et al. (Eds.): ICDCIT 2006, LNCS 4317, pp. 41–48, 2006.
© Springer-Verlag Berlin Heidelberg 2006

packets. In the process of diffusion, sensor nodes build up a gradient field between source node and sink. After the sink starts receiving packets with low data rate, it reinforces one particular neighbor in order to obtain data with high data rate. By doing this, one route with high data rate is built. When there are several source nodes, a number of independent paths will be built.

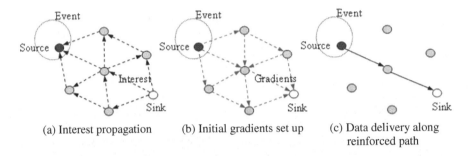

(a) Interest propagation   (b) Initial gradients set up   (c) Data delivery along reinforced path

Fig. 1. Simplified schematic for Directed Diffusion

In area events monitoring application in wireless sensor network implementation, source nodes usually locate in adjacent region. Directed Diffusion algorithm and greedy aggregation tree algorithms all strengthen the path treating source node as a single unit in reinforcement stage [4]. So multipath routing is built, as shown in figure 2(a). Multipath increases the energy consumption of intermediate forwarding nodes. This kind of consumption becomes more when the sink node is away from event area. In such case, if we can gather and aggregate data in the first time, and then transmit back to sink node along single path, as shown in figure 2(b), the energy consumption would be reduced. Based on the above consideration, an energy-aware improved Directed Diffusion algorithm is proposed for area event monitoring.

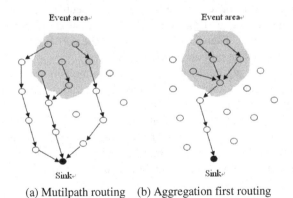

(a) Mutilpath routing   (b) Aggregation first routing

Fig. 2. Different routing schemes for area event monitoring

3   Energy-Aware Improved Directed Diffusion Algorithm

The new improved Directed Diffusion algorithm is still query-based through diffusing interest packets. We have done the improvement in two aspects: built an aggregation tree in event area through the diffusion of new type interest; improve the way how to build the gradient field.

3.1   The Aggregation Tree in Event Area

The improved Directed Diffusion algorithm does not change the query strategy through diffusing interest packets and the naming scheme. On this basis, two types of interest are defined.

Network Interest: this type of interest is created by sink node; it can diffuse throughout the whole network, just like interest in original Directed Diffusion.

Area Interest: this type of interest is translated from network interest by the special source node who receives network interest for the first time. The diffusing hop count and residual energy are inserted into this interest. This type of interest can only diffuse throughout the event area.

The building procedure of the aggregation tree is as follow:

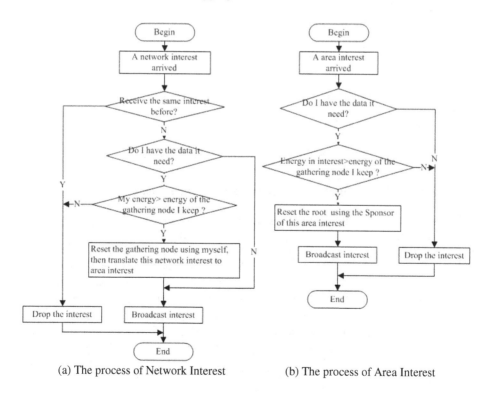

(a) The process of Network Interest   (b) The process of Area Interest

Fig. 3. The building procedure of the aggregation tree

The key issue in the building process of the aggregation tree is how the gathering node is chose. The principle of the selection is that the source nodes those are at the edge of event area, and are of better energy situation become candidates for the gathering node.

Followed the procedure as above, a source node with more energy at the edge of event area becomes the gathering node. As shown in figure 4(a), the first part in bracket is the diffusing hop count of area interest, and second part is residual energy of the node. When the network interest arrives at event area, source nodes 9, 10, 13 receive this interest firstly, then translate into area interest by inserting their own information, and then diffuse their own area interest. Because of the residual energy of node 9 is more, so the area interests of nodes 10,13 is annihilated by the ones of node 9.By doing this, node 9 becomes the gathering node of this event area. According to the diffusing hop count and residual energy, the other nodes choose the node with less diffusing hop count and more residual energy as the next hop. As a result, an energy-aware aggregation tree is built up as shown in figure 4(b).

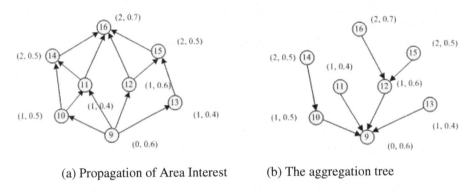

(a) Propagation of Area Interest   (b) The aggregation tree

Fig. 4. The aggregation tree in the event area

3.2 The New Way for Building Transmission Gradient Field

The gathering node is responsible for the transmission of aggregated data to the sink node. So energy efficiency of the route is essential. In EIDD, after election of the gathering node, the gather node sends detecting data to sink node using low data rate. The detecting packet contains the hop to the gathering node and the energy of the nodes it has passed by. The detecting packet arrives at sink node finally throughout different paths. As shown in figure 5(a), with the diffusing of this detecting packet, hop-count gradient field [5] and energy gradient field [6] are both established. Two fields do not coincide with each other. According to the two fields, the sink node send back reinforcement packet to reinforce the special route, as red dotted line in figure 5(b).when the route is reinforced, the gathering begins to transmit aggregated data with high data rate.

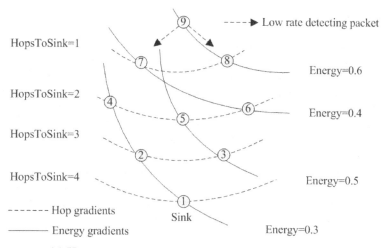

(a) Hop-count gradient field and energy gradient field

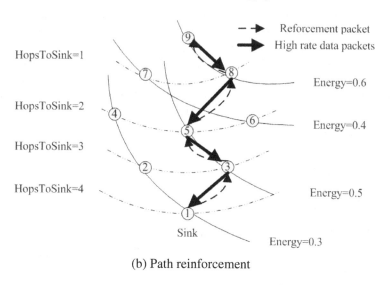

(b) Path reinforcement

Fig. 5. Energy-aware gradient-based routing

4   Evaluation

To evaluate the performance of EIDD, energy simulation platform PowerTOSSIM [7] based on the Mica2 node is adopted. In experiments EIDD is compared with original Directed Diffusion. The analysis consists of three parts: (1) the average energy dissipation per node. (2) Transmission delays under different network scale. (3) The average energy dissipation per packet.

4.1 Main Parameters of the Network Model

In order to study the impact of different network scale, the number of network nodes is changed from 10 to 100, and each node has a fixed communication radius 30m. Nodes are located in a square region, and the region sizes are generated by scaling the square and keep the ratio range constant in order to approximately keep the average density of sensor nodes constant. It allows us to study the impact of network size alone. The event areas are fixed of 70m*70m in size and located in the top right corner. The sink is located in the left corner. In event area, each source node generates one data packet per second. The rate for detecting packet is packet/5s. Interests are generated every 5 seconds, and the interest duration is 100 seconds. The idle time power dissipation is 35mW, the receive power dissipation is 395mW, and the transmit power dissipation is 660mW. Data packet length is 44 byte, and assumes ideal aggregation. Simulation time is set to be the duration of interest.

4.2 Comparative Evaluation

Figure 6 shows the average energy dissipation. From the figure it can be seen that for some sensor fields, EIDD's dissipated energy is only 60% that of DD. Energy savings derives from two reasons: First, in data dissemination stage, EIDD effectively reduces the number of network packets, only the exploratory packets from the root are transmitted throughout the network, while the exploratory packets from other sources are limited in the events region; Second, the data packets form each source are aggregated at the root effectively, so the redundant data is reduced in the network, thus achieves the purpose of saving energy.

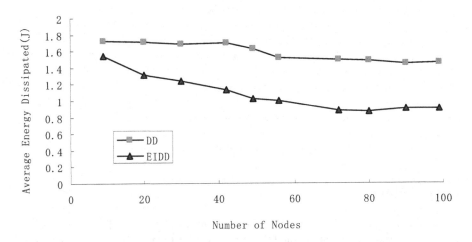

Fig. 6. Average energy dissipated under different network scales

Figure 7 shows the transmission delays of EIDD and DD. This parameter reflects the response speed of enquiries. As can be seen from figure 7, that transmission delay has

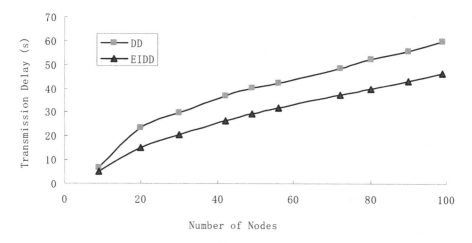

Fig. 7. Transmission Delay under different network scales

increased as a result of the increase of the network size. It is because the hops between sources and the sink also increase with the increase of network scale, which leads to greater transmission delay. The transmission delay of EIDD is lower compared to DD.

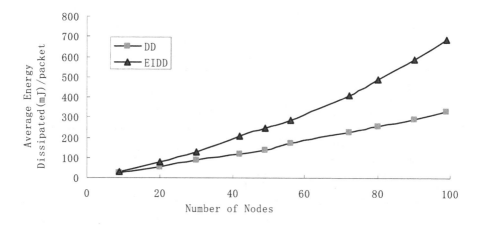

Fig. 8. Average energy dissipated per packet

Greater transmission delay causes shorter data transmission time before interest expired. So the average dissipated energy per packet will increase. Figure 8 shows the average dissipated energy per packet, which is the total energy dissipation divided by the received number of packets. In Figure 8, two curves are rising, but the curve of EIDD grows slower. It is caused by two reasons: Firstly, in the same network size, EIDD has less energy dissipation than DD. Secondly, in the same network size, the transmission delay of EIDD is smaller than DD, so it would generate more data packet in EIDD, and then the sink will receive more packets. For the reasons above, the improved algorithm has high data collection efficiency.

5 Conclusion

In this paper, we devise an Energy-aware Improved Directed Diffusion algorithm for area event monitoring in wireless sensor network. A gathering node is chosen within the event area for data collection and aggregation. The algorithm improves the way of gradient establishments in original DD. A more reasonable transmission path is selected through the establishment of hop gradients and energy gradients. After the simulation, we find that the improved algorithm achieves both energy efficiency and small transmission delay. These results prove that the improved algorithm fits the application of area event monitoring.

Acknowledgement

This research has been sponsored in part by National High Technology Research and Development Program of China (2002AA784030).

Reference

1. Akyildiz, L.F., Su, W., Sankarasubramaniam, Y., Cayirci, E.: Wireless sensor networks: a survey. Computer Networks, (2002) 38(4): 393–422
2. Carle, J., Simplot,D.: Energy efficient area monitoring by sensor networks. IEEE Computer, (2004) 37(2): 40–46
3. Intanagonwiwat, C., Govindan, R., Estrin, D.: Directed diffusion: A scalable and robust communication paradigm for sensor networks. Proceedings of the 6th Annual ACM/IEEE International Conference on Mobile Computing and Networking (MobiCom'00), Boston, MA, August (2000)
4. Krishnamachari, C., Estrin, D., Wicker, S.: The impact of data aggregation in wireless sensor networks. International Workshop on Distributed Event-Based Systems, Vienna (2002)
5. Akkaya, K., Younis, M.: A survey of routing protocols in wireless sensor networks. Elsevier Ad Hoc Network Journal, (2005) 3(3): 325–349
6. Yu, Y., Krishnamachari, B., Prasanna, V.K.: Energy-Latency Tradeoffs for Data Gathering in Wireless Sensor Networks. In IEEE INFOCOM 2004, Hong Kong SAR, PR China (2004)
7. Shnayder, V., Hempstead, M., rong Chen, B., Werner-Allen, G., Welsh, M,.: Simulating the Power Consumption of Large-Scale Sensor Network Applications. Proc. of SenSys'04, Nov. (2004) 188–200

Distributed Node-Based Transmission Power Control for Wireless Ad Hoc Networks

Subhasis Bhattacharjee and Nabanita Das

Advanced Computing and Microelectronics Unit
Indian Statistical Institute
Kolkata, India
{subhasisb_t, ndas}@isical.ac.in

Abstract. Transmission power control at individual nodes is used in wireless ad hoc networks for reducing interference and energy consumption. In this paper, two new distributed node-based power control techniques have been proposed to cope up with two different situations, one for lifetime-critical networks with nodes having less mobility, and the other for networks with mobility-prone nodes. The first algorithm is based on the idea of minimum spanning tree (MST) computation. It takes $O(n)$ rounds (n is the total number of nodes), and results better optimization in terms of node power levels. The lower transmission power of nodes makes it suitable for lifespan-critical networks. But $O(n)$ time complexity limits its application to networks with nodes having high mobility causing frequent topology changes. However, it will be suitable for wireless sensor networks where, after the deployment, nodes become more or less static but lifetime remains to be a critical issue. The second one is based on neighbor pruning scheme that completes transmission power assignment in two rounds of message passing only. Though in terms of the node power levels, the first algorithm performs better, with less computational complexity the second one can easily adapt to the topology changes caused by the mobility of the nodes, and hence is suitable for mobile networks. Simulation studies have been done to compare the performances in terms of different performance metrics.

1 Introduction

In recent times, wireless ad hoc networks have gained much attention as it requires no pre-existing infrastructure for its functioning. A communication session is achieved either through a single-hop radio transmission if the communicating nodes are within one another's transmission range, or by relaying via some intermediate nodes. As the nodes in ad hoc networks are free to move arbitrarily, the network topology may change frequently and unpredictably. Also resources like bandwidth and battery power are limited in many applications. Each node in ad hoc network can potentially change the network topology by adjusting its transmission power. The primary goal of topology control is to design power-efficient algorithms that maintain network connectivity and optimize performance metrics such as network lifetime and/or throughput.

S. Madria et al. (Eds.): ICDCIT 2006, LNCS 4317, pp. 49–62, 2006.
© Springer-Verlag Berlin Heidelberg 2006

For radio transmission, the power required to communicate between nodes varies as the kth power of the distance between them, where $2 \leq k \leq 6$, depending on the condition of the surrounding media [3]. Generally, in ad hoc networks, it is assumed that each node transmits at a constant power level P, covering a range R of transmission. However, it is wasteful from two considerations. Firstly, if distance between two nodes u and v is less than R, u and v can communicate with power less than P. As nodes operate with limited battery power, it is very important to reduce the transmission power of a node to enhance its life. As well as, it can promote appropriate routing algorithms to reduce the total power required for end to end communication. In addition, the greater the power with which a node transmits, the greater the likelihood of the transmission interfering with other transmissions, causing reduction in network throughput.

Various topology control algorithms have been proposed so far for wireless ad-hoc networks considering link-based power control (LBPC) [6]. In those schemes, before each transmission, a node adjusts its power level to be just sufficient to communicate along the specific link. This technique allows to minimize the total power required for the end to end packet delivery when the packet is routed through the least power path. However, in ad hoc networks, the mobility of nodes changes the power requirements of individual links frequently, and to have the current information about it, a node may have to exchange some additional packets causing additional drainage of power. Also, adjustment of transmission power level before each communication poses additional load on the power-starved nodes. Therefore, link-based power control is, in general, not feasible in such networks as it demands much overhead for link maintenance. Hence, in this paper, the focus is given on node-based power control (NBPC), where based on current topology, each node v_i decides a fixed transmission power $p_i \leq P$, same for all its links, that maintains its connectivity with the rest of the network but at the same time helps to reduce the total power required for communication. Since transmission power of a node need not be adjusted before each communication, except in case of topology changes, the overhead is much lower compared to that for link-based power control.

Several algorithms, on NBPC, focused on establishing routes and maintaining these routes under frequent and unpredictable topology changes [7], [8], [9]. A topology control algorithm using heuristics based on a Delauney triangulation of graph is presented in [13]. A centralized spanning tree algorithm for achieving connected and bi-connected static networks, while minimizing the maximum transmission power, is presented in [14]. The distributed algorithms, based on these heuristics, however do not guarantee connectivity. A distributed position-based topology control algorithm, that preserves connectivity, is proposed in [5]. An improved algorithm is presented in [6].

It is evident that for ad hoc networks with static nodes, complex algorithms can be applied to optimize the node powers efficiently, since computation is to be done only during initialization, or in case of failures. Whereas for networks with mobile nodes, the primary objective is fast computation of node powers whenever topology changes, may be at the expense of optimality of solution.

With this fact in mind, two distributed algorithms have been presented in this paper for NBPC, the first one is for lifetime-critical networks suitable with nodes having less mobility, and the second one is for networks with mobile nodes. In both the cases, the objective is to assign each node a transmission power that maintains connectivity and also reduces communication cost in terms of energy. The first algorithm is based on the idea of distributed minimum spanning tree (MST) construction that efficiently minimizes the total sum of node powers in $O(n)$ rounds of time, n is the total number of nodes. However, for ad hoc networks with mobility-prone nodes, this algorithm may result appreciable overhead in recomputing the node power levels in case of topology changes. To cope up with frequent topology changes, second algorithm based on neighbor pruning technique is proposed that completes assignment in two rounds only. Simulation studies have been done and the performances of the proposed schemes are compared with earlier works.

Section 2 presents some preliminary concepts about the network model and performance metrics. Proposed techniques for NBPC have been presented in section 3. Simulation results and comparative study are included in section 4. Finally section 5 concludes the paper.

2   Preliminaries

The following subsections describe the network model considered here along with the performance metrics used for comparing the proposed NBPC techniques.

2.1   Network Model

In this paper, it is assumed that the system initializes with a set V of n ad hoc devices $\{v_1, v_2, \cdots, v_n\}$, deployed over a 2-D region. In the initialization phase, each node transmits with the maximum power P, covering a range R, and discovers its adjacent neighbors. The network, thus discovered by all the n ad hoc devices together, can be represented by a graph, henceforth called the topology graph $G(V, E)$, where V is the set of n ad hoc devices, E is the set of edges and $(v_i, v_j) \in E$ if and only if the Euclidean distance between v_i and v_j is less than R. It is assumed that $G(V, E)$ is always connected.

Fig. 1(a) shows a topology graph $G(V, E)$ with seven nodes.

Definition 1. *In a given topology graph $G(V, E)$, the hop-distance $d(v_i, v_j)$ between two nodes $v_i, v_j \in V$ is the length of the shortest path in hops between them in $G(V, E)$. Two nodes v_i and v_j are said to be h-hop away if $d(v_i, v_j) = h$.*

Definition 2. *The h-hop neighbors of v_i in $G(V, E)$, $N^h(v_i)$ is the set of nodes $V' \subseteq V$, $V' = \{v_{i1}, \cdots, v_{ik}\}$, such that $d(v_i, v_{ij}) \leq h$ for $1 \leq j \leq k$.*

Definition 3. *The h-hop partial graph of v_i, $PG^h(v_i)$ is a subgraph $G'(V', E')$ of $G(V, E)$ induced by the node set $V' = N^h(v_i) \cup \{v_i\}$ and deleting the edges between any two h-hop away nodes of v_i.*

Example 1. For the topology graph $G(V, E)$ shown in Fig.1(a), the 2-hop partial graph of node C, $PG^2(C)$ is shown in Fig.1(b).

Definition 4. *A weighted topology graph $G(V, E, W)$ is the topology graph $G(V, E)$ with a weight $w_{ij} \in W$ for each edge $(v_i, v_j) \in E$, where w_{ij} represents the transmission power cost for the edge (v_i, v_j).*

Example 2. In Fig.1(c) each edge is marked with a weight for the topology graph of Fig.1(a), indicating the transmission power required for communication over that link.

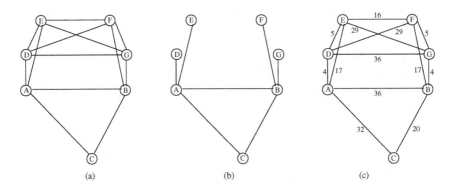

Fig. 1. (a) A topology graph $G(V, E)$, (b) its 2-hop partial graph $PG^2(C)$ and (c) the weighted topology graph $G(V, E, W)$

Given a weighted topology graph $G(V, E, W)$ the objective is to find a *power assignment vector* $\Pi = \{\pi_i \mid 0 < \pi_i \leq P, \forall\ v_i \in V\}$ where π_i is the fixed transmission power assigned to node v_i such that it maintains the connectivity with all other nodes in V as well as conserves power in communicating among nodes when node based power control (NBPC) technique is applied. It is obvious that the power assignment Π will remove some edges as well as will change the weights $w_{ij} \in W$ of $G(V, E, W)$. This modifications are represented by a new graph defined below.

Definition 5. *The power assignment vector Π to a given weighted topology graph $G(V, E, W)$ transforms it to a power graph $G_\Pi(V, E')$ where $E' \subseteq E$ such that an edge $(v_i, v_j) \in E$ is also in E' if $min\{\pi_i, \pi_j\} \geq w_{ij}$, and each edge (v_i, v_j) is associated with transmission cost $w'_{ij} = \pi_i$.*

Example 3. Let $\Pi = \{17, 20, 20, 29, 18, 29, 29\}$ be a power assignment vector for the nodes in the weighted topology graph of Fig.1(c). Fig.2 shows the corresponding power graph $G_\Pi(V, E')$. In Fig.2 each node v_i is labeled with π_i. However, the edge weights w'_{ij} are not shown in the figure for clarity. Note that, the edge $(A, B) \notin E'$ as $\pi_A = 17$ and $\pi_B = 20$ but $w_{AB} = 36$. Also, the edge $(E, F) \in E'$ as $\pi_E = 18$ and $\pi_F = 29$ and $w_{EF} = 16$.

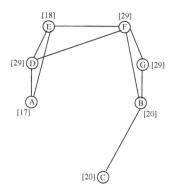

Fig. 2. Power graph $G_\Pi(V, E')$

It is evident that in the power graph $G_\Pi(V, E')$, all the links are bidirectional, i.e. if $(v_i, v_j) \in E'$, $(v_j, v_i) \in E'$, but if $\pi_i \neq \pi_j$, the weights in two directions will be different.

2.2 Performance Metrics

To compare the performances of different power assignment techniques following NBPC, several metrics have been studied so far in the literature. In this paper, the following metrics have been considered for performance evaluation.

Definition 6. *Given a weighted topology graph $G(V, E, W)$, the shortest-path-power for any two nodes v_i and v_j, $SPP(v_i, v_j)$ is defined as the sum of weights on the edges along the shortest path from v_i to v_j.*

Definition 7. *Given a weighted topology graph $G(V, E, W)$, the all-pair-shortest-path-power APSPP is defined as: $APSPP = \sum SPP(v_i, v_j), \forall v_i, v_j \in V$.*

If it is assumed that for message transmission, all source destination pairs occur with equal probability, and routes in general follow the shortest paths, $APSPP$ can be considered as a good measure of the total transmission power required for communication in a round if link based power control is implemented. However, as mentioned earlier, link based power control is not feasible as it needs high overhead in terms of additional communications as well as increased complexity in ad hoc nodes.

In this paper, node based power control techniques are presented where each node determines its power level out of its local neighborhood information. Here follow some definitions for networks with a power assignment vector Π.

Definition 8. *For a power assignment Π of n nodes of a topology graph $G(V, E)$, the Power Sum, i.e., the sum of power levels of all nodes is represented by $S_\Pi = \Sigma_i^n \pi_i$.*

The power sum S_Π is a measure of total power requirement in case of flooding which is an essential mode of communication for topology discovery or route discovery in ad hoc networks.

Definition 9. *Given a power graph $G_\Pi(V, E')$, the shortest-path-power for any two nodes v_i and v_j, $SPP_\Pi(v_i, v_j)$ is defined as the sum of transmission costs on the edges along the shortest path from v_i to v_j.*

Definition 10. *Given a power graph $G_\Pi(V, E')$, the all-pair-shortest-path-power $APSPP_\Pi$ is defined as: $APSPP_\Pi = \sum SPP_\Pi(v_i, v_j), \forall v_i, v_j \in V$.*

In the next section, two different distributed techniques for power assignment are presented and their performances have been compared in terms of the performance metrics described above.

3 Proposed Methodologies for Topology Control

In general, for ad hoc networks the nodes are assumed to be fairly mobile so that the topology changes frequently. However, in some situations like sensor networks, after deployment the nodes become almost stationary. To cope up with these two different mobility scenarios two different distributed techniques, based on two methodologies, namely, the *minimum spanning tree* (MST) construction and the *neighbor pruning* method, have been presented in the following subsections.

MST formation, is the basis of all the algorithms whose objective is to achieve minimum sum of transmission powers S_Π, maintaining connectivity. On the other hand, the neighbor pruning method, is the basis of all the algorithms trying to optimize the total transmission power for end-to-end packet delivery.

3.1 Incremental Spanning Graph

In this paper, the distributed MST construction algorithm ([10], [11]) is adopted with a modification where the selection of edges is based on a dynamically computed weight parameter defined below. The resulting graph is defined as *incremental spanning graph* (ISG). The algorithm starts with each vertex v_i as a distinct component T_i with power assignment $\pi_i = 0$. For each edge $(v_i, v_j) \in E$ of the weighted topology graph $G(V, E, W)$, a weight parameter $w_{ij}^{Tot} = (w_{ij} + w_{ji}) - (\pi_i + \pi_j)$ is defined. There is a designated node in every component called leader. In each round, with the help of other nodes, each leader of a component finds the edge having minimum value of w_{ij}^{Tot} connecting its component to another component in the topology. The components are joined by the selected edge forming a larger component. Joining components in this way helps to minimize the incremental change in power level in each node to achieve connectivity. Let two components T_i and T_j are joined by an edge (v_a, v_b) where $v_a \in T_i$ and $v_b \in T_j$. To support this edge the power levels of nodes v_a and v_b are updated to $\pi_a = w_{ab}$ and $\pi_b = w_{ba}$. Also, node v_a updates weight parameter

w_{ak}^{Tot} for all its neighbors v_k outside the new component. This process of edge selection and component merging continues until a single component is formed containing all n vertices of V. A formal representation of the algorithm is given below.

Procedure ISG
begin
Initialization for each node v_i:
    $T_i = \{v_i\}$ and $\pi_i = 0$
    For each edge (v_i, v_k)
        Set $w_{ik}^{Tot} = (w_{ak} + w_{ka})$

In each round for each component T_i:
    Find edge (v_a, v_b) where $v_a \in T_i$, $v_b \in T_j$, $i \neq j$ s.t. w_{ab}^{Tot} is minimum
    Merge two components, $T_i = T_i \cup T_j$ and *elect the leader*
    If $w_{ab} > \pi_a$ then $\pi_a = w_{ab}$
    If $w_{ba} > \pi_b$ then $\pi_b = w_{ba}$
    For each edge (v_a, v_k) where $v_k \in T_q$ and $q \neq i$
        get updated value of π_k from v_k
        $w_{ak}^{Tot} = maximum \{(w_{ak} + w_{ka}) - (\pi_a + \pi_k), 0\}$
        If $w_{ak}^{Tot} = 0$
            Merge components: $T_i = T_i \cup T_q$
end

The details procedure of leader election and component merging along with time and message complexities can be found in [10] and [11].

Example 4. Fig. 3(a) shows a weighted topology graph $G(V, E, W)$. Fig. 3(b) shows the same graph after initialization, where label $[\pi_i]$ denotes the power level of node v_i and the label w_{ij}^{Tot} denotes the weight of edge (v_i, v_j). Fig. 3(c) shows the modified values of Π and w_{ij}^{Tot} after round 1 of ISG formation. In Fig. 3(c) the dotted lines and the solid lines represent the intra-component and inter-component edges, respectively. The final ISG is shown in Fig. 3(d).

Example 5. Corresponding to $G(V, E, W)$ shown in Fig. 3(a), the ISG generated by the *Procedure ISG* and the MST derived by [2] are shown in Fig. 3(d) and Fig. 4 respectively. Note that for MST, Power Sum $S_\Pi = 56$ which has been improved in ISG as $S_\Pi = 53$.

Remark 1. The time complexity and the message complexity of the proposed algorithm are the same as those of the distributed MST algorithms. Using the technique suggested in [10], it requires $O(n)$ rounds of time and $O(n \log n)$ message communication. However, those have been further improved in [11].

On randomly generated graphs the proposed methodology is compared by simulation with the minimum spanning tree based 2-approximation algorithm presented in [2] with respect to the performance metric S_Π. It is evident from Fig. 5

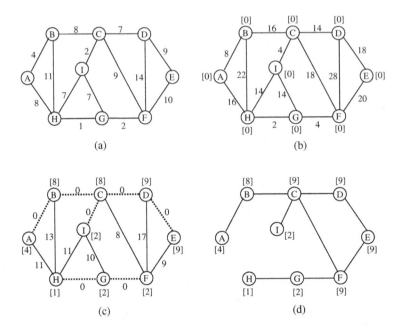

Fig. 3. (a) Weighted topology graph, (b) initial stage of ISG (c) ISG after round 1, and (d) final power assignment

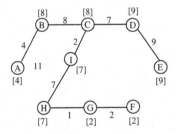

Fig. 4. MST and its power assignment derived by [2]

that with the same time and message complexity, the proposed ISG technique performs better compared to the algorithm in [2].

3.2   Localized Neighbor Pruning

In this method each node v_s collects information to know $PG^2(v_s)$. Given a weighted topology graph $G(V, E, W)$, each node v_s first executes the basic edge relaxation operation (as in Dijkstra's shortest path algorithm) [12] on its 2-hop partial graph $PG^2(v_s)$ to remove those edges from the graph which are not part of a minimum cost path for any pair of nodes. Here, each node v_s maintains two sets of vertices S and Q. Set S contains all nodes for which minimum cost paths

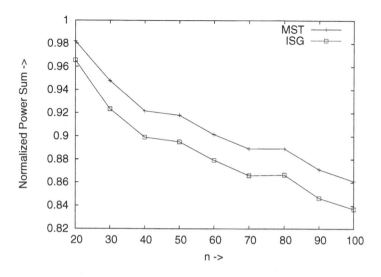

Fig. 5. Comparison of normalized Power Sum S_{Π} for MST and ISG

from v_s are already known and set Q contains all other nodes of $PG^2(v_s)$. It initializes $c[v_s] = 0$ and $c[v_i] = \infty$, $\forall v_i \in PG^2(v_s), i \neq s$, where $c[v_i]$ is the cost of the path from v_s to v_i. Set S is initially empty, and in each step the node with minimum value of $c[v_i]$ is moved from Q to S. $c[v_j], v_j \in Q, \forall v_j \in N^1(v_i)$, is updated to $(c[v_j] + w_{ij})$ if it is less than the existing value of $c[v_j]$. When the set Q becomes empty, each $c[v_i]$ denotes the least cost of the path from v_s to v_i within the given $PG^2(v_s)$.

Once this preprocessing is over, node v_s then removes unnecessary edges in the following two passes and assigns its node power. In the first pass, all edges (v_s, v_i) for which $w_{si} > c[v_i]$ are removed. In the next pass, an edge (v_s, v_i) from the modified $PG^2(v_s)$ is deleted by node v_s, if and only if there exists two edges

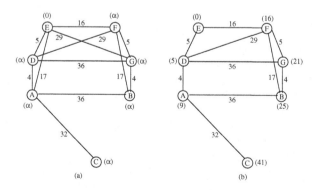

Fig. 6. (a) $PG^2(E)$ for weighted topology graph of Fig. 1(b), and (b) $PG^2(E)$ after assigning $c[v_i]$ to nodes

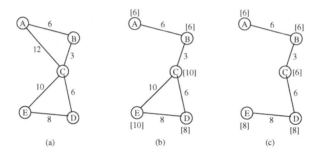

Fig. 7. (a) Weighted topology graph and power assignment after neighbor pruning in (b) 1st pass and (c) 2nd pass of LNP

(v_s, v_k) and (v_k, v_i) each of whose weight w_{sk} and w_{ki} are less than w_{si}. A formal presentation of the algorithm is given below.

Example 6. For the weighted topology graph $G(V, E, W)$ shown in Fig. 1(b), the 2-hop partial graph of node E, $PG^2(E)$ is shown in Fig. 6(a). The initial and final values of $c[v_i]$ are shown as labels $(c[v_i])$ to each node v_i in Fig. 6(a) and 6(b), respectively. Fig. 7 explains the neighbor pruning in pass 1 and 2 respectively of LNP procedure. In Fig. 7(b) and (c), the label $[\pi_i]$ to each node v_i represents node power level after pass 1 and pass 2 of pruning respectively.

Procedure LNP(v_s)
begin
for each vertex v_i in graph $PG^2(V, E)$ // Initialization
    $c[v_i] = \infty$;
$c[v_s] = 0$; $S = \phi$; $Q = V$
while $Q \neq \phi$ // Assigning minimum cost to vertices
    Find node v_i such that $c[v_i]$ is minimum $\forall v_i \in Q$
    $S = S \cup \{v_i\}$
    for each edge (v_i, v_j)
        if $c[v_j] \geq c[v_i] + w_{ij}$
            $c[v_j] = c[v_i] + w_{ij}$
// Neighbor pruning: Pass 1
for each $v_i \in N^1(v_s)$ **if** $c[v_i] < w_{si}$
    Delete the edge (v_s, v_i).
// Neighbor pruning: Pass 2
for each edge (v_s, v_i) in modified $PG^2(v_s)$
    if $\exists (v_s, v_k)$ in modified $PG^2(v_s)$ s.t., $w_{sk} < w_{si}$ and $w_{ki} < w_{si}$
        Delete edge (v_i, v_j)
// Transmission power assignment
$P(v_s) = max\{w_{si}\}$, $\forall v_i$ s.t., edge (v_i, v_j) exists in modified $PG^2(v_s)$
Inform neighbors about $P(v_s)$ and modify 1-hop neighbor set $N^1(v_s)$
end

Remark 2. The LNP procedure at each node v_i takes $O((|E'| + |V'|) \log |V'|)$ time for internal computation where, $|V'|$ and $|E'|$ are the number of vertices and edges in $PG^2(v_i)$. This procedure requires one round to know $PG^2(v_s)$ and one round to inform its power assignment and the modified 1-hop neighbor set. Message complexity is $2|E|$, $|E|$ is the total number of edges.

4   Performance Evaluation

For performance evaluation, a set of performance metrics, namely the power sum S_{Π}, the all-pair shortest path power $APSPP$, which are already defined in section 2.2, and the average hop count H have been considered, and compared with the parameters for link-based power control technique that imposes a lower bound on $APSPP$, and also with the parameters corresponding to the Common-Power algorithm (COMPOW) presented in [4] which gives an upper bound on it.

The COMPOW algorithm assigns a common power level to all the nodes which is the minimum one required to keep the graph G connected. A routing table RT_{P_i} for each admissible power level P_i is constructed by sending and receiving *hello* messages at the power level P_i. Thus the number of entries in RT_{P_i} (those nodes reachable within a finite number of hops) gives the number of reachable nodes with power P_i. The optimum power P_i selected for the node v_i is the smallest power level whose routing table has the same number of entries as that of the routing table at maximum power P. However, the distributed spanning tree construction procedure can also be used to find the minimum common power.

4.1   Simulation Results

The performances of proposed algorithms have been studied by simulation on random graphs. A set of n nodes, where $20 \leq n \leq 100$, are randomly placed in a 500×500 2-D region. Maximum transmission range of each node is varied within the limits $(40 - 350)$ to generate a set of random graphs.

Fig. 8 shows the variation of normalized $APSPP$ with the number of nodes n. It is evident that link based power control (LBPC) always results minimum $APSPP$ as it enables a node to communicate with the power just sufficient for the link under consideration. On the other hand, COMPOW control needs higher $APSPP$ as there all the nodes transmit with a common power needed for connectivity. However, the $APSPP$ values produced by the proposed algorithms ISG and LNP are very close and remains in between those given by LBPC and COMPOW.

Fig. 9 shows the variation of power sum with the total number of nodes n. Since in LBPC the transmission power of a node varies according to the link of communication, power sum S_{Π} does not bear any significance. It is evident that ISG results minimum power sum and COMPOW the maximum, whereas LNP produces S_{Π} in between the two.

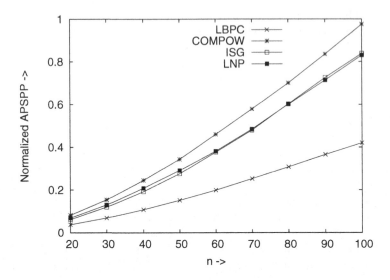

Fig. 8. Normalized $APSPP$ vs n

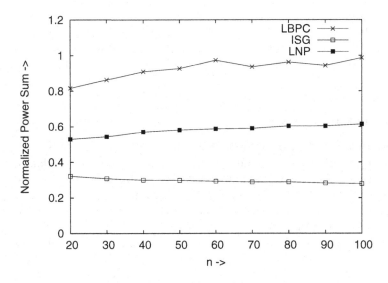

Fig. 9. Power sum S_Π vs n

Fig. 10 shows the variation of average hop count with the number of nodes n. It is obvious that COMPOW results minimum number of hops and ISG results higher values since for the latter the node powers are much less. The average hop counts in LBPC and LNP are almost same; LNP shows better performance for higher n, whereas ISG results highest hop counts and COMPOW the least value for any given n.

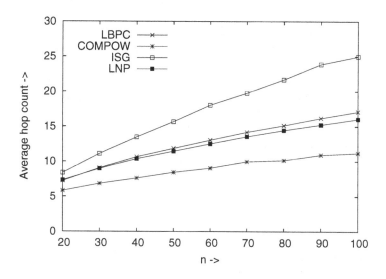

Fig. 10. Hop count H vs n

4.2 Mobility Consideration

For large ad hoc networks with highly mobile nodes, it is evident that the network topology will change frequently. For such networks, ISG technique will not be suitable, since, whenever the mobility of nodes causes a change in the topology, the power graph is to be recomputed. The computation needs $O(n)$ rounds which poses a large overhead on the nodes in terms of message communication and hence the power. Also the network will need so many rounds to gain stability after each time the topology changes. On the otherhand, in such scenarios, LNP technique can perform well, since it needs only two rounds for recomputing the power levels after each time the topology changes.

In summary, ISG technique uses higher complexity in terms of rounds and messages but improves the power sum better. Whereas LNP procedure with less complexity sacrifices a bit in terms of power sum but improves $APSPP$ by the same amount as that by ISG. Also it is to be mentioned that the average hop count is much better in LNP compared to ISG and LBPC as well. So, the ISG algorithm is suitable for NBPC in networks where the lifetime is a more crucial issue than the mobility. On the contrary, for networks where topology changes frequently due to the mobility of nodes, the LNP technique performs better for NBPC by recomputing the node power levels within two rounds only.

5 Conclusion

This paper presents two distributed node-based power control schemes, namely the Incremental Spanning Graph (ISG) technique and Localized Neighbor Pruning (LNP) procedure, appropriate for two different situations, one for lifetime-critical networks with nodes having less mobility, and the other for networks with mobility prone nodes. Simulation studies have been done for performance comparison. The ISG algorithm takes $O(n)$ rounds (n is the total number of nodes) to assign transmission power to individual nodes and results better optimization in terms of sum of transmission powers of individual nodes. The LNP procedure is based on neighbor pruning scheme that completes transmission power assignment in a constant number (2) of rounds of message passing. In spite of lower time complexity, it results comparable communication cost for end-to-end packet delivery. It also improves the hop count appreciably. Therefore, depending on the specific application area the appropriate power control technique is to be applied.

References

1. N. A. Lynch: "Distributed Algorithms", *Morgan Kaufmann Publishers, Inc.*, San Francisco, California.
2. L.M. Kirousis, E. Kranakis, D. Krizanc, and A. Pelc: "Power consumption in packet radio networks", *Theoretical Computer Science*, vol. 243, pp. 289-305, 2000.
3. T. S. Rappaport: "Wireless communications: principles and practice", *Prentice Hall*, 1996.
4. S. Narayanaswamy, V. Kawadia, R. S. Sreenivas and P. R. Kumar: "Power control in ad-hoc networks: theory, architechture, algorithm and implementation of the COMPOW Protocol", *Proc. of the European Wireless Conference*, pp. 156-162, Italy, Feb. 2002.
5. V. Rodoplu and T. H. Meng: "Minimum energy mobile wireless networks", *IEEE J. Selected Areas in Communications*, vol. 17, no. 8, pp. 1333-1344, Aug. 1999.
6. L. Li and J. Y. Halpern: "Minimum energy mobile wireless networks revisited", *Proc. of IEEE Int. Conf. on Communications*, pp. 278-283, June 2001.
7. N. Bambos: "Toward power-sensitive network architectures in wireless communications: concepts, issues, and design aspects", *IEEE Personal Communications Magazine*, pp. 50-59, June 1998.
8. J. Broch, D. A. Maltz, D. B. Johnson, Y. C. Hu, and J. Jetcheva, "A performance comparison of multi-hop wireless ad-hoc network routing protocols", *Proc. of the ACM/IEEE MOBICOM*, pp. 85-97, Oct. 1998.
9. M. S. Corson and A. Ephremides: "A distributed routing algorithm for mobile wireless networks", *Wireless Networks*, vol. 1, pp. 61-81, 1995.
10. R. G. Gallager, P. A. Humblet, and P. M. Spira: "A distributed algorithm for minimum-weight spanning trees", *ACM Trans. on Programming Languages and Systems*, vol. 5, No. 1, pp. 66-77, Jan 1983.
11. J. Garay, S. Kutten, and D. Peleg: "A sub-linear time distributed algorithm for minimum-weight spanning trees", *SIAM Journal of Computing*, vol. 27(1), pp. 302-316, 1998.
12. T. H. Cormen, C. E. Leiserson, R. L. Rivest: "Introduction to algorithms", *MIT Press and McGraw-Hill*, 1998
13. L. Hu: "Topology control for multihop packet radio networks", *IEEE Trans. on Communications*, vol. 41, no. 10, pp. 1474-1481, Oct. 1993.
14. R. Ramanathan and R. Rosales-Hain: "Topology control of multihop wireless networks using transmit power adjustment", *Proc. of IEEE INFOCOM 2000*, pp. 404-413, March 2000.

Ticket-Based Binding Update Protocol for Mobile IPv6[*]

Sangjin Kim[1], Jungdoo Koo[2], and Heekuck Oh[2]

[1] Korea University of Technology and Education,
School of Internet Media Engineering, Republic of Korea
sangjin@kut.ac.kr
[2] Hanyang University, Department of Computer Science and Engineering,
Republic of Korea
{jdkoo, hkoh}@cse.hanyang.ac.kr

Abstract. In this paper, we propose a new ticket based binding update protocol for Mobile IPv6. This protocol uses CGA (Cryptographically Generated Address) to provide mutual authentication between a mobile node and its corresponding node, but differs from previous protocols in the following way. The protocol does not require a mobile node to generate a signature each time it acquires a new IP address. To minimize computational cost of using CGA, the corresponding node issues a ticket that can be used in later update requests. Our initial protocol requires similar computational cost compared to previous protocols based on CGA, but outperforms others when a mobile node has a valid ticket.

Keywords: Mobile IPv6, Binding Update Protocol, CGA.

1 Introduction

1.1 Overview of Mobile IPv6 Binding Update

Mobile IPv6 is an extension to IPv6 to support mobility of nodes transparently and seamlessly. In other words, mobility of a node must be transparent to layers above IP layer, on-going connection must not be broken, and no manual configuration should be required. If the physical movement of a node involves connecting to a different network link that uses a different subnet prefix, an MN (mobile node) needs to acquire a new IP address. Otherwise, the MN will not be reachable. To support this movement seamlessly, Mobile IPv6 nodes use two addresses: a HoA (HOme Address) and a CoA (Care-Of-Address). A HoA is a static and permanent address that can be used to contact an MN regardless of the node's current location. A CoA is a dynamic address that changes with respect to the node's current location. To allow an MN to be reachable regardless of its location, Mobile IPv6 introduce a HA (Home Agent) that plays a role of a stationary proxy. The HA intercepts packets sent to an MN's HoA and forwards it to the node's current CoA when they are not located at their home link. In order to achieve this, an MN must notify its new CoA to its HA each time the node acquires a new one. This process is known as the binding update. In this mode, all traffic from an

---

[*] This work was supported by the Ministry of Information and Communication, Korea, under the HNRC-ITRC program supervised by the IITA.

S. Madria et al. (Eds.): ICDCIT 2006, LNCS 4317, pp. 63–72, 2006.

MN to its CN (Corresponding Node) and vice-versa must be tunneled by the HA. Due to this, inefficient use of network bandwidth is inevitable and this problem is known as the triangular routing problem. To overcome this problem, route optimization mode has been introduced in Mobile IPv6. In this mode, an MN can update its new address with both the HA and the CN. After the update, future traffic can be directly exchanged between an MN and its CN.

If malicious attackers can corrupt the binding update process, it can hijack a session, attempt various DoS (Denial-of-Service) attacks, and bomb neighbors [1]. As a result, binding update must meet the following security requirements.

- **Requirement 1.** A recipient of binding update must be able to securely authenticate the requester. More precisely, the recipient must be able to verify that the claimed HoA is actually assigned to the requester.
- **Requirement 2.** A requester must be able to securely authenticate the recipient.
- **Requirement 3.** Integrity of binding update must be preserved.
- **Requirement 4.** A recipient must be able to securely verify that the requester is located at the claimed CoA.

To achieve these requirements, Mobile IPv6 recommends use of IPsec [2]. The use of IPsec can solve authentication and integrity requirement of binding update but cannot solve the location verification problem. Moreover, we have to consider the following fact. The relationship between an MN and its HA is a long-term relationship and it is normal to assume that there is a prior arrangement between them. Therefore, it is reasonable to assume that IPsec is used to secure binding update messages between an MN and its HA. However, the relationship between an MN and its CN is normally a short-term and it is generally assumed that they do not have any prior arrangements. Furthermore, a certification path to verify each other's certificate may not exists and the cost involved with establishing a security association may be too heavy for mobile nodes. As a result, using IPSec to secure binding updates between an MN and its CN may not be feasible, and it is not an efficient solution.

The location verification problem can be partially solved using the RR (Return Routability) technique [3]. This technique is proposed as a standard way of doing binding updates between an MN and its CN. However, RR technique does not satisfy other security requirements. To solve authentication problem, CGA (Cryptographically Generated Address) technique [4] has been introduced. As introduced in Soliman's book [5], all the requirements stated above can be met using RR and CGA together. In this paper, we propose a new binding update technique which is more efficient than using the basic RR and CGA together.

1.2 Related Work

The basic idea of RR is to test whether a node is reachable using both HoA and CoA before allowing the update to hold [3]. An MN initiates RR by sending HoTI (HOme address Test Init) and CoTI (Care-Of-address Test Init) messages to its CN. HoTI is sent to CN indirectly through HA whereas CoTI is sent directly. In response to these messages, the CN returns two tokens separately in HoT (HOme address Test) and CoT (Care-Of-address Test) messages. The MN combines the two tokens to compute a symmetric key and uses the key in sending the final binding update message. As a result, a node must be able to receive both HoT and CoT, which are sent through different paths, to successfully complete the RR. However, these tokens are not protected, which enables attackers, who can obtain both tokens, to forge binding update messages. Therefore, the security of RR depends on the difficulty of attackers intercepting two tokens that are routed through different routes. As suggest by many researchers, this assumption is too weak. Another issue about RR is that RR does not actually guarantees that the node is located at the claimed CoA. For example, a node can always claim the address of a neighbor.

CGA approach can solve the problem of a node claiming its CoA using another address already used by some other node. In Mobile IPv6, an IP address of a node is normally generated using the stateless address auto configuration method. In this method, a node constructs its address by combining the subnet prefix information and its unique interface ID. In CGA, the public key of a node is used instead of the node's interface ID. As a result, a node can prove its ownership of an address by signing a message using the private key corresponding to the public key included in its address. Since the node itself generates its address dynamically, a node can generate many addresses. However, a node cannot claim the ownership of an address already used by some neighboring node, unless it can obtain the private key of that node. Moreover, once a node has been authenticated using its HoA, all of its CoAs must contain the same public key included in its HoA. This fact can be used to verify the correctness of CoAs claimed by a node. We must note that, due to ingress filtering, claiming an address of a node located at a different link is difficult. Only problem with this approach is the cost of signing and verifying signatures. Previous approaches using CGA [6,7] requires a new signature each time a binding update occurs. This cost may not be tolerable to mobile nodes. However, if a signature is used only once in a while, the cost of generating the signature can be regarded as acceptable. In this paper, we use a ticket to minimize the generation of signatures during binding updates.

1.3 Additional Issues of Binding Update

To alleviate DoS (Denial-Of-Service) attacks, most of the protocols use the following techniques. First, stateless connection is used to protect against connection depletion attack. Second, messages are authenticated to reduce unnecessary maintenance of connection information. Third, puzzles are used to alleviate the possibility of attackers trying to establish multiple connections. In RR, CN does not maintain any state information during the protocol run. In CBID (Crypto-based IDentifiers) protocol [7], client puzzles are used. However, use of cookies and puzzles can be easily added to a protocol. Therefore, a protocol should not be evaluated depending on whether these mechanisms are used or not. However, it would be more efficient if nodes do not require maintaining state information.

Binding update must occur whenever a node acquires a new CoA. The update must also occur when a node returns home. In RR, the full RR procedure can be used when a node moves from its home link to a foreign link or from a foreign link to another foreign link. A node can use only CoTI and CoT instead of full RR if there is a lifetime on the token included in HoT. When a node returns home, the node uses only HoTI and HoT to ask the CN to remove its entry in CN's binding cache. Most of the previous work on binding update do not consider these situations and provide only a single protocol [6,7,8,9].

In most of the previous work, a CN is considered as a stationary host. We also believe that in most cases a CN will be a stationary host. However, we cannot neglect that a CN can also be a mobile host. Therefore, binding update protocols must also provide a suitable protocol to be used when a CN is a mobile host. In ECBU(Extended Certificate-based Binding Update) protocol [8], the HA of CN is introduced when the CN is a mobile node.

1.4   Our Contribution

In this paper, we have proposed a new binding update protocol that satisfy the following requirements.

– CGA is used to provide mutual authentication between an MN and its CN. However, an MN should not have to sign its binding update message each time it obtains a new CoA.
– IPsec should be only used between an MN and its HA.
– A CN should not have to preserve state information during binding updates to alleviate DoS attacks.
– The proposed protocol should satisfy all the security requirements stated previously in section 1.1.
– The proposed protocol should consider that a CN can be a mobile node.
– The proposed protocol should consider various situations such as a node returning home.

Many previous protocols [3,6,7] do not provide mutual authentication. Although the CBID protocol provides mutual authentication, this is done using IPsec [7]. We believe that if an MN and its CN both use CGA, we can construct a secure and efficient protocol without using IPsec between them. The rest of the paper is organized as follows. In section 2, we introduce our protocol in detail. In section 3, we give security and efficiency analysis of our protocol. Finally, we conclude in section 4.

2   The Proposed Protocols

2.1   System Setup

We assume that all IPv6 addresses of both MN and CN are CGAs. Such addresses confirm to the IETF standard RFC 3972. In our protocol, both HoA and CoA are CGAs and they must include the same public key. We also assume that an MN and its HA have previously established a security association required to use the IPsec. Moreover, we assume that an MN trust its HA. We will use the following notation to explain our protocol.

– $M_1 \| M_2$: a bitwise concatenation of message M_1 and M_2.
– K_X: a symmetric key known only to X.
– K_{X-Y}: a symmetric key shared between X and Y.

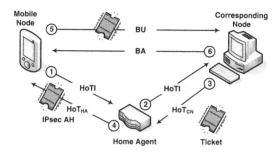

Fig. 1. The TckBU Protocol

- $-K_X, +K_X$: a private and public key of X, respectively.
- $\{M\}.K$: an encryption of M using a key K.
- $H(M)$: a hash value of M computed using a collision-resistant hash function H.
- $\text{MAC}.K(M)$: a message authentication code of M using a key K.
- $\text{Sig.-}K(M)$: a digital signature on M using the private key $-K$.
- N_X: a nonce generated by X.
- T_X: a timestamp generated by X.

2.2 The TckBU Protocol

In this section, we introduce our new ticked-based binding update protocol for Mobile IPv6 called TckBU. The message flow of our protocol is given in Fig. 1. The steps of our protocol is as follows.

- **Message 1, 2.** The MN generates a nonce N_{MN} and associates the nonce with its CN in its binding update list. It then sends the following HoTI message to the CN indirectly through HA:

$$\text{HoTI} = N_{MN}, T_{MN}, +K_{MN}, \text{Sig.-}K_{MN}(H(\text{Auth}_{MN})),$$

where, Auth_{MN} is $\{\text{HoA}||CN_{addr}||N_{MN}||T_{MN}\}$ and CN_{addr} is the address of CN.
- **Message 3.** When the CN receives the HoTI messages, it verifies the validity of $+K_{MN}$ by using it to construct the HoA of MN. The HoA of MN is obtained from the source address field of the IP header of this message. It then uses $+K_{MN}$ to verify the signature. Thus, authenticating the MN. It then generates a symmetric key K_{MN-CN}, which will be used as the ticket key, and a ticket Tck_{MN-CN}, that will be used by the node with HoA. The ticket consists of the following:

$$\text{Tck}_{MN-CN} = \{\text{HoA}||T_{CN}||L_{CN}||K_{MN-CN}\}.K_{CN},$$

where K_{CN} is a symmetric key known only to CN and is used to generate tickets, T_{CN} is a timestamp representing the issuance time of the ticket, L_{CN} is the lifetime of the ticket. After generating the ticket, the CN sends the following message to the

MN's HA (more precisely, the CN sends the following message to the MN, but is intercepted by the MN's HA):

$$\text{HoT}_{CN} = N_{MN}, T_{CN}, \{H(\text{Auth}_{CN}) || K_{MN-CN}\}.+K_{MN},$$
$$+K_{CN}, \text{Sig.-}K_{CN}(H(\text{Auth}_{CN})), \text{Tck}_{MN-CN},$$

where Auth_{CN} is $\{CN_{addr} || \text{HoA} || N_{MN} || T_{CN}\}$. The CN does not require to store any state information regard to this connection. Especially, it does not store tickets it has issued. The HA verifies the validity of $+K_{CN}$ by using it to construct the address of CN. It then uses the $+K_{CN}$ to verify the signature. This verification is done by the HA to reduce the load of the MN. We must note that the ticket key of a ticket is not revealed to HA.

– **Message 4.** The HA sends the following message to the MN using the authentication header of IPsec.

$$\text{HoT}_{HA} = N_{MN}, \{H(\text{Auth}_{CN}) || K_{MN-CN}\}.+K_{MN}, \text{Tck}_{MN-CN}$$

The AH allows the MN to gain assurance that HA have authenticated the CN. The MN looks up its binding update list and tries to match the nonce in the message with the nonce in the database. It then decrypts the ciphertext and verifies $H(\text{Auth}_{CN})$ using N_{MN}.

– **Message 5.** The MN generates another nonce N'_{MN} and associates it with the ticket, CN's address, and the ticket key. The ticket key should be stored securely. It then constructs the following message:

$$\text{BU} = c, N'_{MN}, +K_{MN}, MAC.K_{MN-CN}(c || N'_{MN} || \text{CoA} || CN_{addr} || bu), \text{Tck}_{MN-CN},$$

where c is a counter set to 0 and incremented each time the ticket is used, and bu is a value denoting that this MAC is for binding update. The counter value is also maintained in the binding update list. This message is sent directly to CN. The HoA of MN is included in the header of the packet in the home address destination option field. The CN first verifies $+K_{MN}$ by constructing the HoA and CoA of the MN and comparing it against the HoA and CoA included in the header of the packet. It then verifies the validity of the ticket by decrypting and checking the validation period and the HoA included in the ticket. It then look up its binding cache and obtains the current counter from the cache. Finally, it verifies the MAC using the ticket key. If everything is ok, it stores the nonce, counter, and binding update information in its binding cache.

– **Message 6.** The CN responds to BU by sending the following message:

$$\text{BA} = N'_{MN}, MAC.K_{MN-CN}(N'_{MN} || \text{CoA} || CN_{addr} || ba),$$

where ba is a value denoting that this MAC is for binding acknowledgement. The MN uses the ticket key to verify the MAC. Since N'_{MN} is included in the MAC, the MN can verify that this message is a response to the BU it sent.

A node must initially exchange all the messages to register its newly allocated CoA in CN's binding cache. Once the node has obtained a ticket from the CN, the MN only exchanges message 5 and 6 to update its address. Previous protocols using CGA generate a new signature each time an MN acquires a new CoA. However, in our protocol, a CN verifies the possession of the private key corresponding to the public key included in the HoA before it issues a ticket. Moreover, it verifies the CoA included in the MAC with the HoA included in the ticket. As a result, it is enough for the CN to just verify the MAC without verifying a signature each time the MN acquires a new CoA. An MN also exchanges only these two messages, when it returns home. However, two minor changes are required. First, home address option is not used. Second, the HoA is included in the MAC instead of CoA.

If the CN is a mobile node and it is at a foreign link, the HoTI sent by the requesting MN will be forwarded by the HA of the recipient node. The HA of CN will verify the signature in the HoTI on behalf of CN and sends only the $+K_{MN}$ to CN using AH in IPsec. Nodes including HAs must be able to identify that it has received a HoTI message. The rest of the procedure is the same as when the CN is a stationary host. As a result, a mobile node, whether it is requesting or receiving binding update, must perform one signature generation and one public key encryption/decryption, excluding the cost of verifying AH of IPsec. If the CN is at its home link, the HA will not intercepts messages directed to CN. In this case, CN will have to perform the verification by itself.

3 Analysis

3.1 Security Analysis

We will first argue that our protocols satisfy the security requirements of the binding update protocol.

- **Requirement 1.** The CN authenticates the ownership of HoA using the signature included in HoTI message or using the MAC included in BU message. Moreover, the CN only issues a ticket only when the signature is valid. An attacker requires the private key of MN to forge message 1 and requires the ticket key to forge BU message. The CoA of MN is also verified using the fact that both the HoA and CoA must be generated using the same public key.
- **Requirement 2.** The MN does not directly authenticate the CN. However, we assume that HA is honest and trustworthy entity. Therefore, if an MN receives HoT_{HA} message, the MN can be assured that the intended CN responded correctly to HoTI message. An attacker cannot forge this message without obtaining the private key of the CN. Moreover, the attacker requires the ticket key to forge the BA message.
- **Requirement 3.** A ticket key is required to construct the MAC included in BU messages which preserves integrity of the request. However, the ticket key is known only to the MN and CN. Even the HA does not know the ticket key. If the cipher used in the protocol is secure, using a passive cryptanalysis method to obtain the key from the ticket or from the $\{H(\text{Auth}_{CN})||K_{MN-CN}\}.+K_{MN}$ is infeasible.
- **Requirement 4.** The CoAs of a node must be generated using the same public key that is used to generate the HoA of the node. To claim an ownership of an

address that is already used by another node, a node must obtain a ticket using that node's HoA. However, it is infeasible to obtain a ticket using some other node's HoA without acquiring that node's private key. Therefore, it is infeasible to claim an ownership of an address that is already used by another node.

Now, we will discuss how strong our protocol is against various attacks.

– **DoS Attack.** The CN can be flooded with message 1 containing false signatures or BU message containing illegal MAC. The damage of this kind of attack is severe only when the CN is a mobile host and is located at its home link. Otherwise, the cost of verifying a signature or cost of verifying the ticket will not cause too much harm to its resource. If this kind of attack cannot be tolerated, we could sacrifice communication cost by using two dummy messages and a puzzle included in the second message from CN to MN. The CN can also be flooded with replay of old messages. The replays of HoTI messages are countered using a timestamp and replays of BU messages are countered using a counter.
– **Redirection Attack.** An attacker may try to redirect the mobile node's traffic to some other node including itself. The attacker can be successful at this attack, if he/she can obtain the private key of the victim or the ticket key of the victim's ticket. We assume that both are infeasible if the attacker is attempting a passive cryptanalysis attack. Moreover, even if an attacker acquires these keys, it will not be able to redirect the traffic to another node unless such node is using a CGA generated using the public key of the victim.
– **Neighbor Bombing Attack.** In Mobile IPv6, bombing a node located at a different link is difficult due to ingress filtering. However, it can redirect its traffic to a neighboring node. Since our protocol is based on CGA, it cannot claim an address already used by another node without acquiring that node's private key.

3.2 Efficiency Analysis

In Table 1, we compare our protocol against existing protocols. With respect to the number of messages exchanged, our protocol requires more messages than most of previous protocols. However, after initial binding update occurs, our protocol uses only two messages, which is minimal. Although CAM protocol uses only one message, mutual authentication cannot be provided with just one message.

With respect to computational cost, our protocol requires similar cost to previous CGA-based protocols. However, our protocol performs far better after an MN obtains a ticket. In the protocol proposed by Kang and Park [9], an MN does not generate any signatures during the binding updates. We must note that a CGA in this protocol is computed using the public key of the HA instead of the node's public key. A more serious problem of Kang and Park's is that CGA used by an MN and its CN are different. In extended version of CBID also uses this approach to move the computational burden of an MN to its HA [7]. In this case, the HA must give a different public key to each of its caring node. If this is not the case, an MN can bomb a neighboring node who shares the same key.

Table 1. Comparison of binding update protocols

		non-CGA based		CGA-based				
		[3]*	[8]*	[6]	[7]*	[9]	Ours*	
							Initial	Ticket only
	# of msg.	8**	8	1	4	4	6**	2
MN	signature	0	0	1	1	0	1	0
	exponentiation	0	0	0	2	0	1***	0
	symmetric	1	0	0	0	0	0	0
	MAC	2	2	0	1	2	2	2
CN	signature	0	2	1	1	1	1	0
	exponentiation	0	2	0	2	1	1***	0
	symmetric	1	0	0	0	0	2	1
	MAC	2	6	0	1	3	2	2
HA	signature	0	2	-	-	0	1	-
	exponentiation	0	2	-	-	1	0	-
	symmetric	0	0	-	-	0	0	-
	MAC	0	4	-	-	2	0	-

*: protocols that use IPsec, the cost involving use of IPsec is not counted in this table.
**: tunneling message is counted as 2.
***: encryption/decryption using a public key.

4   Conclusion

In this paper, we have proposed a new ticket-based binding update protocol for Mobile IPv6. Although, tickets have been used for a long time in cryptographic literature, we have no knowledge of ticket concept being used in binding update protocols for Mobile IPv6. The use of tickets can greatly improve the cost of binding update protocols. It can repeatedly provide mutual authentication between an MN and its CN with a very low cost. Our protocol is also based on CGA. CGA is a novel concept that can be used to provide the ownership of an address. Without use of CGA, authenticating the ownership of an address and defending neighbor bombing attacks are difficult. However, the costs of generating signatures hinder its use in mobile environment. Therefore, we have used ticket concept to minimize the need to generate signatures.

References

1. Nikander, P., Arkko, J., Aura, T., Montenegro, G., Nordmark, E.: Mobile IP Version 6 Route Optimization Security Design Background. IETF RFC 4225. (2005)
2. Arkko, J., Devarapalli, V., Dupont, F., Using IPsec to Protect Mobile IPv6 Signaling Between Mobile Nodes and Home Agents. IETF RFC 3776. (2004)
3. Johnson, D., Perkins, C., Arkko, J.,: Mobility Support in IPv6. IETF RFC 3775. (2004)
4. Aura, T.: Cryptographically Generated Addresses (CGA). IETF RFC 3972. (2005)
5. Soliman, H.: Mobile IPv6: Mobility in a Wireless Internet. Addison Wesley. (2004)
6. O'shea, G., Roe, M.: Child-proof Authentication for MIPv6 (CAM). In ACM Computer Communication Review, **31**(2) (2001) 4–8

7. Montenegro, G., Castelluccia, C.: Crypto-Based Identifiers(CBID): Concepts and Application. In ACM Trans. on Infomation and System Security **7**(1) (2004) 97–127
8. Qiu, Y., Zhou, J., Bao, F.: Protecting All Traffic Channels in Mobile IPv6 Network. In Proc. of the IEEE Wireless Communiations and Networking Conf. (2004) 160–165
9. Kang, H., Park, C.: MIPv6 Binding Update Protocol Secure Against Both Redirect and DoS Attacks. In Proc. of the CICS 2005. Lecture Notes in Computer Science **3822**. Springer-Verlag (2005) 407–418

Data Rate Adaptive Route Optimization for Sink Mobility Support in Wireless Sensor Networks

Jeongsik In[1], Jae-Wan Kim[1], Kwang-il Hwang[1], Jihoon Lee[2], and Doo-Seop Eom[1]

[1] School of Electrical Engineering, Korea University, 1, 5-ka, Anam-dong, Sungbuk-ku, Seoul 136-701, South Korea
{windie, kuzzang, brightday, eomds}@final.korea.ac.kr
[2] i-Networking Lab, Samsung Advanced Institute of Technology, San 14-1, Nongseo-Ri, Kiheung-Eup, Yongin, Kyungki-Do 449-712 Korea
vincent.lee@samsung.com

Abstract. Mobile sinks pose several challenges for network protocol design. While moving, a sink should continuously update its topological position information in the sensor nodes to maintain paths. This may require large signaling overhead, resulting in excessive energy consumption. Various schemes have been proposed to reduce the path management overhead. In many of these schemes, the sinks only maintain paths from active sources to reduce the overhead. While reducing the path management overhead, this approach introduces other problems. In this paper, Data Rate Adaptive Route Optimization (DRARO) scheme is proposed. DRARO provides a method for adjusting the route optimization level depending on the amount of data traffic, to minimize overall energy consumption. In addition, DRARO provides ceaseless connection for every sensor nodes and its performance is not affected by the number or movement of the sensing targets.

Keywords: sensor networks, routing, mobility.

1 Introduction

WSNs are a promising research area, encompassing a wide range of applications. WSNs are typically comprised of large numbers of small nodes with sensing, processing, and communication capabilities. The nodes sense the environment and cooperate with each other to respond to users' queries. The sensing targets, i.e. stimuli, of WSNs can be various in characteristics. The network and application models are diverse. Sinks (nodes which gather sensing data) may be stationary or moving while receiving data or waiting for a query response.

Mobile sink can extend the application area of WSNs significantly. Several schemes [1,2,3,4,5] have been proposed for efficient sink mobility support in previous work. These schemes have advantages in some scenarios, and disadvantages in others, as discussed in Sect. 2.

S. Madria et al. (Eds.): ICDCIT 2006, LNCS 4317, pp. 73–80, 2006.
© Springer-Verlag Berlin Heidelberg 2006

In this paper, Data Rate Adaptive Route Optimization (DRARO) scheme is proposed. DRARO is a sink-oriented scheme, in the sense that path setup and maintenance are performed on a per sink basis. In DRARO, every sink maintains paths from every sensor node, regarding every sensor node as a potential source. Thus any sensor node can transmit data to the sinks without requiring any subscription procedure. In addition, the increase in the number of sources or the movement of a stimulus does not incur additional overhead.

A key problem in taking a sink-oriented approach is the excessive per sink overhead required for path management between every source and sink pair. DRARO solves this problem by adopting a low overhead path maintenance scheme and an efficient path optimization scheme. Unlike other routing algorithms, DRARO explicitly separates path maintenance and optimization functions. Path maintenance is performed with minimal overhead, while path optimization is performed only when required. This provides a flexible method to trade off route optimality with signaling overhead, depending on the application requirements or the characteristics of the sensing target, making DRARO suitable for wide range of applications.

In Sect. 2, discussion on related work is presented. In Sect. 3, the proposed scheme is described in detail. In Sect. 4, performance analysis is presented along with simulation results, and Sect. 5 concludes this paper.

2   Related Work

Directed Diffusion (DD) [1] represents early work on data dissemination on WSNs with mobile nodes. It is very flexible for maintaining paths. However, the flexibility is obtained from the periodic data flooding from every source, which can significantly degrade energy efficiency.

In TTDD [2], a source places the information about its data on the *dissemination nodes*, which is selected among the sensor nodes to form a grid structure. A mobile sink can establish a data receiving path from the source through the nearest dissemination node. In SEAD [3] and ONMST [4], a multicast tree is constructed for each source to multicast the data to each sink. The tree is reconfigured as the source or the sinks are moving. The approach the above three schemes follow can be entitled *source-oriented multicast* approach. In this approach, a sink should subscribe to the source to join the multicast tree of the source. The information about the available sources is provided by dissemination nodes [2] or by separate index servers [3,4]. This approach has two major disadvantages. First, sinks are required to query dissemination nodes or index nodes periodically, even when they are not moving. There is no other way for the sinks to be aware of every occurrence of a new source. Second, path management overhead increases as the number of sources increases or the stimuli frequently change their position. In contrast, the proposed scheme is not affected by the number or the changes of sources.

Hybrid Learning-Enforced Time Domain Routing (HLETDR) [5] does not require subscription procedure. Nor does the overhead increase with the number of sources. However, these merits rely on the important condition that the movements of the sinks should have spatiotemporal patterns which can be learned by the sensor nodes over some time period. This requirement can seriously limit the application of the scheme.

3   Data Rate Adaptive Route Optimization (DRARO)

DRARO is designed for efficient sink mobility support in large scale networks. A large number of sensor nodes deployed in a vast area on a 2-dimensional space are considered. Since these nodes communicate through short-range radios, long range data delivery is achieved by multi-hop packet forwarding. In addition, each sensor node is assumed to know its position.

DRARO is composed of two component schemes, Agent-Based Incremental Path Extension (ABIPE) and Directional Route Optimization (DRO). ABIPE is a low overhead path maintenance scheme, and DRO is an efficient route optimization scheme designed to be used in parallel with ABIPE. Figure 1 presents simplified illustrations of the operations of ABIPE and DRO. In ABIPE, a mobile sink elects an agent among its neighbors when it broadcasts a query. As illustrated in Fig. 1 (a), the agent gathers data on behalf of the sink. As the sink moves out of the agent, a new agent is elected to connect the old agents and the sink. In this method, ABIPE can maintain the path from every sensor node to the sink with very low overhead. However, it can lead to severely detouring paths as the figure illustrates. These inefficient paths can be optimized with DRO scheme when required, for example, when there is a large amount of data traffic. In DRO, route optimization is performed along radial lines centered at the last agent, using geographical position information of the sensor nodes. Sensor nodes in the vicinity of the radial lines use the optimized paths, to deliver data packets, instead of the detouring paths. In Fig. 1, route optimization is performed by the fourth agent along six directions.

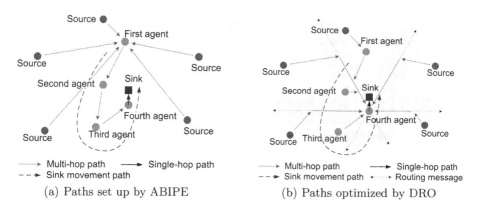

(a) Paths set up by ABIPE   (b) Paths optimized by DRO

Fig. 1. Simplified illustration of ABIPE and DRO

In Sect. 3.1 and 3.2, detailed descriptions of ABIPE and DRO are presented, and in Sect. 3.3, a discussion on data rate adaptation function of DRARO is presented.

3.1 Agent-Based Incremental Path Extension (ABIPE)

In ABIPE, when a sink has a new query, it selects its closest neighbor as its agent. To find the distance to each neighbor, the sink requests HELLO messages from its neighbors. The sink transmits the query to the selected agent, and the agent floods the network with the query on behalf of the sink. During the flooding process, each node in the network can set up the shortest path to the agent using the distance vector algorithm [7]. The query includes the required information for path setup. When a node has data matching the query, it forwards the data to the agent. The agent directly transmits the data to the sink.

When the sink moves out of the radio range of the agent, it elects a new agent. Then the sink transmits a relay request (RREQ) message to the previous agent via the new agent, so that the previous agent can set up a path to the new agent. Thus the previous agent can continue to forward data packets to the sink through the new agent. The overhearing nodes of the RREQ message also update their routing information for the new agent. In this method, the paths from all the sensor nodes to the sink can be maintained with minimal overhead. To route the RREQ from the new agent to the previous agent, simple greedy forwarding can be used [8]. In case the greedy forwarding fails, the message can be delivered along the data forwarding path.

3.2 Directional Route Optimization (DRO)

A newly elected agent can perform path optimization on a request of the sink. An agent which performed path optimization is called an optimizing agent. A sensor node becomes an agent by receiving an RREQ message from the sink. To request path optimization, the sink includes the number of optimizing directions and the coordinates of the previous optimizing agent in the outgoing RREQ message. When the new agent has received the RREQ with path optimization request, it calculates the directions to be optimized, based on the number of directions and the coordinates of the previous optimizing agent. The directions are selected so that any two adjacent directions form the same angle and the previous optimizing agent is placed at the center of two adjacent directions as illustrated in Fig. 1 (b).

After the directions are determined, the new agent sends a path optimize (POPT) message along the directions. In a real network, however, the POPT message cannot be propagated along the straight lines as shown in Fig 1 (b), since the nodes cannot be positioned exactly on the lines. Thus, an algorithm is required to find the next hop node for the message forwarding, given the coordinates of the optimizing agent and the optimizing direction. It is desirable that the next hop node satisfy the two conditions: It should not be too distant from the line and it should extend as far as possible in the optimizing direction. In

DRO, the forwarding node selects a virtual destination point on the optimizing line and selects a node, among its neighbors, which is closest to the virtual destination point. To select the virtual destination point, the forwarding node projects itself on the line, and moves the projection along the line towards the optimizing direction by a pre-determined distance. The distance should be larger than the radio range of the forwarding node.

3.3   Data Rate Adaptive Route Optimization

Overhead required for packet transmissions can be divided into data forwarding overhead and signaling overhead. Data forwarding overhead can be reduced by data path optimizations. However path optimization requires signaling overhead. Trade-off between signaling overhead and path optimality is important to minimize total energy consumption in packet transmissions.

DRARO provides two tunable parameters to adjust the route optimization level, i.e. the number of optimizing directions and the optimization interval. The number of optimizing directions is explained in Sect. 3.2. The optimization interval is the minimum hop distance between two consecutive optimizing agents. A smaller optimization interval triggers more frequent route optimizations, leading to more optimized routes as well as greater signaling overhead.

Many parameters are involved in determining better route optimization level, including the source and sink positions, the expected agent duration, the network dimensions and topology. However, it is too complex, if not impossible, to derive an optimization function including all of these parameters. Thus the route optimization level should be determined based on statistical analyses or simulation results for given network parameters. One of the simplest and extreme applications of the route optimization level adjustment is on-off switching. In the on-off switching method, the route optimization function is turned off when there is no active source, and constant optimization parameters are used when there presents any active source.

4   Performance Analysis

In this section, the performance of DRARO is analyzed with simulation experiments, using Network Simulator 2 (NS2). The performance metrics are throughput, energy consumption, and signaling overhead. In the simulation, default wireless communication modules of NS 2.27 are used with their default parameters. 802.11 DCF is used as the underlying MAC protocol.

Important simulation parameters are summarized as follows. 2000 sensor nodes are randomly distributed on a 5×5 km^2 field. The radio range of the node is 250m. The transmission rate of the physical link is 1 Mbps. The data packet size is 64 bytes and the control packet size is 36 bytes. A sink moves toward random destination point at a constant speed. On arriving at the destination point, it selects another random destination point and continues to move. The simulations are performed for 400 seconds and each result is averaged over 20 random topologies.

RTS/CTS exchange is disabled to speed up the simulation process. Also from a practical point of view, RTS/CTS exchange does not provide benefits for small size packets.

Figure 2 illustrates the impact of the route optimization level on protocol overhead and energy consumption for two source data rates (0.1 packet/s and 1 packet/s for each source node). 10 sources are randomly selected among the sensor nodes. One sink, moving at a speed of 10m/s, gathers data from the source nodes. The route optimization level is determined by the combination of the optimization interval and the number of the optimizing directions. The signaling overhead is presented in the first column, in terms of the amount of control packet forwardings. The data forwarding overhead is presented in the second column, in terms of the amount of data packet forwardings. The total energy consumptions are presented in the third column. In the horizontal axes of the graphs, 'No opt' means no route optimization, and 'Flooding' means that the flooding protocol is used for route optimization instead of DRO. The first and second columns show that the route optimization performance of DRO with 16 directions approximates the performance of the flooding, in spite of the great difference in the amount of signaling overhead. Since the paths constructed by flooding are the shortest paths, the figures indicate that near optimal paths can be constructed by DRO with significantly low overhead compared to that of flooding. The third column shows that as the source data rate increases, higher level of route optimization is required to minimize overall energy consumption. In case the source data rate is 0.1 packet/s, a low level of route optimization (i.e. 4 hops - 8 directions) minimizes energy consumption. For higher levels of

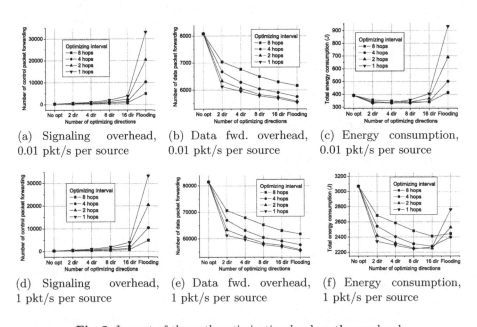

(a) Signaling overhead, 0.01 pkt/s per source

(b) Data fwd. overhead, 0.01 pkt/s per source

(c) Energy consumption, 0.01 pkt/s per source

(d) Signaling overhead, 1 pkt/s per source

(e) Data fwd. overhead, 1 pkt/s per source

(f) Energy consumption, 1 pkt/s per source

Fig. 2. Impact of the path optimization level on the overhead

route optimization, more optimization results in more energy consumption. On the other hand, when the source data rate is 1 packet/s, a higher level of route optimization (i.e. 1 hop - 8 directions) minimizes energy consumption.

Figure 3 shows the impact of the number and the speed of stimuli. A number of stimuli are moving around the field at a constant speed. The number and the speed of the stimuli vary as shown in the graphs. The existence of a stimulus is detected by the sensor node closest to the stimulus, and reported to the sink, moving at a speed of 10m/s, once every second. This models the cooperative detection of the target. However, details of the cooperation are not modeled, since they are independent of the routing scheme. For this and the next results, the optimization interval and the optimizing directions are fixed at 2 hops and 4 directions. Figure 3 shows that the throughput, energy consumption, and overhead are independent of the movements of the stimuli. The throughput, and overhead are independent of the number of the stimuli also. These are the unique features of a sink oriented approach. The energy consumption increases with the number of the stimuli because of the data traffic increase.

Figure 4 shows the impact of the number and the speed of the sinks. The overhead and energy consumption increases linearly with the increase in the number and the speed of the sink. This is inevitable since the signaling and the data forwarding is performed independently for each sink. Figure 4 (a) presents very high throughput even with considerably high sink speed. This is because the sink elects its new agent before it actually moves out of the radio range of the current agent. The time to elect a new agent is determined based on the

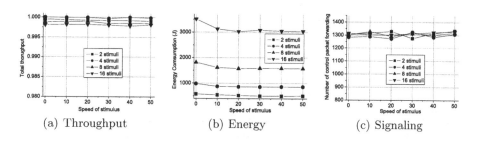

(a) Throughput   (b) Energy   (c) Signaling

Fig. 3. Impact of the number and the speed of the stimuli

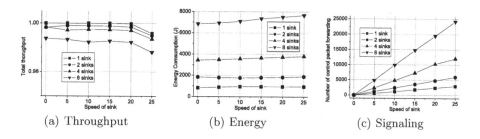

(a) Throughput   (b) Energy   (c) Signaling

Fig. 4. Impact of the number and the speed of the sink

positions of the sink and the current agent. The position estimation cost for the moving sinks are not considered in the above simulations. If this cost is taken into account, the performance will degrade more severely with sink number and speed.

5   Conclusion

In this paper, we have described DRARO, a routing algorithm for large scale wireless sensor networks with mobile sinks. By combining low overhead path maintenance scheme and efficient route optimization scheme, DRARO can efficiently provide ceaseless data forwarding paths for every sensor node, and highly optimized paths for active sources. In addition, DRARO is not affected by the characteristics (number, distributed area, speed, and duration) of stimuli. These merits enable DRARO to cover a wide range of applications.

Acknowledgments. This research was supported by the MIC (Ministry of Information and Communication), Korea, under the ITRC (Information Technology Research Center) support program supervised by the IITA (Institute of Information Technology Assessment).

References

1. Intanagonwiwat, C., Govindan, R., Estrin, D.: Directed Diffusion: A Scalable and Robust Communication Paradigm for Sensor Networks. Mobile Computing and Networks, 2000, pp. 56-67.
2. Ye, F.,Luo, H., Cheng, J. Lu, S., Zhang, L.: A two-tier data dissemination model for large-scale wireless sensor networks. Mobile Computing and Networks, 2002, pp. 148–159.
3. Kim, H., Abdelzaher, T., Kwon, W.: Minimum-Energe Asynchronous Dissemination to Mobile Sinks in Wireless Sensor Networks. Sensys, 2003, pp.193–204.
4. Zhang, W., Cao, G., Porta, T.: Dynamic Proxy Tree-Based Data Dissemination Schemes for Wireless Sensor Networks. IEEE International Conference on Mobile Ad-hoc Sensor System, 2004, pp. 21–30.
5. Baruah, P., Urgaonkar, R., Krishnamachari, B.: Learning-Enforced Time Domain Routing to Mobile Sinks in Wireless Sensor Fields. IEEE International Conference on Local Computer Networks, 2004, pp.525–532.
6. Zhang, W., Cao, G., La Porta, T.: Data Dissemination with Ring-Based Index for Sensor Networks. IEEE international conference on Network Protocol, 2003, pp. 305-314.
7. Perkins, C., Bhagwat, P.: Highly Dynamic Destination-Sequenced Distance-Vector Routing (DSDV) for Mobile Computers. ACM SIGCOMM, August 1994, pp. 234-244.
8. Karp, B., HKung, .T.: GPSR: Greedy Perimeter Stateless Routing for Wireless Networks. Annual International Conference on Mobile Computing and Networking, 2000, pp. 243-254.

Localization Control to Locate Mobile Sensors

Buddhadeb Sau[1], Srabani Mukhopadhyaya[2], and Krishnendu Mukhopadhyaya[3]

[1] Dept. of Maths., Jadavpur University, Kolkata, India
bsau@math.jdvu.ac.in
[2] BIT Mesra, Kolkata, India
srabanim@gmail.com
[3] ACMU, Indian Statistical Institute, Kolkata, India
krishnendu@isical.ac.in

Abstract. Localization is an important issue for Wireless Sensor Networks in a wireless sensor network. A mobile sensor may change its position rapidly and thus require localization calls frequently. It is important to control the number of localization calls, as it is rather expensive. The existing schemes for reducing the frequency of localization calls for mobile sensors uses the technique of extrapolation which involves simple arithmetic calculations. We propose a technique to control the localization that gives much better result. The proposed method involves very low arithmetic computation overheads. We find analytical expressions for the estimated error if the rate of localizations is specified. Simulation studies are carried out to compare the performances of the proposed method with the methods proposed by Tilak et al.

Keywords: Wireless sensor network, localization, mobility, localization control, target tracking.

1 Introduction

A micro-sensor (or simply a sensor) is a small sized and low powered electronic device with limited computational and communication capabilities. A *Wireless Sensor Network (WSN)* is a network containing some ten to millions of such micro-sensors. If the sensors are deployed randomly, or the sensors move about after deployment, finding the locations of sensors (*localization*) is an important issue in WSN. Localization requires communication of several necessary information between sensors over the network and a lot of computations. All these comes at the cost of high energy consumption. So far, research have mainly been focused on finding efficient localization techniques in static sensor networks (where the sensor nodes do not change their positions after deployment) [2,3,4].

Dynamic sensor networks have immense applications giving assistance to mobile soldiers in a battle field, health monitoring, in wild-life tracking [6], etc. When a sensor moves, it needs to find its position frequently. Using Global Positioning System (GPS) may not be appropriate due to its low accuracy, high energy consumption, cost and size. An optimized localization technique of static sensor network is used to find the current position of a mobile sensor. A fast

S. Madria et al. (Eds.): ICDCIT 2006, LNCS 4317, pp. 81–88, 2006.
© Springer-Verlag Berlin Heidelberg 2006

mobile sensor may require frequent localizations, draining the valuable energy quickly.

Thurn et al [5] proposed probabilistic techniques using Monte Carlo localization (MCL) to estimate the location of mobile robots with probabilistic knowledge on movement over predefined map. They used a small number of seed nodes (nodes with known position), as beacons. These nodes have some extra hardware. Hu et al [9] introduced the sequential MCL to exploit the mobility without extra hardware. WSNs generally remain embedded in an unmapped terrain and sensors have no control on their mobility. In [8], the objective is to reduce the number of localization calls. The positions of a sensor at different time instant are estimated from the history of the path of the sensor.

Tilak et al [7] proposed a number of techniques for tracking mobile sensors based on *dead reckoning*. The objective again is to control the number of costly localization operations. Among these techniques, the best performance is achieved by *Mobility Aware Dead Reckoning Driven (MADRD)*. MADRD estimates the position of a sensor, in stead of localizing the sensor every time it moves. Error in the estimated position grows with time. Every time localization is called, the error in the estimated position is calculated. Depending on the value of this error the time for the next localization is fixed. Fast mobile sensors t rigger localization with higher frequency for a given level of accuracy in position estimation.

In this paper, a method is proposed to estimate the positions of a mobile sensor, in stead of localizing the sensor. It gives higher accuracy for a particular energy cost and vice versa. The position of a sensor is required only when the sensor has some data is to be sent. The information of an inactive sensor is ceased to be communicated. Most calculations are carried out at the base station to reduce arithmetic complexity of sensors.

Section 2 describes the problem for tracking mobile sensor. In Section 3 we describe different algorithms for tracking mobile sensors. Section 4 deals with the analysis of the algorithm and different advantages. In Section 5 simulation results are presented. Finally, we present our conclusion in Section 6.

2   Problem Statement and Performance Measures

The position of a sensor is determined by a standard localization method. We assume that the location determined by this localization represents the actual position of the sensor at that moment. The sensors are completely unaware of the mobility pattern. Therefore, the actual position of a sensor S any time t is unknown. The position may be estimated or found by localization call. The absolute error in location estimation may be calculated as:

$$error_{abs} = \sqrt{(x_t - \hat{x}_t)^2 + (y_t - \hat{y}_t)^2}$$

where (x_t, y_t) and $(\hat{x}_t, \hat{y}_t)$ denote the actual and estimated positions at time t respectively. Frequent call of localization consumes enormous energy. To devise an algorithm optimizing both accuracy and energy dissipation simultaneously is very difficult. An efficient, robust and energy aware protocol is required to decide whether the location of the sensor would be estimated with a desired level of accuracy or found by localization with an acceptable level of energy cost.

3   Localization Protocol for Tracking Mobile Sensors

A mobile sensor changes its position with time. A simple strategy for finding its position is the use of standard localization methods at any time. But if the position of the sensor is required frequently, this method is very costly. Tilak et. al tried to reduce the frequency of localizations for finding the position of sensors. They proposed techniques: *Static Fixed Rate* (SFR), *Dynamic Velocity Monotonic* (DVM) and *Mobility Aware Dead Reckoning Driven* (MADRD).

SFR calls a classical localization operation periodically with a fixed time interval. To respond a query from the base station, a sensor sends its position obtained from the last localization. When a sensor remains still or moves fast, in both cases, the reported position suffers a large error. In DVM, localization is called adaptively with the mobility of the sensors. The time interval for the next call for localization is calculated as the time required to traverse the *threshold distance* (a distance, traversed by the sensor, location estimation assumed to be error prone) with the velocity of the sensor between last two points in the sequence of localization calls. In case of high mobility, a sensor calls localization frequently. If a sensor suddenly moves with very high speed from rest, error in the estimated location becomes very high. In MADRD, the velocity is calculated from the information obtained from last two localized points. The predictor estimates the position with this velocity and communicates to the query sender. At the localization point, the localized position is reported to the query sender and the *distance error* is calculated as the distance between the predicted position and reported position. If the error in position estimation exceeds threshold error (application dependent), the predictor appears to be erroneous and localization needs to be triggered more frequently. The calculation of error is necessary every time a localization called. Also, a sensor with high speed calls localizations frequently. We propose a new method, *Mobility Aware Interpolation* (MAINT), to estimate the current position with better tradeoff between the energy consumption and accuracy. The proposed method, MAINT, uses interpolation which gives better estimation in most cases.

3.1   Mobility Aware Interpolation (MAINT)

In some applications of dynamic sensor networks, the base station may need the locations of individual sensors at different times. The location may be required to be attached to the data gathered by the sensors in response to a query. However, the data may not be required immediately. In such cases, the number of localization calls may be reduced by delaying the response. The sensor holds the queries requiring the the location, into a list, `queryPoints` and sends the event to the base station padding the time of occurrence. At the following localization point, the sensor sends these two localized positions to each of the query senders in the time interval between these two localization points which are already in the list. The base station estimates the positions with more accuracy by interpolation with this information. The time interval of localization calls is as simple as in SFR. It eliminates all the arithmetic overheads as opposed to MADRD and the error prone nature in sudden change of speeds. Unnecessary calls of localizations for slow sensors may be avoided. To reduce the energy dissipation, the localization method may be called with higher time interval. The localization may be called immediately after receiving the query for real time applications or some special purpose. Each sensor runs a process with the algorithm described as follows :

Algorithm 1 (MAINT:)

Step-1: Let (x_1, y_1) denotes the last localization point occured at time t_1.
And let queryPoints $= \phi$.

Step-2: While(a query received from a sensor S at time $t > t_1$)
Append S to queryPoints, if $S \notin$ queryPoints.
If (response to the query is immediate) or ($t \geq t_1 + T$) then
/* Call an optimized localization method */
Let $(\hat{x}, \hat{y})$ be the location obtained from the method;
While (queryPoints $! = \phi$) do
Extract a query sender, say S', from queryPoints;
Send t_1, t, (x_1, y_1) and $(\hat{x}, \hat{y})$ to S'
End /* end of while */
Set $t_1 = t$ and $(x_1, y_1) = (\hat{x}, \hat{y})$.
endif
End while

After receiving a message from a sensor, the base station waits until it gets location information of the sender, S. If the processing of the message is immediate, the base station may send location query to the node S. However, the base station extracts localization points from the response obtained from S against the location query and estimates the location of S as follows:

Let (x_1, y_1) and (x_2, y_2) be the localized positions of the sensor s at t_1 and t_2.
if $(t' \in [t_1, t_2])$
Calculate the velocity vector as
$$\dot{x} = (x_2 - x_1)/(t_2 - t_1); \qquad\qquad \dot{y} = (y_2 - y_1)/(t_2 - t_1);$$
Estimate the position of s at time $t' \in [t_1, t_2]$ as
$$x' = x_1 + \dot{x}(t' - t_1); \qquad\qquad y' = y_1 + \dot{y}(t' - t_1);$$

where t' be a time at which the position of S is required by the base station.

4   Energy and Error Analysis

Energy consumption due to a localization call is much higher than other factors in dynamic localization. In the error analysis, we consider energy dissipation only by localization calls. We assume, the energy consumption is proportional to the number of localization calls. Therefore, we measure energy in terms of number of localization calls. Assume that MAINT occurs with a time interval T. The error evaluation is performed *uniformly* over the time interval $[0, T]$.

4.1 Motion Analysis with Random Waypoint Model

The Random WayPoint (RWP) is a commonly used synthetic model for mobility. We carried out the simulation study as well as analysis with RWP mobility model. In Figure 1 the sensor starts from $S_0(x_0, y_0)$ and reaches the point $S_T(x_T, y_T)$ at time T. The sequence of the waypoints attended by the sensor in the time interval $[0, T]$ is $S_0, S_1, \cdots, S_n, S_T$.

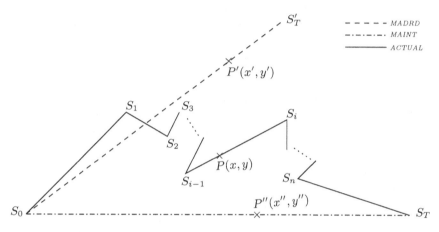

Fig. 1. Figure showing localization calls at two points and the position estimates for the intermediate points by MADRD and MAINT

At any waypoint $S_{i-1}(x_{i-1}, y_{i-1})$ next waypoint $S_i(x_i, y_i)$ is selected randomly with independent and identical uniform distribution over the rectangular area $R = \{(x, y) : 0 \leq x \leq X, 0 \leq y \leq Y\}$. We assume that the occurrence of waypoints follows the Poisson Process. Let t_i be the duration of the interval followed by the waypoint $S_{i-1}(x_{i-1}, y_{i-1})$ and (u_i, v_i) be the velocity components during this period. Therefore, the inter arrival times $t_i : 1 \leq i \leq n$ of the waypoints are independent and identically distributed and follow *exponential distribution* with parameter λ. The sum $T_i = t_1 + t_2 + \cdots + t_i$ is a random variable and follows gamma distribution with parameters λ and i. The number of waypoints n such that $T_n \leq T$ and $T_{n+1} > T$, follows the Poisson distribution with mean λT. Let $P(x, y)$ be the actual position of the sensor at time t, $0 \leq t_{i-1} \leq t \leq t_i \leq T$. Then
$$x = x_{i-1} + (t - T_{i-1})u_i, \quad y = y_{i-1} + (t - T_{i-1})v_i$$
for $i = 1, 2, \ldots, n$ and $T_0 = 0$.

4.2 Error Analysis for Equal Energy Dissipation

Let two consecutive calls of MAINT occurred at 0 and T. We assume, MADRD is called at 0 and T. In this case, both MADRD and MAINT consume equal energy. Let $P'(x', y')$ and $P''(x'', y'')$ are the estimated positions of the sensor at t according to MADRD and MAINT respectively.

Error in MADRD: MADRD is called at S_0 and next at S_T. The velocity used in the estimation by MADRD is (u', v'). The velocity may be calculated from the localization calls at S_0 and the call preceding S_0. Let (x_{-1}, y_{-1}) be the position obtained from localization call by the MADRD preceding S_0 and t_{-1} be the duration. Then $u' = \frac{x_0 - x_{-1}}{t_{-1}}$, $v' = \frac{y_0 - y_{-1}}{t_{-1}}$ where (x_{-1}, y_{-1}) iid as (x_i, y_i) and t_{-1} is iid as t_i. The estimation by MADRD at time t is given by $x' = x_0 + tu'$, $y' = y_0 + tv'$. The expected value of the square of the error at time t is $E[(x - x')^2 + (y - y')^2]$. The average error over the interval $[0, T]$ is

$$Err_{madrd} = \int_0^T E[(x - x')^2 + (y - y')^2] \, dt$$

Error in MAINT: MAINT is also called at S_0 and next at S_T. The velocity (u'', v'') used in the estimation by MAINT may be calculated from the positions of the sensor obtained from the localization calls at S_0 and S_T as $u'' = \frac{x_T - x_0}{T}$, $v'' = \frac{y_T - y_0}{T}$. The estimation by MAINT at time $t \in [t_{i-1}, t_i]$ is given by $x'' = x_0 + tu''$, $y'' = y_0 + tv''$. The average error over the interval $[0, T]$ in MAINT is given by

$$Err_{maint} = \int_0^T E[(x - x'')^2 + (y - y'')^2] \, dt.$$

Comparison of Error between MADRD and MAINT: Actual path of the sensor is continuous and it passes through S_0 and S_T. MADRD extrapolates a path passing through S_0 but not necessarily through S_T. On the other hand, MAINT interpolates the path through S_0 and S_T. Both estimated paths are continuous. MAINT incurs lower average error in the estimation than that in MADRD. Our simulation study shows that the average error in MAINT is uniformly much lower than that of MADRD under RWP mobility model.

5   Simulation Results

Simulation studies were carried out using ns-2 [11] to compare the performance of the proposed technique with that of MADRD. During the simulation, we use the parameters described in Table 1.

In the simulation study, we concentrated mainly on the average error in position for different number of localization counts. Figure 2 shows that MAINT performs uniformly better than MADRD. If we fix the error level, the localization count and hence the energy consumption in MAINT is significantly lower.

Table 1. Relevant parameters used in simulation

Simulation area	$300 \times 300 \, m^2$	Transmit power	0.660 W
Transmission range	10 m	Receive power	0.395 W
Initial Energy	10000 J	Idle power	0.035 W
MAC protocol	802.11	Number of mobile nodes	24
		Number of beacon nodes	36

Also, for comparable numbers of localization count, MAINT has much lower average error. MAINT estimates the position of a sensor with less error and even consuming less energy.

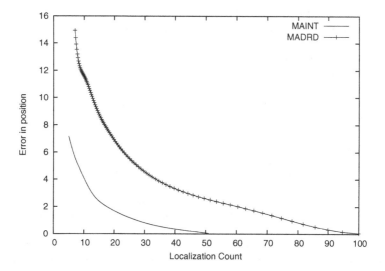

Fig. 2. Figure showing average error and localization counts for MADRD and the proposed technique

MAINT locates a mobile sensor with nearly exact position of the sensor consuming approximately half energy than that of MADRD. MAINT requires higher memory to hold the history of location queries. To reduce the memory requirement, we can hold limited number of most recent query points.

6 Conclusion

The technique, proposed in this paper, uses estimates of the location of a mobile sensor to save on the energy used up in frequent calls for localization. In MADRD, the velocity of a sensor is calculated using the time and location of the last two points of localization. This velocity is later used to extrapolate the position of the sensor at a later time. In comparison, MAINT uses interpolation. The velocity is similarly calculated but not from the last two points, rather from the last localization point and the next localization point. So the position can be estimated only after the next localization takes place. Simulation studies show that MAINT estimates the position of the sensor with much lower error than that of MADRD. Simulation study in this paper was carried out using RWP mobility model. However, analysis of the proposed technique shows that MAINT estimates the path with lower error for any other mobility model. Simulation works using other mobility models like the Gaussian movement model, Brownian motion model etc., are in progress.

References

1. Akyldiz, I.F., Su, W., Sankarasubramaniam, Y., Cayh'ci, E.: Wh'eless Sensor Networks: A Survey. Computer Networks, Vol. 38, No. 4. March (2002) 393–422
2. Bulusu, N., Heidemann, J., Estrin, D.: GPS-less Low Cost Outdoor Localization For Very Small Devices. IEEE Personal Communications Magazine, Vol. 7, No. 5. **October** (2000) 28–34
3. Meguerdichian, S., Koushanfar, F., Qu, G., Potkonjak, M.: Exposure In Wireless Ad-Hoc Sensor Networks. Proc. 7th Int. Conf. on Mobile Computing and Networking (MobiCom'01). Rome, Italy **July** (2001) 139–150
4. Raghunathan, V., Schurgers, C., Park, S., Srivastava, M.B.: Energy-aware wireless microsensor networks. IEEE Signal Processing Magazine, vol. 19, No. 2. IEEE **March** (2002) 40–50
5. Thrun, S., Fox, D., Burgard, W., Dellaert, F.: Robust Monte Carlo Localization for Mobile Robots. Artificial Intelligence (2001)
6. Juang, P., Oki, H., Wang, Y., Martonosi, M., Peh, L.S., Rubenstein, D.: Energy-efficient computing for wildlife tracking: design tradeoffs and early experiences with zebranet. Proc. of 10th Int. Conf. on Architectural Support for Programming Languages and Operating Systems (ASPLOS-X). ACM Press, (2002) 96–107
7. Tilak, S., Kolar, V., Abu-Ghazaleh, N.B., Kang, K.D.: Dynamic Localization Control for Mobile Sensor Networks. IEEE Int. Workshop on Strategies for Energy Efficiency in Ad-Hoc and Sensor Networks(IEEEIWSEEASN-2005).
8. Bergamo, P., Mazzini, G.: Localization in Sensor Networks with Fading the Mobility. IEEE PIMRC. **September** (2002)
9. Hu, L., Evans, D.: Localization in Mobile Sensor Networks. MobiCom'04, **Sept. 26.-Oct.,1** (2004)
10. Bettstetter, C., Wagner, C.: The spatial node distribution of the random waypoint mobility model. In Proceedings of German Workshop on Mobile Ad Hoc networks (WMAN), Ulm, Germany, **March** (2002)
11. Network Simulator : http://isi.edu/nsnam/ns

Static and Dynamic Allocation Algorithms in Mesh Structured Networks

Leszek Koszalka

Chair of Systems and Computer Networks, Faculty of Electronics,
Wroclaw University of Technology, 50-370 Wroclaw, Poland
leszek.koszalka@pwr.wroc.pl

Abstract. The objective of the paper is an evaluation of task allocation algorithms for computer networks with mesh topology. The properties of algorithms have been researched with the designed and implemented experimentation system. The system gives opportunities for simulating allocation processes in the static mode and in the dynamic mode, as well. The investigations have been concentrated on comparing algorithm complexity as the introduced measure of efficiency. The obtained results justify a conclusion that the proposed Window Stack Based Algorithm is very promising.

1 Introduction

In recent years, grid and mesh structures have received increasing attention. Recently, multicomputers and computer networks with nodes connected through high-speed links have become a common computing platform. The mesh topology (structure) for such networks is very reasonable. The mesh has a simple and regular topology as a square or rectangle in 2D space and a cube or rectangular parallelepiped in 3D space. It becomes more and more popular for parallel and distributed computing systems due to its good properties like modularity and also scalability (e.g. [5], [6], [11], and [12]).

It is very important to find free resources for executing incoming jobs in a short time and with productive utilization of available supplies. A good task allocation algorithm should achieve both these objectives. In mesh-connected systems, the allocation algorithm is concerned with assigning the required number of executors to any incoming job i.e. for finding a free sub mesh. If such a submesh is not available (there are no available processors in one coherent area), the job remains in the queue until another just allocated job finishes its execution and releases a proper sub-mesh (*dynamic mode*) or, it is simply dropped (*static mode*).

In the literature, many propositions of algorithms can be found for task allocation purposes (e.g. [2], [4], [5], [6], [7], and [8]). This paper is concentrated on the stack–based allocation algorithms, in particular on algorithms proposed by the author and his co-workers, including BFSBA, SSBA [3], and WSBA initially presented in [1].

In the paper the results of evaluation of properties of those algorithms are presented and discussed. The rest of the paper is organized as follows. Section 2 contains allocation problem statement. Section 3 presents short description of the considered algorithms. In Section 4, a glimpse for the experimentation system is given. Section 5

S. Madria et al. (Eds.): ICDCIT 2006, LNCS 4317, pp. 89 – 101, 2006.
© Springer-Verlag Berlin Heidelberg 2006

and Section 6 present some results of investigations for static mode and dynamic mode, respectively. Final remarks appear in section 7.

2 Problem Statement

Basic Terms. Let us introduce some terms and definitions concerning mesh structured systems (without loss of generality with reference only to 2D meshes).

Mesh is a set of potential executors (nodes in a network) connected in an orderly fashion. The *mesh M (L, W)* is the rectangular mesh composed of the number of $L \times W$ nodes (L denotes length of the mesh and W denotes the width of the mesh) forming a regular two-dimensional matrix.

Node in the row j and column i is denoted as $< i, ,j >$. Rows and columns are counted beginning with left-upper corner of the mesh.

Submesh S(l, w) is a rectangular set of $(l \times w)$ nodes that pertain to the mesh M (L, W). A given submesh is described by $\{< x_1, y_1 >, < x_2, y_2 >\}$, where $< x_1, y_1 >$ and $< x_2, y_2 >$ are the nodes located in its upper left corner and its lower right corner, respectively.

Free submesh is a submesh in which every node is free i.e. it is not at the moment preoccupied with previously allocated tasks.

Busy submesh is a submesh in which at least one node was already assigned to execute a task. The total busy submesh contains only busy nodes.

An example of the rectangular 2D mesh M (16, 12) with four tasks just allocated, including e.g. the task which made the submesh $\{< 6, 2 >, < 9, 5 >\}$ as the total busy submesh, is shown in Fig. 1.

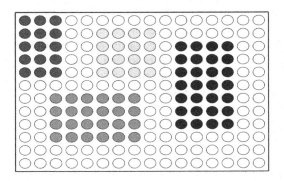

Fig. 1. An example of the mesh with four tasks allocated

Measures of Efficiency. A measure of efficiency called complexity is introduced and used for static mode and dynamic mode. Additionally, for dynamic mode the queue size throughout the allocation process is taken into consideration.

Complexity is a value describing the time needed for carrying out all computations required by a given allocation algorithm. This term is regarded as the total number of elementary operations made during the whole allocation process. This method of time measurement gives opportunities for isolating the complexity of a specific thread – it is especially convenient and reasonable for the dynamic mode.

Assumptions. The following assumptions for allocation process have been taken:

- Any task that is waiting in a queue to be accomplished on the mesh $M(L,W)$ is rectangular. The ith task $i=1,2,...,N$ requires an ordered set of executors i.e. a submesh of known size $S(l_i, w_i)$ or $S(w_i, l_i)$.
- The execution times to tasks are much longer than the predicted total times of their allocations.
- The total number of available nodes in the entire mesh is never smaller than the total number of executors required by tasks in a queue.

Static Mode – problem formulation. An additional assumption is taken: Each allocated task occupies the mesh to the end of the allocation process (its execution time may be considered as infinite). The problem can be stated as follows:

- *given*:   the 2 or 3D mesh, the queue of N tasks with known sizes,
- *to find*:   allocation of tasks within the mesh,
- *such that*: to ensure the possibly smallest complexity i.e. the shortest total allocation time T_N of N tasks.

Dynamic Mode – problem formulation. An additional assumption is taken: Each allocated task does not occupies the mesh to the end of the allocation process. The problem may be stated as follows:

- *given*:   the 2 or 3D mesh, dynamically coming tasks (along with Poisson distribution), the queue of tasks with known sizes,
- *to find*:   allocation of tasks within the mesh and reallocation of submeshes freed after execution of tasks,
- *such that*: to ensure the shortest possible allocation time T_N and the shortest length of queue of tasks to be allocated.

3 Allocation Algorithms

In this section, a preliminary analysis of properties of the considered allocation algorithms is presented. Firstly, known allocation algorithms such as very simple FS, and algorithms from stack-based family: SBA, SSBA, and BFSBA, are characterised. Next, the proposed algorithm WSBA is presented much more in details.

3.1 Description of Algorithms

FS-algorithm (*Full Search*). This algorithm finds a place on the mesh by browsing through all mesh nodes until it finds empty submesh big enough to match incoming task. It involves checking task size (number of processing elements) for every free node found while searching for an empty submesh. This operating routine is assumed to be the least effective but it is important to note that its single task allocation complexity does not really depend on amount of tasks currently operating neither on the mesh nor on their parameters. The main drawback of this algorithm is that it is highly afflicted by fragmentation (the total number of holes within already active area).

SBA-algorithm (*Stack Based Algorithm*). It finds a place on mesh by cross-checking every *Candidate Block (Free Submesh)* with every *Coverage* (the set of nodes such that using one of them as a free node makes a given task to be overlapped with *Busy Submesh*) listed within the algorithm. By using spatial subtraction [6] on a *Candidate Block*, algorithm produces new *Candidate Blocks* and cross checks them with those *Coverages* which have not been cross-checked before. This algorithm is widely documented in [4], [6]-[10]. Complexity of allocating a single task as we may see heavily depends on the total number of tasks within the mesh at the time when new task comes in. It may be concluded that the worst operating case for this algorithm is when high fragmentation occurs and there is the great number of tasks within the mesh.

SSBA-algorithm (*Sorted Stack Based Algorithm*). It is a modification of *SBA*. This algorithm uses sorted *Busy Submeshes* queue for generating *Coverages* which enables it to cut off cross-checking with *Candidate Blocks* earlier. It has two drawbacks which are suspected to increase it complexity even further in conditions which are unfavorable to the standard *SBA*: *Busy Submeshes* queue sorting by insertion on every task allocation and additional checking incorporated in the cut off condition.

BFSBA-algorithm (*Best Fit Stack Based Algorithm*). The main idea if this algorithm is choosing an order of the *Coverages* on the stack, what causes that the fragmentation may be minimized. This algorithm has no visible drawbacks against the *SBA*. It chooses *Candidate Blocks* with the minimal height and with the minimal horizontal position. This operation is not extra time-consuming because it can be done during standard run of the SBA scheme.

3.2 Window Stack-Based Algorithm

The basic idea of the algorithm consists in presenting knowledge of accessible allocation space (i.e. all free nodes available within mesh) in the form of the set of maximum submeshes (*maximum windows*). Maximum windows should have the least as possible common nodes. These windows are placed on the inner stack of the algorithm (window stack) and they are sorted according to left-upper corner, at first along columns, next along rows. After successful allocation, the windows on the stack are updated. The algorithm operates in a loop as a two-step procedure:

Step 1. *Comparing the size of task being allocated with maximum windows on the stack.* Incoming task is always located in the first window on the stack that is big enough to contain it. After successful allocation of a given task go to *Step 2*.
Step 2. *Up-dating all windows on the stack.* It requires following the rules: (i) none of windows would contain the nodes taken by that allocated task, (ii) a window which is contained in the other window has to be popped from the stack, (iii) windows are being cut into maximum windows that do not contain the busy nodes, (iv) the correctly prepared windows are pushed onto the stack in an orderly manner.

In Fig. 2, an example of the states of a mesh is shown, where on the left is the initial state as one-element set of maximum windows and on the right is the four-element set of maximum windows created by algorithm after allocation of three tasks.

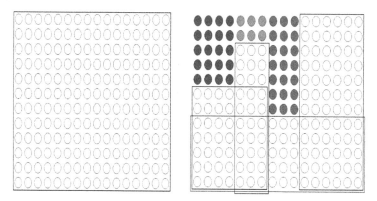

Fig. 2. The WSBA in action – static mode

In Fig. 3, an example of the actualization of the set of maximum windows in the dynamic mode is visualized (in the figures, the blackened nodes are busy). The updating was made at the moment in which one of the tasks was ended and freed the occupied processors (located in submesh *{<7, 2>, <9, 5>}*).

The important feature of the algorithm is that it uses an inner description of free space available on the mesh by keeping a stack holding maximum possible rectangular windows. The algorithm is capable of choosing the right place on the mesh instantly but it has to update the free space description after. Update is based mainly on cutting and sorting free space description. Its main drawback is reallocation process which involves updating all the windows within to required maximum description condition.

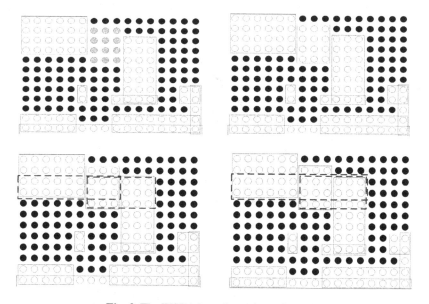

Fig. 3. The WSBA in action – dynamic mode

4 Experimentation System

An experimentation system for testing allocation algorithms in different conditions has been designed. By allowing dynamical task generation and providing a way to simulate task execution process the system gives opportunities for finding algorithm complexity as a direct result of an allocation process. The kernel of the proposed module of the experimentation system for the dynamic mode is shown in Fig. 4. The module is composed of four threads:

- *Task Generator Thread* – to simulate task incoming to the system basing on Poisson process.
- *Algorithm Thread* – to perform all computations needed for finding appropriate free nodes.
- *Processor Mesh Thread* – to allocate tasks within the mesh,
- *Returned Space Buffer Thread* – to return a space occupied by tasks just executed.

The *Generator Thread* and the *Returned Space Buffer Thread* are implemented in queues. There are distinct two situations. In the first situation, a queue contains tasks which are waiting for allocation, thus the length of a queue may also be measured. In the second situation, a queue consists of tasks just executed.

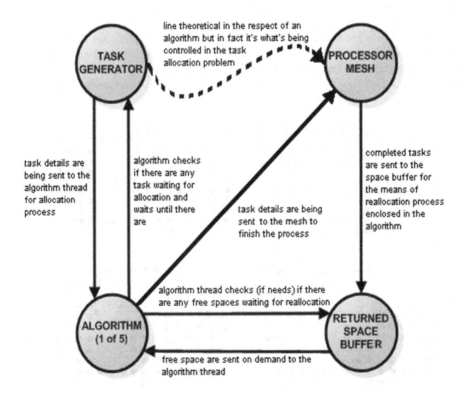

Fig. 4. A concept of dynamic mode testing environment

In order to carry out experiments a simulation environment in JAVA has been created. The Java application was dedicated to work within multi-task environment (MS Windows, Java 1.4.1 SDK).

The experimenter has opportunities to form a design of experiment by determining the parameters, including *for static and dynamic mode:* (i) mesh size, i.e. W and L, (ii) the total number of tasks in a queue, i.e. N, (iii) parameters of probability distribution of sizes of incoming jobs (the random values of w and h are generated separately), (iv) the percentage of mesh utilization i.e. the ratio of : the sum of products w_i and h_i for all N tasks and the product WxL (the total number of nodes available), (v) the allocation algorithm (available *FS, SBA, SSBA, BFSBA,* and *WSBA; for dynamic mode:* (vi) the execution times to the tasks (as random values with uniform distribution within the range defined by experimenter), (vii) the time-instants of joining queue by tasks (as random values with Poisson distribution defined by user).

The chosen implementation environment gives opportunities to visualize the recent state of the mesh during the allocation process. An example of visualization of an allocation process in dynamic mode is shown in Fig, 5.

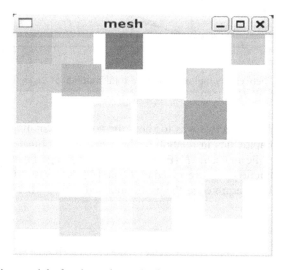

Fig. 5. Visualization module for dynamic mode (intensity of brightness of submesh is corresponded to time left to completing execution of a given task)

5   Investigations - Static Mode

For the static mode, the main goal of the research was to investigate relationship between complexity and parameters such as mesh size and the queue length for the considered allocation algorithms with special attention paid to WSBA-algorithm.

Experiment #S1. The objective was to compare complexities of the considered allocation algorithms. The values of random parameters were generated 100 times for the same mesh size in order to make results (mean values of complexity) more accurate and thus more reliable. In Fig. 6, the advantage of WSBA over other members of SBA-family is confirmed.

The obtained results of experiment allow us to anticipate that with a constantly growing amount of tasks and with relatively big mesh, the WSBA algorithm can remarkable supersede all of its competitors. The WSBA performed as the best but the "runner-up" was FS-algorithm. Thus, when the profit of using WSBA in comparison with FS would be calculated, then one could deduce that the profit of using WSBA in comparison with other algorithms would be not less.

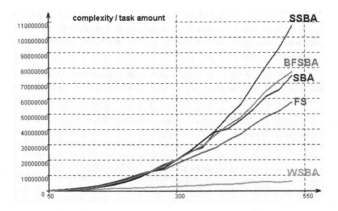

Fig. 6. Relationship between complexity and the total number of tasks for a relatively large square meshes: $100 < (W, H) < 150$

Experiment #S2. The objective was to show the advantage of *WSBA* over *FS* when comparing their complexities in relation to the sizes of task queues and mesh sizes. For these purposes, the index *EAF* (Effectiveness Advantage Factor) defined as the ratio (1) of the completion times received by *FS* and *WSBA*, was utilized.

This index may be interpreted as the profit obtained with WSBA instead of FS.

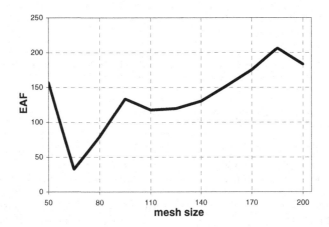

Fig. 7. Profit of using WSBA in relation to mesh size

$$EAF = \frac{T_N(FS)}{T_N(WSBA)} \qquad (1)$$

The series of experiments were made for square mesh with size of L=W=200, and with the sizes of tasks in queue generated using uniform distribution (ranges from 1 to 10 for both length and height).

The obtained results are shown in Fig. 7 and Fig. 8. It may be observed that for relatively big meshes (greater than 100) and for the large total number of tasks (greater than 350) the relationships have increasing tendency, i.e. using WSBA can give the significant profit.

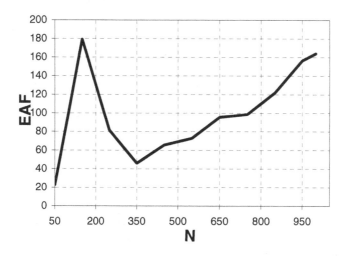

Fig. 8. Profit of using WSBA in relation to the queue size

It may be observed that contrary to *FS*-algorithm, the proposed *WSBA*-algorithm does not have exponential complexity but complexity which is approximately polynomial. This is directly related to the inner free submeshes (throughout the whole allocation process). The task is allocated into the first free submesh that is capable of handling the task, thus placing the task into a mesh and then updating a stack are very fast activities.

Although the WSBA algorithm appeared to be better than the other considered algorithms when operated in the static mode, the properties of WSBA need to be tested when operated in dynamic mode of allocation process.

6   Investigations – Dynamic Mode

In order to make a comparison between algorithms four experiments were conducted.

Experiment #D1. *Comparison between FS and SBA-family (without WSBA).*

It may be observed, in Fig. 9, that SBA family algorithms have all similar complexity during allocation process, so one can take for further tests only one of them which can represent the whole family – SBA is chosen. Such an act is reasonable as complexity charts may become unclear because of all algorithm threads have to asynchronously support reallocation.

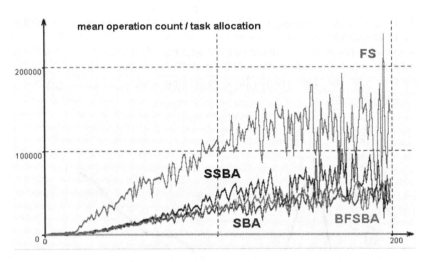

Fig. 9. Complexity in relation to task allocation (without WSBA)

Experiment #D2. *Comparison between FS, SBA and WSBA on the basis of a given allocation process.*

In Fig. 10, it may be observed that overall complexity of the considered algorithms is composed of two major elements. The first is affected by allocation (low values) but the second one is caused by reallocation costs (peaks).

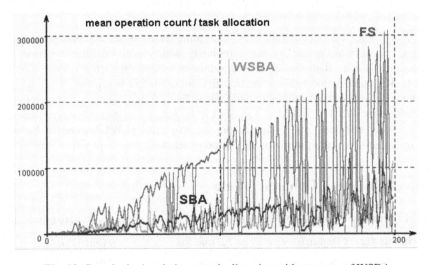

Fig. 10. Complexity in relation to task allocation with presence of WSBA

One can see that WSBA algorithm has the capability to become more efficient than its commercial competitor SBA. Its complexity stays low though its peaks are even higher than those appearing in FS algorithm.

Experiment #D3. *Comparison between FS, SBA and WSBA – mean results.*

In order to make results more reliable series of experiments were repeated what allowed obtaining mean results. The results are presented in Fig. 11. A conclusion taken from this figure is that peaks dominated the WSBA behavior and made it features diminish. In spite of that, one can see that there exist some ranges in which complexity of WSBA is lower than that presented by SBA algorithm.

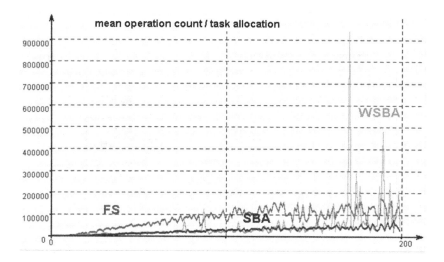

Fig. 11. Mean complexity in relation to task allocation during dynamic allocation process

Experiment #D4. *Investigation of Length of Queue.*

Queue size throughout allocation process may be regarded as a measure to efficiency. The most important in any application of multi-meshed systems is its capability to deal with the tasks as they come for processing. The obtained results (measurements of queue size) are shown in Fig. 12a & 12b. The only conclusion one can come to on their basis is that multitask environment makes such a measurement very difficult. It may be observed that inner tasks managing routines that are being used in such environments make time measurement as well as strict independent thread implementation impossible. Threads supplying allocation and those trigging reallocation in ideal case should run on different units.

The only way to make these measurements reliable is full parallel implementation of the simulation environment.

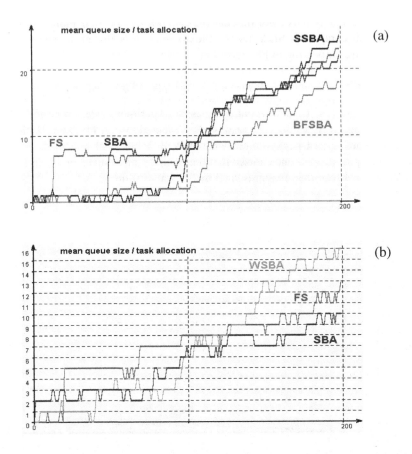

Fig. 12. Task queue behavior: (a) SBA-family, (b) WSBA versus others

7 Final Remarks

The main conclusion resulting from the research is that in the static mode the WSBA may be recommended as the best algorithm when one need to allocate a huge amount of tasks and SBA, BFSBA and SSBA turn out to be useful when the total number of tasks is much smaller.

In order to come to the remarkable conclusion for the dynamic mode it is needed (in author's opinion) to make some modifications of experimentation system (the results presented in Section 6 can be regarded as the first attempt to an evaluation of algorithms in dynamic mode).

In the further future, the research in this area will be concentrated on designing and implementing a distributed mesh allocation algorithm simulation system.

Acknowledgment. I would like to give my appreciation to Mr. M. Kubiak and Mr. T. Larkowski, graduate students at Computer Science and Engineering, Wroclaw University of Technology, for help in implementation of experimentation system.

References

1. Koszalka L., Kubiak M., Pozniak-Koszalka I.: Allocation Algorithm for Mesh-Structured Networks, Proc. of 5th ICN Conference IARIA, ICN5: Management, Mauritius, IEEE Computer Society Press (2006)
2. Chang C., Mohapatra P.: An Integrated Processor Management Scheme for Mesh-Connected Multicomputer System, Proc. of International Conference on Parallel Processing, August (1997)
3. Koszalka L., Lisowski D., Pozniak-Koszalka I.: Comparison of Allocation Algorithms for Mesh - Structured Networks with Using Multistage Experiment, Proc. of ICCSA 2006, Part V, LNCS 3984 (2006) 58-67
4. Chmaj G., Zydek D. and Koszalka L.: Comparison of Task Allocation Algorithms for Mesh-Structured Systems, Computer Systems Engineering, Proc. of 4th Polish-British Workshop (2004) 39-50
5. Sharma D. D., Pradhan D. K.: Submesh Allocation in Mesh Multicomputers Using Busy-List: A Best-Fit Approach with Complete Recognition Capability, Journal of Parallel and Distributed Computing **1** (1996) 106-118
6. Byung S., Das C.R.: A Fast and Efficient Processor Allocation Scheme for Mesh-Connected Multicomputers, IEEE Trans. on Computers **1** (2002) 46-59
7. De M., Das D., Ghosh M.: An Efficient Sorting Algorithm on the Multi-Mesh Network, IEEE Trans. on Computers **10** (1997) 1132-1136
8. Yang Y., Wang J.: Pipelined All-to-All Broadcast in All-Port Meshes and Tori, IEEE Trans. on Computers **10** (2001) 1020-1031
9. Agarwal A.: The MIT Alewife Machine: Architecture and Performance, Computer Architecture (1995) 2-13
10. Kasprzak A.: Packet Switching Wide Area Networks, WPWR, Wroclaw (1997) /in Polish/
11. Liu T., Huang W., Lombardi F., Bhutan L.N.: A Submesh Allocation for Mesh-Connected Multiprocessor Systems, Parallel Processing (1995) 159-163
12. Batcher K., E.: Architecture of a massively parallel processor, Proc. of International Conference on Computer Architecture (1998) 174-179

A Key Management Scheme with Encoding and Improved Security for Wireless Sensor Networks*

Al-Sakib Khan Pathan, Tran Thanh Dai, and Choong Seon Hong

Networking Lab, Department of Computer Engineering, Kyung Hee University
1 Seocheon, Giheung, Yongin, Gyeonggi 449-701, South Korea
{spathan, daitt}@networking.khu.ac.kr, cshong@khu.ac.kr

Abstract. Wireless sensor networks are emerging as a promising solution for various types of futuristic applications both for military and public. Security in wireless sensor networks is very crucial as these networks are expected mainly to operate in the hazardous and hostile environments. Efficient key management could guarantee authenticity and confidentiality of the data exchanged among the nodes in the network. In this paper, we propose an improved and efficient key pre-distribution scheme for wireless sensor networks. Our scheme significantly increases the storage efficiency and security than that of the previously proposed scheme based on LU decomposition. It also ensures node-to-node mutual authentication in a way that an eavesdropper cannot harm the network by monitoring the traffic flows in the network. We also present detailed performance analysis and compare our scheme with the existing schemes.

1 Introduction

Wireless Sensor Network (WSN) is one of the emerging network technologies that would be utilized in abundance in future. WSNs are expected to serve many general purpose applications for the mass public as well as to contribute significantly to military operations, medical, disastrous and emergency situations. However, there are still a lot of unresolved issues in wireless sensor networks of which security is one of the hottest research issues [1], [2]. In fact, security becomes the prime concern when wireless sensors are deployed in hazardous, hostile or more specifically in military reconnaissance scenario. Even if the wireless sensor network has efficient protocols for routing and data passing throughout the network, absence of security simply nullifies the real-world implementation of those in most of the cases. The sensory data collected using acoustic, magnetic, seismic, radar or thermal mechanisms are often considered as secret and not intended to be disclosed in public. Hence, there must be some sorts of mechanisms for node to node data transmission with confidentiality and authenticity of data. Efficient key management schemes could solve this issue. However, the sensors are tiny devices which have low memory, processing power and limited battery power [3], [4], [5], [6]. Due to the resource limitations, the key

---

* This work was supported by MIC and ITRC projects. Dr. C.S. Hong is the Corresponding Author.

S. Madria et al. (Eds.): ICDCIT 2006, LNCS 4317, pp. 102–115, 2006.

management schemes like trusted server, Diffie-Hellman or public-key based schemes used in other networks are not feasible to be applied directly in wireless sensor networks [7], [8], [9], [10].

To address the key agreement problem in WSNs, there are mainly three categories of schemes: key distribution center scheme, public key scheme, and key pre-distribution scheme. Constrained computation and energy resources of sensor nodes often make the first two schemes infeasible for wireless sensor networks [7], [8], [10]. The third category of key management scheme is key pre-distribution scheme, where keying materials are delivered to all sensor nodes prior to deployment. In fact, key pre-distribution seems to be the most feasible solution for key management in these types of networks [8], [9], [10]. The intent of this paper is to propose an efficient key pre-distribution scheme for ensuring better security and resilience of the network. Our scheme uses LU decomposition adopted from [11], [15] but significantly improves the security of the network. In addition to this, we also propose an efficient method to store the keying information in the sensor nodes to effectively utilize the overall network storage.

1.1 Main Contributions of Our Work

1. A new key predistribution scheme based on LU decomposition with significantly better security than the previously proposed schemes
2. Introducing an efficient encoding mechanism to store pre-distributed keying information in the sensors to reduce individual node's and network-wide storage usage
3. Rigorous guarantee of finding common key between any two nodes in the network
4. Detailed performance analysis and comparison of our scheme with previously proposed schemes.

1.2 Organization of This Paper

The organization of this paper is as follows: Following the Section 1, Section 2 mentions the related works, Section 3 presents our proposed scheme, Section 4 deals with the detailed performance analysis and comparisons, and Section 5 concludes the paper with future research directions.

2 Related Works

Eschenauer and Gligor [9] proposed a random key pre-distribution scheme (*often termed as basic probabilistic key sharing scheme*). In this scheme, prior to sensor network deployment, each sensor node is distributed a ring of keys where each key ring consists of randomly chosen k keys from a large pool of P keys, which is generated offline. To agree on a key for communication, two nodes find out one common key within their key rings and use that key as their shared secret key. Choi and Youn [11] proposed a key pre-distribution scheme guaranteeing that any pair of nodes can find a common secret key between themselves by using the keys assigned by LU decomposition of a symmetric matrix of a pool of keys. Chan et al. [7] presented three mechanisms for key establishment using the framework of pre-distributing a random set of keys to each node. The first one is q-composite keys scheme. This scheme is mainly based on [9]. The difference between this scheme and [9] is that q common keys ($q > 1$), instead of just a single one, are needed to establish secure communication between a pair of nodes. The second one is multipath key reinforcement scheme applied in conjunction with the basic scheme to yield improved resilience against node capture attacks by trading off some network communication overhead. The main attractive feature of this scheme is that it can strengthen the security of an established link key by establishing the link key through multiple paths. The third one is random pairwise keys scheme. The purpose of this scheme is to allow node-to-node authentication between communicating nodes. Du et al. [12] proposed a method to improve the basic scheme by exploiting a priori deployment knowledge. They also proposed a pairwise key pre-distribution scheme for wireless sensor networks [8], which uses Blom's key generation scheme [13] and basic scheme as the building blocks. Liu et. al. [10] developed a general framework for pairwise key establishment based on the polynomial-based key pre-distribution protocol in [14] and the probabilistic key distribution in [7] and [9].

3 Proposed Scheme

In this section we propose our scheme. Before stating the details and the analysis part, we briefly mention the terms and preliminaries used in our scheme.

3.1 LU Decomposition

LU decomposition [15] is a procedure for decomposing a square matrix A (dimension $N \times N$) into a product of a lower triangular matrix L and an upper triangular matrix U, such that,

$$A = LU \tag{1}$$

where, L and U have the forms,

$$L_{ij} = \begin{cases} l_{ij} & for \quad i \geq j \\ 0 & for \quad i < j \end{cases} \qquad U_{ij} = \begin{cases} u_{ij} & for \quad i \leq j \\ 0 & for \quad i > j \end{cases}$$

So, for a square matrix of 4×4 equation (1) looks like:

$$\begin{bmatrix} l_{11} & 0 & 0 & 0 \\ l_{21} & l_{22} & 0 & 0 \\ l_{31} & l_{32} & l_{33} & 0 \\ l_{41} & l_{42} & l_{43} & l_{44} \end{bmatrix} \bullet \begin{bmatrix} u_{11} & u_{12} & u_{13} & u_{14} \\ 0 & u_{22} & u_{23} & u_{24} \\ 0 & 0 & u_{33} & u_{34} \\ 0 & 0 & 0 & u_{44} \end{bmatrix} = \begin{bmatrix} a_{11} & a_{12} & a_{13} & a_{14} \\ a_{21} & a_{22} & a_{23} & a_{24} \\ a_{31} & a_{32} & a_{33} & a_{34} \\ a_{41} & a_{42} & a_{43} & a_{44} \end{bmatrix} \tag{2}$$

Now, according to the definition, elementary matrix E is an $N \times N$ matrix if it can be obtained from the identity matrix I_n by using one and only one elementary row operation (e.g., elimination, scaling, or interchange) [16], [17]. Elementary row operations are, $R_i \leftrightarrow R_j$, $cR_i \leftrightarrow R_i$, $R_i + cR_j \leftrightarrow R_i$. If the elementary matrices corresponding to the row operations that we use are, E_1, E_2 ..... E_k, then, $E_k....E_2E_1A = U$. Hence, $A = (E_k....E_2E_1)^{-1}U$ or $L = E_k^{-1} ... E_2^{-1} E_1^{-1}$

3.2 Details of Our Scheme

We divide our scheme into two distinct phases: before deployment key-predistribution and after deployment common pairwise key derivation. We discuss both of these phases in this section.

Phase One: Before Deployment Key-Predistribution. Before deploying the sensors, key-predistribution is done in four distinct but interrelated steps.

Step 1 (Key pool generation). In this step, a large pool of keys P with size s is generated along with their identifiers. This pool of huge number of keys is used for the symmetric matrix formation step.

Step 2 (Symmetric key matrix formation). In this step, a symmetric key matrix A ($N \times N$) is generated where N is the maximum number of sensor nodes that can be deployed and has to satisfy condition (if distinct key is to be used along a row or a column in the symmetric matrix),

$$\frac{N^2 - N}{2} + N = s \tag{3}$$

$$\text{Hence, } N = \left\lfloor \frac{-1 + \sqrt{1 + 8s}}{2} \right\rfloor \tag{4}$$

The two equations (3), (4) denote that, if the size of the key pool P is known, the number of sensor nodes that P can support could be calculated using (4) and vice versa using (3) (Figure 1(left)). Each element A_{ij} of A is assigned a distinct key from key pool P such that $A_{ij} = A_{ji}$ for, i,j = $\overline{1, N}$

Step 3 (LU decomposition). LU decomposition is applied on the matrix A in the step 3. As we know, the results of this decomposition are two matrices L, the lower triangular matrix and U, the upper triangular matrix, both of which are $N \times N$ matrices and follow equation (1) or (2).

Step 4 (LU key pre-distribution and encoded storage). Now, every sensor node is randomly assigned one row from the L matrix and one column from the U matrix, following the condition that, the ith row of L, $L_r(i)$ and the ith column of U, $U_c(i)$ always go together when assigned to a sensor node. Moreover, for storing the row and column information in the sensor, we apply an encoding scheme to increase the efficiency of memory usage throughout the network. It could be noticed that, each row of L or each column of U matrices has two parts; one non-zero-element part and another zero-element part. The zero-element part might contain (N-1) elements at best while in the worst case, zero-element part could be absent in a row or in a column. Figure 1(right) shows the scenario.

For each row of L or each column of U, the first portion consists of nonzero elements. The second portion consists of zero elements (might be absent). Therefore, to store one row of L and one column of U in each sensor, we only need to store each element in the nonzero portion and one value specifying the number of following zeros in the zero-element portion. The non-zero part could actually contain one or more zeros which are treated as non-zero values and stored accordingly. This storing method is extremely effective if the size of network is large or the dimension of the

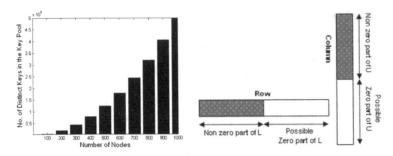

Fig. 1. (left) Number of nodes supported when distinct keys are to be used along a row or a column (right) Structure of L matrix row and U matrix column

matrix A is large. In the analysis, part we examine the effectiveness and efficiency of this encoding mechanism.

Phase Two: After Deployment Pairwise Key Derivation. Let us assume that sensor with id, S_x contains $[L_r(i), U_c(i)]$ and with id, S_y contains $[L_r(j), U_c(j)]$. When S_x and S_y need to find a common secret key between them for communication, they first exchange their columns, and then compute vector products as follows:

$$S_x: L_r(i) \times U_c(j) = A_{ij}$$
$$S_y: L_r(j) \times U_c(i) = A_{ji}$$

As A is the symmetric matrix, $A_{ij} = A_{ji}$

A_{ij} (or A_{ji}) is then used as a common key between S_x and S_y. For the secure exchange of the column information, we apply the following procedure. Let's Suppose given A is,

$$A = \begin{bmatrix} 1 & 2 & 3 & 4 \\ 2 & 5 & 6 & 7 \\ 3 & 6 & 8 & 9 \\ 4 & 7 & 9 & 10 \end{bmatrix}$$

As the procedure stated earlier we calculate the elementary matrices, $E_1, E_2....E_k$ and eventually get,

$$L = \begin{bmatrix} 1 & 0 & 0 & 0 \\ 2 & 1 & 0 & 0 \\ 3 & 0 & 1 & 0 \\ 4 & -1 & 3 & 1 \end{bmatrix} \text{ and } U = \begin{bmatrix} 1 & 2 & 3 & 4 \\ 0 & 1 & 0 & -1 \\ 0 & 0 & -1 & -3 \\ 0 & 0 & 0 & 2 \end{bmatrix} \quad (5)$$

Let us consider that, S_x contains 2nd row of L and 2nd column of U from equation (5). For S_y, it contains 3rd row of L and 3rd column of U. Hence, the sample scenario is:

$$S_x: L_r(i) = [2 \ 1 \ 0 \ 0] \text{ and } U_c(i) = [2 \ 1 \ 0 \ 0]$$
$$S_y: L_r(j) = [3 \ 0 \ 1 \ 0] \text{ and } U_c(j) = [3 \ 0 \ -1 \ 0] \quad (6)$$

When two nodes S_x and S_y want to communicate with each other, they need to regenerate the zeros in the rows and columns assigned to them. Two methods could be used for the secure exchange of information among the nodes.

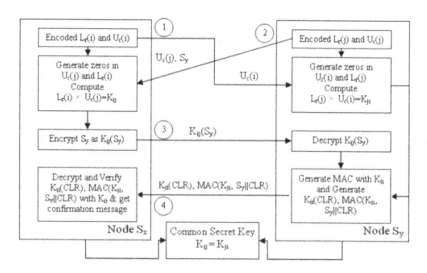

Fig. 2. Secure message exchange (Method 1) in our scheme to derive pairwise secret key

Key Exchange Method 1.

1. S_x sends $U_c(i)$ to S_y.

2. S_y re-generates the zeros in $L_r(j)$ and $U_c(i)$, computes the possible pairwise key, K_{ji} as, $L_r(j) \times U_c(i) = K_{ji}$ (In our example, $K_{ji} = 6$)

3. S_y sends $U_c(j)$ and its id S_y to S_x.

4. Now S_x re-generates the required zeros in the zero-element portion and computes the possible pairwise key K_{ij} as, $L_r(i) \times U_c(j) = K_{ij}$ (In our example, $K_{ij} = 6$. At this stage both of the nodes have calculated the possible pairwise key locally)

5. S_x sends $K_{ij}(S_y)$ to S_y which is the encrypted id of S_y by possible key K_{ij}.

6. S_y uses the key K_{ji} to decrypt $K_{ij}(S_y)$ and eventually finds the value S_y which is its own id. Once, S_y could find the value S_y, it could be sure that S_x is a valid node as the calculated key of S_x matches with the calculated key of S_y. Now, S_y uses its key K_{ji} to generate MAC (Message Authentication Code) and sends $K_{ji}(CLR)$, $MAC(K_{ji}$, $S_y \parallel CLR)$ that is, it agrees with the key of S_x. This CLR message is the confirmation that the node S_y agrees with S_x for the locally computed keys. RC5 [20] could be used to calculate the MAC using the key K_{ji}. RC5 is a symmetric block cipher designed to be suitable for both software and hardware implementation. It is a parameterized algorithm, with a variable block size, a variable number of rounds and a variable length of key. Now as A_{ij} is symmetric, $K_{ij} = K_{ji}$. (For example, following the procedure, in case of equation (6) the common key is 6).

The secure exchange mechanism 1 for our scheme is shown in Figure 2. The circles with numerical values are used to indicate the order of occurrence of the steps.

Key Exchange Method 2. The secure exchange of messages could be done in another way. Instead of four transmissions and receptions, it could also be done in 3 steps in the following way:

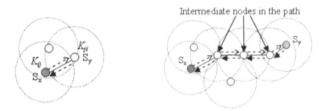

Fig. 3. (left) When two neighbors derive a secure pairwise key (right) Two nodes are not neighbors, but still can derive a pairwise key for node-to-node secure communication

1. $S_x \rightarrow S_y$: S_x, $U_c(i)$
2. $S_x \leftarrow S_y$: S_x, S_y, $U_c(j)$, MAC(K_{ji}, S_x, S_y, $U_c(i)$)
3. $S_x \rightarrow S_y$: K_{ij}(CLR|| S_y), MAC(K_{ij}, K_{ij}(CLR|| S_y))

Here, in the first step, S_x sends [S_x, $U_c(i)$] to S_y. In the second step, S_y generates the zeros in $U_c(i)$, calculates K_{ji} with which it generates a MAC and sends the message, [S_x, S_y, $U_c(j)$, MAC(K_{ji}, S_x, S_y, $U_c(i)$)] to S_x. Now S_x first checks the first part of the message from which it extracts $U_c(j)$, calculates the same secret key as our scheme ensures this ($L_r(i) \times U_c(j) = K_{ij}$) and with this verifies the MAC from S_y. Once it could verify the MAC sent from S_y, it replies back to S_y in the third step with the CLR message and another MAC.

Both of these exchange methods have different advantages. In the last part of analysis, we compare these two secure exchange methods in brief. In our scheme, two neighboring nodes (S_x and S_y) could directly derive the pairwise common key. When the nodes are more than one hop apart, the node S_x sends the messages through its neighbors and the nodes in between S_x and S_y only forward the messages; they do not need to encrypt or decrypt messages while establishing a pairwise common key [Figure 3].

4 Performance Analysis and Comparison

In this section, we investigate the performance of our scheme. We analyze our scheme from the following perspectives: (a) what is the storage-efficiency of this scheme, (b) what is the computational overhead, (c) what level of security it could ensure (d) connectivity of the network and other related analysis. As these factors are dependent on each other; there should be a trade-off among them. In fact, increase of the efficiency of one factor might decrease the efficiency of other. For each of these parameters we mention how our scheme performs in comparison with the previously proposed scheme [11] and then with some of the other schemes. We also mention the limitations of our proposal.

4.1 Storage Analysis

Our scheme outperforms Choi-Youn scheme [11] in terms of network-wide storage efficiency. We propose an efficient method to store the row and column information of L and U matrices which was not present in [11]. In fact in that scheme, when the network size is large, in the worst case, the sensors in the network initially have to memorize the full length of all keying information in rows and columns of L and U matrices respectively. Here, we compare memory usage for keying information storage in [11] and in our proposed scheme. The followings are some notations that will be used later:

- k – length or the number of bits for each keying information in L or U matrix
- N – maximum number of sensor nodes that are to be deployed in the network
- w_i – the total number of nonzero elements in a row of L and in a column of U stored in sensor node with id i
- z – the number of bits needed so that the largest number of zero elements in the zero-element part in a row of L or in a column of U could be represented

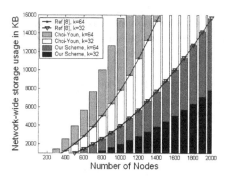 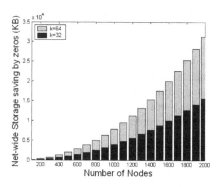

Fig. 4. (left) Network-wide Memory usage in our and other schemes (right) Network-wide storage saving by encoding the zero-element portions when k = 64 and k =32 in our scheme (value of k could vary and it could be smaller)

In [11], the memory needed to store keying information in the network-wide scale,

$$\Gamma_{Choi\text{-}Youn} = 2 \times N^2 \times k \tag{7}$$

In our scheme, the memory usage to store keying information in each individual sensor node is,

$$\gamma_i = (w_i \times k + 2 \times z) \tag{8}$$

It follows that the network-wide memory usage is [Figure 4 (left)],

$$\Gamma_{Our} = \sum_{i=1}^{N} \gamma_i = k \times \sum_{i=1}^{N} w_i + N \times (2 \times z)$$

$$= k \times \frac{N \times (N+1)}{2} + N \times (2 \times z)$$

$$= k \times \frac{N \times (N+1)}{2} + N \times (2 \times ceil \ (\log_2 (N-1))) \tag{9}$$

Here, z = ceil($\log_2$(N-1)) as the largest number of zeros in a row or a column could be represented by the *ceil* (rounded up) value of $\log_2$(N-1), where N is the dimension of the matrix. In our scheme, major memory saving is done by encoding the zeros in the zero-element parts of the L and U matrices. Hence, Network-wide memory saving considering only the encoding of the zero-element portions, could be obtained by (for [11] equation (10) becomes zero) [Figure 4 (right)],

$$\Gamma_{Saving\_zero\_elements} = 2 \times k \times \frac{N \times (N-1)}{2} - N \times (2 \times z)$$

$$= k \times N \times (N-1) - N \times (2 \times ceil (\log_2 (N-1))) \qquad (10)$$

4.2 Computational Resource Utilization

Re-generation of the zeros in the exchanged row and columns incurs some computational overhead which was not present in the previous scheme but this encoding mechanism saves memory resources. The encryption operations and MAC generation also incur extra computations but if there is no encryption of the messages during pairwise key establishment, the eavesdropper could get important information just by listening the traffic flow. In our proposal, both the initiator node and responder nodes perform one encryption and one decryption operations. Besides these, 2 nodes need to generate and verify MACs using their keys. So, our scheme requires more computation at the time of pairwise secret key computation than that of the previously proposed [11], but we show that, for ensuring secrecy of the key and better security of node-to-node communication, this trade-off is necessary.

4.3 Security Analysis

Choi-Youn [11] Scheme is severely vulnerable to man-in-the-middle attack or eavesdropping. While exchanging the information for establishing a pairwise key, there is no effective mechanism to hide the keys and messages exchanged between two nodes. Hence, it is easy for an adversary to listen to the traffic flow and collect the information to extract the key K_{ij} or K_{ji}. In this way, an adversary could capture multiple keys and if it captures the ids of the corresponding nodes, it could be able to launch sybil attack [2]. In many cases, the sensors in a wireless sensor network might need to work together to accomplish a task, hence they can use distribution of subtasks and redundancy of information. In such a situation, if a node pretends to be more than one node using the identities of other legitimate nodes and has captured the secret keys for communicating with the legitimate nodes, this sort of attack could be performed [18], [19]. Compared to this, in our scheme, the key K_{ij} or K_{ji} is never directly exchanged between the two communicating nodes rather these are calculated locally by the individual nodes. Even if the adversary knows the ids of the nodes, it could get little information by eavesdropping the message-exchange between two nodes. As encryption is used in some steps, it becomes harder for the adversary to follow and understand the exchanged messages. The adversary must know some other information like the encryption algorithm used and the information about the rows taken from the matrix L. Let us analyze what happens when a key or a node is captured in our scheme.

If a Key is Compromised. In our scheme, if a key is compromised, only one communication link is affected if distinct keys are used in a row or a column of the generating matrix (A). As two nodes are associated with each communication link (or two nodes at two ends of a communication path), number of nodes affected in such a case is two. However, rest of the links are not affected by this compromise in any way. To stop the illegal communication of the adversary with those nodes, in this scenario, the base station revokes that particular key. Let us consider that, δ ($\delta \geq 1$) denotes the number of times the same key is used along a row or a column in the generator symmetric matrix and ϕ is the number of compromised keys. Hence, if any one of the δ number of same keys (along a row or a column) is compromised, all the links and nodes associated with that particular key, could be affected. When distinct keys are used along a row or a column, $\delta=1$ and in this case, compromise of one key ($\phi=1$) could affect 1 link and 2 nodes. If $\delta=2$ and $\phi=2$, number of links that could be affected is, $\phi \times \delta$ and number of nodes that are vulnerable is $2 \times \phi \times \delta$. In Figure 5, we show the number of nodes and links that could be affected for different values of δ and ϕ. From the figure it is clear that, smaller value of δ is better for the greater resilience of the network (best case, when $\delta=1$).

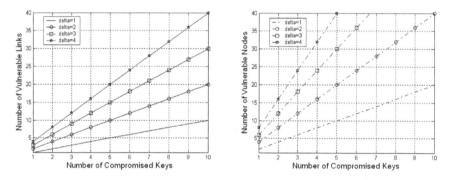

Fig. 5. (left) Number of vulnerable links for different values of ϕ and δ (right) Number of vulnerable nodes for different values of ϕ and δ (delta)

If a Node is Compromised. If a node is compromised along with its id, that is when an attacker knows the id and corresponding row and column information of a legitimate node, our scheme becomes vulnerable as with these information, a key could be derived with any other node in the network. To handle such a case, there is an Intrusion Detection System (IDS) in the network which detects the abnormal behavior of any intruder and accordingly the base station gets involved to revoke that particular id and row-column information so that no other valid node communicates with the rogue node. The details of the IDS is beyond the scope of this paper and will be presented in our future works.

While sending the CLR message from the receiver node to the sender node, (see section 3.2) we encrypt the CLR and use the MAC so that the eavesdropper cannot modify the confirmation message and authenticity is ensured. If no encryption is used, the man-in-the-middle attacker could substitute CLR part from the open message with other invalid information to cause Denial-of-Service [2] attack.

During the pairwise key derivation, we use encryption and different formats of messages in different steps, so that an eavesdropper cannot infer whether or not the same operation is performed on the exchanged messages all the times; thus making it more puzzling for the attacker.

4.4 Key Graph Connectivity

As in our scheme any two nodes in the network can derive a common pairwise key, if the nodes are reachable via a path in the network, that path could surely be used for secure communication between them. If required, all the neighboring nodes could derive pairwise keys among them and thus, the network becomes a fully secured connected graph. However, in this case, if encryption and decryption of messages are done at each hop, the energy consumption and processing overhead of the sensors and the overall network is increased significantly. We assume that, each node does not necessarily need to derive a secret key with all the other nodes, however, this depends on the level of security needed in the network (e.g. military reconnaissance scenario where security is the top priority and some additional costs are affordable).

4.5 Further Analysis

In the L and U matrices, the last row and the last column do not have any zero-element portion. In the worst case, when the dimension of the matrices (N) is very large, a sensor might have to store huge number of elements in the non-zero-element portion without any sort of encoding. A sensor might not be able to store all the non-zero-part-elements for its own storage constraint. In such a case, to avoid the storage-load on a single sensor, the last row and last column could be kept unutilized. Same strategy might be applied for some of the other rows and columns with relatively less number of zeros in the zero-element parts. However, in this case, the number of nodes that could be supported by the symmetric matrix becomes less than that is estimated. This sort of choice of not utilizing some rows and columns depends on the situation at hand and the requirements for deploying the network.

Comparison of Method 1 and Method 2 of secure exchange (as stated in Section 3.2). As with only three transmissions a secure pairwise secret key could be established, in Method 2 communication overhead is less than Method 1 but it is similar in comparison with the exchange method mentioned in [11]. Assuming that encryption, decryption or MAC generation or verification take the same amount of energy and processing costs, the two methods are almost similar in terms of computational cost and processing overhead. Here we are not considering the re-generation of zeros as that operation is same for both of the two methods. As number of transmissions is less in Method 2, the energy consumption is less in Method 2 in comparison to Method 1. Table 1 shows the number of operations in the two methods.

Table 1. Number of operations done in the two secure exchange methods

	Method 1		Method 2	
	Node 1	Node 2	Node 1	Node 2
Encryption	1	1	1	0
Decryption	1	1	0	1
MAC generation or verification	1	1	2	2

Method 1 shows relatively better performance against intended DoS attack by repeated fake transmissions. In fact, when these sorts of attacks happen, our target is to maximize the amount of tasks/operations that the attacker should do so that the attacker requires considerable processing and energy power to harm the network and it eventually gives up attacking after some trials. If the node 1 (S_x) is the attacker in Method 1, in the first step attacker S_x sends arbitrary $U_c(i)$. In reply, without being confirmed about S_x's validity S_y sends: S_y, $U_c(j)$ which does not require any heavy processing. Now attacker should process step 3 (i.e. arbitrarily packet generation or fake encryption of packet), but just after this step S_y could be sure that S_x is a Rogue Node as the decryption of the message $[K_{ij}(S_y)]$ would not produce the id of S_y. Thus this sort of attack is stopped. However, for the same scenario, in Method 2, Attacker S_x sends an arbitrary, S_x, $U_c(i)$. In reply, without being confirmed about S_x's validity S_y sends: S_x, S_y, $U_c(j)$, MAC(K_{ji}, S_x, S_y, $U_c(i)$). That means, S_y in this case, is heavily burdened with processing a lot of tasks for challenging S_x. It has to generate MAC with only one fake transmission from S_x. As with a very little effort S_x could make S_y busy, if S_x transmits the message repeatedly then S_y is always burdened with processing all the requests which would eventually take sufficient energy and computation power of S_y and could result in denial of service by S_y after some time. Blocking the id of S_x might cause another sort of DoS as when the valid S_x wants to communicate later with S_y; it (S_y) could deny accepting the request from S_x. However, Method 1 overcomes this problem by detecting S_x as a rogue node after 2 steps with comparatively less processing overhead. If S_y is the attacker node, Method 2 performs slightly better than Method 1.

Comparison with other schemes. Now we compare our scheme with [9] and [8] in brief. In [9], each sensor node has to memorize the full length of each key in its key ring. It is even worse when many keys in the key ring are assigned to a particular node but they are not utilized after deployment, which is simply the wastage of storage of the tiny resource-constrained sensors. In [9], if one key is compromised by an adversary, it might lead to the compromise of another link between pairs of uncompromised nodes using the same key. In our scheme, keeping the value of δ equal to 1 could keep the rest of the links and nodes unaffected when one key is compromised.

The idea of [9] is that the shared key between any two neighboring nodes is found based on a probability of the occurrence of a key in their key rings. It implies that there still exists some probability that any two neighboring nodes cannot find a common shared key. Therefore, there is a probability that, a node might need to use a multi-link path to establish a pairwise key even with one or more of its neighbors. This surely incurs extra communication overhead on the intermediate connecting nodes. In the worst case, a disconnected key graph might be created. Hence, it means that unsecured communication links could exist in the network. On the contrary, our proposed scheme overcomes this drawback by guaranteeing that any two neighboring nodes could directly derive a pairwise key.

In our scheme, communication overhead for pairwise key establishment is considerably reduced as the traffic in the initial broadcast of each node is reduced. In [9], the information needs to be transmitted is the list of identifiers of the keys stored in a sensor node's key ring. Hence, the traffic is much higher in that case than that of our scheme because in our proposed scheme the only information needed to be broadcast is receiver's (S_y) identifier to query the location of the receiver. Furthermore, there is no need to include a path-key establishment phase like that is in [9].

[8] is basically based on the basic scheme [9]. By showing the disadvantages of [9], we show the disadvantages of [8]. Furthermore, in case of [8], each node has to remember, $m = (\lambda + 1)\tau$ field elements, where λ is the security parameter and τ is the number of key spaces chosen randomly from ω key spaces. As stated in [8], taking $\tau=4$, $\omega=25$ and for example, $\lambda=25\%$ of the total number of nodes in the network, we get the memory requirements presented in Figure 4 (left). It could be noticed from the figure that, when k=32 (i.e. each element is represented by 32 bits) in [8], it requires almost same amount of memory that is needed in our scheme with k=64. Even in such a case, this memory requirement is for ensuring local connectivity, $P_{actual} \geq 0.5$. In fact, the local connectivity is also related with memory requirements. In our scheme, the connectivity is not based on probability rather it is guaranteed that any node can derive a pairwise key to make a direct connection with any other neighboring node.

5 Conclusions

In this paper, we proposed an efficient key management scheme which significantly improves the network-wide memory usage and security. The network-wide memory saved by encoding might be used for processing distributed operations in the network. To point out the major advantages of our scheme: Firstly, it guarantees that any pair of neighboring nodes can directly derive a common secret key between themselves. Secondly, compared to the existing key pre-distribution scheme based on LU decomposition and some other schemes, our scheme is substantially more storage efficient. Thirdly, our scheme is flexible because some security features could be added onto the scheme to make it more robust. Fourthly, it is also scalable because sensor nodes do not need to be deployed simultaneously rather they could be added later on and still they would be able to derive secret keys with any other sensor node in the network. In the future, we will develop an Intrusion Detection System which will run side-by-side our scheme for successful detection of abnormal behavior or the presence of a rogue node in the network. Also we will investigate how the computational costs could be reduced to increase the efficiency of our scheme.

References

1. Karlof, C. and Wagner, D.: Secure routing in wireless sensor networks: Attacks and countermeasures. Elsevier's Ad Hoc Network Journal, Special Issue on Sensor Network Applications and Protocols, September (2003) 293-315
2. Pathan, A-S. K., Lee, H-W., and Hong, C. S.: Security in Wireless Sensor Networks: Issues and Challenges. Proceedings of the 8th IEEE ICACT 2006, Volume II, Phoenix Park, Korea, 20-22 February (2006) 1043-1048
3. Perrig, A., Szewczyk, R., Wen, V., Culler, D., and Tygar, J. D.: SPINS: Security Protocols for Sensor Networks. Wireless Networks, vol. 8, no. 5. (2002) 521-534
4. Jolly, G., Kuscu, M.C., Kokate, P., and Younis, M.: A Low-Energy Key Management Protocol for Wireless Sensor Networks. Proc. Eighth IEEE ISCC 2003, vol.1 (2003) 335 - 340

5. Rabaey, J.M., Ammer, J., Karalar, T., Suetfei Li., Otis, B., Sheets, M., and Tuan, T.: PicoRadios for wireless sensor networks: the next challenge in ultra-low power design. 2002 IEEE ISSCC 2002, Volume 1, 3-7 Feb. (2002) 200 – 201

6. Hollar, S,: COTS Dust. Master's Thesis, Electrical Engineering and Computer Science Department, UC Berkeley (2000)

7. Chan, H., Perrig, A., and Song, D.: Random key predistribution schemes for sensor networks. Proc. 2003 IEEE Symposium on Security and Privacy, 11-14 May (2003) 197-213

8. Du, W., Deng, J., Han, Y. S., Varshney, P. K., Katz, J., and Khalili, A.: A Pairwise Key Predistribution Scheme for Wireless Sensor Networks. ACM Transactions on Information and System Security, Vol. 8, No. 2, May (2005) 228-258

9. Eschenauer, L. and Gligor, V. D.: A key-management scheme for distributed sensor networks. Proceedings of the 9th ACM conference on Computer and Communications, Washington, DC, USA, 18-22 Nov. (2002) 41 - 47

10. Liu, D., Ning, P., and Li, R.: Establishing Pairwise Keys in Distributed Sensor Networks. ACM Transactions on Information and System Security, Vol. 8. No. 1, Feb. (2005) 41-77

11. Choi, S. and Youn, H.: An Efficient Key Pre-distribution Scheme for Secure Distributed Sensor Networks. EUC Workshops 2005, IFIP International Federation for Information Processing, LNCS 3823 (2005) 1088-1097

12. Du, W., Deng, J., Han, Y. S., Chen, S., and Varshney, P.K.: A key management scheme for wireless sensor networks using deployment knowledge". Twenty-third Annual Joint Conference of the IEEE Computer and Communications Societies. INFOCOM 2004, Volume 1, 7-11 March (2004) 586-597

13. Blom. R.: An optimal class of symmetric key generation systems. Advances in Cryptology: Proceedings of EUROCRYPT 84 (Thomas Beth, Norbert Cot, and Ingemar Ingemarsson, eds.), Lecture Notes in Computer Science, Springer-Verlag, 209 (1985) 335-338

14. Blundo, C., Santis, A. D., Herzberg, A., Kutten, S., Vaccaro, U., and Yung, M.: Perfectly-secure key distribution for dynamic conferences. In Advances in Cryptology – CRYPTO '92, LNCS 740 (1993) 471-486

15. Zarowski, C. J.: An Introduction to Numerical Analysis for Electrical and Computer Engineers. Hoboken, NJ John Wiley & Sons, Inc. (US) (2004)

16. Nakos, G., and Joyner, D.: Linear Algebra with Applications, Brooks/Cole USA (1998) 188-194

17. Birkhauser, Linear Algebra, Birkhauser Boston (1997) 33-37

18. Douceur, J.: The Sybil Attack. 1st International Workshop on Peer-to-Peer Systems (2002)

19. Newsome, J., Shi, E., Song, D, and Perrig, A: The sybil attack in sensor networks: analysis & defenses. Proc. of the third international symposium on Information processing in sensor networks, ACM (2004) 259-268

20. Menezes, A., Oorschot, P., and Vanstone, S.: Handbook of Applied Cryptography. CRC Press, Boca Raton (1996)

Key Inheritance-Based False Data Filtering Scheme in Wireless Sensor Networks*

Hae Young Lee and Tae Ho Cho

Sungkyunkwan University, School of Information and Communication Engineering
300 Cheoncheon-dong, Jangan-gu, Suwon, Gyeonggi-do 440-746, Korea
{sofware, taecho}@ece.skku.ac.kr

Abstract. When sensor networks are deployed in hostile environments, an adversary may compromise some sensor nodes and use them to inject false sensing reports. False reports can lead to not only false alarms but also the depletion of limited energy resource in battery powered networks. The interleaved hop-by-hop authentication scheme detects such false reports through interleaved authentication. However, a false report can be forwarded toward the base station significant number of hops before it is detected and dropped. In this paper, we propose an enhanced interleaved authentication scheme called the key inheritance-based filtering that prevents forwarding of false reports. The keys of each node used in the message authentication consist of its own key and the keys inherited from its upstream nodes. Every authenticated report contains the combination of the message authentication codes generated by using the keys of the consecutive nodes in a path from the base station to a terminal node. The proposed scheme can detect a false report at the very next node of the compromised node that injected the false report before it consumes a significant amount of energy.

1 Introduction

Recent advances in MEMS (micro-electro-mechanical systems) and low power highly integrated digital electronics have enabled the development of low-cost sensor networks [1,2]. Sensor networks consist of small nodes with sensing, computation, and wireless communications capabilities [3]. Sensor networks are expected to interact with the physical world at an unprecedented level to enable various new applications [4]. In many applications sensor nodes are deployed in open environments, and hence are vulnerable to physical attacks, potentially compromising the node's cryptographic keys [5]. False sensing reports can be injected through compromised nodes, which can lead to not only false alarms but also the depletion of limited energy resource in battery powered networks (Fig. 1) [4].

To minimize the grave damage, false reports should be dropped en-route as early as possible, and the few eluded ones should be further rejected at the base station [6].

---

* This research was supported by the MIC (Ministry of Information and Communication), Korea, under the ITRC (Information Technology Research Center) support program supervised by the IITA (Institute of Information Technology Assessment).

S. Madria et al. (Eds.): ICDCIT 2006, LNCS 4317, pp. 116–127, 2006.

The digital signature-based technique can be used to authenticate and filter false report [7]. However, this technique has high overhead both in terms of computation and bandwidth [8], which makes it unsuitable for sensor networks [9]. Therefore, researchers have proposed several symmetric cryptography-based security solutions. Ye *et al.* [4] proposed a statistical en-route filtering scheme in which a report is forwarded only if it contains the message authentication codes (MACs) generated by multiple nodes, by using keys from different partitions in a global key pool. Zhu *et at.* [10] proposed the interleaved hop-by-hop authentication scheme that detects false reports through interleaved authentication. Zhang *et al.* [11] proposed the interleaved authentication scheme in braided multipath routing sensor networks. Other techniques for filtering false reports can be found in [7,12,13]. While each of these designs has its own merits, a false report can be forwarded toward the base station significant number of hops before it is detected and dropped.

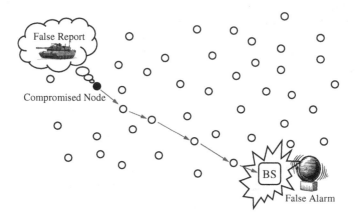

Fig. 1. False sensing report can be injected through compromised node (filled circle), which can lead to not only false alarms but also the depletion of limited energy resource

In this paper, we propose an enhanced interleaved authentication scheme called the key inheritance-based filtering that prevents forwarding of false reports. The keys of each node used in the message authentication consist of its own key and the keys inherited from its *upstream* (toward the base station) nodes. Every authenticated report contains the combination of MACs generated by using the keys possessed by the consecutive nodes in a path from the base station to a terminal node. If no more than a certain number t nodes are compromised, the proposed scheme can detect a false report at the very next hop node of the compromised node that injected the false report before it consumes a significant amount of energy. Here t is a security threshold value determined based on the security requirements of the application.

To increase the impact of their attacks, adversaries often inject a large number of false reports [13]. The number of false reports is often several orders of magnitude greater than that of authenticated reports [4]. The proposed scheme is particularly useful for these scenarios in energy saving by early detecting false reports. The effectiveness of the proposed scheme is shown with the simulation result at the end of the paper.

The remainder of the paper is organized as follows: Section 2 briefly describes the interleaved hop-by-hop authentication scheme as background knowledge. Section 3 introduces the proposed scheme in detail. In Section 4 we study the security of the proposed scheme. Section 5 reviews the simulation result. Finally, conclusion and future work is discussed in Section 6.

2   The Interleaved Hop-by-Hop Authentication (IHA) Scheme

In this section, we briefly describe the interleaved hop-by-hop authentication (IHA) scheme [10] in which nodes are *associated* and every report is verified based on the pairwise keys shared with the associated nodes. Fig. 2 [10] shows such association that can achieve $(t + 1)$ resilience, where $t = 2$. Nodes u_1, u_2, $\cdots$, u_6 are intermediate nodes on the path from the base station BS to the cluster head CH and node v_1 and v_2 are the cluster nodes. Basically, an intermediate node has an *upper* and a *lower* *associated* node of $t + 1$ hops away from it. An intermediate node that is less than $t + 1$ hops away from CH has one of the cluster nodes as its lower associated node, For example, u_2 has v_2 as its lower associated node.

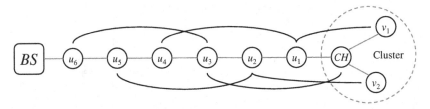

Fig. 2. An example showing the definition of *association* in the IHA ($t = 2$). BS is the base station and CH is a cluster head. Basically, an intermediate node between BS and CH has an *upper* and a *lower associated* node of $t + 1$ hops away from it.

A report is generated collaboratively by $t + 1$ cluster nodes (including the cluster head) when they sensed an event. When an intermediate node receives a report, it verifies the authenticity of the report by comparing the MAC generated by its lower associated node with the MAC reproduced by itself using the pairwise key shared with the associated node. For example, node u_1 compares the MAC generated by v_1 with the MAC reproduced by itself using the pairwise key shared with v_1. Upon success, it replaces the verified MAC with the MAC generated by itself using the pairwise key shared with its upper associated node. For example, u_1 replaces the verified MAC (by generated by v_1) with the MAC generated by itself using the pairwise key shared with its upper associated node u_4.

In the IHA, if every node knows the IDs of the nodes that are $t + 1$ hops away from it, a false report can be forwarded up to t hops before it is detected and dropped. If not, a false report can travel up to $(t - 1)(t - 2)$ hops [10].

3   A Key Inheritance-Based Filtering (KIF) Scheme

In this section, we introduce the key inheritance-based filtering (KIF) scheme in detail.

3.1   Assumptions

We assume that every sensing report is generated if the $t + 1$ consecutive nodes on the path from the base station to a terminal node sensed an *event* (e.g., an increase in the temperature being monitored by the nodes), where t is a design parameter. One of these nodes is elected as a cluster head and collects sensor readings from them. The issues of electing a node as the cluster head are out of the scope of this paper. Sensor nodes are similar to the current generation of sensor nodes (e.g., the Berkeley MICA motes [14,15]) in their computational and communication capabilities and energy resources. We assume that every node has space to store several hundred bytes of keying materials. We assume that if a node is compromised, all the information it holds will also be compromised. However, the base station will not be compromised. We also assume that adversaries cannot compromise any node during the key inheritance phase.

3.2   Threat Model and Design Goal

In this paper, we focus on massive attacks of false data injection. That is, adversaries inject a large number of false reports to increase the impact of their attacks. We assume that the compromised nodes can collude in their attack. Our goal is to design a filtering scheme that can detect a false report at the very next node of the compromised node that injected the false report if no more than t nodes are compromised.

3.3   Notation and Definition

The following notations appear in the rest of this paper.

- N_i is the principal (such as a communicating node) of $i \in \mathfrak{I}$ hops away from the base station. For a non-positive integer i, N_i is the base station (e.g., N_{-5} = the base station).
- K_i is the symmetric key at an index $i \in \aleph$.
- $MAC(K)$ is the MAC of a message generated with a symmetric key K.
- E_i is the endorsement generated by a node N_i.

Definition 1.   For two nodes N_i and N_j ($i < j$) on the same path, if N_i and N_j have a shared key K_k and all the intermediate node between N_i and N_j except the base station do not have any key at the index k, we say N_j *inherited K_k from N_i*.

Definition 2.   For two nodes N_i and N_j ($j = i + 1$) on the same path, if N_j has a key K_k and N_i has another key at index k, we say K_k *is N_j's own key*.

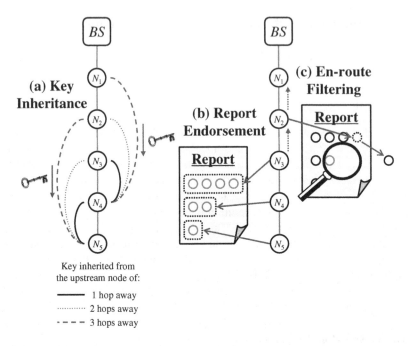

Fig. 3. The KIF involves 3 phases: *key inheritance, report endorsement,* and *en-route filtering.* In the key inheritance phase, every node on a path inherits the keys from its upstream nodes (a). In the report endorsement phase, multiple nodes generate a report collaboratively (c). In the en-route phase, every forwarding node authenticates the report and replaces the un-matching MAC in the report with the MAC generated by itself (c).

3.4 Scheme Overview

The KIF involves the following three phases:

1. In the *key inheritance* phase, the base station prepares the $(t^2 + 3t + 4) / 2$ keys for the path to a terminal node. Every node on the path inherits the $t + 1$ keys from its $t + 1$ upstream nodes (Fig. 3(a)) and a new key is assigned to the node as its own key. It thus has $t + 2$ keys.
2. In the *report endorsement* phase, $t + 1$ nodes generate a report collaboratively when they sensed an event. More specifically, every participating node generates $t + 2$ MACs over the event then sends these MACs to its cluster head. The cluster head collects the MACs from all the participating nodes then put them into a report (Fig. 3(b)). Finally, it forwards the report toward the base station. Every report contains $(t^2 + 3t + 4) / 2$ MACs.
3. In the *en-route filtering* phase, every forwarding node verifies the MACs in a report based on its keys. Upon success, it replaces the one different MAC in the report to the one generated by itself (Fig. 3(c)). Finally, it forwards the report toward the base station.

3.5 The Basic Scheme

In this section, we illustrate the basic idea in the KIF.

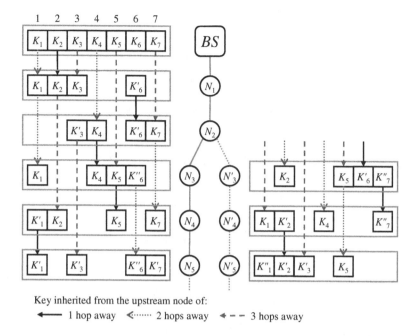

Key inherited from the upstream node of:
← 1 hop away   ◄······ 2 hops away   ◄− − 3 hops away

Fig. 4. An example of inheriting keys in the *key inheritance* phase when $t = 2$. The base station *BS* has seven keys to inherit for the nodes in the path. Every node on the path inherits the three keys with no repeated indexes from its three upstream nodes and a key other than the seven keys from *BS*. Thus, it has four keys.

3.5.1 Key Inheritance

In this phase, the base station prepares the k keys $\{K_1, K_2, \cdots, K_k\}$ to inherit for each path, where $k = (t^2 + 3t + 4) / 2$.[1] For a node N_i on the path, it inherits the $t + 1$ keys with no repeated indexes from its $t + 1$ upstream nodes $\{N_{i-1}, N_{i-2}, \cdots, N_{i-t-1}\}$, one key at a random index from each of them. Note that N_i is the base station if $i \leq 0$. The base station assigns a new key K_j ($1 \leq j \leq k$) to N_i as its own key. Thus, it has $t + 2$ keys. In practices, these key inheritance and assignment can be achieved using by end-to-end authentication protocols such as SNEP [9].

Fig. 4 shows an example of the key inheritance when $t = 2$. To start with, the base station *BS* generates the seven keys $\{K_1, K_2, \cdots, K_7\}$ for the path. Then, every node on the path inherits the three keys with no repeated indexes from its three upstream nodes and a new key is assigned to the node as its own key. For example, Node N_3

---

[1] Since node $N_1, N_2, \cdots, N_{t+1}$ inherit $t+1, t, \cdots, 1$ keys, respectively, from the base station, the base station should have $(t^2 + 3t + 2)/2$ keys to inherit. The other key is the base station's own key.

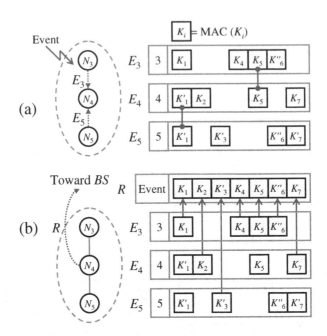

Fig. 5. An example of the report endorsement ($t = 2$). When the three nodes sensed an event, each node sends an endorsement to the cluster head N_4. An endorsement is authenticated by comparing the MACs for the overlapping indexes (a). If the three endorsements are authenticated, N_4 prepares a report R and puts the collected MACs into R (b). Finally, it forwards the report toward the base station BS.

inherits K_1, K_4, and K_5 from N_1, N_2, and BS ($= N_0$), respectively, and a new key K''_6 is assigned to N_3 as its own key.

3.5.2 Report Endorsement

When the $t + 1$ consequent nodes N_i, N_{i+1}, $\cdots$, N_{i+t} on a path sensed an event, each node generates the $t + 2$ MACs over the event using its $t + 2$ keys. It then sends an endorsement to the cluster head. Note that the issues of electing a node as the cluster head are out of the scope of this paper. Every endorsement contains these $t + 2$ MACs. If the cluster head collected $t + 1$ endorsements (including its endorsement), it checks if there are $t + 2$ MACs in each endorsement. It then verifies the authenticity of the endorsement by comparing the MACs already generated by itself with the MACs contained in the endorsement for the overlapping indexes. The endorsement is authenticated only if at least one of the former MACs matches exactly with one of the latter MACs for the overlapping index. For example, an endorsement is authenticated if the fifth MAC generated by the cluster head matches with the fifth MAC contained in the endorsement (Fig. 5(a)). If $t + 1$ endorsements are authenticated, the cluster head prepares a report. For each index, it puts the MAC generated by the most upper node into the report. Finally, it forwards the report toward the base station.

Fig. 5 shows an example of the report endorsement in the KIF when $t = 2$. When the three nodes N_3, N_4, and N_5 on a path sensed an event, each node sends an endorsement to its cluster head. Suppose that node N_4 is elected as the cluster head. N_4 collects and verifies the authenticity of the endorsements. Because $MAC (K_5)$ in $E_3 = MAC (K_5)$ in E_4 and $MAC (K'_1)$ in $E_5 = MAC (K'_1)$ in E_4 (Fig. 6(a)), they are authenticated. N_4 prepares a report R and puts the collected MACs into R as shown in Fig. 5(b). For each index, it puts the MAC generated by the most upper node into R. Finally, it forwards R towards the base station BS.

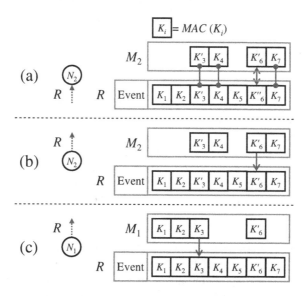

Fig. 6. An example of the en-route filtering ($t = 2$). When the forwarding node N_2 receives the report R, it reproduces the four MACs over the event in R. Because $MAC (K''_6) \neq MAC (K'_6)$ and the other MACs match exactly for the overlapping indexes (a), N_2 replaces $MAC (K''_6)$ to $MAC (K'_6)$ then forwards R (b). R is also forwarded by N_1 because $MAC (K_3) \neq MAC (K'_3)$ and the other MACs match (c).

3.5.3 En-route Filtering

When a forwarding node receives a report from its *downstream* (toward a terminal node) node, it first checks if there are $(t^2 + 3t + 4) / 2$ MACs in the report. Then, it reproduces the $t + 2$ MACs using its keys and verifies the authenticity of the report by comparing the result with the MACs in the report for the overlapping indexes. The report is authenticated only if one of the former MACs differs from one of the latter MACs and the $t + 1$ of the former MACs match exactly with that of the latter MACs for the overlapping indexes. If the report is authenticated, the node replaces the different MAC with its reproduced MAC. Finally, it forwards the report toward the base station.

Fig. 6 shows an example of the en-route filtering in the KIF when $t = 2$. When the forwarding node N_2 received the report R, it reproduces the four MACs {$MAC (K'_3)$,

MAC (K_4), MAC (K'_6), MAC (K_7)} over the event in R. Because MAC $(K'_6) \neq MAC$ (K''_6) and the other MACs match exactly for the overlapping indexes (Fig. 6(a)), R is authenticated. Thus, it replaces MAC (K''_6) in R to MAC (K'_6) then forwards R toward the base station (Fig. 6(b)). R is also authenticated by N_1 (MAC $(K_3) \neq MAC$ (K'_3) and the other MACs match). Therefore, N_1 replaces MAC (K'_3) in R to MAC (K_3) then forwards R toward the base station (Fig. 6(c)).

The base station can verify the authenticity of the report by comparing the $(t^2 + 3t + 4) / 2$ reproduced MACs with the MACs in the report. If one of the former MACs differs from one of the latter MAC and the others match exactly, the report is authenticated.

4 Security Analysis

If the $t + 1$ consequent nodes N_i, N_{i+1}, $\cdots$, N_{i+t} on a path generates an authenticated report, the report contains the $(t^2 + 3t + 4) / 2$ MACs: the $t + 1$, t, $\cdots$, 2, and 1 MACs generated using by the $t + 1$ keys with no repeated indexes inherited from N_{i-1}, the t different keys inherited with no repeated indexes from N_{i-2}, $\cdots$, the two different keys with no repeated indexes inherited from N_{i-t-1}, and N_i's own key, respectively. The report will be authenticated by N_{i-1} because it contains the $t + 1$ MACs generated using by the $t + 1$ keys inherited from N_{i-1}, That is, the $t + 1$ MACs in the report match with the $t + 1$ MACs reproduced by N_{i-1} and the MAC generated using by N_i's own key differs from the MAC reproduced (Definition 2). If adversaries compromised t nodes among these nodes, they compromise only the t keys inherited from N_{i-1}. Therefore, any false report injected by the adversaries will be detected by the very next node N_{i-1} (if N_1 is compromised, false reports can be detected by the base station). For example, if an adversary compromises node N_3 and N_4 in Fig 5, she can inject a false report, {E, MAC (K_1), MAC (K_2), M^f_3, MAC (K_4), MAC (K_5), MAC (K''_6), MAC (K_7)}, through them, where M^f_3 is a forged MAC at the key index three. However, the false report may be detected by N_2 since two of its MACs, {M^f_3, MAC (K''_6)}, differ from the MACs reproduced by N_2, {MAC (K'_3), MAC (K_4), MAC (K'_6), MAC (K_7)}. That is, the false report may be filtered since it does not have the MAC generated by using K'_3, which node N_5 inherited from N_2.

KIF is not designed to address other attacks that a compromised sensor node may launch, such as dropping authenticated reports and replaying authenticated reports. However, certain techniques can be applied to solve or alleviate these problems. For example, multipath forwarding can alleviate dropping of authenticated report [16]. Replayed reports can be detected if each node can use a cache [17,18] to store the signatures of recently forwarded reports [4].

5 Simulation Result

To show the effectiveness of the KIF, we have compared the KIF with the IHA through the simulation. Each node takes 16.25, 12.5 μJ to transmit/receive a byte and each MAC generation consumes 15 μJ [4]. The size of an original report is 24 bytes. The size of a MAC is 1 byte. In the IHA, a false report can travel up to $(t-2)(t-1)$ hops before it is detected [10]. Fig. 7 shows the average energy consumption caused by a false report when t is between 1 and 10. As shown in the figure, the KIF consumes less energy against a false report compared to the IHA and as t increases the difference between two schemes becomes larger.

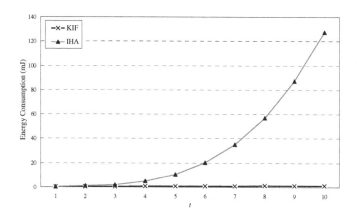

Fig. 7. The average energy consumption caused by a false report. The KIF consumes less energy against a false report compared to the IHA and as t increases the difference between two schemes becomes larger.

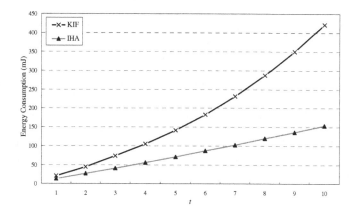

Fig. 8. The average energy consumption caused by an authenticated report. The KIF consumes more energy than the IHA.

Fig. 8 shows the average energy consumption caused by an authenticated report when t is between 1 and 10. The IHA consumes less energy than the KIF. However, as shown in Fig. 9, the KIF saves energy when the amount of false traffic is high.

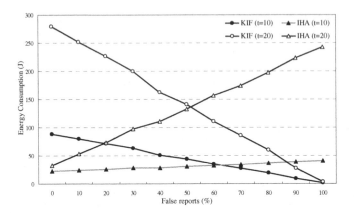

Fig. 9. The average energy consumption caused by one thousand reports. The KIF saves energy when the amount of false traffic is high.

6   Conclusion and Future Work

In this paper, we proposed an enhanced interleaved authentication scheme called the key inheritance-based filtering that prevents forwarding of false reports. The keys of each node used in the message authentication consist of its own key and the keys inherited from its upstream nodes. Every authenticated report contains the combination of the MACs generated by using the keys possessed by the consecutive nodes in a path from the base station to a terminal node. If the number of compromised nodes is no more than the security threshold value, the KIF guarantees that a false report can be detected at the very next node of the compromised node that injected the false report. Since adversaries often inject a large number of false reports to increase the impact of their attacks the KIF's early detection capability is particularly effective against these attacks in saving energy.

The KIF and IHA can be combined to further enhance the energy usage since the former is effective in saving energy when massive attacks of false data injection occur and the latter has low computation and communication overhead if the mass of the attacks is small. For example, we can change from the IHA to the KIF if the amount of false traffic exceeds a certain threshold value. Our future research will be focused on combining these two schemes. We will also study on the key management issues regarding the IHA.

Reference

1. Akyildiz, I.F., Su, W., Sankarasubramaniam, Y., Cayirci, E.: A Survey on Sensor Networks. IEEE Commun. Mag. 40(8) (2002) 102-114
2. Akkaya, K., Younis, M.: A Survey on Routing Protocols for Wireless Sensor Networks. Ad hoc Netw. 3(3) (2004) 325-349
3. Chi, S.H., Cho, T.H.: Fuzzy Logic based Propagation Limiting Method for Message Routing in Wireless Sensor Networks. Lect. Notes Comput. Sc. 3983 (2006) 58-67

4. Ye, F., Luo, H., Lu, S.: Statistical En-Route Filtering of Injected False Data in Sensor Networks. IEEE J. Sel. Area Comm. 23(4) (2005) 839-850
5. Przydatek, B., Song, D., Perrig, A.: SIA: Secure Information Aggregation in Sensor Networks. In Proc. of SenSys (2003) 255-265
6. Yang, H, Lu, S.: Commutative Cipher Based En-Route Filtering in Wireless Sensor Networks. In Proc. of VTC (2003) 1223-1227
7. Zhang, W., Cao, G.: Group Rekeying for Filtering False Data in Sensor Networks: A Predistribution and Local Collaboration-based Approach. In Proc. of INFOCOM (2005) 503-514
8. Hu, Y., Perrig, A., Johnson, D.: Packet Leashes: A Defense against Wormhole Attacks in Wireless Ad Hoc Networks. In Proc. of INFOCOM (2003) 1976-1986
9. Perrig, A., Szewczyk, R., Tygar, J.D., Wen, V., Culler, D.E.: SPINS: Security Protocols for Sensor Networks. Wirel. Netw. 8(5) (2002) 521-534
10. Zhu, S., Setia, S., Jajodia, S., Ning, P.: An Interleaved Hop-by-Hop Authentication Scheme for Filtering of Injected False Data in Sensor Networks. In Proc. of S&P (2004) 259-271
11. Zhang, Y., Yang, J., Vu, H.T.: The Interleaved Authentication for Filtering False Reports in Multipath Routing based Sensor Networks. In Proc. of IPDPS (2006)
12. Yang, H., Ye, F., Yuan, Y., Lu, S., Arbaugh, W.: Toward resilient security in wireless sensor networks. In Proc. of MobiHoc (2005) 34-45
13. Zhang, Y., Liu, W., Lou, W., Fang, Y.: Location-Based Compromise-Tolerant Security Mechanisms for Wireless Sensor Networks. IEEE J. Sel. Area Comm. 24(2) (2006) 247-260
14. Hill, J., Szewczyk, R., Woo, A., Hollar, S., Culler, D., Pister, K.: System Architecture Directions for Networked Sensors. In Proc. of ASPLOS (2000) 93-104
15. Crossbow Wireless Sensor Networks. http://www.xbow.com/
16. Karlof, C., Wagner, D.: Secure Routing in Wireless Sensor Networks: Attacks and Countermeasures. In Proc. of SPNA (2002) 28-37
17. Ye, F., Zhong, G., Lu, S., Zhang, L.: Gradient Broadcast: A Robust Data Delivery Protocol for Large Scale Sensor Networks. Wirel. Netw. 11(2) (2005)
18. Intanagonwiwat, C., Govindan, R., Estrin, D.: Directed Diffusion: A Scalable and Robust Communication Paradigm for Sensor Networks. In Proc. of MOBICOM (2000) 56-67

Anonymous Agreed Order Multicast: Performance and Free Riding

Jerzy Konorski

Technical University of Gdansk
ul. Narutowicza 11/12, 80-952 Gdansk, Poland
jekon@eti.pg.gda.pl

Abstract. We argue that some group communication protocols should be concerned about agreed delivery order (ADO) of exchanged messages, but not about membership control and occasional ADO violations. A LAN-oriented protocol called *Distributed Precedence Graph* (DPG) is outlined and investigated via simulation. Site anonymity permitted by DPG invites selfish *free riding* site behavior i.e., participation in the benefits of DPG (delivery of messages in agreed order) while shirking from the costly obligations (multicast of control messages). Such behavior, known from P2P and MANET systems, has been alien to agreed order multicast. We study free riding relative to the group size and message reception miss rate, and propose a simple disincentive.

1 Introduction

A group communication protocol (GCP) governs multiple-destination traffic flows that may strongly interact with one another. GCPs have been an object of extensive research since the early 1990s, owing both to the rapid expansion of cooperative work applications and the deployment of IP multicast [4], as well as to their theoretical appeal. In a generic model, a group of *member sites* exchange one-to-group *messages* via a communication network. In each member site, a GCP instance *admits* messages from, and *delivers* received messages to, the local application instance, whereas the network provides *multicast* and *reception* primitives.

GCP decides when to multicast an admitted message and when to deliver a received one, subject to prescribed group-wide message ordering. We focus on *agreed delivery order* (ADO) and *agreed order multicast*. For any instant t, let $D_{n,t}$ denote the sequence of messages so far delivered at site n. ADO ensures that for any t, n, and n', if $D_{n,t}$ and $D_{n',t}$ are of equal length then $D_{n,t} = D_{n',t}$, otherwise the shorter one is a prefix of the longer one. The difference between $D_{n,t}$ and $D_{n',t}$ measures the current lag of n with respect to n' or vice versa. Eventually, all sites "catch up" to produce a uniform and complete ADO sequence D. When a message has been delivered at all sites, D extends by one message, and the rate at which this occurs measures the *group throughput*. Examples of agreed order multicast are TOTEM [1], LANSIS [5], NEWTOP [6], TRANS [11], TO [13], and PSYNC [14].

We show how the natural synchronism of broadcast LANs enables anonymous (membership insensitive) agreed order multicast. We study the group throughput

S. Madria et al. (Eds.): ICDCIT 2006, LNCS 4317, pp. 128–135, 2006.
© Springer-Verlag Berlin Heidelberg 2006

under a *Distributed Precedence Graph* (DPG) protocol [9]. Next we describe selfish *free riding* site behavior; although familiar in the P2P and MANET folklore, it has not been considered in a GCP context. We propose a simple disincentive to free ride.

In Sec. 2 we state the communication model and *strong ADO* property, and motivate membership insensitivity and tolerance of occasional ADO violations. In Sec. 3 we outline DPG and in Sec. 4 investigate its performance via simulation. Sec. 5 deals with free riding. Sec. 6 concludes the paper and suggests further research.

2 Communication Model and Message Ordering

Consider N member sites exchanging one-to-all messages and assume that: (i) the sender of a message is also a recipient, (ii) *independent* reception misses occur – a message may be missed at one site and received at others, (iii) a noncooperative GCP instance may refuse to re-multicast a message for a "catch up," and (iv) member sites may undergo alternate presence and absence spells (e.g., due to loss of connectivity).

Let M_SET be the set of messages in a group session. ADO requires that there exist a total order on M_SET such that for any $m, m' \in M\_SET$ with m' following m,

$$\forall_{n=1,...,N} \ m \text{ and } m' \text{ occur in } D_n \text{ and } m' \text{ follows } m \text{ in } D_n, \tag{1}$$

where D_n is the sequence of messages delivered at site n. If the membership varies over time, *Virtual Synchrony* [2] stipulates that agreed order be preserved as long as the sites view each other as members.

A GCP breaks up into ADO and membership control (MC) protocols. Since ADO entails large message latencies and overhead, *quasi-ADO* can be considered instead, allowing rare ADO violations. MC is not possible if the sites are anonymous; neither is it critical for "collective output" applications, interested in performing some task rather than keeping a record of message recipients. Take a distributed resource sharing system, where sites exchange resource requests and the output depends on keeping consistent FIFO order of local request queues [10]. Fig. 1 shows that ADO violations worsen the performance, but are not fatal; the initial part of the curve even shows that the cost of maintaining a low ADO violation rate outweighs its benefits.

We define *strong ADO* that has a flavor of Extended Virtual Synchrony [12] for it preserves ADO across membership changes, though MC is not guaranteed.

Definition 1. Strong ADO holds if

(i) (1) holds provided that no membership changes occur, otherwise
(ii) each member site n delivers messages consistently with a common total order during its presence spells; let D_n be the sequence of delivered messages, then there exists a total order on M_SET such that for $m, m' \in M\_SET$ with m' following m,

$$\forall_{n=1,...,N} \text{ if } m \text{ and } m' \text{ occur in } D_n \text{ then } m' \text{ follows } m \text{ in } D_n. \tag{2}$$

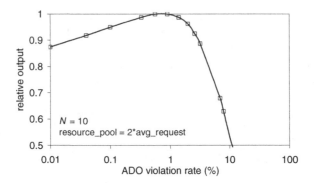

Fig. 1. Performance of distributed resource sharing

3 DPG Protocol

In this section we specify the LAN service abstraction and outline DPG-n, DPG protocol instance at site n. DPG permits anonymous member sites to maintain strong quasi-ADO except for arbitrarily improbable scenarios. For proof see [10].

3.1 Network Service Model

The *one-channel* (1C) LAN service abstraction was specified in [13] (it can model some wide-area network environments too [10]). 1C states that there exists a total order "$\rightarrow$" on M_SET such that for any $m, m' \in M\_SET$ with $m \rightarrow m'$,

$$\forall_{n=1,...,N} \text{ if } m \text{ and } m' \text{ occur in } R_n \text{ then } m' \text{ follows } m \text{ in } R_n, \tag{3}$$

where R_n is the sequence of messages received at site n. Clearly, "$\rightarrow$" is the multicast order (re-multicasts not included). The if-then structure of (3) reflects reception misses. A performance-oriented enhancement of 1C can be proposed as follows.

Definition 2. Let "$\Rightarrow$" be the *contiguity* suborder (transitive reduction) of "$\rightarrow$": $m \Rightarrow m'$ means that $m \rightarrow m'$ and there exists no m'' such that $m \rightarrow m''$ and $m'' \rightarrow m'$. The network service is *1C with Contiguity Inference Device* (CID) if at each member site and for any pair of consecutively received messages m and m', $m \rightarrow m'$ is always inferred in accordance with (3) and sometimes also $m \Rightarrow m'$ as specified below:

(i) if $m \Rightarrow m'$ is inferred at a site then indeed $m \Rightarrow m'$,
(ii) if $m \Rightarrow m'$ then the inference about m and m' ($m \Rightarrow m'$ or only $m \rightarrow m'$) may vary from site to site, depending on the local conditions.

For example, if received messages m and m' are separated by a minimum message transmission duration then $m \Rightarrow m'$ is inferred; still, reception of two contiguous messages may be separated by a longer interval.

3.2 DPG Data Structures and Operation

To maintain strong ADO, DPG-n, updates a *message precedence graph* G. Two types of protocol data units (PDU) are defined: a *message* PDU carries a first-time message multicast; a *report* PDU helps recover missed messages via re-multicast ("catch-up"). A unique random *tag* is appended to each PDU, valid only for the PDU lifetime and not reflecting the sender's identity. "X" designates a PDU tagged with X. A report PDU contains the current G at DPG-n, a list of tags of missed messages whose re-multicast DPG-n is requesting, and a list of messages DPG-n is re-multicasting at another site's request.

Strong quasi-ADO approximates the multicast order "$\rightarrow$". DPG-n maintains a correspondence between the vertices of G and received PDU tags, written as X, Y, Z, U etc., (X, Y) being an arc going from X into Y. Some arcs are *marked*. If $X \in G$ then DPG-n has received X or has been notified of its reception at some other site via a report PDU; if $(X, Y) \in G$ then messages X and Y were multicast in this order, as inferred by the local CID or based on received report PDUs. By exchanging report PDUs, member sites assist one another in a "catch-up."

Reception of a message PDU containing Z causes the extension of G by vertex Z and arcs (X, Z) for all X with no outgoing arc in G. If Z is a message then its body is stored (also when n is the sender of Z). DPG-n maintains the latest received PDU tag L_Rec and marks arc (L_Rec, Z) if CID infers $L\_Rec \Rightarrow Z$ at the instant of Z reception. The current G included by DPG-n in report PDUs permits DPG instances at the other sites to update their precedence graphs as follows. Suppose DPG-n currently storing graph G has received a graph G' in a report PDU. First it computes $G \cup G'$ and marks each arc that was marked in G or G'. Next, it *linearizes* G so as to take advantage of the acquired knowledge of "$\rightarrow$". Linearization continues until there are neither *replaceable* nor *removable* arcs in G.

An arc (X, Y) is considered replaceable if there exists a vertex $Z \in G$ such that either $(X, Z) \in G$ and (X, Z) is marked, or $(Z, Y) \in G$ and (Z, Y) is marked $((X, Y)$ is then replaced by (Z, Y) or (X, Z) respectively), and removable if there exists a directed path from X to Y in G consisting of more than one arc $((X,Y)$ is then removed from G). Fig. 2 gives an example that illustrates how occasional inference of $m \Rightarrow m'$ (reflected by the markings in G) permits to quickly approximate "$\rightarrow$".

DPG-n stores L_Deliv, the latest delivered message tag. X is *deliverable* when (L_Deliv, X) is marked or when all Y_i where $(L\_Deliv, Y_i) \in G$ have seen reception of sufficiently many report PDUs while included in G. In the latter case, the Y_i are ignored if they are report PDUs, otherwise if $(Y_1, Y_2) \in G$ then Y_1 is delivered first, and if there is no directed path between Y_1 and Y_2 then they are delivered in arbitrary static order e.g., of ascending tags. Delivery of X follows if the message body has already been stored; otherwise a dummy message is delivered with the understanding that all member sites that have received X are currently absent. Subsequently, L_Deliv along with the outgoing arcs is removed from G, and X becomes the new L_Deliv.

All DPG instances collectively attempt to maintain a nearly periodic report PDU "heartbeat." A DPG flow control mechanism keeps the size of G manageable and ensures that messages are admitted and delivered roughly at the same pace.

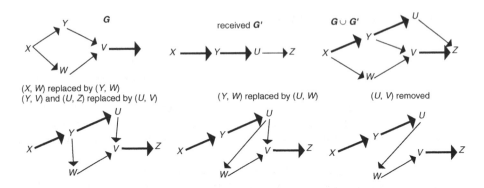

Fig. 2. Linearization example (*marked arcs drawn thick*)

4 DPG Performance

Group throughput is interrelated with message latencies via flow control and must be traded off for ADO violation rate. In a simulation experiment, the network was idealized to marginalize inter-site delays. Transmission overhead due to PDU tags, precedence graphs, and message lists was assumed negligible. No background traffic was allowed. Each member site always had a message ready for multicast and free buffers ready for reception. We believe such a setting provides a convenient framework in which to compare different GCPs. Other simulation details are listed in Table 1.

Table 1. Simulation setting

number of member sites, N	5..30 (always present)
CID	ideal (always infers contiguity if true) or none
"catch-up,", flow control, and report PDU "heartbeat" settings	produce 1% ADO violation rate and one report PDUs per five message PDUs
reception miss rate, c	0..0.2

For $N = 10$, Fig. 3 (left) plots the group throughput (normalized to the LAN bandwidth) against c. At large c, admission and delivery of messages are slow to keep the ADO violation rate low. At low c, ideal CID speeds up delivery: a report PDU often makes for marking more arcs in G, and its quick linearization. This is less effective at larger c, since report PDUs are themselves prone to reception misses.

The impact of ideal CID depends more on c than on N – Fig. 3 (right). DPG ensures a relatively stable group throughput for various N and a constant c. For a large c, ideal CID even slightly improves the throughput as N grows; this is due to a growing chance of two contiguous messages being received at some site, which then disseminates the knowledge about their contiguity across the group. A more realistic model would feature some probability of contiguity inference (between 0 for the "no CID" and 1 for the "ideal CID" cases).

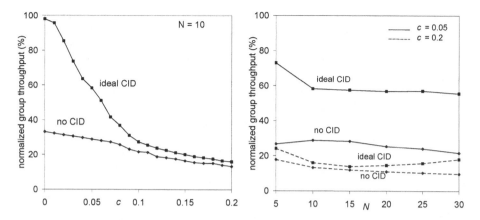

Fig. 3. DPG group throughput against: reception miss rate (*left*), group size (*right*)

5 Free Riding on DPG

The prediction of the DPG performance may change significantly if selfish behavior is factored in. A selfish site will not adhere to DPG if it runs counter its individual objective (*payoff*); for a general motivation see [7]. Agreed order multicast has drawn little attention in this context, ADO being the apparent common goal. However, site anonymity (hence, membership insensitivity) permitted by DPG, invites *free riding* i.e., participation in the benefits (delivery of messages in ADO), while shirking from the costly obligations (multicast of report PDUs in support of "catch-up"). Similar behavior has been noted in P2P systems (downloading shared files without contributing one's own) [8] and MANETs (injection of source packets without forwarding transit packets) [3]. Let a site's payoff be defined as the difference between the rates of message and report PDU multicast i.e.,

$$payoff = message\_rate - \alpha\ report\_rate, \tag{4}$$

where α is an arbitrary weight. The second component in (4) is particularly justified by battery lifetime considerations in a wireless network.

The presence of selfish sites (*invaders*) was simulated for $N = 10$ and probability of contiguity inference if true $P\_infer = 1$ (ideal CID) or 0.5. Fig. 4 (left) depicts the incentive to free ride – the relative difference between the invader's payoff and that of a cooperative site adhering to DPG. The incentive strengthens with c and weakens with P_infer due to the increased number of report PDUs cooperative sites have to contribute to keep the ADO violation rate low. The incentive further strengthens with the number of invaders since the number of report PDUs the remaining sites have to contribute becomes then even larger. When c approaches 0.2, the incentive becomes as high as 60% to 100%.

To disincentivize free riding, DPG can be complemented with a *privilege/veto mechanism*. First, when the report PDU "heartbeat" dictates that a report be multicast, a site does so with a probability P_report independently of the other sites. In the presence of invaders, this leaves the possibility of no report being multicast (a gap in the "heartbeat"), in which case the sender of the latest one is privileged to multicast $M > 1$ successive messages (*privilege messages*), whereas the other sites must back off. Secondly, a site may veto a received privileged message if, prior to its delivery based on subsequent updates of G, it deems the sender's privilege undeserved (e.g., the sender was not the last site to multicast a report before the gap or more than M privileged messages have been multicast). The veto is communicated via a report PDU using the message tag as a reference. One veto is enough to prevent local delivery of a message, a provision that may be assumed strong enough to discourage multicast of unjustified privilege messages. Note that a missed report PDU does not trigger a veto, but can trigger an unjustified privilege message multicast; the latter, however, will be vetoed by any site that did not miss the report. Also note that unnecessary vetoes are possible; however, unless the protocol collapses as the number of invaders approaches N, they should be rare given the ADO violation rate is kept reasonably low. Finally, it is not in the interest of a cooperative site *not* to veto an unjustified privilege message, since it would give more incentive to invaders.

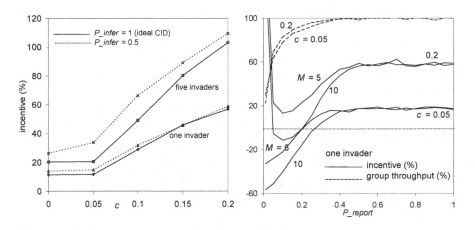

Fig. 4. Group throughput and incentive to free ride for $\alpha = 0.5$ against: c (*left*), P_report (*right*)

A report PDU preceding a gap in the "heartbeat" and subsequent privilege messages can be linked up e.g., using a public hash function and a hash-chain commitment scheme: each PDU contains a hash of the next privilege message in line; its validity can thus be easily verified upon reception.

Fig. 4 (right) depicts the incentives (4) and group throughput (normalized to a fully cooperative setting) against P_report for $N = 10$, $P\_infer = 0.5$, and one invader (qualitatively similar plots arise for more invaders). As P_report decreases, so do the group throughput and incentive. The latter in fact goes negative for small enough P_report, indicating a desirable region of resiliency against selfish behavior. (A sudden increase of the incentives for very small P_report is due to the fact that neither the invaders nor cooperative sites then multicast messages, but the latter still do multicast report PDUs.) Note that in the desirable region, the group throughput remains at an acceptable 70% to 80% of the cooperative maximum.

6 Conclusion

Some GCPs concerned about ADO need not be concerned about MC. We have discussed a membership-insensitive, quasi-ADO protocol on top of 1C with CID, and investigated its performance. The impact of CID, reception miss rate, and free riding was pointed out. To keep the paper short, group membership was assumed constant.

Systematic game-theoretic studies of DPG with free riding will permit to optimize P_report relative to N and c, as well as give more insight into the noncooperative game that arises among invaders. The proposed privilege/veto mechanism suggests a kind of a *timing game* [7], for which more sophisticated invader strategies can be envisaged than just refraining from multicasting report PDUs.

Acknowledgment. This work was supported in part by the Ministry of Education and Science, Poland, under Grant 1599/T11/2005/29.

References

1. Amir, Y., Moser, L.E., Melliar-Smith, P.M., Agarwal, D.A., Ciarfella, P.: Fast Message Ordering and Membership Using a Logical Token-Passing Ring. In: *Proceedings of the 14th ICDCS* (1993) 551-560
2. Birman, K.P., Schiper, A., Stephenson, P.: Lightweight Causal and Atomic Group Multicast. ACM Trans. on Comp. Systems 9 (1991) 272-314
3. Buttyan, L., Hubaux, J. P.: Stimulating Cooperation in Self-organizing Mobile Ad Hoc Networks. ACM/Kluwer Mobile Networks and Applications 8 (2003) 579-592
4. Diot, C., Dabbous, W., Crowcroft, J.: Multipoint Communication: A Survey of Protocols, Functions and Mechanisms. IEEE J. on Selected Areas in Comm. 15 (1997) 277-290
5. Dolev, D., Kramer, S., Malki, D.: Early Delivery Totally Ordered Multicast in Asynchronous Environments. In: *Proceedings of the* 23rd FTCS (1993) 544-553
6. Ezhilchelvan, P.D., Macedo, R.A., Shrivastava, S.K.: Newtop: A Fault-Tolerant Group Communication Protocol. In: *Proceedings of the 15th ICDCS* (1995) 336-356
7. Fudenberg, D., Tirole, J.: Game Theory. MIT Press (1991)
8. Golle, P., Leyton-Brown, K., Mironov, I, Lillibridge, M.: Incentives for Sharing in Peer-to-Peer Networks. In: *Proceedings of the the 3rd ACM Conf. on Electronic Commerce* (2001) 264-267
9. Konorski, J.: Membership-Insensitive Totally Ordered Multicast: Properties and Performance. Lecture Notes in Computer Science, Vol. 1815. Springer-Verlag. Berlin Heidelberg New York (2000)
10. Konorski, J.: Distributed Network Protocols for Anonymous Stations in Cooperative and Noncooperative Settings. Gdansk University of Technology (2006)
11. Melliar-Smith, P.M, Moser, L.E., Agrawala, V.: Broadcast Protocols for Distributed Systems. IEEE Trans. on Parallel and Distributed Systems 1 (1990) 17-25
12. Moser, L.E., Amir, Y., Melliar-Smith, P.M., Agarwal, D.A.: Extended Virtual Synchrony. In: *Proceedings of the 14th ICDCS* (1994) 56-65
13. Nakamura, A., Takizawa, M.: Priority-Based and Semi-Total Ordering Broadcast Protocols. In: *Proceedings of the 12th ICDCS* (1992) 178-185
14. Peterson, L.L., Bucholz, N.C., Schlichting, R.D.: Preserving and Using Context Information in Interprocess Communication. ACM Trans. on Comp. Systems 7 (1989) 217-246

On Reliability Analysis of Forward Loop Forward Hop Networks

Soumen Maity[1] and S. Ramsundar[2]

[1] Department of Mathematics, Indian Institute of Technology Guwahati
Guwahati 781 039, Assam, India
soumen@iitg.ernet.in
[2] Computer Science & Engineering, Indian Institute of Technology Guwahati,
Guwahati 781 039, Assam, India
sundark@iitg.ernet.in

Abstract. A common technique to improve the reliability of loop (or ring) networks is by introducing link redundancy; that is, by providing several alternative paths for communication between pairs of nodes. With alternative paths between nodes, the network can now sustain several node and link failures by bypassing the faulty components. However, faults occurring at strategic locations in a ring can prevent the computation by disrupting I/O operations, blocking the flow of information, or even segmenting the structure into pieces which can no longer be suitable for any practical purpose.

An extensive characterization of fault-tolerance in FLFH networks is given in this paper. The characterization has revealed several properties which describe the problem of constructing subrings and linear arrays in the presence of node failures in the FLFH network for a specific link configuration. Also in this paper, bounds are established on the degree of fault tolerance achievable in a redundant FLFH network when performing a computation that requires a fixed number of operational nodes. Also the bounds on the size of the problems guaranteed to be solved in the presence of a given number of faults in the network are derived.

1 Introduction

Loop (or ring) networks are commonly used for the interconnection of computers that are in close proximity. Reliability is a severe problem in single-loop networks; any single node or link failure can disrupt communication. A way to provide higher reliability in loop networks is to introduce redundancy. The idea here is to design regular multi-connected loop network so that several alternative paths for communication exists between nodes. In other words, each node is connected to two or more nodes in the network. With alternate paths between nodes, the network can sustain several node and link failures. Several ring networks, suggested in [1,4,12,14], are based on this principle. Although reliability can be improved in these networks, it is still possible that faults occurring in strategic locations in the network can logically disconnect the ring structure.

S. Madria et al. (Eds.): ICDCIT 2006, LNCS 4317, pp. 136–144, 2006.
© Springer-Verlag Berlin Heidelberg 2006

Disconnection of a ring does not mean that the entire structure is unusable. In fact, it still might be possible to find one or more subrings or linear arrays in the original ring in spite of the failure of some nodes.

In this paper, the inherent limits to reconfigurability of FLFH networks are studied by using (i) the properties of catastrophic fault patterns, and (ii) the necessary and sufficient conditions for construction of subrings and linear arrays in presence of faults. In particular, bounds on the size of the problems one can be guaranteed to solve in the presence of a given number of faults in the network are derived.

The organization of this paper is as follows. In Section 2, basic concepts are introduced and basic conditions on FLFH network are discussed. In Section 3, properties of catastrophic fault patterns are discussed followed by the bounds on the sizes of connected components, such as subrings and linear arrays. An algorithm to get the optimal linear array in the generalized FLFH network is given is Section 4. Finally, limits to reconfiguration of FLFH topologies are studied in Section 5.

2   Preliminaries

The basic components of such a ring network are the processing elements (PEs) namely P_0 to P_{n-1}. We sometimes refer to a processor P_i as processor i. There are two kinds of links : *regular* and *bypass*. A regular link connects P_i to $P_{(i+1) \mod n}$, its direction is from P_i to $P_{(i+1) \mod n}$, while the bypass links connect non-neighbors. The bypass links are used strictly for reconfiguration schemes, otherwise they are redundant. From now on we use $\aleph(n, G)$ to denote that the ring network $\aleph$ has n PEs and has a redundancy set G. We now formally introduce the following definitions:

Definition 1. A FLFH network $\aleph(n, G)$ consists of a set $V = \{P_0, P_1, \ldots, P_{n-1}\}$ of n PEs and a set $G = \{1, 2, \ldots, g\}$ of g unidirectional links. We say $\aleph(n, G)$ has link redundancy or link configuration G if, the directed links are from p_i to $p_{i+t \pmod n}$ for $1 \leq i \leq n$ and $1 \leq t \leq g$.

We now define a redundant linear array and show its relationship with the FLFH network.

Let $S = \{LCU, A, RCU\}$ represent a redundant linear array in which LCU and RCU denote Left and Right Control Unit respectively and $A = \{P_0, P_1, \ldots, P_{n-1}\}$ denotes a redundant linear array of PEs. The LCU and RCU which interface with the linear array A are responsible for all the I/O functions. All the links are unidirectional. There exists a regular link from P_i to P_{i+1}, $0 \leq i < n-1$. Any link connecting P_i to P_j where $j > i$ is a bypass link. The length of a bypass link, connecting P_i and P_j, is the distance in the array between P_i and P_j; i.e., $|j - i|$. Note that for each $P_i \in A$ with $i > N - g$ there exists a link from P_i to RCU. Similarly, LCU is connected to $P_1, P_2, \ldots, P_g$. Every P_i has in-degree (also out-degree) g, LCU has out-degree g, and RCU has in-degree g.

There is very close relationship between a FLFH network and a redundant linear array: a ring is essentially a redundant linear array in which end points of the array are connected to each other in a wrap-around manner rather than to *LCU* or *RCU*. We will denote the array A on n PEs by simply $A(n)$.

Definition 2. Given a ring network $\aleph(n, G)$, a fault pattern for $\aleph$ is a set of integers $F = \{ f_1, f_2, \ldots, f_m \}$ where $m \leq n$, $f_j \leq f_{j+1}$ and $f_j \in [0, n-1]$. The set F represents the set of faulty PEs in $\aleph$.

There are patterns of faults whose occurrence in $\aleph$ can block the flow of information from one side of the pattern to the other through the faulty region in any fixed direction. In the case of a linear array, the occurrence of one such fault pattern can cause the disconnection of the I/O ports. Such patterns are considered to be catastrophic for a linear array, but we cannot say it is really catastrophic for a ring.

Definition 3. A fault pattern F is *catastrophic* for an array $A(n)$ with link redundancy G if I and O are not connected in the presence of such an assignment of faults.

Definition 4. A fault pattern F is blocking for $\aleph(n, G)$ if it is catastrophic for a redundant linear array A on $n' \geq n$ nodes with redundancy G and vice versa.

Many properties and results of catastrophic fault patterns for linear arrays apply to FLFH networks. In the following we will summarize some known properties of catastrophic fault pattern for linear array and also characterize catastrophic fault pattern for FLFH networks.

3   Fault-Tolerance Analysis of FLFH Networks

In this section properties of catastrophic fault patterns in FLFH networks are discussed. This section also deals with the degree of fault tolerance that can be achieved in a ring in the presence of node failures. An extensive characterization of catastrophic fault patterns for linear array has been given in [6,7,8]. As discussed in [7,8], the only pattern that can be blocking for $A(n)$, where $G = \{1, 2, \ldots, g\}$, is a cluster of at least g faulty nodes.

Definition 5. The *decomposition* of a fault pattern F is a set $B = \{F_1, F_2, \ldots, F_p\}$, where

1. Each F_i is a set of contiguous faulty PEs,
2. $\forall i \neq j, F_i \cap F_j = \emptyset$,
3. $\bigcup_i F_i = F$
4. The cardinality p of the set B should be as minimum as possible.

Definition 6. For a fault pattern F, the *blocking dimension*, given by $D(F)$, is the number of elements in the decomposition of F of cardinality $\geq g$. Each of the F_i those count into blocking dimension is called a *blocking pattern*.

Definition 7. A fault pattern F is said to be *catastrophic* for *FLFH* ring $\aleph(n, G)$ if $\aleph - F$ is not connected, that is, the network becomes disconnected once the faulty processors, and their incident links are removed.

3.1 Properties of Catastrophic Fault Patterns

Theorem 1. *F is catastrophic for a FLFH ring* $\aleph(n, G)$ *if and only if* $D(F) \geq 2$.

Proof: Obviously, for $D(F) = 0$ the ring is not catastrophic. It will be proved that if $D(F) = 1$, then $\aleph - F$ is connected and, thus F is not catastrophic. $D(F) = 1$ means that there cannot be two disjoint blocking fault patterns. Consider two arbitrary non-faulty nodes x and y in $\aleph - F$. We need to show that one of the paths x to y or y to x, should be present. Now a path from x to y does not exit only if there is a blocking fault pattern among x, $x + 1 \pmod{n}$, $x + 2 \pmod{n}, \ldots, y$. Similarly no path exists from y to x, only if there is a blocking fault pattern among y, $y + 1 \pmod{n}$, $y + 2 \pmod{n} \ldots, x$. But, as there is only one blocking fault pattern, one of the paths x to y or y to x exists.

It suffices to show that if $D(F) = 2$ then F is catastrophic. Let $B = \{F_1, F_2, \ldots\}$ be a decomposition of F such that $|F_1| \geq g$ and $|F_2| \geq g$. Let S_1 (S_2) be the set of non-faulty nodes between F_1 and F_2 (F_2 and F_1) in the clockwise direction. Notice that S_1 and S_2 are disjoint and neither of the two are empty, otherwise $D(F) = 1$. Now take $x \in S_1$ and $y \in S_2$. Since F_1 and F_2 are blocking, there is neither a path from x to y nor from y to x.   □

The occurrence of more than one disjoint blocking patterns thus logically disconnects a ring structure. However, disconnection of a ring does not mean that the entire structure is unusable. In fact, it still might be possible to find one or more subrings or linear arrays in the original ring in spite of the failure of some nodes. These subrings and linear arrays can be utilized in computations requiring fewer processing elements. We now deal with the degree of fault tolerance that can be achieved in a ring in the presence of node failures. The degree of fault tolerance is characterized in terms of bounds on the sizes of the subrings and linear arrays it might still be possible to obtain in the presence of faults.

3.2 Subring Results

Theorem 2. *For a FLFH ring* $\aleph(n, G)$ *and a fault pattern F,* $D(F) = 0$ *if and only if there exists a subring* $\aleph(n - |F|, G)$.

Proof: $D(F) = 0$ implies that there is no fault cluster of size g or larger. That is, in the decomposition of F, $|F_i| = \ell_i < g$, $\forall i$. Since $G = \{1, 2, \ldots, g\}$, there exists a link of length $l_i + 1 \in G$ to bypass the fault pattern F_i. It is clear that a ring can be formed on the remaining $n - |F|$ nodes by using regular link of length 1 and links of length $l_i + 1$.   □

Obviously, if there exists a ring on $n - |F|$ nodes, there exists a linear array on $n - |F|$ nodes.

3.3 Linear Array Results

Tyszer [13] had studied the problem of constructing a linar array in the ring when $|F| < 2g$. Tyszer's result is formally described by the following lemma.

Lemma 1. *If $|F| < 2g - 2$, it is possible to create a linear array $A(n - |F|)$.*

We now generalize this result for FLFH network $\aleph(n, G)$. Tyszer's result then follows as a simple corollary of this generalized result. The generalized version is as follows:

Theorem 3. *For a FLFH network $\aleph(n, G)$ and a fault pattern F, there exists a linear array $A(v)$ regardless of the number of faults $|F|$, where*

$$v = \frac{n - |F|}{Max\ \{1, D(F)\}}$$

Proof: If $D(F) = 0$, then the theorem follows from Theorem 2. Let $D(F) > 0$. Let $F_{i1}, F_{i2}, \ldots, F_{iD(F)}$ be the blocking fault patterns in the decomposition of F. Removal from $\aleph$ of these blocking patterns will disconnect the ring into $D(F)$ connected components, $C_1, C_2, \ldots, C_{D(F)}$. Let n_i denote the number of non-faulty elements in C_i. Without loss of generality, let $n_1 \geq n_i, \forall i, 1 < i \leq D(F)$, that is, C_1 is the connected component containing the largest number of non-faulty elements. Then, $n_1 \geq \frac{N - |F|}{D(F)}$, by pigeon hole principle. Without loss of generality, let C_1 be

$$S_1, F_2, S_2, F_3, \ldots, S_{q-1}, F_q, S_q.$$

where F_i's are non-blocking fault patterns in the decomposition of F and all nodes in F_i are to the left of the nodes in S_i (which consists solely of non-faulty nodes), and all nodes in S_i are to the left of the nodes in F_{i+1}; all operations are modulo n. An array on these S_i's can be constructed as follows:

1. Connect every node in S_i using regular link.
2. Connect S_i to S_{i+1} using a bypass link of length $l_{i+1} + 1$, this is clearly possible since $l_{i+1} = |F_{i+1}| < g$.

□

Note that $|F| < 2g - 2$ implies that $D(F) \leq 1$. Thus, by Theorem 3, there exists a linear array of $n - |F|$ working PEs. In other words, the result by Tyszer, follows as a simple corollary of Theorem 3.

4   Optimal Linear Array Formation Strategy for Generalized FLFH Networks

In this section, we consider generalized FLFH networks with an arbitrary link structure, and study the problem of optimal linear array construction in the presence of a set of blocking fault patterns. We consider optimality with respect to the size of the reconfigured array.

A generalized FLFH network is similar to the FLFH network defined before with the only difference being that the redundancy set is not constrained to have all the elements from 1 to g. So any proper subset of $G = \{1, 2, \ldots, g\}$ will be a redundancy set for a generalized FLFH network. We now introduce the following definitions:

Definition 8. A generalized FLFH network $\aleph(n, G)$ consists of a set $V = \{P_0, P_1, \ldots, P_{n-1}\}$ of n PEs and a set $G = \{g_1 = 1, g_2, \ldots, g_k\}$, $1 < g_2 < g_3 \ldots < g_k$, of k unidirectional links. We say $\aleph(n, G)$ has link redundancy or link configuration G if, the directed links are from p_i to p_{i+g_t} (mod n) for $1 \leq i \leq n$ and $g_t \in G$, $1 \leq t \leq k$.

In generalized FLFH networks, a cluster of atleast g faulty nodes is not the only blocking fault pattern. For example, consider the fault pattern $F = \{0, 2, 8\}$ in the generalized FLFH network $\aleph(10, G)$ with $G = \{1, 3\}$ as shown in Figure 1. It can be noted that F is a blocking pattern but it is not a cluster of 3 faulty processors. We know that a fault pattern F is blocking for $\aleph(n, G)$ if it is catastrophic for a redundant linear array A on $n' \geq n$ nodes with redundancy G and vice versa. The fault pattern in Figure 1 is a catastrophic fault pattern for a linear array with unidirectional link redundancy $G = \{1, 3\}$, occurring as a blocking pattern in generalized FLFH network with $G = \{1, 3\}$. Thus the number of blocking fault patterns in FLFH network $\aleph(n, G)$ is the same as the number of catastrophic fault pattern for linear array with link redundancy G. A count on the number of catastrophic fault patterns in linear array with link redundancy $G = \{1, 2, g\}$, $g > 2$, is given in [7].

Definition 9. Given a generalized FLFH network $\aleph(n, G)$ and a fault pattern F, we construct a graph $H = (V, E)$ as follows: The set V of vertices is the set of working processors, and the set E of edges are the directed links between two working processors. We preserve the direction of the link, in the edge representing it. We call the graph H the *Auxiliary graph* of $\aleph$ for the fault pattern F.

By definition of Auxiliary graph it follows that a fault pattern F is a blocking fault pattern for for generalized FLFH $\aleph$, if and only if the corresponding auxiliary graph H is directed acyclic graph (DAG)[3]. We use the concept of derived graph to solve our problem.

We say that a linear array formed is *optimal* if it contains maximum possible working PEs. Obviously, the linear array should be a single connected component. If the fault pattern F cuts the network into disconnected components, such a linear array will be entirely within a component. Now we use the directed acyclic graph property of the auxiliary graph to show that we can find the optimal linear array in polynomial time. We may have several connected components of the auxiliary graph H. Then in each of the connected components we can find the all pairs longest path to get the optimal linear array. The longest path problem is solvable in linear time for directed acyclic graph, as given in [3].

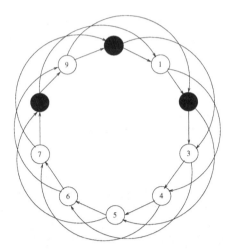

Fig. 1. A blocking fault pattern

5   Limits to Reconfigurability of Generalized FLFH Network

In this section, we are concerned about the guaranteed fault tolerance in a redundant ring network in the presence of PE failures. It is assumed that some form of reconfiguration mechanism is built into the network and is triggered on the occurrence of one or more PE failures. The guaranteed level of fault tolerance is related to the limits to reconfigurability. In order to quantify the limits to reconfigurability of redundant rings, we focus on performing computations that require a fixed number of connected non-faulty PEs. As seen earlier, it still might be possible to find one or more subrings or linear arrays in the original ring in spite of the failure of some nodes. These subrings and linear arrays can be utilized in computations requiring fewer processing nodes. In this section, we derive bounds on the size of the problems one can be guaranteed to solve in the presence of a given number of faults in the network.

Definition 10. A ring problem X of size $|X| = m$ is a problem whose solution requires a ring of size at least m.

Definition 11. An array problem X of size $|X| = m$ is a problem whose solution requires a linear array of size at least m.

Definition 12. A generalized FLFH ring network $\aleph(n, G)$ is "(k, m)-Ring Intolerant" if in the presence of k faults, it is not possible to solve all ring-problems of size m or greater.

Definition 13. A generalized FLFH ring network $\aleph(n, G)$ is "(k, m)-Array Intolerant" if in the presence of k faults, it is not possible to solve all array-problems of size m or greater.

An obvious but useful property linking ring intolerance and array intolerance is the following.

Lemma 2. *If a generalized FLFH ring network $\aleph(n, G)$ is (α, β)-Array Intolerant then it is also (α, β)-Ring Intolerant.*

Theorem 4. *A generalized FLFH ring network $\aleph(n, G)$ is "$(\alpha g_k, \beta)$-Array Intolerant", where $\alpha \geq 1$ and $\beta = \lceil \frac{n}{\alpha} \rceil - g_k + 1$.*

Proof: If we can show that αg_k faults can be arranged in such a way that none of the linear arrays is of size β, then we are done. Let $F_1, F_2, \ldots, F_\alpha$ be α identical blocking fault patterns, each consisting of exactly g_k faults. There is a total of αg_k faults in $\aleph$. Now place the $F_1, F_2, \ldots, F_\alpha$ in $\aleph$ in such a way that F_i's are equally spaced. The number of non-faulty PEs between F_i and F_{i+1}, is $\leq \lceil \frac{n}{\alpha} \rceil - g_k$. This implies that in occurrence of αg_k faults in $\aleph$, an array may be formed on $\lceil \frac{\aleph}{\alpha} \rceil - g_k$ non-faulty PEs, but one cannot guarantee $\lceil \frac{n}{\alpha} \rceil - g_k + 1$ sized linear array. Therefore, it follows that $\aleph$ is $(\alpha g_k, \beta)$-Array Intolerant. $\square$

In other words, it is always impossible to solve an array-problem of size $|X| = m$ in presence of αg_k faults if $m > \lceil \frac{n}{\alpha} \rceil - g_k$. The intolerance of a generalized FLFH ring network can therefore be shown and rephrased in terms of the largest subring and largest linear array possible in it, in presence of faults.

6   Conclusions

A characterization of fault-tolerance of FLFH networks is given in this paper. It is shown that some of the existing results follow as simple corollaries to the ones established in this paper. The characterization has revealed several properties which describe the problem of constructing subrings and linear arrays in the presence of node failures in the FLFH network for a specified link configuration. Also in this paper, bounds on the degree of fault tolerance that can be achieved in a FLFH network when performing a computation (on a linear array as well as on ring) that requires a fixed number of operational nodes are established. Bounds on the size of the problems one can guarantee to solve in the presence of a given number of faults in the network are also derived. Efficient reconfiguration strategy for generalized FLFH network is also shown. Currently, work is underway for similar analysis of FLBH (Forward Loop Backward Hop) networks.

References

1. B. Arden and H. Lee, Analysis of chordal ring networks, *IEEE Trans. Computers*, **C-30**, 4 (1981), 291-295.
2. J. Bruck, R. Cypher and C.-T. Ho, Fault-tolerant meshes and hypercubes with minimal number of spares, *IEEE Trans. Computers*, **C-42**, (1993), 1089-1104.
3. T. H. Cormen, Charles E. Leiserson, Ronald L. Rivest, Clifford Stein. 2/e *Introduction to Algorithms*. MIT Press, Cambridge, MA.

4. D. Z. Du, D. F. Hsu, and F. K. Hwang, Doubly linked ring networks, *IEEE Trans. Computers*, **C-34**, 9(1985), 853-855.
5. A. Granov, L Kleinrock and M. Gerla, A highly reliable distributed double loop network architecture, in Proc. *Intl. Symp. on Fault-Tolerant Computing*, Kyoto, Oct. 1980, 319-324.
6. S. Maity, A. Nayak, and B. Roy, On Characterization of Catastrophic Faults in Two-Dimensional VLSI Arrays. *INTEGRATION, The VLSI Journal*, 38(2004), 267-281.
7. S. Maity, B. Roy, and A. Nayak, On Enumeration of Catastrophic Fault Patterns, *Information Processing Letters*, 81 (2002), 209-212.
8. S. Maity, B. Roy, and A. Nayak, Identification of optimal link redundancy for which a given fault pattern is catastrophic in VLSI linear arrays. *Congr. Numer.*, 151(2001), 41-52.
9. H. Masuyama and T. Icimori, Tolerance of doulbe-loop computer networks to multinode failures, *IEEE Trans. Computers*, **C-38**, 5(1989), 738-741.
10. A. Nayak, L. Pagli, and N. Santoro, Efficient construction of catastrophic patterns for VLSI reconfigurable arrays, *INTEGRATION: The VLSI Journal*, 15(1993), 133-150.
11. J. M. Peha, F. A. Tobagi, Comments on tolerance of double-loop networks with multinode failures, *IEEE Trans. Computers*, **C-41**, 11(1992), 1488-1490.
12. C. S. Raghavendra, Fault tolerance in regular network architectures, *IEEE Micro 4*, 6(1884), 44-53.
13. J. Tyszer, A multiple fault-tolerant processor network architecture for pipeline computing, *IEEE Trans. Computers*, **C-37**, 11(1988), 1414-1418.
14. H. F. Wedde and P. H. L. Tjoie, Long-term reconfiguration of double ring networks under real time constraints, in *Proc. Real-Time Systems Symp.*, 1987, 104-111.

A Dynamic Paging Scheme for Minimizing Signaling Costs in Hierarchical Mobile IPv6 Networks

Myung-Kyu Yi

Dept. of Computer Science & Engineering Korea University,
1,5-Ga, Anam-Dong, SungBuk-Gu, Seoul 136-701, South Korea
`kainos@disys.korea.ac.kr`

Abstract. In this paper, we propose a dynamic paging scheme for minimizing signaling costs in Hierarchical Mobile IPv6 (HMIPv6) networks. To minimize signaling overhead, in our proposal, an idle mobile node does not register when moving within a paging area in HMIPv6 networks. Moreover, the size of the paging area is determined dynamically according the changes of mobility and calling patterns of mobile nodes. An analytic model is applied to determine the optimal size of a paging area. The cost analysis presented in this paper shows that our proposal offers considerable performance advantages to existing HMIPv6 schemes.

1 Introduction

With the recent advances in portable devices and wireless networks, mobile users want to access web sites and transmit and receive e-mail from virtually anywhere. In order to communicate, all mobile devices must be configured with an IP address in accordance with the IP protocol and its addressing scheme. The problem occurs when an Mobile Node (MN) roams away from its home network and is no longer reachable using normal IP routing. This results in the active sessions of the device being terminated. A natural solution is to use IP layer mobility. Mobile IPv6[1] is the IETF proposed standard solution for handling terminal mobility among IP subnets. It allows users to keep the same IP address, stay connected, and maintain ongoing applications while roaming between IP networks.

In a basic Mobile IPv6 (MIPv6) operation, each MN is identified by two IP addresses: its Home Address (HoA) and its Care-of Address (CoA). The HoA is a static address that is used to identify higher layer connections. The CoA is a temporary IP address for routing purpose when the MN is attached to a foreign link. When an MN moves from its home link to a foreign link, it first forms a CoA based on the prefix of the foreign link. Then, the MN informs its Home Agent (HA) and any active correspondent node (CN) by sending a Binding Update (BU) message. The BU message contains the MN's HoA and its CoA. The HA needs to store this information in order to forward packets address to the MN's home address. Therefore, data packets addressed to the MN are routed to its home network, where the HA now intercepts and tunnels

S. Madria et al. (Eds.): ICDCIT 2006, LNCS 4317, pp. 145–158, 2006.

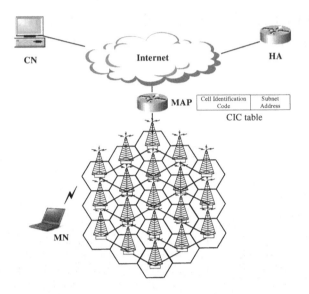

Fig. 1. Wireless cellular network model

them to the CoA toward the MN. When the MN moves back to its home link, it will notify the HA to delete the binding.

In MIPv6, however, the CoA of an MN changes whenever it moves from one IP subnet to another. This could lead to frequent registrations with the HA. Thus, Hierarchical Mobile IPv6 (HMIPv6)[2] is proposed by IETF to reduce signaling cost. The HMIPv6 is a mobility management protocol aimed at reducing wireless signalling and improving handover performance while moving within a particular domain. It uses a new MIPv6 node called the Mobility Anchor Point (MAP) to handle Mobile IP registration locally. When an MN moves into a new MAP domain in HMIPv6 networks, it needs to configure two CoAs: an Regional Care-of Address (RCoA) on the MAP's link and an on-link CoA (LCoA). While the LCoA is simply referred to as the CoA in MIPv6, the RCoA is auto-configured by the MN when receiving the MAP option. Then, the MN registers with its MAP and HA by sending a BU message. If the MN changes its LCoA within a local MAP domain, it only needs to register the new LCoA with the MAP. The RCoA does not change as long as the MN moves within an MAP domain. Therefore, the HA and external CNs need not be informed about local mobility within an IPv6 network. In HMIPv6, all packets addressed to the MN's RCoA are intercepted by the MAP and tunnelled to the MN's LCoA.

To maintain connectivity with the Internet, an MN must generate location updates every time it changes its location, even if it is currently in idle mode. Such mobility-related signaling leads to significant wastage of an MN's battery power when the MN is fast moving. To solve these problems, several IP paging schemes[3,4,5] have been proposed to reduce signaling costs for location updates in Mobile IP. Paging is a technique can improve the scalability of IP mobility protocol by reducing the number of message sent. However, existing IP paging schemes[3,4] do not consider the HMIPv6 scheme which can reduce the amount of signaling required and improve handoff speed for mobile connections. In [4,5], the size of the paging area is only configured manually by administrators or paging servers. In this paper, therefore, we propose the extension to the base HMIPv6 specification for dynamic paging support. Typically, IP paging schemes require the cost of broadcasting a paging message in the cells covered by the paging area. To reduce the total amount of signalling, in our proposal, the size of the paging area is determined dynamically according the changes of mobility and calling patterns of MNs. Our work has focused on addressing the dynamic IP paging scheme over HMIPv6 networks.

The rest of the paper is organized as follows. Modelling and system description are presented in Section 2. Section 3 describes the proposed protocol of location update and packet delivery. Section 4 shows the evaluation of the proposed system's performance and analysis of results. Finally, our conclusions are presented in Section 5.

2   System Model

In our proposal, an IP-based cellular network consists of based stations and routers interconnected by wired link as shown in Fig. 1. Base stations and routers are both IP-based but base stations have wireless interfaces. Wireless networks are connected to the Internet by the access router and the MAP. In our proposal, each MAP is in charge of the paging process for that paging area.

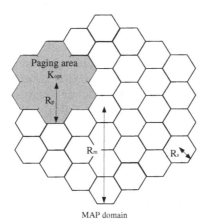

Fig. 2. Paging area model

We assume that the IP-based cellular network is divided into cells of the same size. Each cell has a Cell Identification Code (CIC), which identifies the cells and their relative orientation as similar to [6]. Each cell periodically broadcasts its identification code. We assume that each MAP has a CIC table, which consists of cell identification and network prefix. Therefore, when an MN performs a registration with the MAP by sending a BU message with its LCoA, the MAP knows the exact location of the MN and current CIC by comparing with its CIC table. Since the MAP always knows the network topology within an MAP domain, it can compute the optimal size of the paging area K_{opt} for each MN based on the changes of mobility and calling patterns as shown in Fig. 2. More detailed illustration for the optimal size of the paging area K_{opt} will be addressed in the next section.

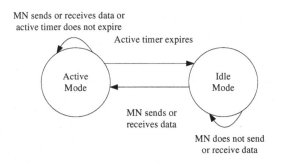

Fig. 3. An MN's mode transition diagram

In order to save battery power consumption at MNs, as shown in Fig. 3, we assume that each MN is allowed to enter a power saving idle mode when it is inactive for a period of time as same to [4,5]. When an MN is in active mode, it operates in the same manner as in HMIPv6 scheme. However, if an MN does not send or receive data for a certain period of time, the active timer will expire and the MN will revert to idle mode. During idle mode, the MAP knows the location of the MN with coarse accuracy defined by a paging area composed of several subnets. When an MN is in idle mode, it does not need to register its location when moving within a paging area. Whenever the MN sends or receives data, it returns to active mode and its active timer is reset. To support IP paging protocol, we propose to

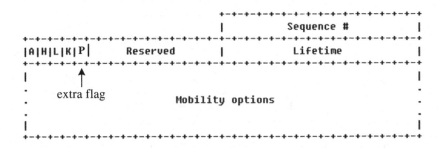

Fig. 4. Modified binding update message

extend the HMIPv6 BU message with an extra flag "P" taken from the reserved field as shown in Fig. 4. When this flag is set, it means that an MN is in idle mode.

3   Protocol Overview

This section describes the location update and packet delivery procedure.

3.1   Location Update Procedure

Fig. 5 presents the procedure for a location update by sending a BU message. When an MN is in active mode, it operates in exactly the same manner as the existing HMIPv6 scheme. If an MN attaches to a new link, the MN creates new LCoA and RCoA. The MN then sends a BU message to the MAP using its RCoA and LCoA. If the MAP accepts the local BU, it sends a Binding Acknowledgement (BA) message to the MN. After registering with the MAP, the MN must register its new RCoA with its HA and CNs by sending a BU message as in HMIPv6. The RCoA does not change as long as the MN moves within a MAP domain.

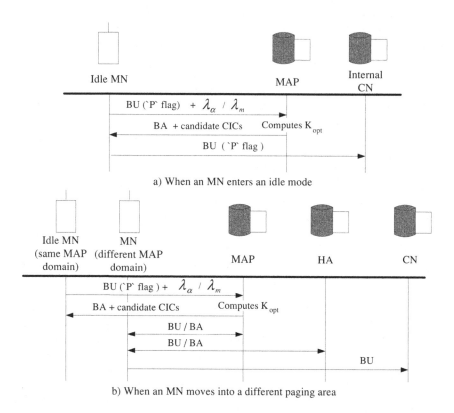

Fig. 5. Location update procedure

If the active timer expires and the MN does not send or receive data, the MN enters an idle mode. Whenever an MN enters an idle mode, it performs the following operations:

1) The idle MN sends a $BU_{[RCoA,LCoA]}$[1] message to the MAP with "P" flag set. At the same time, the idle MN sends its average packet arrival rate λ_α and average subnet residence time $1/\lambda_m$ to the MAP.
2) Then, the MAP changes the operational mode in its binding cache for the MN to idle mode.
3) Since the MAP can extract the MN's network prefix from the MN's LCoA, it knows exact location of the MN and current CIC from its CIC table.
4) Then, the MAP computes the optimal paging size area K_{opt} of the idle MN. The algorithm for deriving the optimal value K_{opt} will be described in the next section.
5) The MAP sends a BA message to the MN with the list of candidate CICs for the paging area.
6) Finally, the idle MN sends a $BU_{[HoA,RCoA]}$[2] message to the internal CNs[3] with "P" flag set.

After registering with the MAP and internal CNs, the idle MN does not send any other BU messages to the MAP and internal CNs before it moves out of the paging area. However, if the idle MN moves into a different paging area within the same MAP domain, it performs the following operations:

1) Since each base station periodically broadcasts its own CIC together with a beacon signal, the idle MN detects that it has moved into a new paging area by comparing with the list of candidate CICs.
2) The idle MN sends a $BU_{[RCoA,LCoA]}$ meesage with "P" flag set. At the same time, the idle MN sends its average packet arrival rate λ_α and average subnet residence time $1/\lambda_m$ to the MAP.
3) Then, the MAP computes the new K_{opt} of the idle MN.
4) The MAP sends a BA message to the MN with the new list for the candidate CICs for the paging area.

If an idle MN moves into a different MAP domain or changes its operational mode to active mode (i.e., whenever the idle MN sends or receives data), it performs the following operations:

1) The idle MN must perform a normal regional registration with the MAP by sending a $BU_{[RCoA,LCoA]}$ message with "P" flag unset.
2) The MAP changes the operational mode in its binding cache for the MN to active mode.

---

[1] BU with the binding between the MN's LCoA and RCoA.
[2] BU with the binding between the MN's HoA and RCoA.
[3] Note that an MN may send a BU containing its LCoA instead of its RCoA to CNs, which are connected to its same link in the current HMIPv6 specification.

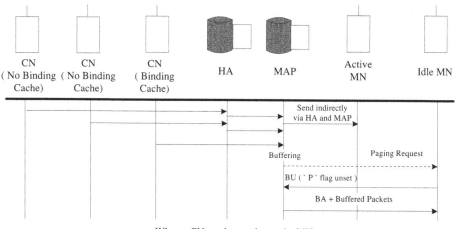

Fig. 6. Packet delivery procedure

3) Then, the idle MN send a $BU_{[HoA,LCoA]}$ message to the internal CNs with "P" flag unset.
4) If the MN moves into a different MAP domain, it performs a registration with the HA and external CNs by sending a $BU_{[HoA,RCoA]}$ message.

3.2 Packet Delivery Procedure

The procedure for a packet delivery under the MN's idle mode is presented in Fig. 6. When a CN sends a packet to the idle MN, it first sends a packet to the MAP via HA using the MN's RCoA. If a CN has a binding cache entry for the idle MN, it first sends a packet directly to the MN's current RCoA without bypassing the HA. Then, the MAP checks the MN's operational mode in its binding cache for the MN. If the MN is in active mode, the MAP sends a packet to the MN using the MN's LCoA. However, if the MN is in idle mode, it performs the following operations:

1) The MAP immediately begins to buffer all packets destined for the idle MN
2) Based on the list of candidate CICs for the paging area, the MAP sends paging request messages for the MN to the candidate access routers.
3) Then, the candidate access routers broadcast the paging request messages to the MN.
4) When the MN receives a paging request message, it sends a $BU_{[RCoA,LCoA]}$ message to the MAP with "P" flag unset.
5) The MAP changes the operational mode in its binding cache for the MN to active mode.
6) Finally, the MAP sends a BA message and then forwards any buffered packets to the MN.

4   Performance Evaluation

4.1   Cost Functions

In this section, we develop an analytic model to derive the cost functions and compare the performance of the proposed scheme called DPHMIPv6 with HMIPv6[2] and PHMIPv6[5] schemes. It is well known that there is a tradeoff between location update and paging in cellular networks. To analyze the performance of the IP-based cellular networks, the total signaling cost including cost of location update and paging is considered as the performance metric.

Analysis of Signaling Cost in HMIPv6. In IP-based cellular networks, the simplest solution is to impose a one-to-one mapping between wireless cells and subnets. For simplicity, therefore, we assume that each cell is assigned a unique subnet address. In the fluid flow model, the direction of an MN's movement in a subnet or MAP domain is uniformly distributed in $[0, 2\pi]$. Let γ and μ be the border crossing rates for an MN out of a subnet and MAP domain, respectively. Let V be the average speed of MNs. From [7], the subnet and MAP domain crossing rates are derived as follows:

$$\gamma = \frac{\pi V}{4R_s} \tag{1}$$

$$\mu = \frac{\pi V}{4R_m} \tag{2}$$

where R_s and R_m are the radius of circular area of a subnet and an MAP domain, respectively. For simplify the analysis, we assume that the subnets are of the same circular shape and size, and form together a contiguous area. Let λ be the border crossing rate for which an MN still stays in the same MAP domain, respectively. Since an MN crossing an MAP domain border must cross a subnet border, the border crossing rate of the MN still staying in the same MAP domain is derived as follows:

$$\lambda = \gamma - \mu \tag{3}$$

The parameters λ and μ are used in our Markov process. In a method similar to those in [7,10], we can model the location update process of the MN by using an embedded Markov chain shown in Fig. 7. In the Markov chain, the system state represents as the number of subnets in the same MAP domain where the MN has travelled around. State K is defined as an MN has passed through K subnets in one MAP domain. The state transition rate λ represents the MN moving rate to the neighboring subnet in the same MAP domain. And the transition rate that the the MN moving to another subnet out of MAP domain is μ.

The equilibrium state probability of state k is denoted as p_k. Thus, p_k can be expressed as:

$$p_k = \left(\frac{\lambda}{\lambda + \mu} \right)^K p_0 \tag{4}$$

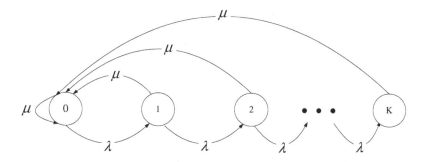

Fig. 7. Imbedded Markov chain model

where p_0 is the equilibrium state probability of state 0. By using the law of total probability, p_0 can be obtained as

$$p_0 = \frac{\mu}{\mu + \lambda}$$
$$p_k = (1 - p_0)^K p_0 \tag{5}$$

We use C_g and C_l to present the location update costs in global binding update and local binding update, respectively. Based on Eq.(5), the average total signaling cost of HMIPv6 scheme after an MN has crossed K subnets is

$$C_{HMIP} = p_0 \cdot C_g + \sum_{j=1}^{K} j \cdot p_j \cdot C_l \tag{6}$$

Analysis of Signaling Costs in PHMIPv6 and DHMIPv6. In PHMIPv6 and DPHMIPv6 schemes, when an MN is in active mode, it operates in the same manner as in HMIPv6 scheme. However, if an MN is in idle mode, it does not register when moving within a paging area. Let α be the probability that an MN in active mode. Using the α, we can get a total signaling cost in DPHMIPv6 as follows:

$$C_{DPHMIP} = \alpha \cdot C_{HMIP} + (1 - \alpha) \cdot C_{idle} \tag{7}$$

Signaling costs in DPHMIPv6 if an MN is in idle mode consist of location update and paging costs as follows:

$$C_{idle} = C_L + C_P \tag{8}$$

When an MN is in idle mode, it only sends a BU message to the MAP only if its operational mode is changed. Then, the MN dose not need to register its location when moving within a paging area. Therefore, the average location update cost of DPHMIPv6 scheme after an MN has crossed K subnets is

$$C_L = p_0 \cdot C_g + 2 \cdot C_l \tag{9}$$

The optimal location area size for an MN, K_{opt} is defined as the value of K that minimizes the cost function. Let us now consider the case when the MN is very fast moving. In that case, the size of the paging area is exactly the same as the size of the MAP domain. Therefore, we can get the maximum size of the paging area as follows:

$$K_{opt}^{max} = \pi \times R_m{}^2 \tag{10}$$

We denote the probability that there are K boundary crossing between two packet arrival by $\alpha(K)$. The probability density of cell residence time has the Laplace-Stieltjes transform $f_m^*(s)$ and mean $\frac{1}{\lambda_m}$. The packet arrival to each MN is a Poisson process with rate λ_α. Based on these parameters, the expression of $\alpha(K)$ as derived in [8] is

$$\alpha(K) = \begin{cases} 1 - \dfrac{1}{\theta}\left[1 - f_m^*(\lambda_\alpha)\right], & K = 0 \\[2mm] \dfrac{1}{\theta}\left[1 - f_m^*(\lambda_\alpha)\right]^2 \left[f_m^*(\lambda_\alpha)\right]^{K-1} & K > 0 \end{cases} \tag{11}$$

where $\theta = \frac{\lambda_\alpha}{\lambda_m}$ is call-to-mobility ratio.

We assume that the cell residence time of an MN has a Gamma distribution with mean $1/\lambda_m$ and variance V_m. The Laplace-Stieltjes transform of Gamma distribution with mean $1/\lambda_m$ and variance V_m is as follows:

$$f_m^*(s) = \left(\frac{\delta \lambda_m}{s + \delta \lambda_m}\right)^\delta, \quad where \; \delta = \frac{1}{V_m \lambda_m^2}. \tag{12}$$

Let R_p be the radius of optimal paging area of an MAP domain. From Eq.(11), we can get the radius of optimal paging area of an MAP domain, R_p, as follows:

$$R_p = \sum_{j=0}^{\infty} j \cdot \alpha(K) \times R_s \tag{13}$$

We consider the worse case scenario that an idle MN moves forward straightly without the change of moving directions within an MAP domain. From (10) and (13), therefore, the optimal size of the paging area, K_{opt}, can be derived as follows:

$$K_{opt} = min\left(\pi \times R_p^2, \; K_{opt}^{max}\right) \tag{14}$$

Let N be the number of cells in a paging area. From Eq.(14), the number of cells in a paging area, N, can be derived as follows:

$$N = \lceil \frac{K_{opt}}{\pi \cdot R_s{}^2} \rceil \tag{15}$$

Let δ_D be the proportionality constant for the packet delivery. Let d_{MAP-MN} be the average distance between the MAP and the MN in terms of the number of hops. In our proposal, when the MN receives a paging request message, it sends a BU message to the MAP with "P" flag unset. Then, the MAP sends a BA message and then forwards any buffered packets to the MN. From Eq.(15), therefore, the paging cost of the DPHMIPv6 scheme, C_P, can be derived as follows:

$$C_P = N \cdot d_{MAP-MN} \cdot \delta_D \tag{16}$$

For simplicity, we consider the worse case scenario that an idle MN has no anchor-cell in PHMIPv6 scheme. In that case, if an idle MN receives a paging request message from the MAP, it sends a paging request message to all access routers that reside in the same MAP domain. From Eq.(15), the paging cost of the PHMIPv6 scheme, C'_P, can be derived as follows:

$$C'_P = \lceil \frac{K^{max}_{opt}}{\pi \cdot R_s^2} \rceil \cdot d_{MAP-MN} \cdot \delta_D \tag{17}$$

Therefore, signaling costs in PHMIPv6 consist of location update and paging costs as follows:

$$C'_{idle} = C_L + C'_P \tag{18}$$

$$C_{PHMIP} = \alpha \cdot C_{HMIP} + (1 - \alpha) \cdot C'_{idle} \tag{19}$$

4.2   Numerical Results

In this section, we will demonstrate some numerical results. Table 1 shows some of the parameters used in our performance analysis that are discussed in [4,8,9].

Fig. 8 shows the effect of the packet arrival rate on the total signaling cost for $\lambda_m = 0.1$, $d_{MAP-MN} = 5$, $K = 50$, and $R_m = 100$. As shown in Fig. 8, the total signaling cost increases as the packet arrival rate λ_α increases. We can see that the performance of the DPHMIPv6, on the whole, results in the lowest total signaling cost compared with HMIPv6 and PHMIPv6 schemes. These results are expected because the DPHMIPv6 scheme tries to reduce the signaling loads when an MN is idle mode. Moreover, the size of the paging area is determined dynamically according the changes of mobility and calling patterns of MNs.

Table 1. Performance analysis parameters

Parameter	Value	Parameter	Value
K	10 - 1000	V	65 mph
α	5%	R_s	10
λ_α	0.01-10	R_m	100 - 1000
λ_m	0.01-10	δ_D	0.1
d_{MAP-MN}	1 - 20	C_g	100
C_l	10	V_m	0.1 - 100

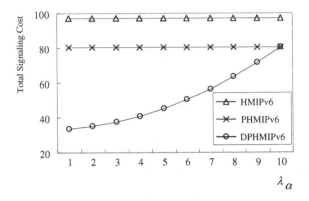

Fig. 8. Effect of λ_α on the total signaling cost

Fig. 9 shows the probability that an MN in active mode α on the total signaling cost for $\lambda_m = 0.1$, $\lambda_\alpha = 0.1$, $d_{MAP-MN} = 5$, $K = 50$, and $R_m = 100$. We can see that the performance of the DPHMIPv6, on the whole, results in the lowest total signaling cost compared with HMIPv6 and PHMIPv6 schemes. For small values of α, the performance of DPHMIPv6 is better than those of HMIPv6 and PHMIPv6 schemes. This is because when α is small, the location update cost is high, which incurs a high signaling cost in HMIPv6. However, the signaling overhead is not incurred when the MN is in idle period time in PHMIPv6 and DPHMIPv6. Moreover, in DPHMIPv6, the size of the paging area for the MN can be adjusted according to the its packet arrival rate and mobility rate.

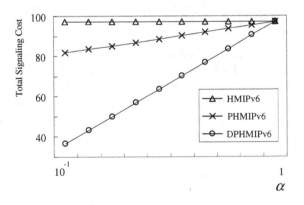

Fig. 9. Effect of α on the total signaling cost

Fig. 10 shows the effect of the radius of circular area of an MAP domain, R_m, on the total signaling cost for $\lambda_m = 0.1$, $\lambda_\alpha = 0.1$, $d_{MAP-MN} = 5$, and $K = 50$. We can see that DPHMIPv6 results in the lowest total cost compared with HMIPv6 and PHMIPv6. These results are expected because DPHMIPv6 tries to reduce the number of BU messages by adjusting the size of the paging area under

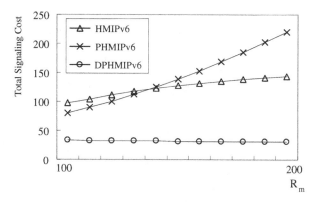

Fig. 10. Effect of R_m on the total signaling cost

the MN's various packet arrival and mobility conditions. From the above analysis of the results, the DPHMIPv6 scheme has a considerable performance advantages over HMIPv6 and PHMIPv6 schemes. So, we conclude that the DPHMIPv6 achieves significant performance improvements by using the dynamic paging scheme based on the changes of mobility and calling patterns of MNs.

5   Conclusions

In this paper, we proposed a dynamic IP paging scheme for HMIPv6 in IP-based cellular networks. Typically, IP paging scheme is designed to reduce location update signaling cost. However, existing IP paging schemes do not consider the HMIPv6 scheme which can reduce signaling load and the delay incurred in registration. Moreover, if an MN moves into a large-scale MAP domain in HMIPv6 networks, the paging cost will be high. To minimize signaling overhead, in our proposal, an idle MN does not register when moving within a paging area in HMIPv6 networks. Additionally, the size of the paging area is determined dynamically according the changes of mobility and calling patterns of MNs. Analytical results using the discrete analytic model shows that our proposal can have superior performance to the HMIPv6 and PHMIPv6 when the session arrival rate to mobility ratio (i.e. SMR $= \lambda_\alpha/\lambda_m$ [5]) is low.

References

1. D. B. Johnson, C. E. Perkins, and J. Arkko,"Mobility support in IPv6," IETF Request for Comments 3775, June 2004.
2. H. Soliman, C. Castelluccia, K. El-Malki, and L. Bellier, "Hierarchical Mobile IPv6 Mobility Management (HMIPv6)", IETF Request for Comments 4140, August 2005.
3. C. Castelluccia, "Extending Mobile IP with Adaptive Individual Paging: A Performance Analysis," Proc. IEEE Symp. Computer and Comm., pp. 113-118, 2000.
4. X. Zhang, J. Castellanos, and A. Campbell, "Design and Performance of Mobile IP Paging," *ACM Mobile Networks and Applications* ,pp.127-141, March, 2002.

5. Myung-Kyu Yi, Chong-Sun Hwang, "A Novel IP Paging Procotol for Minimizing Paging and Delay Costs in Hierarchical Mobile IPv6 Networks," *IEICE Transaction on Information and Systems*, Vol. E87-D, No. 12, pp. 2558-2568, December 2004.
6. Zohar Naor, Hanoch Levy, Uri Zwick, "Cell Identification Codes for tracking mobile users," *Wireless Networks*, Vol. 8, No. 1, pp 73-94, January 2002.
7. Wu, Z.D, "An approach for optimizing binding lifetime with mobile IPv6," in Proceeding of 28th Annual IEEE International Conference on Local Computer Networks, pp. 82-88, Oct. 2003.
8. Lin, Y.-B. "Reducing Location Update Cost in a PCS Network," *IEEE/ACM Transactions on Networking*, Vol. 5, No. 1 , pp 25-33, February 1997.
9. Jiang Xie, Akyildiz, I.F, "A novel distributed dynamic location management scheme for minimizing signaling costs in Mobile IP," *IEEE Transactions on Mobile Computing*, pp 163-175, 2002.
10. Ki-Sik Kong, Sung-Ju Roh, and Chong-Sun Hwang, "Signaling Load of Hierarchical Mobile IPv6 Protocol in IPv6 Networks" , In Proc. of the 9th IFIP Personal Wireless Communications (PWC2004), Lecture Notes in Computer Science (LNCS), Vol.3260, pp.440-450, September 004.

QoS-Aware Routing Based on Local Information for Mobile Ad Hoc Networks

Rong Geng and Zhe Li

Institute of Telecommunications and Information Systems, College of Information Science
& Engineering, Northeastern University, 110004 Shenyang, P.R. China
lizhe@mail.neu.edu.cn

Abstract. In this paper, we propose a novel routing protocol for QoS requirement in mobile ad hoc networks (MANET) called QoS-Aware Routing (QAR) based on local information. QAR takes bandwidth as the metric of the admission scheme, and considers the capability of the available node and path according to node congestion factor and path congestion factor. We simulate our QAR for nodes running the IEEE 802.11 MAC. Results of our simulations show that the packet delivery ratio increases, and the delay of data packet and energy consumed decrease significantly for both static topology and mobile topology compared with DSR that does not provide QoS support.

Keywords: Mobile ad hoc networks (MANET), QoS-aware routing, admission, node congestion factor, path congestion factor.

1 Introduction

Mobile ad hoc networks (MANET) is an autonomous system where all nodes are capable of movement and can be connected dynamically in an arbitrary manner. Without a network infrastructure, network nodes function as routers which discover and maintain routes to other nodes in the network [1]. However, recently, because of the rising popularity of multimedia applications and potential commercial usage of MANET, QoS support in MANET has received a lot of attention. QoS support includes bandwidth, delay, jitter, packet loss ratio and so on [2]. However, QoS routing is difficult in MANET due to several reasons [3]: high overhead of QoS routing in a bandwidth-limited MANET, bandwidth sharing among adjacent nodes, imprecise link information, route maintenance and mobility support. There have been numerous routing protocols to provide QoS support in MANET, for example CEDAR [4]、TBP [5]、QoS-MSR [6] and so on. In the CEDAR routing protocol, it is assumed that the available bandwidth is known. And it chooses core nodes or dominator nodes and uses the core nodes to transfer QoS information (bandwidth) or route. In a sort of ideal model, TBP advances a ticket-based QoS routing protocol which study two sorts of routing problem: delay-constrained least-cost routing and bandwidth-constrained least-cost routing. Extending the MSR to support QoS route discovery mechanism, QoS-MSR protocol collects QoS information (bandwidth or delay). QoS-MSR uses probing mechanism to maintain QoS information. In addition to active probing, passive piggybacking is used in QoS-MSR to obtain QoS information of every node.

S. Madria et al. (Eds.): ICDCIT 2006, LNCS 4317, pp. 159–167, 2006.
© Springer-Verlag Berlin Heidelberg 2006

But all these protocols don't consider the congestion of nodes to QoS routing. In this paper, based on considering wider application and influence of IEEE 802.11 MAC [7], we propose a novel routing protocol for mobile ad hoc networks called QoS-Aware Routing(QAR) based on local information. QAR takes bandwidth as metric of admission scheme, and introduces node congestion factor and path congestion factor as choosing criterion. In QAR, route discovery and route maintenance are the extension of DSR [8] protocol. At the same time, QAR with little modification can be used in other similar reactive protocols.

2 Network Model and Parameter Calculation

2.1 Network Model

We use a directed graph $G(V, E)$ to model the wireless network where V is a finite set of mobile nodes and E is a finite set of bi-direction, wireless radio links between the mobiles nodes. Each node $i \in V$ has unique ID and moves randomly. Each mobile node i has transmission radius with size R, according to wireless transmission model. $N(i)$ is a set of neighbor node j of node i but not including node i. If node j in the transmission radius R of node i, there is a bi-direction, wireless radio links $E[i, j]$ between node i and node j, $E[i, j] \in E$ .Set E varieties with time. The path $p(i, j)$ from source $i \in V$ to destination $j \in V$ is constituted of the no loop sequence of intermediate node m, $p(i, j) = \{i, \cdots, m, \cdots j\}$.

2.2 Estimation of Local Available Bandwidth

In our protocol, we use the local available bandwidth of node $i \in V$ as the access metric to guarantee each node of path $p(i, j)$ to have enough bandwidth of QoS requirement. Therefore estimating the local available bandwidth of intermediate nodes from source to destination is needed. Since local available bandwidth is defined as the unconsumed bandwidth at a given node, each node can determine its own local available bandwidth by passively monitoring network activities. In multi-hop mobile ad hoc networks, estimating the local available bandwidth of node is very hard. Several algorithms have been proposed in [9], [10], [11], etc. We use the method of [9] to estimate the local available bandwidth of node. The idea basic is as follows:

In mobile ad hoc networks, given the network utilization δ and the channel bandwidth $B_{channel}$, the available bandwidth is estimated using the following equation [12]:

$$B_{avail} = (1 - \delta) * B_{channel} \tag{1}$$

where $0 \leq \delta \leq 1$ .There are many techniques to measure the network utilization, but in MANET, channel busy time of MAC is directly related with the network utilization, and the method includes no additional overhead.

In general, the channel at a node can be perceived as either idle or busy. The MAC detects that the channel is free when the following three requirements are met [13]:

- NAV's value is less than the current time;
- Receive state is idle;
- Send state is idle;

In all other cases, the MAC determines that the channel is busy. During every period of time T, the measuring busy time is $Tbusy$. In this way, the local available bandwidth of node can be estimated with formula (2).

$$B_{avail} = (1 - \frac{Tbusy}{T}) * B_{channel} \qquad (2)$$

2.3 Calculation of Node Congestion Factor and Path Congestion Factor

Definition 1. Node congestion factor ($N_{congestion}$): a metric to describe congestion status of a node. The smaller $N_{congestion}$ is, the stronger the node's carrying capacity has.

A variety of metrics can be used for a node to monitor congestion status. In this paper we choose the length of existing packets in send buffer, retransmit number (including RTS and data) and channel busy time as the congestion status metrics of mobile node. Because much longer the length of existing packet in send buffer is, the burthen of node is more heave and the data packets are likely to encounter longer delay and consume more energy. Retransmit number and channel busy time can indicate channel contention and nodes occupied status. In all cases, rising numbers indicate growing congestion. By monitoring the amount of the length of existing packets in send buffer, $Blen_{sample}$, retransmit number, $Rpkt_{sample}$, channel busy time, $Tbusy_{sample}$, during every period of time T, three metrics can be calculated using a weighted moving average, where the estimation of three metrics is updated every T as follows:

$$Blen_{new} = \alpha \times Blen_{sample} + (1 - \alpha) \times Blen_{old} \qquad (3)$$

$$Rpkt_{new} = \beta \times Rpkt_{sample} + (1 - \beta) \times Rpkt_{old} \qquad (4)$$

$$Tbusy_{new} = \gamma \times Tbusy_{sample} + (1 - \gamma) \times Tbusy_{old} \qquad (5)$$

Where α, β and γ are constants, they can be chosen between 0 and 1. The bigger the values are, the current status of node can be reflected better. At the extreme case when the value is equal to 1, we put the current sample as the standard. In our simulation, they are set to 0.7.

Toward the calculated each value $Blen_{new}$, $Rpkt_{new}$ and $Tbusy_{new}$, we use the respectively biggest values of history to unit them to $Blen_{unit}$, $Rpkt_{unit}$ and $Tbusy_{unit}$. According to them, we can calculate the node congestion factor with the following formula:

$$N_{congestion} = a \times Blen_{unit} + b \times Rpkt_{unit} + c \times Tbusy_{unit} \qquad (6)$$

Where a, b and c are used as weighted factor to balance the three metrics. Each node need save $N_{congestion}$ and update it every T second. In our simulation, a, b, c and T are set to 1。

Definition 2. Path congestion factor ($P_{congestion}$): the biggest $N_{congestion}$ of nodes on the path, namely

$$P_{congestion} = \max\{\sum_{m \in p} N_{congestion}(m)\} \qquad (7)$$

$P_{congestion}$ can reflect the congestion status of path. The smaller $P_{congestion}$ is, the stronger the path's capability of transmitting data.

3   QoS-Aware Routing (QAR) Protocol Based on Local Information

At present, advanced QoS routing protocols mostly have taken attention on how to find the shortest path meeting QoS condition, and have not considered the capability of the available path, such as node' congestion of the available path. Based on this point, we advance put forward QoS-Aware routing (QAR) protocol based on local information. This protocol takes bandwidth as the metric of admission control, and considers the carrying capability of the available path according to node congestion factor and path congestion factor. Destination node chooses the path having the least path congestion factor among many available paths. QAR protocol uses source routing, and intermediate nodes do not reply from the cache. Each node hence uses less memory, and avoids overtime information to affect routing.

3.1   Route Discovery

When source node has data to send to destination node, it floods route request to network initiating route discovery. This request packet is extended of DSR routing request packet, acting as RREQ (Source ID, Request ID, Destination ID, QoS constraint, Node congestion, Route record, Max propagation), where the definition of each field is as shown in table 1. For availably controlling the overhead produced by flooding and reducing the transmission of repeated information, QAR protocol uses Source ID and Request ID as the unique mark of RREQ. When a intermediate node (having only ID as <this ID>) receives a RREQ, it judges whether it has already received this packet according to Source ID and Request ID. If this packet is repeated, the intermediate node immediately discards this packet. If the packet isn't repeated, but its hop number is bigger or equal to Max propagation, or this node already has been in Route record, this RREQ is also discarded, otherwise the intermediate node estimates local available bandwidth using formula (2). If the available bandwidth is less than QoS constraint, this RREQ is still discarded.

Table 1. The definition of RREQ in QAR

Field name	Definition
Source ID	ID of the source node
Request ID	Sequence of routing request, setting by the source node
Destination ID	ID of the destination node
QoS constraint	QoS requirement information, here it is bandwidth
Node congestion	Node congestion factor
Route record	The sequence of nodes from source node to destination
Max propagation	Constraint of the maximum hop number

If the intermediate node doesn't discard RREQ, it compares its $N_{congestion}$ which is periodically calculated using formula (6) with Node congestion in RREQ. If the former is bigger than the latter, Node congestion in RREQ is replaced by $N_{congestion}$. In this way, the destination can get the biggest $N_{congestion}$ of path, namely $P_{congestion}$. Finally, the intermediate node inserts itself in Route record, and sends this RREQ using flooding. The procedure of intermediate node is as followed.

The procedure of intermediate node handling RREQ

```
/*When a intermediate node (with a unique identification
= <this ID>) receives a route discovery packet (RREQ)*/
IF (the RREQ have been received)
  Discard this RREQ
ELSE IF (hop number is equal with <Max propagation> or
<this ID> has been in the <route record> )
        Discard this RREQ
    ELSE IF ( B_avail < <QoS constraint>)
            Discard this RREQ
        ELSE IF ( N_congestion > <node congestion>)
```

$$\text{<node congestion>} \quad = \quad N_{congestion}$$

Append <this ID> to <route record>

Update other fields of the RREQ

Broadcast the RREQ to neighbor nodes

END IF

The destination receiving the first RREQ doesn't reply immediately, and waits for RREQ-WAIT time. RREQ-WAIT relates to communication range and load rate and is set to 0.1s in our simulation. In RREQ-WAIT, the destination will receive many RREQs. It will choose the short path with the least $P_{congestion}$ among these RREQs, and replay RREP using the path of selected RREQ. The structure of RREP is same as DSR's. When the source receives RREP, the procedure of route discovery has finished, and communication starts.

3.2 Route Maintenance

The process of route maintenance of QAR is same as DSR. When intermediate node finds the next-hop route breaking off, it empties the information of the path from cache and sends RRER to the source. When the source receives RRER, it starts another procedure of routing discovery. And QAR still uses the scheme of packet salvaging of DSR.

4   Simulation and Analysis

To test the performance of QAR protocol, we ran simulations using ns-2 [14]. We use the modified IEEE 802.11 MAC protocol in RTS/CTS/Data/ACK mode with a channel data rate of 2Mb/s. The node has a radio propagation range of 250 meters, and its initial energy is 100J. Constant bit rate (CBR) flows are deployed for data transmission. The packet size used in our simulations is 512 bytes.

4.1   Performance Metrics

Four performance metrics are introduced for performance evaluations: packet delivery ratio, delay, energy and throughput. Packet delivery ratio is the ratio of the number of data packet received of AGT and the number of data packet originated of AGT. Delay is the average delay of all data packet. Energy is the average energy of all nodes consumed in the simulation. Throughput is the bit of data packet received of AGT.

4.2   Static Topology

We use topologies where 30 static nodes are placed randomly in 1000m×1000m. Five nodes are randomly chosen as sources and five nodes are randomly chosen as destinations. All sources feed the same data rate to their destinations, and the feeding rate varies from 0.1 to 0.6Mbps. We compare QAR with conventional DSR, which has no QoS support. We randomly choose five scenarios and run the simulation for 300s.

The average simulation results are as shown in Fig.1, 2, 3, 4. Fig.1 shows that there is an improvement in packet delivery ratio (by 47.9%) using QAR compared with DSR, due to the node congestion factor that have been introduced, path congestion factor and the access control in QAR. The scheme helps in congestion avoidance. Similarly, the scheme also brings decreased delay and energy consumption. The time used waiting in the buffer and contending for the channel decreased, and the energy used on transmitting packets which will ultimately be dropped is saved. Therefore, delay is decreased by 50.6%, as shown in Fig.2 and energy consumed is decreased by 15.1% as shown in Fig.3. Fig.4 shows that there is an inconspicuous improvement in throughput (by 7.8%) compared with DSR.

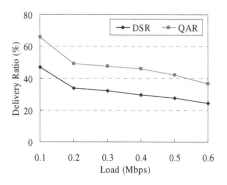

Fig. 1. Packet delivery ratio (static topology)

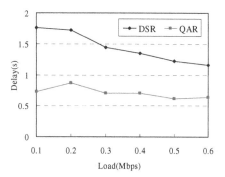

Fig. 2. Delay (static topology)

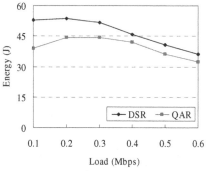

Fig. 3. Energy (static topology)

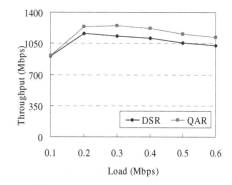

Fig. 4. Throughput (static topology)

4.3 Mobile Topology

We use topologies where 30 mobile nodes are placed randomly in 1000m × 1000m. Each node moves toward a random destination using a speed randomly chosen between 0~10m/s, and arriving a destination, pause time is 2s. Five nodes are randomly chosen as sources and five nodes are randomly chosen as destinations. All sources feed the same data rate to their destinations, and the feeding rate varies from 0.1 to 0.6Mbps. The simulation time is 300s. The simulation results obtained by averaging five different scenarios are as shown in Fig. 5, 6, 7, 8. Fig.5 shows that there is an improvement in packet delivery ratio (up to 173%) using QAR compared with DSR. Fig.6 shows that delay is greatly decreased up to 264% and energy consumed is decreased up to 127% as shown in Fig.7, and we have discussed previously the reason. Fig.8 shows that actually we can get almost equal overall end-to-end throughput for QAR compared with DSR.

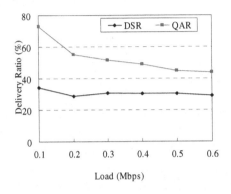

Fig. 5. Packet delivery ratio(mobile topology)   **Fig. 6.** Delay (mobile topology)

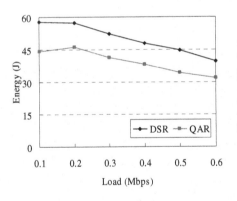
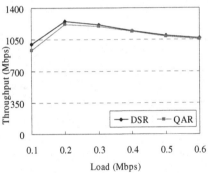

Fig. 7. Energy (mobile topology)   **Fig. 8.** Throughput (mobile topology)

5   Conclusion

In this paper, a new QoS-aware routing (QAR) protocol is proposed for mobile ad hoc network. QAR, including an admission scheme to provide information to the application, introduces bandwidth estimation, node congestion factor and path congestion factor. In the route discovery phase, QAR finds a short path with least path congestion factor, and this path will have stronger capacity of transmitting data.

Simulations show that our QAR can improve packet delivery ratio, while also decrease the delay and energy consumed significantly.

References

1. Zhong Fan: QoS Routing using Lower Layer Information in Ad hoc Networks, IEEE International Symposium, Vol. 1. (2004)135-139
2. Prasabt Mohapatra, Li jian, Gui Chao: QoS in Mobile Ad hoc Networks. Special Issues on QoS in Next-Factorration Wireless Multimedia Communications Systems, IEEE Wireless Communications Magizine (2003)
3. K. Wu and J. Harms: QoS Support in Mobile Ad hoc Networks, University of Alberta, Tech. Rep., (2001)
4. P.sinha, R. Sivakumar, and V.Bharghavan: CEDAR: a Core-Extraction Distributed Ad hoc Routing Algorithm, Seleted Areas in Commun, Vol. 17. (1999)1454-1465
5. S.Chen and K.Nahrstedt: Distributed Quality-of-Service in Ad hoc Networks, IEEE Journal, 17(8), Aug.(1999)1488-1505
6. Shu Wang L, Yang Y T, and Dong O W W: Adapative Multipath Source Routing in Wireless Ad hoc Networks. Proceedings of the IEEE International Conference on Communications, Helsinki, Finland (2001)867
7. IEEE standard for wireless LAN Medium Access Control(MAC) and Physical Layer(PHY) specification, June (1997)
8. David B Johnson and David A Maltz: Dynamic Source Routing in Ad hoc Wireless Networks, in Mobile Computing, Vol. 353. Kluwer Academic Publishers(1996)
9. Chakeres. I. D, Belding-Royer. E. M: PAC: Perceptive Admission Control for Mobile Wireless Networks. Proceedings of OShine, Dallas, Texas, USA, Oct (2004)
10. Yaling Yang, and Robin Kravets: Contention-Aware Admission Control for Ad Hoc Networks. Mobile Computing. IEEE Transactions, Vol. 4. (2005)363-377
11. Shah. S. H, Kai Chen, Nahrstedt. K: Dynamic Bandwidth Management for Single-hop Ad hoc Wireless Networks. Proceedings of the IEEE International Conference on 23-26 March (2003)195-203
12. R. S. Prasad, M. Murray, C. Dovrolis, and K. Claffy: Bandwidth Estimation: Metrics, Measurement Techniques and Tools. Network, IEEE. Vol. 17. (2003)27-35
13. Lei Chen, Wendi B.Heinzelman: QoS-Aware Routing Based on Bandwidth Estimation for Mobile Ad Hoc Networks. IEEE Journal, Vol. 23. (2005)561-572
14. http://www.isi.edu/nsnam/ns

Kalman Filter Based H.264 Motion Vector Recovery for Error Resilient Video Service over Mobile GRID

Ki-Hong Ko and Seong-Whan Kim

Department of Computer Science, Univ. of Seoul, Jeon-Nong-Dong, Seoul, Korea
Tel.: +82-2-2210-5316; fax: +82-2-2210-5275
jedigo@venus.uos.ac.kr, swkim7@uos.ac.kr

Abstract. The goal of mobile GRID is to provide the same QoS to mobile users as experienced by wired users. However, inherent unstable nature of the wireless network causes many challenges. Inherent characteristics make frequency disconnection, delay, and jitter. For the reason, we focus on the error resilience scheme for video communication over mobile GRID environments. We propose an error concealment technique to recover lost motion vectors at the H.264 decoder side. To recover the lost motion vectors, there are two simple techniques: (1) no prediction, where the lost motion vectors are set to zeros, and (2) the prediction using the average or median of spatially adjacent blocks' motion vectors. In this paper, we propose a Kalman filter based scheme for motion vector recovery, and experimented with two test image sequences: Mobile&Calendar and Susie. The experimental results show that our Kalman filter based motion vector recovery scheme improves at average 2 dB PSNR over conventional H.264 decoding with no error recovery. We also improve our scheme using Hilbert curve scan order for Kalman input, and we get 0.512 – 1.652 dB PSNR improvements with better subjective quality over line-by-line scan order.

Keywords: Mobile GRID, Error concealment, Motion vector recovery, Kalman filter, Hilbert curve, H.264.

1 Introduction

Although the goal of mobile GRID is to provide the same QoS as wired GRID, inherent unstable nature of the wireless network causes many problems: frequency disconnection, delay, and jitter [1]. Video transmission over such networks usually requires highly compressed bit stream, and they are more fragile to transmission errors than less compressed video streams. There are many researches to guarantee video quality over transmission errors, and we can classify them into two main categories: (1) forward error concealment (or error resilience coding), which improves robustness of encoded bit stream against the transmission errors; (2) decoder error concealments, which recovers or estimates lost information [2, 3, 4]. In this paper, we propose a Kalman filter based motion vector recovery technique for H.264 video error concealment. Kalman filter is a recursive procedure, in which the process and measurement noise are assumed to be independent and normally distributed [5, 6, 7]. Because motion vectors are usually highly correlated with the adjacent blocks' motion

S. Madria et al. (Eds.): ICDCIT 2006, LNCS 4317, pp. 168–179, 2006.
© Springer-Verlag Berlin Heidelberg 2006

vectors, we can improve the Kalman filter based motion vector recovery using Hilbert curve based sequencing for adjacent motion vector input for Kalman prediction.

This paper is organized as follows. We review the H.264 motion vector prediction scheme and Kalman filter in section 2. In section 3, we propose a Kalman filter based motion vector recovery scheme, and improve the scheme using Hilbert curve scan order for maximizing the correlation between motion vectors in the Kalman prediction input. In section 4, we presented the experimental results, and conclude in section 5.

2 H.264 Motion Vector Prediction and Kalman Filter

H.264 or MPEG-4 part 10 is a digital video codec standard which is noted for achieving very high data compression. It was designed by ITU-T video coding experts group (VCEG) and the ISO/IEC Moving Picture Experts Group (MPEG) as the product of a collective partnership effort known as the joint video team (JVT). Figure 1 shows H.264 decoding process. From NAL (network abstraction layer), the H.264 decoder get a compressed bit stream. The bit stream composed of motion vector information and pixel information. To reconstruct the pixel information, H.264 decoder performs entropy decoding step, which decodes the data elements to produce a set of quantized coefficients X. Inverse quantization and inverse transform step scale and inverse transform these coefficients to give reconstructed frames D'n. Using motion vector information from NAL, H.264 decoder composes a prediction frame, which is directed by motion vector, and the prediction frame is added to D'n to produce uF'n which is filtered to create reconstructed frames. In our scheme, we modified the motion vector recovery to be robust on transmission failure.

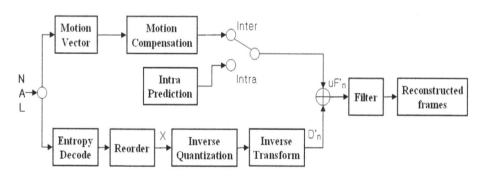

Fig. 1. H.264 decoding process

In this section, we will review the motion vector estimation scheme for H.264 video coding standards, and the basic theory of Kalman filter for better motion vector recovery. H.264 video coding scheme still uses motion vector estimation like other previous video coding schemes: MPEG-1, MPEG-2, and MPEG-4. Moreover, it uses motion vector prediction to exploit the inter-blocks' motion vector correlation, and sends the difference MVD (motion vector difference: MV(E) − MVP(E)) between the estimated motion vector (MV(E)) and predicted motion vector (MVP(E)). In H.264 standard, we can use variable block size motion estimation: 16x16, 8x16, 16x8, 8x8, 4x8, 8x4, or 4x4 block based. As shown in Figure 2, we can predict the motion vector MVP(E) of the current block E from the three neighboring blocks: A, B, and C. Depending on the size of neighboring blocks, we can use different prediction scheme [8]. Figure 2(a) shows that the size of all neighboring blocks is same. Figure 2(b) shows that E has two 16x8 partitions E_1 and E_2. Figure 2(c) shows that E has two 8x16 partitions E_1 and E_2. Figure 2(d) shows that the sizes of E's neighbor blocks are different. Figure 2(e) shows that E has four 8x8 partitions E1, E2, E3, and E4 and the sizes of E's neighbor blocks are different. Figure 2(f) shows that E has two 8x4 partitions E_1 and E_2. Two special cases are (1) if we do not have B and C, we use A's motion vector for MVP(E); (2) if the current block's mode is SKIPPED, we compute median(MV(A), MV(B), MV(C)) for MVP(E). At the encoder side, H.264 computes the motion vector MV using motion vector estimation and the motion vector prediction MVP(E) using the guideline as shown in Figure 2. From MV and MVP(E), we compute MVD, which is the difference between MV and MVP(E), and send only the MVD for coding efficiency.

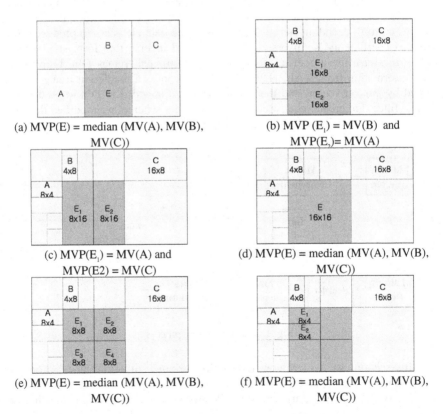

(a) MVP(E) = median (MV(A), MV(B), MV(C))

(b) MVP (E_1) = MV(B) and MVP(E_2)= MV(A)

(c) MVP(E_1) = MV(A) and MVP(E2) = MV(C)

(d) MVP(E) = median (MV(A), MV(B), MV(C))

(e) MVP(E) = median (MV(A), MV(B), MV(C))

(f) MVP(E) = median (MV(A), MV(B), MV(C))

Fig. 2. H.264 motion vector prediction [7]: MV (motion vector estimation), MVP (motion vector prediction)

In our scheme, we used Kalman filter for better motion vector recovery. A Kalman filter is a recursive procedure to estimate the states s_k of a discrete-time controlled process governed by the linear stochastic difference equation, from a set of measured observations t_k. The mathematical model is expressed as in Equation (1).

$$s_k = As_{k-1} + w_{k-1}$$
$$t_k = Hs_k + r_k$$

(1)

The NxN matrix A represents a state transition matrix, w_k is an Nx1 process noise vector with $N(0, \sigma_w^2)$, t_k is Mx1 measurement vector, H is MxM measurement matrix, and r_k is Mx1 measurement noise vector with $N(0, \sigma_r^2)$. To estimate the process, Kalman filter uses a form of feedback control as shown in Figure 3 [5]. We define $\hat{s}_k^-$, $\hat{s}_k$, p_k^- and p_k as the priori state estimate, posteriori state estimate, priori estimate error covariance, and posteriori estimate error covariance, respectively. K is the Kalman gain.

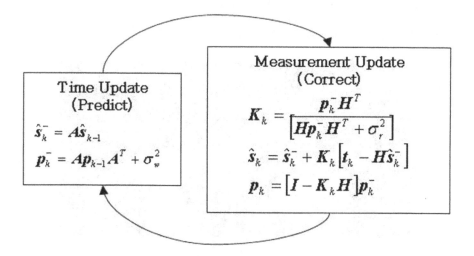

Fig. 3. Kalman filter cycle [5]

3   Kalman Filter Based Motion Vector Recovery

We propose a motion vector recovery procedure for the motion vector transmission errors. Figure 4 shows the modified H.264 decoder with Kalman filter based motion vector recovery for MVD (motion vector difference) loss. From NAL (network abstraction layer) packets, we can normally get MVD and residual textures. When we fail to decode MVD, we can estimate the MVD using the previous MVD information. We used the previous MVD information for Kalman filter prediction.

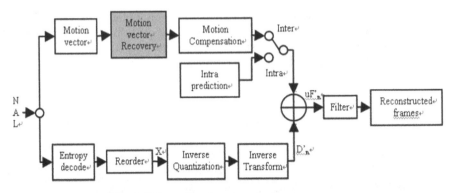

Fig. 4. Kalman filter based motion vector recovery

We used line-by-line scanning pattern (Figure 5(a)) for $[sx_0, sx_1,...,sx_{k-1}, sx_{k...}]$ sequencing. However, we can use a different scanning as shown in Figure 5(b), to maximize the inter-correlation between MV (motion vector) estimates. Hilbert curve is a one dimensional curve which visits every point within a two dimensional space. If we don't get MVD because of the error occurrence, we predict MV to recover the lost MV [9, 10, 11].

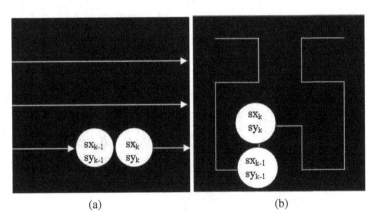

Fig. 5. Kalman prediction input sequencing design using (a) line-by-line scan order and (b) Hilbert curve scan order

In our Kalman prediction model, we define the state s = [sx, sy] as the MV estimate, and we can establish a state model as in Equation (2). Likewise, we define the measurement t = [tx, ty] as in Equation (3). We used MVP(E) for the measurement input [tx, ty].

$$sx_k = a_1 sx_{k-1} + wx_{k-1} \qquad sy_k = b_1 sy_{k-1} + wy_{k-1} \qquad (2)$$
$$wx_{k-1} \sim N(0, \sigma_w^2) \qquad wy_{k-1} \sim N(0, \sigma_w^2)$$
$$\sigma_w^2 = E[(wx)^2] = E[(wy)^2]$$

$$tx_k = sx_k + rx_k \quad ty_k = sy_k + ry_k \tag{3}$$
$$rx_k \sim N(0, \sigma_r^2) \quad ry_k \sim N(0, \sigma_r^2)$$
$$\sigma_r^2 = E[(rx_k)^2] = E[(ry_k)^2]$$

To recover lost motion vectors, we use the following procedure. In Time Update step, we compute a priori MV estimate $[\hat{s}x_k^-, \hat{s}y_k^-]$ from the previous block's MV estimate $[\hat{s}x_{k-1}, \hat{s}y_{k-1}]$, and also a priori error covariance as in Equation (4). In Measurement Update step, we compute the current block's MV estimate $[\hat{s}x_k, \hat{s}y_k]$ and the corresponding error covariance using Equation (5). We set $\sigma_w^2 = 0.75$, $\sigma_r^2 = 0.25$. We assume that there are higher correlation between horizontally adjacent blocks, and set $a_1 = b_1 = 0.98$.

Algorithm: Motion vector recovery using Kalman filter

Step 0: **Initialization:**
$$\begin{bmatrix} sx_0 \\ sy_0 \end{bmatrix} = \begin{bmatrix} 0 \\ 0 \end{bmatrix}, \quad \begin{bmatrix} px_0 \\ py_0 \end{bmatrix} = \begin{bmatrix} 0 \\ 0 \end{bmatrix}$$

Step 1: **Time Update:**
$$\begin{bmatrix} \hat{s}x_k^- \\ \hat{s}y_k^- \end{bmatrix} = \begin{bmatrix} a_1 & 0 \\ 0 & b_1 \end{bmatrix} \begin{bmatrix} \hat{s}x_{k-1} \\ \hat{s}y_{k-1} \end{bmatrix} \tag{4}$$
$$\begin{bmatrix} px_k^- \\ py_k^- \end{bmatrix} = \begin{bmatrix} a_1 & 0 \\ 0 & b_1 \end{bmatrix} \begin{bmatrix} px_x \\ py_{k-1} \end{bmatrix} \begin{bmatrix} a_1 & 0 \\ 0 & b_1 \end{bmatrix}^T + \sigma_w^2$$

Step 2: **Measurement Update:**
$$\begin{bmatrix} \hat{s}x_k \\ \hat{s}y_k \end{bmatrix} = \begin{bmatrix} \hat{s}x_x^- \\ \hat{s}y_k^- \end{bmatrix} + \begin{bmatrix} Kx_k \cdot (tx_k - \hat{s}x_k^-) \\ Ky_k \cdot (ty_k - \hat{s}y_k^-) \end{bmatrix} \tag{5}$$
$$\begin{bmatrix} px_k \\ py_k \end{bmatrix} = \begin{bmatrix} (1 - Kx_k \cdot px_x^-) \\ (1 - Ky_y \cdot py_y^-) \end{bmatrix}$$
$$\begin{bmatrix} Kx_k \\ Ky_k \end{bmatrix} = \begin{bmatrix} px_k^- / (px_k^- + \sigma_r^2) \\ py_k^- / (py_k^- + \sigma_r^2) \end{bmatrix}$$

---

4 Experimental Results

We evaluated our motion vector recovery schemes with the standard test sequences: Mobile&Calendar and Susie. We compared H.264 motion vector prediction with MVD loss (scheme 1), Kalman filter based motion vector prediction with line-by-line scan input (scheme 2), and Kalman filter based motion vector prediction with Hilbert curve scan input (scheme 3). We used H.264 video compression (no B frame mode and I frame every 15 frames), and randomly insert motion vector loss in each frames. We generated a random error pattern for the lost motion vectors as shown in Figure 6.

(a) Mobile&Calendar: 56th frame.

(b) Susie: 117th frame.

Fig. 6. Lost motion vector error profile for Mobile&Calendar and Susie

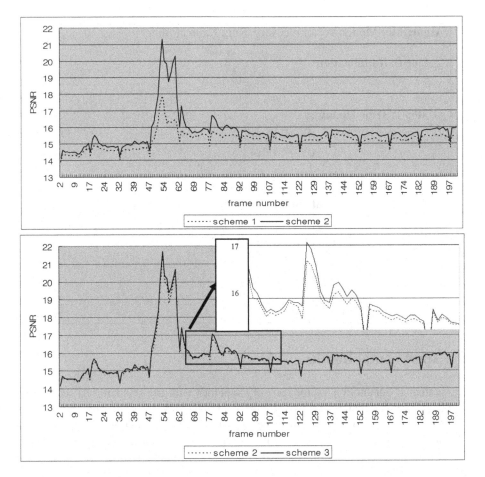

Fig. 7. PSNR after motion vector recovery: (top) scheme 1 and scheme 2, (bottom) scheme 2 and scheme 3 for Mobile&Calendar sequence with average error rate=9.9%

Figure 7 shows PSNR (luminance only) for scheme 1, scheme 2, and scheme 3 after motion vector recovery in Mobile&Calendar sequences. As shown in Figure 7, scheme 2 is better than scheme 1 with 0.179 dB – 3.894 dB improvements, and scheme 3 shows 0.002 dB – 0.594 dB improvements over scheme 2.

Figure 8 shows PSNR (luminance only) for scheme 1, scheme 2, and scheme 3 after motion vector recovery in Susie sequences. As shown in Figure 8, scheme 2 is better than scheme 1 with 0.292 dB – 7.403 dB improvements, and scheme 3 shows -0.446 dB – 1.652 dB improvements over scheme 2.

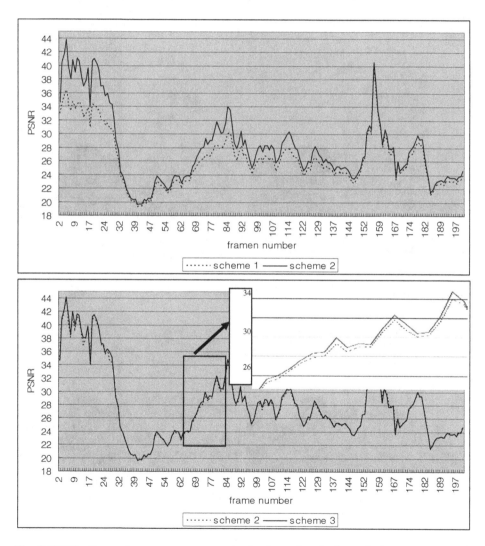

Fig. 8. PSNR after motion vector recovery: (top) scheme 1 and scheme 2, (bottom) scheme 2 and scheme 3 for Susie sequence with average error rate = 8.93%

Figure 9 and Figure 10 compare the image quality for scheme 1, scheme 2, and scheme 3 in Mobile&Calendar and Susie sequences. As shown in Figure 9 and Figure 10, scheme 2 and scheme 3 are better than scheme 1 in subjective quality, and scheme 3 is usually better than scheme 2. However, scheme 2 is better than or equal to scheme 3 when there is much motion. In that case, we cannot get the advantages of Hilbert curve to maximize the local inter-correlation between adjacent blocks' motion vectors.

(a)   (b)

(c)   (d)

Fig. 9. Subjective comparison for Mobile&Calendar: (a) No error, (b) scheme 1: PSNR =16.377 dB, (c) scheme 2: PSNR=18.772 dB, (d) scheme 3: PSNR=19.365 dB

For detailed subjective quality, we enlarged the image regions. Figure 11(b) shows the region, in which scheme 2 is better than scheme 3 (calendar details in (b) are better than (c)). In this case, the area of calendar's number in Figure 11(b) are better

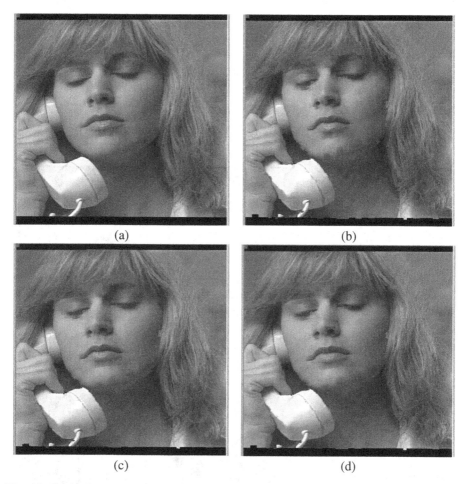

Fig. 10. Subjective comparison for Susie: (a) No error, (b) scheme 1: PSNR=26.497 dB, (c) scheme 2: PSNR=27.976 dB, (d) scheme 3: PSNR=28.357 dB

than in Figure 11(c), because the real motion of calendar in Mobile&Calendar moves from left to right. Therefore it makes scheme 2 outperforms scheme 3. Figure 11(e) shows the region, in which scheme 2 is better than scheme 3 (face details in (e) are better than (f)). In this case, the area of Susie's noise and eye in Figure 11(e) are better than in Figure 11(f), because the real motion of Susie's face moves from left to right. Therefore it makes scheme 2 outperforms scheme 3.

Figure 12(c) shows the region, in which scheme 3 is better than scheme 2 (edge details along the ball is missing in scheme 2). In this case, the motions of ball and train move from right to left, which is inverse direction to usual line-by-line scan order. Figure 12(f) shows that the edge details are preserved in the scheme 3 case because the motion of phone moves from down to up.

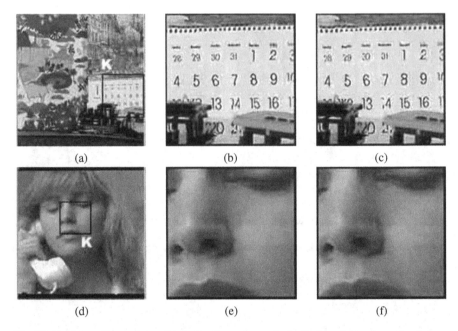

(a)   (b)   (c)

(d)   (e)   (f)

Fig. 11. Regions where scheme 2 is better than scheme 3. (a, d) show the regions, (b, e) show the result from scheme 2, (c, f) show the result from scheme 3

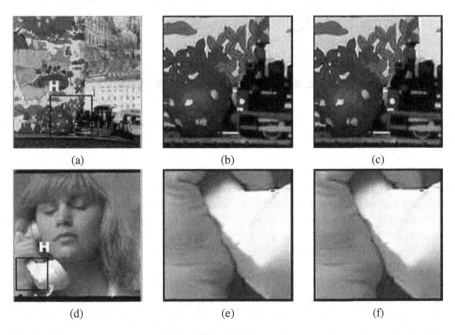

(a)   (b)   (c)

(d)   (e)   (f)

Fig. 12. Regions where scheme 3 is better than scheme 2: (a, d) the regions, (b, e) show scheme 2 enlarged, (c, f) shows scheme 3 enlarged

5 Conclusions

In the mobile GRID, inherent unstable nature of the wireless network causes many problems. This unstable feature makes frequent disconnection, delay, and jitter. For this reason, the mobile GRID needs a mechanism to support stable QoS for video communication environments. To support comparable QoS for video communication service as wired GRID environments, we use error resilient video decoder technique. In this paper, we proposed a Kalman filter based motion vector recovery technique over H.264 video coding standard. To use Kalman filtering model for the motion vector recovery, we used H.264 motion vector prediction for Kalman measurement input. To exploit the inter-correlation between adjacent blocks' motion vectors, we used Hilbert curve scan order for Kalman filter input sequencing. H.264 motion vector recovery using Kalman filtering shows comparable results, and we showed that Hilbert curve scan order for Kalman input sequencing shows better performance than line-by-line scan input sequencing more than $0.179 - 3.894$ dB, $-0.445 - 1.652$ dB for Mobile&Calendar and Susie image sequences, respectively.

References

1. Zhang W., Zhang J., Ma D., Wang B., Chen Y.: Key technique research on GRID mobile service. Proc. 2nd Int. Conf. Information Technology (2004)
2. Lam, W.M., Reibman, A.R., Liu, B.: Recovery of Lost or Erroneously Received Motion Vectors, Proc. ICASSP'93, Minneapolis, MN 417-420
3. Wang, Y., Wenger, S., Wen, J., Katsaggelos, A.K.: Error Resilient Video Coding Techniques, Vol. 17. IEEE Signal Processing Magazine (2000) 61-82
4. Wang, Y., Zhu, Q.F.: Error Control and Concealment for Video Communication: a Review, Vol. 86. Proc. IEEE (1998) 974-997
5. Welch, G., Bishop, G.: An Introduction to The Kalman Filters, available in http://www.cs.unc.edu/~welch/kalman/index.html
6. Gao, Z.W., Lie, W.N.: Video Error Concealment by using Kalman-Filtering Technique, Proc. IEEE ISCAS-2004, Vancouver Canada (2004)
7. Kuo, C.M., Hsieh, C.H., Jou, Y.D., Lin, H.C., Lu, P.C.: Motion Estimation for Video Compression using Kalman Filtering, Vol. 42. No. 2. IEEE Trans. on Broadcasting (1996) 110-116
8. Richardson, I.E.G.: H.264 and MPEG-4 Video Compression, John Wiley & Sons (2003) 170-176
9. Voorhies, D.: Space-Filling Curves and a Measure of Coherence, Graphics Gems II, James Arvo, Academic Press (1999) 26-30
10. Bially, T.: Space-Filling Curves: Their Generation and Their Application to Bandwidth Reduction, IEEE Trans. Info. Theory (1969), vol. IT-15: 658-664
11. The Hilbert curve available in http://www.compuphase.com/hilbert.htm

Throughput and Delay Analysis Considering Packet Arrival in IEEE 802.11

Sinam Woo[1], Woojin Park[1], Younghwan Jung[1], Sunshin An[1],
and Dongho Kim[2]

[1] Department of Electronics and Computer Engineering,
Korea University, Seoul, Korea
{snwoo, progress, youngh, sunshin}@dsys.korea.ac.kr
[2] Department of Computer Engineering,
Halla University, Wonju, Kangwon, Korea
imi@hit.halla.ac.kr

Abstract. In recent years, Wireless Local Area Networks (WLANs) have become extremely popular. IEEE 802.11 protocol is the dominating standards for WLANs employing the Distributed Coordination Function (DCF) as its Medium Access Control (MAC) mechanism. In the literature, several papers have stuided performance of IEEE 802.11 protocol and assume that a station always have a packet available for transmission. This paper[1] presents a Markov chain model to compute IEEE 802.11 DCF performance taking into account the packet arrival rates. Throughput and packet delay analysis are carried out in order to study the performance of IEEE 802.11 DCF under various traffic conditions. We present the analytical results of throughput and packet delay through network size and arrival rates. Results indicate that throughput and packet delay depends on the number of stations and packet arrival rates.

Keywords: Throughput, Delay, Wireless, WLAN.

1 Introduction

Wreless Local Area Networks (WLANs) are gaining great popularity and are rapidly deployed all over the world. WLANs are flexible and easy to implement as no cables are required. Various wireless communication standards have been developed and the dominating protocol is IEEE 802.11.

IEEE 802.11 specifications include both the Medium Access Control (MAC) and the Physical Layer (PHY). MAC is based on the Carrier Sense Multiple Access with Collision Avoidance (CSMA/CA) scheme and it incorporates two medium access methods: Distributed Coordination Function (DCF) and Point Coordination Function (PCF). DCF is an asynchronous data transmission function, which is best suited to delay-insensitive data. On the other hand, the optional PCF is utilized, when time-bounded services are required according to

---

[1] This research was supported by SK Telecom in Korea.

S. Madria et al. (Eds.): ICDCIT 2006, LNCS 4317, pp. 180–191, 2006.

the communication needs. DCF mechanism describes two techniques to transmit data packets: a two-way handshaking (DATA-ACK) called basic access and an optional four-way handshaking (RTS-CTS-DATA-ACK) called RTS/CTS access method. In the basic access, the transmitter sends a data packet (DATA) and the receiver responds with an acknowledgement (ACK) after the successful reception of the data. The RTS/CTS mode requires the exchange of short frames between the transmitter (RTS) and the receiver (CTS), prior to data packet transmission.

In the literature, several papers have studied the performance of IEEE 802.11 protocol using analytical model and assume that analytical models are under high traffic conditions. Bianchi [1] proposed a Markov chain model to evaluate the performance of the DCF on a channel with no errors. The key assumption of the model is that at each transmission and regardless of the number of retransmission suffered, the packet collides with a constant probability. Wu [4] modified Bianchi's Markov chain to calculate throughput taking into account the packet's retransmission limit as specified in the standard. Chtzmisios et al [3] employed Wu's Markov chain to develop a mathematical model that calculates additional performance metrics, the average packet delay, and the packet drop probability and the packet drop time. Xiao [7] studies backoff-based priority scheme and calculates saturation throughputs, saturation delays, and frame dropping probability through analytical model.

In this paper, we extend the study of throughput and packet delay by considering the packet arrival and utilize a discrete-time Markov chain model carrying out a similar analysis with [1] and [7]. Our model assumes that network consists of n contending stations transmitting in ideal conditions: no errors occur in the channel and no hidden stations exist. We also consider that every station can immediately send packet if it has a packet available for transmission and the collision probability of a transmitted packet is constant and independent of the retransmission.

This paper is organized as follows. Section 2 introduces the DCF of IEEE 802.11 MAC and focuses on the backoff procedure. Section 3 describes the mathematical model to calculate the throughput and the packet delay. Section 4 provides various analysis results. Finally, section 5 concludes the paper.

2   Distributed Coordination Function

IEEE 8021.11 DCF is based on a Carrier Sense Multiple Access with Collision Avoidance (CSMA/CA) scheme and employs a binary exponential backoff technique. Under DCF, before initiating a transmission, each station senses the channel to determine its state: idle or busy.

If the medium is sensed to be idle for a time interval greater than the Distributed Inter-Frame Space (DIFS), the station proceeds with the packet transmission. If the medium is sensed busy, the station waits until the ongoing transmission is over. The station then defers for a randomly selected backoff interval, initializing its random backoff timer, which is decremented as long as the channel is sensed idle. The backoff timer is frozen when a transmission is detected and is reactivated when the channel is sensed idle again for more than one DIFS. Moreover, each station is allowed to transmit only when its backoff timer reaches zero and at the beginning of each slot time. After the successful reception of a packet, the destination station sends back an immediate positive acknowledgement (ACK) after a time interval equal to Short Inter-Frame Space (SIFS). If the source station does not receive an ACK, the data packet is assumed to have been lost and a retransmission is scheduled. Every station maintains a station short retry count that indicates the number of retransmission attempts of a data packet.

If the retry count reaches the specified limit, retry attempts stop and the packet is discarded. Before initiating a packet transmission, the backoff timer value for each station is uniformly chosen in the interval $[0, W_i - 1]$ where Wi is the current contention window size(CW) and i is the backoff stage. The value of W_i depends on the number of failed transmissions of the packet. After each retransmission due to a packet collision or error, W_i is doubled up to a maximum value, $W_m = 2^m W_{min}$ where m is the number of backoff stages and W_{min} is the minimum contention window size. Once W_i reach W_m, it will remain at this value until it is reset to W_o either after the successful transmission of a data packet or when retry limit reaches the maximum value.

3   Throughput and Delay Analysis

An analytical model based on Bianchi's model [1] and Wu's model [4] under high traffic conditions is proposed. In this paper, we extend an analytical model considering various traffic conditions. In our analysis, we ignore the effect of frame errors due to bit errors introduced by channel noise. Therefore, frames are received in error only when they encounter collisions due to other simultaneous transmissions. We assume that network consists of a finite number of contending stations n and that each station immediately sends a packet only when it has packets available for transmission, after the completion of each successful transmission. And the maximum backoff window size is recommended with a default value 1024 in IEEE 802.11 specification. The initial backoff window size is recommended with a default value, 32 in 802.11b and 16 in 802.11a. The default long retry limit is 4 and the default short retry limit is 7 [3]. In this paper, we modify the backoff window size and retry limit for simplicity.

3.1   Markov Chain Definition

Consider a fixed number n of contending stations and each packet needs to wait for a random backoff time before transmitting. $n(t)$ is defined as a random process representing the number of packets in the system at time t, $s(t)$ is defined as a random process representing the backoff stage of the station at time t, and $b(t)$ is defined as a random process representing the backoff time counter for a given station at time t. Let p denote the probability that a station in the backoff stage senses the channel busy and λ be the arrival rate in a slot time.

Therefore, three-dimensional Markov chain with state space (i, j, k), where i stands for the number of packets taking values from $(0, 1, \ldots N)$, j stands for the backoff stage, which is uniformly chosen in the range $(0, 1, \ldots, L)$ and k stands for the backoff counter taking values from $(0, 1, \ldots, W_j - 1)$, where $L = log(W_{max}/W_{min})$ is the retry limit and $W_j = 2^j W_{min}$ is the backoff counter in the backoff state j. The state transition diagram is shown in Fig. 1. Let

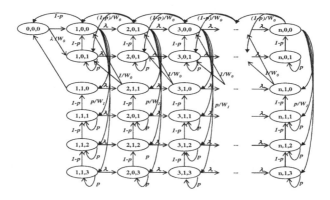

Fig. 1. Markov Chain Model for arrival rate and backoff window

$P_{(i,j,k)(i',j',k')}$ be the transition probability of the number packets from i to i', the backoff stage going from j to j', and the backoff counter going from k to k'. The transition probabilities in Fig. 1.

$$P_{(i,j,k)(i,j,k)} = p, \qquad i \in (1, N), j \in (0, L), k \in (1, W_j - 1)$$

$$P_{(i,j,k)(i,j,k-1)} = 1 - p, \qquad i \in (1, N), j \in (0, L), k \in (1, W_j - 1)$$

$$P_{(i,j,0)(i-1,0,k)} = (1 - p)/W_0, \ i \in (2, N), j \in (0, L - 1), k \in (0, W_j - 1)$$

$$P_{(i,j,0)(i,j+1,k)} = p/W_{j+1}, \qquad i \in (1, N), j \in (0, L - 1), k \in (0, W_j - 1)$$

$$P_{(i,L,0)(i-1,0,k)} = 1/W_0, \qquad i \in (2, N), k \in (0, W_0 - 1) \tag{1}$$

$$P_{(i,j,k)(i+1,j,k)} = \lambda, \qquad i \in (1, N - 1), j \in (0, L), k \in (0, W_j - 1)$$

$$P_{(0,0,0)(1,0,k)} = \lambda/W_0, \qquad k \in (0, W_0 - 1)$$

$$P_{(1,j,0)(0,0,0)} = 1 - p, \qquad j \in (0, L - 1)$$

$$P_{(1,L,0)(0,0,0)} = 1$$

Let $\pi_{i,j,k} = \lim_{t \to \infty} Pn(t) = i, s(t) = j, b(t) = k$ be the stationary distribution of the Markove chain. We now show that the stationary probabilities are calculated recursively through the following algorithm.

1. Set $\pi_{1,0,0} = C$
2. Compute the following, repeating from $i = 0$ to n
   (a) when there are a packet in a queue
       i. if $i = 1, j = 1, k \neq 0$, then compute

$$\pi_{i,j,k} = \sum_{m=0}^{W_j-k-1} \frac{p(1-p)^m}{W_j(1-p+\lambda)^{m+1}} \pi_{i,0,0} \qquad (2)$$

ii. if $i = 1, j = 1, k = 0$, then compute

$$\pi_{i,j,0} = \frac{1}{1+\lambda} \sum_{m+0}^{W_j-1} \frac{p(1-p)^m}{W_j(1-p+\lambda)^m} \pi_{i,0,0} \qquad (3)$$

iii. if $i = 1, j = 0, k \neq 0$, then compute

$$\pi_{i,j,k} = \frac{1+\lambda}{2-2p+\lambda} \pi_{i,j,0} \qquad (4)$$

iv. if $i = 0, j = 0, k = 0$, then compute

$$\pi_{0,0,0} = \frac{1-p}{\lambda} \pi_{1,0,0} + \frac{1}{\lambda} \pi_{1,1,0} \qquad (5)$$

   (b) when there are more than a packet($i \neq n$) in a queue
       i. if $1 < i < n, j = 1, k \neq 0$, then compute

$$\pi_{i,j,k} = \sum_{m=0}^{W_j-k-1} \frac{\lambda(1-p)^m}{(1-p+\lambda)^{m+1}} \pi_{i+1,j,k+m} + \sum_{m=0}^{W_j-k-1} \frac{p(1-p)^m}{W_j(1-p+\lambda)^{m+1}} \pi_{i,0,0} \qquad (6)$$

ii. if $1 < i < n, j = 1, k = 0$, then compute

$$\pi_{i,j,k} = \frac{1}{1+\lambda} \sum_{m=0}^{W_j-1} \frac{\lambda(1-p)^m}{(1-p+\lambda)^m} \pi_{i+1,j,m} + \frac{1}{1+\lambda} \sum_{m=0}^{W_j-1} \frac{p(1-p)^m}{W_j(1-p+\lambda)^m} \pi_{i,0,0} \qquad (7)$$

iii. if $1 < i < n, j = 0, k = 0$, then compute

$$\pi_{i,j,k} = \lambda \sum_{m=0}^{W_j-1} \pi_{i-1,j,m} + \lambda \sum_{m=0}^{W_{j+1}-1} \pi_{i,j+1,m} \qquad (8)$$

iv. if $1 < i < n, j = 0, k \neq 0$, then compute

$$\pi_{i,j,k} = \frac{1+\lambda}{2-2p+\lambda} \pi_{i,j,0} + \frac{\lambda}{2-2p+\lambda} \pi_{i-1,j,k} - \frac{\lambda}{2-2p+\lambda} \pi_{i-1,j,0} \qquad (9)$$

   (c) when queue is full
       i. if $i = n, j = 1, k \neq 0$, then compute

$$\pi_{i,j,k} = \sum \pi_{i-1,j,k+m} + \sum \pi_{i,0,0} \qquad (10)$$

ii. if $i = n, j = 1, k = 0$, then compute

$$\pi_{i,j,k} = \sum \lambda \pi_{i-1,j,m} + \sum \pi_{i,0,0} \qquad (11)$$

iii. if $i = n, j = 0, k \neq 0$, then compute

$$\pi_{i,j,k} = \frac{\lambda}{1-p} \pi_{i-1,j,k} \qquad (12)$$

iv. if $i = n, j = 0, k = 0$, then compute

$$\pi_{i,j,k} = \lambda \sum_{m=0}^{W_j-1} \pi_{i-1,j,m} \qquad (13)$$

3. Calculate the total sum of all the transition probabilities

$$P = \sum_{i=0}^{n} \sum_{j=0}^{L} \sum_{k=0}^{W_j-1} \pi_{i,j,k} \qquad (14)$$

4. Normalize by letting

$$\pi_{i,j,k}/P \rightarrow \pi_{i,j,k} \qquad (15)$$

Thus, by equation (2) and (13), all the value $\pi_{i,j,k}$ are calculated as the value C and the collision probability p. All the value $\pi_{i,j,k}$ is normalized by (15).

Let τ be the probability that a station transmits during a slot time. A station transmits when its backoff counter reaches zero, as it were, the station is at state $(i, j, 0)$. Therefore, we have

$$\tau = \sum_{i=1}^{N} \sum_{j=0}^{L} \pi_{i,j,0} \qquad (16)$$

3.2   Throughput Analysis

Let P_{tr} be the probability that there is at least one transmission in the slot time and let n be the number of stations. Since n stations contend on channel, each station transmits with probability τ

$$P_{tr} = 1 - (1 - tau)^n \qquad (17)$$

Let P_s be the probability that a successful transmission occurs in a slot time. The P_s that an occuring packet transmission is successful is given by the probability that exactly one station transmits and the remaining $n - 1$ stations defer transmission. We have

$$P_s = n\tau(1 - \tau)^{n-1} \qquad (18)$$

Let S be the normailzed throughput which is defined as the fraction of the time the channel is used to transmit payload. $E[P]$ is the average packet payload size and all packets have the same size. The probability that the channel is idle for a slot time is $1 - P_{tr}$, and the probability that the channel is neither idle nor successful for a slot time is $1 - (1 - P_{tr}) - P_s$. Hence, we have

$$S = \frac{E[payload\,transmitted\,in\,a\,slot\,time]}{E[length\,of\,a\,slot\,time]}$$

$$= \frac{P_s E[P]}{(1-P_{tr})/sigma+P_s T_s+(P_{tr}-P_s)T_c} \tag{19}$$

Here, T_s is the average time that the channel is sensed busy because of a successful transmission, T_c is the average time that the channel has a collision, and σ is the duration of an empty slot time. Assuming that all stations use the same channel access mechanism and a systme is run via the basic access mechanism. T_s and T_c are defined as follows.

$$\begin{aligned} T_S &= T_H + T_{E[P]} + T_{SIFS} + \delta + T_{ACK} + T_{DIFS} + \delta \\ T_C &= T_H + T_{E[P]} + T_{DIFS} + \delta \end{aligned} \tag{20}$$

Let T_H, T_{ACK}, δ be the time to transmit the header ($H = PHY_{hdr} + MAC_{hdr}$), the time to transmit an ACK, and the propagation delay respectively.

3.3 Delay Analysis

Since no hidden nodes are considered, collisions take place becasue two or more contending stations choose the same backoff slot to transmit. The transmission of a frame is finalized when a positive acknowledgement is received. Our analytical model considers delay performance taking into account the retry limit of a data packet transmission and a packet waiting time in a system. Average packet delay includees the waiting delay in a system, the backoff delay, the transmission delay, and the interframe spaces. Also, the average backoff delay depends on the value of a station's backoff counter and the duration when the counter freezes due to busy channel.

Let P_{drop} be the dropping probability. From Fig.1, we observe that a frame can be dropped only in a state $(i, L, 0)$ if a collision occurs. In other words, a frame can be dropped when the retransmission reaches the retry limit. Then we have

$$P_{drop} = \sum_{i=0}^{N} p\pi_{i,L,0} \tag{21}$$

Let $P_{success}$ be the frame successfule probability

$$P_{success} = 1 - P_{drop} = 1 - \sum_{i=0}^{N} p\pi_{i,L,0} \tag{22}$$

Let N be the number of frame available to transmission in a station. *Little's Formula* gives the average delay time in a station. Then we have

$$E[N] = \sum_{i=0}^{n} \sum_{j=0}^{m} \sum_{k=0}^{W_j-1} i\pi_{i,j,k} \tag{23}$$

$$\overline{D} = E[D_{waiting}] = \frac{E[N]}{\lambda}$$

Also, let X be the random variable representing the total number of backoff slots without the counter freezing case. Let B be the randomvariable representing the total number of slots when the counter freezes.

$$E[X] = \sum_{j=0}^{L} \frac{p^j(1-p)}{P_{success}} \sum_{h=0} j \frac{W_h-1}{2}$$

$$E[B] = \frac{p}{1-p} E[X] \tag{24}$$

$E(X)$ and $E(B)$ is the total number of idel and busy slots that a frame encounters during the backoff stage respectively. Let $E(N_{retry})$ be the average number of retries. We have

$$E[N_{retry}] = \sum_{j=0}^{L} \frac{p^j(1-p)}{P_{success}} \tag{25}$$

Let D be the random variable representing the frame delay and let T_o be the time that a station has to wait when its frame transmission collides before sending the channel again. We have

$$E[D] = \overline{D} + E[X]\sigma + E[b]\left[\frac{P_S}{P_{tr}}T_s + \frac{P_{tr}-P_s}{P_{tr}}T_c\right] + E[N_{retry}][T_c+T_o] + T_s \tag{26}$$

where $T_o = T_{ACK_Timeout} + T_{SIFS}$

σ is the duration of an idle slot, $(P_s/P_{tr})T_s + (1 - P_s/P_{tr})T_c$ is the duration of a busy slot, $T_c + T_o$ is a failed transmission slot, and T_s a successful transmission slot respectively. And $T_{ACKTimeout}$ is the duration of ACK timeouts.

Packet payload	8184 bits
MAC header	272 bits
PHY header	128 bits
ACK	112 bits
Channel Bit Rate	$1 Mbit/s$
Propagation Delay	$1\mu s$
Slot Time	$50\mu s$
SIFS	$28\mu s$
DIFS	$128\mu s$
$ACK_{Timeout}$	$300\mu s$

4   Performance Evaluation

In this section we evaluate the proposed analytic model. We adopt IEEE 802.11b as an example and use the system parameters in table 1. Unless specified, the following results have obtained assuming the parameters reported in Table 1. Also the following results are validated when the simulation results in [1] and [7] are compared. For real-time multimedia traffic with sensitive delay requirements, retransmitted frames may be too late to be useful and a smaller retry limit

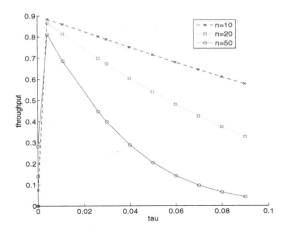

Fig. 2. Throughput versus transmission probability

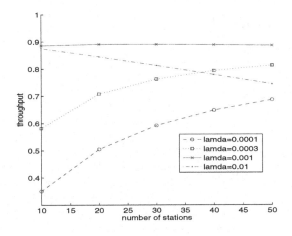

Fig. 3. Throughput versus Number of Station for the basic access scheme

is appropriate. Therefore, we adopt retry limit and backoff window size ($L = 2, W_{min} = 2, W_{max} = 4$). We also can extend the retry limit and the backoff window size due to our proposed model's generality.

Fig.2 shows the theoretically achievable throughput. The figure reports the different throughput obtained in the case of different τ. We see that a small variation in the optimal value of τ leads to a greater decrease in the throughput. Intuitively if the probability τ that a station transmits during a slot time increases, more collisions and lower throughput will be.

Fig.3 and Fig.4 show that the dependency of the throughput and delay is examined on the number of stations in the basic access. The network size has a substantial influence on the packet drop probability due to the increase number

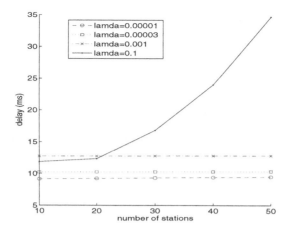

Fig. 4. Delay versus Number of Station at the basic access scheme

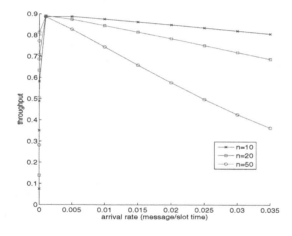

Fig. 5. Delay versus Number of Station at the basic access scheme

of collisions caused from the stations attempt to access the medium. Fig.3 illustrates that the throughput decreases as the number of stations increases and the arrival rates is over 0.001 as more stations trying to transmit packets result in more packet collisions. Fig.4 illustrates that the packet delay increase as the number of stations increase and the arrival rates is over 0.001. This occurs because a station has to wait longer due to the successful transmissions of other stations and more contending stations increase the probability of collisions and the number of retransmissions. To investigate the dependency of the throughput and the delay from the arrival rates, we report the results in Fig.5 and Fig.6.

Fig.5 presents that when the network size is small, the throughput is not significantly increased due to the smaller packet collision. When the network

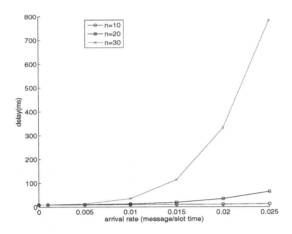

Fig. 6. Delay versus Number of Station at the basic access scheme

size is larger, the throughput degrades more due to the more packet collision. Fig.6 illustrates that the average packet delay is significantly affected from the arrival rates when more colliding stations transmit packets.

5   Conclusion

In this paper, an analytical model using a Markov chain was developed to compute the throughput and the packet delay in IEEE 802.111 protocol. Throughput and delay analysis is carried out in order to study the performance of IEEE 802.11 DCF. Using the analytical model, we develop a throughput and delay analysis under various traffic condition. In the performance evaluation, we have concluded that throughput and packet delay depends on the number of stations than the arrival rates.

Future work can include the throughput and delay analysis including the channel loss. Also we apply the proposed model to the wireless multimedia traffic.

References

1. G.Bianchi, "Performance analysis of the IEEE 802.11 Distributed Coordination Function", IEEE Journal of Sel. Areas Comm., vol. 18, no.3, pp. 535-547, Mar. 2000
2. E.Ziouva and T.Antonakopouls, "CSMA/CA performance under high traffic conditions: Throughput and delay analysis", Computer Comm., vod.25, no.3, pp. 313-321, Feb. 2002
3. P.Chatzmisios, V.Vitas and A.C. Boucouvalas, "Throughput and Delay analysis of IEEE 802.11 protocol", Proc. of IEEE International Workshop on Networked Appliances, pp. 168-174, 2002

4. H.Wu, Y.Peng, K.Long, S.Cheng, J.Ma, "Perfromance of Reliable Transport Protocol over IEEE 802.11 Wireless LAN: Analysis And Enhancement", Proc. Of IEEE INFOCOM, pp.599-607, 2002

5. P. Chazimisios, A.C. Boucouvalas and V.Vitsas, "IEEE 802.11 Packet Delay - A Finite Retry Limit Analysis", Proc. Of IEEE GLOBECOM, vol.2, pp. 950-954, 2003

6. H.Wu, K.Long, S.Cheng, J.Ma, "IEEE 802.11 Distributed Coordination Function (DCF): Analysis and Enhancement", International Conf. on Comm. (ICC), April 2002.

7. Y.Xiao, "Performance Analysis of Priority Schemes for IEEE 802.11 and IEEE 802.11e Wireless LANs", IEEE Trnas. Wireless Comm., vol.4, No.4,July 2005.

8. Z. Tao, S. Panwar, "Throughput and Delay Analysis for the IEEE 802.11e Enhanced Distributed Channel Access", IEEE Trans. Comm., vol. 4, no. 4, Apr. 2006.

A Routing Optimization Algorithm for BGP Egress Selection*

Yaping Liu, Zhenghu Gong, Baosheng Wang, and Jinshu Shu

School of Computer, National University of Defense Technology,
Changsha 410073, Hunan, China
ypliu73@yahoo.com.cn

Abstract. BGP optimal egress selection is one of a recent trend in routing research. Current hot-potato routing has the problem of routing instability. This
paper provides a new algorithm named BGP-RO-ES to minimize hot-potato
disruptions while satisfying multiple constraints of different metrics, such
as traffic engineering, the cost of traffic across the network and the cost of
maintaining lightweight tunnels. The algorithm can be adaptive to different link
failures and can be implemented in current BGP routers with a little change.
Simulation results show that the control stability of BGP-RO-ES can be very
close to that of TIE algorithm and that of RTF_TIE algorithm spending only
half of the cost of maintaining lightweight tunnels.

Keywords: BGP, hot-potato routing, interdomain traffic engineering.

1 Introduction

Hot-potato routing is widely used in the current Border Gateway Protocol (BGP)[1]
routers. However, its main problems are hot-potato disruptions [2], which means
intradomain routing changes can impact interdomain routing and cause abrupt swings
of external routes. Various interdomain traffic engineering algorithms are proposed to
improve the load balance ability of the routing by tweaking BGP routes [3]. They
view the BGP egress selection problem as a static problem ignoring network dynamics. Though *TIE* [4] mechanism considers the issue of link failures, it ignores other
factors (e.g. failure duration [5], the cost of creating and maintaining lightweight
tunnels to ensure consistent forwarding path etc.). In our prior research, a *RTF_TIE*
[6] algorithm is proposed which considers the issue of link failures and failure duration at the same time. However, it also ignores the cost of maintaining lightweight
tunnels and the cost of traffic across the network.

In this paper, we propose a new algorithm *BGP-RO-ES* (BGP Route optimization
for Egress selection) to optimize the route stability for BGP egress selection with
satisfying multiple constraints of different metrics, such as traffic engineering, the
cost of traffic across the network and the cost of maintaining lightweight tunnels. The

---

* This research was supported by the National Grand Fundamental Research 973 Program of
China under Grant No. 2003CB314802 and the National High-Tech Research and Development Plan of China under Grant No. 2005AA121570.

algorithm is a kind of greedy heuristic solutions based on the statistical information about traffic loads, network topology and link failures. Simulation results show that it is effective and flexible comparing with *TIE* and *RTF_TIE*.

2 Problem Statement

To reduce the complexity of modeling all details in the problem, we make some assumptions to focus on the research of the effect by the change of intradomain topology: 1) The BGP speakers are organized in a full iBGP mesh. 2) The eBGP routes and the traffic demands are stable in its optimization time. 3) Only link up/down changes are considered and the change of link metrics caused by IGP engineering is not considered. 4) The default algorithm in the initiate topology is hot-potato routing which can satisfy the requirement of load balance.

We introduce some notations at first. Some main notations are summarized in Table I. The *control stability* (s^{RM})[7] defined in (1) represents the stability of routing. The *metric of the traffic engineering* (*te*) [7] defined in (2) represents the traffic load balance. The *te(δ)* represents the metric of the traffic engineering under transformation δ. The *cost of traffic across the network* (*tcost(δ)*) [8] defined in (3) represents the cost of traffic under δ. We use *icost* to represent the number of selected egress point if the *icostType* is 0 or the number of graph transformations if the *icostType* is 1, which is inconsistency with the forwarding path.

Table 1. Notations

Notation	Description
G	undirected Graph
ΔG	set of the graph transformations
V	set of nodes
L	set of links
P	set of network prefixes
u(*l*)	utilization of the link *l*
Φ(u(*l*))	penalized function of link *l*
$R_i(G,N)$	each region $R_i(G,N)$ is a shortest distance tree rooted in *i*
RI(G,N,v)	*v*'s entry in the routing matrix , if *N* is the egress set for prefix *p*
E	the mapping of prefixes to egress sets
H(G,N,v,δ)	change of routing table of node v under δ
P(δ)	probability of the graph transformation δ
T(δ)	duration time of δ

$$R_i(G,N) = \{v \mid \forall v \in V, m(v,i) \le m(v,i'), \forall i' \in N, i \ne i'\}$$

$$RI(G,N,v) = \{i \mid \forall i \in N, v \in R_i(G,N)\}$$

$$H(G,N,v,\delta) = \begin{cases} 1, & RI(G,N,v) \ne RI(\delta(G),N,v) \\ 0, & otherwise \end{cases}$$

$$s^{RM} = \frac{1}{|P||V|} \sum_{\delta \in \Delta G} \sum_{p \in P} \sum_{v \in V} \frac{H(G,E(p),v,\delta)}{T(\delta)} P(\delta) \tag{1}$$

$$te(\delta) = \sum_{l \in L} \Phi(u(l))(\delta), \delta \in \Delta G \tag{2}$$

$$t\cos t(\delta) = \sum_{p \in P} \sum_{i \in N} \sum_{j \in E(p)} x_{ip}^j \cdot d_{current}(i,j) \cdot t(i,p) \tag{3}$$

$$\sum_{j \in E(p)} x_{ip}^j = 1, \ x_{ip}^j = 0 \ \text{ or } 1$$

The problem of optimization egress selection can be described as minimizing control stability with satisfying the constraints of cost of traffic across the network, the metric of traffic engineering and the *icost* value. The values of parameters (e.g. γ_1, γ_2, γ_3, ω, T) are set by the network administrator.

$$\min s^{RM} \quad \text{s.t}$$

$$\frac{t\cos t(\delta)}{t\cos t_{hot-potato}(\delta)} \le \gamma_1 \tag{4}$$

$$\frac{te(\delta)}{te_{hot-potato}(\delta)} \le \gamma_2 \tag{5}$$

$$\text{if} \quad \frac{te(\delta)}{te_{hot-potato}(\delta)} > \gamma_2, \frac{te(\delta) \cdot P(\delta) \cdot T(\delta)}{te_{hot-potato}(\delta)} \le \omega \cdot T \tag{6}$$

$$i\cos t \le \gamma_3 \tag{7}$$

$$\gamma_1, \gamma_2, \omega > 1, \omega > \gamma_2, \gamma_3 \ge 0$$

3   The BGP-RO-ES Algorithm

In a study of link failures in Sprint's IP backbone, it was observed that most of failures are transient failures [6,9]. This shows that the initial topology is the last state of the topology under some link failures with high probability. Thus our mechanism allows each router to have a ranking of the egress points for each destination prefix. For prefix p, node i uses $m(i,p,e)$ to replace the current distance to select the egress point according to the common sequence in BGP decision process. The value of $m(i,p,e)$ is computed according to (8), in which the $d_G(i,e)$ represents the IGP distance between node i and e in the original graph and the $d_{current}(i,e)$ represents the IGP distance between nodes in the current graph. The $f(i,p,e,\delta,t)$ is a parameter, whose value is 0 or 1.

$$m(i,p,e) = f(i,p,e,\delta,t) \cdot d_G(i,e) + (1 - f(i,p,e,\delta,t)) \cdot d_{current}(i,e) \tag{8}$$

We decompose *BGP-RO-ES* into two parts: offline part and online part, which is as similar as *RTF_TIE*. The offline part computes the parameters (e.g. $f(i,p,e,\delta,t)$) used by the online part. The online part has small change to the current typical BGP decision process. We adopt a greedy approach, during each iteration, choosing values of $f(i,p,e,\delta,t)$ to 0 with satisfying all conditions in this δ for which the value of $s^{RM}_{hot}(\delta)$-$s^{RM}_{fixed}(\delta)$ is largest. We promise that the value of $f(i,p,e,\delta,t)$ is the same for all $e \in E(p)$, so that $f(i,p,e,\delta,t)$ can be represented by $f(i,p,\delta,t)$.

However, some experiences can reduce the complexity of the offline part. We know that if the traffic load is high, the stability of routing is more important and if the traffic load is very low the remainder bandwidth can accommodate unexpected traffic fluctuations. For example, we promise that traffic load is high, if the link utilization is larger than 2/3 and it is light, if the link utilization is smaller than 1/10. We can get the following equation (9) (|L| is the number of links).

$$if \ te(G) \geq 4/3 \, |L| \ or \ te(G) \leq 1/10 \, |L|, \ \gamma_2 = \infty \tag{9}$$

The pseudo code of the offline part is described in *Algotithm.1*. Step *1* initializes all the output values. Step *2* means we use greedy heuristic to solve the problem. The processes in step *3*, *4* and *5* describe how to find the proper solution with satisfying conditions (4), (5), (6) and (7). Comparing with *TIE* algorithm, *BGP-RO-ES* algorithm adds the processes in step *2*, *4* and *5*. Comparing with *RTF_TIE* algorithm, *BGP-RO-ES* algorithm adds the processes in step *2*, *3* and *5*.

Algorithm 1. *BGP-RO-ES* offline part

```
Input:p(δ),T(δ),γ₁,γ₂, γ₃,ω,T,traffic demand,icostType,ΔG
Output: f(i,p,δ,t),type(i,p,δ),timer(i,p,δ)
/* Step 1: init*/
for each i,p,δ, do
 f(i,p,δ,t) =1;type(i,p,δ) =0;timer(i,p,δ) =0;addCost=0;
/* Step 2: sort*/
 sort δ using the value of s^RM_hot(δ)-s^RM_fixed(δ)with decrement;
/* Step 3: satisfy condition (4)*/
if γ₁ is not infinite then
   for each δ in ΔG do /*e is the original egress*/
     if every i,p d_current(i,e)≤γ₁*d_G(i,e)do
        f(i,p,δ,t) = 0; put δ to Q₁;
        update addCost according to icostType;
else Q₁=ΔG; for each i,p,δ do f(i,p,δ,t) =0;
/* Step 4: satisfy condition (5) and (6)*/
if γ₂ is not infinite then
   for each δ in Q₁ do
     if condition (5) and (6) are false do
        for each i,p,δ do f(i,p,δ,t) =1;
        update addCost according to icostType;
     else
        put δ to Q₂;
        if condition (5) is false and (6) are true do
           type(i,p,δ)=1;
           timer(i,p,δ)=ω*T*te_hot(δ)/(p(δ)*te_fix(δ));
else Q₂= Q₁;
/* Step 5: satisfy condition (7)*/
if γ₃ is not infinite then
   while addCost >γ₃ do
     if δ=DEQUEUE(Q₂) is not null then
        for each i,p and f(i,p,δ,t)==0 do
           f(i,p,δ,t) =1; update addCost;
     else
        if addCost >γ₃ then
           return ("can not find a solution");
return results;
```

The outputs of the offline part of *BGP-RO-ES* are control rules. If the event of link failures or link failures' recovery occurs, every BGP router can probe them so that they can set corresponding rules into active state or inactive state. The BGP egress selection process should be modified with a little change to support our control rules. The pseudo code of the online part (Algorithm 2) is composed of three tasks. One task deals with events of link failure or link failure's recovery. The second task is how to select egress point. The difference between it and the standard process in common BGP routers (e.g. CISCO router) is that of step 8). The third task is the timeout process if the actual link failure duration may be much longer than we estimate with statistical information. This task can assure condition (5) or (6) to be satisfied. The online module does not add more complexity to the original process, but need more spaces to save the control rules. The running time of the offline part of *BGP-RO-ES* is $O(|V|^3|\Delta G||P|)$, if we use $|\Delta G|$ to denote the size of ΔG. The running time of the online part of *BGP-RO-ES* algorithm is about $O(1)$.

Algorithm 2. *BGP-RO-ES* online part

```
event process task:                    timeout process task:
if δ then                              if timer(i,p,δ)is timeout
    if δ∈ ΔG then                          then
      set rules in active state;             m(i,p,e) equals to the
      if type(i,p,δ)==1 then                   current IGP distance;
        start timer(i,p,δ);                  notify BGP egress
    if δ recovery then                       decision process to
    if δ∈ ΔG then                            reselect;
      set rules in inactive state;
      if type(i,p,δ)==1 then
        reset timer(i,p,δ);
BGP egress decision process task:
1) Largest weight
2) Largest local preference
3) Local paths over remote paths
4) Shortest AS path
5) Lowest origin type
6) Lowest MED
7) eBGP over iBGP paths
8)if controlRules are active then
      find match rules;
      if found then compute m(i,p,e)according to (8);
      else
         m(i,p,e) equals to IGP distance;
      select Lowest m(i,p,e);
```

4 Simulation

The simulation uses the topology, BGP routing information and traffic data on Jan 1, 2005 of Abilene[10]. Failure links are generated through synthetic methods according to the cumulative distribution function (CDF) in [9]. The average failure duration is used to estimate the value of $T(\delta)$. The $CBGP$[11] is used to simulate the action of BGP in the AS. In the following simulations, the x-axis represents the value of γ_3 and y-axis represents the value of s^{RM}. The value of $icostType$ is set 1 because different values of $icostType$ have very little effect on results.

The first simulation compares the value of s^{RM} among *hot-potato*, *fixed ranking*, *RTF_TIE*, and the routing in this system in which γ_1 is set infinite, γ_2 is set 1.001, ω is set 1.01, and γ_3 is set different values. The Simulation (Fig.1) shows that the value of s^{RM} under *hot-potato* is 1.23 times bigger than that under *RTF_TIE*. In our algorithm, the value of *icost* is half of that under *RTF_TIE* at the cost of the value of s^{RM} 2.3% above that under *RTF_TIE*. In this situation, *hot-potato*, *RTF_TIE* and the current used routing can satisfy condition (5) or (6), but *fixed ranking* routing has about 13% of graph transformations against to condition (5) or (6).

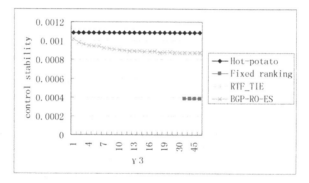

Fig. 1. s^{RM} under different routings ($\gamma_1 = \infty$, $\gamma_2 = 1.001$, $\omega = 1.01$)

In the second simulation, γ_2 is set 1.01, ω is set 1.1. Other parameters are set as the same as in the first simulation. The result (Fig.2) is very similar to Fig.1. The value of s^{RM} under *hot-potato* routing is 1.67 times bigger than that under *RTF_TIE* routing. In our algorithm, the value of *icost* is half of that under *RTF_TIE* at the cost of the value of s^{RM} 16.8% above that under *RTF_TIE*.

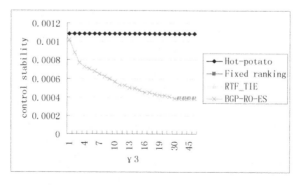

Fig. 2. s^{RM} under different routings ($\gamma_1 = \infty$, $\gamma_2 = 1.01$, $\omega = 1.1$)

In the third simulation we use formula (9) to set the value of γ_2. Other parameters are set as the same as in the first simulation. In the situation, *RTF_TIE* degenerates into *fixed ranking* routing. The result (Fig.3) is the same as in Fig.2. The reason is that the current traffic load is very light. The condition of traffic engineering has no effect.

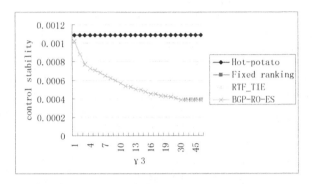

Fig. 3. s^{RM} under different routings ($\gamma_1 = \infty$, $\gamma_2 = \infty$)

The forth simulation (Fig.4) compares the value of s^{RM} among *hot-potato*, *fixed ranking*, *TIE (t=2)*, and the routing in this system in which γ_1 is set 2, γ_2 is set 1.001, ω is set 1.01 and γ_3 is set different values. In the fifth simulation (Fig.5), γ_2 is set 1.01, ω is set 1.1, and other parameters are set as the same as in the forth simulation. The Fig.4 is the same as the Fig.5.The reason is that the *TIE (t=2)* routing can satisfy condition (6) or (7) in these two situations. The results show that the value of s^{RM} under *hot-potato* 1.64 times bigger than that under *TIE*. In our algorithm, the value of *icost* in our algorithm is half of that under *TIE* at the cost of the value of s^{RM} 16.8% above that under *TIE*. The *Fixed ranking* routing can not satisfy condition (4). The results are not as good as upper simulations due to the limitation of condition (4).

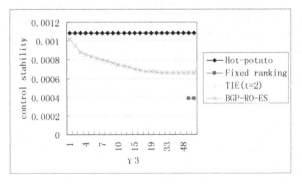

Fig. 4. s^{RM} under different routings ($\gamma_1 = 2$, $\gamma_2 = 1.001$, $\omega = 1.01$)

Simulations show that the *fixed ranking* and *RTF_TIE* routing can not satisfy condition (7) unless the γ_3 is big enough. The control stability of our algorithm can be very close to *TIE* and *RTF_TIE* algorithm with spending only half of *icost*.

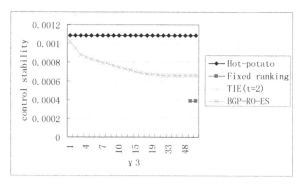

Fig. 5. s^{RM} under different routings ($\gamma_1 = 2$, $\gamma_2 = 1.01$, $\omega = 1.1$)

5 Conclusion

In this paper, we propose an algorithm to optimize the BGP egress selection with multiple constraints considering the network dynamics. Simulation results show that the control stability of our algorithm can be very close to *TIE* and *RTF_TIE* with spending only half of *icost*.

References

1. Y. Rekhter, T. Li, S. Hares, Eds., "A Border Gateway Protocol 4 (BGP-4)", RFC 4271, January 2006.
2. R. Teixeira, A. Shaikh, T. Griffin, and J. Rexford, Dynamics of Hot-Potato Routing in IP Networks, in Proc. ACM SIGMETRICS, June 2004.
3. Steve Uhlig, Implications of characteristics on interdomain traffic engineering, Phd thesis,University catholique de Louvain, 2004.
4. R. Teixeira, T. Griffin, M. Resende, and J. Rexford, TIE Breaking: Tunable Interdomain Egress Selection, in Proc. ACM CONEXT2005, August 2005.
5. Gianluca Iannaccone, Chen-Nee Chuah, Supratik Bhattacharyya and Christophe Diot, Feasibility of IP Restoration in a Tier-1 Backbone, IEEE Network Magazine, March 2004.
6. Yaping Liu, Zhenghu Gong and FengZhao, RTF_TIE: A Tunable Interdomain Egress Selection Algorithm Robust to Transient Link Failures, in Proc. IEEE HPSR2006, Poznan, June 2006.
7. B. Fortz and M. Thorup, Internet traffic engineering by optimizing OSPF weights, in Proc. IEEE INFOCOM, March 2000.
8. T. Bressoud, R. Rastogi, and M. Smith, Optimal configuration of BGP route selection, in Proc. IEEE INFOCOM, 2003.
9. Athina Markopoulou, Gianluca Iannaccone, Supratik Bhattacharyya, Chen-Nee Chuah and Christophe Diot, Characterization of Failures in an IP Backbone, in Proc. IEEE INFOCOM, Hong Kong, March 2004.
10. Abilene Backbone Network. http://abilene.internet2.edu/.
11. C-BGP- An efficient BGP simulator. http://cbgp.info.ucl.ac.be/.

Enhanced OTIS k-Ary n-Cube Networks

Rajib K. Das

Tezpur University, Tezpur - 784028, Assam, India
rkd@tezu.ernet.in

Abstract. This paper presents a variation of OTIS-k-ary n-cube networks (OTIS-Q_n^k) which is called enhanced OTIS-Q_n^k or E-OTIS-Q_n^k. E-OTIS-Q_n^k is defined only for even values of k and is obtained from the normal OTIS-k-ary n cube by adding some extra links without increasing the maximum degree of $2n + 1$. We have established an upper bound of $\lfloor \frac{2nk+5}{3} \rfloor$ on the diameter of E-OTIS-Q_n^k. We have also found the actual diameter using breadth first search for specific values of k and n. It was observed that this upper bound is quite tight, in the sense that it is either equal to the actual diameter or exceeds the diameter by one. We have also defined a classification of the nodes in E-OTIS-Q_n^k based on some properties and shown that the nodes in the same class have the same eccentricity. Finally, we have developed an algorithm for point-to-point routing in E-OTIS-Q_n^k. It is proved that the algorithm always routes by the shortest path.

1 Introduction

The k-ary n-cube network [14] is a popular architecture for multiprocessor systems due to its many desirable properties. The k-ary n-cube possesses an n-dimensional grid structure with k nodes in each dimension. Two popular instances of k-ary n-cube networks are hypercube (where $k = 2$) and torus (where $n = 2$ or 3).

Even though improvement in technology made it possible to realize very powerful multiprocessor systems, the bandwidth limitations imposed by electronic interconnects prove to be a major bottleneck. Optical networks have emerged as an outcome of the search for better alternatives. Optical technologies can provide a large number of high bandwidth channels at a single point, but the electronic interconnects perform better for small distances (say a few millimeter). This has led to the development of hybrid computer architecture like Optical Transpose Interconnection Systems (OTIS).

In the OTIS architecture, the processors are divided into groups and electronic interconnects are used for connections within the same group and optical interconnects are used for intergroup communication. It has been shown in [2] that the bandwidth and the power consumption are optimized when the number of processors in the group equals the number of groups. Several studies of OTIS architecture have been limited to the case where the group size is equal to the number of groups in the system [6], [8], [12]. In such an OTIS system, an

S. Madria et al. (Eds.): ICDCIT 2006, LNCS 4317, pp. 200–211, 2006.

intergroup link connects processor p of group g to processor g of group p. The intra-group links form an interconnection topology called here the *factor* network. Depending on the factor network, we have different OTIS-networks such as OTIS-Mesh, OTIS-Cube, OTIS-star and so on. Among these OTIS-cube and OTIS-mesh are most popular.

A number of algorithms have been developed for the OTIS architecture such as BPC permutations [8], routing, selection and sorting [6], matrix multiplication [9], image processing [10], etc. In [3], a general study of OTIS-Networks where the factor network can be any network, is presented. In [11], a number of results regarding the topological properties of OTIS-k-ary n-cube interconnection networks have been derived.

We note that in each group of an OTIS-k-ary n-cube there is one node whose processor number is the same as the group number. There is no optical link from such a node. In the enhanced OTIS-k-ary n-cube an optical link is provided to such nodes also. The resulting topology is of uniform node degree, lower diameter and better fault-tolerance. The added optical links constitute only a small fraction of the total number of optical links present in the network.

The rest of the paper is organized as follows. In the next section we present the definitions and basic properties. We divide the nodes of E-OTIS-Q_n^k into classes and show that nodes in the same class have the same eccentricity. Later on in this section we establish an upper bound on the diameter of E-OTIS-Q_n^k. Section 3 presents an optimal algorithm for point to point routing.

2   Definition and Basic Properties

Definition 1. *The k-ary n-cube Q_n^k has $N = k^n$ nodes. Each node has a label of the form $x = x_{n-1}x_{n-2}\ldots x_0$, where $0 \leq x_i < k$ for $0 \leq i < n$. Two nodes $x = x_{n-1}x_{n-2}\ldots x_0$ and $y = y_{n-1}y_{n-2}\ldots y_0$ in Q_n^k are connected if and only if there exists i, $0 \leq i < n$ such that $x_i = y_i \pm 1(\bmod\, k)$ and $x_j = y_j$ for $i \neq j$.*

In the remainder of the paper we omit to write mod k in similar expressions.

We can consider $x_{n-1}x_{n-2}\ldots x_0$ as the radix k representation of an integer in the range 0 to $k^n - 1$. We denote the value of that integer also by x.

It is shown in [5] that Q_n^k has degree $2n$ and diameter $n\lfloor k/2 \rfloor$. Given two nodes x and y in Q_n^k, we denote by $H(x, y)$ the Hamming distance between x and y, i.e., the number of digits in which x and y differ.

Definition 2. *Given two integers l, m, where $l, m \in \{0, 1, \ldots k - 1\}$, we define $w(l, m) = \min(|l - m|, k - |l - m|)$*

The length of the shortest path between $x = x_{n-1}x_{n-2}\ldots x_0$ and $y = y_{n-1}y_{n-2}\ldots y_0$ is equal to the *Lee distance* [14] given by $d_L(x, y) \sum_{i=0}^{n-1} w(x_i, y_i)$. The diameter of Q_n^k is $n\lfloor k/2 \rfloor$ because for a pair of nodes x and y, $w(x_i, y_i)$ can be at most $\lfloor k/2 \rfloor$ for each i.

The OTIS-Q_n^k is composed of $N = k^n$ node-disjoint subgraphs $Q_n^{k(0)}$, $Q_n^{k(1)}$, ..., $Q_n^{k(N-1)}$, called groups. Each of these groups is isomorphic to a k-ary n-cube Q_n^k. A node $<g, x>$ in OTIS-Q_n^k corresponds to a node of address x in group $Q_n^{k(g)}$. We refer to g as the group address of node $<g, x>$ and to x as its processor address.

Definition 3. *The OTIS-Q_n^k network is an undirected graph (V, E) given by*
$V = \{<g, x> | g, x \in Q_n^k\}$ *and*
$E = \{(<g, x>, <g, y>) | (x, y)$ *is an edge in* $Q_n^k\} \cup \{(<g, x>, <x, g>) | g \neq x$ *in* $Q_n^k\}$

An intra-group edge of the form $(<g, x>, <g, y>)$ corresponds to an electrical link. The electrical link $(<g, x>, <g, y>)$ is referred to as link i if x and y differ in the ith digit. An inter-group link of the form $(<g, x>, <x, g>)$ corresponds to an optical link.

It is clear that the size of OTIS-Q_n^k is k^{2n}. The degree of a node $<g, p>$ is $2n + 1$, if $g \neq p$ and $2n$, if $g = p$.

The distance between two nodes $<g, x>$ and $<h, y>$, denoted as $d(g, x, h, y)$ is given by [11]

$$d(g, x, h, y) = \begin{cases} d_L(x, y), & \text{if } g = h \\ \min(d_L(g, h) + d_L(x, y) + 2, \\ \quad d_L(x, h) + d_L(g, y) + 1) & \text{otherwise} \end{cases}$$

The diameter of OTIS-Q_n^k is $2n\lfloor k/2 \rfloor + 1$. [11]

2.1   Enhanced OTIS-Q_n^k

In the enhanced OTIS-Q_n^k we want to add optical links to every node of the form $< g, g >$ to make a topology with uniform node degree. Since there are k^n groups and exactly one added link per group, the total number of links added will be $k^n/2$. If k is odd, then k^n is also odd. That is why enhanced OTIS-Q_n^k is defined only when k is even.

Definition 4. *For a node g in Q_n^k where k is even, we define $\bar{g}_i = (g_i + k/2)$ mod k and $\bar{g} = \bar{g}_{n-1}\bar{g}_{n-2} \dots \bar{g}_0$.*

Note that for any node g there is a unique node $\bar{g}$ in Q_n^k and $d_L(g, \bar{g}) = n(k/2)$ is equal to the diameter of Q_n^k. Also, if $h = \bar{g}$, then $\bar{h} = g$.

The enhanced OTIS-Q_n^k is obtained from OTIS-Q_n^k by connecting every node of the form $<g, g>$ to the node $<\bar{g}, \bar{g}>$ by an optical link. We refer to the links of this form as E-links.

The cost of adding these extra edges is minimal as every node still has the maximum degree $2n + 1$. In OTIS-k-ary n-cube all the nodes are not similar in the sense that nodes of the form $<g, p>$, $g \neq p$ have adjacent optical links but nodes of the form $<g, g>$ have no optical links adjacent to them. This drawback is overcome in E-OTIS-Q_n^k. The other benefit of adding these extra links is the reduction in diameter and length of the shortest path between a pair of nodes.

2.2   Classification of Nodes in E-OTIS-Q_n^k

We divide the nodes of E-OTIS-Q_n^k into classes based on the following definitions:

Definition 5. *Given an n digit radix k number $s = s_{n-1}s_{n-2}\ldots s_0$ and a node g in Q_n^k we denote by $g \oplus s$ the node h where $h_i = g_i + s_i(\mathrm{mod}\,k)$.*

It is to be noted that if x and y are adjacent in Q_n^k, so are $x \oplus s$ and $y \oplus s$. Also, if $h = g \oplus s$, then $\bar{h} = \bar{g} \oplus s$.

Definition 6. *A node $< g, x >$ is in the same class as a node $< g \oplus s, x \oplus s >$, where s is an n-digit radix k number.*

Definition 7. *If $p = < g, x >$ then the node $< g \oplus s, x \oplus s >$ is denoted by p^s.*

Next, we show that the nodes in the same class have the same eccentricity. Before proving this result we investigate some properties of the mapping from p to p^s.

Lemma 1. *If p and q are adjacent in E-OTIS-Q_n^k then so are p^s and q^s.*

Proof. Let $p = < g, x >$ and $q = < h, y >$. We consider two cases.

Case I: p and q are connected by an electrical link. Here, $g = h$ and x and y are adjacent in Q_n^k. Then $x \oplus s$ and $y \oplus s$ are adjacent in Q_n^k and hence p^s and q^s are adjacent in E-OTIS-Q_n^k.

Case II: p and q are connected by optical link. If $g \neq x$ then $q = < x, g >$, i.e., $h = x$ and $y = g$. Then $p^s = < g \oplus s, x \oplus s >$ is connected by an optical link to $< x \oplus s, g \oplus s >= q^s$.

If $g = x$, then $q = < \bar{g}, \bar{g} >$. Hence, $p^s = < g \oplus s, g \oplus s >$ is connected by an optical link to $q^s = < \bar{g} \oplus s, \bar{g} \oplus s >$. □

Lemma 2. *If there is a shortest path of length l between nodes $< g, x >$ and $< h, y >$, then there is a shortest path of length l between $< g \oplus s, x \oplus s >$ and $< h \oplus s, y \oplus s >$.*

Proof. Let the sequence of nodes in the shortest path between $< g, x >$ and $< h, y >$ be $p_0, p_1, \ldots, p_l$ where $p_0 = < g, x >$ and $p_l = < h, y >$. We can consider a sequence of nodes $p_0^s, p_1^s, \ldots, p_l^s$. Now, since p_i and p_{i+1} are adjacent, by lemma 1 so are p_i^s and p_{i+1}^s. So, this sequence of nodes constitute a path from p_0^s to p_l^s. Also, this path must be the shortest. Because, if there is a shorter path of length $m < l$ between $< g \oplus s, x \oplus s >$ and $< h \oplus s, y \oplus s >$, we can construct a path of length m between $< g, x >$ and $< h, y >$. □

Lemma 3. *Nodes in the same class have the same eccentricity.*

Proof. Suppose a node $p = < g, x >$ in E-OTIS-Q_n^k is of eccentricity l. We have to show that a node p^s also has eccentricity l for some arbitrary s.

We define $t = t_{n-1}t_{n-2}\ldots t_0$ where $t_i = k - s_i(\mathrm{mod}\,k)$.

Consider an arbitrary node $q = <h, y>$. We show that we can find a path of length at most l between p^s and $q = <h, y>$. Since, p is of eccentricity l, there is a shortest path of length m, $m \leq l$, between p and $q^t = <h \oplus t, y \oplus t>$. By lemma 2, there is a shortest path of length m between p^s and $<h \oplus t \oplus s, y \oplus t \oplus s> = <h, y>$.

To complete the proof note that there is at least one node r which is at distance l from p. By lemma 2 the node r^s is also at distance l from p^s.   □

Lemma 4. *Two nodes $<g, x>$ and $<0, x \oplus s>$ have the same eccentricity, if $s_i = k - g_i$ mod k for $0 \leq i < n$.*

Proof. By lemma 3 the node $<g, x>$ has the same eccentricity as $<g \oplus s, x \oplus s>$. As s is defined $g \oplus s = 0$.   □

From lemma 4, we can infer that any node in some group g, $g \neq 0$ is in the same class as some other node in group 0. So, we have k^n classes corresponding to k^n nodes in group 0. Also, the nodes in the same class have the same eccentricity. It may be noted that the above results are applicable to ordinary OTIS-Q_n^k as well.

2.3   Diameter of E-OTIS-Q_n^k

Lemma 5. *Given two nodes x and y in Q_n^k, where k is even, $d_L(x, y) + d_L(\bar{x}, y) = nk/2$.*

Proof. Let $\bar{x} = z$. Then $z_i = x_i + k/2$ mod k for all i. So, $w(y_i, x_i) + w(y_i, z_i) = k/2$ for all i. Hence, $d_L(x, y) + d_L(z, y) = \sum_i w(x_i, y_i) + w(y_i, z_i) = nk/2$.   □

Lemma 6. *A node $<g, g>$ in E-OTIS-Q_n^k has eccentricity at most $nk/2 + 1$.*

Proof. We consider an arbitrary node $<h, y>$ and two paths between $<g, g>$ and $<h, y>$. Let l_i denote the length of path i.
path 1: $<g, g> \rightarrow <g, h> \rightarrow <h, g> \rightarrow <h, y> :$
$l_1 = d_L(g, h) + 1 + d_L(g, y)$
path 2: $<g, g> \rightarrow <\bar{g}, \bar{g}> \rightarrow <\bar{g}, h> \rightarrow <h, \bar{g}> \rightarrow <h, y> :$
$l_2 = 1 + d_L(\bar{g}, h) + 1 + d_L(\bar{g}, y)$

Let $l_{min} = \text{minimum}(l_1, l_2)$. Then $l_{min} \leq (l_1 + l_2)/2$. Substituting $d_L(\bar{g}, h) = nk/2 - d_L(g, h)$ (lemma 5), we get $l_{min} \leq (nk + 3)/2$. Since l_{min} must be an integer, $l_{min} \leq \lfloor (nk + 3)/2 \rfloor$. As k is even, $\lfloor (nk + 3)/2 \rfloor = nk/2 + 1$.   □

Lemma 7. *A node $<g, \bar{g}>$ has eccentricity at most $nk/2 + 1$.*

Proof. We consider an arbitrary node $<h, y>$ and two paths between $<g, \bar{g}>$ and $<h, y>$. Let l_i denote the length of path i.

path 1: $<g, \bar{g}> \rightarrow <g, h> \rightarrow <h, g> \rightarrow <h, y> :$
$l_1 = d_L(\bar{g}, h) + 1 + d_L(g, y)$
path 2: $<g, \bar{g}> \rightarrow <\bar{g}, g> \rightarrow <\bar{g}, h> \rightarrow <h, \bar{g}> \rightarrow <h, y> :$
$l_2 = 1 + d_L(g, h) + 1 + d_L(\bar{g}, y)$

Here again, $l_{min} = \text{minimum}(l_1, l_2) \leq nk/2 + 1$.   □

Lemma 8. *A node $< g, x >$, has eccentricity at most minimum $(nk/2 + 2 + \lfloor d_L(g,x)/2 \rfloor, nk + 1 - d_L(g,x))$*

Proof. We consider a set of 4 paths between nodes $< g, x >$ and $< h, y >$. Let l_i be the length of path i.

path 1: $< g, x > \to < g, h > \to < h, g > \to < h, y >$:
$l_1 = d_L(x, h) + 1 + d_L(g, y)$
path 2: $< g, x > \to < x, g > \to < x, h > \to < h, x > \to < h, y >$:
$l_2 = 1 + d_L(g, h) + 1 + d_L(x, y)$
path 3: $< g, x > \to < g, g > \to < \bar{g}, \bar{g} > \to < \bar{g}, h > \to < h, \bar{g} > \to < h, y >$
$l_3 = d_L(g, x) + 1 + d_L(\bar{g}, h) + 1 + d_L(\bar{g}, y)$
path 4: $< g, x > \to < x, g > \to < x, x > \to < \bar{x}, \bar{x} > \to < \bar{x}, h > \to < h, \bar{x} > \to < h, y >$
$l_4 = 1 + d_L(g, x) + 1 + d_L(\bar{x}, h) + 1 + d_L(\bar{x}, y)$
    Let $l_{min} = min(l_1, l_2, l_3, l_4)$. Now, $l_{min} \leq (l_1 + l_2 + l_3 + l_4)/4$. Substituting $d_L(\bar{x}, y) = nk/2 - d_L(x, y)$ we get $l_{min} \leq (2nk + 8 + 2d_L(g, x))/4$. Since l_{min} must be an integer we can say $l_{min} \leq nk/2 + 2 + \lfloor d_L(g, x)/2 \rfloor$. This explains the first term for the expression for eccentricity.
    Since, we can reach $< g, \bar{g} >$ from $< g, x >$ in $nk/2 - d_L(g, x)$ steps, applying lemma 7 we have a path from $< g, x >$ to $< h, y >$ of length $nk/2 - d_L(g, x) + nk/2 + 1$. This explains the second term.   □

Table 1 shows the bound on eccentricity as obtained from lemma 6 and 8 for different $d_L(g, x)$ when $k = 6$ and $n = 2$. $d_L(g, x)$ has minimum value zero corresponding to $x = g$ and maximum value $nk/2$ corresponding to $x = \bar{g}$.

Table 1. Bound on eccentricity

$d_L(g,x)$	upper bound on eccentricity	corresponding expression
0	7	$nk/2 + 1$
1	8	$nk/2 + 2 + \lfloor d_L(g,x)/2 \rfloor$
2	9	$nk/2 + 2 + \lfloor d_L(g,x)/2 \rfloor$
3	9	$nk/2 + 2 + \lfloor d_L(g,x)/2 \rfloor$
4	9	$nk + 1 - d_L(g,x)$
5	8	$nk + 1 - d_L(g,x)$
6	7	$nk/2 + 1$

Now, we state the following theorem regarding the diameter of E-OTIS-Q_n^k.

Theorem 1. *The diameter of E-OTIS-Q_n^k is at most $\lfloor \frac{2nk+5}{3} \rfloor$.*

Proof. Consider any node $< g, x >$. By lemma 8 eccentricity of node $< g, x >$ is the minimum of
$l_1 \leq nk/2 + 2 + d_L(g, x)/2$ and
$l_2 \leq nk + 1 - d_L(g, x)$.
    Hence, minimum $(l_1, l_2) \leq (2l_1 + l_2)/3 \leq \lfloor (2nk + 5)/3 \rfloor$ □

Table 2 lists the diameter of OTIS-Q_n^k and E-OTIS-Q_n^k and the bound specified in Theorem 1. In order to find the actual diameter we apply breadth first search. Since, any node $< g, x >$ is in the same class as some other node in group 0, we need to consider only the nodes in group 0 as root nodes for the breadth first search.

It is seen that the bound given by theorem 1 is either equal to the diameter or exceeds the diameter by one.

Table 2. Diameter and upper bound of E-OTIS-Q_n^k

n	k	diameter of OTIS-Q_n^k	diameter of E-OTIS-Q_n^k	upper bound $\lfloor \frac{2nk+5}{3} \rfloor$
2	4	9	6	7
3	4	13	9	9
4	4	17	12	12
2	6	13	9	9
3	6	19	13	13
2	8	17	12	12
3	8	25	17	17

3 Shortest Path Routing

First we give a routing algorithm for shortest path routing in OTIS-Q_n^k. For a source node $< g, x >$ and destination node $< h, y >$, this algorithm always gives a path of length $d(g, x, h, y)$ defined in section 2.

If $(g = h)$ the shortest path between $< g, x >$ and $< h, y >$ is of length $d_L(x, y)$. Otherwise, $d(g, x, h, y)$ is minimum of
$l_1 = d_L(g, h) + d_L(x, y) + 2$ and
$l_2 = d_L(x, h) + d_L(g, y) + 1$

Let us call the paths corresponding to l_1 and l_2 as path 1 and path 2 respectively. Now we make the following observations

Obs 1. If $g = x$ or $h = y$, then l_2 is shorter than l_1

Obs 2. If $h = x$, then l_2 is shorter than l_1

Obs 3. If $l_1 < l_2$ then we must have $g \neq x$ and $h \neq x$.

We can verify **Obs 1** and **2** just by substituting in the expressions for l_1 and l_2. Now we give the algorithm **Route** (g, x, h, y) to route from $< g, x >$ to $< h, y >$ in an OTIS-Q_n^k.

Route (g, x, h, y) {
If $g = h$ then traverse group g to move to $< g, y >$
    else if $d_L(g, h) + d_L(x, y) + 2 < d_L(x, h) + d_L(g, y) + 1$ then **route1** (g, x, h, y)
        else **route2** (g, x, h, y) }

route1 (g, x, h, y) {
go by optical link to $< x, g >$
traverse group x to $< x, h >$
go by optical link to $< h, x >$
traverse group h to $< h, y >$ }

route2 (g, x, h, y) {
traverse group g to $< g, h >$
go by optical link to $< h, g >$
traverse group h to $< h, y >$ }

Here **route1** and **route2** corresponds to path 1 and 2 respectively. Algorithm **route1** is valid only if $g \neq x$ and $h \neq x$. Note that when we follow path 1, we have $g \neq x$ and $h \neq x$ by obs. 3. For traversing a group, say for going from $< g, x >$ to $< g, h >$, routing algorithm for Q_n^k as given in [11] can be followed.

3.1 Routing in E-OTIS-Q_n^k

The E-links which are added to an OTIS-Q_n^k to get E-OTIS-Q_n^k are of the form $(< p, p >, < \bar{p}, \bar{p} >)$. We show that any shortest path in E-OTIS-Q_n^k can contain a link of this form at most once.

Lemma 9. *In any shortest path from a node $< g, x >$ to a node $< h, y >$, a link of the form $(< p, p >, < \bar{p}, \bar{p} >$ can be present at most once.*

Proof. We prove by contradiction. Let us suppose a shortest path from $< g, x >$ to $< h, y >$ contains more than one E-link. Suppose the first two occurrences of such E-links are of the form $(< p, p >, < \bar{p}, \bar{p} >)$ and and $(< q, q >, < \bar{q}, \bar{q} >$.
Suppose the path is

$$< g, x > \rightarrow < p, p > \rightarrow < \bar{p}, \bar{p} > \rightarrow < q, q > \rightarrow < \bar{q}, \bar{q} > \rightarrow < h, y > \qquad (A)$$

The length of the partial path from $< g, x >$ to $< p, p >$ is
$d_L(g, p) + d_L(x, p) + 1$, if $g \neq p$
$d_L(x, p)$, if $g = p$.
Similarly length of the partial path from $< \bar{p}, \bar{p} >$ to $< q, q >$ is $d_L(\bar{p}, q) + d_L(\bar{p}, q) + 1$. Hence length of the partial path from $< g, x >$ to $< \bar{q}, \bar{q} >$ is greater than or equal to $d_L(g, p) + d_L(p, x) + 2d_L(\bar{p}, q) + 2$
We can reach $< \bar{q}, \bar{q} >$ from $< g, x >$ without using any E-link and length of that path is at most $d_L(g, \bar{q}) + d_L(x, \bar{q}) + 1$.
Now $d_L(g, p) + d_L(p, x) + 2d_L(\bar{p}, q) + 2$
$= d_L(g, p) + d_L(p, \bar{q}) + d_L(x, p) + d_L(p, \bar{q}) + 2$ [as $d_L(\bar{p}, q) = d_L(p, \bar{q})$]
$\geq d_L(g, \bar{q}) + d_L(x, \bar{q}) + 2$
$> d_L(g, \bar{q}) + d_L(x, \bar{q}) + 1$
Hence, path (A) cannot be a shortest path, which is a contradiction.   □

Now we can claim that the shortest path between $< g, x >$ and $< h, y >$ either won't have any E-link or will have only one E-link. In the later case the path will be of the form

$$< g, x > \rightarrow < b, b > \rightarrow < \bar{b}, \bar{b} > \rightarrow < h, y > \qquad (B)$$

Let $C_i(g, x, h, y)$ be the number of times electrical link i is used in the path (B). We call it the the cost associated with the ith digit. We can write $C_i(g, x, h, y) = C_i(g, x, b, b) + C_i(\bar{b}, \bar{b}, h, y)$.

Lemma 10. $C_i(g, x, h, y) = w(g_i, b_i) + w(x_i, b_i) + w(\bar{h}_i, b_i) + w(\bar{y}_i, b_i)$.

Proof. The path from $< g, x >$ to $< b, b >$ is as
$$< g, x > \rightarrow < g, b > \rightarrow < b, g > \rightarrow < b, b >$$
We need to change the ith digit $w(x_i, b_i)$ times while going from $< g, x >$ to $< g, b >$, and $w(g_i, b_i)$ times while going from $< b, g >$ to $< b, b >$. Thus, $C_i(g, x, b, b) = w(g_i, b_i) + w(x_i, b_i)$. Similarly, $C_i(\bar{b}, \bar{b}, h, y) = w(\bar{b}_i, h_i) + w(\bar{b}_i, y_i)$. Since, $w(\bar{b}_i, h_i) = w(b_i + k/2, h_i) = w(b_i, h_i + k/2) = w(b_i, \bar{h}_i)$, we have $C_i(g, x, h, y) = w(g_i, b_i) + w(x_i, b_i) + w(\bar{h}_i, b_i) + w(\bar{y}_i, b_i)$.   □

We are interested in finding optimum b_i such that $C_i(g, x, h, y)$ is minimum.

Definition 8. *Let i_1, i_2, i_3 and i_4 are integers, all in the set $\{0, 1, \cdots, k-1\}$. For a $j \in \{0, 1, \cdots k-1\}$, define $f(j) = w(j, i_1) + w(j, i_2) + w(j, i_3) + w(j, i_4)$ and the set $S(i_1, i_2, i_3, i_4) = \{j | f(j) \text{ is minimum }\}$.*

The following lemmas are related to the above definition.

Lemma 11. *The set $S(i_1, i_2, i_3, i_4)$ will contain at least one integer of the set $\{i_1, i_2, i_3, i_4\}$.*

Proof. In this proof we refer to the set $S(i_1, i_2, i_3, i_4)$ by just S.

Either $S = \{0, 1, \cdots, k-1\}$ or $S \subset \{0, 1, \cdots, k-1\}$. In the former case S contains all of i_1, i_2, i_3 and i_4. In the later case, there exists some $v \in S$ such that either $v + 1 \notin S$ or $v - 1 \notin S$. We claim that v must be one of i_1, i_2, i_3 and i_4.

We prove by contradiction. Suppose v is none of i_1, i_2, i_3 and i_4. Consider two sets $V_+ = \{v+1, v+2, \cdots, v+\frac{k}{2}-1\}$ and $V_- = \{v-1, v-2, \cdots, v-\frac{k}{2}+1\}$. We consider the following cases.

Case 1. None of i_1, i_2, i_3 and i_4 is equal to $\bar{v}$. Then two of them must belong to V_+ and two of them to V_-. Because, if V_+ contains 3 of i_1, i_2, i_3 and i_4, then $f(v+1) = f(v) - 2 < f(v)$ and v cannot belong to S. Similarly if V_- contains 3 of them, then $f(v-1) = f(v) - 2$.

When V_+ contains two of i_1, i_2, i_3 and i_4, and V_- contains the other two, we have $f(v+1) = f(v-1) = f(v)$. Then both $v+1$, and $v-1$ are in S, which violates the definition of v.

Case 2. At least one of i_1, i_2, i_3, and i_4 is equal to $\bar{v}$. Suppose only $i_1 = \bar{v}$ and the other three are not equal to $\bar{v}$. If two of i_2, i_3 and i_4 belong to V_+ and the other belong to V_-, then $f(v-1) = f(v)$ but $f(v+1) = f(v) - 2 < f(v)$. Then v cannot belong to S. Similarly, if more than one of i_1, i_2, i_3 and i_4 are equal to $\bar{v}$, it can be shown that v cannot be in S.

Combining Case 1 and 2, we conclude that it is not possible for v to be none of i_1, i_2, i_3 and i_4.   □

Lemma 12. *If $b_i \in S(g_i, x_i, \bar{h}_i, \bar{y}_i)$ then $C_i(g, x, h, y)$ is minimum.*

Proof. Follows from lemma 10 and definition 8.   □

Now we state the following algorithm (**RTE**). It returns two values : the length of the shortest path involving an E-link and the optimal b.

RTE (g, x, h, y)
{
(1)   sum1 $\leftarrow$ 0; sum2 $\leftarrow$ 0;
(2)   for $i = 0$ to $n - 1$ do $b_i \leftarrow$ **find-b_i**(g_i, x_i, h_i, y_i)
(3)   if (sum1+sum2 $= n$) then $b \leftarrow \bar{h}$
(4)   return $(d(g, x, b, b) + 1 + d(\bar{b}, \bar{b}, h, y), b)$
}

find-b_i (g_i, x_i, h_i, y_i)
{
$B[0] \leftarrow g_i$; $A[0] \leftarrow w(g_i, x_i) + w(g_i, \bar{h}_i) + w(g_i, \bar{y}_i)$;
$B[1] \leftarrow \bar{h}_i$; $A[1] \leftarrow w(\bar{h}_i, g_i) + w(\bar{h}_i, x_i) + w(\bar{h}_i, y_i)$
$B[2] \leftarrow x_i$; $A[2] \leftarrow w(x_i, g_i) + w(x_i, \bar{h}_i) + w(x_i, \bar{y}_i)$
$B[3] \leftarrow \bar{y}_i$; $A[3] \leftarrow w(\bar{y}_i, g_i) + w(\bar{y}_i, x_i) + w(\bar{y}_i, \bar{h}_i)$
$j \leftarrow$ **min-index** $(A[], 4)$
if $j = 0$ and $A[0] = A[1]$ then sum1 $\leftarrow$ sum1 $+ 1$;
if $j = 1$ then sum2 $\leftarrow$ sum2 $+ 1$;
return $(B[j])$
}

min-index $(A[], m)$
{
minimum $\leftarrow A[0]$; $j \leftarrow 0$
for $t = 1$ to $m - 1$ do
        if $A[t] <$ minimum then
                minimum $\leftarrow A[t]$; $j \leftarrow t$;
return (j)
}

We assume that the variables sum1 and sum2 are accessible to both **RTE** and **find-b_i**. The terms $d(g, x, b, b)$ and $d(\bar{b}, \bar{b}, h, y)$ in line (4) of **RTE** correspond to **route** (g, x, b, b) and **route** $(\bar{b}, \bar{b}, h, y)$ respectively and 1 is due to the use of an E-link $< b, b >$ to $< \bar{b}, \bar{b} >$.

The length of the path (B) $= \sum C_i(g, x, h, y)+$ number of optical links in the path. By lemma 12, if $b_i \in S(g_i, x_i, \bar{h}_i, \bar{y}_i)$ then $C_i(g, x, h, y)$ is minimum. The function find-b_i is used to compute the optimal b_i. According to lemma 11, the optimal b_i is one of g_i, x_i, $\bar{h}_i$ and $\bar{y}_i$. In the function find-b_i, two arrays $A[]$ and $B[]$ are created as above and the array $A[]$ is passed to the function **min-index**. The function **min-index** returns the index t for which $A[t]$ is minimum and then **find-b_i** returns $B[t]$. So, the b_i's as set in line (2) of **RTE** are optimal considering the cost $C_i(g, x, h, y)$ for all i. Line (3) of **RTE** is for a possible reduction in number of optical links.

Now, if $b = g$, there is no optical link in the path from $< g, x >$ to $< b, b >$ and if $b = \bar{h}$, there is no optical link in the path from $< \bar{b}, \bar{b} >$ to $< h, y >$. Now, $A[0] = C_i(g, x, h, y)$, if $b_i = g_i$ and $A[1] = C_i(g, x, h, y)$, if $b_i = \bar{h}_i$. When $A[t]$ and $A[u]$ are both minimum but $t < u$, the function **min-index** will return t.

Hence, if g_i is an optimal choice for b_i for all i, b will be set to g in line (2) of **RTE** and there will be no optical link in the path from $< g, x >$ to $< h, y >$. When $b \neq g$, we cannot avoid optical link in the path from $< g, x >$ to $< b, b >$. We check the values sum1 and sum2 to find out if b can be made equal to $\bar{h}$. sum1 is the number of cases when both g_i and $\bar{h}_i$ are optimal choices for b_i. sum2 is the number of cases when only $\bar{h}_i$ is an optimal choice for b_i. If sum1 + sum2 $= n$, we can set $b = \bar{h}$ and avoid optical link in the path from $< \bar{b}, \bar{b} >$ to $< h, y >$.

Lemma 13. *The algorithm RTE always gives the shortest path involving an E-link.*

Proof. By lemma 9, a shortest path involving an E-link, cannot have more than one E-links. The algorithm RTE uses only one E-link $< b, b >$ to $< \bar{b}, \bar{b} >$. From the above discussion it is clear that the choice of b made by algorithm **RTE** is an optimal one. Hence, the proof.   □

Now we state the algorithm for routing in E-OTIS-Q_n^k which we call **Eroute**.

Eroute (g, x, h, y)
{
$L_1 \leftarrow d(g, x, h, y)$
$(L_2, b) \leftarrow$ **RTE**(g, x, h, y)
if $L_1 \leq L_2$ then **route** (g, x, h, y)
else
        route (g, x, b, b)
        follow E-link to $< \bar{b}, \bar{b} >$
        route $(\bar{b}, \bar{b}, h, y)$
}

Theorem 2. *The algorithm* **Eroute** *always routes by the shortest path.*

Proof. The shortest path between two nodes $< g, x >$ and $< h, y >$ either does not have an E-link or has only one E-link. In the former case, the length of the shortest path is L_1 and routing for ordinary OTIS-Q_n^k can be followed. In the later case, the length of the shortest path is L_2 as found by **RTE**.   □

The computation complexity of the algorithm **Eroute** is $O(n)$ since we have to find optimal b_i for $i = 0$ to $n - 1$ and the time to compute each b_i is $O(1)$. The number of hops in the path is at most $\lfloor \frac{2nk+5}{3} \rfloor$. Also, the number of optical links in the computed shortest path is at most 3.

4   Conclusion

We have proposed the architecture enhanced OTIS-k-ary n-cube whose maximum degree is the same as that of OTIS-k-ary n-cube. The OTIS structure is an attractive option for multiprocessor systems as it offers the benefits from both optical and electrical technologies. In [11], a number of properties of k-ary n-cube networks including basic topological properties, embedding, routing, broadcasting, and fault tolerance have been studied. The obtained results [11] confirm the suitability of OTIS-Q_n^k for multiprocessor interconnection networks. E-OTIS-Q_n retains OTIS-Q_n as a subgraph and thus has almost all the desirable properties of OTIS-cube but contains some additional optical links of the form $< g, g >$ to $< \bar{g}, \bar{g} >$. The advantage gained by adding those extra links are, namely, uniform node degree, reduction in diameter, and reduced inter-node distances. The optical links added constitute a fraction $(1/k^n)$ of the total number of optical links present in E-OTIS-Q_n^k. We have proved an upper bound of $\lfloor \frac{2nk+5}{3} \rfloor$ on the diameter of E-OTIS-Q_n^k. We also find the actual diameter for different values of n and k by using breadth first search and find that this bound is quite tight. Our conjecture is that the diameter of E-OTIS-Q_n^k is equal to $\lfloor \frac{2nk+4}{3} \rfloor$. Also, an algorithm for shortest path routing has been developed. It is proved that the algorithm always routes by the shortest path.

References

1. Nugent, S. F.: The iPSC/2 direct-connect communication technology. In: Proceedings of 3rd Conference on Hypercube Concurrent Computers and Applications 1 (1988) 51–60
2. Krishnamoorthy, A., Marchand, P., Kiamilev, F., Esener, S.: Grain-size considerations for optoelectronic multistage interconnection networks. Applied Optics. **31** (1992) 5480–5507
3. Day, K., Al-Ayyoub, A. E.: Topological properties of OTIS-networks. IEEE Transactions on Parallel and Distributed Systems. **13** (2002) 359–366
4. Vanvoorst, B., Seidel, S., Barscz, E.: Workload of an iPSC/860. In: Pro. Scalable High-performance Computing Conference. (1994) 221–228
5. Day, K., Al-Ayyoub, A. E.: Fault diameter of k-ary n-cube networks. IEEE Transactions on Parallel and Distributed Systems. **8** (1997) 903–907
6. Rajasekaran, S., Sahni, S.: Randomized routing, selection, and sorting on the OTIS-Mesh. IEEE Transactions on Parallel and Distributed Systems. **9** (1998) 833–840
7. Wang, C. -F., Sahni, S.: OTIS optoelectronic computers. Parallel Computation Using Optical Interconnections. eds. Li, K., Pan, Y., Zhang, S. Q. (1998) 99–116
8. Sahni, S., Wang, C. -F.: BPC permutations on the OTIS-Mesh optoelectronic computer. In: Proc. Fourth Int'l Conf. Massively Parallel Processing Using Optical Interconnections. (1997) 130–135
9. Wang, C. -F., Sahni, S.: Matrix multiplication on the OTIS-Mesh optoelectronic computer. IEEE Transactions on Computers. **50** (2001) 635–646
10. Wang, C. -F., S. Sahni, S.: Image processing on the OTIS-Mesh optoelectronic computer. IEEE Transactions on Parallel and Distributed Systems. **11** (2000) 97–109
11. Day, K.: Optical transpose k-ary n-cube networks. Journal of System Architecture : the Euromicro Journal. **50** (2004) 697–705
12. Zane, F., Marchand, P., Paturi, R., Esener, S.: Scalable network architectures using the Optical Transpose Interconnection Systems (OTIS). Journal of Parallel and Distributed Computing. **60** (2000) 521–538
13. Das, R. K.: Routing and topological properties of Enhanced OTIS Cube. In: Proc. ADCOM 2005 (2005)
14. Bose, B., Broeg, B., Kwon, Y., Ashir, Y.: Lee distance and topological properties of k-ary n-cubes. IEEE Transactions on Computers. **44** (1995) 1021–1030

Multimedia Traffic Distribution Using Capacitated Multicast Tree

Yong-Jin Lee

Department of Technology Education
Korea National University of Education
San 7, Darak-Ri, Chungwon-Gun, Chungbuk, 363-791, Korea
lyj@knue.ac.kr

Abstract. This study deals with the capacitated multicast tree (CMT) problem, which consists of finding a set of minimum cost multicasting trees rooted at a source node satisfying the traffic requirements at end-nodes. This paper proposes a dynamic programming based algorithm with two phases. In the first phase, the algorithm generates feasible solutions to satisfy the traffic capacity constraint. It finds the optimal multicast trees using matching procedure in the second phase. The proposed algorithm for the CMT problem can be used for efficient multimedia traffic distribution in local area network. Performance evaluation shows that the proposed algorithm has good efficiency for small network with light traffic.

1 Introduction

Most local area networks are currently connected to the Internet via a gateway node such as router or switching hub. Typically, the total traffic volume of end-user nodes that can be served by a port of the gateway node is limited. So, the local area network consists of a gateway node (source) and several trees that cover all end user nodes to satisfy the constraints on traffic volume. When there is the incoming multimedia traffic from the Internet, gateway node should find all the multicast trees to distribute the multimedia traffic to end-user nodes in a local area network quickly. This problem is called as the capacitated multicast tree (CMT) problem. Two methods are available in the literature to solve the problem: heuristic [1,2] and exact [3,4,5,6]. Since the CMT problem is NP-complete [7], optimal solutions for a large problem cannot be obtained in a reasonable amount of computing time. Therefore, heuristic methods have been developed to obtain approximate solutions for large problems. For a small problem where the number of nodes is less than thirty, several exact methods have been reported in the literature. Chandy [3] finds the solution using the branch and bound method, but suffers from the drawback of solving the unconstrained minimum multicasting tree at every stage. Gavish [4] finds a solution for the problem using linear programming relaxation for the case where the distance matrix is symmetric. Gavish [5] formulates the CMT problem using mixed integer programming, and solves using the Bender's decomposition procedure, but the execution time is too large

S. Madria et al. (Eds.): ICDCIT 2006, LNCS 4317, pp. 212–220, 2006.
© Springer-Verlag Berlin Heidelberg 2006

even for only ten nodes. Kershenbaum [6] presents a solution using the depth first rule as the branch rule, but the execution time increases sharply as the number of nodes increases. To summarize, most of existing exact methods use the branch and bound technique. However, in this paper, we use the dynamic programming technique.

Similar problems are MCLP (Minimum Cost Loop Problem) and QoS (Quality of Service) routing problem. MCLP [8] is to find the minimal cost loops rooted at source node. QoS routing problem is to select feasible paths that satisfy various QoS requirements of applications in a network. Multiple additively constrained QoS routing problem is referred as multiple constrained path selection (MCPS) [9,10]. Delay constrained least cost (DCLC) path selection problem [11,12] is to find a path that has the least cost among the paths from source to destination, and the delay of it remains under a given bound. In order to solve the above problems, network configurations such as link connectivity, link cost, and delay should be given. On the other hand, the proposed CMT problem is to find the network configuration composed of several multicasting trees to satisfy the traffic constraint. Since the problem definition of the CMT problem is different from those of MCLP, MCPS and DCLC, direct application of MCLP, MCPS and DCLC solutions to the CMT problem is not possible.

The objective of this paper is to formulate and develop an exact algorithm to solve the CMT problem using new approach. Our proposed algorithm solves the CMT problem in two phases: In the first phase, the algorithm uses dynamic programming to generate feasible solutions to satisfy the traffic capacity constraint. In the second phase, it finds capacitated minimum multicast trees based on the matching procedure.

To investigate the feasibility of the algorithm for real networks, we carry out a performance evaluation of the algorithm. Computational complexity analysis and performance evaluation results demonstrate that our proposed exact algorithm can be effectively applied to the small network with light traffic volume. To shorten the execution time, heuristic methods [1,2] can be used for large networks. The main contributions of this paper are: (i) formulation of the CMT problem, (ii) proposing and evaluation its exact solution by using novel approach, and (iii) depending on the size of the local area network, determining the threshold in choosing between heuristic methods and the exact algorithm.

The rest of the paper is organized as follows. Section 2 describes the mathematical formulation of the CMT problem. Section 3 presents our proposed dynamic programming based modeling and exact algorithm. Section 4 evaluates the computational complexity of our proposed algorithm using an analytical model. Finally, concluding remarks are given in Section 5.

2 Formulation of the Capacitated Multicast Tree Problem

The CMT problem is concerned with finding a set of minimal multicasting trees that are used to form the broadcast trees for real time traffic distribution, such as multimedia.

The end-user nodes are linked together by a tree connected to a port in the source node, where the links connecting the end user nodes have finite capacity, i.e. they can handle limited amount of traffic. This translates to restricting the number of end user nodes served by a single tree. The solution of the CMT problem results in a collection of trees that serve all end user nodes with a minimal connection cost.

We now consider the modeling of the CMT problem. Assume that there is graph, $G=(V, A)$, where $V = \{0,1,2,..,n\}$, traffic requirement at node is λ_i ($\lambda_i \leq \Delta, i \in V- \{0\}$) and link cost between node i and node j is $d_{ij} ((i, j) \in A)$. Δ represents maximum traffic served by single tree. Index 0 represents the source node. The problem formulation is described by Eq. (1).

$$Minimize \ \sum_{i,j} d_{ij} x_{ij}$$

$$S.T.$$

$$\sum_{i \in tree(\alpha)} \lambda_i x_{ij} \leq \Delta$$

$$\sum_{i,j} x_{ij} = n$$

$$x_{ij} = 0 \ or \ 1$$

(1)

The objective of the CMT problem is to find a collection of least-cost multicasting trees rooted at node 0. $tree(\alpha)$ ($\alpha=1,2,..,lcnt$) is the multicasting tree whose one of nodes is connected the source node. $lcnt$ is the number of trees that covers n nodes. A particular case occurs when each λ_i is equal to one. In that case, the constraint means that no more than Δ nodes can belong to any tree of the solution. In Eq. (1), x_{ij} represents link between node i and j (i,j: $i=1,2,..,n$; $j=1,2,..,n$). If link (i, j) is included in any tree ($tree(\alpha)$) of the solution, then x_{ij} is set to 1.

3   Solution of the Capacitated Multicast Tree Problem

In the previous section, we develop solution for the problem. Our solution consists of two phases: subtree generation and matching as described below.

3.1   Subtree Generation Phase

To generate the feasible subtrees of the CMT problem using dynamic programming, we define stage variables and state variables. Stage variable, k ($k=1,2...$), is the number of nodes to form a subtree rooted at the source node to the given node j. State variables, j and S are the node index to be connected and the set of node indexes included in the subtree in order to connect node j, respectively. Then, using the principle of optimality, we obtain the recurrence relation as shown in Eq. (2).

$$If \sum_{q \in S} \lambda_q + \lambda_j \leq \Delta,$$

$$\Psi_k^{(j,S)} = \underset{q \in S, q \neq j}{Min} \ [\Psi_{k-1}^{(q,S-\{q\})} + d_{qj}], \qquad\qquad k = 1$$

$$\Psi_k^{(j,S)} = \underset{q \in S, q \neq j}{Min} \ [\Psi_{k-1}^{(q,S-\{q\})} + d_{qj}, \ \sum_{q \in S, q \neq j} \Psi_1^{(q,\{j\})} - (k-1)d_{j0}], \qquad k \geq 2$$

$$(S \subseteq N_j)$$

$$else$$

$$\Psi_k^{(j,S)} = \infty$$

In Eq. (2), $\Psi_k^{(j,S)}$ represents the least cost to connect node j with the subtrees of which the number of nodes included in S is k. $\Psi_k^{(j,S)}$ is set to infinity when the sum of all the traffic exceeds Δ. Since the boundary condition represents the cost to connect from the source node to node j directly without intermediate nodes, it is defined by Eq. (3).

$$\Psi_0^j = d_{0j} \qquad\qquad (3)$$

To obtain a feasible solution, we compute $\Psi_1^{(j,S)}$ for all (j,S) satisfying $\sum_{q \in S} \lambda_q + \lambda_j \leq \Delta$ by using $\Psi_0^{(j,S)}$. Then, $\Psi_2^{(j,S)}$ is computed using $\Psi_1^{(j,S)}$. By repeating

the procedure, we reach the phase where for all (j,S), $\sum_{q \in S} \lambda_q + \lambda_j > \Delta$.

Since $\Psi_k^{(j,S)}$ are infinity for all (j,S) at such a phase, we set $L=k$. This means that the tree cannot be extended any more. So, subtrees obtained at the previous stage k $(0,1,2,..,L-1)$ are feasible solutions. In Eq. (2), $\sum_{q \in S, q \neq j} \Psi_1^{(q,\{j\})} - (k-1)d_{j0}$ represents

the case where the tree diverges. For example, assume that there are five nodes including source node (index 0) and all the links between nodes are connected. Now, we connect node 2 and source node. For $k = 3$, Eq. (2) can be expressed as: $\Psi_3^{(2,\{1,3,4\})} = $ Min $[\Psi_2^{(1,\{3,4\})}+d_{12}, \Psi_2^{(3,\{1,4\})}+d_{32}, \Psi_2^{(4,\{1,3\})}+d_{42}, \Psi_1^{(1,\{2\})}+\Psi_1^{(3,\{2\})}+\Psi_1^{(4,\{2\})} - 2d_{02}]$ and corresponding feasible connections are depicted in Fig. 1. For (a), (b), and (c) of Fig. 1, since the optimal connection of the circle was already obtained in the previous stage $(k=2)$, it is sufficient to consider only S to connect node 2. Now, we consider the situation where the tree branches off. In Fig. 1(d), since $\Psi_1^{(1,\{2\})} + \Psi_1^{(3,\{2\})} + \Psi_1^{(4,\{2\})} = \Psi_0^2 + d_{21} + \Psi_0^2 + d_{23} + \Psi_0^2 + d_{24} = 3\Psi_0^2 + d_{21} + d_{23} + d_{24} = 3d_{02} + d_{21} + d_{23} + d_{24}$, we

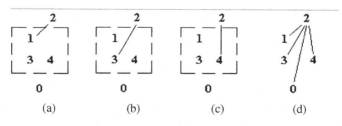

Fig. 1. Feasible connections for $\Psi_3^{(2,\{1,3,4\})}$

have included d_{02} three times. Hence, the cost of Fig. 1(d) becomes $\Psi_1^{(1,\{2\})} + \Psi_1^{(3,\{2\})} + \Psi_1^{(4,\{2\})} - 2d_{02}$. From the above inferences, in the kth stage, the branch cost to node j becomes $\sum_{q \in S, q \neq j} \psi_1^{(q,\{j\})} - (k-1)d_{0j}$.

3.2 Matching Phase

At stage k of the subtree generation phase, $\Psi_k^{(j,S)}$ represents the cost of the tree that is composed of the same elements as $j \cup S$, but the order of elements included in the set is different. Among $\Psi_k^{(j,S)}$, the minimum cost, $\Omega_k^{P(m)}$ is computed. That is, the cost for $P(m)$ at stage k, $\Omega_k^{P(m)}$ is defined as Eq. (4). The value of $\Omega_k^{P(m)}$ from Eq. (4) represents the cost of the tree, which is composed of the same node indexes with different order. Node set corresponding to $\Omega_k^{P(m)}$ is the optimal policy(R_m). R_m is the set of node indexes included in the tree rooted at the source node. Of course, node 0 is not included in R_m. Finally, since n nodes have to be included in any tree (R_m) rooted at the source node without duplicate inclusion in the optimal solution, the optimal solution can be obtained by substituting $\Phi(R_m)$ for $\Omega_k^{P(m)}$ from Eq. (4).

$$\Omega_0^j = \Psi_0^j \qquad\qquad\qquad\qquad k = 0$$

$$\Omega_k^{P(m)} = Min[\Psi_k^{(j,S)}] \qquad\qquad\quad k = 1,2,..,L\text{-}1 \qquad (4)$$

$$\forall (j,S) \text{ such that } P(m) - \{\{j\} \cap S\} = \varnothing$$

There can be several collections composed of the element, R_m satisfying the split condition of set N'. Thus, the global optimal value, G, is the least value among the cost, $\Phi(R_m)$ corresponding to R_m. Properties of the CMT algorithm are as follows:

Lemma 1. Subtree generation phase of the CMT algorithm has the finite stages.

Proof. The finish time of subtree generation phase depends on the relationship between $\Sigma_{i=1}^n \lambda_i$ and Δ. In the worst case ($\Sigma_{i=1}^n \lambda_i \approx \Delta$), we might generate maximum feasible subtrees. In such a case, k is close to n. The maximum of k (= L) can be nearly same as n-1, but more than or equal to n. If L is equal to n, we will find single loop. This is against our assumption ($\Sigma_{i=1}^n \lambda_i > \Delta$). Thus, we can finish the feasible subtree generation phase in at most n-1 stages.   ■

Lemma 2. CMT algorithm produces the optimal solution.

Proof. In the subtree generation phase, we enumerate the feasible subtreess by using the optimality principle of dynamic programming. So, there can be no other feasible subtrees except our solutions. In the matching phase, we first find partitions of which unions compose of the node set, N' = {1,2,..,n}. Next, we generate tress composed of theabove partitions. These trees are found by adding the index of the source node to indexes of both end nodes included in the partition and are sub-optimal solutions. Then, we select the least cost solution among sub-optimal solutions. Therefore, it is natural forthe selected solution to be the global optimal solution.   ■

Because there can be several collections to satisfy the condition, G can be expressed by Eq. (5).

$$\forall R_m \text{ such that } \cup R_m = N' \text{ and } R_i \cap R_j = \varnothing \ (i \neq j),$$
$$G = \text{Min} \ [\Sigma \Phi(R_m)] \tag{5}$$

3.3 Optimal CMT Algorithm

From the above model, the optimal CMT algorithm is described as the following.

ALGORITHM Optimal CMT algorithm
procedure subtree generation phase
00 **begin**
01 **for** $k = 0$ and **for all** j such that $j \notin N'$ **do**

02         $\Psi_0^j \leftarrow d_{0j}$

03 **end for**
04 **while** $\Psi_k^{(j,S)} \neq \infty, \ \forall \ (j,S)$ **do**

05   **if** $\sum\limits_{q \in S} \lambda_q + \lambda_j \ \leq \ \Delta$ **then**

06   **if** $k = 1$, **then**

07                 $\Psi_k^{(j,S)} \leftarrow \underset{q \in S, q \neq j}{Min} \ [\Psi_{k-1}^{(q,S-\{q\})} + d_{qj}]$

08   **else**

09   **for all** k such that $k = 1, 2, .., S$ and $S \subseteq N_j$ **do**

10                 $\Psi_k^{(j,S)} = \underset{q \in S, q \neq j}{Min} \ [\Psi_{k-1}^{(q,S-\{q\})} + d_{qj}, \ \sum\limits_{q \in S, q \neq j} \Psi_1^{(q,\{j\})} - (k-1)d_{j0}]$

11   **end for**
12   **end if**
13   **else** $\Psi_k^{(j,S)} \leftarrow \infty$
14   **end if**
15 **end while**
16 L $\leftarrow k$
17 **end**

procedure matching phase
00 **begin**
01 **for** $k = 0$ and **for all** j such that $j \notin N'$ **do**

02         $\Omega_0^j \leftarrow \Psi_0^j$

03 **end for**
04 **for all** k such that $k = 1, 2, .., L-1$ **do**
05         $m \leftarrow 1$

06   **for all** j such that $j < \underset{q \in S}{\text{Min}}\{q\}$ **do**

07             $P(m) \leftarrow \{j\} \notin S$
08             $m \leftarrow m+1$

```
09    end for
10 end for
11 for all k such that k=1,2,..,L-1 do
12    m ← 1
13    for all (j, S) such that P(m) - {j∉ S} = ∅ do
14        Ω_k^{P(m)} ← Min[Ψ_k^{(j,S)}]
15        m ← m+1
16    end for
17 end for
18 for all m do
19    for all R_m such that ∪R_m = N' and R_i∩R_j = ∅ (i≠j) do
20            find Φ(R_m)
21    end for
22 end for

23 for all m  do
24    G ← Min [ΣΦ(R_m)]
25 end for
26 find the set of optimal trees corresponding to G.
27 end
```

4 Performance Evaluation

In this section, we evaluate the performance of the algorithm in terms of its computational complexity. We first consider the amount of computation in the stage variable (k). It is maximum when the traffic requirement at each node is one ($\lambda_i = 1$, $\forall i$) and the maximum traffic per single loop is Δ. First, for any stage (k), $\Psi_k^{(j,S)}$ must be computed for $k \times {}_nC_{n-1}$ different (j,S) pairs. Since such computation requires k additions and $k-1$ comparisons, where $k = 1$ to L, the number of additions and comparisons in the subtree generation phase are $n(n-1)2^L$ and $n(n-2)2^L$, respectively. In addition, the upper bound for number of additions and comparisons in the subtree generation phase are $n(n-1)2^L$ and $n(n-2)2^L$, respectively.

Fig. 2 represents the number of computations of CMT algorithm for two different cases (heavy traffic- $\Delta \approx 1/2\sum_{i=1}^n \lambda_i$ and light traffic- $\Delta \approx 1/5\sum_{i=1}^n \lambda_i$). In the light traffic and $n=30$, the number of adds and multiplications are 111,360 and 107,520 respectively. These values are so small compared to the performance of modern computer. However, in the heavy traffic and $n=30$, the number of adds and multiplications are increased to 2.85×10^7 and 2.75×10^7 respectively.

Table 1 shows the memory amount of CMT algorithm for two different cases (heavy traffc- $\Delta \approx 1/2\sum_{i=1}^n \lambda_i$ and light traffic- $\Delta \approx 1/5\sum_{i=1}^n \lambda_i$). For each case, ten problems were randomly generated and executed on workstation. CMT algorithm shows the best efficiency when the sum of the traffic requirements is much less than Δ. That is, whenthe number of nodes is 10, mean execution times for light and heavy traffic

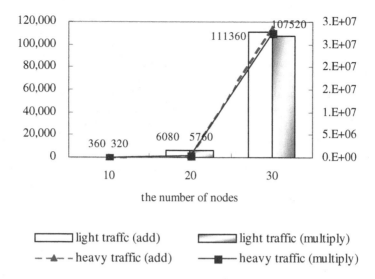

Fig. 2. The number of computations

cases are 0.3 and 0.2 seconds, respectively. On the other hand, when the number of nodes is 30, mean execution times for light and heavy traffic cases are 60 and 200 seconds respectively. As the number of nodes becomes large, memory access time increases remarkably. The reason is why $k \times {}_nC_{n-1}$ storage spaces are required in each stage k to store $\Psi_k^{(j,S)}$. However, the current main memory cannot maintain all the results from the previous computation. If we can use the huge main memory, we will reduce the computation time. In addition, the reason for the less execution time in the light traffics is that since L value in CMT algorithm becomes small in light traffic case, the amount of computations for CMT algorithm also becomes small. To summarize, the proposed CMT algorithm is affected by the traffic volume and Δ, and is effective in the case when the number of nodes is less than thirty and the traffic volume is light. Since the execution time increases rapidly for more than thirty nodes or heavy traffic case, it is desirable to use the heuristic method for the network with large nodes or heavy traffic.

Table 1. Storage space requirements

n case	10	20	30
light traffic	36	77,520	46,823,400
heavy traffic	1,260	1,847,560	232,6762,800

5 Conclusions

The CMT problem is used to discover multicasting trees for real-time multimedia traffic distribution from the source node to end nodes in local area network. In this paper, we have presented the problem formulation and an exact algorithm for the CMT problem. The proposed exact algorithm minimizes the total cost to discover the capacitated multicasting trees rooted at a source node. It consists of generating the feasible trees using dynamic programming and finding the minimum multicasting trees by using the matching procedure. The algorithm can be applied to any network regardless of its configuration. Computational complexity analysis and performance evaluation show that the proposed algorithm is effective for small network with the light traffic volume. Future work includes of developing algorithms for the network with the stochastic traffic requirements.

Acknowledgement

This work has been supported in part by the '05 research grant from Korea National University of Education.

References

1. Lee, Y. and Atiquzzaman, M.: Least Cost Multicast Multicasting Tree Algorithm for Local Computer Network. Lecture Notes in Computer Science, Vol. 3619. (2005) 268-275.
2. Lee, Y. and Atiquzzaman, M.: Least Cost Heuristic for the Delay-Constrained Capacitated Minimum Multicasting Tree Problem. Computer Communications, Vol. 28, No. 11. (2005) 1371-1379.
3. Chandy K and Lo T. The Capacitated Minimum Multicasting Tree Networks. Networks 3. (1973) 173-181.
4. Gavish B. Augmented Based Algorithm for Centralized Network Design. IEEE Trans. on. Comm, Vol. 33, No. 12. (1985) 1247-1257.
5. Gavish B. Topological Design of Centralized Computer Networks Formulations and Algorithms. Networks, Vol. 12. (1982) 55-357.
6. Kershenbaum A and Boorstyn R. Centralized Teleprocessing Network Design. Networks, Vol. 13. (1983) 279-293.
7. Papadimitriou C. The Complexity of the Capacitated Tree Problem. Networks, Vol. 8. (1978) 217- 230.
8. Lee, Y. and Atiquzzaman, M.: Optimal Multicast Loop Algorithm for Multimedia Traffic Distribution. Lecture Notes in Computer Science, Vol. 3824. (2005) 1099-1106.
9. Cheng, G. and Ansari, N.: On Multiple Additively Constrained Path Selection. IEE Proc. Communications, Vol. 149, No. 5. (2002) 237-241.
10. Cheng, G. and Ansari, N.: Finding All Hop(s) Shortest Path. IEEE Communications Letters, Vol. 8, No. 2. (2004) 122-124.
11. Cheng, G. and Ansari, N.: Achieving 100% Success Ratio in Finding the Delay Constrained Least Cost Path. Proc. of IEEE GLOBECOM '04. (2004) 1505-1509.
12. Juttner, A., Szyiatowszki, Mecs, I., and Rajko, Z.: Lagrange relaxation based method for the QoS ruoting problem. Proc. IEEE INFOCOM '01. (2001) 859-869.

Application-Level Checkpointing Techniques for Parallel Programs*

John Paul Walters[1] and Vipin Chaudhary[2]

[1] Institute for Scientific Computing
Wayne State University
jwalters@wayne.edu
[2] Department of Computer Science and Engineering
University at Buffalo, The State University of New York
vipin@buffalo.edu

Abstract. In its simplest form, checkpointing is the act of saving a program's computation state in a form external to the running program, e.g. the computation state is saved to a filesystem. The checkpoint files can then be used to resume computation upon failure of the original process(s), hopefully with minimal loss of computing work. A checkpoint can be taken using a variety of techniques in every level of the system, from utilizing special hardware/architectural checkpointing features through modification of the user's source code. This survey will discuss the various techniques used in application-level checkpointing, with special attention being paid to techniques for checkpointing parallel and distributed applications.

1 Introduction

When programmers seek to write code resilient to failures, the typical course of action is to resort to application checkpointing. Application checkpointing is the act of saving the state of a computation such that, in the event of failure, it can be recovered with only minimal loss of computation. This is especially useful in areas such as computational biology where it is not unusual for an application to run for many weeks before completion [1]. In such cases it is possible for the program's running time to exceed the hardware's failure rate. If the application cannot be recovered from some intermediate point in the computation, it is reasonable to expect that the application may never finish. A high-level overview of the necessary components of checkpointing could be written as:

1. Interrupt the computation.
2. Save the address space to a file.
3. Save the register set to a file.

---

* This research was supported in part by NSF IGERT grant 9987598 and the Institute for Scientific Computing at Wayne State University.

S. Madria et al. (Eds.): ICDCIT 2006, LNCS 4317, pp. 221–234, 2006.

Other attributes could also be saved, including sockets, open files, and pipes. But the items listed above suffice to accurately restore a computation.

The problem is compounded when considering clusters of machines, all of which fail independently at some given rate. If the application makes use of the entire cluster, then the failure of a single machine will halt progress of the entire application. In these cases programmers would like to make use of application checkpointing schemes in the distributed environment, but the problem can no longer be solved by simply taking a snapshot of each process as there may be messages in transit that none of the individual processes would lay claim to.

Consider also the case of grid computing. In this case, all of the complexities of computing in the distributed manner apply (messages in transit, synchronizing multiple processes) but new problems arise as well. In a grid environment individual machines may be under the control of different administrative domains. Indeed the identity of any particular node responsible for running a programmer's code may be unknown to the programmer. In such cases, checkpoints cannot simply be saved to local filesystems, but must be funneled to a known location. Furthermore, the heterogeneous nature of the grid makes it exceedingly possible that machines of different architectures are allocated to the programmer upon resuming the application. One solution to this problem would be to mandate a certain architecture for the application. While such a solution would work, a better solution would handle checkpoint resumption on heterogeneous architectures.

To address the problems above, a series of checkpoint techniques have been developed that provide programmers with varying degrees of checkpointing transparency. The four major categories are as follows [2,3]:

1 Hardware-level, additional hardware is incorporated into the processor to save state [3].
2 Kernel-level, the operating system is primarily responsible for checkpointing running programs [4,5,6].
3 User-level, a checkpointing library is linked into a program that will be responsible for checkpointing the program independent of the programmer [7,8].
4 Application-level, the checkpointing code is inserted directly into the application by a programmer/preprocessor.

This survey will present the major techniques used in application-level checkpointing with special attention being paid to distributed/grid applications. In figure 1, a taxonomy of common application-level checkpointing schemes is presented, including a classification of the specific implementations discussed in this survey.

A related problem is the issue of process and thread migration [9,10,11,2]. While this survey does not specifically address the issue of process migration, it is worth noting that many of the challenges associated with application checkpointing arise in the case of process migration as the two problems are nearly identical in nature.

Application–Level

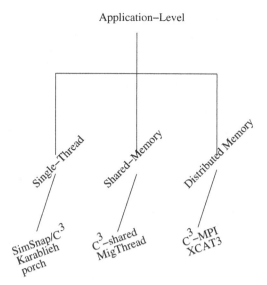

Fig. 1. A taxonomy of application-level checkpointing schemes

2   Application-Level Checkpointing

Application-level checkpointing represents the highest degree of abstraction from the process itself. Unlike the more transparent techniques of kernel-level check-pointing and user-level checkpointing, application-level checkpointing requires more programmer interaction. It would seem then that application-level schemes are at a disadvantage when compared to their user-level and kernel-level coun-terparts. But application-level checkpointing carries with it several distinct ad-vantages over the lower-level techniques, including its overall portability.

2.1   Introduction

The essence of application-level checkpointing is to place the checkpointing bur-den on the application itself, rather than the operating system or a set of user-level libraries that are linked into the program. In order to accomplish the self-checkpointing, the program source must be modified to support checkpoint-ing. Unlike other techniques (such as user-level checkpointing), application-level checkpointing seeks to abstract the application state to the application-level. Thus, the process state is not saved through low-level system calls. Instead, compiler assistance (typically in the form of a pre-processor) is used in a tech-nique called "code instrumentation" [12,1,13,14,15,16,17,18,19].

Ideally, the use of application-level checkpointing would not require additional effort from the programmer. That is, the programmer should not be held respon-sible for adding the checkpointing code himself. To avoid this, the pre-processor scans the original code provided by the programmer, inserts the necessary check-pointing constructs, and outputs the checkpoint-enabled code. The new code should function no different than the original, with the exception of the addition of the checkpointing functionality.

As mentioned above the application-level code must represent the low-level program status (program counter, etc.) in terms of higher level constructs. For instance, application-level stacks are implemented to keep track of a program's place when nested inside function calls. Each time the application enters a function, the function ID (another application-level construct) is pushed onto the checkpointing stack. Similarly, when an application leaves a function, the function ID is removed from the checkpointing stack.

Since the application does not make use of the low-level representation of the process, checkpointing code must be inserted such that a program simply executes the checkpointing code at appropriate times during its execution. Of course, this means that the code can no longer be checkpointing at arbitrary points (via interruption). Furthermore, when the application is restored the application-level scheme cannot simply restore the program-counter to return the application to the appropriate point. Instead, a series of jump statements are used to allow the application to simply initialize variables but skip the checkpointed computations in order to recover from a failure.

While the above may seem to be a disadvantage to the application-level scheme, such a technique allows for three distinct advantages: language independence/portability, checkpoint size, and checkpoint heterogeneity. We now consider each of these in turn.

At the user-level, the checkpointing schemes rely heavily on system calls provided by the operating system in order to gain access to low-level process information. Furthermore, these system calls are not necessarily available in all languages. Most user-level techniques appear to assume that the "C" language is the only one used by programmers, including the area of scientific computing. This doesn't mean that user-level techniques cannot be used in different languages, but that the techniques must be adapted depending on the environment. Application-level checkpointing schemes, on the other hand, have the potential to be implemented independent of the language provided that the basic language constructs are present.

The checkpoint size is also of great concern when checkpointing large applications. Using standard user-level checkpointing techniques or kernel-level techniques typically save nearly the entire process state including data that need not be saved in order to recover the application. For example, in [1] the authors note that in "protein-folding applications on the IBM Blue Gene machine, an application-level checkpoint is a few megabytes in size whereas a full system-level checkpoint is a few terabytes." Of course the example just presented is rather drastic, but the advantage remains clear - application-level checkpointing has the capacity to dramatically reduce checkpoint size. The advantage to smaller checkpoint sizes is even more clear when checkpointing grid-based applications.

The third major advantage is that of heterogeneity. This too is particularly advantageous in grid-enabled applications. In such an environment, one may not have access to sufficient homogeneous resources. In fact, one may not even have access to the same grid resources in subsequent application runs. For this reason, heterogeneous checkpointing becomes a distinct advantage. It potentially allows a programmer to take advantage of many more resources that would otherwise go unused. But the real advantage occurs when a node fails. In such a case it may happen that the only available nodes to replace the failed one are heterogeneous to the failed node. In such a case, using a heterogeneous checkpointing scheme, a new node can be selected without regard for its system software or architecture. Furthermore, application-level schemes allow a larger portion of the application to be checkpointed and restored to heterogeneous systems, including pointers.

Of course, there are disadvantages to the application-level technique. For example, applications can only be checkpointed if their source code is available to the pre-processor. Another shortcoming to application-level checkpointing is the difficulty in representing a running program's state. As discussed previously, an application-level technique cannot depend on low-level system calls to discern a running program's state. Similarly, multi-threaded applications must take special care in order to ensure thread synchrony, given that multiple threads will not reach a checkpoint simultaneously.

The final major shortcoming of the application-level technique relates to the issue of heterogeneity. While the application-level scheme may naturally lend itself to portability, one major problem is the manner in which data should be represented. Since different architectures represent data types in different sizes (not to mention different endianness), a technique to convert data on one architecture to meaningful data on another is needed. One standard solution is to use a machine independent technique, the classic example being XDR (External Data Representation) [20]. Some newer application-level schemes have used an XML-based format as well [21]. The major shortcoming to using an intermediate format technique is that all data must be converted twice, once during the checkpoint and again during the restore. Depending on the amount of data that needs converting as well as the frequency at which checkpoints are taking, this extra conversion could be significant. Another technique is to appeal to the lowest precision in the group [22] or to save all checkpoint data in a precision that is higher than that of any of the machines within the group. Both of these techniques suffer from the disadvantage that a conversion is required, even if the checkpoint is being restored to the machine on which it was taken. In addition, the technique of saving in the lowest precision of the group requires knowledge of the group members before checkpointing takes place. In many situtations, particularly grid scenarios, this information may be unavailable. And saving in a precision that is higher than any member of the group not only requires knowledge of the group, but would also lead to inflated checkpoint sizes.

A third technique to data conversion seeks to eliminate the conversion step altogether if at all possible. Ine one such technique, called "receiver makes right," the originator of the data simply checkpoints the data in its own precision. This technique has been used in [14] as well as in PVM [23]. In this case, the receiver is charged with ensuring that the data conversion takes place when necessary. In many cases, such as when a checkpoint is restored to the same machine on which it was taken, the data conversion can be skipped altogether. In the case of large checkpoints, the time savings could be significant. Should the receiver's architecture differ such that data conversion is necessary, the checkpoint data can be converted.

At the outset, the "receiver makes right" scheme seems like the logical choice. However, data conversion issues arise in the case of architecture differences. For example, a 32 bit data type can be adapted to fit in to a 64 bit data type on another architecture with relative ease. But how to handle the case of adapting a 64 bit data type to a 32 bit data type is non-trivial. In such a case, the possibility exists that the conversion simply cannot proceed as the resulting inaccuracy would be unacceptable.

We next consider three types of application-level checkpointing techniques: single-threaded, multi-threaded, and cluster/grid-enabled application-level checkpointing. Each of these categories carries with it its own difficulties, with each building upon the previous. We begin with single-threaded checkpointing.

2.2   Single-Threaded Application-Level Checkpointing

In [17] a technique similar to PORCH [22] is discussed. The goal is to provide a heterogeneous checkpointing scheme capable of checkpointing "real" programs, including pointers and unions, both of which are known to cause portability problems. They make use of a pre-processor to transform a programmer's code into a functionally similar, but checkpointable, program.

To address the data conversion issues, [17] uses a technique similar to the "receiver makes right" method. Data is always saved in the accuracy of the machine on which the checkpoint is performed. They force the restoring process to first determine its own accuracy and then perform any necessary conversion. Each process can determine its accuracy at runtime, which they claim makes their technique portable to any architecture. The accuracy of a particular architecture is determined by exploiting properties of computer arithmetic developed by [24].

There are several different techniques used to save the state of variables in [17]. Global variables are saved using a series of macros that are generated by the pre-processor. To handle stack variables, the pre-processor encapsulates all local (stack) variables within a particular scope inside a structure. Just as in the case of the global variables, a series of macros are generated in order to facilitate saving the particular variable, which in this case is a structure of variables.

The program itself will likely make calls to additional functions. In order to facilitate rebuilding the execution stack a data structure called the "state stack" is used. Each element of the "state stack" contains three fields. The first is a pointer to the structure containing the local variables. The second is a pointer to a function (generated by the pre-processor) that is capable of saving the state of the local variables. The final field is a label to the callout position of the current scope. The callout of a function is simply the point at which a new function is called from the current scope [17].

In order to facilitate the restoring of an application, an application-level abstraction of the program counter is needed. This is accomplished by making use of the labels described above. Before each function call (with the exception of checkpoints) a label is inserted. A label is also inserted after a checkpoint [17]. This label is used in the nodes that are pushed onto the "state stack" described above. Such a technique allows a restored application to skip unnecessary computation. Upon restoration, the function simply rebuilds its state stack. This is done by restoring the local variables on each node of the state stack and then skipping directly to the next function call (using the labels). Function calls are then entered in the correct order and their variables restored accordingly.

One common difficulty in application checkpointing, particularly heterogeneous checkpointing, is how to handle pointers and other dynamically allocated data. Karablieh, Bazzi, and Hicks solve this problem by the introduction of a memory refractor, which essentially introduces an additional level of indirection to achieve portability [17]. The memory refractor itself is an array of data structures and is divided into three parts including the global variables, stack, and heap variables [17]. All variables, including non-pointers are kept in the memory refractor. In doing so, the authors are able to effectively abstract the specific memory location from the particular variable by introducing an index for each variable. Pointers then point to the memory refractor entry for a variable, rather than a specific memory location. This, according to [17] allows for portable pointers as well as rebuilding pointers upon recovery. Karablieh, Bazzi and Hicks acknowledge that this is not necessarily the most efficient scheme, but suggest that the portability and heterogeneity of their technique outweighs its inefficiency.

In [18] a novel use for application-level checkpointing is discussed. Rather than exploiting application-level checkpointing for its fault-tolerance and load-balancing characteristics, Szwed et al. describe its use in fast-forwarding applications towards architectural simulation. One can consider fast-forwarding, in their sense, to be roughly equivalent checkpointing/restarting. The difference in this case is that application is restored to a simulator from natively executing code. This acts roughly as an accelerator where researchers can use native execution to "fast-forward" to the more interesting code segments. At a certain point in the code a checkpoint is then taken which is then restored to a simulator. The simulator then continues the computation without modification to the simulator itself. According to [18], such a technique is useful for performing time-consuming cycle accurate simulations on only a particular code segment of interest.

To perform the checkpointing and migration necessary for the simulator, Szwed et al. make use of the Cornell Checkpoint Compiler (C^3) [25,26]. C^3 consists of two components: a source-to-source compiler (pre-processor) and a runtime library. As would be expected, the pre-processor is used to convert the source code of an application into a semantically equivalent version, capable of self-checkpointing [18]. The runtime library includes checkpointable versions of several key "C" library functions.

The C^3 system also makes use of a "position stack" that acts similar to the "state stack" used in [17]. In [18], a label is still inserted after every checkpoint and before every function that might lead to a checkpoint. The authors perform a call-graph analysis in order to determine which function calls could lead to a checkpoint.

The most unique aspect of C^3 is the method used to restore variables and pointers. C^3 depends on variables being restored to their original memory locations in order to properly restore pointers. To do this, C^3 contains its own versions of the standard "C" memory functions. The most notable of these is the "memory allocator." In this case the memory allocator not only ensures that data is restored to its original address, but also manages heap data in the memory pool. The memory pool is what allows the allocator to restore pointers. Upon restart, the allocator requests from the operating system that the exact same pool of memory be allocated to the process. In doing so, variables can be simply copied from the checkpoint file back into memory without requiring any additional pointer indirection such as in [17].

2.3   Shared-Memory Application-Level Checkpointing

Of course, application-level checkpointing is not limited to single-threaded applications. Indeed there are many different application-level checkpointing schemes targeted at shared memory applications. Here we will discuss two such techniques, a variation on the C^3 scheme, and *MigThread*. These techniques represent two different approaches to the application-level checkpointing scheme as well as different assumptions related to the underlying architectures.

We begin with *MigThread* [27]. In this case, Checkpoints are inserted by the programmer, and it is the programmer's responsibility to ensure program correctness when executing the checkpoint. That is, in order to ensure that an accurate global state is checkpointed, the programmer should enclose the checkpoint in any necessary barriers. The standard technique of using a pre-processor as well as a runtime support module is used in *MigThread* as well.

What's unique about *MigThread* is its heterogeneity and its ability to checkpoint/restart individual threads on remote (possibly heterogeneous) machines. The key to its heterogeneity is its data conversion technique, dubbed "course-grain tagged receiver makes right" (CGT-RMR). This technique allows the sender (or checkpoint initiator) to save the checkpoint data in its own native format. Any conversion that needs to be done will be performed by the receiver upon restarting the checkpoint. This reduces the number of conversions required, possibly to zero if the architecture of the restored checkpoint is the same as when the checkpoint was taken. Data is identified by a series of tags that are generated automatically by the pre-processor and inserted into the user's source code.

One advantage to the technique used by *MigThread* is that is can handle both pointers and dynamic memory without requiring the use of a memory refractor as in [17]. Variables are collected into two different structures, depending on whether they're pointers or non-pointers. This is done at both a global level and at the function level. Upon restoring a checkpoint, the pointers within the pointer structure can be traced and updated according to their new memory locations.

As mentioned above, *MigThread* also supports the checkpointing of individual threads. This is done by invoking the application on the target/restore machine and indicating that a particular thread should be restored. The thread specified through a configuration file is then restored independent of any additional threads. This can be particularly useful in load balancing applications.

A variation on the C^3 system that is capable of checkpointing shared memory systems is dedescribed in [1]. In particular, this system is designed to operate using the OpenMP multi-threading compiler directives [28].

In the shared memory implementation of C^3, variables are saved similarly to the technique described in [18]. Most importantly, the memory pool is still used in order to restore pointer variables to their original locations. This has important implications, as the authors note. In particular, the C^3 checkpoints are generally not portable to heterogeneous architectures due to the fact that the C^3 system performs no data conversion, not even converting between little and big endian.

The most interesting features of C^3 system are its synchronization constructs. The problem is that calls to checkpoint a thread are hints and may not occur each time a thread comes across a checkpoint. Given that no assumptions can be made as to the rate at which threads progress it is possible for two or more threads to deadlock at a checkpoint. For example, consider a two-threaded application where the first thread reaches an application barrier while the second reaches a checkpoint barrier. In such a scenario, neither thread will progress as the first is waiting for the second at the application barrier, and the second is waiting for the first at a checkpoint barrier.

The solution to this problem, according to [1] is to ensure that a checkpoint never crosses an application barrier. In order to do this, C^3 intercepts calls to the OpenMP API and introduces a global **checkpointFlag** variable. When a thread wishes to take a checkpoint it first sets the **checkpointFlag** variable to true and then proceeds to the first checkpoint barrier. Threads that are waiting at an application barrier poll the **checkpointFlag** variable. If they find that it is set to true, the threads waiting at the application barrier immediately begin a checkpoint before returning to the application barrier.

Locks are another problem that must be addressed. The problem is that one thread may hold a mutex and wish to checkpoint, while a second thread may wish to first aquire the mutex before checkpointing. In order for the second thread to perform the checkpoint, the first thread must release its mutex. A proper checkpoint library should ensure that when the application is restored the mutex will be returned to the first thread. To ensure that this occurs, threads are charged with maintaining a table of their own mutexes. Upon restore, each thread checks its table and releases any mutexes that it should not hold.

2.4 Grid/Cluster Application-Level Checkpointing

We now turn to the final type of application-level checkpointing, in particular checkpointing for cluster and grid-based applications. There are a variety of techniques that have been used in order to perform checkpointing in distributed systems, most of which focuses on message-passing systems. In particular, [29] presents a survey of many techniques that are applicable both to user-level and application-level checkpointing. In this section, two typical coordinated check-pointing algorithms will be discussed. But it is worth noting that, according to [29], other techniques also exist including message logging. In [30] an additional technique is used that essentially turns a distributed system into a shared memory system. The advantage of this technique is that techniques used to checkpoint parallel or shared-memory systems can also be adapted. The disadvantage is that most distributed systems do not allow a task to read and write to the remote address space of another task.

The first checkpointing protocol for message passing systems that will be examined again utilizes the C^3 system. This time, however, the focus is not on the C^3 system itself, but rather the protocol used to guarantee an accurate and consistent global state for MPI programs [26]. A coordinated checkpointing protocol is one in which processes checkpoint together, typically by utilizing a initiator that is responsible for coordinating the protocol. Non-coordinated checkpointing protocols are also possible, some of which are described in [29]. The main problem with the non-coordinated technique is the possibility of their experiencing the "domino effect" due to inconsistent global states. The "domino effect" can lead to the failure of every checkpoint, eventually requiring that the application be restarted [31].

The coordinated technique used in C^3 uses an initiator that is responsible for initiating and coordinating the checkpoint protocol. In C^3 the initiator is simply process 0. When the application is instrumented with the C^3 system more checkpoints are inserted than may be needed. It is therefore the initiator's responsibility to begin the checkpoint when necessary.

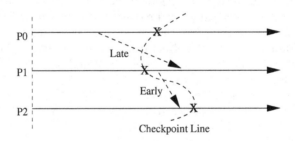

Fig. 2. Illustration of late and early messages

The primary problem with checkpointing message-passing systems is in dealing with both late and early messages. This is a problem in application-level schemes (particularly MPI due to the "tag" that is placed on a message) as there is no guarantee of FIFO message delivery. A late message is one that crosses a checkpoint line in the forward direction. That is, a process sends a message, a checkpoint is taken, and the destination process receives the message after the checkpoint. The problem in this case is that upon resuming from the intermediate checkpoint, the first process will have already sent the message before the checkpoint and will not resend it after the checkpoint. But the receiving process, which did not receive the message until after the checkpoint, will not receive the message on restart as the sending process will not have re-sent it. Therefore, the global state will be inconsistent.

A similar problem occurs if a message crosses a checkpoint line in the reverse direction. In this case, however, a process will have taken a checkpoint and proceeded to send a message to another process which has not yet taken the checkpoint. Upon restarting from the checkpoint, the receiving process will have already received the message, while the sending process will again re-send the message, resulting in duplicate messages being sent. In order to maintain a consistant global state, such duplicate messages should be suppressed.

Both late and early messages are illustrated in figure 2. An arrow indicates a sent message, where the source is the arrow's origin with the arrow pointing at the destination.

In [26] a 4-phase protocol for C^3 is described that solves the problem of late and early messages. The first phase begins the protocol when the initiator sends a **pleasecheckpoint** message to all processes indicating that a checkpoint should take place when the process reaches its next checkpoint location. Processes at this state are still free to send and receive messages freely.

Phase two begins once a process reaches a checkpoint location. It saves its state including all early messages and begins waiting for, and recording, late messages. When all messages have been received (this is done by comparing the messages sent/received from each process similar to that described in [5]), the process sends a **readytostoprecording** message to the initiator, but still continues to record.

When the initiator receives the **readytostoprecording** from all processes it responds with a **stopRecording** message directed to all processes (phase 3). Phase 4 terminates the protocol when the application stops recording to its checkpoint file. A process stops recording when either it receives the **stopRecording** message from the initiator or when it receives a message from a process that has already stopped recording (since there is no guarantee of FIFO message delivery, etcetera). At this point the process then sends a **stoppedRecording** message back to the initiator. Once the initiator receives the **stoppedRecording** message from all processes the checkpoint can be written to disk and the protocol terminated [26].

In XCAT3 [21] a slightly different protocol is used to checkpoint grid-based applications. Unlike the non-blocking technique used in [26], Krishnan and Gannon describe a blocking approach to grid-based checkpointing. The primary difference between blocking and non-blocking coordinated checkpointing is that in the blocking case a consistant global state is achieved by emptying the communication channel before checkpointing. A high-level description of such a protocol consists of three phases.

1. Empty communications channel.
2. Individual processes checkpoint their local state.
3. Computation resumes.

The checkpointing protocol requires changes to the *XCAT3* architecture, particularly in implementing the application coordinator. The application coordinator essentially serves the same function as the initiator but also provides some additional grid-specific services. In particular, the coordinator provides references into the grid file storage service. This is particularly important in a grid-scenario as a global filesystem such as NFS is not necessarily available, and a checkpoint saved only to local storage would likely prove useless. Therefore a more resilient storage mechanism is needed. In the *XCAT3* system this is provided by a "master storage service" [21].

In the *XCAT3* system a checkpoint is initiated by a user who instructs the application coordinator to being a checkpoint. Upon receiving this, the application coordinator sends a **freezeComponent** message to each mobile component ID. One can think of the mobile component ID as a remote process. When the mobile component receives the **freezeComponent** message it waits for all "remote invocations" to complete.

Once the application coordinator receives a **componentFrozen** message from each component the coordinator can be certain that all communication has been terminated. The coordinator then sends each remote component a reference to an individual storage service on the master storage service as part of a **storeComponentState** message.

Upon receiving the **storeComponentState** message each remote component stores its complete computation state at the location given by the individual storage service. After storing the individual checkpoint at the individual storage service, a storageID is generated and returned to the component. The components then return the storageID to the application coordinator.

The application coordinator stores references to the storageID into its own stable storage so that the checkpoints can be easily located. Upon committing the references to stable storage, the application coordinator sends a **unfreezeComponent** message to each component and computation resumes.

3   Conclusions

Given the current interest in grid-based systems and the potential (indeed likelihood) for a grid to be composed of an array of different architectures and operating systems, it seems likely that the focus of checkpointing researchers will be aimed more towards distributed and grid-based checkpointing than shared-memory or single process checkpointing. With that in mind, it is the opinion of these authors that application-level checkpointing will be the focus of checkpointing for the near futur due primarily to its support for heterogeneity.

References

1. Bronevetsky, G., Marques, D., Pingali, K., Szwed, P., Schulz, M.: Application-level checkpointing for shared memory programs. In: ASPLOS-XI: Proceedings of the 11th international conference on Architectural support for programming languages and operating systems, ACM Press (2004) 235–247

2. Milojicic, D.S., Douglis, F., Paindaveine, Y., Wheeler, R., Zhou, S.: Process migration. ACM Comput. Surv. **32**(3) (2000) 241–299
3. Sorin, D.J., Martin, M.M.K., Hill, M.D., Wood, D.A.: Safetynet: improving the availability of shared memory multiprocessors with global checkpoint/recovery. In: ISCA '02: Proceedings of the 29th annual international symposium on Computer architecture, IEEE Computer Society (2002) 123–134
4. Duell, J.: The design and implementation of berkeley lab's linux checkpoint/restart (2003) http://old-www.nersc.gov/research/FTG/ checkpoint/reports.html.
5. Sankaran, S., Squyres, J.M., Barrett, B., Lumsdaine, A., Duell, J., Hargrove, P., Roman, E.: The LAM/MPI checkpoint/restart framework: System-initiated checkpointing. In: Proceedings, LACSI Symposium, Sante Fe, New Mexico, USA (2003)
6. Gao, Q., Yu, W., Huang, W., Panda, D.K.: Application-transparent checkpoint/restart for mpi programs over infiniband. In: ICPP'06: Proceedings of the 35th International Conference on Parallel Processing, Columbus, OH (2006)
7. Plank, J.S., Beck, M., Kingsley, G., Li, K.: Libckpt: Transparent checkpointing under unix. Technical Report UT-CS-94-242 (1994)
8. Bozyigit, M., Wasiq, M.: User-level process checkpoint and restore for migration. SIGOPS Oper. Syst. Rev. **35**(2) (2001) 86–96
9. Dimitrov, B., Rego, V.: Arachne: A portable threads system supporting migrant threads on heterogeneous network farms. IEEE Transactions on Parallel and Distributed Systems **9**(5) (1998) 459
10. Mascarenhas, E., Rego, V.: Ariadne: Architecture of a portable threads system supporting thread migration. Software- Practice and Experience **26**(3) (1996) 327–356
11. Itzkovitz, A., Schuster, A., Wolfovich, L.: Thread migration and its applications in distributed shared memory systems. Technical Report LPCR9603, Technion, Isreal (1996)
12. Jiang, H., Chaudhary, V.: Process/thread migration and checkpointing in heterogeneous distributed systems. In: Proceedings of the 37th Annual Hawaii International Conference on System Sciences. (2004) 282
13. Karablieh, F., Bazzi, R.A.: Heterogeneous checkpointing for multithreaded applications. In: Proceedings. 21st IEEE Symposium on Reliable Distributed Systems. (2002) 140
14. Jiang, H., Chaudhary, V., Walters, J.P.: Data conversion for process/thread migration and checkpointing. In: Proceedings. 2003 International Conference on Parallel Processing. (2003) 473
15. Beguelin, A., Seligman, E., Stephan, P.: Application level fault tolerance in heterogeneous networks of workstations. J. Parallel Distrib. Comput. **43**(2) (1997) 147–155
16. Jiang, H., Chaudhary, V.: On improving thread migration: Safety and performance. In Sahni, S., Prasanna, V.K., Shukla, U., eds.: Proceedings 9th International Conference on High Performance Computing HiPC2002. Volume 2552 of Lecture Notes in Computer Science., Berlin, Germany, Springer-Verlag (2002) 474–484
17. Karablieh, F., Bazzi, R.A., Hicks, M.: Compiler-assisted heterogeneous checkpointing. In: Proceedings. 20th IEEE Symposium on Reliable Distributed Systems. (2001) 56
18. Szwed, P.K., Marques, D., Buels, R.M., McKee, S.A., Schulz, M.: Simsnap: fast-forwarding via native execution and application-level checkpointing. In: INTERACT-8 2004. Eighth Workshop on Interaction between Compilers and Computer Architectures. (2004) 65

19. Strumpen, V.: Compiler technology for portable checkpoints (1998)
20. Lyon, B.: Sun external data representation specification. Technical report, SUN Microsystems, Inc., Mountain View (1984)
21. Krishnan, S., Gannon, D.: Checkpoint and restart for distributed components in xcat3. In: Proceedings of the Fifth IEEE/ACM International Workshop on Grid Computing. (2004) 281
22. Ramkumar, B., Strumpen, V.: Portable checkpointing for heterogeneous architectures. In: Twenty-Seventh Annual International Symposium on Fault-Tolerant Computing, IEEE Computer Society (1997) 58–67
23. Zhou, H., Geist, A.: "Receiver makes right" data conversion in PVM. In: Conference Proceedings of the 1995 IEEE Fourteenth Annual International Phoenix Conference on Computers and Communications, IEEE Computer Society (1995) 458–464
24. Zhong, H., Nieh, J.: The ergonomics of software porting: Automatically configuring software to the runtime environment (2006) http://www.cwi.nl/ftp/steven/enquire/ enquire.html.
25. Bronevetsky, G., Marques, D., Pingali, K., Stodghill, P.: Collective operations in application-level fault-tolerant mpi. In: ICS '03: Proceedings of the 17th annual international conference on Supercomputing, ACM Press (2003) 234–243
26. Bronevetsky, G., Marques, D., Pingali, K., Stodghill, P.: Automated application-level checkpointing of mpi programs. In: PPoPP '03: Proceedings of the ninth ACM SIGPLAN symposium on Principles and practice of parallel programming, ACM Press (2003) 84–94
27. Jiang, H., Chaudhary, V.: Compile/run-time support for thread migration. In: Proceedings International Parallel and Distributed Processing Symposium, IPDPS, IEEE Computer Society (2002) 58–66
28. Dagum, L., Menon, R.: Openmp: an industry standard api for shared-memory programming. In: IEEE Computational Science and Engineering, IEEE Computer Society (1998) 46–55
29. Elnozahy, E.N.M., Alvisi, L., Wang, Y.M., Johnson, D.B.: A survey of rollback-recovery protocols in message-passing systems. ACM Comput. Surv. 34(3) (2002) 375–408
30. de Camargo, R.Y., Goldchleger, A., Kon, F., Goldman, A.: Checkpointing-based rollback recovery for parallel applications on the integrade grid middleware. In: Proceedings of the 2nd workshop on Middleware for grid computing, ACM Press (2004) 35–40
31. Agbaria, A., Freund, A., Friedman, R.: Evaluating distributed checkpointing protocols. In: Proceedings. 23rd International Conference on Distributed Computing Systems. (2003) 266

A Generalized Linear Programming Based Approach to Optimal Divisible Load Scheduling

D. Ghose[1] and H.J. Kim[2]

[1] Department of Aerospace Engineering, Indian Institute of Science, Bangalore, India
[2] CIST, Korea University, Seoul, South Korea
dghose@aero.iisc.ernet.in, khj-@korea.ac.kr

Abstract. In this paper we propose a general Linear Programming (LP) based formulation and solution methodology for obtaining optimal solution to the load distribution problem in divisible load scheduling. We exploit the power of the versatile LP formulation to propose algorithms that yield exact solutions to several very general load distribution problems for which either no solutions or only heuristic solutions were available. We consider both star (single-level tree) networks and linear daisy chain networks, having processors equipped with front-ends, that form the generic models for several important network topologies. We consider arbitrary processing node availability or release times and general models for communication delays and computation time that account for constant overheads such as start up times in communication and computation. The optimality of the LP based algorithms is proved rigorously.

1 Introduction

The divisible load scheduling literature deals with the processing of massive loads that can be partitioned into smaller load fractions and distributed to processing nodes over a network subject to communication delays. This area has become an important topic of research since its inception by Cheng and Robertazzi [1]. Another paper that independently introduced several concepts related to processing of divisible loads is by Agrawal and Jagadish [2]. Since then this area has expanded to encompass various issues of concern to the practitioners of distributed computing [3,4,5,6,7]. Some papers address the problem of distributing loads under practical constraints such as different release times [8,12,13], and constant communication start-up times [9,10,11]. Almost all the algorithms that exist in the literature on divisible load scheduling are based on iterative or closed form solutions of simply formulated problems. When practical aspects are taken into account, the closed-form solutions either do not exist or are too complicated to generalize to large networks. In these cases heuristic algorithms are used.

In this paper, we propose a linear programming (LP) approach for divisible load problems, which can not only be extended to large networks, but also accounts for several practical considerations. The earliest application of LP to divisible load scheduling was by Agrawal and Jagadish [2] followed by Drozdowski [4]. However, these notable efforts have not exploited the complete power of LP.

S. Madria et al. (Eds.): ICDCIT 2006, LNCS 4317, pp. 235–248, 2006.

One difficulty in applying LP to these problems is due to the non-linearity introduced by the non-zero arbitrary processor availability or release times and the affine nature of the communication and computational time models. Because of these, one needs to develop algorithms that are *based* on LP, but require further justification and proof that they indeed converge to the optimal solution. This is one of the major objectives of our paper.

Scheduling of divisible loads is characterized by some aspects that are unique to it. In most of divisible load scheduling literature, the computation and communication time models are assumed to be linear. This linearity aids closed-form solutions. In some cases affine models, where the constant part is the start-up time, has been assumed. A cursory glance of the literature [8,9,10,11,12,13] will reveal that, with affine models, there are no closed-form solutions available for general network parameter values. Moreover, the load distribution conditions become very complicated even for simple cases. Affine models also prevent the use of linear programming approach directly. However, as we shall prove with some rigor, our approach, which is based on an LP formulation, is guaranteed to converge to the optimal solution irrespective of the network parameter values. This is a major step forward in solving large scale divisible load scheduling problems.

An important concept, which is one of the most elegant contributions of the existing closed-form analytical work in the literature, is the optimality principle, that says that all processors that participate in the load computation activity must stop computing at the same time instant for the load distribution to be optimal [3]. This principle is universally used in the DLT literature to derive closed-form solutions. We will not use it in the LP formulation, but the optimal solution will adhere to this principle automatically. There would be some processors that would be "inefficient" and should not be given any load for computation. Identification of these processors are done by using the load distribution conditions [3] when they are available. Unfortunately, there are no such conditions available when affine models are used. Even in the LP formulation the affine models do not allow the simultaneous identification of these processors *and* yield the optimal load distribution both at the same time. This is where we need to design an effective algorithm that uses the LP formulation as a tool.

In this paper we will consider cases that are combinations of the following: (a) *Generic topology:* Linear network/tree network (b) *Communication and Computation time models:* Start-up time/No start up time (c) *Processor availability:* Arbitrary processor release times/zero processor release times.

2   Some Notations and Definitions

z_i = Ratio of the time taken by a communication link i, to the time taken by a reference link, to communicate a given amount of load (thus, z is inversely proportional to the speed of the communication link).

w_i = Ratio of the time taken by a processing node or workstation P_i, to the time taken by a reference processor, to compute a given amount of load (thus, w is inversely proportional to the speed of a processing node).

T_{cm} = Time taken by a reference link to communicate one unit of load.

T_{cp} = Time taken by a reference processing node to process or compute one unit load.

L = The total load to be distributed and processed.

α_i = The amount of load assigned to a processing node P_i, with $\alpha_i \in [0, L]$.

I = The set of processors under consideration.

$T^*(I)$ = Processing time obtained by solving the LP for the processor set I.

$\alpha^*(I)$ = $\{\alpha_i^*(I)|_{i \in I}\}$ = The load distribution vector obtained by solving the LP for the processor set I, with $\alpha_i^*(I)$ being the load allocated to Processor P_i.

α = $\{\alpha_i|_{i \in I}\}$ = Any arbitrary load distribution vector for the processor set I.

$T(\alpha)$ = Processing time of the network with processor set I when α is the load distribution. It is defined as $T(\alpha) = \max_{i \in I}\{T_i(\alpha)\}$.

$T_i(\alpha)$ = Finish time of Processor P_i when load α is given to the network with P_i getting load α_i.

r_i = The release time of Processor P_i.

t_{cm_i} = The communication startup time for the link to the Processor P_i.

t_{cp_i} = The computation setup time for the Processor P_i.

Note that $T^*(I)$ is just the optimal value of the variable T in the LP formulation when the LP is solved. It is not necessarily the optimal processing time of the network. That is, $\min_\alpha T(\alpha)$ need not be the same as $T^*(I)$.

Some symbols used to classify the LP formulations and algorithms are: L (linear), T (star or single-level tree), F (with front-end), NF (without front-end), S (simple; no release time constraints, zero communication and computation start-up times), R (Release time constraints present), C (Non-zero communication and computation start-up times). For example, LP(T-F-S) would mean a LP formulation for a tree network, with each processor equipped with front ends, and a simple case which does not consider any release time constraints or communication and computation start up times.

3   Star Or Tree Network

The single-level tree architecture is a generic model for divisible load scheduling for a wide variety of distributed networks. Figure 1 represents the generic model of such a general architecture and also a special case of a bus based system.

It is assumed that all the processors are equipped with communication co-processors or front-ends so that the main processor can continue with computations while the front-end handles the load communication part. We consider several cases here. and present linear programming (LP) formulations that will be used for obtaining the optimal load distribution for the given network. In general, for a set of processors I arranged in a given topology, the LP formulations will have the following decision vector,

$$\{\alpha_i|_{i \in I}, T\} \tag{1}$$

which, on solution of the LP, will produce the optimal decision vector

$$\{\alpha_i^*|_{i \in I}, T^*\} \tag{2}$$

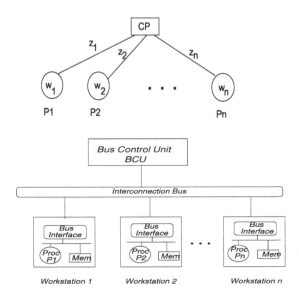

Fig. 1. A general single-level tree or star architecture and a bus based system

Then, by definition,

$$\alpha_i^*(I) = \alpha_i^*, \ i \in I; \ T^*(I) = T^* \tag{3}$$

Note that, the optimal decision vector is not necessarily the solution to the optimal load distribution problem. It is only the solution to the LP formulation. To obtain the optimal load distribution we need to do some more work. This is where the LP based algorithm becomes important. In the LP formulation, we will assume that the processors in I are consecutively numbered from 1 to n and this is also the sequence of load distribution. This numbering is only an artifice to make the equations easily understandable, since otherwise the notations become too cumbersome. This assumption, however, does not detract from the generality of the approach in any way.

No Release Time Constraints; No Communication or Computation Startup Time. The timing diagram that leads to the LP problem formulated below is given in Figure 2.
LP(T-F-S)

$$\min T$$

$$\text{subject to (Proc. } P_i) : \quad \sum_{j=1}^{i} \alpha_j z_j T_{cm} + \alpha_i w_i T_{cp} \leq T, \quad \text{for } i = 1, \dots, n$$

$$\alpha_i \geq 0, \ i = 1, \dots, n; \quad \sum_{i=1}^{n} \alpha_i = L$$

Number of constraints (apart from the usual positivity constraints and the normalization constraint) is n. The solution of this LP problem will directly yield the

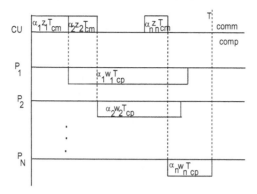

Fig. 2. Timing diagram for LP(T-F-S)

optimal solution. Hence, in this case, $\min_\alpha T(\alpha) = T^*(I)$. Some of the processors may get zero load in the optimal solution. These are the "inefficient" processors identified in [3] and are "dropped".

Most problems in the divisible load scheduling literature involving single level tree architectures and single installment load scheduling can be solved using this simple formulation. For example, the problems given in [3] can be easily solved.

Arbitrary Release Times; No Communication or Computation Startup Time. The timing diagram is given in Figure 3. Note that a processor can start computing only from its release time.

LP(T-F-R)

$$\min T$$

$$\text{subject to (Proc. } P_i) : \quad \sum_{j=1}^{i} \alpha_j z_j T_{cm} + \alpha_i w_i T_{cp} \leq T,$$

$$r_i + \alpha_i w_i T_{cp} \leq T, \qquad \text{for } i = 1, \ldots, n$$

$$\alpha_i \geq 0, \ i = 1, \ldots, n; \quad \sum_{i=1}^{n} \alpha_i = L$$

Number of constraints here is $2n$. Before we analyze this case further, note that by putting $r_i = 0$, for all i, we get back the equations for (T-F-S) case. The second equation for each processor is automatically subsumed in the first equation. So, in subsequent cases, we will assume the arbitrary release time case as the basic framework for developing the equations for the other cases.

The result of LP(T-F-R) cannot be used directly to obtain the optimal load distribution or processing time in a general case. This is because some of the processors may have such a large release time that the other processors would have finished their computation much before this time. In that case the LP problem may have multiple solutions in terms of α, and T^* would be,

$$T^* = \max\{r_1, r_2, \ldots, r_n\} \tag{4}$$

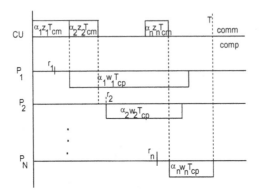

Fig. 3. Timing diagram for LP(T-F-R)

and the processor that has the maximum release time will not get any load to process. In fact, its release time would determine the value of T in the LP solution through its corresponding constraint. Hence, if (4) holds, then the solution of the LP problem has to be used carefully. However, it may also happen that

$$T^* > \max\{r_1, r_2, \ldots, r_n\} \tag{5}$$

but one of the processors still gets zero load. This may happen because the processor is inefficient in the sense of the load distribution conditions given in [3]. In this case, however, the LP solution will give the optimal load distribution.

The above observations, which will be used to design an LP based algorithm, are formally stated below.

Lemma 1. *If LP(T-F-R), with processor set I, yields a solution such that $T^*(I) = r_k$, for some $k \in I$, then reformulating the LP problem with the set of processors as $I \setminus \{k\}$ will yield a solution such that $T^*(I \setminus \{k\}) \leq T^*(I)$.*

Proof. From the inequality in the LP formulation, corresponding to processor P_k, we get $\alpha_k^* = 0$. Removing P_k from the reformulated LP, and solving it, we will get $\alpha^*(I \setminus \{k\})$ and $T^*(I \setminus \{k\})$. Then, $T^*(I) \geq \max\{T_1^*(I), \ldots, T_{k-1}^*(I), T_{k+1}^*(I), \ldots, T_n^*(I)\} \geq T^*(I \setminus \{k\})$, where, $T_i^*(I) = \max\{\sum_{j=1}^{i} \alpha_j^*(I)z_j T_{cm} + \alpha_i^*(I)w_i T_{cp}, r_i + \alpha_i^*(I)w_i T_{cp}\}$. The first inequality is obvious and the second is true because the load distribution $\alpha(I \setminus \{k\}) = \{\alpha_i^*(I)|_{i \in I \setminus \{k\}}\}$ cannot give a lower value of T than the LP solution of $T^*(I \setminus \{k\})$. ∎

Lemma 2. *The solution of LP(T-F-R), with processor set I, yields the optimal load distribution if $T^*(I) > r_k$, for all $k \in I$.*

Proof. By the very definition of LP, $T^*(I)$ can be obtained as below:

$$X_i(\alpha^*(I)) = \sum_{j=1}^{i} \alpha_j^*(I)z_j T_{cm} + \alpha_i^*(I)w_i T_{cp}$$

$$Y_i(\alpha^*(I)) = r_i + \alpha_i^*(I)w_i T_{cp}$$
$$T^*(I) = \max_{i \in I} \{\max\{X_i(\alpha^*(I)), Y_i(\alpha^*(I))\}\} \tag{6}$$

Given an arbitrary load distribution $\alpha = \{\alpha_i|_{i \in I}\}$, in a network with processor set I, the processing time $T(\alpha)$ can be obtained as follows:

$$T_i(\alpha) = \begin{cases} \max\{X_i(\alpha), Y_i(\alpha)\}, & \text{if } \alpha_i > 0 \\ \\ 0, & \text{if } \alpha_i = 0 \end{cases} \tag{7}$$

$$T(\alpha) = \max_{i \in I}\{T_i(\alpha)\} \tag{8}$$

According to the lemma, if $T^*(I) > r_k$ for all k, then $\alpha^*(I)$ also minimizes $T(\alpha)$. That is, $T(\alpha^*(I)) \leq T(\alpha)$ for all α. We will prove this statement by contradiction. Let us assume that there exists an $\hat{\alpha}$, so that

$$T(\hat{\alpha}) < T(\alpha^*(I)) \tag{9}$$

Since $\alpha^*(I)$ is the solution to the LP problem, it should satisfy,

$$\max_{i \in I}\{\max\{X_i(\hat{\alpha}), Y_i(\hat{\alpha})\}\} \geq \max_{i \in I}\{\max\{X_i(\alpha^*(I)), Y_i(\alpha^*(I))\}\} \tag{10}$$

Let us collect the indices of the non-zero elements of $\hat{\alpha}$ vector in a set $\hat{I}$, and those of the $\alpha^*(I)$ vector in a set $\tilde{I}$. Both $\hat{I} \subset I$ and $\tilde{I} \subset I$ are non-empty sets. Then (9) can be written as,

$$\max_{i \in \hat{I}}\{T_i(\hat{\alpha})\} < \max_{i \in \tilde{I}}\{T_i(\alpha^*(I))\} \tag{11}$$

One of the following two cases may arise:
Case I: The maximum of the LHS of (10) is attained for an index $p \in I \setminus \hat{I}$. Then the LHS of (11) also attains its maximum at the same index p.

IA: Let the RHS of (10) attain its maximum for an index $q \in I \setminus \tilde{I}$. Then the RHS of (11) also attains its maximum at the same index q. Then, from (10) and (11),

$$T_p(\hat{\alpha}) \geq T_q(\alpha^*(I)); \quad T_p(\hat{\alpha}) < T_q(\alpha^*(I)) \tag{12}$$

which is a contradiction.
IB: Let the RHS of (10) attain its maximum for an index $q \in \tilde{I}$. Then the RHS of (11) will attain its maximum at a different index $\bar{q}$ and

$$T_q(\alpha^*(I)) \geq T_{\bar{q}}(\alpha^*(I)) \tag{13}$$

Further, from (10) and (11),

$$T_p(\hat{\alpha}) \geq T_q(\alpha^*(I)); \quad T_p(\hat{\alpha}) < T_{\bar{q}}(\alpha^*(I)) \tag{14}$$

These inequalities, taken together, lead to a contradiction.

Case II: The maximum of LHS of (10) is attained for an index $\bar{p} \in \hat{I}$. Then, $\hat{\alpha}_{\bar{p}} = 0$ and

$$T_{\bar{p}}(\hat{\alpha}) = \max\{X_{\bar{p}}(\hat{\alpha}), Y_{\bar{p}}(\hat{\alpha})\}|_{\hat{\alpha}_{\bar{p}}=0} = \max\left\{\sum_{i=1}^{\bar{p}-1} \hat{\alpha}_i z_i T_{cm}, r_{\bar{p}}\right\} = r_{\bar{p}} \quad (15)$$

This last equality is justified since if $\sum_{i=1}^{\bar{p}-1} \hat{\alpha}_i z_i T_{cm} > r_{\bar{p}}$ then the nearest processor P_j before or after processor $P_{\bar{p}}$, having a non-zero $\hat{\alpha}_j$, will have a finish time greater than $\sum_{i=1}^{\bar{p}-1} \hat{\alpha}_i z_i T_{cm}$. That such a $\hat{\alpha}_j$ will exist is ensured by the fact that $\tilde{I}$ is a non-empty set. In fact, if P_j is before $P_{\bar{p}}$ then its finish time will be $\sum_{i=1}^{\bar{p}-1} \hat{\alpha}_i z_i T_{cm} + \hat{\alpha}_j w_j T_{cp}$ and if it is after $P_{\bar{p}}$ then its finish time will be $\sum_{i=1}^{\bar{p}-1} \hat{\alpha}_i z_i T_{cm} + \hat{\alpha}_j z_j T_{cm} + \hat{\alpha}_j w_j T_{cp}$. This contradicts the assumption that $T_{\bar{p}}(\hat{\alpha})$ is the maximum of the LHS of (10). Now from (10) and (15) we have,

$$T_{\bar{p}}(\hat{\alpha}) = r_{\bar{p}} \geq T^*(I) \quad (16)$$

which contradicts the initial assumption in the lemma that for all k, $T^*(I) > r_k$. Hence the proof of the lemma. □

These two lemmas can now be used to obtain an LP based algorithm that guarantees an optimal solution.

Algorithm(T-F-R)

Step 1: Consider the network with processor set I and formulate LP(T-F-R).
Step 2: Solve LP(T-F-R) and identify processors k for which $T^*(I) = r_k$.
Step 3: If such processors exist then eliminate them and reconstitute the processor set as $I \leftarrow I \setminus \{k\}$ and go to Step 1. Otherwise (if no such k exists), go to the next step.
Step 4: Accept the solution of LP(T-F-R), with $\alpha_k = 0$ for all P_k that have been eliminated in the LP formulation, as the optimal load distribution and the optimal time performance.

Theorem 1. *Algorithm(T-F-R) guarantees convergence to optimal load distribution in a finite number of steps.*

Proof. From Lemma 1, we can see that every looping through Steps 1 to 3, in Algorithm(T-F-R), either reduces the value of T or leaves it unchanged. The looping occurs for a finite number of steps since there are a finite number of processors. When no more processors are eliminated (this is bound to happen because when there is only one processor left, all the conditions are automatically satisfied), Lemma 2 will ensure optimality of the solution. □

This algorithm gives exact solutions to the class of problems given in [8,13] which propose only heuristic algorithms restricted to bus networks. Another major point that emerges from our solution is that even for arbitrary processor release times, optimal single installment strategies exist and it is not *necessary* to use multi-installment strategies. In fact, [8,13] do not give solutions in terms of single installment strategies. Of course, in the case of finite buffer capacity (which we do not consider in this paper), as given in [13], multi-installments may become a necessity if the number of processors are restricted.

Arbitrary Release Times; Non-zero Communication and Computation Startup Times. The timing diagram is the same as in Figure 3, except that each communication and computation block should also include the constant startup time, which could be different for different processors and links.

LP(T-F-R-C)

$$\min T$$

$$\text{subject to (Proc. } P_i): \quad \sum_{j=1}^{i} \left(t_{cm_j} + \alpha_j z_j T_{cm} \right) + t_{cp_i} + \alpha_i w_i T_{cp} \leq T$$

$$r_i + t_{cp_i} + \alpha_i w_i T_{cp} \leq T, \quad \text{for } i = 1, \ldots, n$$

$$\alpha_i \geq 0, \; i = 1, \ldots, n; \quad \sum_{i=1}^{n} \alpha_i = L$$

In this case, the non-linearity is induced by the inclusion of the constant terms r_i, t_{cm_i}, and t_{cp_i}. The corresponding results are as follows:

Lemma 3. *If the LP(T-F-R-C), with processor set I, yields a solution such that $T^*(I) = r_k + t_{cp_k}$, for some $k \in I$, then reformulating the LP problem with the set of processors as $I \setminus \{k\}$ will yield a solution such that $T^*(I \setminus \{k\}) \leq T^*(I)$.*

Proof. Similar to Lemma 1, and is omitted. ⬜

Lemma 4. *If LP(T-F-R-C), with processor set I, yields a solution such that $T^*(I) > r_i + t_{cp_i}$, for all $i \in I$ but, for some (maybe more than one) $k \in I$, we get $\alpha_k^*(I) = 0$, then reformulating the LP problem with the set of processors as $I \setminus \{k'\}$ will yield a solution $T^*(I \setminus \{k'\}) \leq T^*(I)$, where k' is the largest of all the indices k that satisfy the $\alpha_k^*(I) = 0$ condition.*

Proof. In this case, the processor $P_{k'}$ gets zero load because its communication-cum-computation speed is so slow that giving it any non-zero load will hold up the processing performance of the subsequent processors $k' + 1, \ldots, n$. However, it does not affect the communication and computation performance of the processors $P_1, \ldots, P_{k'-1}$. Thus, eliminating this processor will not affect the time performance of its predecessor processors, but will improve the time of its follower processors since the communication overhead $t_{cm_{k'}}$ will no longer exist. This immediately leads to the result in the lemma. ⬜

This Lemma is significant as it is analogous to the optimal load distribution condition derived in [3]. However, note that the condition given in [3] has been derived assuming a much simpler case where the release times and constant start up and setup times are all zero. An equivalent condition with nonzero values for these is likely to be extremely complicated and is, in fact, still an open problem. The LP formulation takes care of this condition in a simple way.

Lemma 5. *The solution of LP(T-F-R-C), with processor set I, yields the optimal load distribution if (i) $T^*(I) > r_k + t_{cp_k}$, for all $k \in I$ and (ii) $\alpha_k^*(I) > 0$ for all $k \in I$.*

Proof. The proof of the lemma is similar to Lemma 2. We omit details. ⬜

These generalize Lemmas 1 and 2 and form the basis for the following algorithm.

Algorithm(T-F-R-C)

Steps 1, 2, and 3 are the same as Algorithm(T-F-R).
Step 4: Identify all processors k for which $\alpha_k^*(I) = 0$. *(These are the processor-link pairs that are inefficient in the sense that giving them load will hold up the computation of their followers that are faster).*
Step 5: If such processors exist then find the maximum k that satisfies this condition. Eliminate this processor and reconstitute the processor set as $I \leftarrow I \backslash k$ and go to Step 1. Otherwise (if no such k exists), go to step 6.
Step 6: Same as Step 4 in Algorithm(T-F-R).

Theorem 2. *Algorithm(T-F-R-C) guarantees convergence to optimal load distribution in a finite number of steps.*

Proof. As in Theorem 1, follows directly from Lemmas 3, 4, and 5.   []

This algorithm gives exact solutions to the class of problems related to star networks considered in [9,10,11] in all its generality (that is, when the startup times for both communication and computation have different values for different processors, heterogeneous network, release times, etc.).

4   Linear Networks

The generic linear network, shown in Figure 4(a) represents several important network topologies that are formed out of standard grid, ring, or mesh topologies (Figure 4(b)) depending on the application. For example, a network of sensors where decision-making requires data fusion that depends on exchange of data between adjacent sensors/computers collecting data from overlapping footprints, the classical agreement problem in the communication-control based decision-making literature , and image processing tasks where edge information needs to be exchanged, are some applications where the linear topology is a logical choice. In our model we further assume that the boundary processor (P_0) acts as the control unit (CU) and the load scheduler, and is also involved in computations.

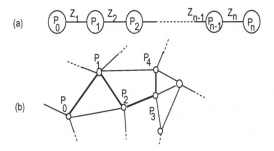

Fig. 4. (a) Linear network: Generic topology (b) General topology

No Release Time Constraints; No Communication or Computation Startup Times. The timing diagram is shown in Figure 5.
LP(L-F-S)

$\min T$

subject to (Proc. P_0) : $\alpha_0 w_0 T_{cp} \leq T$

(Proc. P_i) : $\sum_{j=0}^{i-1} \left(L - \sum_{k=0}^{j} \alpha_k \right) z_{j+1} T_{cm} + \alpha_i w_i T_{cp} \leq T, \quad i = 1, \ldots, n$

$\alpha_i \geq 0, \ i = 0, 1, \ldots, n; \ \sum_{i=0}^{n} \alpha_i = L$

Number of constraints is $n + 1$. A solution to LP(L-F-S) will give the optimal load distribution directly. According to results available in [3], all processors will have some non-zero load to process.

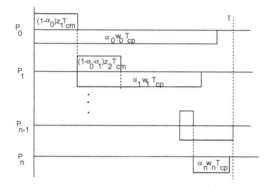

Fig. 5. Timing diagram for LP(L-F-S)

Arbitrary Release Times; No Communication or Computation Startup Time. The timing diagram is shown in Figure 6.
LP(L-F-R)

$\min T$

subject to (Proc. P_0) : $r_0 + \alpha_0 w_0 T_{cp} \leq T$

(Proc. P_i) : $\sum_{j=0}^{i-1} \left(L - \sum_{k=0}^{j} \alpha_k \right) z_{j+1} T_{cm} + \alpha_i w_i T_{cp} \leq T,$

$r_i + \alpha_i w_i T_{cp} \leq T, \quad i = 1, \ldots, n$

$\alpha_i \geq 0, \ i = 0, 1, \ldots, n; \ \sum_{i=0}^{n} \alpha_i = L$

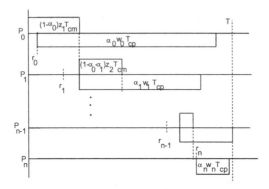

Fig. 6. Timing diagram for LP(L-F-R)

Number of constraints is $(2n+1)$. In this case, unlike in the star (tree) network, no processors can be "dropped" in the sense that they are an inherent part of the network and continue to take part in the communication process. However, some processors may get zero load to compute, and this will give rise to a situation analogous to the tree network case. The corresponding results we need in order to design the LP based algorithm are the following:

Lemma 6. *If LP(L-F-R), with processor set I, yields a solution such that $T^*(I) = r_k$ for some $k \in I$, then reformulating the LP problem with the set of processors as $I \setminus \{k\}$, but with the link between P_{k-1} and P_{k+1} assigned a speed parameter of $\hat{z}_{k+1} = z_k + z_{k+1}$, will yield a solution such that $T^*(I \setminus \{k\}) \leq T^*(I)$.*

Proof. From the inequality in LP(L-F-R), corresponding to processor P_k, we get $\alpha_k^* = 0$. Removing P_k from the reformulated LP, and solving it, we will get a load distribution $\alpha^*(I \setminus \{k\})$ and a processing time $T^*(I \setminus \{k\})$. Note that if we define a load distribution α for this new network as, $\alpha(I \setminus \{k\}) = (\alpha_1^*(I), \ldots, \alpha_{k-1}^*(I), \alpha_{k+1}^*(I), \ldots, \alpha_n^*(I))$, then the corresponding $T((I \setminus \{k\})) \leq T^*(I)$. Hence, an optimal load distribution obtained by solving the new LP will definitely satisfy $T^*(I \setminus \{k\}) \leq T^*(I)$.   □

Lemma 7. *The solution of LP(L-F-R), with the processor set I, yields the optimal load distribution if $T^*(I) > r_k$, for any $k \in I$.*

Proof. The proof is similar to Lemma 2.   □

The LP based algorithm is the same as Algorithm(T-F-R), except Step 3 which will now be,

Step 3: If such processors exist then reconstitute the processor set as $I \leftarrow I \setminus \{k\}$, with the link between P_{k-1} and P_{k+1} assigned the speed parameter $z_k + z_{k+1}$. Otherwise (if no such k exists), go to the next step.

There is a slight abuse of notation here since, if Step 3 is executed several times, the consecutive links may no longer have consecutive numbers if the original numbering is retained. However, renumbering the nodes at every pass through Step 3 will take care of this aspect. Alternatively, a simple mechanism of identifying the relative position of the nodes will also serve the purpose.

A theorem similar to the T-F-R case proving convergence can also be stated.

This algorithm gives exact solution to the class of problems considered in [12], where only heuristic solution was proposed using multi-installment strategy.

Arbitrary Release Times; Non-zero Communication and Computation Startup Time. The timing diagram is the same as Figure 6, except that each communication and computation block also includes the startup times.

LP(L-F-R-C)

$\min T$

subject to (Proc. P_0) : $r_0 + t_{cp_0} + \alpha_0 w_0 T_{cp} \leq T$

(Proc. P_i) : $\displaystyle\sum_{j=0}^{i-1} \left[t_{cm_{j+1}} + \left(L - \sum_{k=0}^{j} \alpha_k \right) z_{j+1} T_{cm} \right] + t_{cp_i} + \alpha_i w_i T_{cp} \leq T$

$$r_i + t_{cp_i} + \alpha_i w_i T_{cp} \leq T, \quad i = 1, \ldots, n$$

$$\alpha_i \geq 0, \ i = 0, 1, \ldots, n; \quad \sum_{i=0}^{n} \alpha_i = L$$

Lemma 8. *If LP(L-F-R-C), with processor set I, yields a solution such that $T^*(I) = r_k + t_{cp_k}$, for some $k \in I$, then reformulating the LP problem with the set of processors as $I \setminus \{k\}$, but with the link between P_{k-1} and P_{k+1} assigned a speed parameter of $\hat{z}_{k+1} = z_k + z_{k+1}$ and communication startup time $\hat{t}_{cm_{k+1}} = t_{cm_k} + t_{cm_{k+1}}$, will yield a solution $T^*(I \setminus \{k\}) \leq T^*(I)$.*

Proof. Similar to Lemma 6.   ⬚

Lemma 9. *The solution of the LP formulation with the processor set I yields the optimal load distribution if $T^*(I) > r_k + t_{cp_k}$, for all $k \in I$.*

Proof. Similar to Lemma 2.   ⬚

The LP based algorithm is same as Algorithm(T-F-R), except Steps 2 and 3.

Step 2: Solve LP(T-F-R) and identify processors k for which $T^*(I) = r_k + t_{cp_k}$.
Step 3: If such processors exist then reconstitute the processor set as $I \leftarrow I \setminus \{k\}$, with the link between P_{k-1} and P_{k+1} assigned the speed parameter $z_k + z_{k+1}$ and communication startup time $\hat{t}_{cm_{k+1}} = t_{cm_k} + t_{cm_{k+1}}$. Otherwise (if no such k exists), go to the next step.

A similar theorem, as in the previous section, proving convergence, can be stated as well.

5   Conclusions

This paper gives a rigorous mathematical framework for analyzing the optimality of linear programming (LP) based load distribution strategies applicable to divisible loads under various general conditions. This is a significant extension to the simplified strategies proposed so far in the literature on divisible loads. Future extension of this work will deal with the case when the network processors are not equipped with front-end processors and communication off-loading cannot be assumed.

Acknowledgements. Partially supported by the Information Technology Research Center (ITRC), Ministry of Information and Telecommunications, Korea.

References

1. Cheng, Y. C., and T. G. Robertazzi, Distributed computation with communication delays, *IEEE Trans. on Aerospace and Electronic Systems*, 24, pp. 700-712, 1988.
2. Agrawal, R., and Jagadish, H.V., Partitioning techniques for large-grained parallelism, *IEEE Trans. on Computers*, Vol. 37, No. 12, pp. 1627-1634, 1988.
3. Bharadwaj, V. et al., *Scheduling Divisible Loads in Parallel and Distributed Systems*, IEEE Computer Society Press, Los Almitos, California, 1996.
4. Drozdowski, M., *Selected Problems of Scheduling Tasks in Multiprocessor Computer Systems*, Poznan University of Technology Press, Series Monographs, No. 321, Poznon, Poland, 1997.
5. Bharadwaj, V. et al., Divisible load theory: A new paradigm for load scheduling in distributed systems, *Cluster Computing*, Vol. 6, No. 1, pp. 7-17, 2003.
6. Robertazzi, T., Ten reasons to use divisible load theory, *IEEE Computer*, Vol. 36, No. 5, pp. 63-68, 2003.
7. Ghose, D. et al., Adaptive divisible load scheduling strategies for workstation clusters with unknown network resources, *IEEE Trans. on Parallel and Distributed Systems*, Vol. 16, No. 10, pp. 897-907, 2005.
8. Bharadwaj, V. et al., "Scheduling divisible loads in bus networks with arbitrary processor release times, *Computer Math. Applic.*, Vol. 32, No. 7, pp. 57-77, 1996.
9. Blazewicz, J., and M. Drozdowski, Distributed processing of divisible jobs with communication startup costs, *Discrete Applied Mathematics*, Vol. 76, No. 1, pp. 21-41, 1997.
10. Bharadwaj, V. et al., On the influence of start-up costs in scheduling divisible loads on bus networks, *IEEE Trans. on Parallel and Distributed Systems*, Vol. 11, No. 12, pp. 1288-1305, 2000.
11. Bharadwaj, V. et al., Design and analysis of load distribution strategies with start-up costs in scheduling divisible loads on distributed networks, *Mathematical and Computer Modeling*, Vol. 32, No. 7-8, pp. 901-932, 2000.
12. Bharadwaj, V., and W.H. Min, Scheduling divisible loads on heterogeneous linear daisy chain networks with arbitrary processor release times, *IEEE Trans. on Parallel and Distributed Systems*, Vol. 15, No. 3, pp. 273-288, 2004.
13. Bharadwaj, V., and G. Barlas, Scheduling divisible loads with processor release times and finite size buffer capacity constraints, *Cluster Computing*, Vol. 6, No. 1, pp. 63-74, 2003.

Improving the Deployability of Existing Windows-Based Client/Server Business Information Systems Using ActiveX

Jonathan Jiin-Tian Chyou and Bill Yu-Fan Cheng

Department of Management Information Systems, National Chengchi University
No. 64, Sec. 2, Zhinan Rd., Taipei City 11605, Taiwan
jchyou@mis.nccu.edu.tw, bill@mail.hit.edu.tw

Abstract. Today, increasingly large and complex business information systems (BISs) are being built as client/server (C/S) applications. Unfortunately, for the most common C/S BISs, that is, the Windows-based C/S BISs (WinBISs), client programs must be manually deployed to each end-user machine bringing about a heavy BIS maintenance load. ActiveX, if used properly, is more cost- effective than alternatives in improving the deployment of existing WinBISs. Yet, ActiveX has three shortcomings, namely insecurity, complexity, and bulkiness. The purpose of this paper is to overcome the shortcomings of ActiveX, and then develop an ActiveX-based solution to automate the deployment of existing WinBISs. We first propose a downloadable architecture, which supports the development of automatically-deployed BISs. Then we propose an architecture transformation process, which transforms existing WinBISs into the downloadable architecture. Additionally, we show an example of how to use the downloadable architecture and the architecture transformation process. The example also provides evidence to support the feasibility of such architecture and process.

Keywords: ActiveX, Deployability, Information System Deployment, Information System Architecture, Information System Architecture Transformation.

1 Introduction

In order to compete successfully in global markets, businesses must achieve excellence in managing their information management operations. Business information system (BIS) is seen as one of the key strategies that businesses should adopt in their efforts to achieve information management excellence. It comes as no surprise, therefore, that the academic and industrial community continually attempt to develop technologies that will make it easier, faster, and less expensive to build and maintain high-quality BISs. ActiveX [10] [15] is an excellent example of these technologies. At present, ActiveX has been widely applied in system software and tool programs, such as Macromedia's Flash player, Microsoft's online update service, and Trend Micro's HouseCall online antivirus program, all of which are well-known applications of ActiveX. Unfortunately, the relative success in system software and tool programs has not been matched by the same degree of success in BISs. However, the ActiveX in fact, has potential to

S. Madria et al. (Eds.): ICDCIT 2006, LNCS 4317, pp. 249–263, 2006.

contribute to businesses to achieve information management excellence, and therefore ActiveX's new possible applications in BISs are worthy of continued study.

Furthermore, remarkable advances of personal computer (PC) technologies have drastically affected the building of BISs. There has been a shift of BIS from massive mainframe, centralized architecture, and text-based user interface to PC, client/server (C/S) architecture, and graphical user interface. Today, increasingly large and complex BISs are being built as C/S applications. Unfortunately, for the most common C/S BISs, that is, the Windows-based C/S BISs (WinBISs), client programs must be manually deployed to each end-user machine bringing about a heavy BIS maintenance load. ActiveX, if used properly, is more cost-effective than alternatives in improving the deployment of existing WinBISs, that is to say, ActiveX will enable developers to leverage their existing knowledge, skill, tools, experience, and code set to automate the deployment of existing WinBISs, meaning costly and risky rewrites of existing WinBISs can be avoided.

But ActiveX is no magic solution, and thus it still has three shortcomings, namely insecurity, complexity, and bulkiness. These shortcomings resulted in fewer applications and less research of ActiveX in BISs. The purpose of this paper is to overcome the shortcomings of ActiveX, and then develop an ActiveX-based technology to automate the deployment of existing WinBISs. Section 2 discusses ActiveX's shortcomings and their solutions. Section 3 clarifies the assumptions of the proposed technology. Section 4 describes the first part of the technology, namely the downloadable architecture, which supports the development of automatically- deployed BISs. Section 5 describes the second part of the technology, namely the architecture transformation process, which transforms existing WinBISs into the downloadable architecture. Section 6 shows an example of how to use the proposed technology. The example also provides evidence to support the feasibility of the proposed technology. Section 7 discusses related works, while section 8 concludes the paper.

2   Overcoming the Shortcomings of ActiveX

Here, we discuss ActiveX's shortcomings and their solutions. Firstly, one of the biggest controversies about ActiveX is security. An ActiveX component can go to the end-user's local hard disk and have full access to system files, which creates the possibility of a hacker writing a component that reads and writes directly to that hard disk. The next time the end-user visits the hacker's Website, the component could pass a virus to the hard disk or do some other irreparable harm to the end-user's machine [10]. However, while the lack of a Java-like SandBox security mechanism in ActiveX is a problem for Internet-based BIS, it is not as much of a problem for Intranet- or Extranet-based BISs. Both the client program and database are located on a closed network, so security and trust relationships are not an issue.

Secondly, ActiveX is too complex a Web component technology that is difficult and even frustrating to understand and use. Fortunately, a visual basic (VB) -like visual programming tool (VB-like tool), such as VB, Delphi, and PowerBuilder, abstracts complex ActiveX technology and makes it easy to use. With VB-like tools, developers now have the ability to develop ActiveX-based BISs as easily and quickly as they created WinBISs, hence by using their previous expertise and tools, costly and risky rewrites of existing WinBISs can be avoided.

Furthermore, ActiveX components are binary objects, so they tend to be pretty large. They can take 3-5 minutes to download to end-user machines. However, unlike Java applets, ActiveX components usually need to be downloaded only once. Still, for someone who has never been to a Website with ActiveX components, this waiting could be tedious. Also, just as with other programs, when developers update their ActiveX component, end-users have to download it again. One simple way to reduce the size of ActiveX components for faster download is file compression. The most effective way to minimize this speed bump is decomposition. There are two types of decompositions. The first type of decomposition is to separate common code from application-specific code into shared dynamic-link libraries (DLLs). This method offer four benefits: (a) the ActiveX component is smaller since it contains only the code unique to it; the common code is in DLLs; (b) an end-user machine with several DLL-enabled ActiveX components installed on it needs only a single copy of DLLs, which are shared by all the ActiveX components; (c) only minimal DLLs will be necessary to download, as if the correct version already exists on the end-user machine, they will not be downloaded; and (d) the download of DLLs can be avoided, when the DLLs are installed on end-user machines in advance. The second type of decomposition is partitioning a program into a set of smaller independent pieces from a functional perspective. Thereafter, each piece is made into a small ActiveX component rather than an entire program made into a massive ActiveX component. The benefits of using this method are: (a) the ActiveX component is much smaller, and its size is independent of program size and complexity; (b) enables an incremental program deployment, thus each launch of the program only requires pertinent code, which includes one ActiveX component and its dependent DLLs, be downloaded and installed. Non-pertinent code is delayed until their first use; (c) enables a partial program update. When a program is modified, some code may be independent of the changes and hence need not be downloaded and re-installed; and (d) enhances the possibility of code reuse due to high cohesion and loose coupling features of ActiveX components.

3 The Assumptions of the Proposed Technology

This section lists the assumptions of the downloadable architecture and the architecture transformation process. These assumptions are based on the section 2.

1. The assumptions of the downloadable architecture:

   (1) Downloadable BIS, that is, BIS using the downloadable architecture will be restricted to use in Intranet or Extranet only.
   (2) Developers will create ActiveX components with an ActiveX-enabled version of VB-like tools, such as Delphi 2006 and VB 6.0.

2. The assumptions of the architecture transformation process:

   (1) The assumed transformation subjects are the VB like tool-created, Intranet- or Extranet-based WinBISs.

(2) The tool for creating ActiveX components is assumed the same as that for WinBIS. For example, the Delphi 3.0-created WinBIS is transformed into the downloadable architecture by using Delphi 2006.

4 The Downloadable Architecture

To overcome the shortcomings of the C/S architecture, the improved C/S architecture namely downloadable architecture is proposed. It allows developers to develop downloadable BISs to be downloaded, installed and run on end-user machines dynamically and automatically from a central location. A BIS architecture shows how a BIS is realized by a collection of elements together with the interactions among these elements [17]. We discuss these matters in more detail below.

4.1 Elements of the Downloadable Architecture

Like the C/S architecture [16], the downloadable architecture consists of three types of building blocks: client program (required), application server (optional), and database (required). One characteristic in which the downloadable architecture differs from the C/S architecture is automatic deployment of client programs. The client programs of the C/S architecture implemented as Windows programs have to be deployed manually. Instead, the client programs of the downloadable architecture are implemented as ActiveX-enabled Websites called program warehouses, and will be deployed automatically. Please compare Figure 1 with Figure 2.

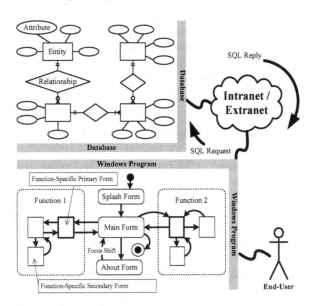

Fig. 1. Architectural Overview of Two-Tier Windows-Based C/S BISs

A program warehouse consists of a home page, a menu page, a message page, one or more package carriers, one or more component packages, and zero or more DLL packages. The home page, the menu page, the message page, and the package carrier all are simple Webpages. The home page is used to inspect the end-user environment, customize the Website for the end-user, split up the browser window into frames, and other such Website initialization processes. The menu page is used to list all available functions of the client program. The message page is used to display information about the system. The package carrier is used to deliver a component package and zero or more DLL packages to the end-user machine. In addition, the package carrier also performs some user interface processes to increase the usability of the client program. The component package and the DLL package both are CAB-format compressed files (CAB files) that include one or more downloadable files. The component package contains an ActiveX component (OCX file) and its installation instructions (INF file), but the DLL package contains only an ActiveX component's dependent DLL. Each of the ActiveX

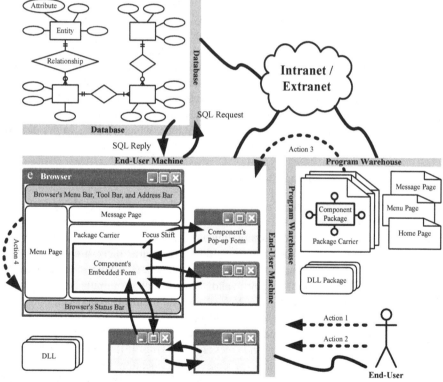

Action 1= End-user opens the home page of the program warehouse.   **Action 2=** End-user selects a desired function by clicking a menu item on the menu page.
Action 3= Browser checks whether a recent enough version of the function-specific component exists in the end-user machine.
　　　　　If it does not exist, the component package and related DLL packages be downloaded, extracted, and installed.
Action 4= Browser creates and initializes a component instance.

Fig. 2. Architectural Overview of Two-Tier Downloadable BISs

components is composed of an embedded form and zero or more pop-up forms, to implement a function of the client program that appears as a menu item on the menu page.

4.2 Interactions Among Elements

Downloadable BIS is a Web-based system, and can be accessed through an ActiveX-enabled Web browser from anywhere with Intranet or Extranet connectivity. Here, we outline the interactions among elements (see Figure 2). Firstly, an end-user visits the program warehouse, and then the menu page is displayed within the end-user's browser. Secondly, the end-user selects the desired function from the menu page, and then a function-specific package carrier is downloaded to the end-user machine. Thirdly, the browser analyzes the package carrier to retrieve the component's globally unique identifier (GUID), the component's minimum required version, and the component package's download location. Using this information, the browser checks whether a recent enough version of the component exists in the end-user machine. If it does not exist already, the browser downloads the component package, extracts the included component and component's installation instructions, and then installs the component against the installation instructions. Fourthly, the browser parses component's installation instructions to retrieve each dependent DLL's file name, each dependent DLL's minimum required version and each dependent DLL package's download location. Using this information, the browser checks whether a recent enough version of the DLL exists in the end-user machine. If it does not exist already, the browser downloads the DLL package, extracts the included DLL, and then installs the DLL against the component's installation instructions. Finally, the browser instantiates and initializes the component before a component instance, which embeds in the package carrier, is displayed within the browser.

4.3 Communications Among Elements

The downloadable architecture is loosely coupled, meaning one element can be understood without examining the other, and one element often can be changed without changing the other. Nevertheless, communication among elements of downloadable architecture is unavoidable. In downloadable architecture, there are five types of communication: communication between ActiveX component instances, communication between AtiveX component instance and Web script, communication between client-side Web script and server-side Web script, communication between client-side Web scripts, and communication between server-side Web scripts. The inter-module communication methods provided by high-level programming languages, such as global variable, procedure call, and message passing [5], cannot work in the downloadable architecture. The interprocess communication methods provided by operating systems, such as RPC, DCOM, and CORBA [10] [18], also cannot work in the downloadable architecture (note that there is no overlap between lifetimes of ActiveX component instances). Moreover, most of the session state maintenance methods provided by Web technologies, such as ASP/PHP session variable, URL-encoded variable, hidden form variable [13], are partial solutions. In fact, session cookie [13] is the only solution that supports all such types of communication.

4.4 Web Browser's Security Settings

For security reasons, by default, most Web browsers will block or warn against the download and installation of ActiveX components. Thus, it is necessary to configure the browser's security settings to enable ActiveX components.

5 The Architecture Transformation Process

This section presents a simple and systematic process, which transforms existing WinBISs into the downloadable architecture, for the purpose of deployability improvement. We will first outline the process from beginning to end. We will then discuss some activities of the process in detail.

5.1 The Client Program Architecture Transformation Process

To be precise, such BIS architecture transformation involves only the client programs. It is for this reason that we simply propose a client program architecture transformation process (see Figure 3). Repeat this process for each client program of the WinBIS, until they are all transformed into the program warehouse, and then the WinBIS is transformed into the downloadable architecture. The process covers the various project management and engineering activities. The process begins with the activity that prepares a plan for the project. This activity and the activity that monitors and controls the project against the plan are both typical project management activities. Engineering activities are repeatedly performed. The first engineering activity is to make the home page, menu page and message page. The next is to make the ActiveX component using a VB-like tool. The third is to make the installation instructions file.

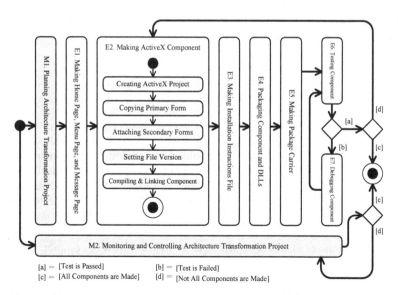

Fig. 3. Client Program Architecture Transformation Process Model

The fourth is to package the component and its dependent DLLs. The fifth is to make the package carrier. The sixth is to test the component and its dependent elements that include the installation instructions file, the package carrier, and DLLs. Finally debug the component and its dependent elements if the test fails. Please note that signing CAB files that include component packages and DLL packages with a valid digital certificate are not necessary for Intranet- or Extranet-based downloadable BISs. A digital signature is a way to tell the end-user to accept the CAB files. It is an indication of the author of the CAB files. In an environment where everybody knows this CAB file is safe, and they are likely to accept it, the developer can ask the end-user to configure the browser's security settings to accept and download unsigned CAB files.

5.2 Making ActiveX Component

The code of specific function of the WinBIS transforms into an ActiveX component by using a VB-like tool. Such ActiveX component-making activity consists of the following steps (see Figure 1, 2 & 3). Additional information about the VB-like tools can be found in the related documents.

1. Create a new ActiveX component project. Such a project in VB is called "ActiveX control project", while in Delphi it is called "ActiveForm project". After that, the VB-like tool brings up a blank form that will embed in the package carrier. Such embedded form in VB is called "UserControl form", in Delphi is called "Active form", and in this paper is called "embedded form".
2. Open the primary form (namely the first display form) of the specific function of the WinBIS. Then copy all components and code of the primary form (except the VB-like tool generated code) to the embedded form via the clipboard. Following this, write code for communication with Web scripts and other ActiveX components, as well as to manipulate the Web browser.
3. Add all secondary forms (namely any form except the primary form) of the specific function of the WinBIS to the project.
4. Specify the file version of the ActiveX component.
5. Compile and link the project to produce the ActiveX component.

5.3 Making the Installation Instructions File (INF File)

An INF file is a text file, which can be created or modified using any text editor in which the user can control the insertion of line breaks. It provides installation instructions that the browser uses to download and install a component and DLLs required by the component. Moreover, an INF file is made up of different named sections. Some sections have predefined names and some sections have name defined by the writer of the INF file. A line with a square bracket ([]) signals the start of a new section. The word inside the square bracket is the section name. All the lines that follow are considered the same section, until the next section starts. Note that we will confine our discussion to the needs of the downloadable architecture. For complete information about the INF files, refer to the related documents [15].

The downloadable architecture uses three types of sections to control the download and installation of a component and its dependent DLLs. We discuss these sections in more detail below. In addition, Figure 4 shows an example of the INF file for the

UsrCngProfile component. This INF file can be modified to download and install any ActiveX component by changing UsrCngProfile's information to the desired ActiveX component's information.

The [Add.Code] Section. This section provides a complete list of all the files that end-users have to download and install. FileName=SectionName is used in this section to specify a required file, and to map the file to a section of the same name. During the actual installation process, the browser will install each file needed in reverse order, as stated in this section. Hence, the developer needs to esure that the component (OCX file) is listed first in this section, followed by dependent DLLs, with the least-dependent DLL at the bottom of the list.

The Component Section. This section contains all the information necessary to download and install the component, and should be named the same as the component's file name. The following lines are required in this section.

1. clsid={12345678-1234-1234-1234-123456789ABC}. This line specifies the string representation of the GUID of the component, enclosed in braces { }.
2. file=thiscab. This line indicates the component is located in the same CAB file as the INF file.
3. FileVersion=a,b,c,d. This line specifies the minimum required file version of the component.
4. RegisterServer=yes. This line asks to register the component.

The DLL-Specific Section. Each DLL-specific section contains all information necessary to download and install a dependent DLL of the component, and should be named the same as the dependent DLL's file name. The following lines are required in each DLL-specific section.

1. file=URL. This line indicates where the DLL package can be downloaded from.
2. FileVersion=a,b,c,d. This line specifies the minimum required file version of the DLL.
3. DestDir=11. This line asks to place the DLL into the \Windows\System directory.

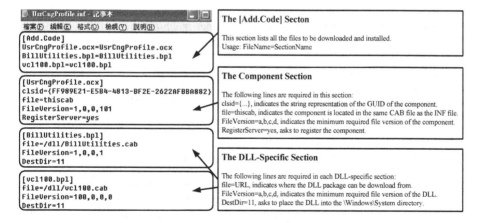

Fig. 4. Example Installation Instructions File

5.4 Packing Component and DLL

Each component and its installation instructions must be packaged in a CAB file, called a component package. Each component's dependent DLL must also be packaged in a CAB file, called a DLL package. Developers can use the Cabarc.exe command line utility which comes with the Microsoft Cabinet Software Development Kit (Cabinet SDK), to create these two CAB files. The Cabinet SDK can be downloaded from this location: http://msdn.microsoft.com/library/default.asp?url=/library/en-us/dncabsdk/ html/cabdl.asp.

Component packages are created using the n command, followed by the name of the component package to be created, followed by the name of the INF file, in turn followed by the name of the OCX file, for example: "cabarc n UsrCngProfile.cab UsrCngProfile.inf UsrCngProfile.ocx". DLL packages are created using the n command, followed by the name of the DLL package to be created, finally followed by the name of the DLL file, for example: "cabarc n BillPackage.cab BillPackage.bpl". For detailed instructions on using the Cabarc.exe utility, see the Microsoft Cabarc User's Guide (Cabarc.doc) included in the DOCS folder of the Cabinet SDK.

5.5 Making Package Carrier

To put it more precisely, package carriers have three functions: (a) to create and initialize an instance of a function-specific ActiveX component that the end-user wants to use; (b) to specify the minimum required file version of the component, and the download location for the component package; and (c) to perform some user interface processes to increase the usability of the downloadable BIS.

The easiest way to create and initialize an instance of ActiveX component, as well as to specify the file version of the component and the download location for the component package is to use the OBJECT html tag (see Figure 5). The important attributes of the OBJECT tag are summarized below.

1. CODEBASE: Specifies the download location for the component package. As an option, developers can specify the file version of the component by attaching a number sign (#) and file version at the end of the CODEBASE path. If #version is not specified and a version of this component is already installed on the end-user machine, no download occurs. If #version is specified and an earlier version of the component is already installed on the end-user machine, the component package will be downloaded. If the component is not present on the end-user machine, the component package will be downloaded whether #version is specified or not.
2. CLSID: Specifies the string representation of the GUID of the component. The format is "CLSID:12345678-1234-1234-1234-123456789ABC".
3. ID: Specifies a document-wide name of the component instance that client-side Web scripts can reference.

Unfortunately, Microsoft has made changes to the way that IE handles ActiveX components. Microsoft lost in a key Web browser patent ruling. The ruling forced Microsoft to redesign IE to get around such patent. Therefore end-users cannot directly interact with ActiveX component instances created by the OBJECT tag. End-users can interact with such component instances after activating their user interfaces, by either clicking it or using the TAB key to set focus on it and then pressing the SPACEBAR or the ENTER key [14]. For this reason, we will make use of an external script file to create and initialize an ActiveX component instance rather than using the OBJECT tag. ActiveX component instances created from external script files immediately respond to end-user interaction and do not need to be activated. Figure 6 contains an example of creating and initializing an ActiveX component instance using the external script file.

Additionally, package carriers perform three types of user interface processes that include (a) displaying an icon and a text string that identify the function to the end-user; (b) showing the end-user the component is being downloaded and installed; and (c) avoiding showing a disabled ActiveX component instance. Figure 6 demonstrates such user interface processes.

```
<OBJECT
  CODEBASE=/UsrCngProfile/UsrCngProfile.cab#version=1,0,0,101
  CLSID=CLSID:FF989E21-E5B4-4813-BF2E-2622AFBBA882
  ID=ax>
</OBJECT>
```

Fig. 5. Example of Creating an ActiveX Component Instance Using the OBJECT Tag

```
<!-- UsrCngProfile.asp - Example Package Carrier, is implemented using JavaScript and ASP -->
<%@ LANGUAGE=JavaScript %>

<HTML>
<HEAD>
  <META HTTP-EQUIV=Content-Type CONTENT=text/html;CHARSET=big5>
  <STYLE>
  BODY {color:green;margin:0;margin-left:10}
  </STYLE>
</HEAD>

<!-- names the package carrier -->
<BODY ID=UsrCngProfileAsp>

<!-- avoids to show a disabled component instance -->
<%
if ( Request.Cookies("LoginName") == "" )
%>
  <TABLE><TR><TD><IMG SRC=/img/stop.gif></TD><TD>Please Login First</TD></TR></TABLE>
<%
else
{
%>
  <!-- begin to display information about the component is being downloaded and installed -->
  <TABLE><TR>
  <TD><IMG SRC=/img/fun05.gif></TD>
  <TD ID=FunTitle>My Profile − Downloading <IMG SRC=/img/processing.gif></TD>
  </TR></TABLE>

  <!-- creates a component instance by using an external script file -->
  <SCRIPT LANGUAGE=JavaScript SRC=UsrCngProfile.js></SCRIPT>

  <SCRIPT LANGUAGE=JavaScript>
  //finish to display information about the component is being downloaded and installed
  function showLoaded(){if(document.readyState=="complete")FunTitle.innerText="My Profile";}
  document.onreadystatechange=showLoaded;

  //initializes the component instance
  ax.tabIndex=0;
  ax.focus();
  ax.color=0xE0FFFF;
  </SCRIPT>
<%
}
%>
</BODY>
</HTML>
```

```
// UsrCngProfile.js - External Script File, is implemented using JavaScript.

var obj=document.createElement("object");                            //creates a component instance
UsrCngProfileAsp.appendChild(obj);                                   //inserts the component instance into the package carrier
obj.codeBase="/UsrCngProfile/UsrCngProfile.cab#version=1,0,0,101";   //sets the URL for the component package
obj.classid="CLSID:FF989E21-E5B4-4813-BF2E-2622AFBBA882";           //sets the GUID of the component
obj.id="ax";                                                         //names the component instance
```

Fig. 6. Example Package Carrier

6 Case Study: A Windows-Based C/S Book Management System

In this section we will give an example of using the downloadable architecture and the architecture transformation process in a WinBIS. Additionally, we hope this example can provide evidence to support the feasibility of such architecture and process. This is a typical two-tier WinBIS which supports the management of books. The single client program of the system is developed with Delphi 3.0. The database of the system, on the other hand, is managed using SQL Server 2000. The client program provides fifteen functions that can be grouped into three categories: reader service, daily operation, and data management. From a form perspective, the client program is composed of eighty-eight forms that can be classified into five types: splash form, main form, about form, function-specific primary form, and function-specific secondary form. Moreover, from the relationship between function and form, each function is implemented as both a function-specific primary form and zero or more function- specific secondary forms.

6.1 Deployability Improvement of the Book Management System

In order to improve the deployability of this system, we go through the architecture transformation process, to transform its only client program from a Windows program into a program warehouse. First, we make the home page, menu page, and message page. The home page split up the browser window into three frames. The menu page is loaded into the left frame; the message page into the right-top frame; while the end-user selected package carrier is loaded into the right-bottom frame. Next, we make the ActiveX component (with Delphi 2006), INF file, component package, DLL packages, and package carrier for all fifteen functions of the client program one by one. Detailed account of the making process of two of fifteen ActiveX components are given below.

The Log In/Out ActiveX Component. The Log In/Out function allows an end-user to login or logout of the system. In the old system, this function is implemented as three forms: the log in/out form (primary form), the warning form, and the information form. The log in/out form is custom-made; the warning form and the information form are made with existing dialog subroutines. In the new downloadable system, this function is implemented as an ActiveX component, which is composed of an embedded form and two pop-up forms. To create this ActiveX component, first we create a new ActiveX component project. Then we open the log in/out form, and copy and paste all its components and code into the embedded form (except the VB-like tool generated code). We then modify the global variable related code in response to the change from global variables to session cookies. Following this, we write code to refresh the message page. We then specify the file version of the ActiveX component. Finally, we compile and link the project to produce the ActiveX component. The size of the ActiveX component's package is 24.49 KB; the total size of seven dependent common DLLs' packages is 1284.79 KB. Hence, an end-user will download 1309.28 KB code, when he/she first uses this function, if we cannot pre-install the DLLs on his/her machine.

The Book Data Management ActiveX Component. The Book Management function allows an end-user to insert, delete, modify, and retrieve book data. In the old system, this function is implemented as thirteen forms: the search form (primary form), the search results form, the book edit form, the delete results form, the load picture form, the export picture form, the abstract edit form, the find form, the replace form, the font form, the print form, the warning form, and the confirmation form. The load picture form, the export picture form, the abstract edit form, the find form, the replace form, the font form, the print form are made with existing dialog components; the warning form and the confirmation form are made with existing dialog subroutines; the remainders are custom-made. In the new downloadable system, this function is implemented as an ActiveX component, which is composed of an embedded form and twelve pop-up forms. To create this ActiveX component, first we create a new ActiveX component project. Then we open the search form, and copy and paste all its components and code into the embedded form (except the VB-like tool generated code). We then write code to check if the end-user is logged in (using session cookies), and if not, to disable the ActiveX component. Following this, we attach other three custom-made forms to the project. We then specify the file version of the ActiveX component and finally, we compile and link the project to produce the ActiveX component. The size of the ActiveX component's package is 46.68 KB; the total size of seven dependent common DLLs' packages is 1284.79 KB; the size of dependent text editor DLL's package is 17.81 KB. The Log In/Out function must be performed before this function. Hence, an end-user will download 64.49 KB code, when he/she first uses this function, if we cannot pre-install the DLLs on his/her machine.

6.2 On-Line Testing

You can test the downloadable book management system via the Internet. The URL is http://ax.bill.idv.tw; the id is test; the password is test again. But please note:

1. You have to configure the browser's security settings to enable ActiveX components and session cookies. Moreover, if behind a firewall, you have to configure the firewall to open the TCP port 2433 and UDP port 1434.
2. Downloadable BISs are restricted to use in Intranet or Extranet only. In fact, you will manipulate the downloadable book management system via the Internet. Bear in mind that file download speed and database access efficiency on the Internet are very different from the Intranet/Extranet.
3. The Web server (Internet Information Services 5.0) and the database management system (SQL Server 2000) both operated in a humble environment: (a) AMD Athlon 1.0G CPU; (b) 768 MB SDRAM; and (c) 2 Mbps/256 Kbps ADSL. In general, businesses will provide more desirable operating environment for downloadable BISs.

7 Related Work

Information system deployment is a complex process which covers all the activities that have to be carried out from the end of the development itself on developer sites to the actual installation and maintenance of the information system on end-user machines [3] [7]. It is worth noting that until recently the research community focused on the development and evolution of information systems. Very little research work dealt with the delivery, installation and maintenance of information systems on end-user machines

[4]. On the whole, there are two ways to ease the deployment load of existing information systems. The first way is to deploy information systems using better deployment tools. Another way is to transform the architecture of information systems for the purpose of deployability improvement. Over the past few years, several research works have been devoted to the study of deployment tools, such as [6], [7], [9], [20]. Carzaniga et al. [3] and Jansen et al. [11] characterizing a variety of deployment tools to help our understanding of such deployment tools. Similarly, several research works have focused on the architecture transformation of information systems, such as [1], [2], [8], [12], [19]. However, there has been no research on the ActiveX-based architecture transformation of WinBISs for the purpose of deployability improvement. Incidentally, practical and well-defined ActiveX-based BIS architecture has never been described so far. Thus, we need not only to develop the architecture transformation process, but also to define the downloadable architecture.

8   Conclusion

For WinBISs, client programs must be manually deployed to each end-user machine bringing about a heavy BIS maintenance load. If all client programs were to be stored in a central warehouse, and thereafter the client programs were to be downloaded, installed and run on end-user machines dynamically and automatically, then the BIS maintenance load would be effectively eased. In this paper, we have proposed an ActiveX-based technology to realize this idea. The innovative applied technology can easily and effectively improve the deployability of existing WinBISs bringing about a remarkable ease in the BIS maintenance load, and is a contribution to the information systems field.

References

1. Babiker, E., Simmons, D., Shannon, R., & Ellis, N. (1997). A Model for Reengineering Legacy Expert Systems to Object-Oriented Architecture. Expert Systems with Applications, 12(3), 363-371.
2. Bodhuin, T., Guardaboscio, E., & Tortorella, M. (2002). Migrating COBOL Systems to the Web by Using the MVC Design Pattern. Proceedings of the 9th Working Conference on Reverse Engineering, Richmod, VA, 329-338.
3. Carzaniga, A., Fuggetta, A., Hall, R.S., Heimbigner, D., Van der Hoek, A., & Wolf, A.L. (1998). A Characterization Framework for Software Deployment Technologies, (Tech. Rep. CU-CS-857-98). Boulder: University of Colorado, Deptartment of Computer Science.
4. Coupaye, T., & Estublier, J. (2000). Foundations of Enterprise Software Deployment. Proceedings of the European Conference on Software Maintenance and Reengineering 2000, Zurich, Switzerland, 65-73.
5. Dershem, H.L., & Jipping, M.J. (1995). Programming Languages: Structures and Models. Boston: PWS.
6. Dolstra, E., Visser, E., & de Jonge, M. (2004). Imposing a Memory Management Discipline on Software Deployment. Proceedings of the 26th International Conference on Software Engineering, Scotland, UK, 583-592.
7. Hall, R.S., Heimbigner, D., & Wolf, A.L. (1999). A Cooperative Approach to Support Software Deployment Using the Software Dock. Proceedings of the 21th International Conference on Software Engineering, Los Angeles, 174-183.

8. Hassan, A.E., & Holt, R.C. (2005). A Lightweight Approach for Migrating Web Frameworks. Information and Software Technology, 47(8), 521-532.

9. Hnetynka, P. (2005). A Model-Driven Environment for Component Deployment. Proceedings of the 3rd ACIS International Conference on Software Engineering Research, Management and Applications, Mount Pleasant, MI, 6-13.

10. Hoque, R., & Sharma, T. (1998). Programming Web Components. New York: McGraw-Hill.

11. Jansen, S., Ballintijn, G., & Brinkkemper, S. (2005). A Process Model and Typology for Software Product Updaters. Proceedings of the 9th European Conference on Software Maintenance and Reengineering, Manchester, UK, 265-274.

12. Klusener, A.S., Lammel, R., & Verhoef, C. (2005). Architectural Modifications to Deployed Software. Science of Computer Programming, 54(2-3), 143-211.

13. Kristol, D.M. (2001). HTTP Cookies: Standards, Privacy, and Politics. ACM Transactions on Internet Technology, 1(2), 151-198.

14. Microsoft (2006a). Activating ActiveX Controls. http://msdn.microsoft.com/workshop/author/dhtml/overview/activating_activex.asp.

15. Microsoft (2006b). ActiveX Controls. http://msdn.microsoft.com/library/default.asp?url=/workshop/components/ activex/activex_node_entry.asp.

16. Orfali, R., Harkey, D., & Edwards, J. (1999). Client/Server Survival Guide. Hoboken, NJ: Wiley.

17. Shaw, M., DeLine, R., Klein, D.V., Ross, T.L., Young, D.M., & Zelesnik, G. (1995). Abstractions for Software Architecture and Tools to Support Them. IEEE Transactions on Software Engineering, 21(4), 314-335.

18. Silberschatz, A., Galvin, P.B., & Gagne, G. (2004). Operating System Concepts. Hoboken, NJ: Wiley.

19. Tahvildari, L., Kontogiannis, K., & Mylopoulos, J. (2003). Quality-Driven Software Reengineering. The Journal of Systems and Software, 66(3), 225-239.

20. Van der Hoek, A., & Wolf, A.L. (2003). Software Release Management for Component-Based Software. Software: Practice and Experience, 33(1), 77-98.

An Automatic Approach to Displaying Web Applications as Portlets

Fernando Bellas[1], Iñaki Paz[2], Alberto Pan[1],
Óscar Díaz[2], Víctor Carneiro[1], and Fidel Cacheda[1]

[1] Department of Information and Communications Technologies,
University of A Coruña, A Coruña, 15071, Spain
{fbellas, apan, viccar, fidel}@udc.es
[2] ONEKIN Research Group,
University of the Basque Country, San Sebastián, 20018, Spain
{inaki.paz, oscar.diaz}@ehu.es

Abstract. Wrapping existing Web applications into portals allows to protect investment and improves user experience. Most current portlet-based portal servers provide a bridge portlet that allows to "portletize" a single Web page, that is, wrapping the whole page or a set of regions as a portlet. They use an annotation-based approach to specifying the page's regions that must be extracted. This approach does not scale well when a whole application is to be portletized, since it requires to manually annotate each page. This paper describes the design of a bridge portlet that automatically adapts pages according to the space available in the portlet's window. The bridge portlet delegates page adaptation to a framework that uses a chain of user-configurable "transformers". Each transformer implements an automatic page adaptation technique. Experiments show that our approach is effective.

Keywords: Portlet, Portal, Web content adaptation, Web wrappers.

1 Introduction

Moving an application to the Web implies facing its multi-channel character. The very same functionality can be offered through a variety of "channels", e.g. as a Web application to be accessed from a desktop or a small-screen device (e.g. PDA, smart phone, etc), or as a portlet available through a portal. Although the functionality remains the same, the characteristics of each channel determine the implementation. The pressure to have a Web presence, and the pace at which technology evolves, make most organization support the desktop-oriented Web application first, and at latter stages, care about adapting it for small-screen devices and portals.

Portlets are interactive Web mini-applications, local or remote to the portal, that render markup fragments that the portal can integrate into a page (usually shared by other portlets). Integrating a Web application as a portlet improves the user experience, since the portal can automatically apply user profiles when accessing the Web application. For example, if the application requires authentication, the portal

S. Madria et al. (Eds.): ICDCIT 2006, LNCS 4317, pp. 264–277, 2006.

can store authentication parameters to automatically authenticate the user in the application when she or he logs in the portal. However, in principle, to integrate a Web application, a specific portlet must be developed.

This paper focuses on "portletizing" existing Web applications, that is, wrapping them as portlets. Current portal servers (e.g. BEA WebLogic Portal, IBM WebSphere Portal, Oracle Portal, etc) only provide support to portletize a single Web page, that is, wrapping the whole page or a set of regions as a portlet. The administrator uses a tool that allows him/her to access the Web page and specify the regions she or he is interested in. Usually, the administration tool generates a file, sometimes called an annotation file [10], that specifies the location of those regions (e.g. by using XPath expressions). The portal server provides a portlet (hereafter, the "bridge portlet") that navigate automatically to the Web page [1, 8], extracts the regions specified in the corresponding annotation file, and returns a fragment containing those regions (see Fig. 1). However, this kind of portletization only allows to portletize one page and the space available in the portlet's window (window state) is not taken into account.

[6] raises the issues involved in "deep portletization". This implies portletizing the whole bulk of pages that comprise the Web application. Their approach also relies on annotations.

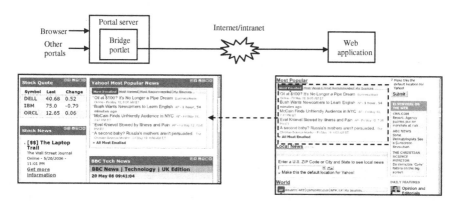

Fig. 1. Using a bridge portlet to wrap the "Most Popular" region from the "Yahoo! News" main page

Annotation-based approaches account for a fine-grained, accurate adaptation of the Web application to the portlet setting, since particular regions of the Web pages can be extracted. However, it requires to manually annotate each page to specify the regions of interest and how they will be displayed in function of the window state. Furthermore, annotations must use an addressing language (e.g. XPath) to accomplish such tasks. Changes in the Web pages (e.g. adding or removing an HTML tag) may easily invalidate addressing expressions. This leads to a maintenance nightmare.

Among the distinct issues involved in portletizing a Web application [6], this paper presents an automatic approach to displaying Web applications as portlets. In our approach, Web pages are displayed according to space available in the portlet's window. In the *solo* state, all the content of the page is displayed. In the *maximized* state, only the body block (all regions except header, footer, and sidebars) is shown. In the *normal* state, the body block is segmented. We present the design of a bridge portlet that adapts pages accordingly. The bridge portlet delegates page adaptation to a framework that uses a chain of "transformers". Each transformer implements an automatic page adaptation technique, valid no matter the application. A specific chain is used for each possible window state. To validate our approach, we implemented a prototype and portletized 50 Internet Web applications.

This approach does not allow to achieve the fine-grained, accurate adaptation that can be obtained with an annotation-based approach. However, it brings two key benefits, namely, it avoids having to annotate each page, and enhances resilience to Web page modifications (XPath expressions are not used).

The main contributions of our work are:

- A visualization model to automatically display Web applications as portlets.
- The design of a bridge portlet that implements this model.
- A new technique to automatically identify the main blocks of a Web page, and in particular to extract the body block.

The rest of the paper is organized as follows. Section 2 gives an overview of portlet technology. In section 3 we present a sample scenario. Section 4 discusses the design of the bridge portlet. Section 5 presents experimental results. In section 6 we compare our approach with related work. Finally, section 7 presents conclusions.

2 Overview of Portlet Technology

The classic approach to integrating a Web application into a remote portal consists in defining a Web service (SOAP/REST) that exposes part of the application's business logic. The problem with this approach is that any portal wishing to integrate such an application must re-implement the user interface. It would be easier if the service was a remote portlet, returning HTML markup fragments rather than plain data. The Web Services for Remote Portlets (WSRP) specification [14] standardizes the interfaces of the Web services a portlet producer must implement to allow another application (typically a portal) to consume its portlets, regardless of the technology the producer and consumer use (e.g. J2EE, .NET, etc). Portlet URLs embedded into fragments point to the portal. Whenever the user clicks on a link, the portal receives the HTTP request, invokes an operation on the portlet's producer that returns the markup fragment corresponding to this interaction, and finally composes a page that includes the response of this portlet and those of the remaining portlets in the page.

The Java Portlet Specification (JSR 168) [12] standardizes a Java API for implementing local, WSRP-compatible portlets. Java portlets run in a portlet container, a portal component that provides portlets with a runtime environment. Fig. 2 shows the typical architecture of a Java portal server [2]. The WSRP producer component provides an implementation of the WSRP interfaces, so other consumers can access local portlets. The WSRP consumer is implemented as a local portlet that acts as a generic proxy of any WSRP producer.

The WSRP standard defines portlet modes and window states. Portlet modes refer to the types of functionality a portlet can perform. In *view* mode, the portlet renders fragments that support its functional purpose (e.g. displaying weather forecasts). In *edit* mode, the portlet lets the user customize the behavior of the portlet (e.g. specifying the default temperature unit). The *help* mode provides help information. Finally, the *preview* mode allows to view the portlet before adding it to a portal page.

Window states act as an indication of the space available in the portlet's window. The *normal* state indicates the portlet is likely sharing the page with other portlets. When the state is *minimized*, the portlet should not render visible markup. In the *maximized* state, the portlet has more space compared to other portlets in the page. Finally, the *solo* state indicates the portlet is the only portlet in the page.

The portal decorates the fragments returned by a portlet with buttons to let the user select the portlet mode and window state.

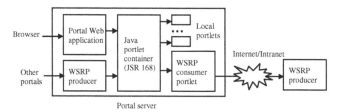

Fig. 2. Typical architecture of a standards-based Java portal server

3   A Sample Scenario

This section uses the "Yahoo! Weather" service (*http://weather.yahoo.com*) as a sample scenario to illustrate our vision of how a Web application could be automatically displayed as a portlet (*view* mode). According to the expected behavior in the standard window states, our bridge portlet automatically adapts Web pages to the space available in the portlet's window. It also tries to keep the original look-and-feel. Fig. 3 shows the responses generated by the bridge portlet.

Fig. 3(a) shows the first page of the application when the user has selected the *solo* window state. Since the portlet is the only one in the portal page, the bridge portlet decides to show the original content. As the fragment returned by the portlet must be inserted into the portal page, the portlet extracts the markup contained inside the *<body>* tag of the original page, and rewrites the URLs that must be navigable inside the portlet's window.

Fig. 3(b) shows the same page when the user selects the *maximized* window state. In this state, the portlet is supposed to have a lot of space in the page, but less than in the *solo* window state. The content of Web pages is often structured in five high-level blocks: header, footer, left side bar, right side bar, and body (the content region of the page). From the point of view of the actual content, the body block is the most important one, since the rest of blocks are usually dedicated to navigational issues and miscellaneous information. In consequence, to save space, the bridge portlet detects the high-level blocks, extracts the body block, and rewrites the URLs that must be navigable inside the portlet's window.

Fig. 3(c) shows the same page when the user selects the *normal* window state. Since the portlet is supposed to share the page with other portlets, the bridge portlet must reduce even more the amount of markup it generates. To do so, it applies the same transformations as in the *maximized* window state and returns a fragment that contains the first part of the body block.

Fig. 3(d) illustrates the situation when the user enters *La Coruna* in the form and clicks on the *Search* button. The portlet had rewritten the form's URL previously to point to itself. In consequence, this interaction causes a request directed to it. The portlet fetches the corresponding page and proceeds as in the previous case.

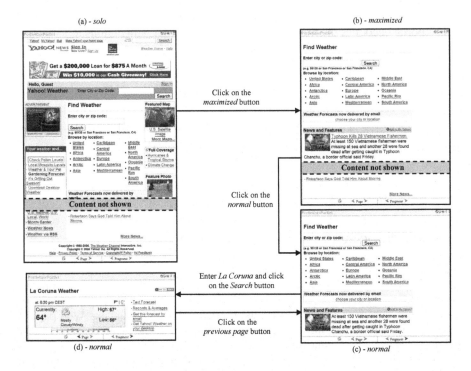

Fig. 3. Displaying "Yahoo! Weather" as a portlet (*view* mode). To save space, figures (a) and (b) do not show all the content generated by the bridge portlet.

To keep the application navigable, the bridge portlet includes five *navigability buttons* (enabled or disabled as appropriate) at the bottom of all generated fragments. Such buttons are links that point to the bridge portlet. The *previous/next fragment* buttons allow the user to navigate through the fragments of a page when the window state is *normal*. For example, if the user clicks on the *next fragment* button in Fig. 3(c), the bridge portlet returns the next fragment of the body block.

The *previous/next page* buttons allow the user to navigate through the pages already visited. Each page is displayed in the previously selected fragment. For example, if the user clicks on the *previous page* button in Fig. 3(d), the bridge portlet returns the markup corresponding to Fig. 3(c). For convenience, a *home page* button is also included to let the user go directly to the initial page.

Note that the *previous/next page* buttons of the browser do not cause the same effect as the *previous/next page* buttons included by the bridge portlet. The former allow to navigate sequentially through all the pages previously returned by the portal. The latter allow the user to navigate through the pages already visited in an individual portlet, without affecting the pages displayed by the rest of portlets.

4 Design and Implementation of the Bridge Portlet

4.1 Architecture

The fragments shown in Fig. 3 can be generated by using a chain of transformations that depends on the current window state. For example, when the window state is *maximized*, as in Fig. 3(b), the fragment can be generated by (1) detecting the high-level blocks of the original page and extracting the body block, and (2) including the navigability buttons. When the window state is *normal*, as in Fig. 3(c), an additional transformation, that splits the body and extracts the appropriate fragment, can be applied between the two transformations used in the *maximized* window state.

The above observation gives rise to the framework depicted in Fig. 4. *TransfomerChainManager* allows to obtain a particular chain (*TransfomerChain*) of transformation strategies to be applied to a page in a given window state. All transformation strategies implement the *Transformer* interface. The *transform* method in *TransfomerChain* allows to execute the chain of transformations on a given page. By default, the framework provides three transformers:

- *BodyExtractor*. It returns the body block by detecting the high-level blocks of the original page and discarding the header, the footer, and the side bars.
- *GeneralSegmenter*. It divides the page into rectangular sections and returns the requested section. The area (in square pixels) of the rectangular sections is specified by a configuration parameter, and represents the approximate size of the portlet's window the user wishes in the *normal* window state.
- *PageNavigabilityTransformer*. It inserts the navigability buttons.

The default implementation of the *TransformerChainManager* returns the empty chain when the window state is *solo*, the *{BodyExtractor→PageNavigability-Transformer}* chain when the window state is *maximized*, and finally, the *{BodyExtractor→GeneralSegmenter→PageNavigabilityTransformer}* chain for the *normal* window state.

Except in the *minimized* window state, when the bridge portlet receives a request for a page, it calls: (1) *getPage* on *PageManager* to retrieve the page, (2) *getTransformerChain* on *TransformerChainManager* to obtain the particular chain of transformers to be applied in the current window state, (3) *transform* on *TransformerChain* to generate the fragment by applying the chain of transformations, and finally (4) *postProcessPage* on *PagePostProcessor*. When the window state is *minimized*, the bridge portlet returns an empty fragment (this is the default behavior inherited from *javax.portlet.GenericPortlet*).

The *Page* object returned by *PageManager* provides "getter" methods to access certain information of the page, such as JavaScript code, CSS styles, and the fragment that contains all the tags inside the *<body>* tag. Transformers work with this fragment, since the rest of tags cannot be included in the portal page. Internally, this fragment is represented as a DOM tree. All transformers work with the standard DOM API. Since some transformers (currently *BodyExtractor* and *General Segmenter*) need to know the visual information of each node, we use a mechanism of DOM Level 3 that allows to attach information to nodes. In particular, each node has an attached object providing visual information of the rectangular region it defines. This information includes the *X* and *Y* coordinates of the left upper corner of the rectangle, and its width and height.

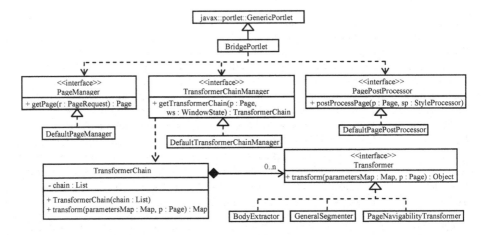

Fig. 4. Bridge portlet's framework

The implementation of *PagePostProcessor* has to rewrite the URLs that must be navigable inside the portlet's window, include CSS styles and JavaScript code defined inside the *<head>* tag of the original page, and rename all JavaScript functions/variables and CSS styles to avoid collisions with the rest of portlets included in the same page and with the portal itself.

Finally, it is worth noting that since the bridge portlet has been designed as a framework, new transformers and chains of transformers can be easily added. For example, transformers could be implemented for extracting specific areas delimited by XPath expressions (when a fine-grained, accurate adaptation approach is required) or allowing the user to create bookmarks to specific screens (customization).

4.2 Implementation of *BodyExtractor*

We only discuss the implementation of *BodyExtractor*, since this is the only transformer that makes use of heuristics. *BodyExtractor* uses four "block removers": *HeaderRemover*, *FooterRemover*, *LeftSideBarRemover*, and *RightSideBarRemover*. The implementation of all block removers is orthogonal. Each remover tries to find a region (a group of nodes) that visually can be considered as the block it is trying to remove. To do so, each remover uses the visual information included in nodes. A region can be classified as a particular block in function of its shape (width/height ratio) and its position. For example, the header block has a flat shape (high width/height ratio) and is placed at the top of the page. Each remover uses four configuration parameters. Three of them refer to the shape and position of the block it is trying to find. The other allows to specify if the remover is enabled or disabled.

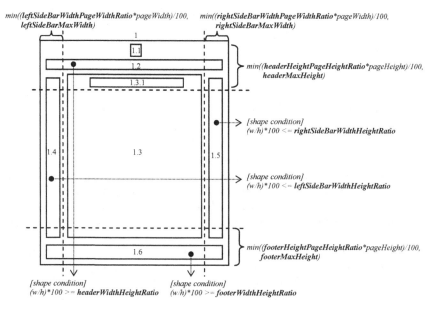

Fig. 5. *BodyExtractor*'s virtual blocks and shape conditions. In the figure, *node 1* is the outer rectangle and configuration parameters are in bold type.

Since the implementation of all removers is orthogonal, we will only describe the implementation of *HeaderRemover*. The algorithm used by *HeaderRemover* makes use of two concepts: the *virtual header* and the *shape condition* (see Fig. 5). The *virtual header* is the region where the header is supposed to be contained (if it exists). This region is placed at the top of the page. It has the same width as the page and a height computed as *min((headerHeightPageHeightRatio*pageHeight)/100, headerMaxHeight)*. *headerHeightPageHeightRatio* is a configuration parameter that specifies the ratio of the virtual header height to the page height. For example, a value of 35% means that the virtual header height is 35% of the page height. However, for long pages this parameter places the bottom line of the virtual header too down. To overcome this problem, we have added a second parameter, *headerMaxHeight*, which specifies the maximum height of the virtual header in pixels (e.g. 400 pixels).

The *shape condition* is the condition a node must fulfill to be considered as flat. A node is considered as flat if *(w/h)*100 >= headerWidthHeightRatio*. *w* and *h* are the width and height (in pixels) of the rectangular region defined by the node. *headerWidthHeightRatio* is a configuration parameter that specifies the minimum width/height ratio the region must fulfill to be considered as flat. For example, a value of 200% means that the region must be at least 2 times wider than higher.

Taking into account these two concepts, *HeaderRemover* implements the following algorithm (see Fig. 5):

1. It computes the virtual header.
2. It finds the deepest node (node 1) that contains the virtual header.
3. It considers the direct children (nodes 1.1, 1.2, 1.3, 1.4, 1.5, and 1.6) of the node containing the virtual header, and chooses the child node that fulfills the following conditions:
   • It is inside the virtual header (nodes 1.1 and 1.2).
   • It is the closest to the bottom line of the virtual header.
   • It fulfills the shape condition.
4. The node found in the previous step (node 1.2) and the sibling nodes placed above it (node 1.1) are considered as the header, and in consequence, they are removed. Those sibling nodes may not fulfill the shape condition, but they are removed by consistency (visually they are placed above it).

Note that the previous algorithm would never consider node 1.3.1 as part of the header, even though it is inside the virtual header and has a flat shape. This is because its father (node 1.3), which is a direct child of the node containing the virtual header (node 1), is not inside the virtual header. Intuitively, this means that a region inside the virtual header, but which it is also inside another region that probably corresponds to the body block, is not removed.

Finally, note also that the previous algorithm does not remove anything if it does not find a node fulfilling the conditions imposed by the third step. This is important because the pages of the Web application may not have the block the remover is trying to remove (e.g. pages could have a left side bar, but not a right side bar).

4.3 Prototype

To validate our approach we implemented a prototype of the bridge portlet. The portlet's windows shown in Fig. 3 (section 3) were obtained with this prototype. The implementation uses the standard Java Portlet API, and in consequence, it can be deployed in any standard Java portal server. In particular, we used eXo Platform [7]. A demo is available at *http://www.tic.udc.es/~fbellas/portletizer*.

Since the nodes of the DOM tree contained in the *Page* object returned by *PageManager* must provide visual information, the implementation of *PageManager* must use an HTML parser providing this information. For simplicity, *DefaultPageManager* uses Jiffie [13], which is a Java library that allows to access Internet Explorer's COM interfaces. The *PageManager* interface hides the parser to the rest of classes in the framework.

To portletize a Web application, the portal user creates an instance of the bridge portlet, adds it to a portal page, and selects the *edit* mode. In the *edit* mode, the bridge portlet displays a configuration wizard that allows to specify:

• The URL of the first page of the application (e.g. *http://weather.yahoo.com* in the sample scenario). This is the only field that must be explicitly filled.
• A set of URL patterns for the URLs that must be navigable inside the portlet's window. The bridge portlet rewrites the URLs matching these patterns to point to itself. In the sample scenario, if we wish to keep the search form and the "browse by location" links navigable, we could specify */search/weather2* for the search form, and */regional/** and */forecast/** to browse by location. URL patterns can be specified in "absolute URL" or "absolute path" (as in the example) notation.

- The configuration of *BodyExtractor* and *GeneralSegmenter*. The configuration wizard provides default values (see section 5).

The above information is stored as the portlet's preferences [12], and in consequence, each portlet instance has its own configuration of *BodyExtractor* and *GeneralSegmenter* (tuned for the application to portletize if necessary).

The prototype does not allow to display directly the portletized Web application in the *solo* window state, since such a window state is not supported by the Java Portlet Specification, but only by the WSRP standard. However, such a mode can be simulated by selecting the *maximized* window state, and then selecting the *edit* mode and disabling *BodyExtractor*'s removers in the configuration wizard.

Finally, to concentrate our efforts in evaluating the core of our approach, we have omitted the implementation of diverse aspects, such as cookie management, rewriting of URLs embedded in JavaScript code, collisions with the CSS styles used by the portal or other portlets, and correct treatment of FRAMEs/IFRAMEs.

5 Experiments

We evaluated the accuracy of page adaptation. Taking aside implementation bugs, the accuracy depends exclusively on the performance of *BodyExtractor*, since this is currently the only transformer that makes use of heuristics. To this end, we portletized 50 Internet Web applications. Since portlets are supposed to be interactive mini-applications, we chose Web applications providing concrete services (e.g. weather forecasts, news, translation, search, etc), and for each service, apart from its main page, we specified patterns to rewrite URLs corresponding to two or three types of pages. The sample scenario is a case in point. We specified patterns for the URL corresponding to the search form and the "browse by location" links. This way, the resulting portletized Web application represents a mini-application that allows the user to know the weather by typing a city in the form or browsing by location.

From these 50 Web applications, we selected randomly 15 of them. We used this subset (the training set) to experimentally choose appropriate default values for *BodyExtractor*'s configuration parameters. We tried to choose values that produced good results for most of the applications in the training set. Table 1 shows the default values we finally used. Table 2 contains the results for the training set with the default configuration. We used a very strict criterion. *Perfect* means that the body block was correctly extracted in all portletized pages, that is, the outer blocks (header, footer, and side bars) were completely removed. *Acceptable* means that some region of some of the outer blocks was not removed in some page. *Error* means that some region of the body block was removed or that some of the outer blocks was not removed (no region inside such a block was removed) in some page. In all cases, we discarded the errors caused by the known limitations in the implementation of our prototype.

As Table 1 shows, 80% of the applications were displayed perfectly with the default configuration. Two applications were displayed acceptably because they contained pages with regions that although visually are part of one of the outer blocks, they are not placed as supposed by *BodyExtractor*'s removers. In consequence, they cannot be extracted, even adjusting the configuration parameters. For example, the pages of "Yahoo! Most Viewed News" (*news.yahoo.com/ms/1776*) include a tabbed navigation bar in the header that corresponds to the region 1.3.1 in Fig. 5. In consequence, *HeaderRemover* does not remove this bar since it supposes it belongs to the body block. Finally, one application was displayed with errors, since part of the body block was removed. This was because its pages visually do not contain footer. However, they contain regions inside the virtual footer that fulfill the conditions to be considered as footer. This result could be improved to *Perfect* by disabling *FooterRemover*.

Table 1. *BodyExtractor*'s default configuration. All removers were enabled.

Parameter	Val.	Parameter	Val.	Parameter	Val.
headerHeightPageHeightRatio	35%	headerMaxHeight	400	headerWidthHeightRatio	200%
footerHeightPageHeightRatio	35%	footerMaxHeight	400	footerWidthHeightRatio	200%
leftSideBarWidthPageWidthRatio	35%	leftSideBarMaxWidth	300	leftSideBarWidthHeightRatio	33,3%
rightSideBarWidthPageWidthRatio	55%	rightSideBarMaxWidth	600	rightSideBarWidthHeightRatio	75%

Table 2. *BodyExtractor*'s results for the training set. $P \equiv perfect$, $A \equiv acceptable$, $E \equiv error$.

Service	Res.	Service	Res.
news.yahoo.com/ms/1776	A	weather.lycos.com	P
weather.yahoo.com	P	www.wired.com/technology.html	P
weather.msn.com → Weather at a given location	P	www.yellowpages.com	P
www.freetranslation.com/free	P	music.msn.com/default.aspx	P
www.wordreference.com	E	news.bbc.co.uk/2/hi/europe/default.stm	A
moneycentral.msn.com/detail/stock_quote	P	www.allmovie.com → Horror category	P
movies.go.com/newandupcoming	P	news.bbc.co.uk/sport	P
www.cmt.com/news	P		

P	80%	A	13.3%	E	6.7%

By using the default configuration we obtained with the training set, we portletized the remaining 35 Web applications (the test set). Table 3 shows the results. More than 70% of the applications were displayed perfectly. Four applications (11.4%) were displayed acceptably and six with errors (17.1%). For these ten applications, we tried to improve their results by modifying the configuration. After this, 88.6% of applications could be displayed perfectly and the rest were displayed acceptably. In particular, one *Acceptable* result could be improved to *Perfect*. The other three could not be improved. Five *Error* results could be improved to *Perfect* and one to *Acceptable*. In the seven applications where we modified the default configuration, we only had to modify one parameter in six of them, and two parameters in the other. In all cases, we used the same configuration for all the portletized pages in each Web application. This was because (as expected) they shared a similar layout.

The *Acceptable* results that could not be improved by adjusting *BodyExtractor*'s configuration parameters were caused by the presence of regions, visually inside one of the outer blocks, but that were not placed as supposed by *BodyExtractor*'s removers (similar to the case of "Yahoo! Most Viewed News"). For these cases, we could have added a configuration parameter to each *BodyExtractor*'s remover to allow the removal of all regions inside the virtual block, independently of their nesting with other regions. Enabling this parameter and adjusting one of the parameters that define the height or width of the block to remove (e.g. *headerMaxHeight* in the case of *HeaderRemover*) would allow to remove those regions. However, this would be a very precise kind of tuning, probably less resilient even than the use of XPath expressions to extract the body block. If we really want to improve the result for this kind of applications, it is better to resort to an annotation-based approach by adding a transformer to the framework that extracts the body block by using XPath expressions.

Table 3. *BodyExtractor*'s results for the test set. $P \equiv perfect$, $A \equiv acceptable$, $E \equiv error$, $X \rightarrow Y$ $\equiv X$ (A or E) with default configuration and Y (P or A) with specific configuration.

Service	Res.	Service	Res.
autos.yahoo.com/usedcars/find.html	P	www.infospace.com → Symbol lookup	E→P
movies.yahoo.com/feature/comingsoon.html	P	www.hollywood.com/movies/coming_soon.aspx	A→P
finance.yahoo.com/lookup	P	www.xe.com/ucc	E→P
astrology.yahoo.com/astrology → Aries	P	www.becas.com/c/index.html	P
www.bbc.co.uk/weather	P	www.oanda.com/convert/classic	P
yp.yahoo.com (restaurants)	P	www.periodismo.com/c	P
education.yahoo.com/reference/dict_en_es	P	home.skysports.com/Football	P
www.google.com	E→P	www.eurosport.com/formula1	A
search.yahoo.com	E→P	www.soundgenerator.com/news/index.cfm	A
www.elrincondelprogramador.com	P	www.technewsworld.com/perl/section/internet	P
www.guiacampsa.com	P	entertainment.lycos.com/movies/comingSoon.php	E→A
world.altavista.com	P	www.msnbc.msn.com/id/3032847	P
dictionary.reference.com/translate/text.html	P	health.msn.com/encyclopedia/default.aspx	P
www.encyclopedia.com	P	astrocenter.astrology.msn.com/msn/DeptHoroscope.aspx	P
encarta.msn.com → Dictionary	P	movies.msn.com/movies/lifecycle.aspx	P
encarta.msn.com → Thesaurus	P	sports.excite.com/index.html	P
dictionary.cambridge.org	P	www.nme.com/news	A
www.quote.com/qc/lookup/symbol_search.aspx	E→P		

With default configuration	P	71.4%	A	11.4%	E	17.1%
With specific configuration	P	88.6%	A	11.4%	E	0%

In summary, we can extract the following conclusions:

- With *BodyExtactor*'s default configuration, more than 70% of applications were displayed perfectly, and more than 80% were displayed perfectly or acceptably.
- For the applications that were displayed acceptably or erroneously using the default configuration, more than half were displayed perfectly by adjusting usually only one configuration parameter, while the rest were displayed acceptably.
- We used the same configuration for all the portletized pages in each application.

6 Related Work

Since our bridge portlet has to automatically adapt Web pages to the space available in the portlet's window, the research area most related to our work is that of automatic Web content adaptation to small-screen devices.

Gupta et al. [9] describe Crunch, an HTTP proxy that tries to extract the relevant content in Web pages. In particular, Crunch uses a filter that removes "link lists", which are regions for which the ratio of the number of links to the number of non-linked words is greater than a specific threshold. Usually side bars contain long link lists. Compared with our *BodyExtractor*, this filter is too trivial to effectively extract the body block, since it removes link lists contained in regions inside the body block, and in general, it does not remove headers, footers, and regions inside side bars with a low percentage of links.

Chen et al. [5] present an adaptation technique that, among other things, allows to detect the high-level blocks of a Web page. To do so, they traverse the DOM tree and classify nodes into one of the high-level blocks by considering their position and shape (height/width ratio). The design of our *BodyExtractor* is inspired by this idea, even though our approach is very different. To determine if a node belongs to one of the high-level blocks, they use a dynamic threshold based on the height/width ratio of the node. For example, to determine if a node belongs to the header, the threshold gives the maximum value the Y coordinate of the node can has (the wider the node, the higher the threshold). The algorithm that computes the thresholds requires training and cannot be tuned for a particular application. Our approach seems more appropriate in a portlet setting, where the user portletizes a number of applications (using the default configuration), and if necessary, she or he can use the *edit* mode to tune the configuration for a particular application. Furthermore, they do not take into account the nesting of nodes, and in consequence, nodes inside the body block can be easily classified as belonging to one of the outer blocks. In the portletization case, this would produce an *Error* result, since part of the body block would be removed.

Buyukkokten et al. [4] present a browsing system, PowerBrowser, that allows to transform a Web page into a hierarchy of text blocks, "called Semantic Textual Units", which exclude images and formatting information. In principle, these techniques could be reused to implement an alternative transformer to our *GeneralSegmenter*. However, such techniques do not keep the original look-and-feel.

Bickmore et al. [3] describe five adaptation techniques that split a Web page into a set of hierarchically-linked subpages. Our *GeneralSegmenter* is similar to their "indexed segmentation" technique. The rest of techniques assume a page layout based on section headers (*<h1>* - *<h6>* tags), tables, and text blocks. However, this layout is rarely used today. Furthermore, they destroy the original look-and-feel.

Hwang et al. [11] make minor improvements to the previous techniques and add a new one: "generalized outlining". This technique is applicable to pages containing items that follow a common layout pattern (e.g. a list of news items). It splits the page into an index page and an individual page for each item. The index page contains a summary and a link for each item. To detect repeated layout patterns, it uses a grouping function, which detects items that structurally share a common prefix, that is, items starting with the same sequence of HTML tags. To summarize each item, the summarizing function returns the content corresponding to the prefix. In principle, this technique could be an alternative to our *GeneralSegmenter* for this type of pages. However, it has some limitations. On the one hand, if items have optional elements (e.g. an image) at the beginning, the grouping function will not find a common prefix. On the other hand, if items are rendered by using the same sequence of HTML tags, the summarizing function will return the whole item. We are investigating other techniques to achieve this kind of splitting.

7 Conclusions

In this paper we presented an automatic approach to displaying a Web application as a portlet in function of the space available in the portlet's window. We illustrated this approach with a sample scenario and presented the design of a bridge portlet that adapts Web pages accordingly. The bridge portlet delegates page adaptation to a framework that uses a chain of user-configurable transformers. Experiments show that more than 70% of the Web applications evaluated were displayed perfectly with the default configuration, and more than 80% were displayed perfectly or acceptably. For the applications that were displayed acceptably or erroneously, more than half were displayed perfectly by adjusting usually only one configuration parameter, and the rest were displayed acceptably. While our approach is not as accurate as an annotation-based approach, it is much more maintainable.

Acknowledgments. This work was partially supported by the Spanish Science and Technology Ministry and European Social Funds (FEDER) under projects TSI2005-07730 and TIC2002-01442. Alberto Pan's work was partially supported by the "Ramon y Cajal" program of the Spanish Science and Technology Ministry.

References

1. Anupam, V., Freire, J., Kumar, B., Lieuwen, D.F.: Automating Web Navigation with the WebVCR. International World Wide Web Conference (2000) 503–517
2. Bellas, F.: Standards for Second-Generation Portals. IEEE Internet Computing, Vol. 8, No. 2 (2004) 54-60
3. Bickmore, T.W., Girgensohn, A., Sullivan, J.W.: Web Page Filtering and Re-authoring for Mobile Users. Computer Journal, Vol. 42, No. 6 (1999) 534–546
4. Buyukkokten, O., Kaljuvee, O., Garcia-Molina, H., Paepcke, A., Winograd, T.: Efficient Web Browsing on Handheld Devices Using Page and Form Summarization. ACM Transactions on Information Systems, Vol. 20, No. 1 (2002) 82–115
5. Chen, Y., Xie, X., Ma, W.-Y., Zhang, H.: Adapting Web Pages for Small-Screen Devices. IEEE Internet Computing, Vol. 9, No. 1 (2005) 50–56
6. Díaz, O., Paz, I.: Turning Web Applications into Portlets: Raising the Issues. IEEE/IPSJ International Symposium on Applications and the Internet (2005) 31–37
7. eXo Platform. http://www.exoplatform.org
8. Freire, J., Kumar, B., Lieuwen, D.F.: WebViews: Accessing Personalized Web Content and Services. International World Wide Web Conference (2001) 576–586
9. Gupta, S., Kaiser, G.E., Grimm, P., Chiang, M.F., Starren, J.: Automating Content Extraction of HTML Documents. World Wide Web Journal, Vol. 8, No. 2 (2005) 179 – 224
10. Hori, M., Ono, K., Abe, M., Koyanagi, T.: Generating Transformational Annotation for Web Document Adaptation: Tool Support and Empirical Evaluation. Journal of Web Semantics, Vol. 2, No. 1 (2004) 1–18
11. Hwang, Y., Kim, J., Seo, E.: Structure-Aware Web Transcoding for Mobile Devices. IEEE Internet Computing, Vol. 7, No. 5 (2003) 14–21
12. Java Community Process: Java Portlet Specification - Version 1.0. http://jcp.org/aboutJava/communityprocess/final/jsr168/index.html
13. Java InterFace For Internet Explorer (Jiffie). http://jiffie.sourceforge.net.
14. OASIS: Web Services for Remote Portlets Specification - Version 1.0. http://www.oasisopen.org/committees/tc_home.php?wg_abbrev=wsrp

Allocating QOS-Constrained Applications in a Web Service-Oriented Grid

Yash Patel and John Darlington

London e-Science Centre, Imperial College, London SW7 2AZ
{yp03, jd}@doc.ic.ac.uk

Abstract. The success of web services has influenced the way in which Grid applications are being written. Web services are increasingly used as a means to realise service-oriented distributed computing. Grid users often submit their applications in the form of workflows with certain Quality of Service (QoS) requirements imposed on the workflows. These workflows detail the composition of web services and the level of service required from the Grid. This paper addresses workload allocation techniques for Grid workflows. We model a web service as an $M/M/k$ queue and obtain a numerical solution for missed deadlines (failures) of Grid workflow tasks. The approach is evaluated through an experimental simulation and the results confirm that the proposed workload allocation strategy performs considerably better in terms of satisfying QoS requirements of Grid workflows than scheduling algorithms that don't employ such workload allocation techniques.

Keywords: Workload, $M/M/k$ queue, Response time distribution, QoS, Workflows.

1 Introduction

The term Grid computing [11] is commonly used to refer to a distributed infrastructure that promotes large-scale resource sharing in a dynamic multi-institutional virtual organization. Recently, the Grid architecture has made a noticeable shift toward a service-oriented framework [14]. Web services are now constantly used as an enabling technology for realising service-oriented Grid computing. A web service is a platform-independent software component that is described by using a service description language [9] and provides functionalities to publish its interfaces to some directory or registry of services. The service-oriented concept lends itself to an architecture that requires interoperability across heterogeneous platforms and exposes all or part of its applications on different machines, platforms, and domains. The Open Grid Services Architecture (OGSA) [3] is developed to provide an extensible framework of services that support Grid functionalities by combining the realms of web services and Grid technologies.

Complex scientific experiments within a Grid are increasingly specified in the form of workflows [6], which detail the composition of distributed resources such as computational devices, data, applications, and scientific instruments. These resources in turn could be exposed in the form of a web service. Users who submit a workflow to the Grid

S. Madria et al. (Eds.): ICDCIT 2006, LNCS 4317, pp. 278–290, 2006.

will often have constraints on how they wish the workflow to perform. These may be described in the form of a Quality of Service (QoS) document which details the level of service they require from the Grid. This may include requirements on such things as the overall execution time for their workflow; the time at which certain parts of the workflow must be completed; cost to the user. In order to determine if these QoS constraints can be satisfied it is necessary to store performance information of resources and applications within the Grid. Such information could also be performance data related to execution of web services; information about speed and reliability; mean service time and mean arrival rate. Here we see that existing Grid middleware for resource descriptions [25] and performance repositories [12] may be used for the storage and retrieval of this data.

Scheduling within Grid is mainly based on two techniques. Either scheduling is performed based on real time information such as waiting time in the queue, residual processing time; or on average-based metrics such as mean service rate, mean arrival rates. Real time information based algorithms generally perform better than average-based strategies [26]. However, obtaining real time information from a distributed system such as Grid, leads to high overheads. Moreover obtaining extremely volatile information such as service load, exact waiting times from geographically distributed web services can lead to substantial delays and consequently to inaccurate scheduling decisions. Also, it may not be possible to obtain instantaneous information at any arbitrary point in time from some web services. Thus, it is necessary to develop approaches which are not dependent on obtaining accurate instantaneous information. The use of average-based strategies seems to be an appropriate approach. Average-based scheduling, for jobs based on FCFS (First Come First Served) rule in a Grid, consists of distributing the workload received by a central entity such as a brokering service, which sends jobs to underlying service providers. This process is referred to as workload allocation strategy in this paper. The workload allocation scheme determines the proportion of workload directed to a matching web service. Once the workload gets collected in the queue of a web service, jobs are executed using a FCFS rule. A thread is immediately assigned from the thread pool for executing a job waiting in the queue, if the pool is not empty.

This paper is organised as follows. Section 2 presents related work and compares our work with others in the field. Section 3 describes the Grid model (figure 1) considered and assumptions held in this paper. Workload allocation strategy in terms of minimising workflow task failures is obtained numerically in Section 4 and the performance of the workload allocation strategy is evaluated in Section 5. Finally, we conclude the paper in Section 6.

2   Related Work

Various application domains and projects such as OMII-BPEL, GridCC are using web services as a means for enabling loosely coupled and extensible systems [22] [13] [21]. Many web services flow specification languages are emerging, such as BPEL4WS [1], WSCI [5],and BPML [4].

In a distributed system such as Grid, job scheduling is performed at both global and local level [15] [24]. At global level, workload is distributed to resource clusters

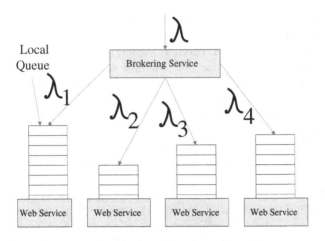

Fig. 1. Grid Model

and within them, the local schedulers dispatch jobs to the underlying resources via a scheduling strategy. Kao et al. [8] use two homogenous non real time servers to provide a service that will satisfy QoS requirements of jobs. However they don't extend their approach to a distributed system such as Grid. Zhu et al. extend the work of Kao et al. by considering more than 2 servers that aim to satisfy QoS requirements of jobs [23]. The performance of scheduling based on minimising failures to meet waiting time requirements (the maximum time a job can wait before execution) of jobs is also evaluated in [23]. However, their work is confined to a single service with n processing nodes only and does not consider a distributed system such as Grid.

Performance-based workload allocation schemes are presented in [7] for enterprise application environments. Their work takes into account both system and application-oriented statistics, and dynamically calculates a workload allocation weight for each server. However the strategies used, require real time system and application information, in order for the workload allocator to calculate appropriate weights, which can lead to high overheads and intolerable delays.

Our work focuses on developing a workload allocation strategy which minimises failures of QoS-constrained workflows in a Grid. The Grid is modelled as a collection of web services, managed by a brokering service (figure 1), where jobs in the form of workflows arrive with certain QoS requirements imposed on the workflows. Relevant Grid components such as performance repository, workflow management system and others are not shown in figure 1, in order to focus on the central topic of the paper.

3   The Model

We model each web service as an $M/M/k$ queue [16], which performs some functionality (service type). The number of service types is n and the number of web services matching a service type i is N_i. Web service j with service type i, has a mean service rate of μ_{ij}. Each web service has its associated queue, where jobs get collected. Jobs to this queue are dispatched via a brokering service. The brokering service receives jobs in the form of workflows, which are composed of individual tasks. When a workflow task finishes, further tasks must be started. Hence the brokering service dispatches tasks (jobs) of new and old workflows to appropriate web services using a workload allocation strategy developed in the next section. The jobs are executed by the web service in the order they are received. Hence essentially the queue associated with a web service is a FCFS queue. Whenever a job is received, a thread from a thread pool is assigned to execute it. The thread can only be assigned if the pool is not empty, otherwise jobs in the queue have to wait until a thread finishes execution and returns back to the pool. The jobs received by the brokering service follow a uniform distribution of deadline requirements, as assumed in [8] [23] [17]. Workflows have overall deadline constraints, which are explicitly specified by the end-user. There could also be other constraints such as cost, reliability, network constraints. A full list of constraints is beyond the scope of this paper. However for simplicity, we keep the QoS requirements of workflows limited to overall deadline constraints. Deadlines for individual tasks of workflows are calculated by the brokering service using a formula given in the experimental evaluation. We define a workflow failure as failure in meeting the overall workflow deadline. Failure in meeting deadlines of intermediate workflow tasks is not a workflow failure.

4   Theoretical Analysis of Minimisation of Workflow Task Failures

In this section we obtain a numerical solution for failures of tasks of workflows, to be executed on web services and a non-linear program for computing workload allocation to web services. The non-linear program minimises the failures of tasks of workflows. Its solution yields the workload proportions for web services.

4.1   Workload Allocation Based on Failure Minimisation of Workflow Tasks

In this section, a workload allocation strategy using minimisation of failures of tasks of workflows for a web service is developed. The Grid consists of n different web service types, where each web service is modelled as an $M/M/k$ queue with infinite customer capacity, meaning the number of jobs that can wait in the queue of a web service is infinite. Hence essentially a web service is indeed an $M/M/k/\infty$ queue. Web service j of service type i has k_{ij} processing threads, where each processing thread has a mean service rate of μ_{ij}. We consider that the brokering service receives jobs, with an arrival rate of λ, out of which λ_i corresponds to web services of service type i. Out of λ_i, λ_{ij} is allocated to j^{th} web service of service type i. Thus the arrival rate can be expressed as the sum of workload proportions of web services, given by equations 1 and 2.

$$\lambda = \sum_{i=1}^{n} \lambda_i \tag{1}$$

$$\lambda_i = \sum_{j=1}^{N_i} \lambda_{ij} \tag{2}$$

Let $r_{ij}(t)$ and $R_{ij}(t)$ be the PDF (Probability Density Function) and CDF (Cumulative Density Function) of the response time of web service j of service type i respectively for an $M/M/k$ queue. Response time of a job consist of its waiting time in the queue of a web service and its service time. The PDF of the response time for an $M/M/k$ queue is given by equation 3 [16]. By definition, CDF of the response time can be represented by equations 5 and 6.

$$r_{ij}(t) = (1 - \frac{k_{ij}\rho^{k_{ij}}}{k_{ij}!(k_{ij} - \rho)(\sum_{j=0}^{k_{ij}-1} \frac{(k_{ij}\rho)^j}{j!} + \frac{(k_{ij}\rho)^{k_{ij}}}{k_{ij}!(1-\rho)})})e^{-\mu_{ij}t}$$

$$- \frac{\mu_{ij}\rho^{k_{ij}}(e^{-\mu_{ij}(k_{ij}-\rho)t} - e^{-\mu_{ij}t})}{(\sum_{j=0}^{k_{ij}-1} \frac{(k_{ij}\rho)^j}{j!} + \frac{(k_{ij}\rho)^{k_{ij}}}{k_{ij}!(1-\rho)})(k_{ij} - 1)!(1 - k_{ij} - \rho)} \tag{3}$$

$$\rho = \frac{\lambda_{ij}}{k_{ij}\mu_{ij}} \tag{4}$$

$$R_{ij}(t) = P(T \le t) \tag{5}$$

$$R_{ij}(t) = \int_0^t r_{ij}(t)dt \tag{6}$$

We assume a uniform distribution of deadlines of jobs to be allocated to web services, as assumed in [8] [23] [17]. This is not a restriction and general distributions could be accomodated as well, while still keeping the analysis effective. Let the lower and upper bounds of the uniform distribution of deadline of jobs to be allocated to web services of type i be L_i and U_i. Its PDF $d_i(t)$ is given by equation 7.

$$d_i(t) = \frac{1}{U_i - L_i} \tag{7}$$

Now we can compute expected failures for web service j of service type i, using the following integral, given by equation 8, where $Failures_{ij}$ are workflow task failures for web service j of service type i. Equation 8 is an integral that computes a continuous expectation. It computes expected failures for an arrival rate of λ_{ij}. The term $1 - R_{ij}(t)$ is the probability of jobs to finish in time greater than t and the term $d_i(t)$ is the probability of the number of jobs requiring t time to finish. Thus the product of the two terms compute a failure probability, which when multiplied with λ_{ij} yields the expected number of failures.

$$Failures_{ij} = \lambda_{ij} \int_{L_i}^{U_i} d_i(t)(1 - R_{ij}(t))dt \tag{8}$$

Solving the integral, we obtain expected failures for web service j of service type i, given by equation 9.

$$Failures_{ij} = 1 - y_1 + y_2\mu_{ij}(k_{ij} - \rho) - \frac{y_2}{\mu_{ij}}$$

$$+(\frac{1}{U_i - L_i})(\frac{y_1}{\mu_{ij}} + \frac{k_{ij} - \rho}{\mu_{ij}})(e^{-\mu_{ij}L_i} - e^{-\mu_{ij}U_i})$$

$$-(\frac{y_2}{U_i - L_i})(e^{-\mu_{ij}L_i(k_{ij}-\rho)} - e^{-\mu_{ij}U_i(k_{ij}-\rho)}) \tag{9}$$

$$y_1 = \frac{1 - (\frac{1}{\sum_{j=0}^{k_{ij}-1} \frac{(k_{ij}\rho)^j}{j!} + \frac{(k_{ij}\rho)^{k_{ij}}}{k_{ij}!(1-\rho)}}) \frac{k_{ij}\rho^{k_{ij}}}{k_{ij}!(k_{ij}-\rho)}}{\mu_{ij}} \tag{10}$$

$$y_2 = \frac{\mu_{ij}(\frac{1}{\sum_{j=0}^{k_{ij}-1} \frac{(k_{ij}\rho)^j}{j!} + \frac{(k_{ij}\rho)^{k_{ij}}}{k_{ij}!(1-\rho)}})\rho^{k_{ij}}}{(k_{ij} - 1)!(1 - k_{ij} - \rho)} \tag{11}$$

In case of arbitrary distribution of deadlines of jobs, the distribution of deadline allocations of jobs matching service type i can be expressed mathematically given by equation 12.

$$P(d_1) = p_1, \ P(d_2) = p_2, \ ......, \ P(d_m) = p_m \tag{12}$$

The sum of probabilities of m jobs is equal to one. The terms d_1 to d_m are the deadline allocations of jobs. We can express expected failures for web service j of service type i as equation 13.

$$Failures_{ij} = \lambda_{ij} \sum_{i=1}^{m} P(t)(1 - R_{ij}(t)) \tag{13}$$

Thus total failures expected is the sum of expected failures for all web services, given by equation 14.

$$Failures = \sum_{i=1}^{n} \sum_{j=1}^{N_i} Failures_{ij} \tag{14}$$

The objective is to minimise total failures. We can now write the minimisation problem represented by equations 15 to 19.

$$minimise[\sum_{i=1}^{n} \sum_{j=1}^{N_i} Failures_{ij}] \tag{15}$$

subject to

$$\forall i, \sum_{j=1}^{N_i} \lambda_{ij} = \lambda_i \tag{16}$$

$$\sum_{i=1}^{n} \lambda_i = \lambda \tag{17}$$

$$\forall j, 0 \leq \lambda_{ij} \leq \lambda_i \tag{18}$$

$$\forall i, 0 \leq \lambda_i \leq \lambda \tag{19}$$

The above problem can be solved using appropriate non-linear optimisation techniques. We solve it as constrained Lagrange multiplier problem [7]. The problem is decomposed into n Lagrange multiplier problems and solved individually. This is because λ_i is already known initially and the problem is to decompose it into arrival rates for web services by minimising failures of tasks of workflows. We use GAMS [2] language to model the non-linear problem and use dicopt [18] as the optimisation solver by Carnegie Mellon University, to solve it.

5   Experimental Evaluation

In this section we present experimental results for the workload allocation technique described in this paper.

5.1   Setup

Table 1 summarises the experimental setup. We have performed 3 simulations, the first with workflow type 1, second with workflow type 2 and in the third simulation, workload is made heterogenous. The workflows experimented with are shown in figure 2. Workflow type 1 is quite simple compared to type 2, which is a real scientific workflow. In the first two simulations, the workflows are all similar, but having different overall workflow deadlines. In the third simulation, workload is made heterogenous (HW), meaning any of the three workflows shown as heterogenous workload, in figure 2 could be submitted. Apart from that, the workflows have different overall workflow deadlines. We have performed 10 runs in each different setup of a simulation and averaged out the values. Initially 500 jobs allow the system to reach steady state, the next 1000 jobs are used for calculating statistics such as mean execution time of workflows, mean workflow failures and mean utilisation of a web service. The last 500 jobs mark the ending period of the simulation. The simulation is developed on top of simjava 2 [10], a discrete event simulation package. The Grid size is kept small in order to get an asymptotic behaviour of workflow failures, as coefficient of variation (CV) of workflow task execution time or arrival rates (λ) of workflows are increased. Deadlines of individual tasks of workflows are calculated using equation 20. In order to compute deadlines of workflow tasks, we put no restriction on the nature of their execution time distributions (general distributions with finite mean and variance) and compute deadlines in a way such that 95% of jobs would execute in time under the calculated deadline. Equation 21 is the

Table 1. Simulation parameters

Simulation	1	2	3
Web Services per task	6-24	3-12	6-24
Arrival Rate (λ) (per sec)	1.5-10	0.1-2.0	1.5-3.6
Task Mean (μ) (sec)	3-12	3-10	3-12
Task CV = σ/μ	0.2-2.0	0.2-1.4	0.2-2.0
Workflows	Type 1	Type 2	HW
Workflow deadline (sec)	40-60	80-100	40-60
Threads per web service	1-5	1-3	1-5

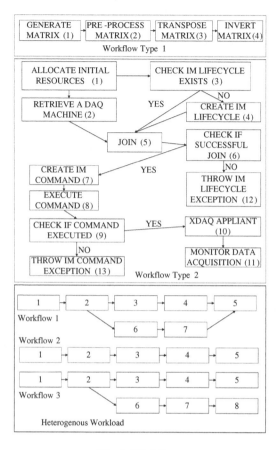

Fig. 2. Workflows

cumulative density function of execution time distribution associated with a workflow task. Such bounds or confidence intervals on the execution time can be computed using various techniques such as Chebyshev inequality [19], Monte Carlo approach [20] and Central Limit Theorem [19] or by performing finite integration, if the underlying execution time PDFs are available in analytical forms. Deadline calculation takes care of all possible execution paths in a workflow. $deadline_W$ is the overall workflow deadline for any possible path in a workflow, as shown in table 1. We provide an example for the first task of workflow 2 in figure 2. Mean of the execution time (μ) and coefficient of variation of the execution time (CV) are specified in table 1 with respect to a reference machine. Equation 20 is scaled with reference to $deadline_W$, as it is for the first task of the workflow. Subsequent workflow tasks' deadlines are scaled with reference to the remaining workflow deadline.

$$deadline_1 = \frac{X_1}{X_1 + X_2 + X_3 + X_4 + X_5} deadline_W \qquad (20)$$

$$P(0 \leq x \leq X_i) = 0.95 \qquad (21)$$

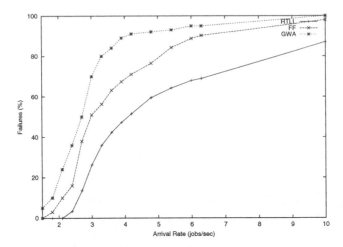

Fig. 3. Failures vs λ, CV = 0.2 (Simulation 1)

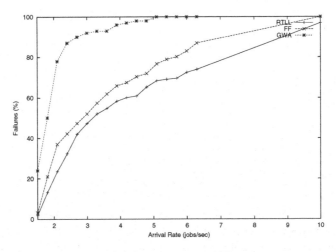

Fig. 4. Failures vs λ, CV = 1.8 (Simulation 1)

5.2   Results

We compare our workload allocation scheme (FF) with traditional job dispatching strategies like global weighted allocation (GWA) and real time based least loaded algorithm (RTLL). The GWA scheme calculates the proportion of workload based on the processing speed of a web service. Hence, higher the processing speed, higher the workload proportion for the web service. The least-loaded scheme selects the web service which can satisfy the deadlines of jobs. The workflows don't have any slack period, meaning that they are scheduled without any delay as soon as they are submitted. The main comparison metrics between the schemes are mean execution time of workflows, workflow failures and utilisation of web services as we increase λ and CV. However

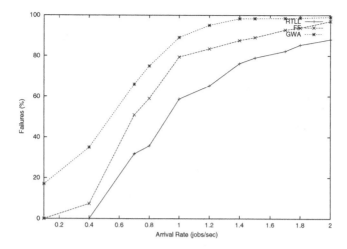

Fig. 5. Failures vs λ, CV = 0.2 (Simulation 2)

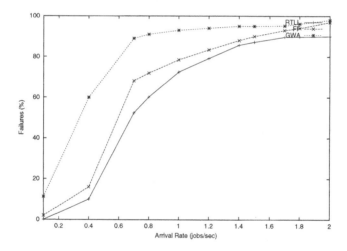

Fig. 6. Failures vs λ, CV = 1.4 (Simulation 2)

we will keep our discussion limited to failures as the main comparison between the schemes is their ability to satisfy QoS requirements.

5.3 Effect of Arrival Rate and Workload Nature

Referring to figures 3 and 4, for low arrival rates, FF performs similar to RTLL. However its performance compared to RTLL drops as λ increases. However FF significantly outperforms GWA. This trends continues, but the advantage gets reducing as arrival rates increase. This can be explained as follows. When arrival rates increase, more work needs to be scheduled in less time and the average response time is an increasing function of arrival rate, as is evident from equation 9 in section 4. Hence failures due

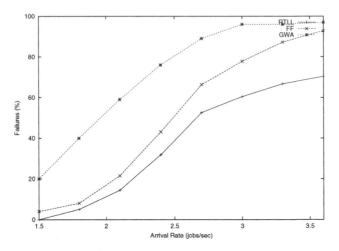

Fig. 7. Failures vs λ, CV = 0.2 (Simulation 3)

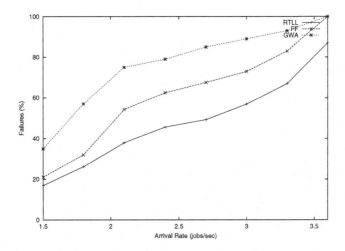

Fig. 8. Failures vs λ, CV = 1.8 (Simulation 3)

to missing deadline assignments increase and as a consequence workflow failures increase. For both low and high CVs, at low arrival rates, FF performs similar to RTLL. Referring to figures 5 and 6, for low arrival rates, FF is outperformed slightly by RTLL. However its advantage over GWA is significant. Referring to figures 7 and 8, the situation is similar to the above cases. Hence heterogenous workload does not change the behaviour of the schemes.

5.4   Effect of CV of Execution Time of Workflow Tasks

For both low and high CVs of execution time of jobs, the nature of graphs are similar, however failures increase as CV increases. In case of heterogenous workload, the graphs climb more steeply compared to the case of type 1 workflow. In all cases FF significantly outperforms GWA. This shows that the variability of execution time does not significantly affect the nature of graphs for different schemes. However the advantage of a particular scheme over others reduces as failures reach limiting values asymptotically. As CV is increased, failures increase because workflow jobs take longer time to execute and thus tend to complete near their assigned deadlines or even fail to meet their deadlines.

6   Conclusion and Future Work

The effectiveness of the workload allocation strategy is proved through theoretical analysis. The strategy is also evaluated through experimental simulation. Results confirm that workload allocation strategy performs considerably better than the algorithms that do not use these strategies. When the arrival rates are low, the workload allocation technique performs similar compared to scheduling algorithms based on real time performance information. Workflow and workload nature also don't change the performance of the scheme notably. Moreover execution time variability does not change the performance of the workload allocation strategy significantly for both low are high arrival rates.

As future work we would like to model web services as $G/G/k$ queues and perform theoretical analysis. The reason behind modelling web services as $G/G/k$ queues is that $M/M/k$ queues don't often exist in real world situations. We would like to perform experiments with workflows having a slack period, meaning they can wait for some time before getting serviced.

References

1. BPEL   Specification,   http://www-106.ibm.com/developerworks/webservices/library/ws-bpel/2003.
2. General Algebraic Modeling System (GAMS). *http://www.gams.com/*.
3. Open Grid Services Architecture Homepage. *http://www.globus.org/ogsa*.
4. A. Arkin et al. Business Process Modeling Language (BPML), Version 1.0. 2002.
5. A. Arkin, S. Askary, S. Fordin, W. Jekel et al. Web Service Choreography Interface (WSCI) 1.0. *Standards proposal by BEA Systems, Intalio, SAP, and Sun Microsystems*, 2002.
6. A. Mayer et al. Workflow Expression: Comparison of Spatial and Temporal Approaches. *Workflow in Grid Systems Workshop*, 2004.
7. Arfken, G. Lagrange Multipliers. *Mathematical Methods for Physicists, Orlando, FL: Academic Press*, pages 945–950, 1985.
8. B. Kao and H. Garcia-Molina. Scheduling Soft Real-Time Jobs over Dual Non-Real-Time Servers. *IEEE Trans. Parallel and Distributed Systems, vol. 7, no. 1*, pages 56–68, 1996.
9. Christensen E., Curbera F., Meredith G. and Weerawarana S. Web Services Description Language. *http://msdn.microsoft.com/xml/general/wsdl.asp*, 2000.
10. F. Howell et al. SimJava. *http://www.dcs.ed.ac.uk/home/hase/simjava*.
11. I. Foster and C. Kesselman, editors. *The Grid: Blueprint for a New Computing Infrastructure*. Morgan Kaufmann, July 1998.
12. G. Nudd and S. Jarvis. Performance-based middleware for Grid computing. *Concurrency and Computation: Practice and Experience*, 2004.

13. GRIDCC Collaboration. Grid Enabled Remote Instrumentation with Distributed Control and Computation. *http://www.gridCC.org*.
14. I. Foster et al. Grid Services for Distributed Systems Integration. *Computer*, 35(6), 2002.
15. Krauter, K., Buyya, R., Maheshwaran, M. A Taxonomy and Survey of Grid Resource Management Systems. *Technical Report 2000/80: Mannitoba University and Monash University*, 2000.
16. L. Kleinrock. Queueing Systems. *John Wiley and Sons*, 1975.
17. Ligang He, Stephen A. Jarvis, Daniel P. Spooner, Hong Jiang, Donna N. Dillenberger and Graham R. Nudd. Allocating Non-real-time and Soft Real-time Jobs in Multiclusters . *IEEE Transactions on Parallel and Distributed Systems, 17(2):99-112*, 2006.
18. M. A. Duran and I. E. Grossmann. An Outer-Approximation Algorithm for a Class of Mixed-Integer Nonlinear Programs. *Mathematical Programming*, 36:307–339, 1986.
19. Milton Abramowitz and Irene A. Stegun. Handbook of Mathematical Functions with Formulas, Graphs, and Mathematical Tables. 1972.
20. N. Metropolis and S. Ulam. The Monte Carlo Method. *Journal of the American Statistical Association*, 1949.
21. OMII. Open Middleware Infrastructure Institute. *http://www.omii.ac.uk*.
22. Tuecke, S., Czajkowski, K., Foster, I., Frey, J., Graham, S., Kesselman, C. Grid Service Specification draft 3. *http://www.gridforum.org/ogsi-wg*, 2002.
23. W. Zhu and B. Fleisch. Performance Evaluation of Soft Real-Time Scheduling on a Multicomputer Cluster. *Proc. 20th International Conference Distributed Computing Systems (ICDCS 2000)*, pages 610–617, 2000.
24. Weissman, J. B., Grimshaw, A. S. A Federated Model for Scheduling in Wide Area Systems. *Proceedings of the IEEE High Performance Distributed Computing*, 1996.
25. Xuehai Zhang and Jennifer M. Schopf. Performance Analysis of the Globus Toolkit Monitoring and Discovery Service, MDS2. In *Proceedings of the International Workshop on Middleware Performance (MP 2004)*, Apr. 2004.
26. X.Y. Tang and S.T. Chanson. Optimizing Static Job Scheduling in a Network of Heterogeneous Computers. *Proc. 29th International Conference on Parallel Processing*, pages 373–382, 2000.

Multicontext-Aware Recommendation
for Ubiquitous Commerce

Joonhee Kwon[1] and Sungrim Kim[2]

[1] Department of Computer Science, Kyonggi University,
San 94-6, Yiui-dong, Yeongtong-ku, Suwon-si, Kyonggi-do, Korea
kwonjh@kyonggi.ac.kr
[2] Department of Internet Information, Seoil College,
49-3, Myonmok-dong, Jungrang-Ku, Seoul, Korea
srkim@seoil.ac.kr

Abstract. Recommender systems address a variety of ubiquitous commerce needs. In ubiquitous commerce, contextual information must be incorporated into the recommendation process. The total amount of information is larger due to the greater number of contexts in multicontext environments. Multicontext therefore requires a more accurate and rapid recommendation method. This paper proposes a multicontext-aware recommendation for ubiquitous commerce using consumer's preferences and behavior as a weighting factor. The recommendation method is described and an application prototype is presented. Several experiments are performed and the results verify that the proposed method's recommendation performance is better than other existing method.

1 Introduction

The trend toward ubiquitous computing does not represent simply a change in the way people access and use information. In the end it will have a profound effect on the way people access and use services, enabling new classes of services that only make sense by virtue of being embedded in the environment. Ultimately these technologies will lead us to a world of ubiquitous commerce [5].

Recommender systems are used by electronic commerce to suggest items to their consumers. The items can be recommended based on an analysis of the past buying behavior of a consumer as a prediction for his future buying behavior [10]. However, in ubiquitous commerce, it may not be sufficient to consider only consumers and items. It is also important to incorporate the contextual information into the recommendation process [1].

The total amount of information consumers can obtain from a recommender system is restricted to a limited amount of information. However, the total amount of information can increase, due to the greater number of contexts in multicontext-aware environments. This requires an accurate and rapid composition method of recommendations for multi-context. Previous studies focusing on context-aware recommendations have typically supported only a single context. Although there have been some studies on multi-context, the composition of information over contexts is fixed at the design time and no attempt is made to dynamically compose via current

S. Madria et al. (Eds.): ICDCIT 2006, LNCS 4317, pp. 291–304, 2006.
© Springer-Verlag Berlin Heidelberg 2006

contexts. However, the information a consumer can obtain from recommender systems will vary dynamically over contexts. In this paper, a new multicontext-aware recommendation for ubiquitous commerce is proposed.

One of the main considerations of recommendation methods in multi-context environments is that information needs to be composed in accordance with the dynamic changes of each context. Traditional approaches to recommender systems have taken into account only preferences. Because these approaches use only preferences, there are limitations to recommending while using dynamically changed attention. In this paper, not only the consumer's preferences but also behavior as an attention factor is used in the dynamic composition process for a recommendation. Our proposed method recommends the more accurate information for the target context rapidly.

The discussion will proceed as follows. Section 2 will give an overview of related work. Section 3 will discuss the recommendation method. Section 4 will describe a shopping application prototype. Section 5 will discuss the experiments. Finally, Section 6 will conclude the paper.

2 Related Work

Recommendation services are well known for their use in the electronic commerce applications. Here, they furnish personalized environments for selling items such as books, and CDs. Many online consumers utilize recommendation services, such as, for example, Amazon, CDnow, Barnes & Noble Booksellers, and IMDB [11]. However, traditional approaches to recommender systems have not taken into account the context when making recommendations. This seriously limits the relevance of the results.

Recently, many researchers have actively tried to expound upon the potential of context-awareness. Most previous works in the area of context-aware recommendation are based on the match of a context to a consumer's preferences [6,13]. They work only with a specific single context. Although there are a few focusing on multi-context, the composition of information over contexts is fixed at the design time and no attempt is made to dynamically compose via current contexts. Moreover, these methods are not concerned about recommending information rapidly with the change of a consumer's continuous contexts.

Other approaches to context-aware recommendations concentrate on recommending information rapidly in ubiquitous computing. In [3], rapid recommendation based on a context-aware cache is proposed. The context-aware cache tries to capture the information the consumer is most likely to need in future contexts. It makes for a more immediate retrieval and reduces the cost of retrieving information by doing most of the work automatically. In [7], the recommendation method locally stores the recommendation information that the consumer is likely to need in the near future based on consumer's context history in order to retrieve information rapidly. Moreover, using a type of multi-agent architecture, it allows for rapid recommendations and solves problems with the limitations of client's device storage. These approaches do not consider multi-context, however.

3 Multicontext-Aware Recommendation Method

The proposed method for the multicontext-aware recommendation is conceptually comprised of three main tasks, as shown in Figure 1. The first step is to extract the candidate recommendation information from recommendation rules related to the context values from the shopping records for each context. These rules are extracted using association rule mining [2]. Some recent studies have considered the use of association rule mining in personalized recommender systems [8]. Following this, the recommendation information in the near future is extracted using the current context value and recommendation information rules. The detailed method is shown in [7].

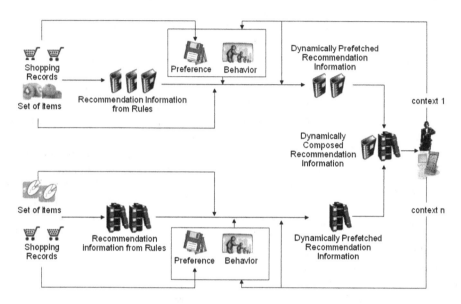

Fig. 1. Multicontext-Aware Recommendation Method

In the second step, the recommendation information appearing in the very near future is prefetched dynamically using a context value, preferences and behavior for each context. The recommendation information extracted in the first step can cause the consumer's device storage capacity and transmitting rate to increase. To solve these problems, only the recommendation information that can be used in the very near future is stored, and this process is then repeated.

In the realm of ubiquitous service, there are a significant number of contexts vying for a consumer's attention [10]. Attention is defined as focused mental engagement on a particular message or piece of information [4]. The degree of attention may be determined using preferences and behavior; however, previous approaches have only used preferences. In this paper, attention is used as a weighting factor in the dynamic extraction process of a recommendation. The amount of recommendation information needed for a context with a high weight is larger than that needed for context with a low weight.

Our weighting mechanism works as follows: N is the number of context types, and C_n denotes the n-th context. PW_n denotes the preferences weight, BW_n denotes the behavior weight and AW_n denotes the attention weight with respect to C_n. It is possible to compute AW_n using the following formula with a single adjustable parameter α $(0 \leq \alpha \leq 1)$:

$$AW_n = (\alpha * BW_n) + ((1-\alpha) * PW_n), \quad \text{where } 0 \leq BW_n, PW_n, AW_n \leq 1$$

$$PW_n = \frac{\text{the total number of } C_n \text{ in consumer's shopping records}}{\text{the total number of consumer's shopping records}}$$

$$BW_n = \frac{\text{the minimum degree of consumer's behavior in } C_n}{\text{the maximum degree of consumer's behavior in } C_n}$$

The degree of a consumer's behavior is determined by a behavior policy. An example of a behavior policy states that the degree of the consumer's behavior may be determined using the walking velocity in the location context. In the second step, the minimum degree of consumer's behavior is used in the BW_n, because the degree of consumer's behavior in the near future is not estimated. The BW_n is tuned using current degree of consumer's behavior in final step.

Moreover, the center and the periphery are adopted in our recommendation method. This approach, based on calm technology, engages both the center and the periphery of a consumer's attention, and in fact moves back and forth between the two. The periphery denotes what people are attuned to without attending to explicitly [12]. When driving, attention is centered on the road, but not the music on the radio. However, music of interest is noticed immediately, showing that people can be attuned to music in the periphery, and can quickly attend to it. In this paper, while the consumer is in the center, all information extracted by attention weight is recommended, but when the consumer is in the periphery, only information extracted by attention weight above the threshold is recommended.

Our dynamic prefetching mechanism works as follows: the recommendation information of contexts that will appear in the very near future is prefetched from results of the first step using the context values and attention weight. The total amount of recommendation information that a consumer can obtain is restricted to a limited amount of information, called R_{max}. This means that the amount of the recommendation information of C_n does not exceed R_{max}. Thus, the amount of recommendation information to be prefetched is set to R_{max} multiplied by AW_n.

When a consumer's mobile device storage does not have enough space to store new recommendation results generated from the above step, replacement policy is needed. Reference types of cache are categorized into three types: sequential, looping, and other references. In this paper, it is assumed that the reference type is sequential; meaning that consecutive block references occur only once. Sequentially-referenced blocks are never re-referenced; hence, the referenced blocks need not be retained. Therefore the proposed method uses the MRU (Most Recently Used) replacement policy [14].

In the final step, the recommendation information is composed dynamically. The dynamic composition does not mean a simple merging of results from the second step. As BW_n is changed according to current degree of a consumer's behavior and the total amount of the results from the second step can exceed R_{max}.

Because BW_n is changed according to current degree of a consumer's behavior in the final step, the AW_n is needed to recalculate. If the current AW_n is larger than the AW_n resulting from the second step, the information is additionally delivered from the candidate recommendation information. The AW_n is recalculated using the following BW_n in the final step.

$$BW_n = \frac{\text{the current degree of consumer's behavior in } C_n}{\text{the maximum degree of consumer's behavior in } C_n}$$

When the total amount of recommendation information from the second step exceeds R_{max}, the recommendation information for each context is rescaled into the range $[0, R_{max}]$ by min-max normalization.

4   Shopping Application: Location- and Audio-Aware Recommendation

In this section, a location- and audio-aware shopping application prototype is presented that utilizes the proposed method. In this application prototype, the existing method in [3] and the proposed method are compared. To present the existing method in multicontext-aware environments, the composition of information over contexts is fixed at the design time.

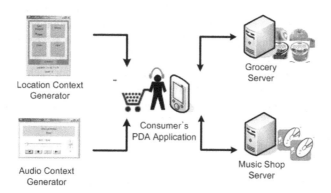

Fig. 2. The overview of shopping application prototype

Figure 2 shows the overview of the location- and audio-aware shopping application prototype. Each component communicates with web services in wireless LAN. The servers and the context generators were implemented in Visual C# .Net and Microsoft SQL-Server on a Pentium IV desktop computer. The consumer's PDA application was implemented using a Microsoft Pocket PC emulator on a Pentium M laptop computer. The location context generator is utilized to become aware of the consumer's location context virtually. The audio context generator was used to become aware of the consumer's audio context virtually. After this step, the consumer's PDA application recommends desired items based on the consumer's location and the audio context.

The following are some assumptions in this paper. First, the maximum degree of consumer's behavior is set to 2. For the location context, the degree of the consumer's behavior is determined using the walking velocity. More precisely, a fast (or slow) velocity is considered as the degree of a consumer's behavior is 0.4 (or 2). For the audio context, the degree of a consumer's behavior is determined using the volume of the music. That is, turning up (or down) the volume is considered, and the degree of consumer's behavior is set to 0.4 (or 2). Second, the maximum number of recommendation information allowed in the consumer's PDA storage is set to 8. In the existing method, the number of recommendation information for each context allowed in the consumer's PDA storage is set to 4. Third, the maximum amount representing the number of information recommended in the consumer's PDA is set to 8. In the existing method, the amount of information recommended for each context in the consumer's PDA is set to 4. Fourth, the estimated remaining time is 5 (or 15) minutes when the degree of a consumer's behavior for the location context is 0.4 (or 2). The estimated remaining time is 10 minutes for the audio context. Finally, when the system logs a consumer in, the current time is at 10:00 A.M.. It is assumed that α is 0.5 in AW_n, and that the threshold of AW_n is 0.3 in the periphery. When shopping in the grocery store a person's attention is centered on the location context, and not on the audio context.

The consumer's, Jane shopping scenario was simulated based on the above assumptions. Figure 3 shows part of the recommendation rules. The candidate recommendation information is extracted from the recommendation rules and sorted by confidence of item in descending order as shown in Figure 4. The recommendation information in grocery store is the cheapest source for each item and the recommendation information in music shop is the top sellers for each item.

She enters a grocery store, while listening to blues music on the internet with a PDA attached with the proposed method. The system logs her in, responds with a welcome message, and then proceeds to present a recommended shopping list based on her contexts.

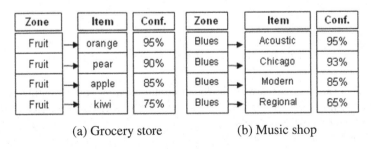

Zone	Item	Conf.	Zone	Item	Conf.
Fruit	orange	95%	Blues	Acoustic	95%
Fruit	pear	90%	Blues	Chicago	93%
Fruit	apple	85%	Blues	Modern	85%
Fruit	kiwi	75%	Blues	Regional	65%

(a) Grocery store   (b) Music shop

Fig. 3. Recommendation rules

Zone	Item	Source	Zone	Item	Source	Zone	Item	Source
Fruit	orange	USA	Dairy	cheese	gouda	Vegetable	cabbage	USA
Fruit	pear	domestic	Dairy	butter	low fat	Vegetable	potato	domestic
Fruit	apple	domestic	Dairy	cream	lurpak	Vegetable	onion	domestic
Fruit	kiwi	Australia	Dairy	yogurt	denmark	Vegetable	carrot	Australia

(a) Grocery store

Genre	Item	Source	Genre	Item	Source
Blues	Acoustic	John Lee Hooker	R&B	Classic R&B	A Time To Love
Blues	Chicago	Bring 'Em In	R&B	Funk	Stevie Wonder
Blues	Modern	Hope and Desire	R&B	Motown	Give Love at Christmas
Blues	Regional	Sippiana Hericane	R&B	Neo-Soul	Baduizm

(b) Music shop

Fig. 4. Candidate recommendation information

The sequence of contexts that will appear in the near future determined from the current contexts is shown in Figure 5. In our prototype, the sequence of location context was determined by the nearest distance and the sequence of audio context was already known using a list of registered music.

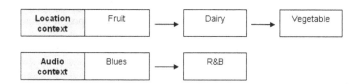

Fig. 5. Sequence of contexts

The result of the prefetched information is shown in Figure 6. The prefetch order for the recommendation information is sorted by the estimated time of the context in an ascending order. The existing method extracts all information about fruits and blues in Figure 6(a). Compared with Figure 6(a), only the information according to the attention weight for each context is prefetched in Figure 6(b).

	Information prefetched
Fruit	orange, pear, apple, kiwi
Blues	Acoustic, Chicago, Modern, Regional

	Estimated Time	BW	PW	W
Fruit	10:00	0.2	0.1	0.15
Blues	10:00	0.2	0.4	0.3
Dairy	10:05	0.2	0.3	0.25
Vegetable	10:10	0.2	0.2	0.2

	Information prefetched
	Orange
	Acoustic, Chicago
	Cheese, Butter
	Cabbage, Potato

(a) Existing method   (b) Proposed method

Fig. 6. Result of information prefetched

At this point, she walks quickly in the "fruit" zone, while listening to "blues" music. Figure 7 shows the results of recommendation information from Figure 6.

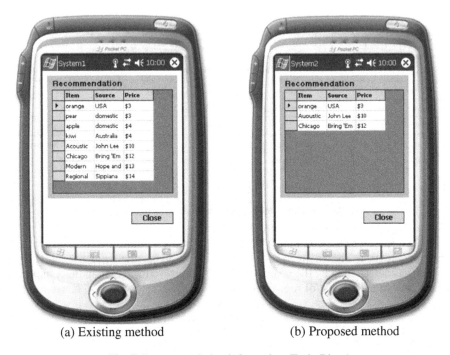

(a) Existing method   (b) Proposed method

Fig. 7. Recommendation information (Fruit, Blues)

Next, she walks with the same velocity in the "dairy" zone, while listening to "blues" music. Figure 8(b) shows the results of the recommendation information from Figure 6. Compared with Figure 8(b), Figure 8(a) shows the recommendation information about dairy delivered from server. It results in communication with the server become necessary.

Next, she listens to "R&B" music with an attention weight of 0.2 while walking slowly in the "dairy" zone. In Figure 9(b), information about cream needs to be delivered from the server, because the value of BW has changed to 1. The information about the R&B music is not recommended because listening to music is in the periphery and AW is below the threshold. Compared with Figure 9(b), Figure 9(a) shows the recommendation information about the R&B delivered from the server. It results in communication with the server becoming necessary.

As shown in our shopping prototype, the advantage of the proposed method is as follows: it recommends the more accurate information for the target context by providing only information that the consumer will find useful using attention. Additionally, it may reduce additional communication overhead with the server by not providing excessive information on context with low attention and context in periphery of attention.

(a) Existing method   (b) Proposed method

Fig. 8. Recommendation information (Dairy, Blues)

(a) Existing method   (b) Proposed method

Fig. 9. Recommendation information (Dairy, R&B)

5 Experiments

In this section, experimental evaluations in multicontext-aware environments are presented. The consumer's PDA application as well as the servers was experimented with in Section 4. Both the existing methods, called *System1* and the proposed method, called *System2* were considered.

In the experiments, the number of contexts was set to 3, and α in attention weight AW_n was set to 0.5. All context values for each context were changed every 5sec. The values of the items for each context were generated from a value of 1 to a value of 50. The candidate recommendation information for each context was randomly generated from the set of items. The number of recommendation rules for each context was set to 20, and the candidate recommendation information was randomly generated from the set of items. The maximum number of information to be recommended in the consumer's PDA was set to 15. In *System1*, the amount of information recommended for each context in the consumer's PDA was set to 5.

5.1 Experiment 1: Relevance and Completeness

In this section, we focused on the accuracy of recommendation information. For comparison, the acceptance ratio of AW_n was varied by 25%, from 0% to 100%. For the performance evaluation, the experiment was conducted 100 times using a set of multi-context data and a set of purchased items. The context values with AW_n in Table 1 for each context were generated randomly. The maximum amount of recommendation information allowed in the consumer's PDA storage was set to 8Kbytes.

Table 1. Parameters for the set of multi-context data (Experiment 1)

Data Set	Attention Weight
D1-1	$0 \leq AW_1, AW_2, AW_3 \leq 1$
D1-2	$0.7 \leq AW_1 \leq 1$ $0 \leq AW_2, AW_3 \leq 0.15$

The accuracy of recommendation information was evaluated using the relevance and completeness. The set of information recommended to a consumer was denoted by R, and the set of items purchased by P. |S| denotes the cardinality of a set S; thus, the relevance and completeness are defined in [9] as shown below.

$$Relevance = \frac{|R| \cap |P|}{|R|}$$

$$Completeness = \frac{|R| \cap |P|}{|P|}$$

P was generated for each context, as listed in Table 2.

Table 2. Parameters for the set of items purchased

Parameter	Description
$\|P\|$	$12 \leq \|P\| \leq 18$
P	$P1 \cup P2$
P1	$\|P1\| = \|P\| * AW_n *$ acceptance ratio of AW_n , where P1 is selected from candidate recommendation information
P2	$\|P2\| = \|P\| - \|P1\|$, where P2 is selected from the set of items except a candidate's recommendation information

Figure 10 and Figure 11 show the average relevance and completeness of recommendation information for each context using the data sets D1-1 and D1-2. Several the same observations are found in these results. First, the average relevance and completeness in *System2* consistently performed better than that in *System1*. Second, as the acceptance ratio of AW_n increases, the difference between *System1* and *System2* increased.

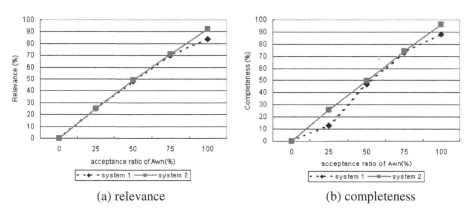

(a) relevance   (b) completeness

Fig. 10. Average relevance and completeness in data set D1-1

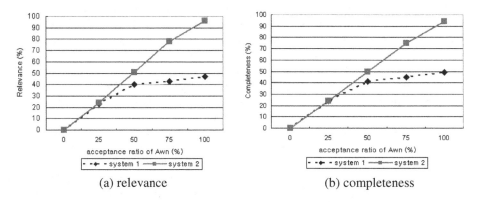

(a) relevance   (b) completeness

Fig. 11. Average relevance and completeness in data set D1-2

Significantly, in Figure 11, unlike Figure 10, the performance difference between *System1* and *System2* was raised. For *System2*, the average relevance and completeness was near 100% when the acceptance ratio of AW_n increased. However, the average relevance and completeness for *System1* did not exceed 50%. This is due to the fact that the amount of information recommended for each context was fixed. The amount of recommendation information needed for context C_1, with a high AW_n, is larger than that needed in contexts C_2 and C_3 with low AW_n. However, in *System1*, the recommendation information is not composed in accordance with the dynamic changes of C_1.

5.2 Experiment 2: Recommendation Time

In this section, we focused on the rapidness of recommendation. We tested the average recommendation time for each context whenever the consumer's cache size was varied. For comparison, we varied the cache size by 2Kbytes from 2Kbytes to 20Kbytes. The context values with AW_n in Table 3 for each context were generated randomly. For the performance evaluation, the experiment was conducted 100 times using a set of multi-context data. In wireless LAN, download velocity was from 6.0Mbps to 6.1Mbps and upload velocity was from 5.8Mbps to 5.9Mbps.

Table 3. Parameters for the set of multi-context data (Experiment 2)

Data Set	Attention Weight
D2-1	$0 \leq AW_1, AW_2, AW_3 < 0.1$
D2-2	$0.1 \leq AW_1, AW_2, AW_3 < 0.2$
...	...
D2-10	$0.9 \leq AW_1, AW_2, AW_3 < 1.0$

Figure 12 shows the average recommendation time whenever the consumer's cache size was varied. Figure 12(d) presents average recommendation time in AW_n from 0.3 to 1, unlike Figure 12(a), Figure 12(b) and Figure 12(c). This is due to the fact that the 7 experimental results in AW_n from 0.3 to 1 are almost the same.

We observe a decrease in recommendation time when the cache size increases as shown in Figure 12. Significantly, in low AW_n, performance of *System2* is better than that of *System1* and the performance difference between *System1* and *System2* is higher when cache size is small.

In Figure 12(a) and Figure 12(b), we can observe that the performance of *System2* is better than that of *System1*. It is simply because that in low AW_n, the amount of recommendation information in *System2* is reduced, while *System1* recommends fixed set of information regardless of degree of consumer's attention. Figure 12(c) also shows the performance of *System1* and *System2* is almost the same. However, in Figure 12(d), the recommendation time of *System2* is slower than that of *System1*. This is due to the fact that *System1* and *System2* recommends the same amount of information and *System2* needs additional process to compose information dynamically when AW_n is higher than 0.3. However, the overall performance of *System2* is better

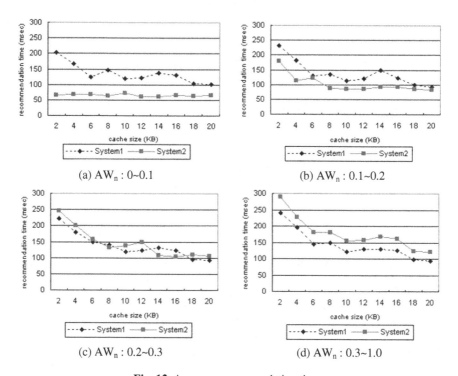

Fig. 12. Average recommendation time

than that of *System1* as the difference between the performance of *System1* and *System2* in Figure 12(d) is negligible than it in Figure 12(a) and Figure 12(b).

6 Conclusion

Recommender systems address a variety of ubiquitous commerce needs. In ubiquitous commerce, it may not be adequate to consider only consumers and items. It is also important to incorporate the contextual information into the recommendation process. The total amount of information is increased due to the greater number of contexts, and this requires an accurate and rapid recommendation method. However, previous works on context-aware recommendation generally support only a single context. A new multicontext-aware recommendation method is suggested that uses preferences and behavior. Both preferences and behavior were utilized to fine-tune the composition recommendation for each context. The composition of the most significant information for each context was changed dynamically over time such that it accurately reflected the consumer's preferences and behavior.

The main contributions of this paper are described as follows. First, a new multicontext-aware recommendation method was presented using a consumer's preferences and behavior. Second, a location- and audio-aware shopping prototype that utilizes the proposed method was illustrated. Finally, that the proposed method is capable of recommending accurately and rapidly was validated through experiments.

References

[1] G. Adomavicius, R. Sankaranarayanan, S. Sen and A. Tuzhilin, "Incorporating Contextual Information in Recommender Systems Using a Multidimensional Approach", ACM Transactions on Information Systems, Vol. 23, Issue 1, 2005.

[2] R. Agrawal, T. Imielinski and A. Swami, "Mining Association Rules in Large Databases", In Proceedings of ACM SIGMOD Conference on Management of Data, Washington D.C., p.207-216, May 1993.

[3] P. J. Brown and G. J. F. Jones, "Context-aware Retrieval: Exploring a New Environment for Information Retrieval and Information Filtering", Personal and Ubiquitous Computing, 2001, Vol. 5, Issue 4, p.253-263, December, 2001.

[4] T. H. Davenport, "May We Have Your Attention, Please?", Ubiquity Vol. 2, Issue 17, 2001.

[5] A. Fano and A. Gershman, "Issues and Challenges in Ubiquitous Computing: The Future of Business Services in the Age of Ubiquitous Computing", Communications of the ACM, Vol. 45, Issue 12, 2002.

[6] G. Kappel, B. Proll, W. Retschitzegger and W. Schwinger, "Customisation for Ubiquitous Web Applications - A Comparison of Approaches", International Journal of Web Engineering and Technology, Vol.1, No.1, p.79-111, 2003.

[7] J. Kwon, S. Kim and Y. Yoon, "Just-In-Time Recommendation using Multi-Agents for Context-Awareness in Ubiquitous Computing Environment", Lecture Notes in Computer Science 2973, p.656-669, Mar, 2004.

[8] B. Mobasher, R. Cooley and J. Srivastava, "Automatic Personalization Based on Web Usage mining", In Communications of the ACM, Vol. 43, No. 8, p.142-151, 2000.

[9] D. S. Phatak and R. Mulvaney, "Clustering for Personalized Mobile Web Usage", In Proceeding of the IEEE FUZZ, p.705-710, 2002.

[10] P. Tarasewich, "Designing Mobile Commerce Applications", Communications of the ACM, Vol. 46 , Issue 12 , p.57- 60, 2003.

[11] J. Wang and M. J. T. Reinders, "Music Recommender System for Wi-Fi Walkman", Mathematics and Computer Science, Delft University of technology, no. ICT-2003-01, 2003.

[12] M. Weiser and J. S. Brown, "The Coming Age of Calm Technology", Xerox PARC, October 5, 1996.

[13] G. Yap, A. Tan and H. Pang, "Dynamically-optimized Context in Recommender Systems", Proceedings of the 6th International Conference on Mobile Data Management, p.265-272, May, 2005.

[14] J. Yoon, S. L. Min and Y. Cho, "Buffer Cache Management: Predicting the Future from the Past", Proceedings of the International Symposium on Parallel Architectures, Algorithms and Networks, p.105-110, 2002.

An Improved E-Commerce Protocol for Fair Exchange

Debajyoti Konar[1] and Chandan Mazumdar[2]

[1] Institute of Engg & Management, Salt Lake, Kolkata - 700 091, India
konar.d@gmail.com
[2] Jadavpur University, Kolkata – 7000032, India
chandanm@cse.jdvu.ac.in

Abstract. In this paper, an improved fair exchange protocol for e-commerce has been presented. The new protocol builds upon a previously published one by Ray & Ray [12]. After discussing the protocol and related fairness, four weaknesses have been found, viz., Fairness Problem: Advantage Merchant, Fairness Problem: Advantage Customer, Possibility of Man in the Middle Attack and Possibility of Malicious Bank. Our modified fair exchange e-commerce protocol is able to handle these weaknesses. The proposed protocol does not involve third party to ensure the fairness.

1 Introduction

Local and global trading of shares, insurance policies, other financial products, music, books, software, etc. through E-commerce transaction is growing rapidly. These digital goods can be marketed through the website of the company concerned. Any person or agency can go through the details of a product and can purchase by ordering the same and paying online. Two or more parties involved in a commercial transaction can identify their activities as a sequence of some message exchanges. The fairness of these exchanges is the way that guarantees that either all the parties obtained what they want or none do [2, 14]. The issue of fairness is becoming increasingly important along with the growth of E-commerce. Also these E commerce protocols should be robust enough to handle the fairness issues as the customer and the vendor or the merchant may be in different locations, which are at long distance.

Non-repudiation services for transmission of messages are defined in terms of *non-repudiation of origin* (NRO) and *non-repudiation of receipt* (NRR).The service NRO is to protect the recipient from originator's repudiation regarding the origin of the message and NRR is to protect from the denial of the receipt of the message [2, 13]. A straight forward approach for fair exchange problem used in several ISO proposal is to use a third party to ensure the fairness, which obviously can be named as *Trusted Third Party* (TTP) approach [13, 14]. However there are several methods where TTP is not being used and in these cases '*gradual release of secrets*' (GRS) is being used to achieve the fairness [2, 3, 5]. Whatever may be the approach of the fair exchange protocol (either of TTP approach or GRS approach), an analysis of fairness is recommended, as E-commerce protocols are required to provide mutual guarantees to protocol participants regarding fairness. The security properties of several key-exchange protocols and authentication protocols have been analyzed widely for a considerably

S. Madria et al. (Eds.): ICDCIT 2006, LNCS 4317, pp. 305–313, 2006.
© Springer-Verlag Berlin Heidelberg 2006

long time. Finite-State Analysis has also been used to analyze several protocols [6, 8, 9]. Due to the growing requirement of fairness of protocols, the fair exchange protocols are being developed, analyzed and modified in recent past [4, 7, 10, 14].

In this paper we considered a fair exchange protocol, proposed by Ray &Ray [12], which allows a customer to exchange payment for a digital product of a merchant with fairness in exchange and anonymity of each party. We also considered a work by Adam Barth and Andrew Tappert in which they modeled the protocol in the Reactive Modules language of Mocha [1] to test claims made by Ray & Ray by formalizing as propositional logic invariants and alternating-time temporal logic (ATL) formulas. We have analyzed the protocol, proposed by Ray & Ray and discover some weaknesses in the protocol. We present a modified protocol to handle those weaknesses and also propose some future scope of work.

Section 2 of this paper contains the description of the protocol, proposed by Ray & Ray. In section 3, we analyze the protocol to show that a few types of attacks can nullify the claims of Ray & Ray. A modified protocol is presented in section 4. The features of the modified protocol are discussed in section 5. Section 6 concludes the paper.

2   Anonymous Fair Exchange Protocol by Ray and Ray

The protocol engages customer (C), customer's bank (CB), merchant (M) and merchant's bank (MB) as participating parties. The protocol allows the presence of third party (TP) during a prelude phase. In this protocol a merchant (M) who wishes to sell a digital product m registers itself with a third party (TP) by sending the product details for advertising on the web. The customer (C) downloads the encrypted product from TP and sends the purchase order to the merchant (M), using a pseudo identifier, together with a one time public key, C_{ipub}. M responds by sending the product encrypted with a key, $K_1 X K_2$, together with encrypted information about the account that s/he wishes to be credited. The key $K_1 X K_2$ has a mathematical relation with K_1 and using the theory of cross-validation [14], the customer (C) can verify that the product s/he is about to receive is the one he will be paying for.

2.1 Prelude

1. M registers with TP
2. M keeps a public key with TP i.e. M → TP: [m, K_1], M_{ipub}
3. C selects a product to purchase, i.e., TP → C: [m, K_1], M_{ipub}
4. *C generates a one-time public/private key (C_{ipub}, C_{iprv}) to use during the current transaction T_i*

2.2 Protocol Description

1) C → M: PO [CC(PO), C_{iprv}] [C_{ipub}, M_{ipub}]; /*C places the purchase order to M*/
2) M → C: [*Abort*, M_{iprv}]; /* M aborts*/
   Or
   M → C: [CC(PO), M_{iprv}] [m.r, $K_1 X K_2$] [CC([m.r, $K_1 X K_2$]), Miprv] [r, K_1] [CC([r, K_1]), M_{iprv}] [M_{acct}, MB_{pub}] [CC([M_{acct}, MB_{pub}]), M_{iprv}];

/*Accepcting the purchase order, M sends encrypted product and account in formation*/

3) C → CB: [[MTI, C_{prv}], CB_{pub}]; /* C asks for pay-order or payment token*/

4) CB → C: [[P, B_{cprv}], C_{pub}]; /* CB sends pay-order or payment token to C*/

   Or

   CB → C: [Failure, C_{pub}]; /*CB fails to send pay-order or payment token to C*/

5) C → M: [[P, B_{cprv}], M_{ipub}]; /* C sends payment (pay-order) to M*/

   Or

   C → M: [Abort, C_{iprv}]; /* C aborts denying payment*/

6) M → MB: [[P, B_{cprv}], MB_{pub}]; /*M sends pay-order to MB for clearance*/

7) MB → M: [ack, MB_{prv}]; /*MB sends acknowledgement of payment-clearance to M*/

8) M → C: [K_2^{-1}, C_{ipub}] [$CC(K_2^{-1})$, M_{iprv}] [r^{-1}, C_{ipub}] [$CC(r^{-1})$, M_{iprv}];
   /*M sends decryption key to C*/

It is clear from the description, in the protocol, eight message exchanges are involved without using any third party as a participant. Message 1 allows the customer (C) to place the purchase order for a desired digital product to the merchant (M) whereas by message 2, the merchant (M) responds by signing the purchase order on acceptance and sending the encrypted (with cross-key $K_1 \ X \ K_2$) product and his /her account information, encrypted with his/her bank's (MB) public key. In message 3 customer (C) ask for a pay-order (token) from his/her bank (CB) and receives the pay-order from bank (CB) through message 4. After receiving pay-order, customer (C) sends it to merchant (M) by using message 5. In message 6, merchant (M) deposits the pay-order with his/her bank (MB) and after getting the acknowledgement regarding the encashment of pay-order from his/her bank (MB) by message 7, merchant (M) sends the decryption key to the customer (C) by using message 8. Now, the customer (C) can obtain the digital product by decrypting the encrypted digital product, which is already available from message 2. In [12], the authors, Ray and Ray, propose the involvement of third party (TP) only by The customer (C) and the protocol assumes resilient private channels with TP. After completing the message exchanges 1,2,3 & 4, the customer (C) obtain the pay- order from his/her bank (CB) and now s/he can call upon the third party (TP) to force resolution of the transaction. The involvement of third party (TP) in this phase is as follows:

C → TP: *message 1, message 2*, [P, B_{cprv}]

TP → M: "Please send product decryption key"

Case 1 (if M already has [P, B_{cprv}])

M → TP: K_2^{-1}, r^{-1}

TP → C: K_2^{-1}, r^{-1}

Case 2 (if M does not have [P, B_{cprv}])

M → TP: "I did not receive payment token"

TP → M: [P, B_{cprv}] and Resume base protocol with message exchange 6

Case 3 (if timeout occurs)

No response from merchant (M)

TP → C: K_1^{-1}

3 Analysis

The authors claim their protocol allows anonymous fair exchange of money for a digital good and also the identities are protected by single-transaction public/private key pairs. In addition, the authors claim that the customer is being assured of obtaining correct product by their protocol. Here we considered the extension of the protocol with third party and also several potential attacks to analyze the protocol and to verify the claims.

3.1 Fairness Problem: Advantage M

As we mentioned, the protocol believes that the third party may be involved in the transaction only by the invocation of customer (C), the customer sends message 1, message 2, pay-order [P, B_{cprv}], which s/he has received from his /her bank (CB) to the third party (TP). The third party then asks the merchant (M) to send decryption key to the customer. The merchant now can ignore the third party's message, can comply or can reply the third party that s/he has not received payment. In the last case, the third party (TP) forwards the pay-order to the merchant (M) and assumes s/he will continue the protocol, but clearly s/he may not do so and may continue to deny that s/he has received payment.

3.2 Fairness Problem: Advantage C

On the other hand, after message 2 the merchant (M) is committed to transaction in the eyes of the third party (TP) and can not abort the transaction, which leads to a favour to the customer (C) because after receiving [P, B_{cprv}] from CB, the customer (C) is in a position to either force the transaction to occur by invoking third party (TP) or abort by denying payment.

3.3 Malicious Bank: A Possible Attack

In the protocol, guarantee of anonymity leads to a fabrication attack i.e., to play the role of customer, an employee of the customer's bank can create a pay-order and in that case the bank will be considered as malicious bank. As per the description of the protocol, the pay-order contains simply an account to be credited, an amount to credit and a nonce to prevent the replay attacks, all encrypted under a key B_{cprv}, which is a shared private key among banks. So an employee of the customer's bank (considered as malicious bank) can create [[P, B_{cprv}], M_{ipub}] to play the role of customer. Neither merchant (M) nor merchant's bank (MB) can learn the identity of the creator of pay-order (P). This leads to a weakness of the protocol.

3.4 Man in the Middle: A Possible Attack

In the protocol we may have a man-in-middle attack. As customer (C) generates fresh public-private key pair in the prelude, to play the role of customer (C) any intruder may generate its own public-private key pair and may replace C_{iprv}/C_{ipub}. This C_{iprv}/C_{ipub} pair, which is never signed by any participating party of the protocol, occur only in messages exchange 1 and 8 as:

1. C → M: PO [CC(PO), C_{iprv}] [C_{ipub}, M_{ipub}]
8. M → C: [K_2^{-1}, C_{ipub}] [CC(K_2^{-1}), M_{iprv}] [r^{-1}, C_{ipub}] [CC(r^{-1}), M_{iprv}]

So, to learn about the digital-good the intruder may intercept the messages of the customer (C) to relay those to the merchant and forward the responses to the customer (C). Here the intruder can learn the product only, by an interception attack. This attack may disclose the customer's private preference of goods, which leads to breach of privacy. This is a weakness, which requires modification and this situation occurs, as the merchant never confirms the public key, sent by the customer.

4 The Modified Protocol

Considering the above analysis in 3.1, 3.2, 3.3 & 3.4 we propose the modification on the protocol. The proposed modified protocol engages the customer (C), customer's bank (CB), merchant (M) and merchant's bank (MB) as participants without using third party not even in prelude. This protocol is also based on the theory of cross-validation [12]. It is assumed that the key distribution scheme for the proposed protocol is secure.

4.1 Protocol Description

Here the merchant advertises his/her product (*m*) with all of its details in its own website so that the customer can download it. The protocol starts when the customer enters into the merchants website to have the details of the product and being satisfied with the product decides to purchase it. After that the protocol may be described as follows:

1) M → C: [m, K_1], M_{ipub}; /*C selects a product m from M's website*/
2) C → M: PO [CC(PO), C_{iprv}] [C_{ipub}, M_{ipub}]; /*C places the purchase order to M*/
3) M → C: [Abort, M_{iprv}]; /* M aborts*/
   Or
   M → C: [CC(PO), M_{iprv}] [m.r, K_1xK_2] [CC([m.r, K_1xK_2]), M_{iprv}] [r, K_1]
   [CC([r, K_1]), M_{iprv}] [M_{acct}, MB_{pub}] [CC([M_{acct}, MB_{pub}]), M_{iprv}]
   [CC(C_{ipub}), M_{iprv}];
   /*Accepting the purchase order, M sends encrypted product and account information
        including customer's public key encrypted with his/her private key*/
4) C → CB: [[MTI, C_{prv}], CB_{pub}]; /* C instructs CB to prepare pay-order and to send it to MB*/
5) CB → MB: [[P,B_{cprv}],MB_{pub}]; /*CB sends the pay-order to MB*/
   Or
   CB → C: [Failure, C_{pub}]; /*CB fails to send pay-order and informs C*/
6) CB → C: [P,CB_{prv}]; /*CB sends a copy of payment details to C*/
7) C → M: [P, M_{ipub}]; /*C forwards the copy of payment details to M*/
   Or
   C → M: [Abort, C_{iprv}]; /*C aborts if message 5 is failure message*/
8) MB → CB: [ack, MB_{prv}]; /*MB sends acknowledgement of payment-clearance to CB*/

9) MB → M: [ack, MB$_{prv}$]; /*MB sends a copy of acknowledgement of payment-clearance to M*/

10) M → MB: [rcpt(ack), M$_{prv}$]; /*M sends a receipt of acknowledgement to MB*/

11) CB → C: [[ack, MB$_{prv}$], CB$_{prv}$];
   /*CB forwards a copy of acknowledgement of payment-clearance to C*/

12) C → CB: [rcpt(ack), C$_{prv}$]; /*C sends a receipt of acknowledgement to CB*/

13) M → C: [K$_2^{-1}$, C$_{ipub}$] [CC(K$_2^{-1}$), M$_{iprv}$] [r^{-1}, C$_{ipub}$] [CC([r^{-1}), M$_{iprv}$];
   /*M sends decryption key to C*/

14) C → M: [rcpt, C$_{iprv}$]; /*C sends receipt of decryption key to M*/

15) M → C; [[bill_memo, [ack, MB$_{prv}$]], M$_{iprv}$];
   /*M sends final bill/memo and payment receipt to C*/

In the protocol, there are 15 message exchanges within the participating parties. First message exchange is to download [[m, K$_1$], M$_{ipub}$] from the website of the merchant (M). Message 2 allows the customer (C) to place the purchase order for a desired digital product to the merchant (M) whereas by message 3, the merchant (M) either aborts the transaction or responds by signing the purchase order on acceptance and sending the encrypted (with cross-key K$_1$xK$_2$) product and his /her account information, encrypted with his/her bank's (MB) public key. Unlike the protocol, proposed by Ray & Ray, in this message the merchant (M) also includes the customer's public-key under his/her private-key ([CC(C$_{ipub}$), M$_{iprv}$]). Thus, the customer can detect the man-in-middle attack. In message 4 customer (C) issues a payment instruction (MTI) to his/her bank (CB) mentioning the merchant's account information (M$_{acct}$, MB$_{pub}$), exact amount to be paid to the merchant's bank account. Through message 5, customer's bank (CB) sends the pay-order to merchant's bank (MB) and sends copy of payment details to the customer (C) by message 6 or sends a failure message to the customer (C). Then the customer (C) forwards the copy of payment details to merchant (M) just to say that pay-order has been sent to the specified bank account. The customer (C) aborts the transaction, if from message 5 s/he receives a failure message through message 7. After clearance of pay-order, sent by customer's bank (CB), the merchant's bank (MB) sends the acknowledgement against the payment (credited to the merchant's account) to the customer's bank (CB) and also to the merchant (M) to inform that the payment has been credited to his/her account consecutively by messages 8 and 9. In message 10, the merchant (M) sends the receipt of payment acknowledgement to it's bank (MB). The customer's bank (CB) forwards the copy of payment acknowledgement to the customer (C) by signing it with private key, which is an alternative document of acceptance of payment by the merchant. The customer (C) also sends the receipt of the same to the customer's bank (CB). These facts are being reflected in messages 11 and 12 respectively. As the merchant (M) already knows that the specified payment has been credited to his/her account, s/he sends the decryption key, which will be used to get the digital product, to the customer (C) by using message 13. Finally, by messages 14 and 15, the customer (C) sends the receipt of decryption key (i.e., actually the receipt of digital product) to the merchant (M) by signing it with his/her private key and after receiving the receipt the merchant (M) sends the detailed bill/memo along with a copy of the payment acceptance (signed by the merchant's bank), both signed by its private key.

4.2 Symbols of the Protocol

Symbols	Interpretation
B_{acct}	B's bank account
m	The digital product or good
PO	Purchase Order for product m
T_i	Transaction involving purchase of m
A_{prv}, A_{pub}	A's private and public keys
A_{iprv}, A_{ipub}	A's private and public keys for T_i
$A \rightarrow B:X$	A sends X to B
$[X,K]$	Encryption of X with key K
CC(X)	Cryptographic checksum of X
MTI	Money Transfer Instruction
ack	Acknowledgement
$rcpt$	Receipt message
$rcpt(ack)$	Receipt of acknowledgement
$bill\_memo$	Descriptive bill/memo for the purpose of accounting

5 Features of the Proposed Modified Protocol

Our proposed protocol holds the features, by which the correctness of the product is being ensured to each party without using any third party. As fairness is the more pertinent issue in the e-commerce protocol, in our proposed modified protocol, to achieve the true fairness, we have tried to handle the weaknesses which we have discovered in the protocol proposed by Ray & Ray. Here, we discuss only those features of our protocol as follows:

5.1 Handling the Fairness Problem: Advantage M

In the protocol, proposed by Ray & Ray, we have identified a weakness in fairness, i.e., advantage of the merchant (M) in 3.1. In our proposed modified protocol we are not using any third party. Here the customer (C) is getting the information from his/her bank that the exact payment has been sent to the merchant's account through message 6. Again, by message 11 s/he (C) is getting signed copy of the acknowledgement from his/her bank (CB) regarding the encashment of the payment into merchant's account, signed by merchant's bank (MB), which customer's bank (CB) is getting from merchant's bank (MB) through message 8. These facts lead to a situation where merchant (M) is not in advantage like the protocol, proposed by Ray & Ray. As the customer (C) have two important documents, viz, [[ack, MB_{prv}], CB_{prv}] & [P,CB_{pub}], which can legally prove that s/he has done the payment to merchant's account in merchant's bank and s/he can seek justice from legal authority in case of denial of acceptance of the payment from merchant (M).

5.2 Handling the Fairness Problem: Advantage C

In our proposed modified protocol the customer (C) is issuing the payment instruction to his/her bank (CB) and the bank is sending the payment to merchant's bank. Also, here, the customer (C) cannot invoke the third party (TP), as our protocol is not using any third party. The above facts lead to a situation where, the customer is not in a position to either force the transaction by invoking third party (TP) or abort by denying payment, which solves the fairness problem regarding advantage of the customer (C), mentioned in 3.2.

5.3 Handling the Malicious Bank Attack

In the protocol, proposed by Ray & Ray, any malicious bank (in essence, an employee of the customer's bank) can create $[[P, B_{cprv}], M_{ipub}]$ to play the role of customer. Neither merchant (M) nor merchant's bank (MB) can learn the identity of the creator of pay-order (P). In our proposed modified protocol, through message 4, customer's bank (CB) sends the pay-order to merchant's bank (MB) and sends copy of payment details to the customer (C) by message 6. After receiving the copy of payment details customer (C) sends the same to merchant (M) just to say that pay-order has been sent to the specified bank account through message 7. So, if any malicious bank (in essence, an employee of the customer's bank) creates the pay-order, it will go to merchant's bank and be credited to merchant's account. After getting the payment acknowledgement the merchant will send the decryption key to the customer. So, for a malicious bank, it's not possible to have the decryption key. The above facts leads to a situation where any malicious bank will not be not at all interested to be involved in the transaction, which certainly protects the transaction from the malicious bank attack, mentioned in 3.3.

5.4 Handling the Man in the Middle Attack

In the protocol, proposed by Ray & Ray, any intruder may intercept the messages of the customer (C) to learn the digital-good. This possibility occurs, as the merchant never confirms the public key, sent by the customer. In our proposed modified protocol, the merchant (M) either aborts the transaction or includes the customer's public-key encrypted by his/her private-key ($[CC(C_{ipub}), M_{iprv}]$), while sending message 3. Here, the merchant (M) is signing the public key of the customer (C) with its own private key and sending it to the customer (C). If there is any intruder, the customer (C) can not get its own public key C_{ipub} signed by the merchant's private key (M_{iprv}). So the customer can detect the man-in-middle attack, mentioned in 3.4.

6 Conclusion

In this work we have discussed the protocol, proposed by Ray & Ray. After analyzing the protocol four weaknesses have been found, viz., Fairness Problem: Advantage M, Fairness Problem: Advantage C, Possibility of Man in the Middle Attack and Possibility of Malicious Bank Attack. Then we presented a modified fair exchange e-commerce protocol which is able to handle the weaknesses of the protocol proposed by Ray & Ray. Our proposed protocol is also based on the theory of cross-validation and holds the properties, by which the correctness of the product is being ensured to each party. Here we have not used any third party in the protocol, involving 15 message exchanges among the participating parties. As fairness is the more pertinent issue in the e-commerce protocol, we have considered it as a major concern in this work.

Though in the presented protocol we have not used any third party, a role of a trusted third party (TTP) may be considered in future. In future scope of work, we are going to extend the protocol with a trusted third party (TTP), which will be acceptable to all and will be a participant of the protocol, not be invoked only by one participant for his/her interest. Any statutory authority of clearance of payment (like the Reserve Bank of India or the Federal Reserve of USA) may be an example of that TTP.

We believe our work in this paper will extend the area of applicability of fair non-repudiation protocol in E-commerce so that customers and merchants can participate in such transaction with more assurance.

References

1. Rajeev Alur, Thomas A. Henzinger, F.Y.C. Mang, Shaz Qadeer, Sriram K. Rajamani, and Serdar Tasiran: "Mocha: Modularity in model checking." *Proceedings of the 10th International Conference on Computer-aided Verification.* Lecture Notes in Computer Science (1427), Springer-Verlag, 1998, pp. 521-525. (http://www-cad.eecs.berkeley.edu/~mocha/)
2. N.Asokan, V. Schunter, M.Waidner: "Optimistic Protocols for Fair Exchange", *Proc. Of 4th ACM Conference on Computer and Communication Security, Zurich,1997*
3. N.Asokan, V. Shoup, M.Waidner: " Asynchronous Protocols for Optimistic Fair Exchange", *Proc. IEEE Symposium on Research in Security and Privacy*, 1998, pp. 86-99.
4. Feng Bao, G. Wang, J. Zhou, H.Zhu: " Analysis and Improvementof Micali's Fair Cotract Signing Protocol", *Proc. Australian Conference on Information Security and Privacy, Sydney, Australia, 2004, Lecture Notes in Computer Science* (3108), pp. 176-187.
5. Shimon Even, Oded Goldreich, Abraham Lempel: " A Randomized Protocol for Signing Contracts"; *Communications of the ACM* 28/6,1985,pp. 637-647.
6. R. Kemmerer, C. Meadows, J. Millen: "Three Systems for Cryptographic Protocol Analysis", *J. Cryptography*, 7(2),1994, pp. 79-130.
7. S. Kremer, O. Markowitch, J. Zhou: "An Intensive Survey of Fair exchange Protocols",*J. Computer Communications*, 25(17), 2002, pp. 1606-1621.
8. C. Meadows: "The NRL Protocol Analyzer: An Overview", *J. Logic Programming*, 26(2),1996, pp. 113-131.
9. C. Meadows: "Analyzing the Needham-Schroeder Public Key Protocol: A Comparison of Two Approaches", *Proc. European symposium on Research in Computer Security, Springer-Verlag*, 1996, pp. 365-384.
10. Silvio Micali: "Simple and Fast Optimistic Protocols for Fair Electronic Exchange", *Proc. ACM Symposium on Principles of Distributed Computing, Boston, U.S.A.*,2003, pp. 12-19.
11. J. Onieva, J. Zhou, J. Lopez: " Non-repudiation Protocols for Multiple Entities", *J. Computer Communications*, 27(16), 2004, pp. 1608-1616.
12. Indrakshi Ray and Indrajit Ray. "An Anonymous Fair-Exchange E-Commerce Protocol." *Proceedings of the First International Workshop on Internet Computing and E-Commerce, San Francisco, CA, April*, 2001.
13. Steve Schneider: " Formal analysis of a Non-repudiation Protocol", *Proc. 11th IEEE Computer Security Foundations workshop, Rockport, U.S.A.*, 1998, pp. 54-65.
14. J. Zhou: "Achieving Fair Non-repudiation in Electronic Transactions", *J. Organizational Computing and Electronic Commerce*,11(4), 2001, pp. 253-267.

Requirements-Driven Modeling of the Web Service Execution and Adaptation Lifecycle

N.C. Narendra[1] and B. Orriens[2]

[1] IBM India Research Lab, Bangalore, India
narendra@in.ibm.com
[2] Tilburg University, The Netherlands
b.orriens@uvt.nl

Abstract. The increasing popularity of Web services for application integration has resulted in a large body of research on Web service composition. However, the major lacuna so far in Web service composition is the lack of a holistic requirements-driven approach for modeling the entire Web service lifecycle, i.e., composition, joint execution, midstream adaptation in response to failures or changing requirements, and finally re-execution until successful completion. In this paper we present such an approach based on our earlier work on context-driven Web service modeling. In particular, we separate requirements into two parts – functional and extra-functional requirements (FRs and EFRs, respectively). We express FRs as commitments made by individual Web services towards the composite Web service, and EFRs as rules that constrain the behavior of the individual Web services while they execute against their FRs. We also show how midstream adaptation in Web service execution - caused either by changes in user requirements or execution failures – can be managed in our approach. We believe that ours is the first such approach towards a comprehensive modeling of requirements for composite Web service executions, and especially during adaptation.

1 Introduction and Motivation

Web services have emerged as a major technology for deploying automated interactions between distributed systems. Web services are suitable candidates for enabling application integration between independent businesses because of their platform- and language-independent interfaces that feature them. Composition primarily concerns requests of users that cannot be satisfied by any available Web service, whereas a composite service obtained by combining a set of available Web services might be used [3].

However, Web services' joint execution also needs to be modeled, thereby driving the need for representing composite Web services as workflows. The workflow model can represent each Web service execution as a task. Web service execution is also expected to model the changes in business process execution that are a constant feature in most business organizations today. Hence the need to explicitly model - and develop techniques for dealing with – adaptation in Web services execution, becomes crucial. These changes could be caused by several factors, such as execution failure of

S. Madria et al. (Eds.): ICDCIT 2006, LNCS 4317, pp. 314–324, 2006.
© Springer-Verlag Berlin Heidelberg 2006

a particular Web service, or even the user's requirements changing midstream. To that end, a requirements-driven approach to modeling the entire Web service execution lifecycle – composition, joint execution, midstream adaptation, and finally, re-execution until successful completion – becomes crucial. In this paper, we leverage from our previous work [11, 14] to develop such a requirements-driven approach. We also show how our approach is able to accomplish the primary objectives of representing Web service executions in terms of the requirements that they satisfy; and maintaining traceability between Web service requirements and executions, especially during adaptation.

We do not provide a formal definition of requirement in this paper; rather, we simply define a requirement as a need to be fulfilled, either originating from a user of the composite service, or from an external authority. The former requirement is called a *functional requirement* (FR) and the latter, *extra-functional requirement* (EFR). The key difference between the two is the following: the FRs represent the core functionality that should be met by the composite services, whereas the EFRs are requirements to be met by the composite service in addition to the FRs.

Sometimes, adding an EFR may conflict with an FR. For example, one FR would be to ensure that the customer is able to open a bank account within 7 days. However, new reporting & checking requirements may force additional services to be instantiated in the workflow, which may delay the opening by an extra 2 days. However, in this paper, we restrict our attention to only those situations where no conflicts exist among requirements.

This paper is organized as follows. We introduce our running scenario in Section 2, which we will be using throughout the rest of the paper in order to illustrate our ideas. We present the other preliminaries in Section 3 – workflow, adaptive workflow, our context-driven Web services architecture. In Section 4, we introduce and describe the two types of user requirements – FRs and EFRs. Section 5 shows how our Web services architecture is enhanced via our requirements-driven modeling approach; this also includes discussion on adaptation. We present related work in Section 6. The paper concludes in Section 7 with suggestions for future work.

2 Running Scenario

Our scenario, inspired by the e-procurement scenario from [10], is an online book purchase scenario depicted in Figure 1.

Upon receiving an order from a customer, the book prices are calculated and informed to the customer. In addition, the customer's purchase order is received only after the customer's credit check proves successful. Once the purchase order is received, the online merchant arranges for shipping of the books from several suppliers, who in turn ship the books to the customer. In parallel, the invoice is sent to the customer, from whom the payment is also received. In Figure 1, the online merchant is the composite service. The participating service instances are: credit check, shipper arrange, invoice management, shipper, payment service. The other tasks in the workflow – receive book request, send prices to customer, notify customer, receive purchase order - are carried out by service instances instantiated by Web service providers that belong to the composite service. The shipping part of the workflow is highlighted in yellow color – the reason for this will become apparent when we discuss

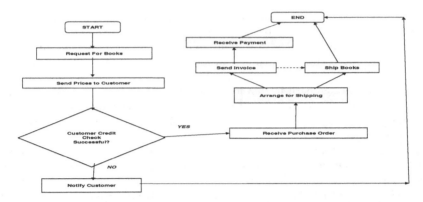

Fig. 1. Book Purchase Workflow

adaptation of this workflow later in Section 6. In Figure 1, a soft-sync edge (to be explained later) from Send Invoice to Ship Books is displayed. This imposes the constraint that Ship Books task can commence only after Send Invoice task has been started.

3 Preliminaries

3.1 Workflow

Our basic workflow model is based on our earlier adaptive workflow research [13], which is derived from the workflow model of [1]. We assume that each workflow instance is a directed graph $W = <N,E>$, where N is the set of nodes and E is the set of edges. Each edge e in E is a tuple of the form $<n_{begin}, n_{end}>$, where the edge is directed from n_{begin} to n_{end}. We first define two unique nodes – START and END nodes; for each workflow, there will be only one of each kind. A START node has no predecessor, and an END node has no successor. The workflow graph is assumed to obey two simple conditions: every node in the graph is reachable from the START node, and the END node is reachable from every node in the graph. Nodes are of two kinds – *work nodes* and *route nodes*. Work nodes are nodes that actually perform the activities in the workflow. Route nodes are nodes whose only function is to evaluate rules (i.e., boolean conditions) and, depending on the result of the evaluation, these nodes direct the flow of control to specific work nodes or route nodes.

Edges are of four kinds – *forward edge, loop edge, soft-sync edge and strict-sync edge*. Forward edges depict the normal workflow execution, which is in a forward direction. Loop edges are backward pointing edges that are used to depict the repeated execution of loops. The "sync" edges, which are of two types, are used to support synchronizations of tasks from different parallel branches of a loop. A "soft-sync" edge is used to signify a "delay dependency" between two nodes n_1 and n_2, i.e., n_2 can only be executed if n_1 is either completed or cannot be triggered anymore. This type of synchronization does not require the successful completion of n_1. A "strict-sync" edge between n_1 and n_2 requires that n_1 successfully complete before n_2 executes.

Clearly, the use of such edges must satisfy some conditions. First, redundant control flow dependencies between nodes and loops should be avoided. In addition, a sync edge may not connect a node from inside a loop body with a node not contained within that loop.

3.2 Adaptive Workflow

In [13], we have developed a 3-tier model for adaptive workflow. This model has been derived out of the fundamental observation that a workflow definition is to be modeled in order to meet one or more business goals. Each execution of a workflow definition is, therefore an *instance* of the workflow definition. We call the workflow definition itself a workflow *schema*, which has been created via a process of workflow *planning* driven by business goals. Hence the three tiers in our model are *planning*, *schema* and *instance* tiers [13]. At instance level, only the workflow instances need to be modified. At schema level, the workflow definition will need to be modified – this would arise if certain business practices change. At planning level, the workflow goals themselves would change, leading to radical changes in the workflow schema.

3.3 Context Ontologies for Web Service Composition and Execution

Modeling Web services execution is quite different from that in "traditional" (i.e., monolithic) workflow, due to semantic heterogeneities between Web services originating from different Web service providers. This gap arises, since the different Web services have been created and operate in different *contexts* – context being defined as the information that characterizes the interaction between a Web service and its external environment [7]. In order to bridge this gap, we have proposed the use of *ontologies* [11] to represent the contexts of the Web services so that the contexts can be reconciled for composition and execution. We represent this context information thus: *C-context* for *composite service*, *W-context* for *Web service provider*, and *I-context* for individual *service instances* that are created by the Web service providers. Some sample C-context arguments are: *label*, *previous Web services*, *current Web services*, *next Web services*, *begin time*, *status per Web service instance*, and *date*; similarly, some sample W-context arguments are *label*, *number of service instances allowed*, *number of service instances running*, *next service instance availability*, *status per service instance per composite service*, and *date*; whereas, some sample I-context arguments are *label*, *status*, *previous service instances*, *next service instances*, *regular actions* (this argument illustrates the actions that a Web service instance executes according to a certain context, and this helps track the execution trace of a Web service instance), *begin-time*, *end-time (expected & effective)*, *reasons of failure*, *corrective actions* (this argument is in relation to *regular actions* argument), and *date*.

Our conceptual architecture is as depicted below in Figure 2, and operates as per two operations – *consolidation* and *reconciliation*. Consolidation occurs when a Web service accepts an invitation of participation (1), and creates an instance with an I-context (2). The transfer of details from the I-contexts of the same Web service instances to the W-Context of their associated Web service is featured by a consolidation of these details before this W-context is updated (3,4). Reconciliation occurs during execution; an instance transfers its I-context details to the C-context of the

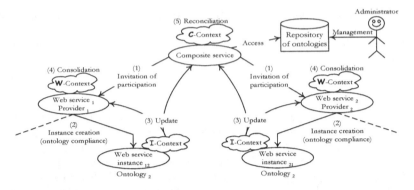

Fig. 2. Context and Ontology Use in Web Services Composition

composite service, after performing a reconciliation of the data to address the afore-mentioned semantic heterogeneity (3,5).

We therefore see a natural mapping to the 3-tier adaptive workflow model described in Section 3.2: planning⟷C-context, schema⟷W-context and instance⟷I-context. We are currently implementing these ideas in our *ConWeSc* (Context-based Semantic Web Services) prototype [11].

3.4 Rule-Driven Modeling of Composite Web Services

Our layered rule-driven modeling approach is leveraged from [14], and is based on the conceptual model shown below in Figure 3.

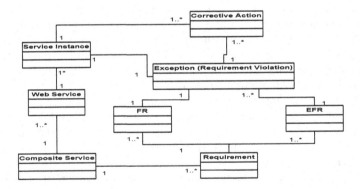

Fig. 3. Conceptual Model of Web Service Requirements vis-à-vis Executions

In order to ease the representation and modeling of requirements we adopt a modularization facility called *facets* in this paper, which has been introduced in [14]. The identified facets are: *what, how, where, who, when* and *why*. The *what* facet emphasizes the informational view in the requirement, the *how* facet emphasizes the functional view of the requirement (i.e., how the requirement is to be met), whereas the *where* facet emphasizes the locational/geographical view in the requirement. The *who* facet is concerned with the participants affected by the requirement. The temporal aspect is covered in the *when* facet, while the *who* facet covers the rationale behind the requirement. For any requirement, all facets may not be needed; however, the composite service designer can choose to use those facets as appropriate.

We can therefore use our 3-tier context-ontology structure to represent this information at the appropriate C/W/I-context levels. Our augmented contextual information can then consist of the following additions:

- At I-context level: FRs for this instance, EFRs for this instance, dependencies (the other instances that this instance depends on for its execution – this information is aggregated and stored at the sub-workflow level in the W-context)
- At W-context level: FRs for this sub-workflow, EFRs for this sub-workflow, sub-workflow specification (stores aggregate dependencies information from the I-context; this information is in turn further aggregated and stored at the workflow level in the C-context)
- At C-context level: overall FRs for the workflow, overall EFRs for the workflow, workflow specification, specification assignments (specifies the assignment of Web service providers to their appropriate sub-workflows).

4 Modeling Requirements

4.1 Modeling Functional Requirements (FRs)

At the C-context layer, we model FRs as high-level business commitments [12] among the participants in the composite service, including the user. At the W-context layer, we translate this into the sub-workflow specifications derived from the FRs (to be described in more detail below). At the I-context layer, each sub-workflow specification is then translated into workflow tasks.

For our running scenario, an example FR would be the fulfillment of the customer order upon successful credit check. In this FR there are two parties involved, being the online merchant and the customer; both representing the **who** facet. The merchant sends a Customer Order Fulfillment to the customer, which represents the **what** facet; which is done after the customer credit check has been successfully completed (constituting the FR's when facet). This constraint is expressed as:

```
shipment(?merchant,?customer,?books)   :-
    credit_check(?customer).
```

where we use POSL (http://www.ruleml.org/submission/ruleml-shortation.html), a simplified notation for RuleML (http://www.ruleml.org/) here to express such constraints.

Representing the **where** facet here are eBook.com, the name of our fictional online merchant, and MyCompany, to which we assume the customer belongs. A constraint that may be placed in this regard is that the merchant's location is in the same region as the customer's shipping address, expressed as:

```
shipment(?customer,?books; region->customer_address) :-
    location(region->merchant_address).
```

In the **how** facet we find links to previously executed workflows for this FR, if any – as per Figure 3, the following tasks can be stored here: {Send Invoice, Ship Books}. Finally, in the **why** facet the business rationale for this workflow can be recorded. From Figure 1, we see that the tasks that satisfy this FR, are {Receive Purchase Order, Arrange for Shipping, Send Invoice, Ship Books}.

4.2 Modeling Extra-Functional Requirements (EFRs)

An example of a C-level EFR in our running scenario, could be to only process orders that can be fulfilled by suppliers within a certain geographical region. The W-level EFR would comprise constraints specific to the operation of a Web service and its instances in the composition. Some of these would either be derived from the C-level EFR, or would be EFRs specific to the Web service in question. An example of the latter, in our running scenario, is that a product shipper can only ship a product after ensuring a pre-specified minimum inventory after the shipment, most probably via replenishment. An example of the former in our running scenario, would be for a shipper to derive its W-level EFR from the C-level EFR to ensure that it only ships products to customers within the pre-specified geographical region.

The I-level EFR contains constraints that affect the workflow execution sequence, and which are derived from the C-level and W-level EFRs. These are primarily ordering constraints that can be expressed via the control flow and data flow dependencies in our workflow model. An example of an I-level EFR in our running scenario would be the soft-sync constraint between the Send Invoice and Ship Books tasks.

For our running scenario, the example EFR could be the aforementioned soft-sync edge constraint, which is described as follows:

what – Ordering Constraint
who – Send Invoice, Ship Books
when – shipping of the book is to start only after the invoice has been prepared

```
preparation(?invoice) :-
      Ship(?customer,?books)
```

where – from shipper's location to customer's shipping address

```
shipment(?customer,?books; region->customer_address) :-
    location(region->shipper_address).
```

how – as per Figure 3, this would store the related task information, such as a sync edge from Send Invoice to Ship Books
why – linkage to overall business context, storing business-related rationale for this EFR

5   Requirements-Driven Web Service Execution and Adaptation

As per Figure 3, we see that each commitment – representing an FR – is represented by a task sequence. As the workflow execution proceeds, the reconciliation operation

(Section 2.3) is implemented, which results in updation and transfer of I-context details to the composite service. As soon as the appropriate task sequence completes, the appropriate FR information is updated; once the last task in the task sequence is executed, the FR is tagged as having been fulfilled.

The approach for monitoring and tagging EFRs is also similar, but with some differences. Each task could have one or more EFRs associated with it, as per the business needs, as depicted in Figure 3. When a task executes, the reconciliation operation updates the I-context details to reflect successful compliance with the EFRs for the task. For example, in our running scenario, the EFR for the "Arrange for Shipping" task is that it should only contact those shippers with proven track records as per certain policies specified by the online merchant. When the task executes, the I-context is updated with the details of the shippers who are being shortlisted for shipping the books. At this stage, the composite service can check whether the EFR is being met.

Adaptation in Web service executions is needed when there either the user's requirement changes, or to deal with an exception. Two adaptation types are possible: forward [1,2] and backward [15] adaptation. Backward adaptation involves rolling back workflow tasks until the system reaches a state before the occurrence of the exception. Forward adaptation on the other hand, treats an exception as an alternate behavior, starting from which the workflow execution is corrected and then resumed until successful conclusion. In this paper, due to lack of space, we highlight our forward adaptation approach via Figure 4.

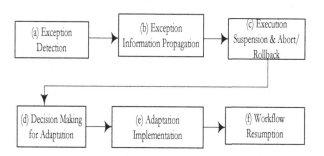

Fig. 4. Adaptation Steps

Our strategy consists of the following steps. First, the composite service designer announces the failure of a Web service instance. The FRs and EFRs violated by this exception are also identified. Second, the exception information is propagated to the other instances (concurrently executing and yet to execute). In Figure 1, these are colored in yellow, and represent those instances affected by the failure of the Arrange for Shipping task. Third, these affected instances are suspended, and their execution is rolled back, pending adaptation; as per Figure 3, the appropriate FRs and EFRs are tagged as not having been met, due to this rollback. Fourth, the composite service designer then redesigns the part of the workflow, so that it meets the FRs and EFRs that are yet to be fulfilled.

6 Related Work

The work reported in [8] proposes extensions to BPEL for accommodating adaptation in Web services execution, and for run-time modifications. However, their approach does not take into account the heterogeneity of Web service instances and assumes a more monolithic structure similar to that of traditional workflows. More generally, exception handling in workflow systems is an actively pursued area of research [2, 4, 5]. Techniques for exception handling range from providing specific exception handlers and policies/rules for different types of exceptions [4, 5, 9], to user-driven interventions during exception handling [4]. However, to the best of our knowledge, none of these techniques provide a context-based framework for automating workflow adaptation.

Rule-based web service modeling has steadily been receiving increasing attention from both industry and academia. From the field of web services relevant work includes for example WS-Policy (http://www-106.ibm.com/developerworks/library/specification/ws-polfram/) from industry, and [6] from the scientific community. Coming more from the area of rule based development proposals such as RuleML (http://www.ruleml.org/), SWSL (http:// www.daml.org/services/swsf/1.0/swsl/), SWRL (http://www.daml.org/2003/11/swrl/), WSPL [5], APPEL (http://www.w3.org/TR/P3P-preferences/) and others have been made for rule and policy specification languages to capture FRs and EFRs. However, as far as we are able to assess these different works focus by and large on design of requirements; leaving it unclear how execution and in particular automated adaptation can be facilitated, especially in light of requirements traceability during adaptation.

7 Conclusions

In this paper, we have considered the important, but still unsolved, problem of modeling Web service executions, especially in the face of adaptation. By leveraging from our earlier work, we first gave a definition of the Web service execution lifecycle. We later described our requirements-driven modeling approach for the lifecycle, by classifying requirements into *functional* (those that are needed for meeting core functionality requirements) and *extra-functional* (those that are needed for meeting regulatory and other business-related requirements in addition to core requirements) requirements. We also showed how our approach can help in maintaining traceability between the requirements and Web service executions, especially during adaptation. We believe that ours is the first overall & holistic approach towards modeling Web service executions.

Future work will involve enhancing our ConWeSc prototype in order to implement our approach. We are also investigating formalizing our model via the commitment-based approach introduced in [12, 16].

Acknowledgement. The authors wish to thank Marlon Dumas for feedback on earlier versions of this paper. The first author also wishes to thank his manager, Guruduth Banavar, for supporting his work.

References

[1] Reichert, M., and Dadam, P.: ADEPT$_{flex}$ – Supporting Dynamic Changes of Workflows without Losing Control. *Journal of Intelligent Information Systems 10 (2): 93-129*, 1998.

[2] Narendra, N.C., and Gundugola S.: Automated Context-Aware Adaptation of Web Service Executions. In *Proceedings of 4th ACS/IEEE Conference on Computer Systems and Applications (AICCSA-06)*, IEEE Computer Society Press, to appear, 2006

[3] Berardi, D., Calvanese, D., De Giacomo, G., Lenzerini M., and Mecella M.: A Foundational Vision for E-Services. In *Proceedings of the Workshop on Web Service, E-Business, and the Semantic Web (WES'2003) held in conjunction with the 15th Conference on Advanced Information Systems Engineering (CaiSE'2003)*, Klagenfurt/Velden, Austria, 2003.

[4] Li, J., Mai, W., Butler, G.: Implementing Exception Handling Policies for Workflow Management System. In *Proceedings of Tenth Asia-Pacific Software Engineering Conference, 2003*; also available from http://csdl.computer.org/comp/proceedings/apsec/2003/2011/00/20110564abs.htm

[5] Casati, F., Ceri, S., Paraboschi, S., Pozzi, G. : Specification and implementation of Exceptions in Workflow Management Systems. *ACM Transactions on Database Systems*, Vol. 24, No. 3, pp. 405-451, September 1999.

[6] Casati, F., Shan, E,, Dayal, U., Shan, M.: Business-Oriented Management of Web Services. *Communications of the ACM, Vol. 46, No. 10, pp. 55-60, 2003*

[7] Dey, A.K., Abowd, G.D., and Salber, D.: A Conceptual Framework and a Toolkit for Supporting the Rapid Prototyping of Context-Aware Applications. *Human-Computer Interaction Journal, Special Issue on Context-Aware Computing*, 16, 1, 2001.

[8] Karastoyanova, D., and Buchmann, A.: Extending Web Service Flow Models to Provide for Adaptability. In *Proceedings of OOPSLA '04 Workshop on "Best Practices and Methodologies in Service-oriented Architectures: Paving the Way to Web-services Success"*, Vancouver, Canada, 24 October 2004; also available from http://www.informatik.tu-darmstadt.de/GK/participants/dimka/Publications/WS-flow-Adaptability-OOPSLA04.pdf

[9] Hamadi, R., and Benatallah, B.: Policy-based Exception Handling in Business Processes. *Technical Report UNSW-CSE-TR0428, University of New South Wales, Sydney, Australia, August 2004*

[10] Kuo, D., Fekete, A., and Greenfield, P.: Towards a Framework for Capturing Transactional Requirements of Real Workflows. In *Proceedings of the Second International Workshop on Cooperative Internet Computing (CIC'02)*, August 2002, HongKong; also available from http://www3.ict.csiro.au/vgn/images/portal/cit_16537/28/46/89618ICT_pdf_1080615392283.pdf

[11] Maamar, Z., Narendra, N.C., and Sattanathan, S.: Towards an Ontology-based Approach for Specifying and Securing Web Services. *Information and Software Technology Journal, 2006*, forthcoming.

[12] Jain, A.K., Aparacio IV, M., and Singh, M.P.: Agents for Process Coherence in Virtual Enterprises. Communications of the ACM, volume 42, number 3, March 1999, pages 62-69; also available from http://www.csc.ncsu.edu/faculty/mpsingh/papers/mas/cacm-99-virtual-enterprises.pdf

[13] Narendra, N.C.: Design Considerations for Incorporating Flexible Workflow and Multi-Agent Interactions in Agent Societies. *Journal for Association of Information Systems*, 1, 2003

[14] Orriens, B., Yang, J., and Papazoglou, M.: A Rule-driven Approach for Developing Adaptive Service Oriented Business Collaboration. In *Proceedings of 3ʳᵈ International Conference on Service Oriented Computing (ICSOC 2005), Amsterdam, The Netherlands,* December 2005

[15] Rinderle, S., Bassil, S., and Reichert, M.: A Framework for Semantic Recovery Strategies in Case of Process Activity Failures. In *Proceedings of International Conference on Enterprise Information Systems (ICEIS) 2006,* May 2006

[16] Wan, F., and Singh, M.P.: Formalizing Multi-party Agreements via Commitments. In *Proceedings of the 4th International Joint Conference on Autonomous Agents and Multiagent Systems (AAMAS), Utrecht, July 2005*; also available from http://www.csc.ncsu.edu/faculty/mpsingh/papers/mas/aamas-05-wan-singh.pdf

Modified Raymond's Algorithm for Priority (MRA-P) Based Mutual Exclusion in Distributed Systems

S. Kanrar[1] and N. Chaki[2]

[1] Department of Computer Science, Narasingha Dutta College, Howrah, India
`sukhen2003@yahoo.co.in`
[2] Department of Computer Science, University of Calcutta, Calcutta, India
`nabendu@ieee.org`

Abstract. The traditional approaches towards implementing mutual exclusion can not be applied for distributed systems where nodes are loosely coupled. The existing algorithms typically follow either a symmetric or a token based approach. While the symmetric algorithms tend to increase the network traffic, token based approach offers solutions at a lower communication cost. Raymond has designed an efficient token based mutual exclusion algorithm. However, one major limitation of Raymond's algorithm is the lack of fairness in the sense that a token request that is generated later may be granted ahead of another request that was made earlier. In this work, we have proposed a modification of Raymond's algorithm. The new token based algorithm not only overcomes the fairness problem, but also handles the priority of the requesting processes.

Keywords: Distributed mutual exclusion, Fairness, Token based algorithm, Critical Section, Priority.

1 Introduction

This paper is an extension of the Modified Raymond's Algorithm (MRA) that we have proposed earlier. The problem of mutual exclusion in distributed systems has drawn considerable attention over the years and several algorithms have been proposed. There has been two broad approaches of designing the algorithms, namely token based algorithms and symmetric algorithms. Section 2 of the paper presents a brief review of contemporary works on mutual exclusion in the distributed system.

As we study the existing token based approaches, it has been observed that the fairness aspect in terms of responding to the token request in a FIFO order, is often not ensured. This has been discussed with appropriate example in section 3. MRA solves the fairness problem of Raymond's algorithm. Another important aspect of mutual exclusion algorithms is to handle the priorities of the processes [2, 8, 12, 13, 14]. In this paper, we have proposed a new token based algorithm named Modified Raymond's Algorithm for Priority (MRA-P) that ensures fairness besides allowing higher priority jobs ahead of others. Before that, however, we have also included the MRA algorithm in section 4 for the sake of completeness.

S. Madria et al. (Eds.): ICDCIT 2006, LNCS 4317, pp. 325–332, 2006.
© Springer-Verlag Berlin Heidelberg 2006

2 Review Work

A good number of algorithms have been proposed to address the issue of mutual exclusion [1, 2, 3, 4, 5, 6, 7, 8, 9, 10, 11, 12, 13, 14] for distributed systems. These algorithms may be broadly classified into two groups. The algorithms in the first group are symmetric [1, 6, 7, 8, 11] while the rest are token based [2, 3, 4, 5, 9, 10] algorithms. The possession of a system-wide unique token gives a node the right to enter the critical section. Lamport proposed one of the first distributed mutual exclusion algorithms [6]. The algorithm is symmetric and requires 3*(N-I) messages. Other symmetric algorithms [1, 8] reduced the number of required massages to 2*(N-l) messages per critical section entry. Suzuki and Kasami proposed a broadcast Algorithm [5], based on which, Singhal proposed a heuristically aided algorithm [9]. The maximum number of messages for these algorithms is of the order of N.

In token-based approach, a tree-based logical topology has been assumed by many researchers [10, 11, 12]. The basic notion underlying these algorithms is path reversal. Token based mutual exclusion algorithms provide access to the CS using a single token foe each CS. Requests for CS entries are typically directed to whichever node is the current token holder. Housn and Trehel proposed a Distributed mutual exclusion token based algorithm by prioritized groups [4]. The tree's root is the site that last held the token. Priority between routers is carried out by a comparison mechanism.

Some of the mutual exclusion algorithms [3] have been proposed for a prioritized environment suitable for real-time applications but impose a higher message passing overhead than our approach. Goscinski [14] proposed a priority-based algorithm based on broadcast requests using a token-passing approach. Chang [13] and others developed extensions to various algorithms for priority handling that use broadcast messages [9, 15]. In Raymond's [2] token based mutual exclusion algorithm, requests are sent over a static spanning tree of the network, toward the token holder. This algorithm is resilient to non-adjacent node crashes and recoveries.

3 The Fairness Issue

One of the concerns with many of the mutual exclusion algorithms is fairness. The commonly accepted definition of fairness in the context of mutual exclusion is that requests for access to the CS are satisfied in the order of their timestamps. However, for a large number of algorithms, a process Pi may be allowed to enter its CS over the demand of process Pj even if process Pj's request for CS is raised earlier. The situation has been illustrated with an example in figure 1 for Raymond's algorithm.

Initially, P_5 is the root node and holder of the token. The processes P_4, P_1 and P_2 respectively place the 1st, 2nd and the 3rd requests to enter the respective critical sections. Figure 1 illustrates contents of the local queues after the requests by P_4, P_1 and P_2 are placed. Let's assume that P_5 exits from the CS now. According to Raymond's algorithm, the token is transferred to P_3 that is now the root of the tree. P_5, further, sends a request to P_3 since its local queue is not empty. The local queue at P_3 will add the process id of P_5. P_3 passes the token to P_4 and also sends a request to P_4. P_4 removes 4 from its local queue and enters the CS leaving only 3 in the queue.

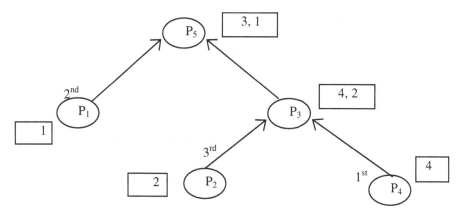

Fig. 1. Fairness in a Tree based Topology

After P_4 completes its CS, it removes 3 from its local queue, passes the token back to P_3 and reverses the edge (P_4, P_3). Once again, P_3 becomes the root. Now, P_3 removes 2 from its local queue and passes the token to P_2 along with a request to return the control. Thus, P_2 enters the CS ahead of P_1 even though P_1's requests for the token earlier then P_2. If we continue with the example, we will find that P_1 too will be allowed to enter it CS, but not before the fairness condition is violated as explained above. The Modified Raymond's Algorithm (MRA) that ensures fairness in allocation has been discussed briefly in section 4 of this paper for the sake of completeness.

4 The MRA Algorithm

The modified Raymond's algorithm (MRA) assumes an inverted tree structure as the logical topology. The edges in an inverted tree are directed from child to parent node. and each node Pi, other than the root node, has exactly one out-edge (Pi. Pj).

A process is allowed to enter into critical section only after it gets the token. The process P_{hold} that holds the token is also the root of the tree. The root changes each time the token is transferred to some other process. Double ended queues are maintained locally for each process. We further propose to maintain a request queue with P_{hold} that would store the ids of processes that have so far requested for the token.

Local double queue (LDQ): Every process Pi maintains a local double ended queue (LDQi). A process Pj wishing to enter the CS, enter its own id, j, in the LDQj. It further sends a request for the token along with LDQj on its outgoing edge.

When a process Pm receives a token request from another process Pn, it adds the ids from LDQ, into LDQm followed by its own id, i.e. m in this case. The revised local queue LDQ_m thus formed, is sent along with the token request to parent node, if no such request is pending.

Request queue (RQ): Process P_{hold} maintains a request queue that stores the process ids for the token requesting processes in an FIFO order. The RQ is transferred to the new root of the tree along with the token.

Algorithm to Enter CS

Step 1: A Process P_i wishing to enter CS,
1.1 P_i enters its id i in the LDQ_i;
1.2 P_i sends a request for the token {i} on its out-edge along with LDQ_j;

Step 2: When a process $P_j \neq P_{hold}$ receives a token request from another process P_k
2.1 P_j adds the ids from LDQ_k into LDQ_j followed by its own id.j;
2.2 LDQ_j, is sent out with {i}, where the request is originally from P_i;
2.3   If a request from P_j is pending, then only token request {i} is sent out;

Step 3: When a process $P_j = P_{hold}$ receives a token request {i} from process P_k,
3.1 P_j adds the ids from LDQ_k into LDQ_j followed by its own id, i.e., j;
3.2   The processor id i is added to the RQ;

Step 4: On completing the execution of a CS, $P_j = P_{hold}$, performs the following:
4.1 P_j scans the first id k from RQ;
4.2   It extracts entries starting from k to the first occurrence of j from LDQ_j;
4.3   The extracted sequence of ids is reversed from j to k;
4.4   Edge P_m to P_j is reversed, where m is the id that follows j in the sequence;
4.5 P_m is the new P_{hold} and root - the token and RQ is passed to P_m from P_j;
4.6   If LDQ_j is not empty and the last id left in it is j, then
      4.6.1 P_j places a token request to P_m along with the reduced LDQ_j;
      4.6.2   The ids from LDQ_j are added to LDQ_m followed by m;
    else
      4.6.3   LDQj is emptied;
    Endif.

Step 5: The newly designated process $P_m = P_{hold}$ performs the following
5.1   If the first id of RQ is m, then
      5.1.1   The first id of RQ i.e., m, in this case, is removed from the RQ;
      5.1.2   The entry m is removed from the top of LPQm;
      5.1.3 P_m enters its CS;
    else
      5.1.4 Repeat through the step 4;
    Endif.

5   Handling the Priority

In this section, we are going to alter the algorithm proposed in section 4 so that priorities in the processes may be handled. We need to maintain an additional data structure in all the nodes as introduced below.

Priority queue (PQ): Every process Pi maintains a priority queue PQi. A process Pi wishing to enter the critical section, sends a request for the token along with LDQj and its priority status on its outgoing edge. When a process Pm receives a token request from another process P_n, there are three possibilities.

1. The priority queue of P_m is empty: Pm enters the priority of P_n in PQ_m.
2. The priority queue of P_m is not empty and priorities of two processes are not the same: Pm enters both the priorities in PQ_m with the higher priority entered first.
3. The priority queue of P_m is not empty and priorities of the two processes are same: Pm adds the priority of P_n in its PQ_m.

The MRA algorithm as presented in section 4, is modified to utilize the priority queues such that a higher priority process gets the token first even if a lower priority process has placed its request earlier. However, the fairness property shall be maintained when two equal priority processes want to get the token.

Algorithm to Enter CS Following Priority of Processes

Step 1: A Process Pi wishing to enter the CS,
    1.1 Pi enters its id i in the LDQi and priority in PQi;
    1.2 Pi sends a token request {i} with LDQ_j and the priority of Pi;
Step 2: When a process Pj ≠ Phold receives a token request from process Pk,
    2.1 Pj it adds priority in PQj in ascending order;
    2.2 According to priority, Pj adds the ids into LDQj followed by its own id j;
    2.3 The revised LDQj and PQj, is sent out with token request {i};
    2.4 If a request from Pj is pending, then only token request {i} is sent out;
Step 3: When a process Pj = Phold receives a token request {i} from process Pk,
    3.1 Pj adds priority in PQj in ascending order;
    3.2 According to priority, Pj adds the ids into LDQj followed by its own id j;
    3.3 The token requesting process id i is added to the RQ;
Step 4: On completing the execution of CS, $Pj=P_{hold}$ performs the following
    4.1 Pj scans the first id k from RQ;
    4.2 Pj extracts from k to the first j in LDQj and removes first element of PQj;
    4.3 The extracted sequence of ids are reversed from j to k;
    4.4 Directed edge from Pm to Pj is reversed, where m is the id that follows j;
    4.5 Phold = Pm;
    4.6 Pass RQ to Pm from Pj along with the token;
    4.7 If LDQj is not empty then
        4.7.1 Pj places a token request to Pm along with the reduced LDQj;
        4.7.2 The id of LDQj is added to the head of LDQm followed by m;
    Endif.
Step 5: The newly designated root Pm = Phold performs the following
    5.1 If the first id of RQ is m, then
        5.1.1 Remove the first id of RQ i.e. m, in this case, from the RQ;
        5.1.2 Remove first element of PQ;
        5.1.2 The entry m is removed from the top of LDQm;
        5.1.3 Pm enters its CS.;
    elseif the first id of RQ is not m, then
        5.2.1 Scan and extract the first k from LDQm;
        5.2.2 Extract entries of LDQm starting from k to m;
        5.2.3 Reverse edge Pm to Pk, if extracted sequence is of length 2;
        5.2.4 Hand over the token and RQ to this new root Pj;
    Endif.

6 Illustrating the MRA-P Algorithm

In figure 2, four of the processes have requested for the token that is currently held by $P_{hold} = P_5$. The processes have different priorities. Lesser the priority of a process, higher is the integer value representing its priority level. A process with highest priority is of priority value 1. In figure 2, we have shown the priority values only for the four processes P_1, P_2, P_4 and P_6 and these are 1, 3, 3 and 2 respectively. Processes P_4, P_1, P_2 and P_6 have placed requests to enter the respective critical sections, in that order. However, according to their priorities, the order in which the processes are to be allowed to enter the respective critical sections is P_1, P_6, P_4 and P_2. We further assume that process P_5 remains in its CS until all four requests are made and the local queues at the nodes are updated.

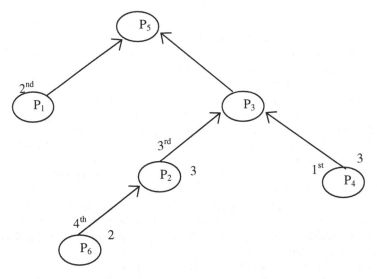

Fig. 2. Process Priority in Inverted Tree Topology

Figure 3 is a tabular representation that illustrates how the content of the LDQs and PQs maintained at different nodes and that of RQ with P_{hold} change in successive iterations as explained above. The token requests from P_4, P_1, P_2 and P_6 have been placed in step 1, step 2, step 3 and step 4 respectively. The RQ in step 4 is {1, 6, 4, 2} and is maintained at $P_5=P_{hold}$. In step 5, process P_5 has come out of its CS and the RQ is transferred to P_1 before it enters its CS. Similarly, P_6 enters the CS in step 9.

The token comes back to P_5 in step 10 (not shown in Table 1). Process P_4 enters its critical section next in step 11 and P_2 does so in step 13 after the token comes back to P_5 once again in step 12 (not shown in Table 1). The steps in which the processes enters its CS are marked by placing a * in the RQ entries in the appropriate cell. The token is finally left with P_2 and all the data structures are left empty [step 13]. In an identical situation, when the same four processes P_4, P_1, P_2 and P_6 requested for token in the same order, the Raymond's algorithm fails to ensure the fairness. The MRA algorithm, although handles the fairness issue successfully, does not consider priorities of requesting processes. The MRA-P algorithm proposed in this paper, however, solves both the issues effectively.

Table 1. A tabular illustration of the MRA-P

Pi	Queue	Step 1	Step 2	Step 3	Step 4	Step 5	Step 6	Step 9	Step 11	Step 13
P_6	RQ	-	-	-	-	-	-	*4,2	-	-
	PQ_6	-	-	-	2	2	2	-	-	-
	LDQ_6	-	-	-	6	6	6	2,6	-	-
P_5	RQ	4	1,4	1,4,2	1,6,4,2		6,4,2		-	-
	PQ_5	3	1,3	1,3,3	1,2,3,3	2,3,3	2,3,3	3,3	3	-
	LDQ_5	4,3,5	1,5,4,3,5	1,5,4,3,5,2,3,5,	1,5,6,2,3,5,4,3,5,2,3,5	6,2,3,5,4,3,5,2,3,5	6,2,3,5,4,3,5,2,3,5	4,3,5,2,3,5	2,3,5	-
P_4	RQ	-	-	-	-	-	-	-	*2	-
	PQ_4	3	3	3	3	3	3	3	-	-
	LDQ_4	4	4	4	4	4	4	4	3,4	-
P_3	RQ	-	-	-	-	-	-	-	-	-
	PQ_3	3	3	3,3	2,3,3	2,3,3	2,3,3	-	3	-
	LDQ_3	4,3	4,3	4,3,2,3	6,2,3,4,3,2,3	6,2,3,4,3,2,3	6,2,3,4,3,2,3	5,3,4,3,2,3	5,3,2,3	-
P_2	RQ	-		-	-	-	-	-	-	*
	PQ_2	-		3	2,3	2,3	2,3	3	3	-
	LDQ_2	-		2	6,2,2	6,2,2	6,2,2	3,2,2	2	-
P_1	RQ	-	-	-	-	*6,4,2	-	-	-	-
	PQ_1	-	1	1	1	-	-	-	-	-
	LDQ_1	-	1	1	1	2,6	-	-	-	-

7 Conclusion

The proposed algorithm maintains safety, i.e., no two processes enter their critical sections at the same instance as because there is only one token in the system and a process must hold the token before it is allowed to enter the critical sections. The algorithm also maintain liveness, in the sense that once a process comes out of the critical section, it look at the request queue maintained in the same node to check if some other process has requested for the token. The token is passed on accordingly. The proposed algorithm exchanges minimal information to select the next process that would enter the critical section and it maintains simple data structure in the nodes. However, the most significant improvement that has been achieved in this paper, is that the competing processes are given token first considering their priorities and then following the order in which the requests have been entered.

We present a new fair and prioritized algorithm for mutual exclusion in a distributed environment. Our approach uses a token-based model working on a logical tree structure, which is self-modified as tokens are passed along the edges. We have used a set of local queues whose union would resemble a single global queue. The MRA-P algorithm has a message complexity O(n). Comparing MRA-P and other non-prioritized algorithms, however, the proposed algorithm uses greater number of message exchanges and would therefore result in longer response times. This suggests that MRA-P should be used only when strict priority ordering is required.

References

1. Ricart, G., and A. K. Agrawala, "An optimal algorithm for mutual exclusion in computer networks", Communications of the   ACM, Vol.24(1), pp.9-17, 1981.
2. Raymond, K., "A tree-based algorithm for distributed mutual exclusion", ACM Transaction on Computer System, Vol.7, pp. 61-77, 1989.
3. Mueller, F., "Prioritized Token-Based Mutual Exclusion for Distributed Systems", Proceeding of 12th Intern. Parallel Proc. Symposium and 9th Symp. on Parallel and Distributed Processing, March 30 – April 3,Orlando, Florida, pp.791—795, 1998
4. Housni, A., Trehel, M., "Distributed mutual exclusion token-permission based by prioritized groups", Proc. of ACS/IEEE International Conference, pp. 253 – 259, 2001.
5. Suzuki and T. Kasami, "An optimality theory for mutual exclusion algorithms in computer science", Proc. of IEEE Int Conf erence on Dist. Comp. Syst., pp.365-370, Oct. 1982.
6. Lamport. L, "Time, Clocks, and the ordering of events in a distributed system", Communications of the ACM, 21(7), pp.558-565, 1978
7. Neilsen. M, Mizuno. M, "A Dag–Based Algorithm for distributed mutual exclusion", Proc. of the 11th IEEE International Conference on Distributed Computing System, May 1991.
8. O. S. F. Carvalho and G. Roucairol, "On mutual exclusion in computer network", Communications of the ACM, 26(2), pp.146-147, 1983.
9. M. Singhal, "A heuristically-aided algorithm for mutual exclusion for distributed systems", IEEE Transactions on Computers, 38(5), pp:70-78, 1989.
10. M. Trehel, M. Naimi, "A distributed algorithm for mutual exclusion based on data structures and fault tolerance", Proc. of 6th Intl. conf. on Computers & Communication, pp. 35-39, 1987.
11. J. M. Bernabeu-Auban and M. Ahamad., "Applying a path-compression technique to obtain an efficient distributed mutual exclusion algorithm", LNCS, vol. 392, pp.33-44, 1989.
12. M. Naimi, M. Trehel, A. Arnold, "A log(N) distributed mutual exclusion algorithm based on path reversal", Journal of Parallel and Distributed Computing, Vol. 34(1), pp 1-13, 1996.
13. Y.Chang; "Design of mutual exclusion algorithms for real-time distributed systems"; Journal of Information Science and Engeneering; Vol.10, pp. 527–548, 1994.
14. A. Goscinski; "Two algorithms for mutual exclusion in real-time distributed computer systems"; Journal of Parallel and Distributed Computing, Vol. 1, pp. 77–82, 1990.
15. I. Suzuki, T. Kasami; "A distributed mutual exclusion algorithm"; ACM Transactions of Computer Systems, Vol. 18(12), pp. 94–101, Dec. 1993.

Efficient Remote User Authentication and Key Establishment for Multi-server Environment

Somanath Tripathy and Sukumar Nandi

Indian Institute of Technology Guwahati, India
{som, sukumar}@iitg.ernet.in

Abstract. With the rapid development of communication technologies, resources are distributed over multiple servers in the network. These resources are usually restricted to authorized users. To provide access control and secure communication in the network, remote user authentication and key establishment is found to be most important. A Reversible Cellular Automata based remote user authentication and key establishment scheme using smart card is proposed in this paper. The scheme is simple, less computational and robust against various known attacks.

1 Introduction

The present distributed computing environment allows service providers to share their services through networks. As the resources are not free for all, access control is necessary. Remote user authentication and key agreement are two important parameters for access control in these scenarios. Remote user authentication scheme is introduced by Lamport [11]. A potential user must supply his identity ID_i and password pw_i to the server. The server uses a password list as an access control mechanism to authenticate legitimate users. However, cost of maintaining and protecting a password table leads to a tremendous problem for larger networks. Hwang and Li in [6] proposed a password based remote user authentication scheme using smart cards to eliminate the usage of password list. The scheme is robust against replay attacks as well. However, Chan and Cheng [2] pointed out impersonation attack against Hwang and Li scheme [6]. Many smart card based remote user authentication protocols have been proposed and analyzed [4, 8, 9, 14, 17]. Most of these schemes have used multiple instance of computational intensive (encryption/ hash based) operations. Recently, Cellular Automata based remote user authentication scheme [16] reduces the overloaded intensive computations. All these schemes proposed for client server model are not applicable to multi-server environments. Neural network based password authentication scheme for multiple-server networks [10], consumes more time for training the neural networks. Besides this, constructing and maintaining neural networks at each servers is not cost effective. Public-key crypto system based remote user authentication protocols [12, 20, 21] involve exponential modulo operations. These need high computation and communication bandwidth. To avoid those expensive operations Juang et.al [7] proposed

S. Madria et al. (Eds.): ICDCIT 2006, LNCS 4317, pp. 333–346, 2006.

a scheme using symmetric encryption/ decryptions and hash operations. Each server needs to maintain a common secret between each individual user, which is given by registration center (RC). Computing this common secret for a user and a server requires extra time for RC. Also, storing of secret tokens at each servers do not scale well for larger networks. Chang and Lee in [3] proposed an efficient scheme to avoid such difficulties. This scheme allows user to change its password freely. Unfortunately, an attacker can be able to change the password of a legitimate user without knowing the corresponding password. Apart from that, if secret parameter of registration center is revealed accidentally in any of the above schemes, whole system would be broken. Usage of multiple instances of computational intensive operations (encryption/ decryption, hash operation) degrades performance of the system as well.

This paper proposes an efficient remote user authentication and key exchange mechanism suitable for multiple server environments avoiding above limitations. One of the major contribution of our work is to introduce a simple computational model called one-dimensional second order Reversible Cellular Automata (RCA), for designing remote user authentication and key establishment. This protocol employs minimum instances of hash operation based on their suitability in terms of performance and security levels [5]. Another contribution of this paper is the concept of a cache based nonce to avoid synchronization issues of time stamping. The cache is a good random number generator because it is the fastest changing memory location, within the computer. This makes the correlation between successive nonce unpredictable for an adversary.

The paper is organized as follows. We discuss briefly about CA and second order RCA in next section. Detail explanation of our proposal is given in section 3. Section 4 verifies our protocol and analyze the security features of proposed scheme. Section 5 shows the effectiveness of our proposed approach by comparing its security features and implementation requirements with some existing schemes and we conclude our paper in section 6.

2   Cellular Automata (CA) Preliminaries

Cellular automaton (CA) is a dynamical system, consisting of a large number of cells in which each cells are updated synchronously at discrete time steps according to a local update rule. This local rule is a function of the present configurations of itself and its neighbors. For instance, in a 2-state 3-neighborhood CA, the evolution of ith cell (x_i) can be formulated as a function of the present state of $(i-1)^{th}, i^{th}$, and $(i+1)^{th}$ cells; $x_i^{(t+1)} = f(x_{i-1}^{(t)}, x_i^{(t)}, x_{i+1}^{(t)})$, where f denotes the next state function. Therefore, there are $2^{2^3} = 256$ possible different next state functions, and each of them can be specified by a decimal number called the rule number(RN). Table 1 shows the next states computed according to rule 30 and rule 45. The topmost row shows all the possible (8) configurations at instant t. The states at the instant of time $(t+1)$ are computed according to the rules as given in subsequent rows of that table. The vector

Table 1. Next state configuration for CA rules 30 and 45

Neighborhood State:	111	110	101	100	011	010	001	000	RN
Next State:	0	0	0	1	1	1	1	0	30
Next State:	0	0	1	0	1	1	0	1	45

$X^{(t)} = (x_1^{(t)}, x_2^{(t)}, \ldots, x_n^{(t)})$ is called the configuration at time t of the n-cell CA. $X^{(0)}$ is called initial configuration of that CA. In practice, we consider the finite cell CA, so the boundary conditions need to be considered. We consider periodic boundary conditions where, if $i \equiv j \bmod n$, then $x_i^{(t)} = x_j^{(t)}$ (more details about CA please refer [13] and [18]).

2.1 Reversible Cellular Automata (RCA)

Reversible Cellular Automata (RCA) is a CA in which the previous configurations can be deduced from the current configuration. Here, we discuss a class of RCA in which the configuration at time $t + 1$ depends on the configuration of two consecutive time steps $(t - 1$ and $t)$. Such an RCA is called second order RCA [18]. The configuration of the ith cell on clock cycle $t + 1$ is determined by the states of the ν-neighborhood configuration at clock cycle t and the self configuration at $t - 1$ clock cycle. For example a 3-neighborhood RCA configuration can be expressed as

$$x_i^{(t+1)} = f(x_{i-1}^{(t)}, x_i^{(t)}, x_{i+1}^{(t)}) \oplus x_i^{(t-1)} \tag{1}$$
$$x_i^{(t-1)} = f(x_{i-1}^{(t)}, x_i^{(t)}, x_{i+1}^{(t)}) \oplus x_i^{(t+1)} \tag{2}$$

Logic diagram of such an RCA using elementary CA rule 30 is depicted in Figure 1. ξ_i and y_i respectively denote for $x_i^{(t+1)}$ and $x_i^{(t-1)}$. Depending on two initial configurations (Y, X) at time steps *t-1* and *t*, the next configuration (ξ) is evolved. Again, using two consecutive configurations (ξ, X) the initial configuration Y can be deduced. We denote this operation as follows.

$$\xi = RCA(Y, X) \tag{3}$$
$$Y = RCA(\xi, X) \tag{4}$$

In general, the application of one-dimensional Cellular Automata (CA) to design cryptographic primitives [19] have been confined to design pseudo random generator, hash digest, stream ciphers and block ciphers. Recently, we exploit the feature of rule-30 based second order RCA for designing remote-user authentication [16]. This protocol is suitable for client-server model, where server needs to authenticate user before providing the services. The same kind of RCA is used in this paper, towards designing mutual authentication and key establishment for multiple-server environments.

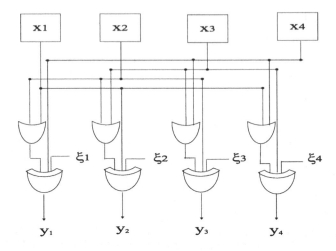

Fig. 1. Logic structure of 4-cell periodic boundary RCA

3   The Proposed Scheme

The proposed authentication and key exchange protocol for multiple server environment does not maintain any password lists. It minimizes the usage of computational intensive operations (encryption/ decryption and hash operations) and communication overheads considering the limited computational capability of smart-card devices. Security of this scheme has driven from the properties of one way hash functions and the RCA based operation. As discussed earlier, the next (previous) configuration of an RCA depends on both its previous (next) and its current configurations, and is difficult to predict if two consecutive configurations are unknown. We choose rule 30 based periodic boundary second order RCA as one of the basic component in our scheme, as rule 30 based CA is non-linear and can be used as pseudo random pattern generator [18]. This makes an attacker difficult for predicting the two subsequent configurations used, from a given output.

The proposed scheme uses the concept of nonce to thwart replay attacks without needing synchronization. Exploiting the randomness of cache contents in a processor, cache based nonce are used in this work . The following notations are used through out the paper.

UID_i: Identity of user U_i
pw_i: Password of user U_i.
PID_j: Identity of service provider P_j
RC: Registration Center.
Sx: Common secret among RC and all service providers.
TS_{Sx}: Time stamp on secret Sx
$E_k(.)$: The encryption function with key k
$D_k(.)$: The decryption function with key k

$\oplus$:   EXOR operation

$H(.)$:   Strong one-way Hash function.

KS: The session key

N_i, N_j: Nonce

$LH(Z)$:   Left half bits of Z

$RH(Z)$:   Right half bits of Z

3.1   Operational Details of the Proposed Scheme

All servers and the registration center (RC) are assumed to be trust worthy. At first, RC obtains a time stamp(TS_{Sx}) from a trusted time stamp authority and chooses a secret (Sx). Then, it sends its own secret (Sx and time stamp (TS_{Sx}) to all the servers under its control via secure channels. The complete operation of our proposed scheme comprises of three basic operational phases viz. the registration phase, the login and authentication phase, and the password change phase are discussed subsequently.

The Registration Phase: Each user should register with the RC in order to access services from the servers (under the control of this RC) in future. During registration time, user U_i provides its identity UID_i and the password pw_i along with a registration request to the RC through a secure channel. The RC computes T_i using its secret Sx and time stamp TS_{Sx} in equation (5)

$$T_i = H(UID_i \oplus Sx \oplus TS_{Sx}) \oplus pw_i. \tag{5}$$

RC returns a smart card encoded with $< UID_i, T_i, H(.) >$. Hereafter, U_i can access services from any server in the corresponding system at any time, performing the login and authentication phase using its smart card.

The Login and Authentication Phase: U_i enters the corresponding password pw_i and requests to access the server P_j. Then the login and authentication phase executes at both the ends as depicted in Figure 2, is explained hereafter.

Step 1. U_i computes $S_i = T_i \oplus pw_i$; generates a random nonce N_j, and calculates the followings.

$$\alpha_i = RCA(N_j, S_i) \tag{6}$$
$$\beta_j = N_j \oplus UID_i \oplus PID_j \tag{7}$$
$$\beta_i = LH(H(\beta_j)) \tag{8}$$

Next, U_i sends $< \alpha_i, \beta_i, UID_i >$ to P_j. Holds the β_j value associated with P_j in its buffer for a valid period.

Step 2. P_j computes S_i of the corresponding UID_i using equation (9), and determines N_j from α_i using the computed S_i value in equation (10).

$$S_i = H(UID_i \oplus Sx \oplus TS_{Sx}) \tag{9}$$
$$N_j = RCA(\alpha_i, S_i) \tag{10}$$

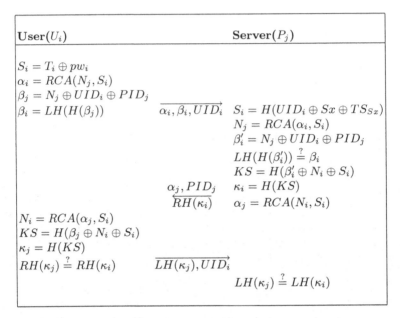

Fig. 2. Proposed Login and Authentication phase

Then, it computes $\beta_i' = N_j \oplus UID_i \oplus PID_j$, compares $LH(H(\beta_i'))$ with received β_i, and rejects the request if unmatch. Otherwise, the server generates a cache based nonce N_i, computes KS (the session key), α_j and κ_i as written below.

$$KS = H(\beta_i \oplus N_i \oplus S_i) \tag{11}$$

$$\alpha_j = RCA(N_i, S_i) \tag{12}$$

$$\kappa_i = H(KS) \tag{13}$$

P_j sends $< \alpha_j, RH(\kappa_i) >$ to U_i keeping $LH(\kappa_i)$ corresponding to UID_i in its buffer for a valid period.

Step 3. After getting response from P_j, U_i computes N_i from α_j using

$$N_i = RCA(\alpha_j, S_i). \tag{14}$$

It accesses β_j associated with the P_j from its buffer, and determines the session key KS and κ_j as follows.

$$KS = H(N_i \oplus \beta_j \oplus S_i) \tag{15}$$

$$\kappa_j = H(KS) \tag{16}$$

If $RH(\kappa_j) = RH(\kappa_i)$ (received from the server), U_i assures the legitimacy of P_j, and sends $LH(\kappa_j)$ to P_j. Otherwise it rejects the connection.

Step 4. P_j accesses the ($LH(\kappa_i)$) value associated with UID_i from its buffer, and compares it with the received $LH(\kappa_j)$. P_j assures the user U_i, if $LH(\kappa_i) = LH(\kappa_j)$.

U_i and P_j invalidate their corresponding buffer contents and use KS as session key.

The Password Change Phase: Our protocol allows a a card holder to change the corresponding password after verifying the legitimacy to avoid unauthorized changing of password. User U_i needs to perform the following steps for changing its password pw_i.

Step 1. User submits the corresponding password pw_i, and selects the password change option.

Step 2. U_i computes γ_1 and γ_2 using equation (17) and (18) after generating a random number N_i. .

$$S_i = T_i \oplus pw_i; \gamma_1 = RCA(N_i, S_i) \tag{17}$$

$$\gamma_2 = H(N_i) \tag{18}$$

Sends $< \gamma_1, \gamma_2, UID_i >$ to any server or RC for verifying the authenticity of user.

Step 3. Server computes the corresponding S_i using equation (9) and, determines N_i' from γ_1 using equation (19).

$$N_i' = RCA(\gamma_1, S_i) \tag{19}$$

User is allowed to change the current password by executing step 4, if $H(N_i') = \gamma_2$. Otherwise the request is rejected.

Step 4. User gives a new password pw_{new}. T_i is updated by $T_{i_{new}} = T_i \oplus pw_i \oplus pw_i^{new}$. Hereafter, U_i uses the new password (pw_i^{new}) to login any server or RC.

In this phase some additional computations (in step 2 and step 3) are needed to execute this phase. The computation overhead is acceptable because of rare occurrence of this phase.

4   Analysis of the Proposed Scheme

This section comprises of two parts, verification of basic security properties, and robustness against various known attacks.

4.1   Protocol Verification

Mutual authentication and key establishment are the two basic properties of an authentication protocol. To verify our scheme, we use BAN logic and the notations used in [1].

- $U \mid\equiv P$: U believes P

- $U \xleftrightarrow{KS} P$: KS the shared key between U and P

- $U \mathrel{|\!\!\sim} KS$: U said KS

- $\sharp(N)$: Freshness of N

- $U \Rightarrow KS$: U Sees KS.

Consider an instance of protocol execution: user U_i establishes a session key KS with service provider P_j. We claim the validity of our protocol by proving following four formula.

1. $U_i \models P_j \models U_i \xleftrightarrow{KS} P_j$

2. $P_j \models U_i \models U_i \xleftrightarrow{KS} P_j$

3. $P_j \models U_i \xleftrightarrow{KS} P_j$

4. $U_i \models U_i \xleftrightarrow{KS} P_j$

Before analyzing the protocol depicted in Figure 2, we first write it in the idealized form as follows.

1. M1: $U_i \to P_j$: $\{N_j\}_{S_i}$

2. M2: $P_j \to U_i$: $\{N_i\}_{S_i}, \sharp(KS)$

3. M3: $U_i \to P_j : \sharp(KS)$

As per our proposed scheme, secret token S_i is encoded on the smart card of corresponding user U_i and it can be easily computed by P_j. Also, there is no direct way to find S_i from the information over flow ($\alpha_i = RCA(N_i, S_i)$). Therefore, we denote $RCA(N_i, S_i)$ in BAN logic notation $\{N_i\}_{S_i}$. $LH(\kappa_i)$ and $RH(\kappa_i)$ used in the protocol, check integrity and confirm the existence of KS. Also these values, verify freshness of N_j, N_i and therefore, freshness of KS. The assumptions of the scheme are follows

1. $U_i \models U_i \xleftrightarrow{S_i} P_j$

2. $P_j \models U_i \xleftrightarrow{S_i} P_j$

3. $U_i \models \sharp(N_j)$

4. $P_j \models \sharp(N_i)$

5. $U_i \mathrel{|\!\!\sim} KS$

6. $P_j \mathrel{|\!\!\sim} KS$

U_i and P_j sends encrypted nonce through the message flows M1 and M2, which can be decrypted by their partner. These nonce values are used to generate the session key KS. Applying nonce verification postulates [1], we can write

$$U_i \mid\equiv P_j \mid\sim (KS) \tag{20}$$

$$\frac{U_i \mid\equiv \sharp(N_j)}{U_i \mid\equiv \sharp(KS)} \tag{21}$$

$$\frac{U_i \mid\equiv P_j \mid\sim (KS), U_i \mid\equiv \sharp(KS)}{U_i \mid\equiv P_j \mid\equiv KS}. \tag{22}$$

$Therefore, \; U_i \mid\equiv P_j \mid\equiv U_i \xleftrightarrow{KS} P_j.$ □

Similarly, from message flow M3, P_j verifies the freshness and existence of KS and proceeding the similar steps as above, it can be showed that
$P_j \mid\equiv U_i \mid\equiv U_i \xleftrightarrow{KS} P_j.$ □

As the nonce $N_j(N_i)$ under jurisdiction of $U_i(P_j)$, and both of them are used in the KS computation we can write

$$P_j \mid\Rightarrow KS \tag{23}$$

$$U_i \mid\Rightarrow KS \tag{24}$$

$$\frac{P_j \mid\equiv U_i \mid\Rightarrow KS, P_j \mid\equiv U_i \mid\equiv KS}{P_j \mid\equiv KS} \tag{25}$$

$Therefore, \; P_j \mid\equiv U_i \xleftrightarrow{KS} P_j.$ □

$$\frac{U_i \mid\equiv P_j \mid\Rightarrow KS, U_i \mid\equiv P_j \mid\equiv KS}{U_i \mid\equiv KS}. \tag{26}$$

$Therefore, \; U_i \mid\equiv U_i \xleftrightarrow{KS} P_j.$ □

4.2   Security Analysis

Security of our proposed scheme relies on the one way property of hash function (OWHF) and reversibility of second order RCA.

P1: Let H be a one-way hash function.
- It is infeasible to derive the value M from a given $H(M)$ [15].
- It is infeasible to find different values M and M' such that $H(M) = H(M')$ [15].

P2: Assume a second order n-cell RCA, $\xi = RCA(X, Y)$.
- $\forall \xi \; \forall X \in Z_{2^n} \; \exists !Y$ such that $RCA(X, Y) = \xi$; because of the reversible property. Given only ξ, each of the 2^n choices for X could be valid, and therefore the probability of a guess being correct is $< 2^{-n}$.

Security of the proposed scheme is analyzed using above properties **P1** and **P2**.

Security of the User's Secret Token S_i: It is difficult to derive S_i from the information overflow (α_i and α_j) because of the property ($P2$). If attacker obtains the information encoded in smart card (T_i) by chance. Still, he fails to compute S_i due to lack of corresponding password pw_i.

Security of the Common Secret Among RC and Servers Sx: Let the common secret (among servers and RC) Sx is revealed by chance. Still, it is hard for the intruder to compute the time-stamp information TS_{Sx} because of ($P1$). If he clones a new card with computing the secret token S_A using the revealed secret Sx. Server will not accept the legitimacy of secret S_A as attacker uses a post dated time stamp TS_{Sx}'.

Stolen Card Attack: If the smart card of a legitimate user (UID_i, pw_i) has stolen, the attacker impersonates the corresponding user (UID_i). Attacker attempts through a password ($pw_a \neq pw_i$). Card computes $S_a \neq S_i$ and logs in by sending $< \alpha_i^a, \beta_i^a, UID_i >$. But, server rejects the request as $LH(H(\beta_i')) \neq \beta_i^a$. Let attacker tries with different password and said to be succeed, if server authenticates. This attack is similar to on-line dictionary attack, and it can be avoided by restricting the number of attempts. The card self distracts after few consecutive fails. Off-line dictionary attack is not possible because no password related information flows in our proposed protocol.

If attacker attempts to change password of a card, he needs to provide the current password. Server or RC permits him to change the password once, he proves his legitimacy. But, he fails because of lack of the current password. Therefore, attacker can not change password of a stolen card also.

Replay Attack: The information ($\beta_j, LH(\kappa_i)$) used to check freshness of the message, sustains for a valid period in the buffer and computed from cache based nonce. Therefore, the replayed information can be identified and connection can be closed.

Reflection Attack: The proposed scheme withstands against reflection attack by sending different information (integrity checkers) in different directions. Let the attacker sends the message $< \alpha_i, PID_j, RH(\beta_i) >$ in step 2 to U_i as response of step 1. U_i obtains N_i from α_j and computes $KS = H(UID_i \oplus PID_j \oplus S_i)$. U_i will reject the message as $RH(H(KS)) \neq RH(\beta_i)$.

Non-forgery: Let an intruder impersonates a legal user to log in a server exploiting an executed session. Assume, he replayed the message flow $< \alpha_i^p, \beta_i^p, UID_i >$ to server P_j. Server accepts and sends, $< \alpha_j, RH(\kappa_j), PID_j >$. But, as the attacker dose not know the corresponding S_i, he can not compute the corresponding $LH(\kappa_i)$ because of the property ($P2$) and therefore fails to complete the protocol.

Forward Secrecy: If attacker knows a session key KS by chance, he can not determine the corresponding S_i because of the property ($P1$). Also, the previous session keys can not be determined due to lack of S_i. Therefore, the proposed scheme maintains Forward secrecy.

Denial of Service (DOS) Attack: Attacker may try to open a large number of half open connections with a particular server, so that the buffer of server becomes full. Then the server denies for service to a legitimate user. This can be executed by another legitimate user only, since illegitimate one be stopped on the fist message flow. Server avoids this form of attack, by restricting the user to request for another session before completion of the previous session (i.e before the corresponding information expires from the buffer).

5 Discussions

In this section, we compare our scheme with some existing efficient proposals to justify the efficiency. Comparison is based on both security properties and implementation requirements. Common features like single registration, mutual authentication, secure key establishment etc. are excluded from the comparison.

5.1 Security Properties

The proposals proposed in [20] and [21] use computational intensive operations like modular exponentiation to achieve better security. Unfortunately, DOS like generous attacks are not considered in these proposals. These schemes incorporate time stamps that need clock synchronization. But clock synchronization among users and servers is a tremendous problem for larger network. Moreover, if the secret (private key) of RC is revealed accidentally, attacker can be able to impersonate any user or server and therefore breaks the system.

Juang et.al [7] proposed a scheme avoiding the modular exponentiation operations, which does not require any clock synchronization among users and servers. Major disadvantage of this scheme is that each server needs to maintain a list of secret tokens for each users. Thus this scheme does not scale well for larger networks. Also, this proposal does not have any user password change phase. Later Chang et.al [3] proposed a scheme to avoid this difficulty. This scheme allows a user to change the password without checking of validity of the card owner. Attacker can exploit this flaw to change the password of other's card and disallow the card owner to use it. Moreover, if the common secret among server and RC is revealed by chance attacker could able to compute secret tokens for each user. Table 2 results the comparison of security features of our proposed scheme and existing schemes. Following abbreviations are used in this table.

UPF: The scheme allows user to change its password
SYNC: The scheme needs synchronization among servers and users.
DOS: The scheme is resistant against DOS attacks.
S_{RC}: Status of the scheme when secret of the RC compromises.

5.2 Implementation Requirements

Both the communication overhead and computational burdens have a significant impact on the adaptability of the smart card based proposal. A brief comparison

Table 2. Security Features Comparison

Schemes	Proposed	[21]	[7]	[3]
UPF	Yes	No password	No	Flaw
SYNC	No Need	Need	No Need	No Need
DOS	Yes	No	No	No
S_{RC}	Operative	Breaks	Breaks	Breaks

of both the computation and communication overhead of various existing schemes and our proposed scheme is given in Table 3. The complexity in registration phase and password change phase are ignored, as these phases occur rarely. We use the following notations in Table 2.

Comp.: Computation complexity
Comn.: Communication over head
H: Computation complexity of a single instance of hash operation
E: Computation complexity of a single instance of symmetric encryption/ decryption.
ME: Computation complexity of modular exponentiation.
l: Length of security parameters.

Table 3. Implementation complexity Comparison

Scheme	Comp.		Comn.	
	User	Server	$U_i \rightarrow P_j$	$P_j \rightarrow U_i$
Proposed	3*H	3*H	2*l+2*ID	$\frac{3}{2}$*l +ID
Yang [21]	5*ME+ H +E	4*ME+H+E	l+ID	3*l+ID+T
Juang [7]	3*E + 3*H	4*E + 2*H	4*l+2*ID	3*l+ID
Chang [3]	3*E + 4*H	3*E + 4*H	3*l +2*ID	3*l +ID

Size of l would be at least 1024-bit in Yang's scheme [21] as security of this scheme relies on traditional factorization problem. Therefore, theses like schemes need high communication band-width. Security of rest other schemes under our comparison is based on symmetric key encryption and hash based operations. So, the higher level of security can be achieved by choosing size of $l = 160$-bit. It is clear from the Table 2, that our scheme consumes least communication bandwidth of size $(3 + \frac{1}{2})l + 3ID$-bits ($l = 160$-bits) compared against all other schemes.

The proposed scheme requires no encryption/ decryption operations nor computational intensive modular exponentiation. It uses only three instances of hash operations at either ends to complete the protocol. Our scheme uses few more RCA based operations that are simple bitwise procedures which, can be executed independently for every bit. Inherent parallelism of RCA based operations, provide for a very fast and efficient implementation. Moreover, providing a small silicon space for RCA speed can be increased to a greater extent. Therefore, performance of the proposed scheme is expected to be substantially higher then other existing schemes.

6 Conclusion

In this paper, we have proposed a smart card based remote user authentication and key establishment protocol for multi-server environment. Major contribution of this scheme is to introduce one dimensional RCA, towards designing mutual authentication and key establishment. We have also incorporated a cache-based nonce generation scheme to resist replay attacks avoiding user-server synchronization. The efficiency of our proposed scheme is illustrated considering both security and implementation aspects.

References

1. Burrows, M., Abadi, M., Needham, R.: A Logic of Authentication, SRC research report **39** (1990).
2. Chan, C. K., Cheng, L. M.: Cryptanalysis of a remote user authentication scheme using smart cards. IEEE Trans. on Cons. Ele **46(4)** (2000) 992 - 993.
3. Chang, C. C., Lee, J.: An efficient and secure multi-server password authentication scheme using smart cards. proc of IEEE conf. CW-04 (2004).
4. Fan, C., Chan, Y., Zhang, Z.: Robust remote authentication scheme with smart cards. Comp & Sec **24(8)** (2005) 619-628.
5. Grembowski, T., Lien, R., Gaj, K., Nguyen, N., Bellows, P., Flidr, J., Lehman, T., Schott, B.: Comparative Analysis of the Hardware Implementations of Hash Functions SHA-1 and SHA-512" proc of ISC-2002 **LNCS 2433** (2002) 75-89.
6. Hwang, M. S., Li, L. H.: A new remote user authentication scheme using smart cards. IEEE Trans. on Cons. Ele. **46(1)** (2000) 28-30.
7. Juang, W.S.: Efficient multi-server password authenticated key agreement using smart card. IEEE Trans. On Cons. Ele **50(1)** 2004 251-255.
8. Kai-Chi, L., Cheng, L. M., Fong, A. S., Chi-Kwong, C.: Cryptanalysis of a modified remote user authentication scheme using smart cards. IEEE Trans. on Cons. Ele **49(4)** (2003) 1243-1245.
9. Ku, W. C., Chen, S. M.: Weaknesses and improvements of an efficient password based remote user authentication scheme using smart cards. IEEE Trans. on Cons. Ele. **50(1)** (2004) 204-207.
10. Li, L.H., Lin, I.C., Hwang, M. S.: A remote password authentication scheme for multi-server architecture using neural networks. IEEE Trans. On Neural networks **12(6)** (2001) 1498-1504.

11. Lamport, L.: Password Authentication with Insecure Communication. Comm. of the ACM **24** (1981) 770 - 772.
12. Lin, I. C., Hwang, M. S., Li, L. H.: A new remote user authentication scheme for multi-server architecture. Future Gen. Comp Sys **19** (2003) 13-22.
13. Pal Chaudhuri, P., Chowdhury, D. R., Nandi, S., Chattopadhyay, S: Additive Cellular Automata: Theory and Applications, Volume 1. Wiley-IEEE Computer Society Press (1997).
14. Shen, J. J., Lin, C. W., Hwang, M. S.: A modified remote user authentication scheme using smart cards. IEEE Trans. on Cons. Ele. **49(2)** (2003) 414-416.
15. Stinson, D. R.: Cryptography Theory and Practice, Second Edition, Chapman & Hall CRC Press (2002).
16. Tripathy, S., Chowdhuri, A. R., Nandi, S.: CARA: Cellualr Automata based Remote user authentication proc of COMSWARE-2006 (2006).
17. Yang, C. C, Yang, H. W., Wang, R. C.: Cryptanalysis of Security enhancement for the timestamp based password authentication scheme using smart cards. IEEE Trans. on Cons. Ele. **50(2)** (2004) 578-579.
18. Wolfram, S.: A New kind of Science, Wolfram Media Inc., (2002).
19. Wolfram, S.: Cryptography with cellular automata. proc of Crypto'85, **LNCS vol. 218** (1986) 429-432.
20. Wu, T., Hsu, C.: Efficient user identification scheme with key distribution preserving anonymity for distributed computer network. Comp & Sec **23** (2004) 120-125.
21. Yang, Y., Wang, S., Bao, F., Wang, J., Deng, R.: New efficient user identification and key distribution scheme providing enhanced security, comp & Sec **23** (2004) 697-704.

Materialized View Tuning Mechanism and Usability Enhancement

Tsae-Feng Yu, Thomas Tong, Min Xiao, and Jack Raitto

Oracle Corporation, One Oracle Drive
Nashua, NH 03062, U.S.A
{Tsae-Feng.Yu, Thomas.Tong, Min.Xiao, Jack.Raitto}@oracle.com

Abstract. The materialized view technology has been widely adopted in the data warehouse systems to improve query performance. Two key underlying techniques are materialized view incremental refresh and query rewrite. However, due to the potential complexity of the materialized view defining query and dependency on the materialized view change log, not all materialized views are incrementally refreshable or generally query rewritable. Many restrictions need to be applied and addressed which make the materialized view not easy to use. This paper presents Oracle's tuning mechanism/tool to facilitate the materialized view creation by automatically fixing and/or decomposing the defining query and addressing the change log requirements. The resulting materialized view implemented by a set of recommendation statements achieves the goals of incremental maintenance and broad query rewrite.

Keywords: Data Warehouse, Materialized View, Tuning, Usability, Optimization.

1 Introduction

A materialized view ("MV" or "MView") is a database object that includes the results of a query. It has been widely adopted in the industry and implemented as an important component of database server products by many commercial vendors [3],[4],[5],[6],[7],[8]. Materialized views are often used to pre-compute query results to speed query performance in the data warehouse systems. The use of the materialized views in answering queries is through the mechanism called *query rewrite* which redirects the query access from the table(s) to the MV. On the other hand, to synchronize the data between the MV and its base table(s), a mechanism called *incremental refresh* is to efficiently maintain the MV by applying data changes. The two underlying mechanisms make the MV a popular object in the user applications. Today, the users heavily utilize MVs to achieve efficient reporting and decision support in their data warehouses and even perform real-time applications in transaction processing systems.

Designing a materialized view is a complex problem requiring considerable skill and expertise in order to meet performance goals while minimizing materialized view maintenance costs. These goals can only be achieved by designing a materialized

S. Madria et al. (Eds.): ICDCIT 2006, LNCS 4317, pp. 347–360, 2006.
© Springer-Verlag Berlin Heidelberg 2006

view that can be refreshed incrementally and that can be used to answer the broadest set of request queries possible.

However, due to the potential complexity of the materialized view defining query and the dependency on the change log (e.g., MV log), not all materialized views are incrementally refreshable or generally query rewritable. Many restrictions need to be applied and addressed which make the materialized view not easy to use. For example, when the materialized view log of the base table is missing or insufficient or the materialized view has a UNION set operator in its defining query, the materialized view is not incrementally refreshable. The users often encounter barriers in the MV creation but not knowing how to correct the MV statement. This raises a major usability issue.

Unfortunately, the usability issue of the materialized view has not been paid with enough attention in the past years. Little effort was made to address the need. To improve the usability of the materialized view, ORACLE 9i [7] offered the solution of the EXPLAIN_MVIEW API which explains why the materialized view was not incrementally refreshable or generally rewritable. However, this tool alleviates but does not fix the problem. The users still need to manually modify their MV statements to meet the refresh/rewrite requirements and to work around various restrictions through multiple MV modification attempts. It would be ideal to bridge the usage gap by removing the need for manual correction on the materialized view statements.

In this paper, we present a materialized view tuning technique in form of a package tool, named TUNE_MVIEW [8]. The tool tunes a CREATE MATERIALIZED VIEW statement and generates a set of optimal recommendation statements for the user to implement the materialized view. It offers the following benefits and novel aspects:

1. Automatic enhancement of a user-specified materialized view definition, including:
   a. Automatic addition of columns required to enable MV capabilities such as incremental refresh and/or general query rewrite.
   b. Automatic decomposition of a complex, user-specified MV definition into a set of one or more simpler but more capable MV's definitions.
   c. Automatic transforming a complex SQL form into an equivalent but simpler SQL form, for example:
      i. Transforming SELECT DISTINCT X into SELECT X ... GROUP BY X
      ii. Transforming SELECT X, COUNT(DISTINCT(Y)) ... GROUP BY X into SELECT X,Y, COUNT(*) ... GROUP BY X,Y
2. Automatic conditioning of the MV environment to enhance MV capabilities, including addition of new or enhancement of existing MV logs.
3. Adopting query rewrite and nested MV mechanism to achieve incremental refresh and general query rewrite for complex MV.
4. Application of rewrite equivalences to the decomposition problem (1b), including the use of checksum to ensure the integrity of tune_mview determined rewrite equivalences.

It is observed that there have been a number of research efforts made in [1],[2],[9] to support SQL and database tuning. These works generally analyze query workload and generate recommendations of creating access structures such as indexes and materialized views and/or suggesting the table partitioning alternatives to improve overall database system performance. However, they do not address the need of the general users in automatically tuning materialized view to support incremental refresh maintenance and general query rewrite. Both capabilities in the materialized view are extremely important for the usefulness of the materialized view. Our work aims at the goal of maximizing the MV capabilities while achieving the ease of use. This is a distinct effort in the industry domain which is integrated as part of Oracle's tuning tool.

The rest of the paper is organized as follows. Section 2 presents our materialized view tuning approach and its architecture.   Section 3 provides a number of materialized view tuning examples. Section 4 describes some conclusions.

2   Architecture and Process of Tune Mview

Tuning a materialized view requires various considerations on how to enable materialized view capabilities, including incremental refresh and general query rewrite. Figure 1 depicts the general architecture of our materialized view tuning mechanism. A number of subcomponents are introduced in the framework and each supports specific parts of evaluations and/or tuning tasks.   They will be described individually in the following sections.

2.1   DDL Validator

As shown in Figure 1, when the user submits a CREATE MATERIALIZED VIEW statement to the TUNE_MVIEW, the statement is first validated to determine whether it is tunable. The DDL Validator is the first component of the TUNE_MVIEW that serves for the purpose.   It checks the CREATE statement by analyzing and categorizing the materialized view defining query constructs with a set of property flags such as the aggregation and/or join clauses, special constructs/functions, etc. The flags are used to determine the MV's capabilities and tunabilities. It is noted that, in some cases, the MV is not tunable. For example, if the MV has a complex defining query (e.g., having complex query constructs like non-deterministic functions), it cannot be improved in this API. The DDL Validator will detect the problem and return an error message showing that the CREATE statement cannot be tuned. If the validation is passed, the CREATE MATERIALIZED VIEW statement is forwarded to the next component, the MV SQL Analyzer, for further process.

2.2   MV SQL Analyzer

The MV SQL Analyzer analyzes the defining query of the CREATE MATERIALIZED VIEW statement and generates recommendations that fix/optimize the MV defining query. It processes the MV defining query as a workload query and examines the component clauses including SELECT, FROM, WHERE, GROUP BY, etc. It identifies the missing properties such as depending columns and the way to optimizing the query. Then, the Analyzer transforms the original statement into a number of recommendation statements to fulfil the requested MV abilities such as incremental refresh. The recommendations generally consist of two parts: IMPLEMENTATION and UNDO scripts. The IMPLEMENTATION script has one or more CREATE MATERIALIZED VIEW statements. The statement(s) represent either a modified CREATE MV recommendation (simple defining query modification) or one or more CREATE sub-MV(s) recommendations (in case decomposition is needed). On the other hand, the UNDO script includes one or more DROP MATERIALIZED VIEW statements to reverse CREATE operations in case the execution plan should be restarted. All generated recommendations are recorded in the common Advisor Repository Tables with sequence information.

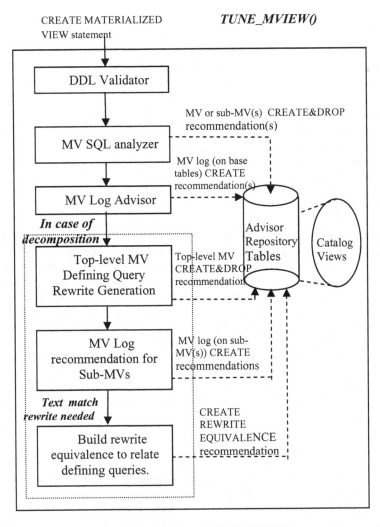

Fig. 1. Architecture of TUNE_MVIEW

It is noted that the MV decomposition strategy is applied when the MV can not be simply fixed through simple query modification. When the decomposition occurs, one or more sub-MVs are generated in the recommendation output. These sub-MVs enable the requested capabilities such as incremental refresh.

2.3 MV Log Advisor

The previously generated CREATE MATERIALIZED VIEW statements are not incrementally refreshable without proper change (MV) logs on base tables. The change logs record row changes done by DML operations on the base tables such as INSERT, DELETE and UPDATE. It is noted that even when the change log on the base table exists, the MV incremental refresh is still not possible if the MV log does not include all the columns referenced in the MV defining query.

To address the log deficiency issue, the **MV Log Advisor** takes the previously generated CREATE MATERIALIZED VIEW statements and checks if some base table logs are missing or need to be amended. Depending on the missing properties, it produces the recommendation statements of CREATE (when the MV log is completely missing) and ALTER MATERIALIZED VIEW LOG FORCE (when the MV log is not sufficient due to missing logging columns) statements. The generated CREATE and/or ALTER MATERIALIZED VIEW LOG statements are orderly recorded in the Advisor Repository Tables.

2.4 MV Decomposition and Rewrite

As mentioned in Section 2.2, if the input CREATE MATERIALIZED VIEW statement cannot be tuned through simple query modification, the decomposition occurs. Typical examples include MVs having set-operators (UNION, MINUS, INTERSECT, etc) and/or inline views (sub-SELECT clause in the defining query). In such cases, the SQL Analyzer divides the defining query into a number of sub-queries to satisfy the requirements (e.g., REFRESH FAST and ENABLE QUERY REWRITE). Each sub-query is then constructed as the defining query of a sub-MV. With the presence of the sub-MVs, the original defining query of the input CREATE MATERIALIZED VIEW statement is then modified to reference these sub-MVs. The input MV becomes a nested MV created on top of one or more sub MVs to enable required MV refresh and rewrite capabilities.

The transformation of the top-level CREATE MATERIALIZED VIEW statement is achieved by the intelligent reuse of our query rewrite engine. The original defining query is submitted to the rewrite engine and gets rewritten in terms of sub-MVs as a modified defining query. The modified defining query then replaces the original defining query and is included in the CREATE MATERIALIZED VIEW statement. In addition, the corresponding DROP statement for the top-level MV is generated. Similar to the recommendations generated by the previous components, the rewritten CREATE MV and its DROP statements are orderly recorded in the Advisor Repository Tables.

2.5 MV Log Recommendations on Sub-MVs

In case of decomposition, the top-level MV referencing sub-MVs could also be incrementally refreshable. In the case, the Sub-MVs essentially serve as the base tables of the top-level MV and will need MV logs to make the top-level MV incrementally refreshable. The MV log recommendation is therefore needed. In the phase, the MV Log Advisor is called again with the top-level MV's defining query and analyses each sub-MV to create the proper MV log. When the MV log is needed, the MV log Advisor generates the CREATE MV LOG statement(s) and records them in Advisor Repository Tables as previously described.

2.6 Rewrite Equivalence Builder

When ENABLE QUERY REWRITE is requested in the CREATE MATERIALIZED VIEW statement and the decomposition occurs, it is necessary to bridge the original defining query and the transformed query (i.e., new defining query). This is to enable the original query to rewrite with the transformed MV. To achieve it, we apply a new mechanism called Rewrite Equivalence to relate the base tables to the new top-level MV. The original MV defining query (i.e., referencing the base tables) is declared as equivalent to the rewritten top-level MV defining query (i.e., referencing sub-MVs) through the BUILD_SAFE_REWRITE_EQUIVALENCE recommendation statement. The equivalence relation is registered in the metadata and used by the query rewrite engine to perform query rewriting. The equivalence statement not only connects two defining queries but also has a checksum value to ensure the genuineness of the system-generated statement. The equivalence statement is also orderly recorded in Advisor Repository Tables.

2.7 Recommendation Statement Ordering and Generation

It is noted that all recommendation statements recorded in the Advisor Repository Tables have operation sequence numbers to ensure the processing orders. The generated IMPLEMENTATION (or CREATE) statements have the following execution order:

1. CREATE OR ALTER MATERIALIZED VIEW LOG FORCE on the base tables.
2. CREATE MATERIALIZED VIEW for sub-MVs (in case of decomposition).
3. CREATE OR ALTER MATERIALIZED VIEW LOG FORCE on the sub-MVs (in case of decomposition).
4. CREATE MATERIALIZED VIEW for top-level MV (in case of decomposition) or directly modified MV.
5. CREATE REWRITE EQUVIVALENCE API call (in case the query rewrite is required).

The generated statements for the DROP (or UNDO) plan have the following dependency order:

1. DROP top-level MV.
2. DROP sub-MVs (in case of decomposition).

After the TUNE_MVIEW is called and finishes its execution, the user can query **catalog views** to access the output recommendations and compose them in a preferred format (e.g., SQL*PLUS scripts) with the following query:

```
SELECT TASK_NAME, SCRIPT_TYPE,
       ACTION_ID, STATEMENT
FROM USER_TUNE_MVIEW
WHERE SCRIPT_TYPE ='IMPLEMENTATION' and
      TASK_NAME = 'MY_TUNEMV_TASK'
ORDER BY ACTION_ID;
```

The user can then execute the IMPLEMENTATION/CREATE script to create the materialized view that has the capabilities of incremental refresh and/or query rewrite. Alternatively, the user can execute the UNDO/DROP script to reserve the CREATE operations that were previously done.

3   Tune Mview Examples

This section presents three examples to illustrate the materialized view tuning work on different cases, including (1) directly fixing the materialized view, (2) tuning the materialized view with decomposition mechanism, and (3) tuning materialized view with optimization.

3.1   Example 1: Fixing the MV Directly

In a simple case, the materialized view creation statement can be fixed directly by modifying the defining query to meet the needs of enabling incremental refresh and general query rewrite. The following example is based on the table definitions below:

Table Name	Column Name	Column Type
STORE	STORE_KEY	Number(38)
	STORE_NAME	Varchar2(20)
	ZIPCODE	Varchar2(20)
	CITY	Varchar2(20)
	COUNTY	Varchar2(20)
	STATE	Varchar2(20)
FACT	STORE_KEY	Number(38)
	TIME_KEY	Date
	PRODUCT_KEY	Number(38)
	DOLLAR_SALES	Number(6,2)
	UNIT_SALES	Number(38)
	DOLLAR_COST	Number(6,2)

The following tune_mview API takes a CREATE MATERIALIZED VIEW statement whose defining query is not incrementally refreshable due to missing columns of COUNT aggregates. It is noted that in order to incrementally refresh SUM(column), a **COUNT(column)** is needed. It is also assumed that both base tables, STORE and FACT, already have sufficient materialized view logs (i.e., no log fixing issues in the case).

```
execute dbms_advisor.tune_mview (:my_task_name,
'CREATE MATERIALIZED VIEW cust_sales_mv
 BUILD IMMEDIATE
 REFRESH FAST
 ENABLE QUERY REWRITE
 AS
 SELECT s.store_name, sum(f.dollar_sales) AS sales,
       sum(f.dollar_cost) as cost
 FROM store s, fact f
 WHERE s.store_key = f.store_key
 GROUP BY s.store_name');
```

After executing the call, two output scripts, IMPLEMENTATION and UNDO, are generated as follows:

(1) The IMPLEMENTATION script:

```
CREATE MATERIALIZED VIEW GROCERY.CUST_SALES_MV
BUILD IMMEDIATE
REFRESH FAST
ENABLE QUERY REWRITE
AS
SELECT GROCERY.STORE.STORE_NAME C1,
   SUM("GROCERY"."FACT"."DOLLAR_COST") M1,
   COUNT("GROCERY"."FACT"."DOLLAR_COST") M2,
   SUM("GROCERY"."FACT"."DOLLAR_SALES")M3,
   COUNT("GROCERY"."FACT"."DOLLAR_SALES") M4, COUNT(*) M5
FROM GROCERY.STORE, GROCERY.FACT
WHERE GROCERY.FACT.STORE_KEY = GROCERY.STORE.STORE_KEY
GROUP BY GROCERY.STORE.STORE_NAME;
```

(2) The UNDO script:

```
DROP MATERIALIZED VIEW GROCERY.CUST_SALES_MV;
```

The original defining query is not sufficient for incremental refresh due to missing columns of COUNT(column). The TUNE_MVIEW analyzes the defining query and adds three additional COUNT columns (M2, M4 and M5) to make the materialized view support incremental refresh and general query rewrite (as seen in the IMPLEMENTATION script output). The UNDO script contains one DROP MATERIALIZED VIEW statement to undo the effect in case of undo action is needed.

3.2 Example 2: Decomposition of MV

In some cases, the materialized view creation statement cannot be fixed directly by modifying its defining query. The defining query may need additional work such as decomposition to enable incremental refresh and general query rewrite. Also, needed for incremental refresh, the materialized view log which captures the changes could be insufficient. Here is an example to show how the TUNE_MVIEW API addresses the MV decomposition and the need of amending change logs. Both examples in Sections 3.2 and 3.3 use the table definitions below:

Table Name	Column Name	Column Type
SALES	PROD_ID	Number(6)
	CUST_ID	Number
	TIME_ID	Date
	COUNTRY_ID	Number(6)
	AMOUNT_SOLD	Number(38)
CUSTOMER	CUST_ID	Number
	CUST_FIRST_NAME	Varchar2(20)
	CUST_LAST_NAME	Varchar2(40)
	CUST_EMAIL	Varchar2(40)
COUNTRY	COUNTRY_ID	Number(6)
	COUNTRY_NAME	Varchar2(50)
	COUNTRY_DESC	Varchar2(1000)

This example shows the materialized views defining query with set operators is decomposed as a number of sub-materialized views. It is assumed that the base tables SALES, CUSTOMER and COUNTRY have materialized view logs but do not have all required column(s). The user is to execute the following statement with a given CREATE MATERIALIZED VIEW statement:

```
execute dbms_advisor.tune_mview (:my_task_name,
'CREATE MATERIALIZED VIEW cust_mv
 REFRESH FAST ON DEMAND
 ENABLE QUERY REWRITE
 AS
 SELECT s.prod_id, s.cust_id, count(*) cnt,sum(s.amount_sold)
        sum_amount
 FROM sales s, customer cs,  country cn
 WHERE s.cust_id = cs.cust_id AND
   cs.country_id = cn.country_id AND
   cn.country_name in ('USA','Canada')
 GROUP BY s.prod_id, s.cust_id
 UNION
 SELECT s.prod_id, s.cust_id, count(*) cnt, sum(s.amount_sold)
        sum_amount
 FROM sales s, customer cs
 WHERE s.cust_id = cs.cust_id AND
       s.cust_id in (1005,1010,1012)
 GROUP BY s.prod_id, s.cust_id');
```

The MATERIALIZED VIEW defining query contains a UNION set-operator which is not supported for incremental refresh. The TUNE_MVIEW then applies the MV decomposition and MV log advisory mechanisms. Two output scripts, IMPLEMENTATION and UNDO, are generated.

(1) The IMPLEMENTATION script consists of the following statements along with two sub-materialized views:

```
-- fix materialized view logs
ALTER MATERIALIZED VIEW LOG FORCE ON "SH"."COUNTRIES"
```

```
ADD ROWID, SEQUENCE("COUNTRY_ID","COUNTRY_NAME")
INCLUDING NEW VALUES;

ALTER MATERIALIZED VIEW LOG FORCE ON "SH"."CUSTOMERS"
ADD ROWID, SEQUENCE("CUST_ID","COUNTRY_ID")
INCLUDING NEW VALUES;

ALTER MATERIALIZED VIEW LOG FORCE ON "SH"."SALES"
ADD ROWID, SEQUENCE("PROD_ID","CUST_ID","AMOUNT_SOLD")
INCLUDING NEW VALUES;
```

-- create sub materialized views
```
CREATE MATERIALIZED VIEW SH.CUST_MV$SUB1
REFRESH FAST ON COMMIT
ENABLE QUERY REWRITE
AS
SELECT SH.SALES.PROD_ID C1, SH.CUSTOMERS.CUST_ID C2,
  SUM("SH"."SALES"."AMOUNT_SOLD") M1,
  COUNT("SH"."SALES"."AMOUNT_SOLD") M2, COUNT(*) M3
FROM SH.SALES, SH.CUSTOMERS
WHERE SH.CUSTOMERS.CUST_ID = SH.SALES.CUST_ID AND
  (SH.SALES.CUST_ID IN (1012, 1010, 1005))
GROUP BY SH.SALES.PROD_ID, SH.CUSTOMERS.CUST_ID;


CREATE MATERIALIZED VIEW SH.CUST_MV$SUB2
REFRESH FAST ON COMMIT
ENABLE QUERY REWRITE
AS
SELECT SH.SALES.PROD_ID C1, SH.CUSTOMERS.CUST_ID C2,
  SH.COUNTRIES.COUNTRY_NAME C3,
  SUM("SH"."SALES"."AMOUNT_SOLD") M1,
  COUNT("SH"."SALES"."AMOUNT_SOLD") M2,
  COUNT(*) M3
FROM SH.SALES, SH.CUSTOMERS,
  SH.COUNTRIES
WHERE SH.CUSTOMERS.CUST_ID = SH.SALES.CUST_ID AND
  SH.COUNTRIES.COUNTRY_ID = SH.CUSTOMERS.COUNTRY_ID AND
  (SH.COUNTRIES.COUNTRY_NAME IN ('USA', 'Canada'))
GROUP BY SH.SALES.PROD_ID,
  SH.CUSTOMERS.CUST_ID,
  SH.COUNTRIES.COUNTRY_NAME;
```

-- create top-level materialized view
```
CREATE MATERIALIZED VIEW SH.CUST_MV
REFRESH FORCE WITH ROWID
ENABLE QUERY REWRITE
AS
(SELECT "CUST_MV$SUB2"."C1" "PROD_ID",
  "CUST_MV$SUB2"."C2" "CUST_ID",
  SUM("CUST_MV$SUB2"."M3") "CNT",
  SUM("CUST_MV$SUB2"."M1") "SUM_AMOUNT"
 FROM "SH"."CUST_MV$SUB2" "CUST_MV$SUB2"
 GROUP BY "CUST_MV$SUB2"."C1","CUST_MV$SUB2"."C2")
```

```
UNION
(SELECT "CUST_MV$SUB1"."C1" "PROD_ID",
  "CUST_MV$SUB1"."C2" "CUST_ID",
  SUM("CUST_MV$SUB1"."M3") "CNT",
  SUM("CUST_MV$SUB1"."M1") "SUM_AMOUNT"
 FROM "SH"."CUST_MV$SUB1" "CUST_MV$SUB1"
 GROUP BY "CUST_MV$SUB1"."C1",
          "CUST_MV$SUB1"."C2");


-- create a rewrite equivalence to link
-- the original query to the created
-- materialized views
EXECUTE
DBMS_ADVANCED_REWRITE.BUILD_SAFE_REWRITE_EQUIVALENCE (
  'SH.CUST_MV$RWEQ',
  'SELECT s.prod_id, s.cust_id, COUNT(*) cnt,
      SUM(s.amount_sold) sum_amount
   FROM sales s, customers cs, countries cn
   WHERE s.cust_id = cs.cust_id AND cs.country_id =
      cn.country_id
      AND cn.country_name IN (''USA'',''Canada'')
   GROUP BY s.prod_id, s.cust_id
   UNION
   SELECT s.prod_id, s.cust_id, COUNT(*) cnt,
          SUM(s.amount_sold) sum_amount
   FROM sales s, customers cs
   WHERE s.cust_id = cs.cust_id AND s.cust_id IN
      (1005,1010,1012)
   GROUP BY s.prod_id, s.cust_id',
  '(SELECT "CUST_MV$SUB2"."C3" "PROD_ID","CUST_MV$SUB2"."C2"
     "CUST_ID",
    SUM("CUST_MV$SUB2"."M3") "CNT",
    SUM("CUST_MV$SUB2"."M1") "SUM_AMOUNT"
   FROM "SH"."CUST_MV$SUB2" "CUST_MV$SUB2"
   GROUP BY "CUST_MV$SUB2"."C3",
            "CUST_MV$SUB2"."C2")
   UNION
   (SELECT "CUST_MV$SUB1"."C2" "PROD_ID","CUST_MV$SUB1"."C1"
     "CUST_ID",
         "CUST_MV$SUB1"."M3" "CNT","CUST_MV$SUB1"."M1"
     "SUM_AMOUNT"
   FROM "SH"."CUST_MV$SUB1" "CUST_MV$SUB1")',-1553577441);
```

(2) The UNDO output is as follows:

```
-- drop sub and top-level materialized views and rewrite
equivalence
DROP MATERIALIZED VIEW SH.CUST_MV$SUB1;
DROP MATERIALIZED VIEW SH.CUST_MV$SUB2;
DROP MATERIALIZED VIEW SH.CUST_MV;
DBMS_ADVANCED_REWRITE.DROP_REWRITE_EQUIVALENCE('SH.CUST_MV$RWEQ'
);
```

The original defining query of cust_mv has been decomposed into two sub-materialized views seen as cust_mv$SUB1 and cust_mv$SUB2. One additional column cnt_amount has been added in cust_mv$SUB1 to make that materialized view cust_mv$SUB1 incrementally refreshable. The original defining query of cust_mv has been modified to reference the two sub-MVs instead where both sub-materialized views are incrementally refreshable. It is noted that one rewrite equivalence relation (i.e., BUILD_SAFE_REWRITE_EQUIVALENCE statement) is built to link the original defining query to the sub materialized views for supporting query rewrite. By doing this, queries accessing the base tables will go through the MV hierarchy path to make use of the top-level MV (i.e., CUST_MV) for rewrite. Also, the last parameter value in the statement is a checksum value to ensure the genuineness of this system-generated query equivalence.

In addition, insufficient materialized view logs (on SALES, CUSTOMER and COUNTRY) are fixed by ALTER MATERIALIZED VIEW LOG FORCE statements to enable incremental refresh of the sub MVs. It is noted that, the ALTER MATERIALIZED VIEW LOG FORCE statement is re-executable which only amends/appends the materialized view log.

3.3 Example 3: Optimizaiton of the MV Defining Query

This example shows the materialized views defining query with set operators is transformed as an optimized defining query. In some cases, Sub-Select queries in the materialized view defining query are of similar shape and their selection predicates can be combined.

We again assume that the base tables SALES and CUSTOMER already have sufficient materialized view logs. The user is to execute the following statement with a given CREATE MATERIALIZED VIEW statement:

```
Execute dbms_advisor.tune_mview (:my_task_name,
'CREATE MATERIALIZED VIEW cust_mv
 REFRESH FAST ON DEMAND
 ENABLE QUERY REWRITE
 AS
 SELECT s.prod_id, s.cust_id, COUNT(*)
   cnt, SUM(s.amount_sold) sum_amount
 FROM sales s, customers cs
 WHERE s.cust_id = cs.cust_id AND s.cust_id IN (2005,1020)
 GROUP BY s.prod_id, s.cust_id
 UNION
 SELECT s.prod_id, s.cust_id, COUNT(*)
   cnt, SUM(s.amount_sold) sum_amount
 FROM sales s, customers cs
 WHERE s.cust_id = cs.cust_id AND s.cust_id IN (1005,1010,1012)
 GROUP BY s.prod_id, s.cust_id');
```

The MV defining query contains a UNION set-operator so that the materialized view itself is not fast-refreshable. However, two sub-Select queries in the materialized view defining query can be combined as one single query.

The IMPLEMENTATION script will be created with an optimized materialized view for support incremental refresh and query rewrite as follows:

```
-- create an optimized MV
CREATE MATERIALIZED VIEW SH.CUST_MV
REFRESH FAST ON DEMAND
ENABLE QUERY REWRITE
AS
SELECT SH.SALES.CUST_ID C1,
   SH.SALES.PROD_ID C2,
   SUM("SH"."SALES"."AMOUNT_SOLD") M1,
   COUNT("SH"."SALES"."AMOUNT_SOLD")M2,
   COUNT(*) M3
FROM SH.CUSTOMERS, SH.SALES
WHERE SH.SALES.CUST_ID = SH.CUSTOMERS.CUST_ID AND
      (SH.SALES.CUST_ID IN (2005, 1020, 1012, 1010, 1005))
GROUP BY SH.SALES.CUST_ID,
         SH.SALES.PROD_ID;
```

The original defining query of cust_mv has been optimized by combining the selection predicates of the two sub-Select queries in CUST_MV.

4   Conclusions

In this paper, we presented a materialized view tuning technique that tunes a CREATE MATERIALIZED VIEW statement to enable incremental refresh and general query rewrite. It enhances the usability of the materialized view so that the user does not require a complete understanding and knowledge on the materialized view nor rely on exhaustive trial and error process. The CREATE MATERIALIZED VIEW statement is automatically fixed and optimized by Oracle's TUNE_MVIEW package procedure.

In addition, this tuning technique also addresses the change log requirement to support materialized view incremental refresh. Missing and insufficient materialized view logs are created or amended by proper recommendations.

To support complex materialized view tuning, an advanced query decomposition mechanism is offered by the SQL Analyzer. It breaks the original MV defining query into a number of incrementally maintainable sub MVs. The query rewrite capability is supported by the query rewrite engine and rewrite equivalence mechanisms.

Best of all, it is by far the only automatic tuning solution for materialized view creation available in the industry.

References

[1] Benoit Dageville, Dinesh Das, Karl Dias, Khaled Yagoub, Mohamed Zait, Mohamed Ziauddin, "Automatic SQL Tuning in Oracle 10g", VLDB conference, Toronto, Canada. (2004)
[2] Daniel Zilio, Jun Rao, Sam Lightstone, Guy Lohman, Adam Storm, Christian, Garcia-Arellano, Scott Fadden, "DB2 Design Advisor: Integrated Automatic Physical Database Design", VLDB conference, Toronto, Canada. (2004)
[3] EBM-Software BV, "X4!-Materialized Views for MySQL", http://x4.olap4all.com/. (2005)

[4] Jonathan Gardner, "Materialized Views in PostgreSQL", http://www.jonathangardner.net/ PostgreSQL/materialized_views/matviews.html (2004)

[5] IBM, "DB2 UDB's High-Function Business Intelligence in e-business", www.redbooks.ibm.com/redbooks/pdfs/sg246546.pdf. (2002)

[6] Microsoft Corporation (2006), "Microsoft SQL Server 2005 Indexed Views", www.microsoft.com.

[7] Oracle Corporation (2002), "Data Warehousing Guide, Oracle9i Release 1", http:// otn.oracle.com/.

[8] Oracle Corporation (2004), "Data Warehousing Guide, Oracle10g Release 1", http:// otn.oracle.com/.

[9] Sanjay Agrawal, Surajit Chaudhuri, Lubor Kollar, Arun Marathe, Vivek Narasayya, Manoj Syamala, "Database Tuning Advisor for Microsoft SQL Server 2005", VLDB conference, Toronto, Canada. (2004)

Research into Verifying Semistructured Data

Gillian Dobbie[1,*], Jing Sun[1], Yuan Fang Li[2,**], and Scott UK-Jin Lee[1]

[1] Department of Computer Science, The University of Auckland, New Zealand
{gill, j.sun, scott}@cs.auckland.ac.nz
[2] School of Computing, National University of Singapore, Republic of Singapore
liyf@comp.nus.edu.sg

Abstract. Semistructured data is now widely used in both web applications and database systems. Much of the research into this area defines algorithms that transform the data and schema, such as data integration, change management, view definition, and data normalization. While some researchers have defined a formalism for the work they have undertaken, there is no widely accepted formalism that can be used for the comparison of algorithms within these areas. The requirements of a formalism that would be helpful in these situations are that it must capture all the necessary semantics required to model the algorithms, it should not be too complex and it should be easy to use. This paper describes a first step in defining such a formalism. We have modelled the semantics expressed in the ORA-SS (Object Relationship Attribute data model for SemiStructured data) data modelling notation in two formal languages that have automatic verification tools. We compare the two models and present the findings.

Keywords: data model, semistructured data, automatic verification.

1 Introduction

Semistructured data is now widely used in both web applications and database systems. There are many research challenges in this area, such as data integration, change management, view definition, and data normalization. Traditionally in these areas a formalism is defined for the database model, and properties of the algorithms can be reasoned about, such as the dependency preserving property of the normalization algorithm in the relational data model. Because research into semistructured data is still in its infancy, many algorithms have been defined in this area and a number of formalisms have been proposed but there is no widely accepted formalism that is generally accepted to reason about the properties of the algorithms. Such a formalism must capture all the necessary semantics required to model the algorithms, should not be too complex, and should be easy to use.

Another area that has been developing steadily is automatic verification. This involves formally specifying a model of a system, and running an automatic model checker or theorem prover that proves or disproves the consistency of the model. In this paper we describe research that we have undertaken in this direction. We have determined the

---

* This work is funded by a Marsden Grant (UOA317) from the Royal Society of New Zealand.
** This work is funded by the Singapore Millenium Foundation (SMF).

S. Madria et al. (Eds.): ICDCIT 2006, LNCS 4317, pp. 361–374, 2006.

semantics that we believe are required to reason about the properties of algorithms, we have modelled them using two different logics and used automatic verification to reason about the properties. This work is a first step towards establishing a widely accepted formalism, and it does highlight some important findings:

- the importance of the model containing enough semantics to express the algorithms over the data, but not excessive semantics
- the model must be broken down into logical sections for understandability and extensibility
- the importance of basing research into semistructured data on previous research in the database area rather than reinventing the wheel.

More specifically, we use a data modelling notation that extends the entity rela-tionship (ER) data model. The ORA-SS (Object Relationship Attribute data model for SemiStructured Data) data model models the schema and instance, so it is possible to model an XML Schema document in an ORA-SS schema diagram and an XML docu-ment in an ORA-SS instance diagram. However the semantics captured in an ORA-SS schema diagram are richer than those that are represented in XML Schema. We have modelled the semantics expressed in the ORA-SS diagrams in OWL (Web Ontology Language), which is based on a description logic, which itself can be translated into first order predicate logic. Because OWL was designed for sharing data using ontolo-gies on the web, it was a natural starting point. OWL has an automatic reasoning tool called RACER (Renamed ABox and Concept Expression Reasoner). We also modelled the semantics expressed in the ORA-SS diagrams in PVS (Prototype Verification Sys-tem), which is a typed higher order logic based verification system with a theorem prover. PVS can express more complex structures than OWL and in part, you get typing for free.

Section 2 clarifies the motivation for the project and describes other research that has offered a formal model for semistructured data. Section 3 provides background for the rest of the paper, highlighting the main features of ORA-SS, OWL and PVS. Section 4 summarizes the modelling of ORA-SS in OWL and PVS. More details of these models can be found in [1,2]. In Section 5 we analyze the two models. We conclude and provide future work in Section 6.

2   Related Work

Much of the work that has addressed challenges in the semistructured data area, such as [LiLi06, LeHo06, EmMo01], have proposed algorithms. However, there is little com-parative analysis of algorithms that are designed for similar tasks. Because there is no widely accepted formalism, it is not possible to reason about the correctness, or show specific properties of the algorithms in a general way. Moreover it is difficult to compare properties of algorithms that are designed for similar purposes. For example it is diffi-cult to compare the properties of the normalization algorithms that have been defined for semistructured data.

The area that our group is specifically interested in is normalization of semistructured data (or XML documents). There has been some very good and very practical work done in this area, such as [3,4,5,6]. If there was a widely accepted data model, with a set of defined operations it would be possible to show properties such as, whether data is lost during the transformations specified and it would also be possible to reason about what constraints are lost in the transformations. The kinds of formal definitions that we have seen to date in the normalization area include [7,5,8,6].

Another area where there are similar transformations are view definitions. It would be helpful to be able to show that given a set of view transformations again no data is lost, and also show that particular operations are reversible. At one level, data integration can be thought of as creating a view over a set of schemas. The unified view that is formed can be defined by a set of operations and the unified view would be better understood if there were some way to state properties of the operations. The operations defined in change management, such as *insert, drop* and *move* can be defined formally. There should be operators for both changes to the data and changes to the schema. A formal definition would not only be useful when defining what changes to allow, but could also help in the defintion of operations and perhaps in detecting the kinds of changes that have occured between different versions of the data or schema.

There was an interesting workshop that highlights the need to bring together people who are working in foundations of semistructured data from different areas that are related to semistructured data [9]. As you can see there have been a number of different approaches to defining foundations for semistructured data (e.g. [10,11], where most model the schema and data as a tree or graph and they are unable to model some of the constraints that can be specified in schema languages such as cardinality of children in relationships in the schema. These works consider limited semantics and do not provide automatic verification.

3   Background

The three key components in this work is the data modelling notation, ORA-SS, the ontology language OWL with the automatic reasoner RACER, and the formal verification language PVS. We briefly describe each of these components in this section.

3.1   ORA-SS (Object Relationship Attribute Model for Semistructured Data)

ORA-SS provides a notation for representing constraints on schemas and instances of semistructured data. The ORA-SS schema diagram extends ER diagrams with hierarchical parent-child relationships, and ordering. Schema diagrams represent relationship types between object classes, cardinality of relationship types, and distinguishes between attributes of object classes and attributes of relationship types. The ORA-SS instance diagram represents the same information as DOM diagrams, namely the relationships between objects and values of attributes. Objects match elements in XML documents, while attributes match leaf elements or attributes. A full description of the ORA-SS data modeling language can be found in [12,13].

We will now highlight some of the salient points in the ORA-SS schema diagram in Figure 1. There is a relationship type between object class *course* and object class *student*. It is a binary relationship type with name *cs*. Each course can have 4 to many

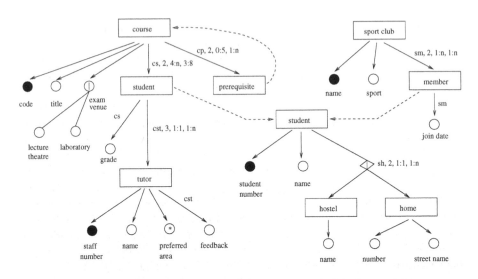

Fig. 1. The ORA-SS schema diagram of a *Course-Student* data model

students and a student can take 3 to 8 courses. Attribute *code* is an identifying attribute of course, and there is a reference between *prerequisite* and *course*, i.e. each prerequisite is in fact another course. The attribute grade belongs to the relationship type *cs*, i.e. it is the grade of a student in a course. Notice that relationship *cst* is a ternary relationship type, i.e. it relates object classes *course*, *student* and *tutor*.

3.2 OWL (Web Ontology Language)

OWL was designed to share data using ontologies over the web, and represents the meanings of terms in vocabularies and the relationships between those terms in a way that is suitable for processing by software.

Description logics [14] are logical formalisms for representing information about knowledge in a particular domain. It is a subset of first-order predicate logic and is well-known for the trade-off between expressivity and decidability. Based on RDF Schema [15] and DAML+OIL [16], the Web Ontology Language (OWL) [17] is the de facto ontology language for the Semantic Web. It consists of three increasingly expressive sub-languages: OWL Lite, DL and Full. OWL DL is very expressive yet decidable. As a result, core inference problems, namely concept subsumption, consistency and instantiation, can be performed automatically. RACER is an automatic reasoning tool for OWL ontologies, which supports min/max restrictions on integers, roles, role hierarchies, inverse and transitive roles.

3.3 PVS (Prototype Verification System)

PVS is a typed higher-order logic based verification system where a formal specification language is integrated with support tools and a theorem prover [18]. It provides formal specification and verification through type checking and theorem proving. PVS has a number of language constructs including user-defined types, built-in types, functions, sets, tuples, records, enumerations, and recursively-defined data types such as lists and binary trees. With the language constructs provided, PVS specifications are represented in parameterized theories that contain assumptions, definitions, axioms, and theorems. Many applications have adopted PVS to provide formal verification support to their system properties [19,20,21].

4   Modelling ORA-SS Diagrams

The ORA-SS notation separates concerns naturally, separating the schema and the instance into individual diagrams. In our modelling we go a step further. We distinguish between:

- constraints that must hold on all schema diagrams
- constraints that must hold on all instance diagrams
- constraints that hold on the relationships between schemas and instances

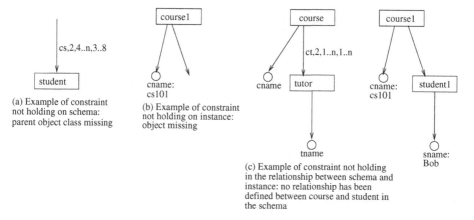

Fig. 2. Examples of constraints not holding in ORA-SS diagrams

The kind of constraint that must hold on the schema is that a child object class must be either related to a parent object class to form a binary relationship or related to another subrelationship type to form an n-ary relationship. The schema in Figure 2(a) violates this constraint. An example of a constraint that must hold on all instance diagrams is that a relationship is between 2 or more objects. Figure 2(b) shows a relationship in an instance diagram, where there is no child object. An example of a constraint that must hold on the relationship between schemas and instances is that if there is a relationship between two objects in an instance, then there must be a relationship type between the related object classes at the schema level. Figure 2(c) shows an instance with a relationship between objects *course1* and *student1*. Assuming that *student1* is a student and not a tutor, then this relationship violates the relationship type in the corresponding schema diagram. Although the mistakes appear obvious in the simple examples in Figure 2, they are harder to see in more complex diagrams or when the data is in a different format, such as XML and XMLSchema.

For each of the models described above, we have a corresponding instance model. There are models for:

- the instance of the schema
- the instance of the instance
- the relationship between the instances of the schema and the instance

In the instance of the schema, it is possible to state constraints such as *course* is an object class. In the instance of the instance, it is possible to state that *course1* is an object, and in the relationship between instances of the schema and the instance it is possible to state that *course1* is a *course*. Figure 3 summarizes the components that make up the ORA-SS model.

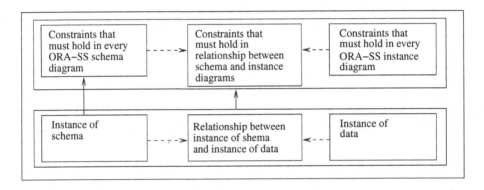

Fig. 3. Components of the Model

4.1   The ORA-SS Ontology in OWL

In OWL, we refer to a model as an ontology. The ORA-SS ontology contains the OWL definitions of all the ORA-SS concepts, such as object class, relationship type, and attributes. The 6 models defined above are captured in the ORA-SS Ontology.

Constraints on the Schema. As each object class and relationship type can be associated with attributes and other object classes or relationship types, we define an OWL class *ENTITY* to represent the super class of both object class and relationship type. The OWL class structure is shown as follows.

$$ENTITY \sqsubseteq \top \qquad\qquad ATTRIBUTE \sqsubseteq \top$$
$$OBJECT \sqsubseteq ENTITY \qquad\qquad ENTITY \sqcap ATTRIBUTE = \bot$$
$$RELATIONSHIP \sqsubseteq ENTITY \qquad\qquad OBJECT \sqcap RELATIONSHIP = \bot$$

It may not seem very intuitive to define relationship types as OWL classes. In ORA-SS, relationship types are used to relate various object classes and relationship types, it might seem more natural to model relationship types as OWL properties. However, there are two reasons that we decide to model relationship types as OWL classes. Firstly, the domain of ORA-SS relationship types can be relationship types themselves, when describing the relationships of ternary and more. Secondly, classes and properties in OWL DL are disjoint. In our model, an OWL relationship type consists of instances which are actually pointers to the pairs of object classes or relationship types that this relationship relates.

In ORA-SS, object classes and relationship types are inter-related to form new relationship types. As mentioned above, since we model relationship types as OWL classes, we need additional properties to connect various object classes and relationship types.

Firstly, this is accomplished by introducing two object-properties, *parent* and *child*, which map a *RELATIONSHIP* to its domain and range *ENTITYs*. The following statements define the domain and range of *parent* and *child*. As in ORA-SS, the domain of a relationship (*parent*) can be either an object class or another relationship type, i.e., an *ENTITY*. The range (*child*) must be an *OBJECT*. These two properties are functional as one relationship type has exactly one domain and one range node. Moreover, we assert that only relationship types can have parents and child but object classes cannot.

$\geq 1\ parent \sqsubseteq RELATIONSHIP$ $\geq 1\ child \sqsubseteq RELATIONSHIP$

$\top \sqsubseteq \forall\ parent.ENTITY$ $\top \sqsubseteq \forall\ child.OBJECT$

$\top \sqsubseteq\ \leq 1\ parent$ $\top \sqsubseteq\ \leq 1\ child$

$OBJECT \sqsubseteq \neg\ \exists\ parent.\top$ $RELATIONSHIP \sqsubseteq \forall\ parent.ENTITY$

$OBJECT \sqsubseteq \neg\ \exists\ child.\top$ $RELATIONSHIP \sqsubseteq \forall\ child.OBJECT$

Secondly, we define two more object-properties: *p-ENTITY-OBJECT* and *p-OBJECT-ENTITY*. These two properties are the inverse of each other and they serve as the super properties of the properties that are to be defined in later ontologies of ORA-SS schema diagrams. Those properties will model the restrictions imposed on the relationship types. The domain and range of *p-ENTITY-OBJECT* are *ENTITY* and *OBJECT*, respectively. Since the two properties are inverses, the domain and range of *p-OBJECT-ENTITY* can be deduced.

$p\text{-}OBJECT\text{-}ENTITY = (^{-}p\text{-}ENTITY\text{-}OBJECT)$

$\geq 1\ p\text{-}ENTITY\text{-}OBJECT \sqsubseteq ENTITY$ $\geq 1\ p\text{-}OBJECT\text{-}ENTITY \sqsubseteq OBJECT$

$\top \sqsubseteq \forall\ p\text{-}ENTITY\text{-}OBJECT.OBJECT$ $\top \sqsubseteq \forall\ p\text{-}OBJECT\text{-}ENTITY.ENTITY$

$ENTITY \sqsubseteq \forall\ p\text{-}ENTITY\text{-}OBJECT.OBJECT$ $OBJECT \sqsubseteq \forall\ p\text{-}OBJECT\text{-}ENTITY.ENTITY$

To define that attributes belong to entities or relationships, first of all, we define an object-property *has-ATTRIBUTE*, whose domain is *ENTITY* and range is *ATTRIBUTE*. Every *ENTITY* must have *ATTRIBUTE* as the range of *has-ATTRIBUTE*.

$\geq 1\ has\text{-}ATTRIBUTE \sqsubseteq ENTITY$ $ENTITY \sqsubseteq \forall\ has\text{-}ATTRIBUTE.ATTRIBUTE$

$\top \sqsubseteq \forall\ .has\text{-}ATTRIBUTE.ATTRIBUTE$

For modeling the ORA-SS candidate and primary keys, we define two new object properties that are sub-properties of *has-ATTRIBUTE*. We also make the property *has-primary-key* inverse functional and state that each *ENTITY* must have at most one primary key. Moreover, we restrict the range of *has-candidate-key* to be *ATTRIBUTE*.

$has\text{-}candidate\text{-}key \sqsubseteq has\text{-}ATTRIBUTE$ $has\text{-}primary\text{-}key \sqsubseteq has\text{-}candidate\text{-}key$

$\top \sqsubseteq \forall\ has\text{-}candidate\text{-}key.ATTRIBUTE$ $\top \sqsubseteq\ \leq 1\ has\text{-}primary\text{-}key^{-}$

$ENTITY \sqsubseteq\ \leq 1\ has\text{-}primary\text{-}key$

Instance of the Schema. The instance of object classes are represented as a subclass of *OBJECT*.

$course \sqsubseteq OBJECT$ $tutor \sqsubseteq OBJECT$

$student \sqsubseteq OBJECT$ $sport\_club \sqsubseteq OBJECT$

$hostel \sqsubseteq OBJECT$ $home \sqsubseteq OBJECT$

$\ldots$ $\ldots$

The instance of relationship types are represented as a subclass of *RELATIONSHIP*.

$cs \sqsubseteq RELATIONSHIP$ $sm \sqsubseteq RELATIONSHIP$ $cst \sqsubseteq RELATIONSHIP$

$sh \sqsubseteq RELATIONSHIP$ $cp \sqsubseteq RELATIONSHIP$

The relationship type *cs* is bound by the *parent/child* properties as follows. We use both *allValuesFrom* and *someValuesFrom* restriction to make sure that only the intended class can be the parent/child class of *cs*.

$cs \sqsubseteq \forall parent.course$ $cs \sqsubseteq \forall child.student\_1$

$cs \sqsubseteq \exists parent.course$ $cs \sqsubseteq \exists child.student\_1$

As discussed in the previous subsection, for each ORA-SS relationship type we define two object-properties that are the inverse of each other.

Example 1. Take *cs* as an example, we construct two object-properties: *p-course-student* and *p-student-course*. Their domain and range are also defined.

$p\text{-}student\text{-}course = (^{-}p\text{-}course\text{-}student)$

$p\text{-}course\text{-}student \sqsubseteq p\text{-}ENTITY\text{-}OBJECT$

$p\text{-}student\text{-}course \sqsubseteq p\text{-}OBJECT\text{-}ENTITY$

$\geq 1\, p\text{-}course\text{-}student \sqsubseteq course$ $\geq 1\, p\text{-}student\text{-}course \sqsubseteq student\_1$

$\top \sqsubseteq \forall p\text{-}course\text{-}student.student\_1$ $\top \sqsubseteq \forall p\text{-}student\text{-}course.course$

One of the important advantages that ORA-SS has over XML Schema language is the ability to express participation constraints for parent/child nodes of a relationship type. This ability expresses the cardinality restrictions that must be satisfied by ORA-SS instances.

Using the terminology defined previously, ORA-SS parent participation constraints are expressed using cardinality restrictions in OWL on a sub-property of *p-ENTITY-OBJECT* to restrict the parent class *Prt*. Child participation constraints can be similarly modeled, using a sub property of *p-OBJECT-ENTITY*.

Example 2. In Fig. 1, the constraints captured by the relationship type cs state that a course must have at least 4 students; and a student must take at least 3 and at most 8 courses. The following axioms are added to the ontology. The two object-properties defined above capture the relationship type between course and student.

$course \sqsubseteq$ $student\_1 \sqsubseteq \forall p\text{-}student\text{-}course.course$

$\quad \forall p\text{-}course\text{-}student.student\_1$ $student\_1 \sqsubseteq \geq 3\, p\text{-}student\text{-}course$

$course \sqsubseteq \geq 4\, p\text{-}course\text{-}student$ $student\_1 \sqsubseteq \leq 8\, p\text{-}student\text{-}course$

The instances of attributes are modelled as a subclass of *ATTRIBUTE*. As OWL adopts the Open World Assumption [17] and an ORA-SS model is closed, we need to find ways to make the OWL model capture the intended meaning of the original diagram. The following are some modeling *conventions*.

– For each *ENTITY*, we use an *allValuesFrom* restriction on *has-ATTRIBUTE* over the union of all its *ATTRIBUTE* classes. This denotes the complete set of attributes that the *ENTITY* holds.

Example 3. In the running example, the object class *student* has student number and name as its attributes.

$$student \sqsubseteq \forall\,has\text{-}ATTRIBUTE.(student\_number \sqcup name)$$

– Each entity (object class or relationship type) can have a number of attributes. For each of the entity-attribute pairs in an ORA-SS schema diagram, we define an object-property, whose domain is the entity and range is the attribute. For an entity *Ent* and its attribute *Att*, we have the following definitions.

$$has\text{-}Ent\text{-}Att \sqsubseteq has\text{-}ATTRIBUTE \qquad \top \sqsubseteq \forall\,has\text{-}Ent\text{-}Att.Att$$
$$\geq 1\,has\text{-}Ent\text{-}Att \sqsubseteq Ent$$

Example 4. In Fig. 1, the object class *sport club* has an attribute name. It can be modeled as follows.

$$\geq 1\,has\text{-}sport\_club\text{-}name \sqsubseteq sport\_club \qquad has\text{-}sport\_club\text{-}name \sqsubseteq has\text{-}ATTRIBUTE$$
$$\top \sqsubseteq \forall\,has\text{-}sport\_club\text{-}name.name \qquad sport\_club \sqsubseteq \forall\,has\text{-}sport\_club\text{-}name.name$$

For an entity with a primary key attribute, we use an *allValuesFrom* restriction on the property *has-primary-key* to constrain it. Since we have specified that *has-primary-key* is inverse functional, this suffices to show that two different objects will have different primary keys. Moreover, for every attribute that is the primary key attribute, we assert that the corresponding object property is a sub property of *has-primary-key*.

Example 5. In Fig. 1, object class *course* has an attribute *code* as its primary key and this is modeled as follows. The hasValuesFrom restriction enforces that each individual must have some *code* value as its primary key.

$$course \sqsubseteq \forall\,has\text{-}primary\text{-}key.code \qquad course \sqsubseteq \exists\,has\text{-}primary\text{-}key.code$$

4.2   The ORA-SS Model in PVS

The PVS model is divided into six files, as shown in Figure 3. We did this because by separating the concerns, it is easier to maintain and modify the model.

Constraints on the Schema. A relationship type is defined as a list of a set of object classes, where there is more than one object class and there are no cycles in the list. That is a relationship type cannot contain the same object class more than once. If there are more than 2 object classes in a relationship type, then the child object class relates to another relationship type.

```
no_cycle_oc(loc: list[set[OC]]): RECURSIVE bool =
    CASES loc OF
        null: TRUE,
        cons(ocs, subloc): (FORALL(subocs: set[OC]):
            member(subocs, subloc) =>disjoint?(ocs, subocs)) AND
            no_cycle_oc(subloc)
    ENDCASES
```

```
MEASURE length(loc)

RelType: TYPE = ocsList: list[set[OC]] | (length(ocsList) > 1)
                AND (no_cycle_oc(ocsList))

Relationship: TYPE = rel: RelType | (length(rel) > 2) =>
                (EXISTS(subRel: RelType): subRel = cdr(rel))
```

In an ORA-SS schema diagram, there are two types of relationship, i.e., a normal relationship where the child participant is a single object class; and a disjunctive relationship where the child participant is a set of disjunctive object classes. The above definition includes both cases. The '*no_cycle_oc*' function is defined as a recursive predicate function to disallow repetition of object classes in a relationship. The relationship type states that for any relationship with more than two elements the tail of the list forms another sub-relationship type.

Every relationship type in an ORA-SS schema diagram has its associated constraints on its participating objects shown using the min:max notation. It constrains the number of child objects that a parent object can relate to and vice versa.

```
parentConstraints(rel: Relationship): [nat, posnat]

parentSet(loRel: list[list[OBJ]], loParent: list[OBJ]):
    RECURSIVE nat =
   CASES loRel OF
      null: 0,
      cons(oRelHead, oRelRest):
        (IF (NOT(oRelHead = null) AND NOT(loParent = null) AND
            loEqual?(cdr(oRelHead), cdr(loParent))) THEN 1
         ELSE 0 ENDIF)
        + parentSet(oRelRest, loParent)
   ENDCASES
MEASURE length(loRel)

correctPC?(rel: Relationship): bool =
   FORALL(oRel: list[ObjRelationship]):
   member(oRel, relInstance(rel)) IMPLIES
     (proj_1(parentConstraints(rel)) <=
       parentSet(nArrayObjRelAll(relInstance(rel)),
       nArrayObjRel(oRel))) AND
     (proj_2(parentConstraints(rel)) >=
       parentSet(nArrayObjRelAll(relInstance(rel)),
       nArrayObjRel(oRel)))
```

The above defines parent constraints as a function where it takes a relationship type as an argument and returns the tuple of natural number and positive natural number which refers to a min:max pair. There is also a function *correctPC?* that checks whether the number of relationship instances for each object of the parent object class or each relationship instance of the sub-relationship type is within the boundaries defined in the relationship or not. The child constraints of the relationship and constraints on attribute values associated with objects and relationships can be defined in a similar way.

An object can have an attribute or set of attributes that have a unique value for each instance of an object class called a candidate key.

```
candidateKeys(oc: OC): list[list[ATT]]

correctCKey?(oc: OC): bool =
  (FORALL(attList: list[ATT]):
   member(attList, candidateKeys(oc)) =>
      noAttRepeat?(attList) AND
      isCKeyObjAtt?(attList, objAttribute(oc))) AND
   noKeyRepeat?(candidateKeys(oc))
```

The above defines the object having a candidate key as a function where it takes an object class as an argument and returns all candidate keys of *OC* as a list of list of attribute. The list of attributes is able to model both candidate key and composite candidate key. The function for checking candidate keys checks two conditions. It checks whether two objects are different when values of the candidate key for each object are different, where the values of the candidate keys belong to the set of attribute values of the object attributes. The function checks the uniqueness of the keys as well as whether the key attributes are actually attributes of the object class. In ORA-SS schema diagrams, an object class has a primary key which is selected from the set of candidate keys. The primary key is defined as a function that takes an object class as an argument and returns a list of attributes which is the primary key of that object class.

Constraints on the Instance. The instances of an object class in a declaration.

```
OC: DATATYPE
  BEGIN
    department: department?
    course: course?
    student: student?
    tutor: tutor?
    home: home?
    hostel: hostel?
  END OC
```

The instances of a relationship are represented as variables (or instances) of relationship types, the degree is represented as a conjecture, and participation constraints are represented as an axiom.

```
dc: Relationship = (:singleton(course),singleton(department):)
dcDegree: CONJECTURE Degree(dc) = 2
dcConstraint_Ax: AXIOM
 parentConstraints(dc)=(1, many) AND childConstraints(dc)=(1, 1)
```

Instances of attributes are modelled in a similar way to instances of object classes. Attributes are assigned to object classes or relationship types in axioms.

```
objAtts: AXIOM
   objAttribute(department) = (:deptName:) AND
   objAttribute(course) = (:code, title, examVenue:)

relAtts: AXIOM
   relAttribute(cst) = (:feedback:) AND
   relAttribute(cs) = (:grade:)
```

There is another axiom that states the primary keys of the object classes.

```
pKeys: AXIOM
   primaryKey(department) = (:deptName:) AND
   primaryKey(course) = (:code:)
```

5   Discussion

In this section we discuss the findings from modeling ORA-SS language in OWL and PVS. OWL is based on Description Logic (DL). An OWL ontology model describes the relationships and constraints among classes. In this sense, it is very similar to that of an ORA-SS schema diagram. OWL provides qualifying number restrictions, role hierarchies, inverse roles and transitive roles. We use qualifying number restrictions for defining the cardinality of relationships, role hierarchies for expressing inheritance of features, and inverse roles to express relationships. These concepts map naturally to some of the features in ORA-SS diagrams. Furthermore, the OWL ontology is designed for creating individuals from a relational model. Thus there is no need to explicitly define the ORA-SS instances in our OWL representation, but to use the OWL individuals directly. Therefore the OWL semantics of the ORA-SS language is simpler.

However, DL has its own limitations. It can be clumsy to model complicated types and predicates. For example, the current OWL notation has no cardinality constraint on the domain, so we had to introduce inverse to check the domain cardinality restriction. On the other hand, PVS is based on high-order logic, which has more expressiveness than that of DL. Therefore, our PVS representation is capable of modeling complicated constraints among schemas such as transformation operators, which may not be trivial using OWL. In addition, PVS is a strongly typed language. It has a type checking facility that can be used to verify typing conditions such as that objects belong to object classes and so on. This means that the specifications are easy to follow because we do not have to write extra theorems for typing. This is very handy because it does syntax checking on the ORA-SS language.

In terms of the automated verification, RACER is a reasoning engine and PVS has a theorem prover. A reasoning engine derives a conclusion from premises expressed in the knowledge base. It behaves more like a model checker, which verifies the consistency of OWL individuals within a finite scope against its ontology model. Because the OWL reasoner is design to handle huge ontology instances, it is very scalable enabling the checking of large XML files. On the other hand, a theorem prover proves mathematical theorems from a specification. It is good at performing a complete proof on certain properties of a model without any scope limitations. Thus PVS is a heavy duty theorem prover that can check more deep constraints such as schema transformation verifications. It provides tools that allow the definition of higher-level proof strategies enabling incremental building and reuse of proofs.

From our own experience, we found that the OWL and PVS approaches are actually complementary to each other. The RACER reasoner is good at detecting inconsistencies (within a finite scope) in an ORA-SS model. If an inconsistency exists it can also provides counter-examples. This is very useful in the sense of debugging errors. On the other hand, PVS theorem prover is good at verifying the total correctness of a property within the model without scope limitations. If a property is proved from PVS that means it should hold for every instance of the model. Hence, by using the RACER and PVS together, we could achieve a complete verification on the ORA-SS models.

6   Conclusion

Much of the research in the area of semistructured data involves algorithms that transform the data and schema, such as data integration, change management, view definition, and data normalization. The work presented in this paper is a first step towards formally defining a data model that is rich enough to capture the semantics that are needed to model and reason about the properties of operations that are capable of describing the algorithms described above. We have modelled the ORA-SS data model using OWL and PVS, and conclude that:

- Semantic Web languages, such as OWL, are extremely good at capturing semantic information about semistructured data.
- Reasoning tools, such as Racer, can be used to check the consistency of the ORA-SS schema and instance diagrams.
- PVS can be used to define a formal mathematical semantics for semistructured data.
- The automated verification provided by PVS empowers our definition of ORA-SS semantics, and if designed well it can be easy to extend.

There are a number of directions that we wish to take this work. Firstly we will study the algorithms that have been defined for the normalization of semistructured data, and derive the basic operations that are necessary to describe the algorithms. Secondly we will extend the OWL and PVS models of ORA-SS diagrams with a formal definition of the basic operations to compare how each model of ORA-SS performs. Thirdly, we will test the success of the models by modelling at least two of the normalization algorithms and comparing the properties of each. Finally we will investigate if the operators that are defined for normalization are general enough to express the general problem of view definitions.

References

1. Li, Y.F., Sun, J., Dobbie, G., Sun, J., Wang, H.H.: Validating Semistructured Data Using OWL. In: Proceedings of the 7th International Conference on Web Age Information Management, LNCS 4016 (2006)
2. Lee, S., Dobbie, G., Sun, J.: PVS Approach to Verifying ORA-SS Data Models. In: Proceedings of the 18th International Conference on Software Engineering and Knowledge Engineering. (2006)

3. Embley, D.W., Mok, W.Y.: Developing XML Documents with Guaranteed "Good" Properties. In: Proceedings of the 20th International Conference on Conceptual Modeling, LNCS 2224 (2001)

4. Wu, X., Ling, T.W., Lee, M.L., Dobbie, G.: Designing Semistructured Databases Using the ORA-SS Model. In: WISE '01: Proceedings of 2nd International Conference on Web Information Systems Engineering, Kyoto, Japan, IEEE Computer Society (2001)

5. Arenas, M., Libkin, L.: A Normal Form for XML Documents. ACM Transactions on Database Systems **29**(1) (2004) 195–232

6. Wang, J., Topor, R.: Removing XML Data Redundancies Using Functional and Equality Generating Dependencies. In: Proceedings of the Australasian Database Conference (2005)

7. Mani, M., Lee, D., Muntz, R.R.: Semantic Data Modeling Using XML Schemas. In: Proceedings of the 20th International Conference on Conceptual Modeling, LNCS 2224 (2001)

8. Vincent, M.W., Liu, J., Liu, C.: Strong Functional Dependencies and their Application to Normal Forms in XML. ACM Transactions on Database Systems **29**(3) (2004) 445–462

9. Neven, F., Schwentick, T., Suciu, D., eds. In Neven, F., Schwentick, T., Suciu, D., eds.: Foundations of Semistructured Data. Volume 05061., Internationales Begegnungs- und Forschungszentrum für Informatik (IBFI), Schloss Dagstuhl, Germany (2005)

10. Milo, T., Suciu, D., Vianu, V.: Typechecking for XML Transformers. J. Comput. Syst. Sci. **66**(1) (2003) 66–97

11. Jagadish, H.V., Lakshmanan, L.V.S., Srivastava, D., Thompson, K.: Tax: A tree algebra for xml. In: DBPL. (2001) 149–164

12. Dobbie, G., Wu, X., Ling, T., Lee, M.: ORA-SS: Object-Relationship-Attribute Model for Semistructured Data. Technical Report TR 21/00, School of Computing, National University of Singapore (2001)

13. Ling, T.W., Lee, M.L., Dobbie, G.: Semistructured Database Design. Springer-Verlag (2005)

14. Nardi, D., Brachman, R.: An introduction to description logic. In Baader, F., Calvanese, D., McGuinness, D., Nardi, D., Patel-Schneider, P., eds.: The description logic handbook: theory, implementation, and applications. Cambridge University Press (2003) 1–40

15. Brickley, D., Guha, R., (eds.): Resource description framework (rdf) schema specification 1.0 (2004) http://www.w3.org/TR/rdf-schema/.

16. Connolly, D., van Harmelen, F., Horrocks, I., McGuiness, D., Patel-Schneider, P., Stein, L., (eds): Reference description of the DAML+OIL ontology markup language (2001) http://www.w3.org/TR/daml+oil-reference.

17. Horrocks I., Patel-Schneider P.F., v.H.F.: From $\mathcal{SHIQ}$ and RDF to OWL: The making of a web ontology language. J. of Web Semantics **1**(1) (2003) 7–26

18. S. Owre and J. M. Rushby and and N. Shankar: PVS: A Prototype Verification System. In Kapur, D., ed.: 11th International Conference on Automated Deduction (CADE). Volume 607 of Lecture Notes in Artificial Intelligence., Saratoga, NY, Springer (1992) 748–752

19. Lawford, M., Wu, H.: Verification of real-time control software using PVS. In P. Ramadge and S. Verdu, ed.: Proceedings of the 2000 Conference on Information Sciences and Systems. Volume 2., Princeton, NJ, Dept. of Electrical Engineering, Princeton University (2000) TP1–13–TP1–17

20. Srivas, M., Rueß, H., Cyrluk, D.: Hardware Verification Using PVS. In: Formal Hardware Verification: Methods and Systems in Comparison. Volume 1287 of LNCS. Springer-Verlag (1997) 156–205

21. Vitt, J., Hooman, J.: Assertional Specification and Verification Using PVS of the Steam Boiler Control System. In: Formal Methods for Industrial Applications: Specifying and Programming the Steam Boiler Control. Volume 1165., Springer-Verlag (1996) 453–472

An Empirical Study on a Web Server Queueing System and Traffic Generation by Simulation

Ho Woo Lee[1], Yun Bae Kim[1], Chang Hun Lee[1], Won Joo Seo[1],
Jin Soo Park[1], and SeungHyun Yoon[2]

[1] Dept. of Systems Management Engineering
Sungkyunkwan University
Suwon, Korea(South)
{hwlee, kimyb}@skku.edu
[2] Network Control Platform Technology Team
BcN System Research Group, ETRI
Daejon, Korea(South)
shpyoon@etri.re.kr

Abstract. In this study, we first analyze the log data of the web-server system at a Korean company and confirm strong self-similarities that have been reported in a wide range of internet data. Then, we propose a simulation approach to generate arrivals of web page requests based on the conventional familiar probability distributions. We also present a forecasting model to generate future arrivals and test the validity of our approach through real data. Finally, we present our software tool that we developed to analyze web log data.

1 Introduction

Since the seminal works of Leland, Taqqu, Willinger, and Wilson [7], it has been reported from various analyses of empirical traffic traces that internet traffic is extremely bursty and possesses characteristics such as self-similarity (see also Paxson and Floyd [13]). Even multifractality has been reported in recent years (Feldmann et al. [4], Kant [6]). Readers are referenced to Crovella and Bestavros [2] and Park et al. [11] for the causes of self-similarity in internet traffic.

Self-similarity is a notion pioneered by Mandelbrot [9]. It designates objects that preserves a certain property with respect to scaling in time and/or space. For more detailed discussions about self-similarity, readers are advised to see Park and Willinger [12]. It is known that the queueing behavior with self-similar arrivals denies the usual "smooth and loose" notion of waiting line phenomena that can be observed in most queueing systems. In the internet queueing, there may be situations in which several hundred customers are waiting for service even when the server is idle 50 % of its time (see Erramilli et al. [3]).

Enormous amount of studies have been carried out to unveil unknown characteristics and mysterious behavior in internet queueing. ON-OFF aggregation, FBM(Fractional Brownian Motion), FGN (Fractional Gaussian Noise) (Mandelbrot [8]), Fractional ARIMA (Hosking [5]) and $M/G/\infty$ input models (Cox [1])

S. Madria et al. (Eds.): ICDCIT 2006, LNCS 4317, pp. 375–388, 2006.
© Springer-Verlag Berlin Heidelberg 2006

were studied to model the arrival processes. But no single formula has been reported so far on the mean queue length and waiting time. Only some limiting properties have been captured.

Even though such terms as self-similarity and heavy tail have been prevailing for many years, many people in Operations Research are still perplexed by any existence of such phenomena. Their first question would be concerned with the extent to which such incidents are pervasive in their daily lives. Their second question would be whether they have to throw away the tools they have acquired in pre-internet era if they want to do something about internet data. This study is aiming at partial answers to those questions. In this study, we empirically demonstrate that the internet traffic is closely related to our conventional and familiar probability distributions. This, in turn, implies that the modeling and analysis of internet traffic is not what OR practitioners should stay away from but something that they can keep in with.

In this paper, we first analyze the log data of the web-server system at a Korean company. The purpose is to confirm the strong self-similarities in diverse faucets of internet systems. Then, we propose a simulation approach to generate arrivals of web page requests based on the conventional probability distributions. We also present a forecasting model to generate future arrivals. We test the validity of our approach through real data. Finally we demonstrate our software tool we developed and used to analyze self-similar data.

This paper is organized as follows. In Section 2, we analyze the web log data of Card2U, Inc., a Korean company located in Seoul, Korea. We first consider the web page requests data and confirm strong self-similarities by graphs. Then, we test the self-similarities by employing the two well-known techniques (V-T plot and R/S plot) and estimate the Hurst parameter. Section 3 starts with the cleaning of the raw data to obtain the data of the first-time page requests (FPR). Assuming that arrivals of the FPRs follow the non-stationary Poisson process, we conclude, after a careful statistical test, that the number of subsequent requests placed by a user is well represented by the geometric distribution. We also test the distribution of the interval lengths of successive page requests during a session and conclude that it is well approximated by the Beta distribution. Section 4 is devoted to the development of the traffic generation scheme and the test of the traffic data generated by simulation based on the results of Section 3. In section 5 we present a forecasting model to generate future arrivals. Section 6 simulates a queueing system to estimate the mean waiting time by using the simulated data and confirm the unusual behavior of the mean waiting time. In Section 6, we present our software tool that we developed to analyze the web log data. Finally Section 8 summarizes the paper.

2   Analysis of the Web Log Data at Card2U, Inc.

In this section, we analyze the web log data of Card2U, Inc. [14]. The log data was collected from July 7, 11:21:32 to July 12, 14:12:14. Table 2.1 shows some important fields of the raw data. The log data contains the host IP address (user IP), requested time (time stamps), requested file, file size, etc.

To extract the meaningful data for the number of web page requests, we cleaned the data by eliminating all files except the ones with .asp and .html extensions. Also we eliminated additional files if a user requests two or more files at the same time. This was to avoid the dual frames.

Table 2.1. Fields contained in the log data collected from Card2U web server

Host IP	Time	Download Time(msec)	Receipt	Volume	Request	File
211.224.193.121	01-07-07 11:21:44	32	306	6021	GET	/img/cong.html
211.224.193.121	01-07-07 11:21:44	32	307	7094	GET	/img/emong.gif
211.123.273.054	01-07-07 11:21:47	31	307	1155	GET	/img/idleft2.asp

Figure 2.1(a)-(d) show the graphs of the total number of page requests in scales of 10, 60, 100 and 1000 seconds respectively. There are obvious cyclic differences in the number of requests between the day time and the night time. Readers can confirm that highly variable patterns are preserved in different time scales. This is believed to be a strong indication for self-similarities.

Figure 2.2(a) shows the V-T Plot to test the self-similarity for the number of page requests in the raw data. The Hurst parameter was estimated to be $H = 0.913$ (Leland et al. [7]). Figure 2.2(b) is the R/S Plot (Mandelbrot and Wallis [10]). The Hurst parameter under this test was estimated to be $H = 0.956$.

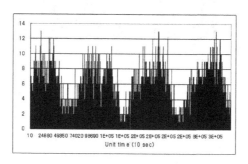

Fig. 2.1(a). Total number of page requests per 10 seconds

3 Development of Traffic Generation Scheme Based on Empirical Data

In this section, we develop a procedural scheme to simulate the web traffic of page requests based on the typical user behavior as follows:

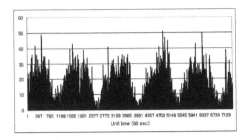

Fig. 2.1(b). Total number of page requests per 60 seconds

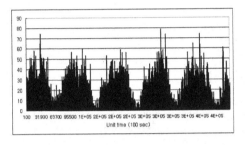

Fig. 2.1(c). Total number of page requests per 100 seconds

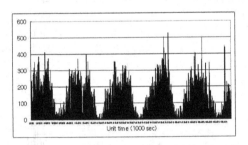

Fig. 2.1(d). Total number of page requests per 1000 seconds

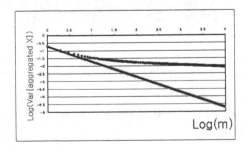

Fig. 2.2(a). Test for self-similarity (V-T plot)

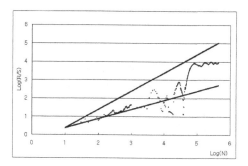

Fig. 2.2(b). Test for self-similarity (R/S plot)

(1) As soon as a user is connected to the web site, a page request is placed. It will be called the first-time page request (FPR)".
(2) Following the FPR, the user will place subsequent page requests (SPR).

The time duration from the FPR to the last SPR placed by a user will be called a session.

3.1   Arrival Process of FPRs

It was shown in Figure 2.1(a)-(d) that the superposed processes of the FRPs and SPRs have strong self-similarity and thus is not a Poisson process. But it is natural to think that the arrivals of FPRs occur "randomly" over a certain period of time. Thus we assume that the FPR arrivals during a 24-hour interval follow the non-stationary Poisson process with arrival rate function

$$\lambda(t) = \lambda_i, \quad t \in (\tau_{i-1}, \tau_i], \ (i = 1, 2, \ldots, N) \tag{3.1}$$

which means that the FPR arrivals follow the stationary Poisson process with constant rate λ_i during the interval $(\tau_{i-1}, \tau_i]$. We will set $\tau_{i+1} - \tau_i = 1$ hour for all i so that the whole day is divided into $N = 24$ intervals of equal length.

In our study of the log data, an arbitrary page request is classified as a FPR if the same requester has been dormant or has not appeared for the past 20 minutes. Figure 3.1 shows the number FPRs per hour and the proportion of the FPRs against the total number of requests.

3.2   Number of Pages Initiated by a FPR During a Session

Let K be a random variable denoting the number of page requests during a session. K includes one FPR and the subsequent SPRs originating from it.

We first empirically derive the distributional form of K and estimate its parameters. The frequency and cumulative distribution function from 8,126 data points is sketched in Figure 3.2. We used ARENA 3.5 Input Analyzer to conclude that K follows the geometric distribution with the following probability mass function

$$Pr(K = k) = q^{k-1}p, \ (k = 1, 2, \ldots). \tag{3.2a}$$

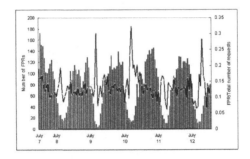

Fig. 3.1. Number of FPRs and its proportion

From the raw data, the mean value was estimated to be

$$E(K) = 1/\hat{p} = 1/0.125 = 8.021. \qquad (3.2b)$$

3.3 Length of Intervals Between Successive Requests During a Session

Let X be a random variable denoting the length of an interval between arbitrary two successive page requests during a session. Figure 3.3 shows the frequency and the cumulative distribution function of the interval lengths.

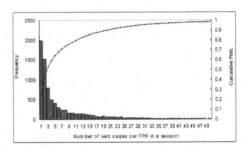

Fig. 3.2. Frequency of the number of subsequent page requests by a FPR during a session and its cumulative distribution function

From the ARENA 3.5 Input Analyzer, we concluded that X is well approximated by the Beta distribution with the following pdf

$$f(x) = \frac{\left(\frac{x}{1200}\right)^{\beta-1} \cdot \left(1 - \frac{x}{1200}\right)^{\alpha-1}}{B(\beta, \alpha)}, \quad (0 < x < 1200), \qquad (3.3a)$$

where

$$B(\beta, \alpha) = \int_0^1 s^{\beta-1} \cdot (1 - s)^{\alpha-1} ds. \qquad (3.3b)$$

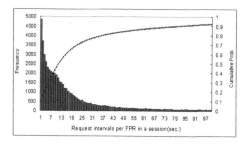

Fig. 3.3. Frequency of the length of intervals between requests during a session

The parameters were estimated as
$$\hat{\alpha} = 20.965, \qquad \hat{\beta} = 0.568 \tag{3.3c}$$
with the sample average
$$\bar{X} = \frac{1200\hat{\beta}}{\hat{\alpha} + \hat{\beta}} = 32.5. \tag{3.3d}$$

3.4 Summary of Steps

If we summarize the steps of generating the arrival process of the page requests,

(Step 0) Collect the log data from a web server system.

(Step 1) Divide the whole time period into appropriate equal length of intervals such that the arrival process of the first-time page requests (FPR) is stationary within each interval.

(Step 2) Extract the FPRs by an appropriate data cleaning. Assume that the arrivals of FPRs follow the stationary Poisson process during an interval.

(Step 3) Estimate the distribution of the number of subsequent page requests (SPR) initiated by a FPR.

(Step 4) Estimate the distribution of the interval length between two page requests.

(Step 5) Simulate the arrivals of the page requests based on the FPR generation scheme of (Step 3) and the probability distributions of (Step 4).

4 Analysis of the Simulated Data and Comparison with Raw Data

Our objectives in this section is two fold:

(1) to check empirically if the simulated arrivals possess the self-similarity, and
(2) to show its queueing behavior.

The self-similarity in the simulated data will be checked first by graphs and then by the V-T plot test. The Hurst parameter will be computed. The queueing behavior of the simulated data will be performed by assigning constant service time to each page request. It had been reported by Erramilli et al. [3] that the mean queue length begins to explode at lower levels of server utilization for higher values of the Hurst parameter. Our queueing simulation is aiming at confirming any existence of such extraordinary queueing behavior in our simulated data.

4.1 Total Number of Page Requests Per Hour

Figure 4.1 shows the comparison of the total number of page requests between the simulated data and the raw data. We see that simulated data follows the daily fluctuation patterns well enough. During the whole simulation period, the total number of simulated web page requests were 77,969 while it was 78,086 in the raw data.

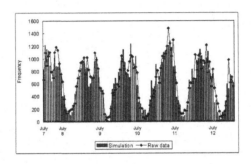

Fig. 4.1. Comparison of the total number of page requests between simulated data and raw data

4.2 Self-similarity Confirmation in the Simulated Data

If the simulated arrivals are to be believed that they approximate the real page request process with high degree of accuracy, it is required that they possess the self-similarity that was shown to exist in our raw data as seen in Figure 2.1(a)-(d). Figure 4.2(a)-(d) show the plots of the total number of simulated page requests counted in different time scales. We can see the same degree of high variabilities as we saw in our raw data. This is a strong indication that the simulated data possess the self-similarity. To test this, we perform the V-T plot test. Figure 4.3 sketches the result of the V-T plot. The Hurst parameter is estimated to be $H = 0.921$. Recalling that the Hurst parameter of the raw data was $H = 0.913$, we can conclude that the simulated data is as strongly self-similar as the raw data.

4.3 Length of the Interval Between Requests

Figure 4.4 shows the comparison of the length of the intervals between two successive page requests in the simulated data and the raw data during the

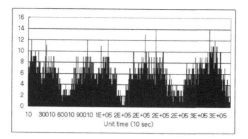

Fig. 4.2(a). Total number of page requests from simulated data (unit time: 10 sec)

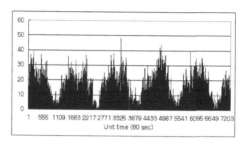

Fig. 4.2(b). Total number of page requests from simulated data (unit time: 60 sec)

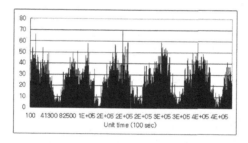

Fig. 4.2(c). Total number of page requests from simulated data (unit time: 100 sec)

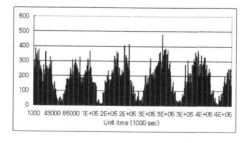

Fig. 4.2(d). Total number of page requests from simulated data (unit time: 1000 sec)

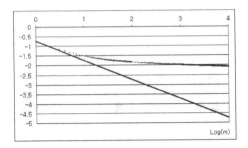

Fig. 4.3. Test of self-similarity of the simulated data (V-T Plot)

time interval from July 7, 20:00 to 21:00. We see that the raw data is well approximated by the simulated data. It was stated in preceding sections that the page request processes are assumed to be stationary during an one-hour interval. This assumption is empirically supported by Figure 4.1 because the simulated probabilities were generated based on the stationarity assumption.

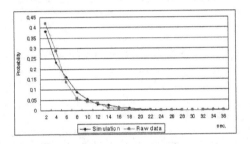

Fig. 4.4. Comparison of the request intervals

5   Forecasting the Future Arrivals

Forecasting the future arrivals heavily depends on the accurate estimate of the FPRs for different time periods. For this purpose, we employ a time-series analysis to catch the time-varying behavior of the FPR process.

Let $\{Z_t, (t = 1, 2, \ldots)\}$ be the number of FPRs during time interval t (in hours). For example, Z_1 is the number of FPRs from July 12, 12:00 to 13:00. We extracted the FPRs from the raw data by collecting the page requests of 24-hour time lag and used SmartForecasts Ver. 3 to plot the autocorrelation function (ACF) and partial autocorrelation function (PACF) in Figure 5.1. From the ACF and PACF, we concluded that the series data is well modeled by ARIMA(1,0,0)(0,1,0). Based on the Box-Jenkins model, Figure 5.2 shows the range of the forecasted number of FPRs with appropriate upper and lower limits. Figure 5.3 sketches the simulated total number of page requests based on the forecasted FPRs, the distribution of the number of subsequent requests (eq. (3.2a)) and the distribution of the request

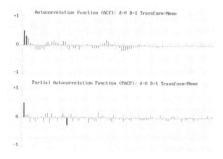

Fig. 5.1. ACF and PACF of the extracted data

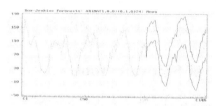

Fig. 5.2. Forecasted range of FPRs per hour

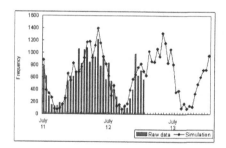

Fig. 5.3. Forecasted total number of page requests per hour

intervals (eq. (3.3a)). We used the mean value of the lower and upper limits as the number of FPRs in the simulation.

6   Queueing Behavior of the Simulated Self-similar Data

With the simulated arrival data of web page requests, we simulate the queueing system under the assumption that the service time is a constant. Figure 6.1 shows extraordinary behavior of the mean waiting time as the traffic intensity increases. As contrasted to the usual behavior of the mean waiting time in the ordinary queueing systems (such as $M/M/1$) in which the mean waiting time begins to explode only when the traffic is heavy (i.e., $\rho \simeq 1$), the figure shows that the mean waiting time begins to increase at lower level of server utilization. This peculiar phenomena in the self-similar queueing systems was reported many times in queueing literature (e.g., see Erramilli et al. [3]).

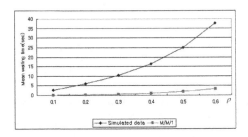

Fig. 6.1. Queueing behavior of the simulated data

7   Development of Software Tool

Testing the self-similarity of the web-log data is a tedious job without an appropriate software tool. We developed a software that can be used to analyze the self-similar data. It was developed based on MS Visual Basic with the support of Visual C++ on an user-friendly GUI environment.

Figure 7.1 shows diverse patterns of the number of arrivals collected in different time scales. This patterns give us useful information on the self-similarity

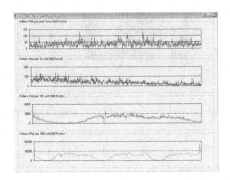

Fig. 7.1. Diverse plot patterns in different time scales

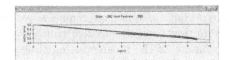

Fig. 7.2. V-T Plot

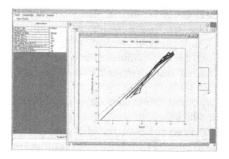

Fig. 7.3. R/S Plot

contained in the log data. Figure 7.2 and Figure 7.3 show V-T plot and R/S plot for self-similarity. The hurst parameters are automatically calculated.

8   Summary

In this paper, we empirically demonstrated that we can use the familiar probability distributions to analyze the internet data. We used the log data of a web server system of a commercial company and first showed that strong self-similarity exists in the arrival process of the page requests. We then developed a traffic generation scheme by using the familiar probability distributions and forecasting technique, and showed that the simulated arrival process well approximates the real arrival process.

Acknowledgement

The first author was supported by the SRC/ERC program of MOST/KOSEF grant R11-2000-073-00000.

The second author was supported by the KOSEF grant R01-2004-000-10948-0.

The first three and the fourth authors are involved in the second phase of the BK-21 (Brain Korea) program funded by the Korean government (MOEHRD).

References

1. Cox, D.R., Long-range dependence: a review, David, H.A. and David, H.T. eds., Statistics: An Appraisal, Iowa State university Press, 1984; 55-74.
2. Crovella, M.E. and Bestavros, A., Self-Similarity in World Wide Web traffic: evidence and possible causes, IEEE/ACM Transactions on Networking 1997; 5(6).
3. Erramilli, A., Narayan, O and Willinger, W., Fractal queueing models, CRC Press, Inc. 1997.
4. Feldmann, A., Gilbert, A.c. and Willinger, W., Data networks as cascades: Investigating the multifractal nature of Internet WAN traffic, Proc. ACM SIGCOMM 1998; 42-55.

5. Hosking, J.R.M., Fractional differencing, Biometrika 1981; 68: 165-176.
6. Kant, K., On aggregate traffic generation with multifractal properties, Global Telecommunications Conference-Globecom'99; 1179-1183.
7. Leland, W. E., Taqqu, M. S., Willinger, W., and Wilson, D. V., On the self-Similar nature of Ethernet traffic (extended version), IEEE/ACM Transaction on Networking 1994; 2(1): 1-15.
8. Mandelbrot, B.B., Fractional Brownian motions, fractional noises and applications, SIAM Rev. 1968; 10: 422-437.
9. Mandelbrot, B.B., The Fractal Geometry of Nature, Freeman, New York, 1982.
10. Mandelbrot, B.B. and Wallis, J.R., Some long-run properties of geophysical records, Water Resources Research 1969; 5: 321-340.
11. Park, K., Kim, G. T. and Crovella, M.E., On the relationship between file sizes, transport protocols and self-similar network traffic, In Proceedings of the Fourth International Conference on Network Protocols(ICNP '96) 1996; 171-180.
12. Park, K. and Willinger, W., Self-similar Network Traffic and Performance Evaluation, John Wiley & Sons, Inc., New York 2000
13. Paxson, V., and Floyd, S., Wide Area Traffic: The failure of Poisson modeling, IEEE/ACM Transaction on Networking 1995; 3(3): 226-244.
14. http://www.card2u.com

Dynamic Primary Copy with Piggy-Backing Mechanism for Replicated UDDI Registry

V.S. Ananthanarayana[1,*] and K. Vidyasankar[2,**]

[1] Department of Information Technology
National Institute of Technology Karnataka, Mangalore, India
anvs@nitk.ac.in
[2] Department of Computer Science
Memorial University of Newfoundland, Canada
vidya@cs.mun.ca

Abstract. As the community using web services grows, the UDDI registry is a crucial entry point that needs to provide high throughput, high availability and access to accurate data. Replication is often used to satisfy such requirements. In this paper, we propose *dynamic primary copy* method, a variant of primary copy method to handle the replicated UDDI registry, and two algorithms implementing this method. In this method, the update is done at the site where the request is submitted. The algorithms use a simple mechanism to handle the conflicting requests on UDDI entities in an efficient fashion. Due to a large volume of update and inquiry requests to UDDI, the number and size of the messages are critical in any replication solution for UDDI registry. Our algorithms reduce both the number and the size of messages significantly. The main difference between the two algorithms is that one of the algorithms handles high degree of conflicting update requests in an efficient fashion without transmitting unnecessary intermediate results.

1 Introduction

Web services are a series of specifications around a very generic architecture [8][1]. This architecture has three components: service requester (SR) - the potential user of the service; service provider (SP) - the entity that implements the service and offers to carry it out on behalf of the service requester; and service registry / service broker with a registry (SBR) - a place which allows service providers to advertise their services and service requesters to query for services. The service broker with a registry is based on the UDDI (Universal Description, Discovery, and Integration) specification [8]. The specification defines how to interact with a service broker and what the entries on the registry look like. Interactions are of two types: registration and look-up. Registration is a procedure whereby new service descriptions are added to the registry. Look-up corresponds to queries sent by SR in search of

---

* Corresponding Author.
** This research is supported in part by the Natural Sciences and Engineering Research Council of Canada Discovery Grant 3182.

S. Madria et al. (Eds.): ICDCIT 2006, LNCS 4317, pp. 389–402, 2006.
© Springer-Verlag Berlin Heidelberg 2006

services. As the community using web services grows, the UDDI registry is a crucial entry point that needs to provide high throughput, low response time, high availability, and access to accurate data. One of the mechanisms to ensure this is by replicating the UDDI registry. However, replication has the challenge of *replica control*, i.e., guaranteeing that the replica are consistent despite updates.

Two types of replication strategies for UDDI replication are discussed in the literature [10][12][5][3]. One is *lazy replication* which propagates updates to replicas through independent transactions after the original transaction commits. Here, the user receives the update acknowledgment before the propagation. This provides fast response. However, data at remote sites do not always reflect the latest updates. In *eager replication*, replicas coordinate first to maintain consistent copies, before the user receives a response. The advantage here is data consistency at all times, and *no lost update* problem in case of failures. Many variations of the above two protocols are discussed in [12] and [5].

In this paper, we propose *dynamic primary copy method*, a variation of primary copy method [4][6], to handle the replicated UDDI registry. In the case of primary copy method, among all replications of the data, one of them is predefined as primary copy and the site which contains that copy is called primary site. Any update request to the data d should be directed to d's primary copy site. In our method, the notion of the 'primary copy' is dynamic (not predefined) and the update is done at the same site where the request is submitted. Our method uses a blend of both eager and lazy replications strategies.

In our approach, update requests are propagated to all sites, each site resolves conflicts among requests in the same way and determines when to execute its request and, after the execution, transmits the result to all sites. We propose a simple and efficient mechanism to identify conflicts.

We show that with large number of replications, as the number of concurrent and conflicting update requests increases, the number of messages exchanged is considerably less when compared with the eager middleware replication protocol [10]. This situation is quite common in the case of Web services where the service providers are *mobile* in nature. We motivate the notion of mobile service providers with the following example. Consider a Web service for defense system scenario, where there is a fixed number of military bases and a large fixed number of military troops. Assume that, data (e.g., troop id) and services (e.g., current location, status of human and non-human resources, current action plan) pertaining to all military troops are maintained at all military bases (replicated information). This information may be queried frequently by the military regiment (e.g., command-in-chief) to formalize the next plan of action. Note that here military troops are SPs, military bases are SBRs and military regiments are SRs. As the military troop proceeds in the battle field, they keep on informing their current status like location, available human and non-human resources, etc., to their nearest military base. This information has to be propagated to other military bases to provide a consistent update. This example explains an application where in there is a possibility of high degree of update requests. However, there is a large number of papers addresses the issue of improving data availability (which is a major concern in mobile applications) for update operations in mobile environment. We are not discussing this issue in this paper.

Due to a large number of (update and inquiry) requests, the number and size of the messages are critical in any replica control algorithm for UDDI registry. In our approach, only relevant information of a request is broadcasted (unlike the entire request with data as in [10]) and so the size of the messages is small. We use a piggy-backing mechanism and combine several messages into one wherever possible, to reduce the number of messages in the algorithm.

We have implemented two algorithms based on the above method. They differ in the way the result of execution of updates is propagated to all other sites. We show that one of the algorithms handles high load of conflicting update requests in an efficient fashion without transmitting unnecessary intermediate update results. In our algorithms, since an update request is executed at the site where it is submitted, there is no need to maintain the knowledge about primary site, which is an overhead.

The organization of the remainder of this paper is as follows. Discussion on UDDI registry API is given in section 2. In this section, we give dependencies among different UDDI data elements with respect to various operations. This is based on UDDI specification given in [11]. We give detailed eager middleware replication strategy in Section 3. Next, in Section 4, we present dynamic primary copy method and two algorithms. Here, we describe a mechanism to handle the dependencies among different data elements of UDDI registry and explain how our algorithms use this mechanism to identify the conflicting requests. Comparison of both the algorithms with respect to the eager middleware replication strategy is given in Section 5 and we conclude in Section 6.

2   UDDI Registry API

The UDDI information model consists of four main data structures (entities) [8]: (i) businessEntity - the organization or business that provides web services; (ii) businessService - a collection of related web services offered by an organization described by a businessEntity; (iii) bindingTemplate - the technical information necessary to use a particular web service; (iv) tModel - represents a reusable concept such as a web service type, a protocol used by web services, or a category system. Every UDDI data structure contains its own unique identifier called *key*, viz., businessKey, serviceKey, bindingKey and tModelKey. The three data structures, businessEntity, businessService and bindingTemplate are related to each other via containment relationship as shown in Figure 1.

The businessService published in one businessEntity can be shared by other businessEntities. This can be done by using the businessService structure as a *projection* to the published businessService. A projected businessService is made a part of a businessEntity by reference as opposed to by containment. One more data structure, publisherAssertion, allows the declaration of relationships between two businessEntity data structures.

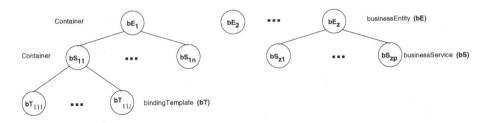

Fig. 1. Relationship between UDDI entities

UDDI defines APIs for publishing service descriptions in the registry and for querying the registry to look for published descriptions.

UDDI Inquiry API includes operations to find registry entries that satisfy search criteria and to get overview information about those entities (*find_business, find_service, find_binding, find_tModel*), and operations that provide details about a specific entry (*get_businessDetail, get_serviceDetail, get_bindingDetail, get_tModelDetail*).

UDDI Publisher API includes operations to add, modify and delete entries in the registry. For creating or modifying entries, APIs used are: *save_business, save_service, save_binding* and *save_tModel*. For deleting entries, APIs used are: *delete_business, delete_service, delete_binding* and *delete_tModel*.

For detailed discussion on inquiry and publisher APIs, please refer [11].

One of the required arguments to be passed to the API is key. Save_xx APIs are complex operations which may lead to the movement of child entities from one entity to another or deletion of existing entities. In the case of save_xx API, the publisher may or may not specify the key of an entity. If (s)he does, (s)he may specify the key of an existing entity or that of a remote entity. Depending on this, there is a possibility of creation of a new entity, movement of an existing entity or just the modification of an existing entity. So, there is a possibility of conflicts during execution of APIs as illustrated in the following examples.

Examples :

In Figure 1, let bEK_i be the key of businessEntity - bE_i, bSK_{ij} be the key of businessService - bS_{ij} and bTK_{ijk} be the key of bindingTemplate - bT_{ijk}.

Ex-1:   Let the publisher issue

r_1 : `save_binding(`bT_{111}`)`. Execution of this request conflicts with execution of inquiry or publisher APIs on any of bT_{111}, bS_{11} and bE_1.

Ex-2:   Let the publisher issue

r_2 : `save_business(`bE_1`)` with businessKey = bEK_1, serviceKeys = bSK_{11},bSK_{12},..., bSK_{1n} and bSK_{21} (i.e., movement of remote businessService bS_{21} from bE_2 to bE_1). Execution of this request conflicts with execution of inquiry or publisher APIs on any of bE_1, bS_{11},..., bS_{1n}, binding templates of bS_{11},..., bS_{1n} and, bS_{21}, its binding templates and bE_2.

Ex-3: Let $\mathbf{bS}_{11}$ be a projected service at $\mathbf{bE}_i$ (i.e., $\mathbf{bE}_i$ has service projection, $\mathbf{bS}_{11}$). So, $\mathbf{bE}_i$ has a businessService (i.e., $\mathbf{bS}_{11}$) with the businessKey, $\mathbf{bEK}_1$ and the serviceKey, $\mathbf{bSK}_{11}$. Let the publisher issue r_3 : save_business($\mathbf{bE}_j$) with businessKey $=$ **Nil** (i.e., $\mathbf{bE}_j$ is a new businessEntity) and serviceKey $= \mathbf{bS}_{11}$. That is, movement of businessService from $\mathbf{bE}_1$ to a new businessService, $\mathbf{bE}_j$. Execution of this request conflicts with execution of inquiry or publisher APIs on any of $\mathbf{bE}_1$, $\mathbf{bS}_{11}$,..., $\mathbf{bS}_{1n}$, $\mathbf{bT}_{111}$,..., $\mathbf{bT}_{11l}$ and $\mathbf{bE}_i$. Note that, the execution of inquiry or publisher APIs on $\mathbf{bE}_i$ conflicts with r_3 because, businessKey of its service projection (i.e., $\mathbf{bS}_{11}$) has to be changed to $\mathbf{bEK}_j$ from $\mathbf{bEK}_i$.

The list of publisher (save_xx and delete_xx) APIs with possible combinations of entities which conflicts with executions of other inquiry and publisher APIs on entities are given in [2].

3   Eager Middleware Replication (EMR)

In this section, we briefly explain EMR protocol proposed in [10]. EMR protocol is a simplified version of eager replication protocol proposed by Jiménez-Peris et.al. [9]. In EMR, the UDDI data is partitioned based on publisher and there is a primary copy for each partition. Knowledge about the site (primary site) which contains the primary copy of the partition should be known a priori to each site. An update request (save_xx or delete_xx API) on data in a partition is a global operation and query (find_xx or get_xx API) is a local operation. A client can submit an update request r_i to any site. This site will multicasts r_i along with the information necessary to update and timestamp to all other sites including the primary site (S_p) corresponding to the partition where the data for r_i belongs to. On receipt of r_i, all the sites other than S_p will send the acknowledgment or request cum acknowledgment (if there is a request to update to the same copy as that of r_i in those sites) to S_p. These acknowledgments are used to fix the order of execution of that request at primary site. Although the update request r_i is received by all sites, only the primary site S_p executes it, commits locally, and multicasts the physical changes to the other sites. Due to multicast of update requests with timestamps, the ordering of update requests at all other sites is the same as that of primary site. They apply the changes received in the same order as that of the primary site.

4   Dynamic Primary Copy with Piggy-Backing Method

In our method, we assume that the registry is divided into pages. Each page contains one or more entities. Lowest granularity of a page is a basic (core) component [8] of an entity. It may be core component of - a businessEntity, a businessService, a bindingTemplate or a tModel. To execute an UDDI API request, there may be a need to access many pages. For example, to execute a request `save_service(bS)`, there is a need to access multiple pages, where the bS data structure (core component) and all its bindingTemplates reside. The request is executed if access to all the pages are granted.

In section 2, we have shown that the publish request not only conflicts with the execution of publish or inquiry request on same or contained entity; but also conflicts with the execution of publish or inquiry request on some remote entities. We call such entities, *overlapping entities*. For example, with reference to r_2 in Ex-2 of Section 2, $bS_{11},\ldots,bS_{1n}$, binding templates of $(bS_{11},\ldots, bS_{1n})$, bS_{21}, its binding templates and bE_2 are entities overlapping with bE_1. Note that there is a dependency between bE_1 and bE_2 because of movement of businessService bS_{21} from bE_2 to bE_1. The idea of overlapping entities is used to handle the conflicting requests.

Handling of conflicting requests: One simple way to identify conflicts is by the common pages which are to be updated. Here, each publish (inquiry) request on an entity can be visualized as update (read) request on the set of pages, where the entity's components are stored. Consider the scenarios shown in Figure 2(a-c), where entities are stored in same or different pages. In Figure 2a,

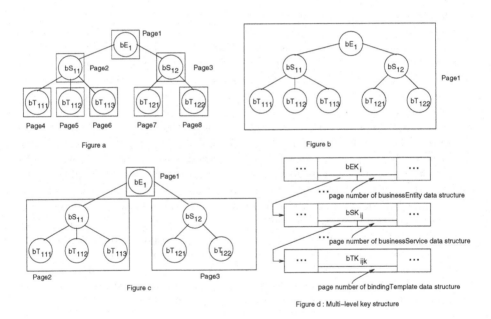

Fig. 2. Storage organization of entities

core component of each entity is stored in a separate page, in Figure 2b, entity components of businessEntity, bE_1 is stored in one page and in Figure 2c, entity components of each businessServices are stored in separate pages. In Figure 2a, as per businessEntity, bE_1 is concerned, `save_business(bE_1)` needs to update the pages, $\{1, 2, 3, 4, 5, 6, 7, 8\}$. We call the set of page numbers corresponding to these pages, *pageset* for the request save_business(bE$_1$). In Figure 2b and 2c, the pageset of save_business(bE$_1$) is {1} and {1, 2, 3} respectively.

Pageset of a request is a set of page numbers, corresponding to the pages of the entity specified in the request, its contained entities, and other new contained entities (e) if any, specified in the request with e's immediate parent.

For example, the request save_service(bS$_{12}$) may contain **bS$_{12}$**'s core component, **bS$_{12}$**'s binding templates to be modified and the binding template, **bT$_{111}$** - i.e., movement of binding template, **bT$_{111}$**, from **bS$_{11}$** to **bS$_{12}$**. In this scenario, the pageset of this request (with respect to the Figure 2a) is {3, 7, 8, 4, 2}.

Now we define conflicting requests as follows:

Two requests r_i and r_j are conflicting, if

1. pageset(r_i) $\cap$ pageset(r_j) $\neq$ {} and
2. at least one of the requests is a publish request.

Conflicts may not be transitive. In Figure 2a, let the requests be

r_4 : save_service(bS$_{11}$)

r_5 : save_business(bE$_1$)

r_6 : save_service(bS$_{12}$)

Here, r_4 is conflicting with r_5, r_5 is conflicting with r_6, but r_4 is non-conflicting with r_6.

Obtaining pageset for a request: In order to get a pageset for a request, we have to first get the page numbers of pages pertaining to the entities defined in the request. One way to achieve this is by maintaining a multi-level key structure corresponding to the keys of entities in UDDI registry as shown in Figure 2d.

Requests consist of entity keys as their arguments. From these keys, we can get the corresponding page numbers and hence the pageset. For every update request, the multi-level key structure should be refreshed to reflect the new status of the UDDI data.

Note that a publish request may lead to changes of other entities in UDDI data. Consider the following request with respect to UDDI data shown in Figure 2(a-c):

r_7 : save_service(bS$_{12}$) with **bS$_{12}$**'s core and containment entities and binding template **bT$_{111}$** of **bS$_{11}$**.

Execution of this request not only changes the structure of **bS$_{12}$** but also changes the structure of **bS$_{11}$**. So, there is an implicit update of **bS$_{11}$** due to r_7. This change should also be propagated along with changes due to r_7.

We assume that the registry is fully replicated at sites, S$_1$, S$_2$,..., S$_n$. Execution of publish requests is based on total ordering. The UDDI pages are updated at the site which receives publish request and then the updated pages are propagated to others. Our method resembles 'primary copy' method in the sense that, the update of pages is done on a copy first and then they are propagated. However, the copy where an update request originates is the 'primary copy' for that update. This means that, if there are two conflicting update requests r_x and r_y with timestamp(r_x) < timestamp(r_y) originated respectively at S$_i$ and S$_j$, then the pages due to r_x at S_i is updated before the update of pages at S_j due to r_y. Hence the pages at S_i become 'primary copy' first, and then the pages at S_j. So, the notion of 'primary copy' is dynamic (not predefined) and the update is done at the same site where the request is submitted. The read operation due to inquiry request is performed *locally* or *globally* using the information available at the site where the request originates.

We propose two dynamic primary copy algorithms to achieve consistency in replicated UDDI. They are:

1. Dynamic Primary Copy with Piggy-backing and Multicasting (**DPCP**$_M$) algorithm and
2. Dynamic Primary Copy with Piggy-backing and Point-to-point (**DPCP**$_P$) algorithm.

Basic idea of handling publish requests by both algorithms: When the publish (update) request r_x is submitted to S_i, S_i (requester) broadcasts r_x with timestamp and waits for the acknowledgments. On receipt of r_x, a site S_j sends an acknowledgment to S_i, if there is no request conflicting with r_x submitted to S_j or there is a conflicting request (w.r.t r_x) submitted to S_j with timestamp greater than r_x. Otherwise S_j defers the acknowledgment to r_x. S_i executes the update request only after the receipt of acknowledgments from all sites. Then, in DPCP$_M$, S_i sends the result of execution to all sites, piggy-backed with deferred acknowledgment, if any, individually for requests received from other sites. In DPCP$_P$, the result of execution with the acknowledgments are delivered only to the next potential waiting requester. If there is no waiting requester, the result of execution is transmitted to all sites. Note that both DPCP$_M$ and DPCP$_P$ algorithms can be used for any replicated database scenario. In this paper, we give detailed algorithms with respect to replicated UDDI registry.

Figure 3 shows the steps involved in handling two conflict publish requests r_x and r_y issued respectively at S_i and S_j and timestamp(r_x) < timestamp(r_y). Both (DPCP$_M$ and DPCP$_P$) algorithms consists of three phases to execute the publish request. They are request phase, acknowledgment phase and update phase. We give detailed explanation of both the algorithms in the rest of the section.

4.1 DPCP$_M$

When a site (requester) receives the publish request on an entity, a pageset for that request is generated. Requester then broadcasts the request, with its unique timestamp and pageset; then it waits for acknowledgments. This is called **request phase**.

On receipt of the request, a site will send the acknowledgment if there is no conflicting request (w.r.t the request received) originated at this site *or* there is a conflicting request originated at this site whose timestamp is greater than the request received. Otherwise the acknowledgment is deferred. This is called **acknowledgment phase**.

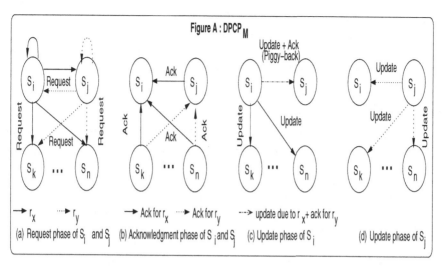

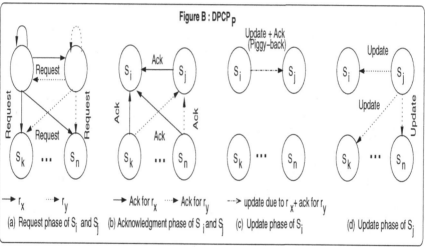

Fig. 3. Handling of publish requests in DPCP$_M$ and DPCP$_P$ algorithms

On receipt of all the acknowledgments, the requester will execute the update request and modify the page(s) pertaining to its pageset. Then, it sends the updated page(s) piggy-backed with the deferred acknowledgment to each of the sites to whom it deferred the acknowledgments. It sends the updated page(s) to others. This is called **update phase**. Note that to handle a publish request the system has to undergo all three phases (Figure 3A).

When a site receives the inquiry request on an entity, e, with the timestamp, TS_e, it is handled locally. The inquiry request on e is delayed, if the site has received or initiated a publish request, which is conflicting with e and e's timestamp is greater than that of these publish requests. Otherwise the inquiry request is processed.

Note that, since each site receives the publish requests with timestamps, all sites will order the conflicting publish requests in the same way. They apply all the changes in correct order. All inquiry requests are legal (i.e., inquiry requests can be reordered so that it will not see any overwritten updates).

4.2   DPCP$_P$

As in DPCP$_M$, this method also has **request phase, acknowledgment phase** and **update phase** (Figure 3B). The request phase and the acknowledgment phase are as in DPCP$_M$. The update phase of DPCP$_P$ is different from that of DPCP$_M$ as discussed below.

On receipt of all the acknowledgments for the publish request r_x at S_i, S_i will execute the publish request and modify the page(s) pertaining to its pageset. Then, S_i sends the updated page(s) piggy-backed with the deferred acknowledgment(s) to the *next deferred site*, say S_j (i.e., to the site where the request with next highest timestamp has originated). If there are no deferred acknowledgments for any S_j, then it multicasts the updated page(s) to all other sites. Note that, the deferred request list for r_x at S_i may contain some requests which are not conflicting with each other and they all could be executed next, after r_x. In this case, S_i sends piggy-backed messages to all of these requester. We explain this with an example. Suppose the publish request r_y from S_j and r_z from S_k are such that (i) they do not conflict with each other, (ii) both conflict with r_x at S_i, and (iii) both have timestamp 'next' to that of r_x. Then S_i sends updates and deferred acknowledgment to r_y of S_j, and updates and deferred acknowledgment to r_z of S_k. Now, suppose there is a request r_w from S_l which conflicts with, and has timestamp greater than, all the three of r_x, r_y, r_z. Then S_i sends deferred acknowledgment to r_w to either S_j or S_k (not to both) along with the respective piggy-backed messages. Due to this situation, the same page with different versions may reach the sites out of order. To apply the updates in order, version information [4] is maintained. at each page. This is an additional overhead for DPCP$_P$ algorithm.

When a site S_j receives an inquiry request i_q (with timestamp, TS_{iq}) and there exists pending remote conflicting publish requests with respect to i_q, then, S_j sends a read request to sites, $S_1, S_2, \ldots, S_k$ ($i \neq k$) - which have the publish requests conflicting with i_q and they have highest timestamp among all other pending publish requests conflicting with respect to i_q, but less than TS_{iq}. After the execution of those publish requests, the sites $S_1, S_2, \ldots, S_k$ will send the result of executions to S_j. S_j incorporates the update in order and executes the inquiry request i_q. So, if there is no pending local or remote publish requests conflicting with the inquiry request, then only the inquiry request is processed. Otherwise the processing of inquiry request is delayed till the appropriate update(s) due to publish request(s) are available. So, in DPCP$_P$ method, the execution of inquiry request may require a remote operation depending on the context.

In DPCP$_P$ method also, all conflicting publish requests are ordered and all inquiry requests are legal.

Note that, unlike $DPCP_P$, there are no messages to be transmitted to handle inquiry request in $DPCP_M$ method.

In Section 5, we will show that the $DPCP_P$ method generates least number of messages when there is a cluster of publish requests with no inquiry requests during the update on overlapping entities.

The characteristic of $DPCP_P$ method is that, with sparse publish request, say one publish request at a time, it resembles $DPCP_M$ method. As the number of publish requests on overlapping entities increases, the intermediate update pages are transmitted only to the potential next deferred site and not to the others. This not only avoids unnecessary updates but also reduces number of messages. In both the approaches, the request message needs to carry only the page numbers and not the 'actual pages to be altered'. This reduces the message size. There is no need to maintain separate algorithm to update the knowledge about the primary sites, in case of failures. This is because UDDI pages are updated at the site which receives publish request and then the updated pages are propagated to others.

For algorithms of the above discussed methods please refer[2].

5   Comparison

In this section, we derive and compare the total number of messages transmitted in eager middleware replication method [10], $DPCP_M$ and $DPCP_P$ methods.

Let n be the number of sites in the system where the registry is replicated and q be the number of sites which received the update requests on the same page at any point of time.

5.1   Eager Middleware Replication Method

We assume that client site will broadcast (instead of multicast) the messages to maintain the ordering of messages generated by itself. In this method, the number of messages at each of q sites is $(n) + (q - 1) + (q)$. The first term, (n) corresponds to the number of REQUEST messages sent, the second term, $(q - 1)$ corresponds to the number of acknowledgments sent and the third term, (q) corresponds to the updated pages received from primary site. The remaining $(n - q - 1)$ sites (i.e., the number of sites excluding client sites and the primary site) will send q acknowledgments and receives q updated pages from the primary site. So, the total number of messages transmitted to update the page requested by q sites (excluding primary site) is :

$$(n + q - 1 + q)q + (q + q)(n - q - 1)$$
$$= 3nq - 3q \qquad\qquad - (1)$$

5.2 $DPCP_M$ Method

In this method, the number of messages at the 1st site (i.e., the site which updates the page first) is $(n) + (n) + (q - 1)$. Here, the first term, (n) corresponds to the number of REQUEST messages broadcasted; the second term, (n) corresponds to the number of ACKNOWLEDGMENT messages received; and the last term, $(q - 1)$ corresponds to the updated pages received from $(q - 1)$ sites. The number of messages at the 2nd site (i.e., the site which updates the page after the 1st site) is $(n) + (n - 1) + (q - 1)$. Here, the first term (i.e., (n)) and the last term (i.e., $(q - 1)$) is same as that of 1st site due to the same reason as given for the 1st site. Since for the 2nd site, the acknowledgment from the 1st site is piggy-backed with the updated page, the number of acknowledgments received by the 2nd site are $(n - 1)$. Similarly, the number of messages at the qth site (i.e., the site which has the highest timestamp on the page under consideration among all q sites) is $(n) + (n - q + 1) + (q - 1)$. The remaining sites (i.e., $(n - q)$) will receive q updated pages from q sites. So, the total number of messages transmitted to update the page by q sites is

$$\sum_{i=1}^{q}[(n) + (n - i + 1) + (q - 1)] + q(n - q)$$
$$= \frac{6nq - q^2 - q}{2} \qquad - (2)$$

5.3   DPCP$_P$ Method

In this method, the number of messages at the 1st site (i.e., the site which has the smallest timestamp on the page under consideration among all q sites) is $(n) + (n) + 1$. Here, the first term, (n) corresponds to the number of REQUEST messages broadcasted; the second term, (n) corresponds to the ACKNOWLEDGMENT messages received; and the last term (i.e., 1) corresponds to the forwarding of the updated page with piggy-back acknowledgment to the 2nd site. The number of messages at the 2nd site (i.e., the site which has the next smallest timestamp on the page under consideration among all q sites) is $(n) + (n - 1) + 1$. The first and the last term are the same as that of the 1st site. Since for the 2nd site, the acknowledgment from the 1st site is piggy-backed with the updated page, the number of acknowledgments received by 2nd site are $(n - 1)$. Similarly the number of messages at the qth site (i.e., the site which has the highest timestamp on the page under consideration among all q sites) is $(n) + (n - q + 1) + 1$. After the qth site, the site which receives the updated page, will send it to all other sites excluding q^{th} site and itself (i.e., $(n - 2)$ messages). So, the total number of messages transmitted to update the page by q sites is

$$\sum_{i=1}^{q}[(n) + (n - i + 1) + 1] + (n - 2)$$
$$= \frac{4nq - q^2 + 3q + 2n - 4}{2} \qquad - (3)$$

It is very clear from above three equations that, as the number of requests on a page increases (i.e, $q > 5$), the number of messages exchanged is significantly less in the case of DPCP method, when compared with Eager Middleware Replication (EMR) method. Or more specifically,

No. of Messages(EMR method) > **No. of Messages**(DPCP$_M$ method), where $q > 5$ and **No. of Messages**(EMR method) > **No. of Messages**(DPCP$_P$

method), where ($q \geq 2$ and $n > 5$) or ($q \geq 3$ and $n < 5$). When $q = 1$, the number of messages transmitted in DPCP_M and DPCP_P is *two* more than EMR method. And also, **No. of Messages**(DPCP_M method) > **No. of Messages**(DPCP_P method), where $q > 1$ and **No. of Messages**(DPCP_M method) = **No. of Messages**(DPCP_P method), where $q = 1$.

Note that to compare with EMR method, we assume that $q < n$.

6   Conclusions

In this paper, we have proposed dynamic primary copy with piggy-backing mechanism for the replicated UDDI registry. We bring out the dependencies among entities with respect to publish requests. Based on this, we defined *overlapping entities* and *conflicting requests*. We proposed a simple mechanism to identify the conflicting requests for UDDI entities. We discussed two replication algorithms, DPCP_M and DPCP_P, which use this mechanism to identify the conflicting requests and allow the concurrent execution of non-conflicting requests. Both algorithms use a piggy-backing scheme to carry the acknowledgments along with the updated information. DPCP_P handles high load of conflicting publish requests in an efficient fashion without transmitting unnecessary intermediate update results. We have shown that, in both algorithms, as the number of update requests increases, the number of messages transmitted is significantly less when compared with the eager middleware replication method [10]. Also, the amount of information the message should carry for an update is less. And, there is no need of knowledge about the primary site, which is an additional overhead.

References

1. Gustavo Alonso, Fabio Casati, Vijay Machiraju: *Web Services : Concepts, Architectures and Applications*, Springer-Verlag, 2004.
2. V.S. Ananthanarayana, K. Vidyasankar: *Dynamic Primary Copy with Piggybacking Mechanism for Replicated UDDI Registry*, Technical Report, Dept. of Computer Science, Memorial University, NL, Canada (Under preparation).
3. T.A. Anderson, Y. Breitbart, H.F. Korth, A. Wool: *Replication, Consistency and Practicality : Are these Mutually Exclusive ?*, ACM SIGMOD 1998, pp 485–495.
4. Philip Bernstein, Vassos Hadzilacos, Nathan Goodman: *Concurrency Control and Recovery in Database Systems*, Addison-Wesley Publishing Company, 1987.
5. Y. Breitbart, R. Komondoor, R. Rastogi, S. Seshadri: *Update Protocols for Replicated Databases*, ACM SIGMOD 1999.
6. P. Chundi, D.J. Rosenkrantz, S.S. Ravi: *Deferred Updates and Data Placement in Distributed Databases*, Int'l Conf. on Data Engg., 1996, pp 469–476.
7. L. Lamport: *Time, Clocks and the Ordering of Events in a Distributed System*, Communications of the ACM 21,7 1978, pp 558–565.
8. H. Kreger: *Web Services Conceptual Architecture (WSCA 1.0) IBM.* Available from *http://ww-4.ibm.com/software/solutions/webservices/pdf/ WSCA.pdf*

9. Jimènez-Periz, R., Patiño-Martìnez, M., Kemme, B., Alonso, G: *Improving Scalability of Fault-tolerant Database Clusters*, In Int. Conf. on Distributed Computing Systems, 2002.
10. Chenliang Sun, Yi Lin, Bettina Kemme: *Comparison of UDDI Registry Replication Strategies*, ICWS 2004, pp 218–225.
11. UDDI.org, *UDDI Version 3.0 Specification*. Available from *http://www.uddi.org/specification.html*
12. Antoni Wolski: *Applying Replication to Data Recharging in Mobile Systems*, in Solid Information Technology Vol. 7, Issue 2, 2001. [http://www.solidtech.com/pdf/sms-wolski.pdf]

Mining Images of Material Nanostructure Data

Aparna Varde[1,3], Jianyu Liang[2], Elke Rundensteiner[3], and Richard Sisson Jr.[2]

[1] Department of Math and Computer Science, Virginia State University, Petersburg, Virginia. USA
[2] Department of Mechanical Engineering, Worcester Polytechnic Institute, Worcester, Massachusetts. USA
[3] Department of Computer Science, Worcester Polytechnic Institute, Worcester, Massachusetts. USA
{aparna, jianyul, rundenst, sisson}@wpi.edu

Abstract. Scientific datasets often consist of complex data types such as images. Mining such data presents interesting issues related to semantics. In this paper, we explore the research issues in mining data from the field of nanotechnology. More specifically, we focus on a problem that relates to image comparison of material nanostructures. A significant challenge here relates to the notion of similarity between the images. Features such as size and height of nano-particles and inter-particle distance are important in image similarity as conveyed by domain experts. However, there are no precise notions of similarity defined apriori. Hence there is a need for learning similarity measures. In this paper, we describe our proposed approach to learn similarity measures for graphical data. We discuss this with reference to nanostructure images. Other challenges in image comparison are also outlined. The use of this research is discussed with respect to targeted applications.

Keywords: Scientific Databases, Image Mining, Notion of Similarity, Interestingness Measures, Data Visualization, Nanotechnology.

1 Introduction

In recent years there has been much interest mining scientific datasets [3, 5, 8, 11, 15]. This presents several challenges pertaining to the complexity of the data types and the semantics of the domain. Scientific data often consists of images which have to be interpreted with reference to context. Discovering knowledge from such data presents issues related notions of similarity, interestingness measures and visualization of the data mining results.

In this paper, we explore such issues in the context of nanotechnology, a popular area in scientific databases today. The field of nanotechnology relates to the design, characterization, production and application of structures, devices and systems by controlling shape, size, structure and chemistry of materials at the nanoscale level. It deals with the understanding and control of matter at dimensions of roughly 1 to 100 nanometers, where unique phenomena enable novel applications [13]. Nanotechnology involves a confluence of several disciplines such as physics, chemistry, biology and materials science.

S. Madria et al. (Eds.): ICDCIT 2006, LNCS 4317, pp. 403–413, 2006.
© Springer-Verlag Berlin Heidelberg 2006

Data from nanotechnology, as in the case of any scientific domain, is of various types such as numbers, plain text, graphs and images. In this paper we focus on images depicting nanostructures of materials. An interesting problem is the comparison of such images in computational analysis. The inferences drawn from comparison are useful in real-world applications such as materials science, biomedicine and tissue engineering [2]. To enable effective comparison, it is essential to preserve the semantics of the images. Accordingly, it is important to define notions of similarity and interestingness measures for comparison with respect to the domain. Moreover, visualization of image comparison results taking into account user interests is also an issue.

In this paper, we focus on one issue, namely, the notion of similarity or distance between the images. Domain experts are able to identify some features crucial in image comparison. For example, the size of the nano-particles within the image, the distance between these nano-particles and the height of the nano-particles in the cross-section of the image are considered to be significant. However, the experts have only subjective notions of similarity, not a precise measure. Hence there is need to learn similarity measures for such images. We describe our proposed approach called LearnMet [14] that has been used in a computational estimation system [15] to learn distance metrics for graphical data. We discuss the issues in enhancing this approach for images. We also discuss some of the other challenges in image comparison.

The rest of this paper is organized as follows. Section 2 gives a background of the domain and the motivation for the given problem. Section 3 describes in detail the problem of comparing nanostructure images along with its associated challenges. Section 4 discusses one particular challenge related to the notion of similarity between the images and a potential method of addressing it. Section 5 summarizes related work. Section 6 states the conclusions.

2 Background and Motivation

The investigation of cell-substrate interactions plays an important role in biomedical and tissue engineering research efforts. Understanding how cells interact with substrates will lead to the ability to optimize substrates for specific biomedical applications [2]. Studies have shown that microscale topography influences cells to assume the shape of underlying patterns and form cytoskeletons oriented to the patterns [4]. There are few studies which have analyzed cell interactions with nanostructured substrates [17].

In order to extensively analyze cell-substrate interactions on the nanoscale, simple, inexpensive, and scalable nanofabrication methods which can accommodate a wide variety of materials must be developed. It is necessary to make this step from the microscale to the nanoscale. Based upon the need for more thorough nanoscale research there is development of simple, inexpensive, and scalable nanofabrication methods which accommodate different types of materials. Bone cells are being cultured on the nanostructures and the cell adhesion, proliferation, differentiation, and mineralization are being monitored using standard cell culture arrays and electrochemical impedance spectroscopy [2].

The results of this research will facilitate the fabrication of biological nanostructures and contribute to the continuing efforts to understand how cells function in the presence of synthetic substrates for biomedical and tissue engineering applications [2, 4].

An important step in this research is the comparison between images depicting the cell responds to various nanostructures used in the given applications. This comparison enables drawing inferences about the impact of the nanostructure on the cells. For example, image comparison at different stages of cell culturing is very important to understand the interaction of the cells with nanostructures. Comparison of different nanostructures at the same stage but obtained under different cell culturing conditions helps to determine how the inter-cellular interactions are affected with the existence of various nanostructures.

The research has potential use in targeted applications. Some of these applications include investigating the adhesion between cells and substrates in biomedical data, studying the alignment of cells and the differentiation between cells. This caters to the broader goals of developing materials for implants in the human body and helping the human skin to heal.

It is desirable to automate the comparison between the nanostructure images for computational analysis. The comparison can be automated using techniques such as clustering [9] and similarity search [8]. However, in order to achieve effective comparison, it is essential to capture the semantics of the images. In other words, it is important to make the comparisons analogous to a domain expert.

The problem of image comparison facing the nanoscience community thus opens potential avenues for data mining research. This problem is discussed in the paper.

3 Comparison of Nanostructure Images

3.1 Goals of Comparison

A nanostructure is a structure with arrangement of its parts in the nanometre scale. Nanostructures of materials are observed to study their properties [13]. Comparing nanostructure images enables us to determine whether the nanostructure play a crucial role in the cells. It helps to answer questions such as:

- What is the difference in nanostructure at various locations of a given sample?
- How does the nanostructure evolve at different stages of a physical / chemical / biochemical process?
- To what extent does processing under different conditions affect the cell-nanostructure interaction at the same stage of a process, such as cell culturing?

This is explained with reference to the figures below depicting images of nanostructures taken with a Scanning Electron Microscope (SEM).

Figure 1 shows a top view of a silicon nanopillar array [2]. Figure 2 is a top view of the same specimen at a different location and more zoomed in. Figure 3 is a top view of a nanopore array etched into silicon [2].

From these images it is observed that Figures 1 and 2 depict different nanostructures due to the difference in location and in the level of zooming. Figures 1 and 3 on the other hand show different nanostructures based on the conditions of the physical process used to obtain them.

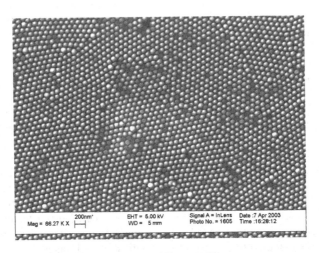

Fig. 1. Top view of Si nanopillar array

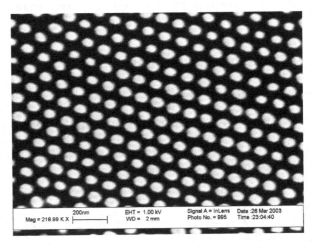

Fig. 2. Top view of Si nanopillar array at a different location of the given sample and more zoomed in

3.2 Issues in Comparison

In order to make nanostructure comparisons, domain experts typically observe certain features of the images, such as:

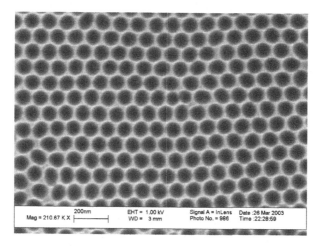

Fig. 3. Top view of nanopore array etched into Si

- Nanoparticle size: This refers to the dimensions of each individual particle in the nanostructure.
- Inter-particle distance: This is the average distance between the particles as seen in a 2-dimensional space.
- Nanoparticle height: This indicates to what extent the particles project above the surface in a cross-section and is recorded as additional data.

When experts manually make such comparisons, these are the subjective notions of similarity. The greater the similarity between these individual features, the greater is the similarity between the nanostructure images as a whole. Thus if two images have the same nanoparticle size, the same inter-particle distance and the same nanoparticle height, then they would be considered similar during visual inspection by domain experts. Also, the experts would manually take into account the effect of aspects such as the level of zooming and the nature of the cross-section (top-view, oblique view etc.) in making such comparisons.

Thus in order to automate image comparison for computational analysis, it is useful to incorporate the reasoning of the experts. However, it is to be noted that this notion of similarity is subjective which is acceptable for visual inspection. In computational analysis, there is a need for objective similarity measures in order to compare these images using processes such as clustering [9]. This motivates the need for learning such domain-specific similarity measures for images.

Another important issue in image comparison is to define interestingness measures. Some knowledge discovered from the comparison can be obvious with respect to the domain. Other knowledge may be less obvious but may not provide any useful information. Thus, based on such criteria, it is essential to define what is interesting to targeted users. These measures again need to be objective so as to facilitate computational analysis. For example, in data mining techniques such as association rules, common interestingness measures are rule confidence and rule support [6]. Likewise, there is a need to define interestingness measures in image comparison.

Having performed analysis by data mining techniques such as similarity search [8] and clustering [9], it is desirable to effectively visualize the data mining results. For instance, users may be interested in observing how a particular feature such as nanoparticle size varies from one specimen to another in evolutions of a physical process such as etching [2].

One possible way to address this would be to model each feature as an *attribute* the content of the feature as the *value* of that attribute. Thus, for example, "nanoparticle size" could be an attribute and "200 nanometers" could be its value.

Tools such as XMDV [16] incorporating techniques such as parallel co-ordinate plots and star-glyphs plots for visualizing multivariate data could then be used. Figure 4 shows an example of a star-glyphs plot for graphical data. Each vertex represents an attribute and the distance from the center of the star represents its value. The number of attributes and their combinations can be customized according to user preferences. Clusters and similarities can be visualized by comparing their shapes and sizes [16].

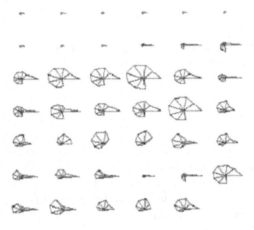

Fig. 4. Example of Star Glyphs Plot

However, such visualization for images poses issues such as feature selection, data post-processing and adaptation of existing techniques to enable the visualization. Addressing these poses challenges.

Hence, in general the following issues can be outlined in comparison of nanostructure images.

- Learning a notion of similarity for the nanostructures
- Defining interestingness measures for comparison between nanostructures
- Visualizing the results of comparison based on user interests

We elaborate on one of these issues, namely, the notion of similarity between the nanostructure images.

4 Notion of Similarity

The problem of similarity measures for complex data types has been approached in several ways [1, 7, 8, 12, 14, 19].

Our earlier work, LearnMet [14] learns domain-specific distance metrics for graphical data. More specifically, we deal with 2-dimensional graphical plots of scientific functions. These graphs plot a dependent versus an independent variable depicting the behavior of process parameters. The graphs have semantics associated with them related to features such as the absolute position of points, statistical observations and critical regions. LearnMet learns distance metrics to capture the semantics of these graphs taking into account such features. We briefly describe the LearnMet approach to learn distance metrics for graphical data and discuss this in the context of images.

4.1 The LearnMet Approach for Graphical Data

In the LearnMet approach experts provide actual clusters depicting the notion of correctness in the domain. A LearnMet distance metric is defined as a weighted sun of components such as position-based, statistical or critical distances [14].

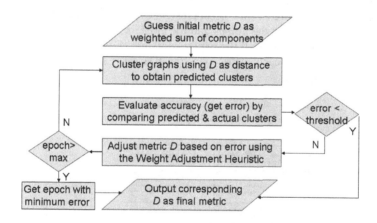

Fig. 5. The LearnMet Approach

In the learning process, predicted clusters obtained with a guessed initial LearnMet metric are iteratively compared with the actual clusters. In each iteration, the metric is refined until the error between predicted and actual clusters is minimal or below threshold. The metric corresponding to the lowest error is the learned metric. This approach is illustrated in the flowchart in Figure 5 and discussed in detail in [14].

4.1.1 Evaluation of LearnMet

The LearnMet approach has been evaluated in the domain of Heat Treating of Materials that motivated its development. A training set of 300 pairs of graphs in Heat Treating is obtained from correct clusters of 25 graphs given by experts. A distinct test set of 300 pairs of graphs is derived from 25 graphs given by experts. Experts give an error threshold of 10%, i.e., 0.1 for estimation. We use the same threshold for clustering. Initial components in the metric are given by experts. Two distinct assignments of initial weights are given by two different experts [14]. The corresponding two metrics are denoted by *DE1* and *DE2* respectively. A third initial metric *EQU* is obtained by assigning equal weights to all components. Several experiments are run by assigning random weights to components in the initial metric [14]. We present two experiments with randomly generated metrics called *RND1* and *RND2*. The initial metrics used in LearnMet experiments are shown in Figure 6.

EXPT	INITIAL METRIC
DE1	$5D_{Euclidean} + 2D_{Mean} + 5D_{Max} + 1D_{LF} + 3D_{BP}$
DE2	$5D_{Euclidean} + 1.5D_{Mean} + 4.5D_{Max} + 3D_{LF} + 3D_{BP}$
EQU	$1D_{Euclidean} + 1D_{Mean} + 1D_{Max} + 1D_{LF} + 1D_{BP}$
RND1	$6D_{Euclidean} + 2.75D_{Mean} + 3.5D_{Max} + 3.25D_{LF} + 1.85D_{BP}$
RND2	$4D_{Euclidean} + 3.2D_{Mean} + 4.3D_{Max} + 1.86D_{LF} + 2.9D_{BP}$

Fig. 6. Initial Metrics in LearnMet Experiments

The learned metric in each experiment is used to cluster graphs in the test set. These clusters are compared with correct clusters over the test set. Euclidean distance (ED) is also used to cluster the graphs and the clusters are compared with the correct clusters. The observations for all the experiments are shown in Figure 7. This figure depicts the accuracy for each metric over the test set. Clustering accuracies of the learned metrics are higher.

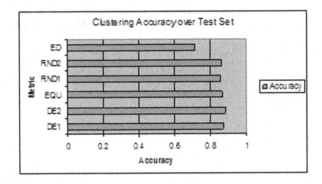

Fig. 7. Test Set Observations

The basic idea in LearnMet can be applied to learn similarity measures for images. However, there are several issues involved here as discussed in the next subsection.

4.2 Learning Similarity Measures for Images

A three-dimensional nanostructure image is more complex than a 2-dimensional graphical plot. The semantics associated with the images is of a different nature.

Some of the features applicable to images can be explicitly identified such as nanoparticle size, interparticle distance and nanoparticle height. However, some aspects are more subtle such as the level of zooming involved in producing the images and the nature of the cross-section for the nanostructure sample. Even among the features identified, the relative importance is not defined apriori. Moreover, it is not always feasible for domain experts to provide actual clusters of images depicting the notion of correctness.

Given these issues, it is non-trivial to directly apply the LearnMet approach for nanostructure images. Considerable enhancement is needed to learn a notion of similarity for images.

Thus, in general it is required that the learning of similarity measures for nanostructure images be done under the following conditions:

- Some features of the image are explicitly defined while others are subtle
- Relative importance of the features is not known apriori
- Actual clusters of images are not provided by domain experts

We propose to address this learning using an approach that involves minimizing the intra-cluster distance and maximizing the inter-cluster distance for each cluster of images. The goal is to learn a similarity measure that achieves this.

The minimum description length principle [10] that minimizes the sum of encoding a theory and examples using the theory is likely to be useful here. The theory in our context could be a cluster representative while the examples could be all the other images in the cluster. This approach involves several challenges such as defining heuristics for iteratively adjusting the similarity measure until the intra-cluster distance is minimal.

Thus, the learning of similarity measures for nanostructure images is proposed to be done in an iterative manner. This forms a topic of our ongoing research.

5 Related Work

Several similarity measures exist in the literature such as Euclidean and Manhattan distances [6], Tri-plot-based measures [12], Edit distances [1] and order-based measures [6, 8, 18]. However, some of them do not apply in the context of the given problem while others alone are not sufficient to define similarity.

In [7] they propose a distance learning method to find the relative importance of dimensions for n-dimensional objects. However, their focus is on dimensionality reduction and not on semantics. In [19] they learn which type of position-based distance is applicable for the given data starting from the formula of Mahalanobis distance. However they do not deal with other distance types concerning images and semantics. In [8] they overview various distance types for similarity search over multimedia databases. However no similarity measure encompassing several types is proposed.

Interestingness measures have been defined in the literature for data mining techniques such as association analysis, clustering and classification [6, 9, 18]. However, there is often a need for interestingness measures to be domain-specific and need to cater to interests of various users. Hence we need to define such measures in the context of our problem.

The XMDV tool [16] incorporates techniques such as parallel co-ordinates plots and star-glyphs plots for visualization of multivariate data. However, the adaptation of this approach to the given problem involves several issues.

6 Conclusions

This paper describes the research issues in mining nanostructure images. The goal is to compare the nanostructures to analyze material properties. The issues in mining relate to the notion of similarity between the images, the interestingness measures in comparison and the visualization of the mining results. This research benefits the nanoscience community. The broader goal is to study properties of materials at the nanoscale level in order to solve problems in the fields of materials science, biomedicine and tissue engineering.

Acknowledgments. The authors thank the researchers from the Nanofacbrication and Nanomanufacturing Group in the Department of Mechanical Engineering and the Database Systems Research Group in the Department of Computer Science at WPI. The support and encouragement of the Department of Math and Computer Science at Virginia State University is also gratefully acknowledged.

References

1. Chen, L., and Ng. R.: On the Marriage of Lp-Norm and Edit Distance. In: VLDB, Toronto, Canada (Aug 2004) 792 - 803.
2. Dougherty, S., Liang, J., Pins, G.: Preceision Nanostructure Fabrication for the Investigation of Cell Substrate Interactions. Technical Report, Worcester Polytechnic Institute, Worcester, Massachusetts (Jun 2006).
3. Fayyad, U., Haussler, D. and Storoltz, P.: Mining Scientific Data. In: Communications of the ACM, 39:11(Nov 1996) 51-57.
4. Flemming, R., Murphy, C., Abrams, G., Goodman, S. and Nealey, P.: Effects of Synthetic Micro and Nanostructured Surfaces on Cell Behavior. In: Biomaterials, 20 (1999) 573-588.
5. Gao, L., and Wang, X.: Continually Evaluating Similarity-Based Pattern Queries on a Streaming Time Series. In: SIGMOD, Madison, Wisconsin (2002) 370-381.
6. Han, J. and Kamber, M.: Data Mining Concepts and Techniques. Morgan Kaufmann, California (2001).
7. Hinneburg, A., Aggarwal, C. and Keim, D.: What is the Nearest Neighbor in High Dimensional Spaces. In: VLDB, Cairo, Egypt (Aug 2000) 506-515.
8. Keim, D., and Bustos, B.: Similarity Search in Multimedia Databases. In: ICDE, Boston, Massachusetts (Mar 2004) 873 – 874.
9. Kaufman, L. and Rosseau, P.: Finding Groups in Data - An Introduction to Cluster Analysis, John Wiley, New York (1988).
10. Rissanen, J.: Stochastic Complexity and the MDL Principle. In: Econometric Reviews, 6 (1987) 85-102.

11. Reich, Y., and Barai, S.: Evaluating Machine Learning Models for Engineering Problems. In: Artificial Intelligence in Engineering, 13 (1999) 257 – 272.
12. Traina, A., Traina, C., Papadimitriou S., and Faloutsos, C.: TriPlots - Scalable Tools for Multidimensional Data Mining. In: KDD, San Francisco, California (2001) 184 – 193.
13. United States National Nanotechnology Initiative. Technical Report, Feb 2006.
14. Varde, A., Rundensteiner, E., Ruiz, C., Maniruzzaman, M., and Sisson Jr., R.: Learning Semantics-Preserving Distance Metrics for Clustering Graphical Data. In: KDD's MDM, Chicago, Illinois (Aug 2005) 107 – 112.
15. Varde, A., Rundensteiner, E., Ruiz, C., Brown, D., Maniruzzaman, M. and Sisson Jr., R.: Integrating Clustering and Classification for Estimating Process Variables in Materials Science. In: AAAI Poster Track, Boston, Massachusetts, July 2006.
16. Ward, M. XMDV Tool: Integrating Multiple Methods for Visualizing Multivariate Data. In: Visualization, Washington DC (Oct 1994) 326 – 333.
17. Webster, T. and Smith, T.: Increased Osteoblast Function on PLGA Composites Containing Nanophase Titania, In: Journal of Biomedical Materials Research (2005) 74A 677-686.
18. Witten, I. and Frank, E.: Data Mining: Practical Machine Learning Algorithms with Java Implementations, Morgan Kaufmann Publishers, California, USA (2000).
19. Xing, E., Ng, A., Jordan, M., and Russell, S.: Distance Metric Learning with Application to Clustering with Side Information, In: NIPS, Vancouver, Canada (Dec 2003) pp. 503-512.

Mining Sequential Support Affinity Patterns with Weight Constraints

Unil Yun

Electronics and Telecommunications Research Institute, Telematics & USN
Research Division, Telematics Service Convergence Research Team
161 Gajeong-dong, Yuseong-gu, Daejeon, 305-700, Korea
yununil@gmail.com

Abstract. In this paper, we present a new algorithm, Weighted Sequential support affinity pattern mining in which a new measure, sequential s-confidence is suggested. By using the measure, sequential patterns with support affinity are generated. A comprehensive performance study shows that WSAffinity is efficient and scalable in weighted sequential pattern mining. Moreover, it generates fewer but important sequential patterns.

Keywords: data mining, sequential pattern mining, support affinity pattern.

1 Introduction

Mining sequential patterns in large databases have had broad applications such as analysis of customer purchase behavior, web access patterns, and biomedical DNA. Sequential pattern growth methods mine the complete set of frequent sequential patterns using a prefix projection growth method to reduce the search space without generating all the candidates. Most algorithms [3, 4, 5, 7, 8, 9, 11, 12] use a support threshold to prune the search space. This strategy provides basic pruning but it is hard to generate the proper number of sequential patterns with a minimum support. In addition, after mining datasets and getting the sequential patterns, spurious sequential patterns with weak support affinity exist although a minimum support is high. It will be better to prune these weak affinity patterns first when the user wants to reduce the number of sequential patterns at the minimum support. WSpan [13] is a weighted sequential pattern mining algorithm that uses the pattern growth approach to adjust the number of sequential patterns when low minimum support is set. However, in WSpan, weak affinity sequential patterns including items with different support levels are mined.

In this paper, we propose an efficient sequential pattern mining algorithm based on a level of support affinity. We define the concept of a sequential support affinity pattern that uses an objective measure, called sequential s-confidence which considers support affinity and prevent the generation of sequential patterns with substantially different support levels. The sequential s-confidence measure is used to generate patterns with similar levels of support. An extensive performance analysis shows that weighted sequential support affinity patterns are extremely valuable patterns, since they have strong affinity in terms of a support. The main contributions of this paper

S. Madria et al. (Eds.): ICDCIT 2006, LNCS 4317, pp. 414–423, 2006.

are: 1) definition of a new measure, a sequential s-confidence, 2) description of weighted sequential affinity pattern mining by using sequential s-confidence, 3) implementation of our algorithm and 4) execution of an extensive experimental study to compare the performance of our algorithm with SPAM [2] and WSpan [13].

2 Problem Definition and Related Work

2.1 Problem Definition

Let $I = \{i_1, i_2... i_n\}$ be a unique set of items. A sequence S is an ordered list of itemsets, denoted as $\langle s_1, s_2, .., s_m \rangle$, where s_j is an itemset which is also called an element of the sequence, and $s_j \subseteq I$. That is, $S = \langle s_1, s_2, ..., s_m \rangle$ and s_j is $(x_{j1}x_{j2}...x_{jk})$, where x_{it} is an item in the itemset s_i. The brackets are omitted if an itemset has only one item. An item can occur at most one time in an itemset of a sequence but it can occur multiple times in different itemsets of a sequence. The size $|S|$ of a sequence is the number of itemsets in the sequence. The length, $l(s)$, is the total number of items in the sequence. A sequence with length 1 is called an 1-sequence. A sequence database, $D = \{S_1, S_2, .., S_n\}$, is a set of tuples $\langle sid, s \rangle$, where sid is a sequence identifier and S_k is an input sequence. A sequence $\alpha = \langle X_1, X_2, .., X_n \rangle$ is called a subsequence of another sequence $\beta = \langle Y_1, Y_2, .., Y_m \rangle$ $(n \leq m)$, and β is called a super sequence of α if there exist an integer $1 \leq i_1 < ... < i_n \leq m$ such that $X_1 \subseteq Y_{i\,1}, ..., \subseteq X_n \subseteq Y_{i\,n}$. A tuple (sid, S) is said to contain a sequence S_a if S is a super sequence of S_a. The support of a sequence S_a in a sequence database SDB is the number of the sequence in SDB that contains S_a. Given a support threshold, min_sup, a sequence S_a is a frequent sequence in the sequence database if the support of the sequence S_a is no less than a minimum support threshold. The problem of sequential pattern mining is to find the complete set of frequent sequential patterns in the database satisfying a minimum support.

2.2 Related Work

In sequential pattern mining, GSP [1] mines sequential patterns based on an Apriori-like approach by generating and testing all candidate subsequences. This is inefficient and ineffective. To overcome this problem, a projection growth based approach, called FreeSpan [6] and PrefixSpan [10] were developed. In SPADE [14], a vertical id-list data format was presented and the frequent sequence enumeration was performed by a simple join on id lists. SPADE can be considered as an extension of vertical format based frequent pattern mining. SPAM [2] utilizes depth first traversal of the search space combined with a vertical bitmap representation to store each sequence. WSpan [13] was the first weighted sequential pattern mining algorithm to consider weight of items within sequences.

3 Weighted Sequential Support Affinity Pattern Mining

We suggest an efficient Weighted Sequential support Affinity pattern mining (WSAffinity) algorithm based on the pattern growth approach. A sequential s-confidence measure is defined to reflect the overall support among items within the sequential pattern. The main approach of the WSAffinity is to push sequential s-confidence into the weighted sequential pattern mining algorithm and prune uninteresting sequential patterns based on the pattern growth approach.

Table 1. Example of a sequence database

Sequence ID	Sequence
10	$\langle$a (abc) (ac) d (cf)$\rangle$
20	$\langle$(ad) abc (bcd) (ae) bcd$\rangle$
30	$\langle$a(ef) b (ab) c (df) ac$\rangle$
40	$\langle$ac (bc) eg (af) acb (ch) (ef)$\rangle$
50	$\langle$ba (ab) (cd) eg (hf)$\rangle$
60	$\langle$a (abd) bc (he)$\rangle$

3.1 The Sequential ws-Confidence

Definition 3.1 Sequential support-confidence (S-confidence)

Support confidence (s-confidence) of a sequential pattern $S = \langle s_1, s_2, ..., s_m \rangle$ and s_j is $(x_{j1}x_{j2}...x_{jk})$, where x_{it} is an item in the itemset s_i, denoted as sequential s-confidence, is a measure that reflects the overall support affinity among items within the sequence. It is the ratio of the minimum support of items within this pattern to the maximum support of items within the sequential pattern. That is, this measure is defined as

$$S\text{-conf}(S) = \frac{\text{Min}_{1 \leq m' \leq m, \, 1 \leq k' \leq legnth(s_{m'})} \{\text{support}((x_{m'k'} \subseteq s_{m'}))\}}{\text{Max}_{1 \leq m'' \leq m, \, 1 \leq k'' \leq legnth(s_{m''})} \{\text{support}((x_{m''k''} \subseteq s_{m''}))\}}$$

Definition 3.2 Sequential support affinity pattern

A sequential pattern is a sequential support affinity pattern if the s-confidence of the sequential pattern is no less than a minimum s-confidence (min_sconf). In other words, a sequential pattern S is a sequential support affinity pattern if and only if |S| > 0 and s-confidence (S) ≥ min_sconf.

Example 1: consider a pattern $S = \{\langle AB \rangle \langle AC \rangle \langle ABC \rangle \langle AE \rangle\}$ and $S` = \{\langle BC \rangle \langle BD \rangle \langle BCD \rangle \langle BF \rangle\}$. Assume that a min_sconf is 0.5, support ({A}) = 2, support ({B}) = 5, support ({C}) = 8, support ({D}) = 4, support ({E}) = 5, and support ({F}) = 6, where support (X) is the support value of a sequential pattern X. Then, the sequential s-confidence (S) is 0.25 (2/8) and s-confidence (S`) is 0.5 (4/8). Therefore, sequential pattern S is not a sequential support affinity pattern but pattern S` is a sequential support affinity pattern.

Property 1. Anti-monotone property of sequential s-confidence

The anti-monotone property of sequential s-confidence is similar to that of the support measure used in frequent pattern mining. If the s-confidence of a sequential pattern S is no less than a min_sconf, sequential s-confidence of every subset of the sequential pattern S is also no less than the min_sconf.

Lemma 1. Sequential s-confidence has the anti-monotonic property

Given a sequential pattern, $S = \langle s_1, s_2, \ldots, s_m \rangle$ and s_j is $(x_{j1}x_{j2}\ldots x_{jk})$, where x_{it} is an item in the itemset s_i, $\text{Max}_{(1 \leq m'' \leq m, 1 \leq k'' \leq \text{length}(S_{m''}))}\{\text{support}(\{x_{m''k''} \subseteq s_{m''}\})\}$ of a sequential pattern S is always greater than or equal to that of a sub-sequence of the sequential pattern S and $\text{Min}_{(1 \leq m' \leq m, 1 \leq k' \leq \text{length}(S_{m'}))}\{\text{support}(\{x_{m'k'} \subseteq s_{m'}\})\}$ of the pattern S is always no less than that of a subset of the sequential pattern S. Therefore, we know that

$$S\text{-conf}(S) = \frac{\text{Min}_{1 \leq m' \leq m, 1 \leq k' \leq legnth(s_{m'})}\{\text{support}(\{x_{m'k'} \subseteq s_{m'}\})\}}{\text{Max}_{1 \leq m'' \leq m, 1 \leq k'' \leq legnth(s_{m''})}\{\text{support}(\{x_{m''k''} \subseteq s_{m''}\})\}}$$

$$\leq \frac{\text{Min}_{1 \leq m' \leq m-1, 1 \leq k' \leq legnth(s_{m'})}\{\text{support}(\{x_{m'k'} \subseteq s_{m'}\})\}}{\text{Max}_{1 \leq m'' \leq m-1, 1 \leq k'' \leq legnth(s_{m''})}\{\text{support}(\{x_{m''k''} \subseteq s_{m''}\})\}}$$

$$\leq \frac{\text{Min}_{1 \leq m'-2 \leq m, 1 \leq k' \leq legnth(s_{m'})}\{\text{support}(\{x_{m'k'} \subseteq s_{m'}\})\}}{\text{Max}_{1 \leq m''-2 \leq m, 1 \leq k'' \leq legnth(s_{m''})}\{\text{support}(\{x_{m''k''} \subseteq s_{m''}\})\}}$$

That is, if the s-confidence of a sequential pattern is greater than or equal to a min_sconf, so is every subset of size m - 1. Therefore, the sequential s-confidence can be used to prune the exponential search space.

Definition 3.3. Weight Range (WR) and Maximum Weight (MaxW)

A weight of an item is a non-negative real number that shows the importance of each item. The weight of each item is assigned to reflect the importance of each item in the sequence database. Weights of items are given within a specific range (weight range) of weights. A Maximum Weight (MaxW) is defined as a value of the maximum weight of items in a sequence database or a projected sequence database.

Weights for items are given with $a_w \leq w \leq b_w$ according to items' importance or priority. The weights with $a_w \leq w \leq b_w$ are normalized as $\min_w \leq w \leq \max_w$ and the normalized weights can be used in the mining process. For example, in market basket data, prices of items are considered as a weight factor and the prices of items can be normalized. Based on the definition, items, itemsets and a sequence have their own weights.

Table 2. Example sets of items with different WRs

Item (min_sup = 2)	$\langle a \rangle$	$\langle b \rangle$	$\langle c \rangle$	$\langle d \rangle$	$\langle e \rangle$	$\langle f \rangle$	$\langle g \rangle$	$\langle h \rangle$
Support	6	6	6	5	4	4	2	3
Weight ($0.7 \leq WR_1 \leq 1.3$)	1.1	1.0	0.9	1.0	0.7	0.9	1.3	1.2
Weight ($0.7 \leq WR_2 \leq 0.9$)	0.9	0.75	0.8	0.85	0.75	0.7	0.85	0.8
Weight ($0.4 \leq WR_3 \leq 0.8$)	0.6	0.8	0.5	0.6	0.4	0.8	0.5	0.6
Weight ($0.2 \leq WR_4 \leq 0.6$)	0.5	0.2	0.6	0.4	0.6	0.3	0.5	0.3

Example 2: Given the sequence database in Table, example sets of items with different weights in Table 2, and minimum support = 2, the set of items in the database, i.e., length-1 subsequences in the form of "item:support" is <a>:6, <b>:6, <c>:6, <d>:5, <e>:4, <f>:4, <g>:2, <h>:3. When WR_3 is used, the weight of a sequence <a (abc) (ac) d (cf)> is 0.66 ((0.6 + 0.8 + 0.5 + 0.6 + 0.8) / 5). Max_W of the different WR is the maximum value of a WR. For example, the Maximum Weight (Max_W) of WR_1, WR_2, WR_3 and WR_4 is 1.3, 0.9, 0.8 and 0.6 respectively.

Definition 3.4. Weighted Sequential Support Affinity pattern

A sequence is a weighted sequential affinity pattern if the following pruning conditions are satisfied.

Pruning condition 1: (Weighted support (support * MaxW ≥ min_sup))

The weighted support of multiplying the sequence's support with a maximum weight among items in the sequence database is no less than a minimum support.

Pruning condition 2: (s-confidence ≥ min_sconf)

The sequential pattern is a sequential support affinity pattern if the s-confidence of a pattern is greater than or equal to a min_sconf.

3.2 Mining Weighted Sequential Support Affinity Patterns

In this section, we show how to mine weighted sequential support affinity patterns by using a prefix-based projection approach. We use the sequence database SDB in Table 1 and apply WR_3 as weights of items from Table 2. Given a minimum support of 2, and min_sconf, 0.7, mining weighted sequential support affinity patterns is performed as follows.

Step 1: Find length-1 weighted sequential patterns

Scan the sequence database once, check the weight of each item and find all the weighted frequent items in sequences. After the first scan of the sequence database, length-1 frequent sequential patterns are <a> : 6, <b> : 6, <c> : 6, <d> : 5, <e> : 4, <f> : 4, <g> : 2 and <h> : 3. The weight list is <a:0.6, b:0.8, c:0.5, d:0.6, e: 0.4, f:0.8, g:0.5, h:0.6> and the maximum weight (Max_W) is 0.8. From pruning by weighted support constraint, item "g" is removed because the weighted support (1.6) of multiplying the support (2) of item "g" with a Max_W (0.8) is less than a min_sup (2). After the projected database is generated from the sequence database, our approach mines weighted sequential affinity patterns from the projected databases recursively.

Step 2: Divide search space

The complete set of weighted sequential patterns can be partitioned into the following seven subsets having prefix: (1) <a>; (2) <b>, (3) <c>, (4) <d>, (5) <e>, (6) <f>, and (7) <h>.

Step 3: Find subsets of sequential patterns

The subsets of sequential patterns can be mined by constructing the corresponding set of projected databases and mining them recursively.

1. Find weighted sequential patterns with the prefix <a>

We only collect the sequences which have the prefix <a>. Additionally, in a sequence containing <a>, only the subsequence prefixed with the first occurrence of <a> should be considered. For example, in sequence <a (abc) (ac) d (cf)>, only the subsequence <(abc) (ac) d (cf)> is considered and in sequence <(ad) abc (bcd) (ae) bcd>, only the sequence <(~d) abc (bcd) (ae) bcde> is collected. The sequences in sequence database SDB containing <a> are projected with regards to <a> to form the <a>-projected database, which consists of six suffix sequences: <(abc) (ac) d (cf)>, <(~d) abc (bcd) (ae) bcd>, <(ef) b (ab) c (df) ac>, <c (bc) e (af) acb (ch) (ef)>, <(ab) (cd) (hf)> and <(abd) bc (he)>. By scanning the <a> projected database once, its locally frequent items are a:6, b:6, c:6, d:5, e:4, f:4, h:3, (~b):4, (~c):1, (~d):1, (~e):1 and (~f):1. In WSAffinity, the pruning conditions defined in definition 3.4 are used. The local items, (~c):1, (~d):1, (~e):1 and (~f):1 are removed by weighted support constraint since the weighted support (0.8) of multiplying the support (1) of the sequences with MaxW (0.8) is less than a minimum support (2). In addition, a local item "e:4" is pruned by sequential s-confidence. The candidate pattern, from a local item "e:4" and a conditional prefix "a" is <ae>:4 and the sequential s-confidence (0.667) of the candidate sequential pattern <ae>:4 is less than the min_sconf (0.7). Moreover, the candidate pattern <ah>:3 is also pruned by sequential s-confidence e The s-confidence of the sequential pattern is 0.5 which is less than the min_sconf (0.7). All the length-2 sequential patterns prefixed with <a> are: <aa>:6, <ab>:6, <ac>:6, <ad>:5 <af>:4 and <(ab)>:4.

Note that previous sequential pattern mining algorithms only consider a support in each projected database so sequences <(ac)>:1 <(ad)>:1 and <(ae)>:1 are only pruned because they are not frequent. The recently developed WSpan algorithm uses weighted support constraint. However, in WSAffinity, before constructing the next projected database, sequential s-confidence is applied to prune sequential weak affinity patterns. The final <a>-projected database is generated as follows: <(abc) (ac) d (cf)>, <(~d) abc (bcd) abcd>, <fb (ab) c (df) ac>, <c (bc) (af) acbcf>, <(ab) (cd) f> and <(abd) bc>. Recursively, all the sequential patterns with prefix <a> can be partitioned into six subsets prefixed with: 1) <aa>, 2) <ab>, 3) <ac>, 4) <ad>, 5) <af> and 6) <(ab)>. These subsets can be mined by constructing respective projected databases and mining each recursively as follows.

1) The <aa> projected database consists of six suffix subsequences prefixed with <(~bc) (ac) d (cf)>, <bc (bcd) abcd>, <(~b) c (df) ac>, < (~f) acbcf>, < (~b) (cd) f>, and <(~bd) bc>. By scanning the <aa> projected database once, its local items are a:4, b:3, c:6, d:4, f:4, (~b):4, (~c):1 and (~f):1. The local items, "(~c):1" and "(~f):1", are pruned by weighted support constraint. The <aa> projected database returns the following sequential patterns: <aaa>:4, <aab>:3, <aac>:6, <aad>:4, <aaf>:4 and <a(ab)>:4. Sequential s-confidence of these patterns is no less than the min_sconf. Recursively, weighted sequential patterns with the prefix <aa> are partitioned and mined.

2) The <ab> projected database consists of six suffix subsequences prefixed with <ab>: <(~c) (ac) d (cf)>, <c (bcd) abcd>, <(ab) c (df) ac>, <(~c) (af) acbcf>, <(cd) f>

and <(~d) bc>. By scanning the <ab> projected database once, we obtain its local items: a: 4, b:4, c:6, d:4, f:4, (~c):2, and (~d):1. Local items, (~c):2, and (~d):1, are pruned by weighted support constraints because the weighted support value (1.6/0.8) of multiplying support (2/1) of the items with a MaxW (0.8) is less than the min_sup (2). In WSAffinity, the sequential candidate pattern, <abf>:4 is removed by sequential s-confidence because the sequential s-confidence (0.67) of pattern <abf> is less than a min_sconf (0.7). The final weighted sequential patterns are <aba>:4, <abb>:4 <abc>:4 and <abd>:4. Recursively, sequential patterns with prefix <ab> are partitioned and mined.

3) The <ac> projected database consists of five suffix subsequences prefixed with <ac>: <(ac) d (cf)>, <(bcd) abcd>, <(df) ac>, <(bc) (af) acbcf>, and <(~d) f>. By scanning the <ac> projected database once, its local items are a:4, b:2, c:4, d:3, f:4, (~d):1 and (~f):1. Sequential candidate patterns, <acb>:2, <a(cd)>:1, and <a(cf)>:1, are pruned by weighted support constraint. The weighted sequential patterns <aca>: 4, <acc>:4 <acd>:3 and <acf>:4 are generated. Recursively, weighted sequential patterns with prefix <ac> are partitioned and mined.

4) The <ad> projected database consists of five suffix subsequences prefixed with <ad>: <(cf)>, <abcd>, <(~f) ac>, <f> and <bc>. By scanning the <ad> projected database once, its local items are a:2, b:2, c:4, d:1, f:2, and (~f):1. Among these candidate patterns, the only weighted frequent item is c:4 which satisfies sequential s-confidence, so <ad> projected database returns one sequential pattern: <adc>:4. Recursively, weighted sequential patterns with the prefix <ad> are partitioned and mined.

5) The <af> projected database consists of two suffix subsequences prefixed with <af>: <b (ab) c (df) ac>, and <acbcf>. By scanning the <af> projected database once, its local items are a:2, b:2, c:2, d:1, and f:2. All local items are pruned because they do not satisfy the pruning condition1 in definition 3.4.

6) The <(ab)> projected database consists of four suffix subsequences prefixed with <(ab)>: <(~c) (ac) d (cf)>, <c (df) ac>, <(cd) f> and <(~d) bc>. By scanning the <(ab)> projected database once, its local items are a:2, b:1, c:4 d:3, f:3, (~c):1 and (~d):1. Local items "a:2", "b:1" "(~c):1 and "(~d):1" are pruned by the weighted support constraint. The candidate pattern "(ab)f" is pruned by the sequential s-confidence. Finally, the sequential pattern generated by the <(ab)> projected database are   <(ab)c>:4 and <(ab)d>:3. Recursively, weighted sequential patterns with prefix <(ab)> are partitioned and mined.

2. Mine remaining weighted sequential patterns

This can be done by constructing the <b>, <c>, <d>, <e>, <f> and <h> projected databases and mining them as shown above.

Step 4: The set of weighted sequential patterns is the collection of patterns found in the above recursive mining process.

You can see that in this example, the number of weighted sequential patterns is fewer than the number of sequential pattern generated in the previous sequential pattern mining algorithms. Table 3 shows examples of pruning candidate patterns.

Table 3. Examples of pruning candidate patterns

Candidate patterns	Weighted support	Sequential s-confidence
<ae> : 4	3.2 (0.8 * 4)	Pruned 0.667 (4/6)
<ah> : 3	2.4 (0.8 * 3)	Pruned 0.5 (3/6)
<acb> : 2	Pruned 1.6 (0.8 * 2)	1 (6/6)
<adb> : 2	Pruned 1.6 (0.8 * 2)	0.83 (5/6)
<(ab)c> : 4	3.2 (0.8 * 4)	1 (6/6)
<(ab)f> : 3	2.4 (0.8 * 3)	Pruned 0.667 (4/6)

4 Performance Evaluation

We report experimental results on the performance of WSAffinity in comparison with recently developed algorithms: SPAM [2] and WSpan [13]. SPAM is currently the fastest among sequential pattern mining algorithms and WSpan is the first weighted sequential pattern mining algorithm. We used datasets generated by the IBM dataset generator. Table 4 shows parameters and their meanings. More detail information can be found in [1]. WSAffinity was written in C++. Experiments were performed on a sparcv9 processor operating at 1062 MHz, with 2048MB of memory on a Unix machine.

Table 4. Parameters for IBM Quest Data Generator

Symbol	Meaning
D	Number of customers in 000s in the dataset
C	Average number of transactions per customer
T	Average number of items per transaction
S	Average length of maximal sequences
I	Average length of transactions within the maximal sequences
N	Number of different items in 000s

4.1 Comparison of WSAffinity with SPAM and WSpan

D1C10T5S8I5 dataset: In this test, weights of items are set as 0.3-0.6. WSAffinity generates fewer sequential patterns than SPAM and WSpan. Particularly, smaller sequential patterns are generated as the sequential s-confidence in Fig. 1, In Fig. 2, we can see that WSAffinity is faster than SPAM and WSpan. In Fig, 1 and Fig 2, the sequential s-confidence is only used to prune weighted sequential patterns with weak support affinity. WSAffinity shows better performance than SPAM and WSpan. Specifically, the performance gaps increase as the minimum s-confidence increases. SPAM generates a huge number of sequential patterns with a minimum support of less than 10%.

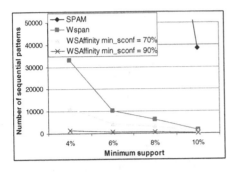

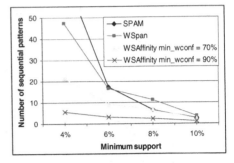

Fig. 1. Num of patterns   **Fig. 2.** Runtime

4.2 Scalability Test

The DxC2.5T5S4I2.5 dataset was used to test scalability with the number of sequences in the sequence database. In this test, we set a minimum support as 0.4% and weights of items from 0.1 to 0.5. From the performance test, WSAffinity scales much better than WSpan and becomes better as sequential s-confidence is increased WSpan shows linear scalability with the number of transactions from 20k to 100k. However, WSAffinity is much more scalable than WSpan. In Fig. 3, we can see that WSAffinity has much better scalability in terms of number of sequences and becomes faster as the sequential s-confidence is increased.

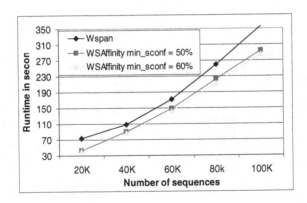

Fig. 3. Scalability test (Min_sup = 0.4%)

5 Conclusion

In this paper, we studied the problem of mining weighted sequential patterns. We introduced sequential s-confidence measure and the concept of weighted sequential support affinity patterns by using the measure. Our main goal in this framework is to push sequential s-confidence into the weighted sequential pattern mining algorithm based on the pattern growth method. The sequential s-confidence can be used to avoid generating spurious sequential patterns that involve items from the different support level. The performance analysis shows better performance than SPAM and WSpan.

References

[1] R. Agrawal, R. Srikant, *Mining Sequential Patterns*, ICDE, 1995.

[2] J. Ayres, J. Gehrke, T. Yiu, and J. Flannick, *Sequential Pattern Mining using A Bitmap Representation*, SIGKDD'02, 2002.

[3] D. Y. Chiu, Y. Wu, A. L.P. Chen, *An Efficient Algorithm for Mining Frequent Sequences by a New Strategy without Support Counting*, ICDE'04, 2004.

[4] M. Ester, *A Top-Down Method for Mining Most Specific Frequent Patterns in Biological Sequence Data*, SDM'04, 2004.

[5] M. Garofalakis, R. Rastogi, K. shim. *SPIRIT: Sequential pattern mining with regular expression constraints*, VLDB'99, 1999.

[6] J. Han, J. Pei, B. Mortazavi-Asi, Q. Chen, U. Dayal, M. C. Hsu, *FreeSpan: Frequent Pattern-Projected Sequential Pattern Mining*, SIGKDD'00, 2000.

[7] H. C. Kum, J. Pei, W. Wang, D. Duncan, *ApproxMAP: Approximate Mining of Consensus Sequential Patterns*, SDM'03, 2003.

[8] H. A. Lorincz, J. F. Boulicaut, *Mining frequent sequential patterns under regular expressions: a highly adaptive strategy for pushing constraints*, SDM'03, 2003.

[9] J. Pei, J. Han, W. Wang, *Mining Sequential Patterns with Constraints in Large Databases*, CIKM'02, 2002.

[10] J. Pei, J. Han, J. Wang, H. Pinto, etc., *Mining Sequential Patterns by Pattern-Growth: The PrefixSpan Approach*, IEEE Transactions on Knowledge and Data Engineering, Oct, 2004.rgrg

[11] H. Pinto, J. Han, J. Pei, K. Wang, *Multi-dimensional Sequence Pattern Mining*, CIKM'01, 2001.

[12] U. Yun, and J. J. Leggett, *WFIM: Weighted Frequent Itemset Mining with a weight range and a minimum weight*, International conference on SIAM Data Mining (SDM`05), April 2005.

[13] U. Yun, and J. J. Leggett, *WSpan: Weighted Sequential pattern mining in large sequence databases*, International conference on IEEE Intelligent Systems (IEEE IS`06), *2006*

[14] M.Zaki, *SPADE: An efficient algorithm for mining frequent sequences.* Machine Learning, 2001.

Lossless Data Hiding for High Embedding Capacity

Hyeran Lee[1] and Kyunghyune Rhee[2]

[1] Department of Computer Science, Pukyong National University,
599-1, Daeyeon3-Dong, Nam-Gu, Busan 608-737, Republic of Korea
hrlee@pknu.ac.kr
[2] Division of Electronic, Computer and Telecommunication Engineering,
Pukyong National University
khrhee@pknu.ac.kr

Abstract. Embedding distortions create problems in some areas such as medical, astronomical, and military imagery. Lossless data hiding is an exact restoration approach for recovering the original image from the stego image. In this paper, we present a lossless data embedding technique with a higher embedding capacity. We propose two lossless data embedding methods; first, a part of the unusable groups U is changed into the usable groups. Secondly, a discrimination function f is modified to improve the embedding capacity, and we are changed the value of an accumulating block in order to improve the embedding capacity. We provide experimental results to demonstrate the effectiveness of our proposed algorithm.

Keywords: Data Hiding, Watermarking, High Capacity, Authentication, Lossless.

1 Introduction

There has been an explosion in the growth of multimedia distribution and communications in the past few years, creating a demand for content protection techniques in which it became very easy to obtain, replicate, and distribute digital content without any loss in quality[1,2]. The digital image has to be provided at the end point in digital form[3]. It is always possible to make illegal copies of digital images. In general, robust watermarks are embedded in the host image such that owner of image is protected by his copyright [4]. A copyright owner distributes his digital image with his invisible watermark embedded in it. Watermarking systems can be classified according to many different criteria. One of them is classified into visible and invisible ones. Visible watermarks cause noticeable changes in the original image when they are embedded, whereas invisible watermarks do not create any perceptible artifacts. Invisible watermarks are divided into robust, fragile, and semi-fragile watermarks. The objective of robust watermarks is to control access and to prevent illegal copying of copyrighted image. It is an important application, especially for digital

S. Madria et al. (Eds.): ICDCIT 2006, LNCS 4317, pp. 424–437, 2006.

image, because digital copies can be easily made, they are perfect reproductions of the original, and they can be easily and inexpensively distributed over the Internet with no quality degradation. In contrast, fragile watermarks can be used to confirm authenticity of a digital content [5]. They can also be used in applications to figure out how the digital content was modified or which portion of it has been tampered with. Semi-fragile watermarks [6] are designed to survive standard transformations, such as lossy compression, but they become invalid if a major change has taken place [7]. In a point of view of data hiding, in most cases, the cover image will experience some permanent distortion due to data hiding and cannot be inverted back to the original image. In some application such as law enforcement and medical image systems, it is desired to reverse the marked image back to the original image after the hidden data are retrieved [8]. We employ the lossless data hiding to satisfy this requirement. In this paper, we present the authentication and the restoration of image using lossless data embedding. We focus on lossless data hiding for high embedding capacity. Fridrich et al. [9] and Honsinger et al. [10] used the spread spectrum approach to add the information payload with the host signal. The methods are robust to a wide range of distortions, but due to use of modulo arithmetic, salt-and-pepper noise are introduced and the embedding capacity is low. Goljan et al. [11] divided the image into disjoint groups (Regular, Singular, and Unusable). The whole image is scanned and Regular-Singular groups are checked whether there is a need to apply the flip operation while embedding information. Though this method involves low and invertible distortions, the capacity is not very high. Our proposed algorithm is modify the above scheme [11] to improve embedding capacity. The rest of the paper is structured as follows. In the next Section, we introduce the lossless data hiding and overflow and Section 3 presents the proposed lossless data hiding method for high embedding capacity. In Section 4, simulation results are shown and lastly, conclusions are given in Section 5.

2   Lossless Data Hiding and Overflow

2.1   Lossless Data Hiding

Watermarking for valuable and sensitive images such as military and medical image presents a major challenge to most of watermarking algorithms. Lossless data hiding embeds invisible data into a digital image in a reversible fashion. As a basic requirement, the quality degradation on the digital image after data embedding should be low. Intriguing feature of lossless data hiding is the reversibility, that is, when the digital image has been authenticated, one can remove the embedded data to restore the original image. The motivation of lossless data hiding is providing a distortion-free data embedding [12]. In sensitive images such as military and medical image, every bit of information is important. Lossless data hiding will provide the original image when the digital image is authenticated.

In scientific research, military, and some other fields, the original media are very difficult and expensive to obtain. Therefore, it is also desired to have the original media inverted back after the hidden data are extracted. The marking techniques satisfying this requirement are referred to as reversible, lossless, distortion-free, or invertible data hiding techniques. We prefer to use the term "lossless data hiding." Celik et al. [6] classified the lossless watermarking techniques in two types. In the first type of algorithms a spread spectrum signal corresponding to the information payload is superimposed on the host signal during encoding. During decoding process, the payload is removed from the watermarked image in the restoration step. The advantage of these algorithms is the use of spread spectrum signal as payload and the increase of the robustness. But the disadvantages are they create salt-and-pepper artifacts in watermarked image due to modulo arithmetic, and offer very limited capacity. In the second type of algorithms some features of the original image are replaced or overwritten with the watermark payload. The original portions of the image that will be replaced by watermark payload are compressed and passed as a part of the embedded payload during embedding. During the decoding process this compressed payload-part is extracted and decompressed. Thus the original image is recovered by replacing the modified portions with these decompressed original features. The advantage of second type of algorithms is they do not suffer from salt-and-pepper artifacts. The disadvantages are they are not as robust as the first type of algorithms, and the capacity, though higher than the first type of algorithms, is still not good enough. However, algorithms of the second type are better than the first type for content authentication where fragility is more important than robustness. Our proposed algorithm belongs to the second type, and we try to solve the problem that capacity is not enough. In [1], lossless data hiding algorithms are classified into three categories: Those for fragile authentication, those for high embedding capacity, and those for semifragile authentication. The first several lossless data hiding algorithms developed at the early stage belong to the first category. In fact, the fragile authentication does not need much data to be embedded in a cover image, so the embedding capacity is relatively small, namely, the amount of embedding data is rather limited. The second category of high embedding capacity needs much larger capacity than those of the first category, however, the visual quality will be deteriorated. Semifragile authentication allows some incidental modification, say, compression within a reasonable extent. For the purpose of semifragile authentication, lossless data hiding algorithms have to be robust to compression. Our proposed algorithm belongs to the second one among the three categories.

2.2 The Problem of Overflow and Underflow

For a given image, after the embedding in image, it is possible to cause overflow and underflow problem, which means the grayscale values of some pixels in the embedded image may exceed the upper bound or the lower bound. In [10], using modulo 256 addition can avoid overflow and underflow. For instance, for an 8-bit gray image, its gray scale ranges from 0 to 255. The overflow refers to the gray scale exceeding 255, whereas the underflow refers to below 0. It is clear that either case will destroy losslessness. In [13], histogram modification is used to prevent the overflow and underflow resulting in the perturbation of the bitplanes of the integer wavelet transform (IWT) coefficients in data embedding. In [12], to avoid overflow and underflow, the algorithm only embeds data into the pixel pairs that will not lead to overflow and underflow, so a two-dimensional binary bookkeeping image is losslessly compressed and embedded as overhead. In general, lossless data embedding algorithms are need an additional overhead to avoid overflow and underflow. However, our proposed lossless data embedding algorithm needs not any overheads, since embedding process of our algorithm makes a change of pixel value within ranges from 0 to 255 for an 8-bit gray scale.

3   Lossless Data Hiding Algorithm for High Embedding Capacity

In this section, a high capacity lossless data hiding method is proposed. We modify the conventional lossless data embedding method[11] to improve the embedding capacity. In our proposed algorithm, we describe two lossless data embedding techniques. In the first technique, a part of the unusable groups U is changed into the usable groups. In the second method, discrimination function f is modified to improve the embedding capacity.

3.1   Method 1

Let us assume that the original image is a grayscale image with $M \times N$ pixels and with pixel values from the set P. For example, for an 8-bit grayscale image, $P = 0, ..., 255$. First, we divide the image into disjoint block of n adjacent pixels $G = (x_1, ..., x_n)$, $G' = (x_3, x_1, x_4, x_2, ..., x_{n-1}, x_n, x_{n-3}, x_{n-2})$. In the G', for example of $n = 4$, all pixels are divided by block of 4 pixels and are permutated with adjacent two pixels such like $(x_3, x_4, x_1, x_2), (x_7, x_8, x_5, x_6), ..., (x_{n-1}, x_n, x_{n-3}, x_{n-2})$. We define so called discrimination function f that assigns a real number $f(x_1, ..., x_n)$, to each pixel block $G = (x_1, ..., x_n)$ such like equation (1). The purpose of this function is to capture the smoothness or "regularity" of the block of pixels G.

$$f(x_1, x_2, ..., x_n) = \sum_{i=1}^{n-1} |x_{i+1} - x_i| \tag{1}$$

We use the discrimination function to classify the type of block. The type of block is classified into three different categories; Regular(R), Singular(S), and Unusable block(U). Finally, we define an invertible operation called "flipping" F. Flipping is a permutation of gray levels that entirely consists of two-cycles.

Thus, F will have the property that $F(F(x)) = x$. An example of the invertible operation F can be the permutation between 0 and 1, 2 and 3, 4 and 5, and so on. Another example is the permutation between 0 and 2, 1 and 3, 4 and 6, and so on. The amplitude of the latter flipping is stronger than the former. The amplitude A of the flipping permutation F is defined as the average change of x under the application of F:

$$A = \frac{1}{|P|} \sum_{x \in P} |x - F(x)| \tag{2}$$

We use the discrimination function f and the flipping operation F to define three types of pixel blocks:

Regular blocks: $G \in R \Leftrightarrow f(F(G)) > f(G)$

Singular blocks: $G \in S \Leftrightarrow f(F(G)) < f(G)$

Unusable blocks: $G \in U \Leftrightarrow f(F(G)) = f(G)$

For the unusable blocks U, we reclassify U blocks into Regular blocks and Singular blocks again to improve the embedding capacity

Regular blocks: $G' \in R \Leftrightarrow f(F(G')) > f(G')$

Singular blocks: $G' \in S \Leftrightarrow f(F(G')) < f(G')$

Unusable blocks: $G' \in U \Leftrightarrow f(F(G')) = f(G')$

The R and S groups are flipped into each other under the flipping operation F, while the unusable groups U do not change their status, $F(R) = S, F(S) = R, and F(U) = U$. As a data embedding method, by assigning binary 1 and 0 to R and S blocks respectively, 1 bit can be embedded into each R or S block. The U block is skipped. The algorithm losslessly compresses the RS-vector C as an overhead for bookkeeping usage in reconstruction of the original image late. If the bit to be embedded does not match the type of block under consideration, the flipping operation F is applied to the block to obtain a match. We take the compressed RS-vector C, append the message bits to it, and embed the resulting bit-stream in the image. We use a theoretical estimate Cap' for the real capacity [8].

$$Cap' = N_R + N_S + N_R \log \left(\frac{N_R}{N_R + N_S} \right) + N_s \log \left(\frac{N_S}{N_R + N_S} \right)$$

For data extraction, the algorithm scans the marked image in the same manner as in the data embedding. From the resultant RS-vector, the embedded data can be extracted. The overhead portion well be used to reconstruct the original image, the remaining portion is the payload. Figure 1 shows embedding process of method 1.

3.2 Method 2

We only describe the difference from the method 1. The discrimination function f is used to capture the smoothness or "regularity" of the block. In the method 2, we changed a discrimination function to be used in the method 2 as shown in equation (3).

$$f'(x_1, x_2, ..., x_{M \times N}) = \sum_{k=0}^{M \times N/b-1} \sum_{j=0}^{b/n-1} \sum_{i=1}^{n-1} |x_{bk+4j+i+1} - x_{bk+4j+i}| \quad (b = 64, 128, 256)$$

(3)

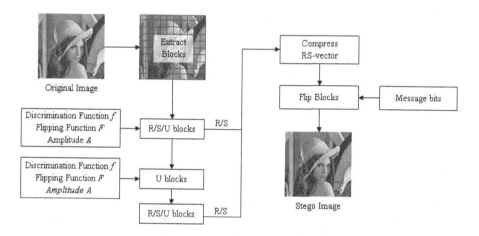

Fig. 1. Embedding process of method 1

As shown in (3) discrimination function f' accumulates the value until the next bth block. In general, the numbers of R and S type are bigger than those of U type in regular image. Similarly the number of R type is bigger than that of S type. The U type of block can change the R and S type using (3). Because the number of R and S type of block are bigger than those of U type in generally, in order to continue this condition, we use accumulating of value of blocks. The increasing of R and S type can improve the capacity, where b is a number of accumulating blocks. The more the value of b is increased, the more capacity is increased. In the method 1, the blocks are classified into three categories R, S, and U. Then the U blocks are reclassified into three categories R, S, and U again to improve the embedding capacity. But in the method 2, the U blocks are not classified again. We used original three block types. The remaining is same as method 1. Figure 2 shows embedding process of method 2.

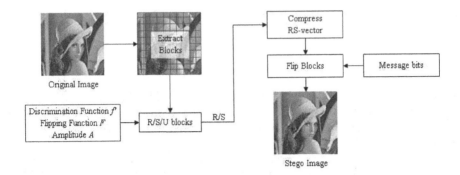

Fig. 2. Embedding process of method 2

4   Experimental Result and Discussions

In this section, we present the experimental results of the proposed algorithm and then compare the results with other algorithms. We apply the proposed method to various standard grayscale test images, including "Lena", "Pepper", "Baboon", "Airplane", "Fishingboat", "Goldhill", "Barbara", "Opera", "Peppers", "Pills", "Pentagon", "Watch", and "Newyork" respectively as shown in Fig. 3. We use grayscale 256×256 pixel images with 8-bit grayscale levels per pixel. We have used JBIG for compression.

4.1   Experimental Results

Table 1 shows the experimental results we have obtained in the proposed method 1. Table 2, 3, and 4 show the experimental results we have obtained in the proposed method 2 with different b value respectively. These results show that the proposed algorithm offers lossless data hiding with higher capacity and imperceptible artifacts.

4.2   Comparison with Other Algorithms

Table 5 shows the experimental results of [11]. Table 6, 7, and 8 are comparing capacity and PSNR offered by [11] and the proposed algorithm. The method [11] divides pixels into R, S, and U blocks. U blocks are not used. On the other hand, our proposed method uses the part of U blocks to embed the data. Figure 9 and 10 are show the graph of comparing capacity and PSNR between the method of [11] and the proposed one, respectively. Hence, the experimental results prove that our proposed algorithm is better, since it gives higher capacity for almost all images and reasonable PSNR value. The capacity of both proposed methods is much better than [11]. Method 2 using accumulating value of blocks is getting better than Method 1.

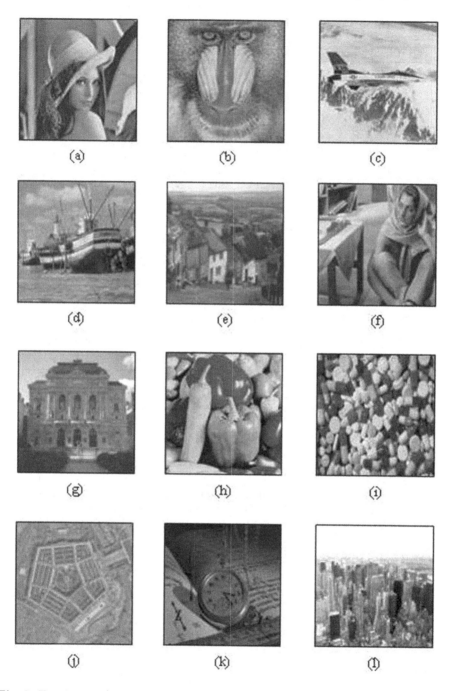

Fig. 3. Test images (256 × 256) (a) Lena, (b) Baboon, (c) Airplane, (d) Fishingboat, (e) Goldhill, (f) Barbara, (g) Opera, (h) Peppers, (i) Pills, (j) Pentagon, (k) Watch, (l) Newyork

Table 1. Estimated capacity Cap' for test images (Method 1)

Test image name	Estimated capacity Cap' for amplitude $a=1,...,7$						
(256× 256)	1	2	3	4	5	6	7
Lena	1211	4068	5870	7408	8099	9272	9738
Baboon	120	337	701	985	1322	1822	2276
Airplane	1032	2501	3540	3875	4102	4107	4172
Fishingboat	494	1306	2076	2738	3325	3799	4060
Goldhill	203	690	1370	1993	2694	3339	3828
Barbara	189	667	1062	1618	1894	2392	2493
Opera	690	1828	2912	3570	3934	4308	4731
Pepper	666	2142	3322	4251	5181	5418	5852
Pills	223	830	1533	2237	2997	3412	3908
Pentagon	189	634	1355	2003	2512	3136	3812
Watch	1000	1764	2193	2507	2759	2729	2936
Newyork	52	199	358	624	754	1067	1355
Average Cap'/MxN	1.71%	3.14%	4.36%	5.32%	6.05%	6.71%	6.62%
Average PSNR(dB)	52.95	46.46	42.66	39.98	37.9	36.23	34.92

Table 2. Estimated capacity Cap' for test images (Method 2, $b=64$)

Test image name	Estimated capacity Cap' for amplitude $a=1,...,7$						
(256× 256)	1	2	3	4	5	6	7
Lena	3944	7670	9618	11266	11938	12380	12086
Baboon	989	2004	3776	5032	6150	7161	8374
Airplane	4519	7197	8755	9731	10663	11142	11158
Fishingboat	2340	5343	7080	9427	10642	11190	11609
Goldhill	1197	3491	5411	7050	8612	10150	11374
Barbara	1008	3268	4405	5901	6357	7375	7895
Opera	3459	6746	9331	10607	11751	11812	11796
Pepper	4342	8543	10852	12081	12994	13400	13470
Pills	2265	5193	7800	9699	11304	11671	12304
Pentagon	1377	3980	6811	8286	9988	10609	11681
Watch	4516	6531	8402	9464	9681	9704	10290
Newyork	274	905	1618	2839	3362	4384	5095
Average Cap'/MxN	3.84%	7.74%	10.66%	12.89%	14.42%	15.38%	16.17%
Average PSNR(dB)	49.51	43.63	40.19	37.72	35.79	34.19	32.91

Table 3. Estimated capacity Cap' for test images (Method 2, b=128)

Test image name (256× 256)	Estimated capacity Cap' for amplitude a=1,...,7						
	1	2	3	4	5	6	7
Lena	6375	11081	13557	14118	14576	14981	15091
Baboon	1852	3094	6580	7504	9040	10155	11140
Airplane	5670	8703	10155	11101	11810	12504	12364
Fishingboat	4096	7962	10177	11709	12374	12915	13416
Goldhill	2040	5273	7088	9010	10476	12247	13185
Barbara	1685	5234	6160	8039	8548	9689	10106
Opera	5166	9078	11753	12341	13260	13223	12982
Pepper	6112	10423	12136	13317	13832	14318	14180
Pills	4159	8182	11141	12195	13447	13811	14074
Pentagon	2396	6385	9518	11108	12635	12691	13702
Watch	6816	9347	11577	12361	12510	12373	12463
Newyork	433	1431	2571	4005	4984	6148	7028
Average Cap'/MxN	5.95%	10.96%	14.29%	16.12%	17.48%	18.45%	19.04%
Average PSNR(dB)	49.87	43.90	40.36	37.86	35.92	34.34	32.99

Table 4. Estimated capacity Cap' for test images (Method 2, b=256)

Test image name (256× 256)	Estimated capacity Cap' for amplitude a=1,...,7						
	1	2	3	4	5	6	7
Lena	7673	12632	14436	14030	15071	15450	15603
Baboon	2843	4360	8075	9242	10673	11352	12468
Airplane	8649	11086	13045	12786	13845	14228	13912
Fishingboat	7777	11388	13181	13858	14282	14462	15164
Goldhill	2952	7075	8691	10697	12192	13334	14103
Barbara	4142	8409	9972	11779	11856	12585	12727
Opera	8501	12439	13734	14082	14885	14887	14746
Pepper	9723	12756	13766	14421	14764	14847	14810
Pills	6285	11529	13510	13781	14871	15315	15292
Pentagon	4348	9399	12187	14123	14431	14395	15121
Watch	10761	13482	14029	15035	14490	14138	14758
Newyork	630	2199	4119	6492	7807	8514	8814
Average Cap'/MxN	9.45%	14.85%	17.64%	19.12%	20.24%	20.79%	21.30%
Average PSNR(dB)	49.92	43.95	40.40	37.90	35.95	34.37	33.02

Table 5. Estimated capacity Cap' for test images [11]

Test image name	Estimated capacity Cap' for amplitude $a=1,...,7$						
(256× 256)	1	2	3	4	5	6	7
Lena	865	2480	3414	4144	4497	5085	5342
Baboon	157	390	850	1084	1472	2011	2485
Airplane	1257	2913	3915	4280	4436	4419	4464
Fishingboat	584	1494	2320	3027	3639	4012	4327
Goldhill	237	776	1501	2152	2918	3574	4069
Barbara	227	795	1226	1795	2092	2594	2703
Opera	842	2070	3235	3897	4246	4596	4960
Pepper	1430	2688	3972	4955	5822	5989	6404
Pills	349	1070	1932	2677	3503	3945	4464
Pentagon	239	754	1567	2251	2834	3479	4174
Watch	1171	1951	2405	2774	3004	2989	3109
Newyork	62	234	391	697	823	1144	1486
Average Cap'/MxN	0.94%	2.24%	3.39%	4.28%	4.99%	5.57%	6.10%
Average PSNR(dB)	49.46	43.54	39.99	37.51	35.6	34.03	32.66

Table 6. Comparing capacity and PSNR offered by [11] and the proposed algorithm (a=1,2)

Test image name	Estimated capacity Cap' for amplitude $a=1,2$					
(256× 256)	$a=1$			$a=2$		
	[11]	M1	M2(b=64)	[11]	M1	M2(b=64)
Lena	865	1211	3944	2480	4068	7670
Baboon	157	120	989	390	337	2004
Airplane	1257	1023	4519	2913	2501	7197
Fishingboat	584	494	2340	1494	1306	5343
Goldhill	237	203	1197	776	690	3491
Barbara	227	189	1008	795	667	3268
Opera	842	690	3459	2070	1828	6746
Pepper	1430	666	4342	2688	2142	8543
Pills	349	223	2265	1070	830	5193
Pentagon	239	189	1377	754	634	3980
Watch	1171	1000	4516	1951	1764	6531
Newyork	62	52	274	234	199	905
Average Cap'/MxN	0.94%	1.71%	3.84%	2.24%	3.14%	7.74%
Average PSNR(dB)	49.46	52.95	49.51	43.54	46.46	43.63

Table 7. Comparing capacity and PSNR offered by [11] and the proposed algorithm (a=3,4)

| Test image name | Estimated capacity Cap' for amplitude $a=3,4$ | | | | | |
| (256× 256) | $a=3$ | | | $a=4$ | | |
	[11]	M1	M2(b=64)	[11]	M1	M2(b=64)
Lena	3414	5870	9618	4144	7408	11266
Baboon	850	701	3776	1084	985	5032
Airplane	3915	3540	8755	4280	3875	9731
Fishingboat	2320	2076	7080	3027	2738	9427
Goldhill	1501	1370	5411	2152	1993	7050
Barbara	1226	1062	4405	1795	1618	5901
Opera	3235	2912	9331	3897	3570	10607
Pepper	3972	3322	10582	4955	4251	12081
Pills	1932	1533	7800	2677	2237	9699
Pentagon	1567	1355	6811	2251	2003	8286
Watch	2405	2193	8402	2774	2507	9464
Newyork	391	358	1618	697	624	2839
Average Cap'/MxN	3.39%	4.36%	10.66%	4.28%	5.32%	12.89%
Average PSNR(dB)	39.99	42.66	40.19	37.51	39.98	37.72

Table 8. Comparing capacity and PSNR offered by [11] and the proposed algorithm (a=5,6)

| Test image name | Estimated capacity Cap' for amplitude $a=5,6$ | | | | | |
| (256× 256) | $a=5$ | | | $a=6$ | | |
	[11]	M1	M2(b=64)	[11]	M1	M2(b=64)
Lena	4497	8099	11938	5085	9272	12380
Baboon	1472	1322	6150	2011	1828	7161
Airplane	4436	4102	10663	4419	4107	11142
Fishingboat	3639	3325	10642	4012	3799	11190
Goldhill	2918	2694	8612	3574	3339	10150
Barbara	2092	1894	6357	2594	2392	7375
Opera	4246	3934	11751	4596	4308	11812
Pepper	5822	5181	12994	5989	5418	13400
Pills	3503	2997	11304	3945	3412	11671
Pentagon	2834	2512	9988	3479	3136	10609
Watch	3004	2759	9681	2989	2729	9704
Newyork	823	754	3362	1144	1067	4384
Average Cap'/MxN	4.99%	6.05%	14.42%	5.57%	6.71%	15.38%
Average PSNR(dB)	35.6	37.9	35.79	34.03	36.23	34.19

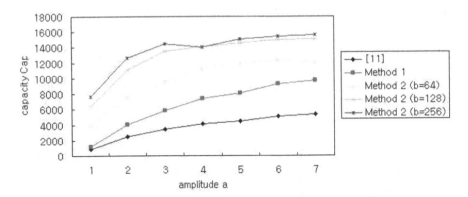

Fig. 4. Comparing capacity offered by [11] and the proposed algorithm (Lena test image)

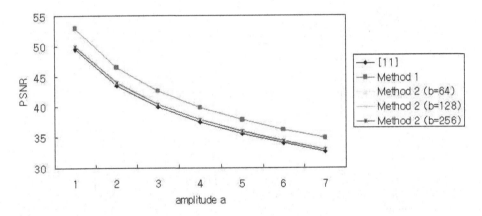

Fig. 5. Comparing PSNR offered by [11] and the proposed algorithm (Lena test image)

Acknowlegement

This work was partially supported by grant No. R01-2006-000-10260-0 from the Basic Research Program of the Korea Science & Engineering Foundation, and the MIC(Ministry of Information and Communication), Korea, under the ITRC(Information Technology Research Center) support program supervised by the IITA(Institute of Information Technology Assessment).

References

1. B. Furht, D. Kirovski : Multimedia Security Handbook *CRC Press*, New York, 2005.
2. E. T. Lin, A. M. Eskicioglu, and R. L. Lagendijk, "Advances in Digital Video Content Protection," *Proceedings of the IEEE*, vol. 93, issue 1 pp. 171-183, January 2005.

3. W. Rosenblatt, W. Trippe, and S. Mooney, : Digital Rights Management, *New York*, 2002.

4. I. J. Cox, J. Kilian, F. T. Leighton, and T. Shamoon, "Secure spread spectrum watermarking for multimedia," *IEEE Transaction Image Processing*, vol. 6, pp.1673-1687, December 1997.

5. P. W. Wong, "A watermark for image integrity and ownership verification," *Proceedings of IEEE International Conference Image Processing*, pp.455-459, 1998.

6. M. U. Celik, G. Sharma, E. Saber, and A. M. Tekalp, "Hierarchical watermarking for secure image authentication with localization," *IEEE Transaction Image Processing*, vol. 11, No. 6, pp. 585-595, 2002.

7. Cox, I. J., Miller, M. L., and Bloom, J.A.: Digital Watermarking *Kaufmann*, San Francisco, 2001.

8. A. Leest, M. Veen, and F. Bruekers, "Reversible image watermarking", *IEEE Proceedings of ICIP'03*, vol. 2, pp.731-734, September 2003.

9. J. Fridrich, M. Goljan, R. Du, "Invertible Authentication," *in proceedings of SPIE Photonics West, Security and Watermarking of Multimedia Contents* , vol. 3971. San jose, California, USA, January 2001.

10. C. W. Honsinger, P. W. jones, M. Rabbani, and J. C. Stoffel, "Lossless recovery of an original image containing embedded data," *United States patent*, 6,278,791, 2001.

11. M. Goljan, J. Fridrich, and R. Du, "Distortion-free data embedding for images," *in 4th Information Hiding Workshop*, pp. 27-41, April 2001.

12. J. Tian, "Reversible watermarking by difference expansion," *in Proceedings of Multimedia and Security Workshop at ACM Multimedia*, December 2002.

13. G. Xuan, Y.Q. Shi, Z.C. Ni, J. Chen, l Yang, Y. Zhen, and J. Zhen, " High Capacity lossless Data Hiding Based on Integer Wavelet Transform," *Proceeding of IEEE international Symposium on Circuits and Systems*, Vancouver, Canada, 2004.

Extension of R-Tree for Spatio-temporal OLAP Operations*

Byeong-Seob You[1], Jae-Dong Lee[2], and Hae-Young Bae[1]

[1] Dept. of Computer Science & Information Engineering, INHA University
Younghyun-dong, Nam-ku, Incheon, 402-751, Korea
bsyou@dblab.inha.ac.kr, hybae@inha.ac.kr
[2] Division of information and computer science, Dankook University
Hannam-ro, Yongsan-gu, Seoul, 140-714, Korea
letsdoit@dankook.ac.kr

Abstract. Spatio-temporal OLAP is an operation providing the spatial hierarchy and the temporal hierarchy for decision making. In this paper, we propose the extended R-tree for spatio-temporal OLAP operations. The proposed method focuses on using a hybrid index of the extended aggregation R-tree and the temporal hash table. The aggregation R-tree is extended for the spatial hierarchy, which is based on the R-tree. It provides a pre-aggregation for fast retrieval of aggregated values. For a temporal hierarchy, the temporal hash table has buckets which are added levels of temporal unit. It is transformed for the temporal hierarchy. It provides pre-aggregation of each temporal unit as year, month and so on. The proposed method supports spatio-temporal analysis since it provides the spatio-temporal hierarchy and the pre-aggregated value.

Keywords: Spatial-Temporal, OLAP, Spatial Data Warehouse.

1 Introduction

In many applications related to traffic, traffic supervision requires historical analysis of traffic information and mobile users require current traffic information [9]. These cases are necessary to integrated analysis of spatial and non-spatial data. Also, these applications require only summarized information [7]. To solve these requirements in spatial data warehouses, some methods using the extended R-tree have been studied [9], [3], and [13]. The aggrega-tion R-tree is extended to store the pre-aggregated values on each entry. The aggrega-tion R-tree provides the fast retrieval of the aggregated value because of using the pre-aggregation [9]. The aggregation R-tree, however, can not pro-vide historical analysis since it has only total aggregated value on each entry. The OLAP-Favored Search composes with the R-tree and the summarized table [3]. The R-tree in the OLAP-Favored Search is extended to store the link to the tuple of the summarized table. The OLAP-Favored Search provides the

---

* This research was supported by the MIC(Ministry of Information and Communication), Korea, under the ITRC(Information Technology Research Center) support program supervised by the IITA(Institute of Information Technology Assessment) .

S. Madria et al. (Eds.): ICDCIT 2006, LNCS 4317, pp. 438–446, 2006.
© Springer-Verlag Berlin Heidelberg 2006

historical analysis in the summarized table. However, this method must access so many data of the summarized table for historical analysis.

In this paper, we propose the hybrid index for providing pre-aggregation with the concept of the spatial hierarchy and the temporal hierarchy in spatial data warehouses. The hybrid index is the efficient index which integrates the temporal hash table into the extended aggregation R-tree. The extended aggregation R-tree has additional informa-tion on the basic R-tree. One is currently aggregated value and the other is a link to temporal hash table. The temporal hash table is linear hash table of year unit. Each bucket has a sorted year unit and a point of the next year unit. Each year unit has the flexible structure so that other time unit could be stored, such as month, day, hour and etc. The hybrid index has some advantages. Firstly, it provides the spatial hierarchy and total pre-aggregation based on the extended aggregation R-tree. Secondly, the temporal hierarchy and the pre-aggregation of each temporal unit based on the temporal hash table are provided. Thirdly, the hybrid index implements efficient and fast decision support.

The rest of this paper is organized as follows. Section 2 describes related work in the aggregation R-tree and the OLAP-Favored Search. Section 3 proposes the hybrid index which keeps aggregated information and supports the spatial hierarchy and the temporal hierarchy. Section 4 contains an experimental evaluation and Section 5 concludes this paper.

2 Related Work

A spatial data warehouse is a system analyzing collected data of spatial and non-spatial data for decision-making process [3], [8]. A spatial data warehouse provides data cubes for efficient decision support [5]. The data cube has the concept hierarchy for efficient decision support [13]. Having spatial data various shapes, it is difficult to construct concept hierarchy on a dimension of spatial data. Previous works solve this problem using spatial index trees, such as Quad-tree [4], R-tree [6], R*-tree [1], R+-tree [11] and etc. Among them, the spatial hierarchy on the R-tree is mainly studied.

The aggregation R-tree is an extended R-tree [9]. Each entry has pre-aggregated value for its minimum bounding rectangle (MBR). The pre-aggregated value is total aggregated value from history to present. The aggregation R-tree can provide the aggregated value of some region. This method, however, can not provide the histori-cally aggregated value and does not support temporal hierarchy. This method can not provide efficient decision support. The OLAP-Favored Search composes the aggregation R-tree with the summarized table [10]. The aggregation R-tree of this method is just extended for the link to the tuple of the summarized table on each entry. The summarized table stores the pre-aggregated value from history to present [2]. This method can provide the historically aggregated value. However, this method after long time would be slower and slower since the summarized table becomes larger and larger. The MV3R-tree is composed of multi version R-tree and 3D R-tree [12]. It supports to find the past location of a moving object. If a query of a various time based on special area is required, all R-tree connected on each time should be retrieved. Because spatial operation requires more cost, a processing cost is increased.

Therefore, the index for efficient analysis of history to present and the efficient support of the spatial hierarchy and the temporal hierarchy is needed.

3   Efficient Spatial Query Processing Using the Hybrid Index with the Pre-aggregated Value

In this section, the structure of the hybrid index in spatial data warehouses for efficient decision support is proposed. The main idea is to integrate the extended aggregation R-tree and the temporal hash table. Each entry of the extended aggregation R-tree has the independent temporal hash table. an extended aggregation R-tree stores a link to tuple of the temporal hash table and values of the aggregate function for data within the MBR. The temporal hash table stores aggregated values of temporal unit for each entry of the extended aggregation R-tree. The hybrid index is built on the object of spatial dimen-sion and the time unit of temporal dimension, therefore its structure has both of the spatial hierarchy based on level of the R-tree and the temporal hierarchy based on temporal units.

It is assumed that every object in some region lies on the arbitrary position and the hybrid index is constructed with those objects. The aggregate function used in the following example of hybrid index is *SUM*.

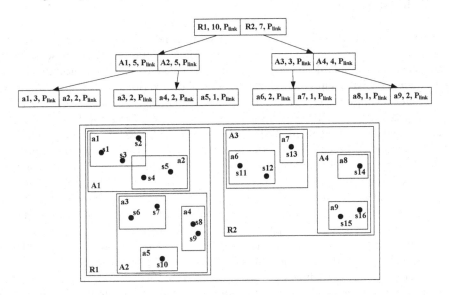

Fig. 1. The Structure of Extended aggregation R-tree

Fig. 1 logically depicts the extended aggregation R-tree of the hybrid index which indexes a set of 9 region segments $r1$, $r2$, ..., $r9$, with MBR as $a1$, $a2$, ..., $a9$ respectively when we assume the virtual region is in a rectangle. There are 3 objects on the region $r1$, objects of $a1$ are $s1$, $s2$, $s3$ respectively. And $a1$ has P_{link} which indicates the independent temporal hash table for the temporal hierarchy. Therefore the total num-ber of objects in $r1$ is 3 and there is an entry ($a1$, 3, P_{link}) in the internal node of the extended aggregation R-tree of the hybrid index. Moving one level up, MBR $A1$ con-tains two regions, $r1$, $r2$. The total number of objects in these regions is 5. And $A1$ has P_{link} which indicates the independent temporal hash table. Therefore there is an entry ($A1$, 5, P_{link}) as a node of level 1 in the extended aggregation R-tree.

The extended aggregation R-tree does not be changed in any case since every region is the standard unit for analysis. So the update of entry has 3 cases according to movement of object. First case is that new object enters in some region. In this case, we find region containing the object from the root node to the leaf node. If we find it in the root level, we add measure value of the object to the aggregated value of the entry and we find region contains the object in the next level. Until we find region of leaf node, we continue the same process. Second case is that the object of some region leaves out in the extended aggregation R-tree. In this case, we find region containing the object from root level to leaf level and we subtract the measure value of the object from the aggregated value of the entry found on each level. This case is the same as the operation of first case except that the add operation is changed into the substract operation. Third case is that one object moves one region to other region. This case is to combine the case which object leaves out of some region and the case which object enters in some region. Therefore we operate first case and second case in sequence.

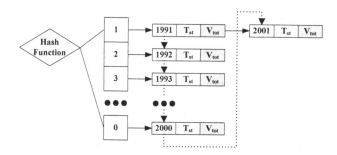

Fig. 2. The Structure of temporal hash table

Fig. 2 shows the temporal hash table of the hybrid index. This temporal hash table is composed of the hash table and 10 buckets. Each bucket has predicate from 1 to 0. The hash function calculates remainder by dividing key value of year unit of temporal data to a variable 10. Since temporal data is occurred in order, it does not have data skew and a key of has table is equally distributed to all buckets well. The range of key value is 1, 2, ..., 9, 0, and this value is the same at the most right number of year unit. Each bucket has a linked list of one or more year structures. The year structure has five fields: key value, time structure, totally aggregated value, next bucket pointer and next year pointer. Key value has year unit and can identify other year unit. Time structure (T_{st}) has aggre-gated values of month and day. In next paragraph, we deal with time structure. Total aggregated value (V_{tot}) is total aggregated value to belong to year unit. For example, if total aggregated value of every month in some year unit is 5, V_{tot} is 60. The next bucket pointer is a pointer indicating the next year structure on the same bucket and the next year pointer is a pointer indicating year structure of temporally next year. If range query is processed, first finds a year bucket on start time of query and we get result data. After result data is gathered from that bucket, we move next bucket according to the next year pointer. Until the year unit of the current bucket is the year on end time of query, it is operated continuously.

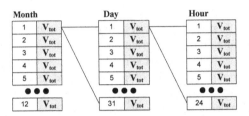

Fig. 2. The Composition of Time Structure

In Fig. 3, we can see the simple structure of the time structure which is composed with month, day and hour. Month has twelve slots as January, February, …, December. Each slot has both the identification and total aggregated value of its days. Therefore there is a slot (M_{id}, V_{tot}). Mid means identification of month and it is the same as month number. V_{tot} means the total aggregated value of days in its month. Day and hour have slots of the same form as month slot. The number of day slot is 31 and the number of hour slot is 24. The number of day in each month is different but the number of day slot is fixed. Fixing the number of slots makes structure simple and provides easy processing. If the number of day in some month is smaller than 31, remained slots is masked.

The temporal hash table must maintain historically aggregated values since historical data is important for trend analysis. Therefore there is only the insert operation in the temporal hash table. We assume that one object enters in an area of the hybrid index and the region containing the object is found on each level of the extended aggregation R-tree. Those entries process the insert operation of each temporal hash table. We calculate key value using the hash function and find the year structure corresponding key value. Next, Total aggregated value of the year structure is increased for the object's meas-ure value. The month slot can be found using the month number since the slot number is the same as the month number. After finding the month slot, total aggregated value of that month slot is increased similarly. The day slot and the hour slot can be treated using the same method as the month slot.

Search operation using the hybrid index has two cases. One is to find the currently aggregated value and other is to find the historically aggregated value. Search algorithm using the hybrid index is as follows.

HybridSearch(N, p, T, U)	
Input:	root node N, search predicate p, temporal range T wanted time unit U
Output:	all slots of both time and aggregated value that satisfies p
SlotList ret = null	

```
IF N is not a leaf THEN
        FOR Each entry E on N
        BEGIN
                IF p.MBR contains E.MBR THEN
                        IF T is current THEN // start time is same to end time
                                add time and the aggregated value to ret
                        ELSE
                                add HashSearch(E.H, T, U) to ret
                IF p.MBR is intersected with E.MBR THEN
                        // invoke HybridSearch on the subtree
                        // whose root node is referenced by E.ptr
                        add HybridSearch(E.ptr, p, T) to ret
        END
ELSE    // N is a leaf
        FOR Each entry E on N
        BEGIN
                IF p.MBR contains E.MBR THEN
                        IF T is current THEN
                                add time and the aggregated value to ret
                        ELSE
                                add HashSearch(E.H, T, U) to ret
        END
RETURN ret
```

The hybrid index executes HybridSearch(N, p, T, U) if the query which has some window area is given. In the extended aggregation R-tree, it compares query window with MBR of each entry of each node from root node N to leaf node. If query window completely contained by MBR of an entry, it adds the aggregated value of entry to result (*ret*). In this case, if the wanted temporal range is current, we get the aggregated value of the extended aggregation R-tree. Otherwise, it calls *HashSearch* function. If query window is intersected with an entry, it invokes *HybridSearch* function on the subtree.

```
                HashSearch(H, T, U)           // can provide until month unit
Input:    temporal hash table H, temporal range T
          wanted time unit U
Output:   all slots of both time and the aggregated value that is contained T
SlotList ret = null
YearStructure Y = year structure found by hash value of year unit on start time
FOR Y.Year <= Year of end time
BEGIN
        IF U is year unit THEN
                add total aggregated value of Y to ret
        ELSE IF U is month unit THEN
                FOR Each month slot M in Y
                BEGIN
                        IF (M.Month >= month of start time) and
                                (Y.Year and M.Month is same to end time
                                or is older than end time)
                                add total aggregated value of M to ret
                END
        Y = year structure of next year
END
RETURN ret
```

HashSearch(H, T, U) is executed by *HybridSearch* function if wanted temporal range is not current. The hash value is calculated by hash function with year value on start time. Using the hash value, the year structure is found. If the wanted time unit is year, it adds total aggregated value of the year structure to result (*ret*). If the wanted time unit is month, it finds month slots which satisfy temporal condition and it adds total aggregated value of them to result (*ret*). Until the year value of the year structure reaches it of end time, the same process is continued.

4   Comparison with Other Approaches

In this section, we evaluate the proposed method by simulating a scenario of a traffic system. We use a system which has a CPU (P4 3.0) and a memory (1GB). The base map for experiment is the road of Seoul in KOREA. Five thousand of cars exist continuously on the hybrid index and almost five thousand of cars move in the area that hybrid index manages. Also, almost five thousand of cars move out of management area of the hybrid index. Test data is randomly inserted in the hybrid index.

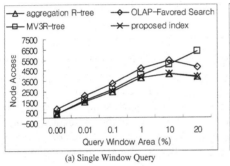 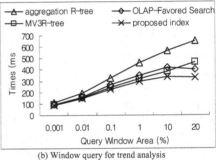

(a) Single Window Query   (b) Window query for trend analysis

Fig. 3. Comparison of performance

First performance evaluation compares the number of node accessed for searching current aggregated information. We survey the number of node accessed for process-ing a hundred of queries (size of query window is same but the position of it is differ-ent). And we repeat this evaluation varying the query window area from 0.001% to 20%.

In Fig. 4 (a), performance of both the aggregation R-Tree and the proposed index is almost same because the technique of search operation for the currently aggregated value is similar. But search operation of the OLAP-Favored Search must read the summarized table after searching the aggregation R-tree. Therefore the OLAP-Favored Search shows bad performance. In case of MV3R-tree, all nodes on R-tree are retrieved because each node does not have pre-aggregation value. So node access count increases steadily along with query window area.

Beyond a threshold size (i.e. 10% of the space) we can observe decreasing the number of node accesses of aggregation R-tree, OLAP-Favored Search, and proposed method index. At the extreme case that the query window covers the whole space, only one access (to the root node) is required since all data are covered by the entry of root area.

Second performance evaluation compares performance with window query for trend analysis. Test environment is the same as first performance evaluation. The period of wanted time is random between 30 days and 50 days.

Fig. 4 (b) shows that the aggregation R-tree has bad performance since all data of the fact table must be read to find historical data. The OLAP-Favored Search searches the historically aggregated value in the summarized table. This method is better than the aggregation R-tree, but is worse than the proposed index. The MV3R-tree has good performance but processing cost continuously increases because of no pre-aggregation. In case of the proposed index, the aggregated value can be found rapidly because the historically aggregated value is constructed by temporal hash table of year unit containing time structure of tem-poral units except year.

5 Conclusion

In this paper, the focus is to design the hybrid index for spatio-temporal OLAP in spatial data warehouses. The hybrid index structure which is composed with the ex-tended aggregation R-tree and the temporal hash table is established. Each entry of the extended aggregation R-tree has the pre-aggregated value of current data and link for historical data. Year structure of the temporal hash table has five fields: the key value for identification of each year structure, the total aggregated value of year unit, time struc-ture for time units on year, the next bucket pointer linking year structures of the same bucket and the next year pointer to guarantee serialization of year unit. Therefore, both the window query for current aggregation and the window query for trend analy-sis do not need to access raw data in fact table since the hybrid index provides histori-cal data and spatio-temporal hierarchy.

The single window query and the window query for trend analysis by the proposed hybrid index resulted more efficiently without processing aggregation and reduced response time. Our method allows the efficient window query and the temporal ori-ented range query for decision support in spatial data warehouses.

References

1. N. Beckmann, H. P. Kriegel, R. Schneider, and B. Seeger, The R*-tree: an efficient and robust access method for points and rectangles. ACM SIGMOD, 1990.
2. N. Colossi, W. Malloy, and B. Reinwald, Relational extensions for OLAP. IBM SYSTEMS JOURNAL, 2002.
3. ESRI, Spatial Data Warehousing for Hospital Organizations, An ESRI White Paper, 1998. http://www.esri.com/library/whitepapers/pdfs/sdwho.pdf
4. R. A. Finkel, and J. L. Bentley, Quad trees: A data structure for retrieval on composite keys. Acta Informatica, 1974.
5. J. Gray, A. Bosworth, A. Layman, and H. Pirahesh, Data Cube: a Relational Aggregation Operator Generalizing Group-by. ICDE, 1996.
6. A. Guttman, R-trees: a dynamic index structure for spatial searching. ACM SIGMOD, 1984.
7. V. Harinarayan, A. Rajaraman, and J. Ullman, Implementing Data Cubes Efficiently. ACM SIGMOD, 1996.

8. R. Kimball, The Data Warehouse Toolkit. John Wiley, 1996.
9. D. Papadias, P. Kalnis, J. Zhang, and Y. Tao, Efficient OLAP Operations in Spatial Data Warehouses. Technical Report: HKUST-CS01-01, University of Science & Technology, Hon Kong, 2001.
10. F. Rao, L. Zhang, X. L. Yu, Y. Li, and Y. Chen, Spatial Hierarchy and OLAP-Favored Search in Spatial Data Warehouse. DOLAP, 2003.
11. T. K. Sellis, N. Roussopoulos, and C. Faloutsos, The R+-Tree: A dynamic index for multi-dimensional objects. VLDB, 1987.
12. Y. Tao and D. Papadis, MV3R-tree: A spatio-temporal access method for timestamp and interval queries. In Very Large DataBase, 2001.
13. L. Zhang, Y. Li, F. Rao, X. Yu, and Y. Chen, An approach to enabling spatial OLAP by aggregating on spatial hierarchy. In Proc. Data Warehousing and Knowledge Discovery, 2003.

Multimedia Data Hiding in Spatial and Transformed Domain

T.S. Das[1], A.K. Sau[2], and S.K. Sarkar[2]

[1] Gurunanak Institute of Technology, Kolkata –700114
tirthasankardas@yahoo.com
[2] Jadavpur University, Kolkata-700032
ayankumarsau@yahoo.com, sksarkar@etce.jdvu.ac.in

Abstract. This paper discusses about the comparative study between spatial and transform domain multimedia data hiding for communication purpose. Still image watermarking can't be used for real time communication. That's why our key objective directs towards the packet communication through still image watermarking. Since still image data hiding technique generally shows low data embedding rate or payload, it is tried to remove that problem also. Moreover, the proposed scheme has to be such one, which can minimize the co-channel interference thereby extracting the multimedia contents with lowest possible error. Based on this analysis, Zigzag modulation and RGB spatial domain and Discrete Cosine Transformed (DCT) domain techniques are proposed which shows better visual and statistical invisibility.

Keywords: Spatial and Transform domain, multimedia data hiding, data embedding rate, interference, Zigzag modulation, RGB, DCT.

1 Introduction

Watermarking is the art of embedding information in a cover-content in a robust and non-perceptible way. So, quality of data hiding technique can be expressed in terms of data embedding rate, imperceptibility and robustness [1]. Digital watermarking algorithms can be thought as digital communication scheme where an auxiliary message is embedded in digital multimedia signals and are available where ever the latter signals move. The decoded message latter on serves the purpose of security in communication, copyright protection etc. Robustness is an essential criterion in digital watermarking schemes along with visual transparency, high data embedding rate etc needed for data embedding and recovery purpose. The spatial domain watermarking generally shows poor robust ness compared to the transform domain techniques. But the data hiding is much easier than that of transform domain. So if a spatial domain data hiding technique gets a secured path than it shows better result in extracted information. Whereas, the transform domain methods are far better against several common signal processing operations as well as deliberate attacks.

The paper is organized as follows: Section 2 describes the watermarking scheme; Section 3 discusses about results and Section 4 presents the conclusion.

S. Madria et al. (Eds.): ICDCIT 2006, LNCS 4317, pp. 447–456, 2006.

2 Watermarking and Detection

An 8-bit gray scale image of dimension 256 X 256 is taken as background cover image (as shown in Fig 1) [2].

2.1 Payload

A. Another 8-bit gray scale image of any dimension is taken as logo image (as shown in Fig.2).
B. A 2 second single channel sound track (8-bit file in WAV format) is taken as second logo (Bit rate: 176Kbps, Audio sample size: 8 bit, Channels: Mono, Audio sample rate: 22 KHz, Audio format: PCM, shown in Fig.3).
C. Text information interested to transmit or for testing a binary texture for error tolerance calculation is taken as third logo.

Fig. 1. 256 X 256 gray scale Cover Image   **Fig. 2.** Logo

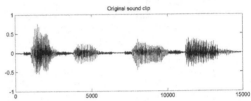

Fig. 3. A single channel sound track

2.2 Lossy Data Compression for Logo

The cover image has 256 gray levels. Since 255-value is very high to modify a pixel of the cover image, so a scaling factor is required to re-quantize the logo image; this in turn reduce the picture quality. Therefore, the number of pixel will remain same but the nearest quantization levels will approximate some pixel values through linear mapping. As a result, the resulting image appears with tolerable quantization noise. However logo image will be visible in spatial or DCT domain in case of high strength of the watermark. In order to avoid that, a noise equivalent to the watermark logo is generated. This can be done by altering the rows and columns of the logo through a secret random number sequence (private key).

2.3 Processing the Sound Track

Single channel 8-bit sound has values of signed integers ranging from −128 to 127, where as 8-bit gray scale image contains unsigned integers. So in order to embed the sound into the picture, it has to be converted into a two dimensional unsigned gray scale image. Here, a bias value is used to change the negative values to positive ones because image pixel does not carry negative value.

2.4 Processing the Text Information

The text watermark is converted into a binary image and then into the gray scale format to control the transparency of the watermark. Here test has been performed for random binary bit pattern or text information to see error tolerance.

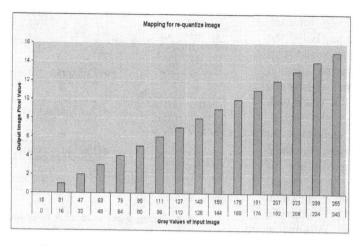

Fig. 4. Mapping function plotted for image re-quantization

Fig. 5. Original & Re-quantized Image

Fig. 6. Equivalent image of the sound clip

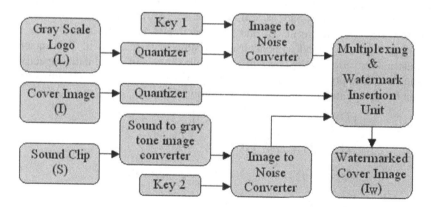

Fig. 7. Block diagram of a Zigzag-space watermark insertion unit

2.5 Zigzag-Space Watermarking

The objective is to embed logo image and sound clip in the same cover image in such a way so that watermarked image appears with a good quality of imperceptibility. If

the embedding informa-
tion contains only the
logo or the sound clip
then there is no question
of interference between
them [3]. But when both
watermarks are simul-
taneously embedded in
the same image then there
exists a possibility of
interference. For mutual
exclusion some algorithm
is required [4] so that the
embedding information

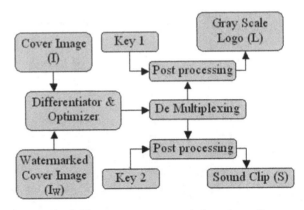

Fig. 8. Zigzag-space watermark detection unit

can be extracted with minimum error. Here, every alternate pixel contains logo and
sound information as shown above. The information is simply added with pixel
intensity value. The logo as well as the Sound both has 8-bit values. So if we simply
add this value then it will corrupt the cover badly. So it needs some gain factor, or
modulation index, which will control this corruption or watermark transparency.
Mathematically we can represent the above algorithm as below:

$$I_m(i, j) = [I(i, j) + M(i, j)]_{i,j=1,1}^{M,N} \tag{1}$$

where $$[M(i, j) = m_L \times L(i, j) + m_S \times S(i, j)]_{i,j=1,1}^{M,N}$$

For i + j = even m_S = 0; i + j = odd, m_L = 0 ; and k = int (i/2); l = int (j/2);

where m_L and m_S are the modulation index for Logo and Sound respectively. For i+j =
even, m_S = 0 and for i+j = odd, m_L = 0. Variables i, j varies maximum limit of x and y
dimension of cover image i.e. M and N respectively. I_m is the loaded cover image
containing logo and sound embedded as invisible watermark in it. This means that
each alternate position of the cover image contains logo and sound data respectively.

The detection process is just the opposite of this watermark embedding process
and can be represented mathematically as follows:

$$[D(i, j) = I_m(i, j) - I(i, j)]_{i,j=1,1}^{MN} \tag{2}$$

$$[D_L(k,l) = D(i, j)]_{i,j=1,1}^{M,N} \tag{3}$$
$$for(i + j) = even; k = int(i/2); l = int(j/2);$$

$$[D_S(k,l) = D(i, j)]_{i,j=1,1}^{M,N} \tag{4}$$
$$for(i + j) = odd; k = int(i/2); l = int(j/2);$$

Multiplying D_L with inverse of modulation index m_L and D_S with inverse of
modulation index m_S logo image and image equivalent of sound clip can be recovered
respectively.

2.6 RGB-Space Watermarking

Insertion algorithm is as simple as modification of list significant bits of the selected layer [6]. Number of bits under change depends upon modulation index m_x (m_L for

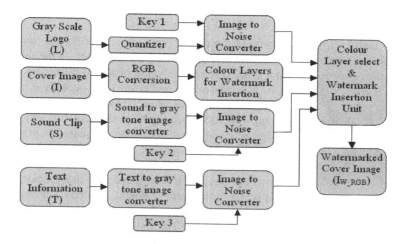

Fig. 9. Block diagram of a RGB-space watermark insertion unit

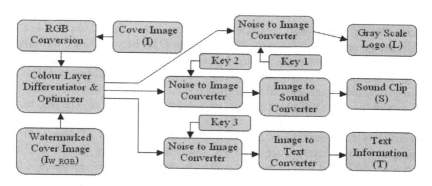

Fig. 10. Block diagram of a RGB-space watermark detection unit

logo, m_S for sound and m_T for text message). 'm_x' can vary from 0 to 1. For $m_x = 0$ no data will be inserted into the carrier layer and for $m_x = 1$, embedded data will totally replace the cover layer values and in that case, maximum distortion will be there in the cover image. The scheme can be expressed in the form of equation as below:

$$[\, I_m(i,j,k) = I(i,j,k) + m_X X(i,j) \,] \, _{i,j,k=1,1,1}^{M,N,3} ;$$
$$X = [L \ S \ T] \text{ for } k = [1 \ 2 \ 3]; \tag{5}$$

where 'L' stands for logo, 'S' stands for sound and 'T' stands for text information and MxN is the size of the cover image. Value of (i,j) corresponds to pixel position and k takes values 1 to 3 for selection of one of the three different colour layers i.e. k = 1 select red colour plane and so on. I_m is the modified host image. In extraction process, the reverse operation of whatever done in case of watermark insertion is performed and can be mathematically expressed as:

$$[X(i,j) = 1/m_X \{I_m(i,j,k) - I(i,j,k)\}]_{i,j,k=1,1,1}^{M,N,3} ; \qquad (6)$$

$$\text{and } X = [L\ S\ T] \text{ for } k = [1\ 2\ 3];$$

Here the logo L (i,j) is not some as the original one rather it will be a re-quantized image loosing some information and sharpness. This loss depends on the modulation

index m_X (greater the value of m_X, loss will be minima). This is because logo and cover layer both have gray scale value from 0 to 1 and these values of Logo are multiplied by m_L to reduce visibility of modification. When modified image is saved as bit map image it quantizes pixel values to 8-bit unsigned integers. Similar thing happens for the sound data also and for this a noise appears in the extracted sound. It is mentioned here that extracted data S (i,j) is not in the form of sound. It needs conversion from image to sound format. Extracted text information T(i,j) is also remain in the form of gray scale image. Threshold is necessary to convert this image to logical black/white text image.

Fig. 11. RGB Lena image

2.7 Watermarking in DCT Domain

Discrete Cosine Transform coefficients of gray scale image are also a two-dimensional space equal to the size of cover image [7]. The values of the coefficients are random, fractional and vary in any direction of zero. Data type of logo, sound or text is different than the coefficients. Thus it's better to change all types of data in the form of gray scale image and calculate their cosine transform. Now these data are of same format as of DCT coefficients of cover image. Large change in DCT coefficients of cover image can distort reconstructed watermarked image. Therefore gain control is necessary. Now coefficients for different types of data need to be separated for proper reconstruction of the inserted watermarks. To do that, whole space has to be divided into number of subspaces. Position of the subspaces is totally depends upon the algorithm and can be used as a security key. The coefficient modification can be done following the equation:

$$CTI_m = CTI + m_x \times CTX \qquad (7)$$

where x stands for logo, sound clip or texture and CT represents DCT coefficients, I is the cover image Cover and I_m is watermarked Cover. Watermark gain control can be done by modulation index m_x. The algorithm for watermark insertion for multimedia data should be as below:

CTI = DCT(Cover Image);[CTIl CTIs CTIt] = Split(CTI);SImg = Convert Sound to Image(Sound Clip);TImg = Convert Text to Image(Text information);CTL = DCT(Logo);CTS = DCT(SImg);CTT = DCT(TImg);for logo ,sound and text CTIx_m = CTIx + α_x.CTx; Where x for logo, sound and text.end for CTI_m = Combine(All CTIx_m);Watermarked Cover = IDTC(CTI_m);

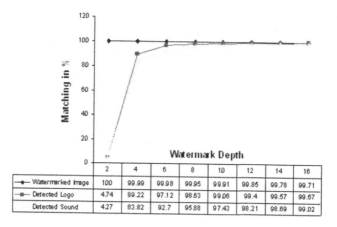

	2	4	6	8	10	12	14	16
Watermarked Image	100	99.99	99.98	99.95	99.91	99.85	99.78	99.71
Detected Logo	4.74	89.22	97.12	98.63	99.06	99.4	99.57	99.67
Detected Sound	4.27	83.82	92.7	95.88	97.43	98.21	98.69	99.02

Fig. 12. Percentage matching of watermarked image with cover image, recovered logo with original and recovered sound clip with original one

Watermark detection procedure is just the reverse of insertion procedure. This watermarking scheme is not a public key system thus require the original unwatermarked cover image. Thus this scheme can also be called a secured watermarking. However the algorithm of extracting watermarks will be as below:

$CTI = DCT(Cover\ Image); CTIW = DCT(Watermarked\ Cover\ Image); Wat = CTIW - CTI; [CTWl\ CTWs\ CTWt] = Split(Wat); Logo = Xpand\ \{IDCT(CTWl)\}; SImg = Xpand\ \{IDCT(CTWs)\}; TImg = Xpand\ \{IDCT(CTWt)\}; Sound\ Clip = Convert\ Image\ to\ Sound(Simg); Text\ information = Convert\ Image\ to\ text(TImg);$

Here *Xpand* function expands recovered image values between maximum and minimum values dynamically. Thus we need not to multiply with inverse modulation index α_x. The splitting algorithm of watermark insertion and extraction must be same to extract multiple watermarks separately. However we can apply some compression algorithm to minimize watermark load rather to minimize distortion of the watermarked image. Here we will also study logarithmic compression of DCT coefficients of watermarks.

3 Results and Discussion

3.1 Zigzag Modulation

The output is obtained with saving watermarked image as gray scale bit map image. There is quantization error incorporated due to this conversion. It would be mentioned here that when gray scale image is saved as bmp image then each pixels value (ranging from 0 to 1 in gray scale format) is quantized as an 8-bit unsigned integer and so some intermediate values are approximated and thus quantization error incorporated in the saved image. We can see from result that detected output is also not much corrupted, almost similar to originals. Number of quantization levels for watermarked is 256, for Logo is 16, for sound it is 16 number of quantization levels for watermarked Cover is 256, for Logo is 8, for sound it is 8. With increasing number

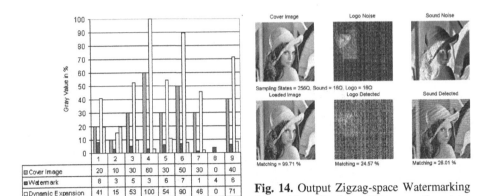

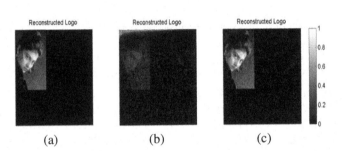

	1	2	3	4	5	6	7	8	9
▣ Cover Image	20	10	30	60	30	50	30	0	40
▣ Watermark	8	3	5	3	6	7	1	4	6
▢ Dynamic Expansion	41	15	53	100	54	90	46	0	71
▢ Expanded Watermark Value	20	20	10	3	11	8	2	0	8

Pixel Position

Fig. 13. Effect of dynamic expansion

Fig. 14. Output Zigzag-space Watermarking for multi-media data with re-quantize states for sound clip 16 and for gray scale logo 16 and saving the loaded cover image with dynamic stretching

Fig. 15. Extracted Logo (a) logarithmic compression (b) logarithmic compression but saving watermarked image in bmp format (c) uncompressed DCT coefficients and saving watermarked image in bmp format

of quantization states of logo and sound, detected output gives better result with decreasing quality of watermarked image. In Fig. 14 output is obtained with saving loaded image as a bmp image. This is obtained using command line " $Ret = mat2gray$ $(Ret);$ ". 'Ret' is an internal variable containing modified data of cover image. The $mat2gray$ $()$ is a dynamic mapping function, mapping output image to gray scale, replacing the maximum value to 1 and minimum value to 0. Detected output contains some data of the cover image, which corrupts detected logo and sound badly. Because maximum value of re-quantization level is 16 for logo, but re-quantized logo pixel may not contain that much value. The dynamic function mat2gray() maps this logo to maximum range 0 to 1 which causes insertion of cover image data into logo and sound region. To fix this problem, a fixed scaling is used. The output has 256 levels for loaded cover, 16 levels for logo or sound. So without using the function 'mat2gray' pixel values are simply divide by 255 to avoid expansion of the pixel values. This fixed scaling helps to avoid data overlap during detection because now we know watermarked data now restricted to a fixed limit (10%). This will be clear from Fig 12. Here watermark data is limited within maximum value of 10. But after dynamic expansion these values change accordingly and values above 10 will be treated as noise during detection. Percentage matching with originals is given in fig. 12 with data table. From the fig18 it's very clear that we can improve quality of embedded logo and sound by the cost of a little quality degradation of cover image.

3.2 RGB Modulation

The picture shown in figure 11 is a RGB color image having all three-color layers contain same values and thus it looks like a gray scale image. Now, red color plain is chosen for logo insertion, green for sound and blue for text embedding. After watermark insertion in the following layers three images are obtained. Combining these three gray images watermarked image is obtained. With close observation, very little change in color can be detected in the watermarked image. This transparency of watermarked data can be changed by proper selection of modulation indexes m_X. Here m_X is taken as 0.04. However all modulation indexes may not be same and in that case modified watermarked image will change its color which not desired. The advantage of this scheme is that the three layers are invariant to each other so watermark data does not interfere to each other. Moreover, an image of same dimension gives three times more space for data embedding than that of a gray image.

3.3 DCT Domain

As per the algorithm DCT coefficients of the logo, image of the sound clip, and image of the text are compressed as a function of $ln()$, so that larger values of the coefficients become smaller, and results are also very effective to minimize distortion but we require to transmit watermarked image. So, we need to write the image in some standard form for data interchange between machines. Now we write the watermarked image in uncompressed standard bit map image (bmp) format. The second sub-image (b) in figure 15 shows the effect. Extracted logo, sound contains very few information of watermarks. This is because when we write a gray scale image in 8-bit bmp format, gray scale values are quantized and this quantization error appears prominently when extracted watermarked data is exponentially uncompressed. The third sub-image (c) in figure 15 with uncompressed DCT coefficients and saving watermarked image in standard bmp format.

Thus we can transmit this watermarked image, and can extract watermarks as well. To reduce noise in extracted logo and sound, filters can be applied. Watermarking in DCT transform domain is more secured than spatial domain because if one can hardly get any information by comparing watermarked with the original one. If someone takes mathematical difference of the two then there will be nothing but noise. Watermarking in DCT domain is more secured than spatial domain because if one can hardly get any information by comparing watermarked with the original one.

4 Conclusions

The Zigzag-space watermarking in spatial domain gives satisfactory output. The maximum change in the pixel value will be 15 out of 255 giving maximum distortion of (15/255) x 100 = 5.88% in output image. For RGB-Space watermarking, cover image has size three times of the gray scale images are in three different layers in RGB space. Each layer is watermarked by three different data, (logo, sound and text).

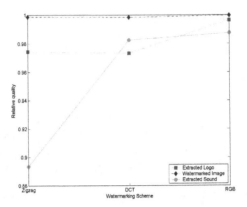

Fig. 16. Relative performance of the algorithms used for multimedia data watermarking in different domain

So this technique gives flexibility for choosing modulation index as high as in Zigzag-space watermarks and more space for data insertion as in Multi-layer watermarking. Also we get an extra layer for embedding text information. There is no chance of data interference as color layers do not interfere each other. Watermarking in DCT domain is also transparent to human visual system provided strength of the watermark is within limit. We get only one band of DCT coefficients of same size of the cover image, so total space is divided for different data insertion. So cover image size should be double than Multi-layer watermarking, thereby decreasing payload capacity. Relative performance of above-mentioned three algorithms is shown in figure 16. The word 'relative' used in the sense that quality of detected signal with respect to the original one. From the figure 16 it is clear that RGB-Space & DCT watermarking gives best result than Zigzag watermarking as far as quality preservation of detected signal and distortion of watermarked image is concerned.

Reference

1. I.J. Cox and M.L. Miller, "A review of watermarking and the importance of perceptual modeling," in *Proc. SPIE Electronic Imaging '97, Storage and Retrieval for Image and Video Databases V,* San Jose, CA, Feb. 1997.
2. R.J. Anderson and F.A.P. Petitcolas, "On the limits of steganography," *IEEE J. Select. Areas Commun.*, vol. 16, pp. 474-481, May 1998.
3. M.D. Swanson, M. Kobayashi, and A.H. Tewfik, "Multimedia data-embedding and watermarking technologies," *Proc. IEEE*, vol. 86, pp. 1064-1087, June 1998
4. J.L. Massey, "Contemporary cryptology: An introduction," in *Contemporary Cryptology: The Science of Information Integrity*, G.J. Simmons, Ed. New York: IEEE Press, 1992, pp. 3-39
5. R. W. G. Hunt, *The Reproduction of Colour in Photography, Printing & Television*, 5th Ed. Fountain Press, England, 1995. ISBN 0863433812
6. Mark D. Fairchild, *Color Appearance Models*, Addison-Wesley, Reading, MA (1998). ISBN 0-201-63464-3
7. Tao B. and Dickinson B., "Adaptive Watermarking in DCT Domain", *Proc. of IEEE International Conf. on Acoustics, Speech and Signal Processing, ICASSP-97*, Vol.4, pp.1985- 2988, 1997

Indexing and Retrieval of Document Images by Spatial Reasoning

P. Punitha, Naveen[*], and D.S. Guru

Department of Studies in Computer Science,
University of Mysore, Manasagangotri, Mysore – 570006, India
punithaswamy@yahoo.com, naveen_msc@yahoo.com,
dsg@compusci.uni-mysore.ac.in

Abstract. In this paper, a new scheme of indexing document images based on B-tree by preserving the nine-directional spatial relationships among the components of a document image is proposed. A technique for labeling of components in document images is also proposed. A procedure for classifying and ranking is also proposed. The experiments are conducted on the MediaTeam document image database that provides diverse collection of document images.

Keywords: Document image indexing/retrieval, Spatial similarity retrieval.

1 Introduction

Creation of large databases of document images in digital libraries has been possible due to the availability of low cost scanners and storage media. The economic feasibility of maintaining such databases has created a tremendous demand for robust ways to represent, access, and manipulate the information that the images contain. A way of representation should capture the knowledge about the image content as much as possible. One way of representing an image is to construct a symbolic image through perception of the binary spatial relationships that exist among these components in the image [1, 3, 7].

Some symbolic image representation techniques based on nine directional codes [1, 2], triangular spatial relationship [5], and 2D-strings and its variants [2, 3] have been proposed. The similarity retrieval using 2D-strings and its variants involves subsequence matching which is non-deterministic polynomial complexity problem. Few attempts for efficient and effective retrieval of symbolic images based on hashing [9, 11, 13], G-tree [12], B-tree [6] have been made. However, the hashing based techniques are not suitable for dynamic databases and the computation of hash addresses takes exponential time. Most of the previous representation and indexing methods based on variants of nine-directional codes and 2D-string representations are limited by the number of objects in the database. The proposed representation and retrieval methods in literature also entail each object present in an image to match an icon in the database, and are ineffectual in handling multiple similar binary spatial

---

[*] Corresponding author.

S. Madria et al. (Eds.): ICDCIT 2006, LNCS 4317, pp. 457–464, 2006.
© Springer-Verlag Berlin Heidelberg 2006

relationships between objects in images [8]. The work [4] reviews techniques for indexing and retrieval of document images.

In this paper, we present a scheme based on nine-directional codes for representing document images. We also propose an efficient B-tree based indexing of document images for efficient retrieval. After retrieving the document images, a classification method and a procedure for ranking of document images in each class are proposed.

2 Labeling and Representation

Let (x_i, y_i)'s be the top-left corners of components in a document image and (w_i, h_i)'s be the widths and heights of components respectively. Width of the document image is calculated as $W = \max(x_i + w_i) - \min(x_i) + 1$. Similarly, the height of the document image is calculated as $H = \max(y_i + h_i) - \min(y_i) + 1$. The ratios w_i/W and h_i/H for all the components present in all the images are calculated and then these ratio tuples of components are grouped into two sets according to the component's category (*text/non-text*). These tuples in two sets are clustered individually into 20 classes using k-means algorithm.p The components in the resulting 20 clusters of text type are assigned component labels from 1 to 20, and the components in 20 clusters of non-text type are assigned the labels from 21 to 40.

Suppose that a document image I contains q components $\{c_1, c_2, \ldots, c_q\}$. The image I can then be encoded by a set of quadruples: $S = \{ T_{ij} \mid \forall\, c_i, c_j \in I \text{ and } 1 \le i < j \le q \}$, where

$$T_{ij} = \begin{cases} (L_i, L_j, D_{ij}, D_{ji}) & \text{if } L_i < L_j \text{ or } (L_i == L_j \,\&\, D_{ij} < D_{ji}) \\ (L_j, L_i, D_{ji}, D_{ij}) & \text{if } L_i > L_j \text{ or } (L_i == L_j \,\&\, D_{ij} \ge D_{ji}) \end{cases} \tag{1}$$

where L_i and L_j are labels of components c_i and c_j respectively in I, D_{ij} is the direction code between components c_i and c_j with c_j as the reference component, and D_{ji} is the direction code between components c_i and c_j with c_i as the reference component. It can be noted that the number of quadruples in S is $q(q-1)/2$.

While determining directional codes we are considering the area of components rather than just points (centroids) of components because such a representation is too sensitive in spatial reasoning. That is, D_{ij} is determined by the direction of the 80% of the ith component to the jth component. Hence the directional codes D_{ij} and D_{ji} need not be complementary to each other.

Let us look at the document image layout shown in fig. 1(a) that contains four components $\{c_1, c_2, c_3, c_4\}$ with corresponding labels $\{1, 2, 3, 4\}$. The nine directional codes are shown in fig. 1(b). The set of quadruples representing the document image is $S = \{(1,2,8,5), (1,3,8,5), (1,4,1,5), (2,3,1,5), (2,4,3,7), (3,4,3,7)\}$.

3 Indexing

Indexing is indeed the mechanism chosen for storing symbolic document images (sets of quadruples) for efficient and effective retrieval. Here we make use of B-tree, an efficient multilevel indexing structure, which outperforms any method based on hashing technique. Due to the fact that, B-tree does not support storage of multivalued data such as quadruples, a unique key is generated for each 4-tuple $(L_i, L_j, D_{ij}, D_{ji})$ using the formula:

$$K = (L_i - 1)\, m\, d^2 + (L_j - 1)\, d^2 + (D_{ij} - 1)\, d + (D_{ji} - 1) \tag{2}$$

where $m = 40$, the number of component labels and $d = 9$, the number of directional codes.

It can be noticed that the computed keys for any two different quadruples are distinct and unique. Let N be the total number of distinct keys due to all n symbolic document images and is denoted by $\{k_1, k_2, ..., k_N\}$. Since, key K can be associated

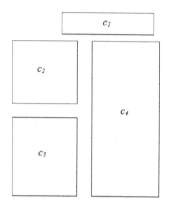

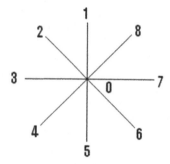

Fig. 1(a). Document Image Layout   **Fig. 1(b).** The nine directional codes

with two or more document images with different frequencies, the list of pairs (i, z_{K_i}) where z_{K_i} is the frequency of K in the image i is formed for each key K. All the keys along with their associated lists are then stored in a B-tree of rank r.

After creating an index of document images using B-tree, the retrieval of similar images from the database for a given query is as trivial as explained in the following section.

4   Retrieval of Similar Document Images

Let Q be a query document image. Let U_Q and T_Q be the distinct number of keys and total number of keys present in Q respectively and thus each distinct key K in Q is associated with a frequency z_{K_Q}. Each distinct key of Q is then searched in B-tree and the associated list of pairs of document image index and frequency is retrieved. The frequency of the query key K is then subtracted from each frequency z_{K_i} (of I_i) associated with K in the extracted list and the differences $d_{K_i} = z_K - z_{K_Q}$ are computed.

Once the lists of document image indices and the corresponding difference in frequencies are obtained for every query key, the following features for each retrieved document image I_i are computed.

- R_i, number of times the document image I_i is retrieved (i.e., number of distinct query keys which are also in I_i)
- D_PLUS_i, sum of the positive differences in frequencies (i.e., positive d_k's associated with I_i) retrieved along with the document image I_i due to various query keys.
- D_MINUS_i, absolute sum of the negative differences (i.e., negative d_k's associated with I_i) in frequencies retrieved along with the image I_i due to various query keys.
- $COMMON_i$, sum of the frequencies of all the query keys due to which the document image I_i is retrieved.

The retrieved document images are categorized into two classes called *most relevant class* and *least relevant class* based on the number of times(R_i) the document image has been retrieved. If a document image I_i, has been retrieved for every distinct query key ($R_i = U_Q$) then it is classified to be a member of the most relevant class, otherwise ($R_i < U_Q$), to be classified as a member of the least relevant class.

Depending on the values of the above defined features, the document images under most relevant category are further classified into four classes viz., *exact match*, document images bearing same components with same spatial scattering as that of the query document image; *super images*, document images containing completely the query image; *sub images*, document images which are contained in the query and *overlapping images*, document images which overlap with the query image.

If a document image I_i has the sum of the positive differences in frequencies retrieved along the document image I_i due to various query keys (D_PLUS_i) as zero, then it indicates that the document image I_i has no key, for which it has been retrieved, with more frequency when compared to that of the query key. Similarly, if the absolute sum of the negative differences in frequencies retrieved along the document image I_i due to various query keys (D_MINUS_i) is zero then the document image has no key, for which it has been retrieved, with less frequency when compared to that of the query key. Thus a document image, which has both D_PLUS_i and D_MINUS_i as zero with the number of distinct keys (U_i) being equal to that of the query document image (U_Q) possesses the same number of keys with the same frequencies as that of the query document image. Therefore, those document images are called *exact match images* and are given top priority in retrieval.

Super images are the document images which contain completely the query document image. These document images may have more number of unique keys (U_i) when compared to that of the query document image (U_Q) and also may have some keys with more frequency than that of the corresponding key in query. However, there is no key with lesser frequency when compared to that of the corresponding key in the query. The document images under this category are given the next priority.

The retrieved document images which satisfy $D\_PLUS_i = 0$ and $D\_MINUS_i \neq 0$ with R_i being U_i do not have any additional unique key and have some keys with lesser frequency when compared to that of the corresponding key in the query document image. These document images become *subset* of the query document image (images completely contained in the query).

The rest of the document images which are retrieved with $R_i = U_Q$ are the images having a sort of *overlap* with the query image, bearing at least one occurrence of each query key. These document images are least preferred among all the images retrieved under most relevant class. However, these document images are given better rank than the images grouped under least relevant class. The above described subclasses of images under the most relevant class are respectively called class1, class2, class3 and class 4 document images.

The document images which are categorized under least relevant class are not retrieved for all the U_Q number of query keys ($R_i < U_Q$) but only for some of the query keys. Similarly to the classification as suggested in most relevant class in the previous subsection, here also we recommend two subclasses; *images contained in query* (*sub images*) and *overlapping document images*, respectively called class 5 and class 6 images.

The document images associated with $D\_PLUS_i = 0$ and $D\_MINUS_i \geq 0$ with R_i being U_i are classified under the *document images contained in the query*. Unlike the document images categorized under, *document images contained in query of most relevant class*, these images will have some missing components when compared to that of the query document image. Indeed, this is the reason why we least prefer these document images compared to the *most relevant images*.

The rest of the images retrieved with ($R_i < U_Q$) are considered to be overlapping document images under *least relevant class*. These *overlapping document images* may even have some additional keys with some missing keys when compared to the query. These are least preferred to any other class of document images.

In order to rank the retrieved document images within each class we use the dissimilarity measure presented in next section.

5 Ranking

Let I_i be a retrieved document image for a query image Q. Let A_i and A_Q be the set of distinct keys describing respectively the document images I_i and Q. Since the keys which are in A_i but not in A_Q and also the keys which are in A_Q but not in A_i indicate the presence of a different component and/or the presence of same component with different spatial relationships, the dissimilarity of I_i with respect to Q is allowed to be directly proportional to the number of such keys in exclusion. Sometimes, there are two document images bearing same number of such keys in exclusion and therefore dissimilarity is directly proportional to the sum of frequencies of keys in exclusion also. In addition to these keys in exclusion, the difference in frequencies (D_PLUS_i and D_MINUS_i) of the keys in common also influences the dissimilarity. However, its impact is less when compared to that of the keys in exclusion as the difference in frequencies of common keys do not imply presence of any additional component either in the retrieved document image or in the query image when compared to each other and hence, it is allowed to have a logarithmic impact. Therefore, we have devised the following dissimilarity measure.

$$V_i = \text{Diss}(I_i, Q)$$
$$= \log(1 + D\_PLUS_i) + E_i * |A_i - A_Q| + \log(1 + D\_MINUS_i) + E_Q * |A_Q - A_i| \quad (3)$$

where E_i is the sum of the frequencies of all the keys which are present only in the retrieved document image I_i but not in the query image Q and is given by

$$E_i = T_i - COMMON_i - D\_PLUS_i + D\_MINUS_i$$

and E_Q is the sum of the frequencies of all the keys which are present only in the query document image Q but not in the retrieved image I_i and is given by

$$E_Q = T_Q - COMMON_i$$

and, $|A_i - A_Q|$ and $|A_Q - A_i|$ are the cardinalities of the set differences which can be directly computed as $U_i - R_i$ and $U_Q - R_i$ respectively.

The dissimilarity measure for each retrieved image is calculated and the images in each class are ranked accordingly. The dissimilarity values computed do not represent the degree of dissimilarities of the retrieved images with respect to Q, but provide a means to rank the retrieved images under the same class.

6 Experimental Results

We have considered 292 document images of different classes (Advertisement, Article and Manual) and their ground truth information of MBRs and categories of components available in the MediaTeam document image database [10] for our experimentation.

We extracted the information about components in all the document images and the ratios w_i/W & h_i/H are calculated as explained in section 2. Then we clustered all *text* components into 20 clusters and are assigned the labels of components as cluster value. Similarly we clustered all *non-text* components into 20 clusters and are assigned the labels of components as cluster value from 21 to 40. After labeling the components in document images, the document images are encoded into symbolic images as sets of quadruples using nine-directional codes as explained in section 2. Using the formula in eqn. (2), keys are computed for all the quadruples and we got 3718 distinct keys. The image and frequency lists are constructed for all distinct keys and the keys are stored in a B-tree thus indexing all the images in the database. Then the document images are retrieved as explained in section 4 from the B-tree for a query document image and the retrieved images are classified into six different classes. The retrieved document images in each class are sorted using the dissimilarity measure proposed in section 5. The top seven retrieved layouts of document images among all classes in the order from class 1 to class 6 for few query images are shown in fig. 2. The ranks and also the classes of retrieved document images are shown below each document image layout in the format $r(c)$, where r is the rank of that image among the retrieved document images to the given query and c denotes the class that the retrieved image belongs to. For the visual perception of components and their spatial relationships in document images, we are presenting the document image layouts instead of exact document images in fig. 2. The symbol 'z' on components of layouts in fig. 2 indicates that those components are of type *non-text*.

In both the figures 2(a) and 2(b) the top left corner images are the query layouts. In fig. 2(a), the retrieved layout with 1(1) (the query itself) is the first retrieved layout for the query under class 1, the remaining are from class 6, and there were no images retrieved in remaining classes. In fig. 2(b), the retrieved layout with 1(1) is the exact match (the query itself) and the remaining are from class 2. From the subjective evaluation, it is evident that the retrieved document images are very much similar to the corresponding query document images.

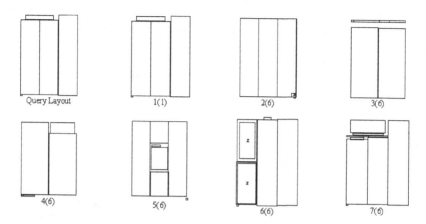

Fig. 2(a). Retrieval results for the query layout at the top left corner

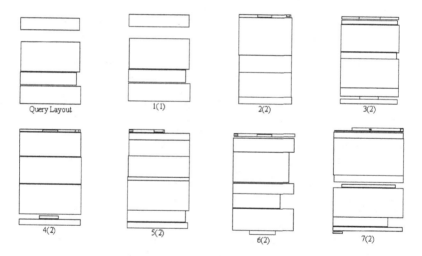

Fig. 2(b). Retrieval results for the top left corner image as the query

8   Conclusion

A novel scheme for indexing, retrieval and rank ordering of the retrieved images in a database of document images has been proposed in this paper. As a necessary step for indexing, a technique of labeling components present in document images and a method of symbolic representation for document images to capture spatial relationships between components have also been proposed. As opposed the conventional searching which is of $O(n \ U_Q \ U_M)$ search time, the proposed retrieval scheme requires $O(U_Q \log_r n)$ search time where U_Q is the number of distinct keys in query image, U_M is the average number of distinct keys that each image contains, n is the total number of document images stored in the database and r is the order of the B-tree. An advantage of the proposed representation and indexing scheme is that it can handle variable number of components in the database and also it can effectively handle multiple similar binary spatial relationships between components in images. It is important to note that there is no irrelevant image among the retrieved document images because an image is retrieved only if it contains at least one key of the query image.

Reference

[1] Chang C. C, "Spatial Match Retrieval of Symbolic Pictures", *Journal of Information Science and Engineering,* Vol.7 No.3, pp.405-422, 1991.

[2] Chang C. C, and Wu T. C, "An exact match retrieval scheme based upon principal component analysis", *Pattern Recognition Letters,* vol. 16, no. 5, pp. 465-470. 1995.

[3] Chang S.K, Jungert E and Li Y, "Representation and Retrieval of Symbolic Pictures Using Generalized 2D Strings", technical report, Univ. of Pittsburg, 1988.

[4] Doermann D, "The Indexing and Retrieval of Document Images: A Survey", Computer Vision and Image Understanding, vol. 70, no. 3, pp. 287-298. 1998.

[5] Guru D S and Nagabhushan P, "Triangular spatial relationship: a new approach for spatial knowledge representation", Pattern Recognition Letters, Volume 22, Number 9, pp. 999-1006, July 2001.

[6] Guru D. S, Punitha P and Nagabhushan P, "Archival and retrieval of symbolic images: An invariant scheme based on triangular spatial relationship", Patter Recognition Letters, vol. 24, no. 14, pp. 2397-2408, 2003.

[7] Lee S.Y and Hsu F.J, "2D C-String: A New Spatial Knowledge Representation for Image Database Systems," *Pattern Recognition,* vol. 23, no. 10, pp. 1077-1087, Oct. 1990.

[8] Punitha P, "IARS: Image Archival and Retrieval Systems", Ph. D. Thesis, Dept. of Studies in Computer Science, University of Mysore, India. (To be awarded).

[9] Sabharwal C. L, and Bhatia S. K, "Image databases and near perfect hash table", Pattern Recognition, vol. 30, no. 11, pp. 1867-1876, 1997.

[10] Sauvola J, and Kauniskangas H, MediaTeam Document Database II, a CD-ROM collection of document images, University of Oulu, Finland, 1999.

[11] Wu T. C and Chang C. C, "Application of geometric hashing to iconic database retrieval", Pattern Recognition Letters, vol. 15, no. 9, 1994.

[12] Wu T. C and Cheng J, "Retrieving similar pictures from iconic database using G-Tree", Pattern Recognition Letters, vol. 18, no. 6, pp. 595-603, 1997.

[13] Zhou X. M and Ang C. H, "Retrieving Similar Pictures from a Pictorial Database by an Improved Hashing Table", Pattern Recognition Letters, vol. 18, pp. 751-758, 1997.

Author Index

Lecture Notes in Computer Science

For information about Vols. 1–4250

please contact your bookseller or Springer